1969

THE UNITED NATIONS

INTERNATIONAL ORGANIZATION AND ADMINISTRATION

may be kept

DAYS

MAURICE WATERS

Associate Professor of Political Science
Wayne State University

THE
UNITED
NATIONS

INTERNATIONAL
ORGANIZATION
AND ADMINISTRATION

THE MACMILLAN COMPANY, NEW YORK
COLLIER-MACMILLAN LIMITED, LONDON

First Printing

Library of Congress catalog card number: 67-17920

THE MACMILLAN COMPANY, NEW YORK
COLLIER-MACMILLAN CANADA, LTD., TORONTO, ONTARIO

PRINTED IN THE UNITED STATES OF AMERICA

Dedicated to my mother and the memory of my father

PREFACE

This book was begun several years ago when I perceived a need for a better understanding of the United Nations than was usually provided in the traditional sources, where a heavy emphasis on organizational structure and problems generally prevails. In many books, even though provocative aspects and questions are introduced, no attempt is made to provide the student with a sense of intimacy regarding the performance of the United Nations. It may be true that there can be no substitute for actual participation, but neither is there, I would argue, any reason why a feeling of distance, vagueness, and uncertainty should prevail regarding the organization as an institution. My own experience at the UN, during the period of my World Affairs Council Fellowship, provided me with a completely different perspective on the organization than I had formerly had.

In my judgment, neither the dreamer's nor the cynic's view needs to be held regarding the organization. That is, I do not believe it necessary to conceive of the UN as the bright path to the rosy future or to define it as an *opéra bouffe* where men play charades with the world's most fundamental problems.

It has also seemed to me that many books on international organization reflect a strong ethnocentric bias, a condition that must be avoided when dealing with such a subject. This bias is perhaps inevitable, except where a person's travels and experience give him an unusually cosmopolitan outlook. A book on the UN ought not to reveal a national bias, and it is hoped that presenting the viewpoints of knowledgeable persons from many countries will lead the reader to perceive the organization from a viewpoint more closely approximating that held by serious students of the subject than he would be likely to get from one scholar.

One gets a good appreciation of the kind of bias he is likely to find in works by American scholars on international organization when he surveys the literature and finds that a preponderance of these studies emphasize the security features of the United Nations' charter. This is perhaps quite natural considering the concerns in the minds of American statesmen and scholars during World War II, when the plans for the postwar organization were being shaped, and considering the views of many in this country when queried about the UN. The United Nations' ability and efforts to meet "threats to the peace" have become the testing ground for judging the organization's efficacy. Such a viewpoint is also found among the popular writers who comment and editorialize on the subject. The prevalence of this attitude was sharply brought home recently when at a session of a conference sponsored by the Cleveland Council on World Affairs the participants voted unanimously that security was the major concern of the UN. Yet it is clear that such a verdict would probably not have been rendered at a comparable meeting held in many other countries, where an emphasis on economic and social problems might get first rating.

This difference in perspective is noted merely to indicate that national views on the UN vary and that since 1945 the UN has been undergoing significant changes in membership and therefore in the nature of the objectives it is expected to seek. Being a democratic and a living organization, it is bound to respond to the demands of its members. Yet an unawareness of this fact and of this change can all too easily lead individuals, scholars and laymen alike, to assess the organization differently and to reach unwarranted conclusions.

A different perspective might enable one to judge the UN's performance in terms of the search for world order. It is, in fact, a basic premise of mine that this is the major objective of the organization and that there are many paths to this end. It is true that some paths may be fraught with greater danger than others in the struggle to attain that order, but it is also true that the Western conception of the UN's *raison d'etre* has been forced to undergo a significant change—one that is still continuing. In fact, one cannot help but conclude that although the UN is an organization of sovereign states, it has, to a degree, taken on a life of its own. The expression "the whole is greater than the sum of its parts" is certainly an apt judgment in this regard.

These articles have been selected because *in toto* they reflect the conviction that the organization does not have a single narrow purpose. I believe that a fair judgment by the student regarding how well the UN is doing and where it is going requires an examination of its many efforts to establish world order, as given by writers representing different cultures and value premises.

A book of readings seemed, therefore, most likely to be able to accomplish these objectives. In addition, it also provides the possibility of giving the reader a greater insight into the various aspects of organizational life and activities, if for no other reason than that it contains a series of separate studies each of which presents its subject in greater depth than a chapter in a book normally allows. And it has permitted the selection of contrasting, and at times opposing, views to be brought to the attention of the student for his consideration, as well as the choice of those articles and reports that have been soundly conceived and highly acclaimed.

The original idea was to present a very simple collection, not because the United Nations is a simple organization, but because I felt that students generally are confused when first introduced to the subject. The array of agencies, programs, and problems often appears to give the beginner intellectual vertigo. One ought not omit a discussion of the major components and activities just for the sake of simplicity, but I believed that if these components were presented within a framework based primarily on two aspects—the internal dimensions and the external activities—the student's comprehension might be enhanced. This would require bringing together in one section those articles relating to the UN's characteristics as an institution—for example, its leadership, rules, organization, and financing—and in a second section those articles analyzing its major problems and programs—for example, its attempts to provide for collective security, disarmament, peace keeping, and economic and social needs. Should such an approach prove successful, I believe that the UN both as a social and political organism and as an ongoing international institution will become more alive and more meaningful to the reader.

It seemed plausible, therefore, to assume that one who sees the organization both in its internal and external operations comes to appreciate it as a living, organic entity.

In short, the book ought to present, vicarious and detached though it may be, an experience in international organization rather than just an intellectual exercise. It ought to provide the reader with good judgment on the processes as well as the problems of international organization, making it unnecessary that he remain a complete outsider to his subject.

Of course, these two foci are not in themselves adequate. Every organization has an ancestry in the realm of ideology and sometimes in the actual practices of states. Hence two sections (Parts I and II) on the history and theory of international organization have been added. Two other sections (Parts III and VI) deal with the constitutional and international law aspects of the United Nations. In Part I the hopes and plans of statesmen and scholars are included, as is a comparison of the League of Nations with the United Nations. In Part II the general characteristics of international organization are analyzed, with a particular focus on the United Nations. In Parts III and VI it was deemed desirable to provide a discussion of the impact of the organization on the shaping of law as well as the effect of law on the organization, and in addition to include a selection examining the role and attitudes of newer members toward the prevailing norms and principles of international law.

Except for this Preface, the introductions have been written with three general objectives in mind. First, it was intended that the basic issues should be singled out to help provide the reader with a focus for that particular section. Second, it was assumed that a few titles of books or articles should be included to aid the interested student in probing the topic in greater depth. And third, it was believed that the inclusion of a few provocative questions would not only create this desire to probe but would also stimulate the student to attempt to think about the nature of the multifarious problems confronting international organization and perhaps to go even further by identifying and questioning the basic assumptions found in the works included here. This is perhaps the ultimate in student participation in an intellectual endeavor, for until it takes place no independent research and analysis will be forthcoming, and the mind is not likely to be led into new pathways that ultimately affect the frontiers of knowledge. The student can begin this exhilarating experience, but only if he rejects the common tendency to behave like a combination of mirror and sponge—reflecting only what he has absorbed. If these introductions and the contents of this reader provide such results, the authors and the editor will surely feel grateful for the part they have played.

It is as much from a sense of pleasure as it is from duty that I would like to express my indebtedness to scholars and students who have provided an intellectual contribution and a generous measure of conscientious and unstinting effort to this endeavor. Of those in the former category, some of whom with great pleasure I still think of as my teachers, I would like to thank Dr. Kenneth Thompson and Professors Hans J. Morgenthau and Quincy Wright. Also, I would like to thank Dean Andrew W. Cordier and Professors Leland M. Goodrich, Daniel Cheever, Richard N. Swift, Harold K. Jacobson, and Urban Whitaker, Jr. On their shoulders lie none of the sins of omission or commission for what lies herein.

To Deans Martin Stearns and Russell Bright and to Professor Norman Wengert go my thanks for their aid in helping to obtain funds and make arrangements to bring the manuscript to completion. A special word of appreciation goes to Professor Max Mark for his support throughout and in particular for his translation of the article by Dr. J. W. Brügel, "The Trusteeship System of the United Nations," which appeared in German in *Europa Archiv*.

Those students and former students who toiled at the many tasks in the library and office and whose efforts I happily acknowledge are Lois Ficker, Frances Formosa, Richard Price, and Anne Marie Stelmaszek. To the first three I give credit for assistance with Chapter 1. Many errors were eliminated through their alertness and good sense. For their many hours of typing and other secretarial assistance my thanks go to Regina Volos and Sandy Zyngier, who performed cheerfully tasks other less charitable persons would have refused. And I extend my appreciation to Donna Monacelli for allowing her office staff to be disrupted for my convenience.

To Robert J. Patterson of The Macmillan Company and Richard Mathewson, former Director of Special Projects of the Office of Public Information, United Nations, for their patience, tolerance, and many efforts to help, I want to provide a special acknowledgement. This leaves unmentioned the many others, particularly those among the United Nations headquarters staff who, as is so often the case, gave generously of their time from days already heavily laden with organizational responsibilities. And finally there are those whose contribution comes in the form of acceptance of absences and deprivations in normal family affairs, a hardship not always understood but accepted out of love—Judy, Robert, George, and especially Elly.

M. W.

CONTENTS

THE UNITED NATIONS

INTERNATIONAL ORGANIZATION AND ADMINISTRATION

PART I

HISTORICAL DEVELOPMENT

CHAPTER 1

THE EVOLUTION OF INTERNATIONAL ORGANIZATION

For over 1,000 years men have dreamed, written, argued, and worked for a world of peace. The first selection in Chapter 1, "From Dreams to Reality" by Maurice Waters, contains a discussion of the plans which have come forth from many lands and have touched on legal, military, and economic approaches and on regional, ideological, and universal hopes for attaining that end. Dreams have ranged from those as abstract and simple as the pleadings of Isidore of Seville in the seventh century to the concrete and complex plans presented by the Organization of American States and the United Nations in the twentieth century.

The success or failure reflected in this enduring desire each reader will have to judge for himself, but it is important to realize the extent of the search that has gone before us. The first article is included to provide an awareness of the nature of that enterprise, although a detailed study must be obtained elsewhere.[1]

[1] See the suggested readings at the end of this introduction.

It is interesting to note that men's concepts of the conditions necessary to establish and maintain peace altered considerably as centuries passed. The emphasis shifted from an essentially legalistic and religious base to a viewpoint showing an increasing appreciation of economic, social, and humane considerations. And as assumptions changed regarding the factors which lead to instability, tension, and war, so did the organizational structures change which men proposed to reach the goal of peace.

As the religious, abstract, and idealistic concerns became less prevalent, men's proposals reflected more practical considerations designed to reconcile two seeming opposites: on the one hand, sovereignty, and on the other, the need to contain dangers to the peace. When such proposals came to fruition, as they gradually did in the nineteenth and twentieth centuries, two approaches predominated. One reflected a faith in functionalism, emphasizing the belief that major world problems could best be solved by assigning them to specialized organizations. Such organizations, dedicated to the eradication of these problems and able to focus their effort and attention on them, would, hopefully, be apolitical.

The second was a multipurpose approach; the organization, reflecting the bicameralism of almost all national legislatures, would consider requests to look into almost all of the major problems confronting societies. Initially it would look into foreign affairs but increasingly it would investigate domestic affairs as well. Although problems of an economic and social nature were given little attention in the Covenant of the League of Nations, it began to be revealed that it was in these problems that the League was most successful. Thus, when the United Nations was created, its charter revealed man's diagnoses of his past successes and errors. The League, it was felt, failed because it was neither strong enough legally nor in terms of concrete forms of power. It was, however, considered to have been on the right track when it attempted to solve man's basic biological and social problems.

Each experience lends itself to the most objective analyses only after the passage of a considerable period of time. But the question that is raised explicitly and implicitly in these first readings is: Is there enough time left to judge wisely? We may ask ourselves specifically what the requirements are for successful collective security. Do they entail a drastic change in the level of armaments? If so, does this mean a radical departure in our present concept of sovereignty? The reader would do well to ponder these questions, for they are basic to an understanding of international organization and politics.

The United Nations, created in 1945, seemed to combine the systems which evolved from all of the preceding concerns and structures. And, because it did, and because of the weariness which prevailed so widely as World War II drew to an end, scholars and statesmen alike thought the turning point in the search for a better world might at last have been reached and an institution created which would finally capture that elusive entity called peace. As the San Francisco speeches of 1945 indicate, hopes were high and views about the prerequisites of peace were widely shared. The speeches twenty years later reveal the extent of the disappointment and the degree of failure in obtaining those prerequisites. As usual, each spokesman blamed the other for the rupture of the entente cordiale. *Whereas President Johnson's 1965 statement contains only general indications of the source of the difficulty—just as President Truman's makes only oblique references to the dangers from those who would deny political freedoms—the speech of Soviet Ambassador Nikolai Fedorenko presents a blunt indictment of the United States as the country bombing and occupying others. But it should be noted that both speakers single out racial discrimination and poverty as continuing causes for dismay and action. To that extent, at least, a common concern was revealed.*

FURTHER READINGS

Documents of the United Nations Conference on International Organization, San Francisco, April 25–June 26, 1945.

Goodrich, Leland M., "From League of Nations to United Nations," *International Organization*, vol. I, February 1947, pp. 3–21.

Hemleben, Sylvester, *Plans for World Peace Through Six Centuries.* Chicago: University of Chicago Press, 1943.

FROM DREAMS TO REALITY

Maurice Waters[*]

International organization in one form or another has a history about as old as that of independent states. The rise of such entities has helped men to perceive the interdependence of their existence despite the artificial division of politics and geography. Throughout the era of the modern nation-state, there has always existed the insecurity arising from potential international chaos or war. Although the nineteenth century dates the advent of efforts to establish international organization as we recognize it today, many of its contemporary principles have endured literally throughout the centuries. For example, the practice of making covenants and defensive alliances and the use of arbitration all precede the creation of international administration.

Problems of international peace have always been present in a system of sovereign states. This is true *a fortiori* when they represent different political philosophies. How to maintain independence and obtain accommodation, to achieve the blessings of security and receive the benefits of liberty, has been the object of attention of moral philosophers and statesmen, political theorists and civic leaders since men's horizons expanded from personal to societal needs. As far back as 1400 years ago, the idea of an organization of states was in the making. Isidore of Seville, 560–636, envisioned a world which being free of disunity would be a "society of nations." Later the first actual blueprint for a union of states was presented by Pierre Dubois, 1250–1321. This union was to be complete with council and court under the rulership of the Holy Roman Emperor. Several plans were formulated in the Medieval period which would have established a Christian community of nations. They were not unrealistic in their aims, but were too closely associated with the political needs of the authors' rulers to be acceptable to others. For example, the *Grand Dessin* of Henry IV and the proposals of King Podiebrad of Bohemia both advanced self-interest, i.e., maintenance and enlargement of their power through techniques of mutual military assistance and internal arbitration.

It is clear, then, that international organizations for the purpose of creating

* Maurice Waters, Associate Professor of Political Science at Wayne State University, is currently Visiting Professor of International Relations at the University of the West Indies. He is the author of *The Ad Hoc Diplomat: A Study in Municipal and International Law*.

the fruits of community and transcending the limitations of sovereignty have been goals of many minds, in the era of the city-state, the dynastic-state and the nation-state.

Neither the League of Nations nor the United Nations should be considered, from either the viewpoint of principle or practice, as typifying a new world of international politics. Rather than a discontinuous history one sees an evolutionary development with virtually every type of international organization having been considered prior to World War I.

Let us now look briefly at the predecessors of our contemporary efforts. Throughout the nineteenth century amidst the setting of balance-of-power, there developed several attempts to resolve international controversies on a multilateral basis. Although these lacked permanency, taking the form of conference rather than of organization, they represent substantial efforts in the direction of meeting problems which remain of major concern. One is still troublesome to international organizations today, namely the problem of achieving agreement on the terms of disarmament. Freedom of movement within a framework of international order was, broadly speaking, the goal of those European powers active in the Concert of Europe.

Although the Concert was formed in a postwar period, the matters discussed transcended the signing of peace treaties. It was this type of multilateral negotiation and decision-making which permits one to say that "more than anything, . . . the Concert system laid the groundwork for the creation of the executive organ [in] international organization" which eventuated in the League of Nations' and the United Nations' Councils.[1] These conferences were undertaken to counteract the instabilities of the balance-of-power.

In the nineteenth century, international organization was not seen as a potential world-state by the authorities but rather as a better way for sovereign states to operate in the pursuit of their own interests in view of the changed industrialized world. Arguments over the dangers to sovereignty, the diminution of nationalism, or the dangers of being engulfed by socialism were not raised as obstacles to such dangerous adventures.

The Concert system fell into disuse after 1822, but the purpose of replacing force with accommodation was revived in 1852 at the Congress of Paris. During the latter part of the nineteenth century, conferences were frequently employed to handle such crises as Russian expansion, the drive to complete the colonization of Africa, and the increasing threats to neutrals posed by the improved technology of war at the disposal of belligerents.

These conferences, including those at the Hague in 1899 and 1907, were convened for the purpose of reformulating states' rights and obligations, and may be characterized as reflecting a need for long-range reform in state behavior and for agreed-upon methods of resolving differences through the use of third parties and the avoidance of war.

[1] Stephen Goodspeed, *The Nature and Function of International Organization* (New York: Oxford University Press, 1959), p. 28.

Aside from largely political efforts which were the concerns of the Concert system, the nineteenth century saw the formation of public international unions. These appeared early in the century and flourished in increasing numbers after 1850. They covered a whole variety of nonpolitical fields. By 1914 about thirty existed and included the Universal Postal Service, the International Bureau of Weights and Measures, the International Sugar Union, the International Opium Commission, and the International Office of Public Health. In each of these areas difficulties arose which were beyond the capacity of any one state to resolve. It soon became evident that this functional approach to intergovernmental and intersocietal problems could pay richer dividends than those approaches traditionally followed.

Simultaneous with their founding came the establishment of a multitude of private associations. As with the public unions, their goals were diverse. "They [were] organized to further the interests of a particular industry, group, or profession, to promote a cause or movement such as calendar reform or world federation, or to carry out a special task in the form of [supporting] religion or administering relief."[2] Among the many which achieved prominence were the World Alliance of YMCA's, the Institute of International Law, the International Union of Tramways, the Inter-Parliamentary Union, and the International Bureau for the Suppression of Traffic in Women and Children.

The twentieth century has witnessed the development of two of the most comprehensive and complex of all organizations which have been part of this evolutionary development. The League of Nations as a concept grew gradually as a result of the conditions of the war.

Despite the great enthusiasm for the war among almost all classes and peoples of Europe, events in the winter of 1914–1915 quickly began to dissipate hopes for an easy and early victory. With the numbing realization which followed, that this would be unlike the last wars Europeans remembered, came a gradual awareness that men would have to create an organization which would provide the means of resolving international disputes and the machinery to enforce it. Various civic groups promulgated ideas even during the war but the leading government officials in both the United States and Britain provided the proposals in 1918 which became the foundation of the League of Nations. In January of that year both Lloyd George and Woodrow Wilson referred in speeches to the need for an international organization to cope with problems of armaments, territorial integrity, trade barriers, etc. The speeches supported and further encouraged the private groups already at work in these and other states to provide plans which it was hoped governments would eventually sanction and join. This was finally achieved January 10, 1920, but not until numerous modifications were accepted and the original harmony had seriously deteriorated in a number of

[2] Stephen Goodspeed, op. cit., p. 30.

angry discussions. Desires for equality by the Japanese, for military security by the French, for selection as the organization's headquarters by the Belgians were expressed and denied.

The Covenant of the League of Nations was a treaty incorporated as a part of another treaty, the Treaty of Versailles, which was the treaty of peace with Germany. Those who signed the latter were thereby signatories to the former (32 in number), although other states not involved in the war could likewise accede to the Covenant (originally 13). And although the provisions of that Covenant established an organization of limited powers with a continued emphasis on state sovereignty, they remained significant throughout the history of the Organization as points of departure for the many debates which ensued. Hence the Covenant was looked upon as providing a constitutional framework for the League's development.

What follows is a brief discussion of the provisions of the Covenant:

Article 1 provided for the means by which states became members and withdrew from the Organization, with the Assembly authorized to admit; Articles 2, 3, and 4 provided for an Assembly and a Council with equality of voting and of representation and the necessity in each organ for unanimity of those present for major decisions to be binding; Articles 6 and 7 provided for a Secretariat, its officers and diplomatic representatives both having the right to diplomatic immunities; Article 8 obligated the Council to prepare plans for the reduction of armaments; Articles 10, 11, and 16, which many authorities feel represented the heart of the League, contained provisions upholding the "territorial integrity" and "political independence" of the members, and somewhat vague obligations of a collective-security nature, in particular aid to those attacked in violation of Covenant provisions; Articles 12, 13, and 14 established the obligation of pacific settlement of disputes and the establishment of a Permanent Court of International Justice to meet that end; Article 22 established the Mandates System and the principle of the rights of the indigenous peoples which the mandatory powers were to uphold and the Council to investigate; and Article 23 was concerned with matters of social well-being of citizens of members and inhabitants of other territories as well.

While the League did succeed in forwarding cooperation in certain economic and technical areas, as an organ of peace and security it failed. The reason for this failure lay in the anachronistic attitudes that led states to continue to make basic decisions affecting war and peace as if the outcome was of limited impact on world affairs. Hopes that the Council would operate, as it was intended to, diminished when the appetites of states exceeded the limitations imposed by the Covenant and the authority wielded by the Council. The Weltanschauung adopted by the greater powers enabled them to disregard their responsibilities to the smaller members as well as to each other. Thus, in the 1930's, the build-up of armaments and the subsequent aggressions could not be stopped by the League, and it consequently lost respect and potency as an instrument of collective security.

Those who laid the groundwork for the United Nations decided that the vast destructiveness of World War II might have been avoided if the League had had the authority and the force commensurate with the task of stopping aggression. Beyond this was the assumption that the incidence of war might be measurably reduced if those economic and social conditions which lead to invidious comparisons, to frustration and hostility, were made the targets of cooperative endeavors. Hence the United Nations system was given a mandate as broad as man's basic needs, although not that full measure of authority necessary to meet them.

Of course, in a broad sense many of the ideas found in both the Covenant and the Charter came from the minds of men of past centuries. One could refer to the writings of such men as Mo Ti of ancient China, of William Penn of England, of Kant and Asoka and Henry IV of Germany, India, and France respectively and of Simon Bolivar of Latin America. In addition one must also give credit to the efforts of those working under the direction of Sumner Welles and more specifically of Leo Pasvolsky, assigned this responsibility by Franklin Roosevelt.

A more formal approach to the establishment of international organization was undertaken in the Summer of 1944, at a conference that continued on through the fall at Dumbarton Oaks, Washington, D.C., and attended in two stages by representatives of the United States, Britain and the Soviet Union, with China taking the place of the Soviet Union in the second phase.

At two subsequent conferences, Yalta (February 4–11, 1945) and Mexico City (February 21–March 8, 1945) additional clarification of positions was reached when in the former the Russians finally gave in to Western insistence that the Security Council veto not apply to procedural votes and in the latter when strong support was forthcoming by the Latins in support of increased importance for the Assembly. They likewise demanded that regional organizations should be permitted to function in the pacific settlement and collective security fields.

The final form of the Charter was worked out at San Francisco in the Spring of 1945 just 75 days after Franklin Roosevelt, the chief architect of the UN, died. One can well imagine the difficulties of providing for a smoothly functioning conference of 3,000 persons, in many cases unknown to each other, and from 46 different nations. The responsibility for working out the routine administration was assigned to Alger Hiss, but the provisions of the Charter which were to obligate the members were the result of the compromises hammered out by the delegates in four working commissions, on General Provisions, on the General Assembly, on the Security Council, and on Judicial Organization.

Some of the most significant changes in the original plans came with the greater emphasis on economic and social matters and with obligations regarding the old League of Nations' Mandates. These modifications came in large measure as a result of pressures from the smaller states, in particular the Australians, Belgians, Canadians, and Uruguayans. From this same source came demands that the powers of the General Assembly be increased and the Security Council veto removed. The former demands were met but not' the latter.

It is well to remember that the United Nations Charter, like the Covenant of the League of Nations, and probably like any major political document which involves the allocation of power, is the end product of a long and complicated series of negotiations, bargaining and compromises.

The United States and Britain wished to follow the precedent of the League Covenant and exclude a great power from voting on a dispute to which it was a party, not only on recommendations for the pacific settlement of disputes, but also on decisions involving enforcement measures. Several of the middle and small members of the international community reluctantly, and of necessity, accepted the veto provisions advocated by the major powers. Australia, representative of many smaller states, supported the abridgment of abolition of great-power voting privileges on decisions other than enforcement. That delegation sought to draw a clear distinction between enforcement and conciliation, and to confine the veto to enforcement measures exclusively. In a dramatic debate Australia led the attack to exclude the veto from decisions relating to peaceful settlement by regarding them as procedural matters. She proposed amendments that provided that in the case of voting on enforcement matters the Security Council had to act in unison or not at all; in matters affecting peaceful settlement, decisions could be taken on the vote of any seven members of the Council.

Uruguay was prepared to accept the Yalta voting formula providing a veto for the great powers because the delegation considered it to be a transitional provision that could be reviewed after ten years. It was strongly believed that the revision or amendment of the Charter should be veto-free after ten years thus adding a dynamic dimension to the inherent static nature of the veto provision—especially on procedural matters. India, upon entering the infant organization, was willing to accept the inclusion of the veto privilege as long as it was supported by the United States and the Soviet Union.

The Conference recognized the role of the major powers in maintaining peace and security. Yet the condition of permanent membership for the great powers on the Security Council did not fail to stir up conflict between the large and small powers. Uruguay accepted this provision because the major powers carried the heaviest burden of the war and now inherited a heavy responsibility for the maintenance of peace. Nevertheless, it was argued that this privileged tenure should not continue indefinitely but only for eight or ten years. Uruguay also proposed that the non-permanent members of the Council be selected by the General Assembly on the basis of regional representation by rotation among the states belonging to each region.

Australia, in partnership with Canada, proposed that such members be selected on the basis of their past military contribution to the cause of world security, and their ability and willingness . . . to assume substantial responsibilities and to make a significant contribution to the maintenance of international security. The essence of the Australian suggestion was incorporated into Article 23 (1) of the Charter.

At Dumbarton Oaks the right of individual and collective self-defense against armed attack was thought to be inherent in the proposals. Nevertheless, Great Britain considered the explicit recognition in Article 51 of significant importance. This explicit recognition was thought to add a legitimacy to political realities and to help dilute charges that measures of individual or collective self-defense were incompatible with the Charter and thus to remove a possible obstacle to Anglo-American co-operation. In the general debate at San Francisco, the Uruguayan delegation defined its position on collective security. An amendment was submitted providing that each state would place part of its military force, based on individual capacity, at the disposal of the organization and that such forces would act by order of the Security Council. Strong support was expressed for the use of force against those states refusing to accept the decisions of the organization. In the main the smaller powers stressed non-intervention and the application of sanctions on deviant states.

It is clear from this brief survey that man's struggle has been for economic, social and physical security, and as he has gradually succeeded in attaining at least a modicum of these wants in domestic affairs he has come to realize that a fuller measure of satisfaction can only be obtained if the same energy and ingenuity is applied to relations between nations. From a period in the nineteenth century when such hopes were primarily the subject of philosophical tracts or international conferences dealing with war-created political issues, to the decades of the 1920's and 1930's when economic and technical problems took their place on organizations' agendas, to the post-World War II period when such interests were compounded by additional concerns for human rights, is truly a long and tortuous road. But it has been laid, although there may be sections in which the roadbed is still rough and uncertain. And it has been built not because international organizations have directed political leaders and their citizens to move in such directions, for no such authority or prestige is theirs. Nor has it been built because a few political leaders have foisted their views upon the rest of mankind. Rather, the explanation may be seen in the flowering of an ideal that has been firmly and universally planted, though its requirements may be neither thoroughly comprehended nor achieved. If it is true that the objectives were once the dreams of a handful of leaders, it is also true that this dream is no longer the property of a few but rather of millions. Perhaps the most significant change that has taken place in the last one hundred years stems from this change in perspective. The result has been that international

THE EVOLUTION OF INTERNATIONAL ORGANIZATION 13

organizations are expected to engage in programs transcending short-range goals reflecting immediate power interests.

Community action for the preservation of the peace is not without problems. Indeed, the values and objectives of international organization can be pointed up in a basic question universal throughout time. How can maximum co-operation be advanced within a world setting where nations are sovereign? This problem has remained an insoluble dilemma since men began to think about international peace. Today, however, more than ever it is in need of solution, for the alternative to peace now is totally new. It is war, of course, but in the form of devastation so complete that one wonders if there will still be a world left if it occurs.

There are some other basic truths about international organization worth noting. It is most important to recognize that international politics and international organization are closely linked. The tendency to think of them as separate and unrelated phenomena must be resisted. Historically, the interests and values, successes and failures of international organizations have reflected the climate of international relations. This relationship emanates from the tendency of state leaders to view an international organization's interests through nationalistic glasses, and thereby to manipulate such institutions for their own ends. The 1960-1962 Congo episode reflects this beautifully. . . . This situation shows that one of the perennial dangers confronting international organization stems from the tendency on the part of state leaders consciously or unconsciously to use and abuse international organizations as if they were adjuncts of their Foreign Offices.

On the other hand, an organization can provide a much-needed forum for international cooperation which would otherwise be missing. "In its institutional aspects especially . . . [it] appears as a framework within which an international process can occur and as an instrument to integrate and even influence international relations."[3]

In a world in which there was only one state or empire, there would be no reason for an international organization. Given the system of sovereign states, the problem of an international organization is to provide the means by which common purposes or goals may be reached through cooperation while deflecting the conflicts which are bound to arise when so many entities seek to advance their separate interests. The theory behind international organization assumes that state behavior can be modified even within the confines of a system of sovereignty. The need to achieve this reconciliation has become increasingly acknowledged but the achievement of this end still eludes our grasp. In that nations are sovereign, they seek freedom to maneuver on the international scene; in that they are members of an international organization, they must agree to limit themselves in accordance with its avowed common purposes. As Dag Hammarskjöld once

[3] Werner Levi, *Fundamentals of World Organization* (St. Paul: University of Minnesota Press, 1950), p. 4.

put it, the existence of the United Nations reflects "a firm faith [on the part] of men and governments to have the common sense to find their way out of the awful labyrinth of seemingly irreconcilable conflicts and insoluble problems in which we are now wandering."[4]

International organization has been confronted with other problems in addition to making "national man" and his needs its compass. The confrontation with the strong image of sovereignty not only may act as a block to the organization's efforts to restrain states in their aggressive behavior, but may also impede the necessity of building an international civil service, objective and dedicated to the cause of the organization. This is not to say that such a *desideratum* is not embraced already by many, but it is clear, especially in light of Nikita Khrushchev's attack on the whole notion of an impartial civil service, that such a viewpoint is not yet universally embraced.

Peace and security are the goals of the United Nations. They have long been sought by man, but today they have a unique character because of a new world setting. In the twentieth century two factors—the increasing interdependence of nations socially, economically and culturally, and the possibility of total war—have made . . . realization of these goals take on a new importance. The United Nations is not a manifestation of only an already existing agreement on the importance of certain values. It has come into existence because of necessity and because of fear. It can make more feasible the solutions to international problems as well as basic human needs because it allows the desires for co-operation to take concrete form and allows conflict to be channelled into orderly paths for solution. In this world of sovereign nation-states, both ends are essential.

SPEECHES AT THE FOUNDING
OF THE UNITED NATIONS*

MR. STETTINIUS [Secretary of State of the United States of America]: Ladies and Gentlemen, it is my honor to recognize the Chairman of the Delegation of the Union of Soviet Socialist Republics, Ambassador Gromyko.

---

[4] *United Nations Bulletin*, May 1, 1954, p. 353.

* Ambassador Andrei Gromyko and President Harry S Truman, "San Francisco 1945 and 1965 Speeches at the Founding and Twentieth Anniversary Meetings of the United Nations." Documents of the United Nations Conference on International Organization, San Francisco, California, April 25–June 26, 1945. United Nations Information Organization, New York, Document 1209, p. 19, June 27, 1945.

MR. GROMYKO: . . . The peace-loving nations who suffered countless sacrifices in this war naturally rest their hopes on the establishment, by collective
efforts, of an international instrument which could prevent the repetition of
a new tragedy for humanity. In accordance with the decisions adopted at
the Dumbarton Oaks Conference, Marshal Stalin said: "To win the war
against Germany means to carry out a great historical deed. But to win the
war still does not mean the insurance of lasting peace and security for the
people in the future. The task is not only to win the war but also to make
impossible the occurrence of a new aggression and a new war, if not forever,
then at least for a long period of time."

Marshal Stalin pointed out that the actions of that Organization would
be sufficiently effective if the great powers who carried the main burden of
the war against Hitlerite Germany would continue to act in the spirit of unanimity and accord. These actions will not be effective if a breach of this
indispensable conditions occurs. . . . We prepared a document which should
become the basis for the actions of the International Organization—its constitution. Naturally, the very best and most perfect Charter in itself is not
yet a guaranty that its provisions will be carried out and insure the preservation of peace. In order to achieve this important and noble task it is also
necessary, in addition to the existing Charter, to have the unity and coordination of actions of members of the International Organization, and first of
all the unity and coordination of actions between the most powerful military
powers of the world. It is also necessary that all members of the International Organization should try to settle all disputes by peaceful means in the
spirit of cooperation and good-will.

✿   ✿   ✿   ✿   ✿   ✿   ✿

The provisions of the Charter, which have been worked out, cover a great
number of questions and problems defining the future activity of the
Organization as a whole and its separate organs. In this connection it is
necessary to point out specially the significance of those provisions of the
Charter which refer to peaceful settlement of disputes and conflicts. The
participants in the Conference paid great attention to this field of their
work. Under the Charter, members of the International Organization obligate themselves to achieve peaceful settlements of the disputes. Let us hope
that this aim will be fully realized.

In conclusion I wish to express confidence that this Conference of the
United Nations will go down in the history of humanity as one of the
most significant events and that our efforts will be beneficial for all peace-
loving peoples of the world, who endured so many hardships and sufferings
as a result of the conflagration set by Hitlerite Germany.

MR. STETTINIUS [Secretary of State of the United States of America]:
Fellow Delegates, the President of the United States of America.

MR. TRUMAN: . . . The Charter of the United Nations which you are now signing is a solid structure upon which we can build for a better world. History will honor you for it. Between the victory in Europe and the final victory in Japan, in this most destructive of all wars, you have won a victory against war itself.

It was the hope of such a Charter that helped sustain the courage of stricken peoples through the darkest days of the war. For it is a declaration of great faith by the nations of the earth—faith that war is not inevitable, faith that peace can be maintained.

If we had had this Charter a few years ago—and above all, the will to use it—millions now dead would be alive. If we should falter in the future in our will to use it, millions now living will surely die.

✿   ✿   ✿   ✿   ✿   ✿   ✿

Out of all the arguments and disputes, and different points of view, a way was found to agree. Here in the spotlight of full publicity, in the tradition of liberty-loving people, opinions were expressed openly and freely. The faith and hope of fifty peaceful nations were laid before this world forum. Differences were overcome. This Charter was not the work of any single nation or group of nations, large or small. It was the result of a spirit of give-and-take, of tolerance for the views and interests of others.

This is proof that nations, like men, can state their differences, can face them, and then can find common ground on which to stand. That is the essence of democracy; that is the essence of keeping the peace in the future. By your agreement, the way was shown toward future agreement, in the years to come.

This Conference owes its success largely to the fact that you have kept your minds firmly on the main objective. You had the single job of writing a constitution—a charter for peace. And you stayed on that job.

✿   ✿   ✿   ✿   ✿   ✿   ✿

What you have accomplished in San Francisco shows how well these lessons of military and economic cooperation have been learned. You have created a great instrument for peace and security and human progress in the world.

✿   ✿   ✿   ✿   ✿   ✿   ✿

If we seek to use it selfishly—for the advantage of any one nation or any small group of nations—we shall be . . . guilty of . . . betrayal.

The successful use of this instrument will require the united will and firm determination of the free peoples who have created it. The job will tax the moral strength and fiber of us all.

We all have to recognize—no matter how great our strength—that we must deny ourselves the license to do always as we please. No one nation, no regional group, can or should expect, any special privilege which harms any other nation. If any nation would keep security for itself, it must be ready and willing to share security with all. That is the price which each nation will have to pay for world peace. Unless we are all willing to pay that price, no organization for world peace can accomplish its purpose.

* * * * * * *

Under this document we have good reason to expect an international bill of rights, acceptable to all the nations involved. That bill of rights will be as much a part of international life as our own Bill of Rights is a part of our Constitution. The Charter is dedicated to the achievement and observance of human rights and fundamental freedoms. Unless we can attain those objectives for all men and women everywhere—without regard to race, language, or religion—we cannot have permanent peace and security in the world.

* * * * * * *

We must set up an effective agency for constant and thorough interchange of thought and ideas. For there lies the road to a better and more tolerant understanding among nations and among peoples.

SPEECHES AT THE TWENTIETH ANNIVERSARY MEETINGS OF THE UNITED NATIONS*

MR. JOHNSON: On my journey across the continent, I stopped in the state of Missouri, and there I met with the man who made the first such pilgrimage here twenty years ago as the thirty-third President of the United States— Harry S. Truman. Mr. Truman sent to this Assembly his greetings and good wishes on this anniversary commemoration. He asked that I express to you for him—as for myself and for my countrymen—the faith which we of the United States hold firmly in the United Nations and in the ultimate success of its mission among men.

* * * * * * *

Today, then—at this time of anniversary—let us not occupy ourselves with parochial doubts or with passing despair. The United Nations—after twenty years—does not draw its life from the assembly halls or the committee rooms. It lives in the conscience and the reason of mankind.

* President of the United States Lyndon B. Johnson and Permanent Representative of the Union of Soviet Socialist Republics Nikolai Fedorenko, UN Monthly Chronicle, Vol. II, No. 7, July 1965.

The most urgent problem we face is the keeping of the peace.

Today, as I speak, clear and present dangers in South East Asia cast their shadow across the path of all mankind.

The United Nations must be concerned.

The most elementary principle of the United Nations is that neighbors must not attack their neighbors—and that principle today is under challenge.

The processes of peaceful settlement today are blocked by wilful aggressors contemptuous of the opinion and the will of mankind.

Bilateral diplomacy has yielded no result.

The machinery of the Geneva Conference has been paralyzed.

Resort to the Security Council has been rejected.

The efforts of the distinguished Secretary-General have been rebuffed.

An appeal for unconditional discussion was met with contempt.

A pause in bombing operations was called an insult.

The concern for peace of the Commonwealth Prime Ministers has received little and very disappointing results.

Therefore, today I put to this World Assembly the facts of aggression, the right of a people to be free from attack, the interest of every member in safety against molestation, the duty of this Organization to reduce the dangers to peace, and the unhesitating readiness of the United States of America to find a peaceful solution.

I now call upon this gathering of the nations of the world to use all their influence, individually and collectively, to bring to the tables those who seem determined to make war. We will support your efforts, as we will support effective action by any agent or agency of these United Nations.

*   *   *   *   *   *   *

The heritage that we share together is a fragile heritage.

A world war would certainly destroy it. Pride and arrogance could destroy it. Neglect and indifference could destroy it. It could be destroyed by narrow nationalism or ideological intolerance—or rabid extremism of either the left or the right.

So we must find the way as a community of nations, as a United Nations, to keep the peace among and between all of us. We must restrain by joint and effective action any who place their ambitions or their dogmas or their prestige above the peace of all the world. And we just must find a way to do that. It is the most profound and the most urgent imperative of the time in which we live.

*   *   *   *   *   *   *

We must stop preaching hatred, we must stop bringing up entire new generations to preserve and to carry out the lethal fantasies of the old generation, stop believing that the gun or the bomb can solve all problems or that a revolution is of any value if it closes doors and limits choices instead of opening both as wide as possible.

Mr. Fedorenko: Delegates of the member states of our world forum have met again in the famed city of San Francisco where the solemn signing of the Charter exactly twenty years ago signified the founding of the United Nations Organization.

The foundations of this world forum were laid in the joint struggle of the peoples of the anti-fascist coalition. The chief factor that made it possible for the new international Organization to emerge was undoubtedly the great victory the twentieth anniversary of which we marked only a short while ago. Fighting for this victory shoulder to shoulder with the Soviet Union, which bore the brunt of the struggle, were the United States, Britain, France, Poland, Czechoslovakia, Yugoslavia and other members of the anti-Hitler coalition.

✻   ✻   ✻   ✻   ✻   ✻   ✻

One cannot but rejoice at the fact that the forces of peace and progress in the United Nations have been growing and getting stronger during the past few years. Twenty years of course are not a long period historically speaking, but they have been replete with events of major significance. The balance of forces in the world has changed. A mighty commonwealth of socialist nations has come into existence. The colonial empires have collapsed. Scores of Asian and African countries which have shaken off the fetters of colonial enslavement have appeared on the world arena. A great purifying anti-colonial thunderstorm of the national liberation revolutions is now sweeping off the last outposts of colonialism.

✻   ✻   ✻   ✻   ✻   ✻   ✻

On the anniversary of our Organization one cannot but look back at the path traversed by the world Organization, and sum up though briefly some results; neither is it possible to pass over in silence the urgent and pressing tasks facing the Organization. If one wishes to speak about the results of United Nations activities, one should in the first place consider them from the viewpoint of implementing the basic provisions of the Charter of the Organization. It should be mentioned in all fairness that the United Nations has to its credit many actions undertaken to achieve the purposes of the Charter—actions aimed at strengthening peace, promoting friendly co-operation among nations and setting peoples free from the yoke of colonial slavery.

✻   ✻   ✻   ✻   ✻   ✻   ✻

But we would be rendering United Nations only lip-service if we did not point out impartially and frankly that the record of its activities is not that of successes and useful deeds alone. . . .

Moreover, the world more than once has witnessed cases of violation of the principles of the Charter by the imperialist powers. And at this time when we have assembled again to mark the anniversary of the United Nations, the United States of America is committing acts of aggression in flagrant violation of the Charter of the United Nations. We see it in Viet-Nam where the war waged by the American imperialist forces is being ominously escalated. We see it in the Dominican Republic, where the revolutionary people have become a victim of armed intervention on the part of the United States, and in other parts of the globe where attempts are being made to suppress the struggle of peoples for freedom and national independence by the use of armed force.

Yesterday in this hall from the lectern above this rostrum of the General Assembly a sermon of a sort was delivered with an appeal to the present session of the General Assembly "to use its influence individually and collectively to compel those, who appear to be determined to conduct war, to sit around the table of negotiations." Is it not common knowledge that the aggressive war in Viet-Nam was unleashed by the United States and that it is not the American cities that are barbarously destroyed, but the peaceful villages of the Democratic Republic of Viet-Nam?

Is it not true that hundreds of tons of bombs and napalm are dropped daily on the people of Viet-Nam but not on the Americans?

What is the moral and political value of yesterday's sermon? Is it not intended to shift responsibility for the crime on the victim of the aggression?

No distortion of facts can help justify the aggression of the United States which poses a serious threat to international peace and security.

Military intervention of the United States in the Dominican Republic has also been a challenge to the Charter of the United Nations. Has not Santo Domingo, which still suffers the tragedy of bloodshed, been occupied by tens of thousands of North American occupation troops who before the eyes of the whole world have trampled underfoot the sovereign rights of this small Latin-American nation—a member state of the United Nations?

All this is proof of the flagrant violation of the United Nations Charter and of the elementary norms of international law.

On this solemn day when we are marking the birth and the 20-year record of activities of our international forum we cannot remain silent.

*   *   *   *   *   *   *

Neither is it possible nowadays to pass over in silence the violation of one of the most important principles of the Charter, that of universality of membership. The great Chinese people who are one of the founders of this Organization still remain outside the United Nations while their legitimate seat is occupied by the Chiang Kai-shek clique. The sooner the United

Nations Organization becomes a truly universal organization of peoples the better will it be for realization of the tasks before it.

*   *   *   *   *   *   *

We must stop the hand of the West German revanchists which is reaching out for the atomic weapons, the hand of the same German militarism against which the peoples had fought and had forged in the course of fighting the foundations of the United Nations Organization.

We must immediately, without delay do away with the remnants of colonial régimes in Southern Rhodesia, Angola, Mozambique and the other remaining outpost of the colonialists. The struggle against racism must continue until its goals have been reached. There is much to be done in the fields of economic and social progress for one cannot remain indifferent to the fact that in our age people in many parts of the globe are suffering from hunger, poverty and disease. We must strive for constructive solutions of a wide complex of problems of international trade, free from discrimination and restrictions, for liquidation of economic and social consequences of colonialism, for industrialization of developing countries and other important problems.

CHAPTER **2**

THE LEAGUE OF NATIONS AND UNITED NATIONS CONTRASTED

In the selection "Covenant and Charter" Herbert Nicholas presents an excellent comparison of the major features of the League and the UN. He indicates how the principle of the concert system of the nineteenth century was revived by the departure from the League's unanimity principle, that international welfare services were given a much greater emphasis in the UN, and that obligations of collective security, although found in both documents, were given a more realistic and at the same time a more difficult expression in the Charter.

The Charter differs from the Covenant in other respects, too. In both, the Assembly's right to concern itself broadly with international problems was established, but in the Charter this right was reduced to making recommendations, and then only when the Security Council was not actively pursuing the same problem. The effect has not only been to increase the importance of the

Council but also to increase the importance of a seat on it, and therefore has led to a demand, recently met, to expand its size. In addition, it has led to an effort to bring into the Assembly many strongly worded resolutions, even though the obligation to honor them is debatable. For further discussion on this point, see Chapter 17.

Two structural changes are also found in the creation of two organs, both defined as principal, that did not exist under the League. But because to all intents and purposes these two, the Economic and Social Council and the Trusteeship Council, must report to the General Assembly, the change in powers is perhaps not so great as it might seem. Yet Nicholas is quite right when he stresses how much greater are the UN's interests in the fate of dependent peoples than was true of the League. The UN not only contains a Trusteeship Council in the place of the League's Mandates Commission but also has accepted responsibility for providing moral pressure on states in behalf of the inhabitants of their own non-self-governing territories. The pressure on the colonial states and on those supervising Trust territories to increase the opportunities for social, economic, and political changes has been tremendous, and the great increase in membership in the UN is a direct reflection of that.

The question must be raised as to what are the likely effects of such provisions, which establish high moral principles, particularly in the economic and social realm, without enforcement provisions. Do they merely highlight the wide gap between the "is" and the "ought," or do they create a pressure that ultimately must give way to concrete measures? One may go further and ask what standard one should employ to judge the efficacy of an international organization like the UN—the views widely expressed by the public; the public positions taken by leading statesmen; the commitments to it (and if so how much) in money, troops, and services by members and non-members; or the frequency with which the organization is asked to help resolve problems confronting the states? These questions emphasize the difficuilty in making valid judgments regarding the extent to which labels of success and failure may be properly applied.

FURTHER READINGS

Brierly, J. L., "The Covenant and the Charter," *British Yearbook of International Law*, Vol. XXIII, 1946, pp. 83–94.

Goodrich, Leland M., and Hambro, Edward, *Charter of the United Nations, Commentary and Documents*, rev. ed. Boston: World Peace Foundation, 1949.

Walters, F. P., *A History of the League of Nations*. New York: Oxford University Press, 1952.

COVENANT AND CHARTER

Herbert G. Nicholas*

In all the excitement that attended the accouchement of the new order, little attention had been paid to the obsequies of the old. In line with the American tactic of emphasizing the novelty of the U.N., the League had been virtually ignored at San Francisco. Its representation there was "unofficial" and had been restricted to "two or three persons": the Acting Secretary-General, Mr. Sean Lester, the Treasurer, Mr. Jacklin, and the senior Director, Mr. Loveday. Mr. Stettinius's speech of welcome to the delegates had pointedly omitted any reference to the League—as if even a word of allusion might set the ghost of Woodrow Wilson's failure walking the stage of the San Francisco Opera House. In the Charter, even where convenience would have dictated identity of nomenclature, pains seemed to have been taken to avoid it—e.g., in the substitution of "Trusteeship" for "Mandate" or "The International Court of Justice" for "The Permanent Court of Justice."

In fact, however, at San Francisco as at Dumbarton Oaks, the delegates paid the League a much more profound tribute than any formal eulogy could have expressed: they copied it. Attention then and since naturally concentrated on the points of difference between the Covenant and the Charter, but the most obvious fact, so obvious as to be taken for granted, is the basic identity of objectives and methods, of plan and structure. "Peace and security" are the main goals, however important and desirable the social and economic aims may be. Voluntary association in accordance with certain agreed codes of behaviour remains the accepted method of procedure. The sovereign state is still the unit of membership. In each body four main organs of basically the same character discharge roughly the same functions—an assembly, to which all members belong; a council, built around a nucleus of great powers; a secretariat, permanent and international, under an elected secretary-general; and a court, as it were adjacent to rather than incorporated in the main structure.

The General Assembly, in composition, is the League Assembly over

* Herbert G. Nicholas, "Covenant and Charter," in *The United Nations as a Political Institution* (London: Oxford University Press, 1959). Chap. II, pp. 14-40, © Oxford University Press, 1959. Published under the auspices of the Royal Institute of International Affairs. By permission of Oxford University Press.

Herbert G. Nicholas is a fellow of New College, Oxford, and Nuffield Reader in the Comparative Study of Institutions at the University of Oxford. He is the author of *The United Nations as a Political Institution* and *Britain and the U.S.A.*

again, the forum in which all member states are represented with equal rights of speech and vote. After San Francisco it was at first widely thought that the U.N. had drawn a clearer line than the League between the functions of its Assembly and its Council, giving the latter a more nearly exclusive responsibility in face of threats to peace and security. Whereas the Covenant had rather sweepingly permitted the League Assembly, like the Council, to "deal . . . with any matter within the sphere of action of the League or affecting the peace of the world" (Article III, paragraph 3), the Charter, while leaving the General Assembly equally wide powers of discussion, sharply restricts it in the making of recommendations. Where matters of peace and security are concerned the Security Council has priority, and the General Assembly may make recommendations only when the Security Council is not dealing with a question or when, for any reason, the Security Council asks the General Assembly to recommend. In fact, as we shall see, this distinction has become, to say the least of it, considerably blurred in practice.

In one direction the Charter enlarged the Assembly's powers. Where economic, social, and mandate questions were concerned the League had entrusted principal responsibility to its Council, charging it with the direction of the League's technical bodies and the supervision of the Mandates Commission. The Charter, virtually restricting the Security Council to "peace and security," gave to the General Assembly an exclusive ultimate authority in the other fields. This, however, must be read against the background of two facts, the first that the Charter also established two specialized Councils, the Economic and Social Council (ECOSOC) and the Trusteeship Council, with proximate authority in their own spheres, and the second that much of the enormous expansion of international activity in the social and economic fields has in fact escaped U.N. control, the separate specialized agencies having sprouted up alongside with a strong independent life of their own.

In procedure the U.N. introduced one important novelty. It abandoned the League's principle of unanimity. In both the Assembly and the Council of the League one hostile vote could prevent a decision (although, as we shall see, the League had its own devices for escaping from this strait-jacket). The U.N. Assembly was empowered, by contrast, to make decisions by majority vote—in the case of "important decisions," by a two-thirds majority. Similarly, the Security Council, as we have seen, reserves its veto for its permanent members; if they concur, an affirmative vote of seven out of its eleven members carries the day.

In structure the Security Council closely parallels its League predecessor, with its core of permanent Great Power members and its elected non-permanent members. The League Council, however, was more fluid, permitting changes in the composition of the Great Power core and the numbers of the elected members, and even the emergence of a category of "semi-permanents." Such fluidity was possible because the League Assembly was given authority to control the Council's composition. The Security Council structure is rooted in the Charter itself, and its form of composition can only be changed by Charter amendment.

More specialized in its function, the Security Council was also designed to be more potent in its operation. It was empowered to decide on behalf of the whole U.N. whether peace is threatened and whether sanctions should be applied, and such decisions, when taken, were to be binding on all members. For this purpose the Security Council was to be equipped with a special organ, a Military Staff Committee composed of the Chiefs of Staff of all the permanent members. This body would make advance plans for the organization and deployment of military forces which member states would place at the disposal of the organization and, when the Council acted, the Committee would serve as its strategic adviser.

The Charter says a good deal more about economic and social objectives than the Covenant did. Nevertheless, by 1939 the League's work in this sphere had so greatly expanded as to lead to a proposal that a new League organization, the Central Committee for Economic and Social Questions, should be created to supervise what the League was doing in this field. This proposal was the seed which in the Charter flowered as ECOSOC, a separate organ of the U.N., "under the authority of the General Assembly," to which it must report. ECOSOC was made responsible for the work of the U.N. in these fields. It was also charged with the task of co-ordinating the work of the specialized agencies, though it was given no coercive powers for this purpose. Its membership was restricted to eighteen, with, in theory, no reserved seats for Great Powers or anyone else.

To look after its mandates and its mandatories the League had established a Commission on which sat nine (subsequently ten) independent experts, in no way official spokesmen of their governments, four of whom were always from mandatory countries. The Permanent Mandates Commission was advisory to the League Council, in which ultimate responsibility was lodged, though in fact the League Assembly also made its voice heard frequently on mandates questions. The U.N. confined ultimate authority to the General Assembly, but, in effect, raised the Mandates Commission to the level of a separate organ under the title of the Trusteeship Council. As under the League, oversight can only be exercised by agreement with the controlling [sic], trusteeship power and moral pressure is the Council's only weapon. The Council was, however, given one power the Commission never enjoyed; it can visit trust territories for itself. Moreover, Chapter XI of the Charter, the Declaration Regarding Non-Self-Governing Territories, though only an unenforceable statement of professions, does impose on all member states who have colonies an administrative code which is morally binding on them. The Trusteeship Council consists not of experts but of representatives of member states—all the administering powers, together with all non-administering members of the Big Five, plus members elected by the General Assembly. The General Assembly elects as many members as are needed to make the numbers of trusteeship and non-trusteeship states equal.

The Charter provided for a Secretariat to serve all these bodies and its provisions in this regard adhered closely to League practice. There was, however, one significant exception: the Secretary-General, under Article 99, was given an explicit political role, by being empowered, of his own initiative, to bring to the attention of the Security Council any matter which might endanger peace and security.

❋   ❋   ❋   ❋   ❋   ❋   ❋

Just as the structure of the U.N. rested upon a League basis, so its philosophical foundations went down into a Geneva subsoil and indeed beyond. In *The League of Nations and the Rule of Law* the late Sir Alfred Zimmern disentangled the ideas which underlay the League Covenant and traced them both to their origins in the earlier history of international organization. It is instructive to examine the Charter in the same way and see what diverse, and at points, discrepant, concepts were combined in it and also how far it re-embodied the ideas of the Covenant and of the working League.

Zimmern found the first influence upon the Covenant in the concept of the Concert of the Great Powers with its roots going back at least as far as the "Congress System" of Castlereagh. The essence of this system was to be found in the regular conferences of the powers whose strength both permitted and obliged them to accept special responsibility for the organization of international order. The League Council was essentially the embodiment of this concept, with the privileged position of its permanent members and its regular meetings.

From the start the thinking of the architects of the U.N. revolved around this concept. The events of 1940–1945, which provided the context for the work of Charter-making, were dominated by "the Grand Alliance," as Churchill called it. The successful prosecution of the war, the indispensable precondition of any successful organization for peace, had depended on a continuous harmonization of Great Power policies through the mechanism of meetings of heads of state, foreign ministers or military chiefs. The harmonization had often been imperfect, but recognition was general, apparently even in Russia, that without it victory would probably not have been achieved. It seemed only logical therefore to build any permanent organization for peace and security upon the same cornerstone.

Consequently the idea of the Concert is to be found at the heart of the Charter. The Security Council gives it structural embodiment, as in the League, with the Great Powers given permanent seats, the five of them being actually named in the constitutional document (Article 23). The veto is the symbol of their privileged position and the constitutional weapon by which they defend it. The other members explicitly recognize their role; they "confer on the Security Council primary responsibility for the maintenance of peace and security, and agree that in carrying out its duties under this responsibility the Security Council acts on their behalf" (Article 24). Moreover, (Article 25) "the Members of the U.N. agree to accept and carry out decisions of the Security Council in accordance with the Charter," even when these decisions involve (Chapter VII) calling upon the members to apply sanctions, up to and including armed force. This indeed was going beyond the Castlereagh concept of the Concert, just as it was going beyond the League Council's potency. It was practically a return, in institutional form, to the Quadruple Alliance system, with the Great Powers acting jointly to keep the peace amongst the rest. To this end the Security Council was to be equipped with its Military Staff Committee; it was to be a permanent policeman of the world.

The Assembly of the League had originally been conceived as a sort of outer circle of conferring powers, without exceptional privileges or responsibilities, meeting less often—perhaps even (so the Foreign Office had originally contemplated) at four-yearly intervals. In fact, as the Covenant took shape, and still more obviously as the League began to function, the Assembly became something very much more than this. Exactly what it was—an annual conference of the whole League world, a "parliament" to the Council's "cabinet," a universal forum for debate and complaint—no one quite liked to say. It was more than some of these labels implied, less than others claimed. It was, indeed, *sui generis*; whether intentionally or not it was the League's nearest approach to a political invention.

The framers of the Charter seem to have approached this section of their work with no clearer concept to guide them than the Wilsonians had had. There was never any shadow of doubt amongst them (not even, apparently, amongst the Russians) that there must be an Assembly; that—provided certain qualifications were met—the U.N. must include, at this level, all the powers, however impotent, and that the obvious model was the Assembly of the League. The exact powers and functions of the General Assembly appear to have been determined, however, not in accordance with any particular theory but as the result of a tug-of-war between (broadly speaking) the Great Powers and the rest. The Great Powers, provided they got their Security Council, were prepared to make concessions to the Assembly elsewhere—e.g., in the social, economic, and trusteeship fields; the other powers aspired to share in as much of the Concert as they could and pressed for as extensive a participation of the General Assembly in all fields as they could obtain. Such black and white terms, of course, do violence to the many shades of opinion that were represented at San Francisco, but it is broadly true to say that the Charter's allocation of power between Council and Assembly reflects some such division of views.

Zimmern and many other writers have traced the development of international organization on its non-political side, in respect of the provision of what he called "World Services," back to the establishment of the Universal Postal Union in 1874. The Covenant, as is well known, incorporated a good deal of "international functionalism," in the role it envisaged for the League in social and economic matters, in its provision of a permanent Secretariat which would collect and provide information, and in the way it enthroned the League (under Article XXIV) as a kind of super-directorate for all existing international bureaux. Functionalism, as we have seen, was a strong influence playing upon the thinking of the Charter-framers, both at Dumbarton Oaks and at San Francisco, and the impact of this "World Services" concept is even more marked in the Charter than it was in the Covenant. Structurally it manifests itself in the Economic and Social Council, and administratively in the co-ordinating role accorded to it in relation to other international organizations (Articles 63 and 64). In fact, however, the concept has been so expanded as almost to be transformed. Just as the nation-state has carried its provision of domestic services far beyond such bare essentials as roads and post offices and now provides for health, employment and higher productivity to such an extent that we speak of "the welfare state," so at the international level by 1945 expectations of what world organization could and should do had passed far beyond the limited, though solid, achievements of the "World Services" side of the League. There was a demand for a sort of "Welfare Internationalism" which would do far more than regulate; it would promote and share; promote health, education, productivity and full employment, share raw materials, technical skills, and perhaps even capital. "Welfare Internationalism" very seldom took the form of a clearly argued and thought-out theory of international action or organization; it was rather the reflection of a diffused set of dissatisfactions and aspirations—unevenly felt, but where felt, as in the so-called "under-developed areas," capable of generating a head of steam which the otherwise indifferent powers could not ignore. The result of this, as far as the Charter was concerned, was what might be expected. Far more than the Covenant, the Charter was lavish with pledges and good intentions. There is not a word in the Covenant to say that people should not starve, but the Preamble to the Charter talks about a determination "to promote social progress and better standards of life" and "the economic and social advancement of all peoples"; the Purposes of the U.N., as defined in Article 1, include "co-operation in solving international problems of an economic, social, cultural or humanitarian character," etc.; the obligations of the organization, as set out in Article 55, include the promotion of "higher standards of living, full employment, and conditions of economic and social progress and development." The catalogue of such phrases is not exhaustive. But compared with the precision of the Charter's provisions in the political field what strikes one about the "Welfare Internationalism" of the Charter is its vagueness, both structurally (as we shall see when we examine the Economic and Social Council) and procedurally, in the lack of clear indications as to the processes by which the organization is to realize its pledges in these fields. Some of this vagueness, of course, is due to the success of the most practical "functionalists" in setting up their own independent agencies outside the U.N., but most of it is due to the comparative novelty of the whole concept and the disposition, in what most of the Charter-framers felt to be a secondary matter, to let verbal inflation be a substitute for hard thinking.

The Concert and World Services concepts between them would have accounted, even by themselves, for most of the U.N. structure as the Charter adumbrates it. But the mode of functioning of the U.N., like that of the League before it, was an expression of other ideas as well, especially where the primary purpose of the two organizations, the maintenance of peace and security, was involved. Zimmern isolated one of these ideas as a distinctively Wilsonian one and gave to it the not altogether happy label of the "Monroe Doctrine System," a name which more accurately describes its ancestry than its functioning. In the Covenant it finds its most explicit expression in Article X, the Article of Mutual Guarantee, by which members "undertake to respect and preserve as against external aggression the territorial integrity and existing political independence" of each other's countries. The Covenant, viewed in this aspect, becomes an extension, to the point of becoming a universalization, of the old-fashioned bilateral treaty of guarantee, by which A undertakes to protect B or (if the two parties are of more equal strength) A and B undertake to protect each other. This is the concept of "one for all and all for one" which later earns the name of Collective Security.

In the Charter, Article 2, §4, affirms: "All Members shall refrain in their international relations from the threat or use of force against the territorial integrity or political independence of any state," a pledge which clearly reproduces half of the undertaking that League members assumed in Article X. What is notably absent is the obligation to *preserve* as well as *respect*— in other words the positive as opposed to the merely negative aspect of the Mutual Guarantee. Why is this? In the British Government's official commentary on the Dumbarton Oaks proposals (Cmd. 6571) this failure to reproduce *in toto* the guarantee of Article X is explained on the ground that, literally interpreted, such a guarantee would freeze the territorial *status quo* "for all time," that the recognition given elsewhere (Article 2, §1) to the general principle of "sovereign equality" protects states against arbitrary molestation, and above all that the Charter contains elsewhere an "absolute" undertaking to prevent war together with much more definite obligations on states to secure that end. The reference is to the authority given to the Security Council by Articles 39, 41, and 42 to act to the full in face of a breach of the peace, threatened or actual, and the powers given to it to call on other members for support. In other words the Guarantee loses something of its complete Mutuality, becoming instead more of a Guarantee by the Strong of the Weak. Such was certainly the main thinking of those who drew up the Charter, particularly the Great Powers. In fact, as events were to show, the failure of the permanent members of the Security Council to agree led to the atrophying of this concept to a point where it virtually reverted, in so far it retained vitality at all, to something like the Mutual Guarantee concept of the League.

Closely allied to the Mutual Guarantee concept in the framing of the League Covenant was what in 1918 the British Judge, Lord Parker, called the principle of the "Hue and Cry" and which found contemporaneous expression in memorandum of Mr. Elihu Root. This was, in essence, the idea that war, as such, was a matter of universal concern, no matter where it occurred, and also a crime against the world community. The world organization should therefore organize a joint and mutual guarantee of all its members, not primarily in defence of their territory and their independence, but against any act of war however arising. This found partial expression in the Covenant's Article XI with its assertion that "Any war or threat of war, whether immediately affecting any of the Members of the League or not, is hereby declared a matter of concern to the whole League." The force of the principle was, however, sensibly abated by the lack of any clear and automatic machinery to give effect to it. Individual states were left free to decide whether or not they would join in the "Hue and Cry" and, by Article XII, resort to war was still permitted under certain limited circumstances.

In 1928 the Pact of Paris, or the Kellog–Briand Pact, sought to carry the idea of "the outlawry of war" a step further. By this the sixty-five states which ultimately adhered to the Pact declared "that they condemn recourse to war . . . and renounce it as an instrument of national policy" and accepted an obligation to settle all disputes or conflicts "by pacific means." As a profession of good intentions the Pact was unexceptionable, but the claim that it "outlawed war" was excessive. War was only "condemned" and "renounced" and no enforcement machinery of any kind was provided. Above all, signatory states made it clear that they did not interpret the Pact as in any way limiting the right of "self-defence," with all the possibilities of broad interpretation therein implied.

It was contended in respect of the "Hue and Cry" concept that it assumed the existence of the rudiments of a world community, and some critics of the League, after its failures over Manchuria and Ethiopia, argued that its experiences then proved that no such rudiments existed. When the U.N. was being framed a slightly different assumption prevailed—that whether or not a world community existed there was a Five Power community with world-wide strength. The logical deduction from this assumption was that the primary responsibility for organizing the Hue and Cry should rest on the Big Five—in other words on that expanded and strengthened manifestation of the Concert which is the Security Council, functioning continuously and equipped with force. Thus in one sense the universal concern over any outbreak of war is narrowed; in the first instance, as in Article 39, it is the Security Council's business to "determine the existence of any threat to the peace," etc., and to "decide what measures shall be taken." On the other hand once the Security Council has made a decision it may call upon all the members, under Article 41, to apply it—and such a call is mandatory; the members are pledged by Articles 25 and 49 to respond. Thus, although the Charter contains no phrase explicitly paralleling Article XI's sweeping assertion that "any war" is "a matter of concern to the whole" membership, the U.N. system is, in effect, organized on that assumption. Furthermore, its founders would have claimed, it goes far beyond the League or the Pact of Paris in the provisions contained in the Charter for giving effect to this belief. As the British official commentary on the Dumbarton Oaks proposals put it: "While the Covenant in certain cases allowed war to be made legally . . . the new organization would not only try to abolish the use of all violence between States but could intervene even when violence is merely threatened."

Wider than the Concert, weaker than the Hue and Cry, there was a third instrument of the pre-1918 world that had provided the League founders with a set of habits and techniques which they sought to incorporate in the Covenant. This was the Hague Conference system. The essence of the system lay in the procedures it developed for the peaceful settlement of disputes by the processes of mediation, conciliation and inquiry, laying down a workable body of rules, and making available a permanent secretariat and a body of arbitrators. The system of itself cannot stop aggression; its function is to facilitate a settlement where the disputants want one and to mobilize public opinion in favour of a peaceful solution even where they do not.

This system was taken over virtually in its entirety by the League and may be found embodied in the Covenant in all those Articles from XII to XV inclusive which set out the agreed processes for settling disputes, either by arbitration, or by judicial settlement through the Permanent Court, or by submission to the Council and ultimately to the Assembly. The Covenant, however, put a novel coping-stone on this structure by Article XVI, providing that any power which flouted this machinery and resorted to war should have invoked against it automatic financial and economic sanctions and conditional military sanctions. (There was a loophole in this procedure, as in the Hue and Cry system; it consisted in the exemption from these procedures of any dispute arising out of a matter solely within the domestic jurisdiction of a member.)

The U.N. took over practically the whole of what the League had incorporated of the Hague Conference system. In Article 1, §1, the Charter announces its purpose "to bring about by peaceful means, and in conformity with the principles of justice and international law, adjustment or settlement of international disputes or situations which might lead to a breach of the peace." The whole of Chapter VI of the Charter, "Pacific Settlement of Disputes," is devoted to an elaboration of the processes which give effect to this purpose, while Chapter XIV outlines the functioning of the International Court in this connexion. The processes set out in Chapter VI run the gamut from direct negotiation between the affected parties, inquiry, mediation, conciliation, arbitration, judicial settlement, and recommendation by the Security Council. The following Chapter VII sets out the ensuing sequence of more militant U.N. action if the dispute, still unsettled after the exhaustion of these processes, becomes a threat to the peace. Although Article 35 permits disputes to be brought before the General Assembly as well, the emphasis in the wording throughout is on *Security Council* action, and clearly the framers expected that in this sphere, as in the sphere of enforcement, the Council would be the prime mover. The Charter does not, of course, any more than the Covenant, give to the world organization any power to impose a settlement of its members' disputes. It provides an elaborate adaptable machinery for settlement which it expects them to use, but no organ of the U.N., not even the Security Council, is empowered to impose a decision. In the event of the dispute developing into a threat to peace and security the Council can certainly act, but again not to impose a decision, but only to preserve the peace. The U.N. is not a world government.

These are the main strands of thought which were woven into the Charter. Subsidiary to them, but still important, are a number of other concepts which found their way, at one level or another, into the Charter, just as in many instances they had found their way into the Covenant. One of these was disarmament. The thinking of the first Hague Conference on this subject became the thinking of Geneva—that armaments were not only an instrument of war but also a cause of war; consequently disarmament was a proper concern of a world organization. In the Covenant this had found expression in Article VIII, by which members, recognizing "that the maintenance of peace requires the reduction of national armaments to the lowest point consistent with national safety and the enforcement by common action of international obligations," gave to the League Council power to produce a disarmament plan which, once accepted by governments, would set upper limits to their forces. The experience of the inter-war years had weakened enthusiasm for disarmament *per se*; the events of the thirties seemed to suggest that it was not armaments as such, but armaments in the wrong hands which endangered peace, that indeed the "peace-loving" nations ought to remain armed if aggression was to be prevented or repulsed. This line of thinking is reflected in the Charter in a much reduced emphasis on disarmament for its own sake. There are two references to the idea: in Article 11 the General Assembly is empowered to consider and make recommendations about the "principles governing disarmament and the regulation of armaments" and in Article 26, in order to establish peace and security "with the least diversion for armaments of the world's human and economic resources," the Security Council is made responsible, with the aid of the Military Staff Committee, for formulating plans "for the establishment of a system for the regulation of armaments." There is here no recognition that peace requires "the reduction of armaments"; the emphasis is more on regulation and much less on disarmament; and nothing is said anywhere about that "interchange of full and frank information" about national armaments which members of the League had sworn to provide (though they notably failed to live up to their promises). Indeed the whole concept of a policing Security Council with a Military Staff Committee implies that adequate force must always be available to the organization. This reflects, of course, the pervasive Churchill–Roosevelt conviction that World War II had been due as much to the weakness of the democracies as to the aggressiveness of the Axis and that the greatest mistake of the victors after World War I had been the precipitate dismantling of their military structure. It is quite possible, too, that the thinking of the Charter on this subject might have been different if the San Francisco Conference had been held after Hiroshima, instead of ending a month before.

We have seen how, so far as structure is concerned, the League's Mandates Commission had been made over, expanded and strengthened, as the U.N.'s Trusteeship Council. The theory of international action in this field had similarly developed in the years between Versailles and San Francisco. Broadly speaking, three sets of ideas can be traced in the Covenant's provisions for a Mandates system: first, the concept of *condominium*, joint supervision of certain disputed areas (such as had been practised in the Congo); second, the concept of trusteeship exercised by an imperial power on behalf of its dependent peoples (as by Britain in India or France in Africa); and third, the concept of the Great Powers as a Concert exercising a collective responsibility to co-ordinate and promote their interests in areas, like the Ottoman Empire or the Congo, which were "unsettled" or "backward." The League system, with its recognition of the power and privilege of the mandatory and its safeguards, sometimes more nominal than real, for the "mandated," represented an imperfect blend of these three concepts. The inter-war years had been marked by a growing demand all over the world for the application of the principle of "self-determination" to dependent peoples. Most of the colonial powers in varying degrees accepted self-government as the goal of their administration, as for example the British in India and the Americans in the Philippines. Little remained after the

Versailles Treaty of any outright imperialist theory that colonies existed merely for the interest of the imperial powers. Argument was confined to the question of in what forms and with what sincerity colonial powers were discharging their responsibilities in their territories. Furthermore, the war had simultaneously weakened the prestige of the imperial powers—particularly in the Far East—and accelerated the drive for self-determination among hitherto dependent peoples. Finally two of the Great Powers at San Francisco were in a crusading anti-imperialist mood (with, of course, appropriate private reservations)—the U.S.A. under the influence of the Legend of 1776 and the promptings of Franklin Roosevelt, and the U.S.S.R. in accordance with the principles of Marxism–Leninism as interpreted by Stalin.

The impact of these forces on the Charter is observable not only in the status of the Trusteeship Council—a separate and "principal" organ—but still more in the extension of the U.N.'s interest to cover not just mandated territories but others as well. Article XXIIIb of the League Covenant had pledged League members to secure "just treatment of the native inhabitants of territories under their control" but this unenforceable expression of good intent was the only mention in the Covenant of colonial peoples, except for those who having lost their wartime masters were put under the mandates system. The Charter, by contrast, contains a lengthy "Declaration Concerning Non-Self-Governing Territories" (Chapter XI). This, admittedly, is no more enforceable than the Covenant's article but its range and precision create a stronger moral pressure on members and demonstrate how far the concept of an international responsibility for dependent peoples had developed since Geneva. In place of the indefinable "just treatment" of the Covenant we have a recognition that the interests of the natives are to be paramount, that their *political,* as well as economic, social, and educational advancement is to be ensured, that "self-government" is to be developed, that "constructive measures of development" are to be promoted and "research" encouraged; above all, that imperial powers are "to transmit regularly to the Secretary-General for information purposes, subject to such limitation as security and constitutional considerations may require, statistical and other information of a technical nature relating to economic, social, and educational conditions." The careful wording of these clauses reveals immediately that the imperial powers did not accept at San Francisco any administrative role for the U.N. in their colonial territories, any more than they admitted the U.N. into the domestic business of their homelands. For all that, these clauses undoubtedly represent the admission of a new concept —the claim of an international organization in principle to interest itself in the affairs of dependent peoples, even those who do not come under the umbrella of its mandates.

The same disposition to expand the concept of what is legitimately of international concern is to be seen in the language of the Charter about "human rights." The League Covenant had admitted, in Article XXIII, to a marginal interest in these fields, but only where labour conditions were concerned (the ILO, of course, was a fuller exemplification of this) and where the traffic in women and children was involved. The Charter, by contrast, not only sounds off in wide terms in its Preamble—"determined . . . to reaffirm faith in fundamental human rights, in the dignity and worth of the human person, in the equal rights of men and women and of nations large and small"—and in its Purposes Article (1, §3)—"to achieve international co-operation . . . in promoting and encouraging respect for human rights and for fundamental freedoms for all without distinction as to race, sex, language or religion"—but also, in Article 55c, commits the U.N. to promoting "universal respect for, and observance of, human rights and fundamental freedoms," etc. Article 62 directs the Economic and Social Council to make recommendations in pursuance of this and finally, Article 68 bids it set up a separate commission "for the promotion of human rights."

Behind this plenitude of language there stood no very clearly defined philosophy of international action such as would explain how an international agency whose members were sovereign states was going to be able to protect the rights of individuals dwelling within the boundaries of those same sovereign states. Still less did the Charter explain how this could be done without infringing Article 2, §7, which expressly forbids intervention "in matters which are essentially within the domestic jurisdiction" of states. Historically, however, the appearance of this concept in the Charter is explicable enough. By 1945 the world had become fully and sickeningly aware of the outrages perpetrated against humanity by the Nazi and Japanese regimes (though much less aware of what went on in the U.S.S.R.). The Nuremberg prosecutions were an indication of the widespread demand for an authority which could go behind national sovereignty and "reasons of state" and bring the perpetrators of such outrages to book. The human rights clauses of the Charter, like so many other clauses, looked backward in a "never again" spirit and drew their inspiration more from a revulsion at the past than from any very clear programme for the future. . . . However this may be, the idea, for all its vagueness—largely because of its vagueness— was popular at San Francisco, not least amongst those countries whose domestic record in the field of civil liberties left most to be desired. Meanwhile, those countries which were sceptical contented themselves with the reflection that these humanitarian clauses were merely recommendatory and did not endow the organization with any powers of enforcement.

The time had been, in the heyday of Cobdenism, when free trade appeared to be, of itself, an adequate solvent of war, as well as an essential ingredient of peace. There remained in 1919 enough vitality in this Victorian concept to secure it some recognition in the League Covenant. The third of Woodrow Wilson's Fourteen Points had called for the "removal, as far as possible, of all economic barriers and the establishment of an equality of trade conditions among all the nations consenting to the peace." This had appeared, considerably modified, as Article XXIIIe of the Covenant: "The Members of the League will make provision to secure and maintain . . . equitable treatment for the commerce of all Members of the League."

After World War II the principal apostle of the Cobdenite faith was Mr. Cordell Hull. That an American Secretary of State, representing a traditionally protectionist power, should preach the gospel of free trade, is explicable largely by the fact that Mr. Hull, like Wilson before him, was both a Democrat and a Southerner, and in each capacity had been engaged in trying to convert his fellow countrymen, as well as the rest of the world, to a belief in the virtues of non-discrimination. Under such impetus the U.S.A. during the war had used its Lend-Lease programme as a powerful lever to exact compliance from its allies in its liberal objectives; each Lend-Lease Agreement contained a clause by which the recipient agreed to the "expansion . . . of production, employment, and the exchange and consumption of goods . . . the elimination of all forms of discriminatory treatment in international commerce . . . [and] the reduction of tariffs and other trade barriers." However, when it came to Charter-drafting, it appeared that even the U.S.A. was not as wholeheartedly committed to these objectives as its language towards its allies made it appear. Strong conservative and protectionist elements made their influence felt in Washington and subsequently at San Francisco, while, of course, Britain, the homeland of Cobdenism, was now more concerned to preserve the Commonwealth preferences than to gamble on her chances in a free-trade world. In any case the almost universal decline in *laissez faire* economics, domestic as well as foreign, meant that the emphasis even amongst the internationalists was now much less on the mere removal of trade barriers and much more on positive action to promote productivity and high levels of employment. The result is to be seen in the Charter in the absence of any reference at all to the desirability of freer trading, as such. In all the plenitude of language in the Preamble, Purposes, and Economic and Social Chapters there is nothing that goes as far even as the Covenant's Article XXIII. Instead, besides the "International Welfare" references to "higher living standards, full employment," etc., already mentioned, there are references to "international co-operation in solving international problems of an economic . . . character" (Article 1), or to "promoting international co-operation in the economic . . . fields" (Article 13), or to "conditions of economic . . . progress and development" (Article 55a). These are broad terms and it is open to members to read into them, if they wish, endorsement for liberal trade policies (as indeed was subsequently done by the promoters of the international Trade Organization and the General Agreement on Tariffs and Trade), but taken all together they constitute only the most shadowy relic of the Cobdenite faith in the world made safe from war by the unhindered enterprise of its producers and traders.

The League, though envisaged as a universal organization, with what might be described as a European–Atlantic core, had admitted into the Covenant a recognition of regionalism, inspired originally by the American sensitivity over the Monroe Doctrine, but persisting in its final form as a legalization of other regional arrangements as well. This was Article XXI; "Nothing in this Covenant shall be deemed to affect the validity of international engagements, such as treaties of arbitration or regional understandings like the Monroe Doctrine, for securing the maintenance of peace." This Article made possible the legalization of such regional alliances as the Little Entente and the Balkan Entente and such arrangements as Locarno. It also opened the door, in some critics' opinion, to a revival of the pre-war alliance system which, in the eyes of leaders such as Wilson, the League had been created to supersede. What is certain is that it represented the persistence into the League period of a reliance on security arrangements originally belonging to a pre-League world.

The League's failure as a universal organization for the preservation of peace and security seemed to one veteran of the inter-war years to point the need for constructing its successor round a frankly regional core. We have seen how at one stage in the evolution of the U.N. Mr. Churchill had advocated an organization built out of a group of regional security systems. At the time and in its original form this idea had been rejected not only by the other Great Power achitects of the U.N. but also, it seems, by Mr. Churchill's Cabinet colleagues at home. Instead, the verdict had been cast in favour of a universal organization of security with a hard core of power and responsibility at the centre. Nothing, however, could obscure the plain fact that over many areas of the world regional arrangements were either in effect or in contemplation, such as gave their members a closer community of interest and feeling and a stronger guarantee of protection than a fledgling universal agency could provide. Recognition of this was initially made at Dumbarton Oaks, where approval was accorded to such bodies, provided their powers of enforcement were to be employed only with "the authorization of the Security Council." At San Francisco the pressures in favour of recognizing regional arrangements were greater even than at Dumbarton Oaks. Not only were there Great Power interests; there were also the pressures coming from smaller states which were members, in fact or in contemplation, of the Inter-American system, the British Commonwealth or the Arab League. They professed concern lest a Security Council with a Great Power veto might prevent swift action by a regional organization; accordingly the Dumbarton Oaks proviso was itself equipped with a loophole—it would not apply where action was being taken against a state which had been an "enemy" in World War II (Article 53). More sweeping, however, was the licence accorded to regional alliances by the addition of an entirely novel Article, No. 51, which does not indeed in so many words contain any reference to regionalism or alliances. What it does, however, is to give explicit authorization to "the inherent right of . . . self-defence," and by recognizing that "self-defence" may be either "individual or collective" goes far to give *carte blanche* to the establishment and free operation of almost any regional arrangement. Whether such a concept is incompatible with the essential purpose of the U.N., however, depends less on the conformity or inconsistency of the two ideas in the abstract than on the applications accorded to them in practice.

PART **II**

THE GENERAL NATURE
OF INTERNATIONAL
ORGANIZATION

CHAPTER **3**

MULTIPURPOSE ORGANIZATION

The kinds of questions which were raised for consideration at the end of the introduction to Part I are germane to the discussion presented by Stanley Hoffmann in this part. He points to the internationalization of politics and of political issues. This development may be attributed in part to the objectives of the major powers as well as to the methods they use to obtain those objectives. And in part it is a reflection of the role of many of the smaller states who are incapable of providing for their own basic needs and wants, but who are uncertain regarding the extent and nature of their relationships with the larger nations.

Hoffmann presents his consideration of what international organization should be. In essence he supports the functionalists' contention that the transference of individual loyalties can come only when an international organization is able to provide those benefits (or, perhaps, to create the impression it does) which are now generally attributable to the state. But he argues that in the case of the new states a "national" stage will have to be reached before the individual can give up the services, protections, and sense of justice which he normally expects from his own state. Hoffmann contends that the economic realm provides the key to this transference. This contention is likely to be less arguable than his view that a federation of states may result in the same centralizing tendencies of present institutions, the net effect being that we have only substituted a larger leviathan for a smaller one.

The author suggests two tests in judging the role of the political organs of the United Nations: (1) Will a proposal increase, decrease, or leave unchanged the level of international tensions? and (2) Is a proposal backed by a sufficient combination of forces and interests to make it feasible? These are interesting questions to raise, but do they really move us forward in improving the performance of the Organization or increasing the effectiveness of its organs? What information can be used to make a priori judgments? If we take the first question for examination, we might assume that there should never have been any resolutions condemning colonialism and criticizing France for its role in Algeria[1] before it agreed to Algeria independence. We might assume this because of the increase in tension which the resolutions created. But, clearly, they greatly helped to reduce the extent of colonialism, which in turn improved the image of the United Nations in the minds of many people and many states. The increased tension from that resolution was short-lived and, one may assume, redounded to the benefit of the Organization. Perhaps the subject of the tension and the parties involved are more important than the mere existence of tension.

As for the test relating to the sufficiency of interests and forces, the picture is again not clear. In the first place, we have seen quite often that success feeds upon itself. However, the degree to which economic development is considered worthy today is related to the results of earlier programs about which feelings were confused at the time. The question is: at what point ought efforts be made on the assumption that the interests and forces backing a project are sufficient? Large-scale economic projects based on low interest rates, like the sunfed idea, have been urged for a long time. It seems quite plausible that, if this program were given wide support, especially by the countries whose money is needed, it would become an acceptable and popular aspect of United Nations programming, and probably would greatly reduce some of the tensions referred to in the first question.

Although Hoffmann's article was written several years ago there is little reason to challenge his argument that the UN benefits our world by acting as a moderating influence on antagonisms of the superpowers and as a center of cooperation between the old nations and the new. The significance of its

---

[1] General Assembly Resolution 1573 (XV), 19 Dec. 1960.

peace-keeping efforts would likewise have to be considered, and the student may want to reflect further upon this peace-keeping function after reading Part V. He will also want to consider whether Hoffmann's stress on the role of the states as the central actors in international politics does not rob the UN of an independence of stature and thus of a significant contribution which ought to be explicitly acknowledged rather than implicitly ignored.

FURTHER READINGS

Alger, Chadwick F., "Comparison of Intranational and International Politics," *American Political Science Review*, June 1963.

Bloomfield, Lincoln, "The United States, the United Nations and the Creation of Community," *International Organization*, Vol. XIV, 1960, pp. 503–513.

Claude, Inis P., *Swords into Plowshares*, 3rd rev. ed. New York: Random House, 1964, Chaps. 1 and 2.

THE ROLE OF INTERNATIONAL ORGANIZATION: LIMITS AND POSSIBILITIES

Stanley Hoffmann*

No field of study is more slippery than international relations. The student of government has a clear frame of reference: the state within which occur the developments which he examines. The student of international relations, unhappily, oscillates between the assumption of a world community which does not exist, except as an ideal, and the various units whose decisions and connections form the pattern of world politics—mainly, the nation-states. International organizations therefore tend to be considered either as the first institutions of a world in search of its constitution or as instruments of foreign policies. The scholar who follows the first approach usually blames, correctly enough, the nation-states for the failures of the organization; but he rarely indicates the means which could be used to bring the realities of world society into line with his ideal. The scholar who takes the second approach stresses, accurately enough, how limited the autonomy of international organizations has been and how little they have contributed to the achievement of their objectives; but because he does not discuss his fundamental assumption—the permanence of the nation-state's driving role in world politics—he reaches somewhat too easily the conclusion that the only prospect in international affairs is more of the same.

It may well be that this conclusion, too, is justified, but it should not be arrived at through a shortcut. The approach which seems the most satisfactory, though not the simplest, should be the following one. First, the objectives defined by the Charter of the United Nations are to be considered as the best moral goals statesmen can pursue; that is, the maintenance of peace and security, the promotion of economic, social and cultural co-operation, respect for human rights, and the establishment of procedures for peaceful change. (Implicit in this assumption is, of course, another one: it is legitimate that statesmen should assign moral ends to their policies, and that states' activities should be submitted to moral judgments, the absence of a single, supranational system of values notwithstanding.) Secondly, the

* Stanley Hoffmann, "The Role of International Organization: Limits and Possibilities," *International Organization*, Vol. 10, 1956, pp. 357-372. Copyright 1956, World Peace Foundation. By permission of *International Organization*.

Stanley Hoffmann is Professor of Government at Harvard University and a member of the Board of Editors of *International Organization*. He is the author of *Contemporary Theory in International Relations*.

means through which these objectives are to be sought are necessarily inter-national agreements; no conquest of the world by one nation, or even by an alliance of nations, could bring them about; consent is indispensable, even if it means that they can only be reached gradually and partially. Thirdly, it cannot be assumed at the outset that the present structure of international society *must* be the permanent framework of action, for it may well be that the objectives cannot be reached within such a framework, as, for instance, the World Federalists have argued. Changes in the structure may thus appear necessary. But one has to avoid utopias; if it is unwise to postulate the perpetuation of the present system, it is equally unwise to advocate ways which an analysis of world politics reveals to be blocked.

The problem which we want to discuss briefly can thus be phrased in the following terms: given the present structure of world society, what *should* and what *can* international organizations do to promote the objectives which we have mentioned?

A short analysis of present world society reveals a number of paradoxes and contradictions.

In the first place, the scene is dominated by two opposite developments. On the one hand, there is the phenomenon usually described as bipolarity of power. On the other hand, at the same time that military and economic strength has become centered, temporarily perhaps, in only two superpowers, there has been a trend toward further political disintegration of the world. As the process of "social mobilisation" of hitherto "passive" peoples progresses, the number of sovereign states has increased, and the continuing break-up of former empires will undoubtedly add new ones. Both developments, contradictory as they appear, make the return to a concert of the great powers impossible; the necessary solidarity and fluidity of power are both gone. And yet, the technological gap between the advanced and the backward nations is greater than ever before.

In the second place, the process of interlocking interests and activities, which internationalists once hopefully described as leading inevitably to a world community, has indeed continued. The distinction between internal and international affairs is now ruled out; it has therefore become impossible to prevent one nation from influencing and intervening in the policies of another. The superb autonomy and specialization of diplomacy is over, and nearly the whole world has become a "Turkish question." At the same time, however, the psychological effect of this development has been rebellion and seeking refuge in a conception made for, and reminiscent of, a more idyllic age: the concept of national sovereignty and independence. The contradiction is nowhere more apparent than in the UN itself. The organization has contributed immeasurably to an internationalization of all problems, and to a kind of equalization of diplomatic standards and practices for all members; but at the same time its operations are based on the principle of equality and the myth of sovereignty. The smaller states use sovereignty as a fortress, and the superpowers as a safeguard of their own freedom of action against friendly or hostile restraints.

In the third place, the two sets of factors previously mentioned have produced a fundamental change in the politics of the two leading powers. The great powers of the nineteenth century used limited means for limited objectives. The relations between these powers could easily be described in equations, or at least in mechanistic terms—balancing process, equilibrium, etc. The superpowers of today have trans-national objectives; each one stands both for a certain organization of the world, and for a certain distribution of social forces and political power in each nation. The means they use, with one important exception (the resort to general war), are also much broader. Their emphasis, in the choice of means, is far less on *national* power, far more on gaining allies. As some theorists have shown, this "multiple equilibrium" opens new channels of influence for the two superpowers and creates, at the expense of both, new procedures of restraint quite different from the restraints imposed on the big powers by the European concert. No big power can "go it alone" and define its interests to the exclusion of other nations' interests; the only, though very real and important, choice it has is between more and less broad international definitions of ends and means, depending on the kind and amount of international power it wants to mobilize.

In the fourth place, the smaller nations are torn between two modes of behavior in which they usually try to indulge simultaneously, as well as between two attitudes toward both the nation-state and the UN. The two modes of behavior represent two levels of world politics. On the one hand, the smaller states try to protect themselves, *collectively*, against the rivalries of the two superpowers. Individually, they would be the victims of the great conflict; together, they have the best chance of restraining the big powers and of gaining a number of advantages in return. Some seek such a common escape in a broad alliance with the United States (Rio Treaty, NATO, SEATO), others in a neutral belt. But in either case, thus protected against the "nationalistic universalism" of the superpowers, they practice traditional nationalism quietly. The smaller nations live in two ages at the same time. As for the two attitudes toward the nation-state and the UN, each one is taken by a different group of states. The new nations focus on the nation-state their highest ambitions of international power, economic development, and social unity. Furthermore, their attachment to the nation-state is proportional to the intensity of their will not to get involved in the big-power conflict: a feeling that neutralists in Europe have echoed and expressed sometimes in impressive theoretical arguments. These nations, at the same time, look on the UN with great enthusiasm; they see in it an instrument for the advancement of the smaller nations (in number and in power), and a mechanism for restraining the superpowers. On the contrary, the older nation-states of continental western Europe are more disabused of the nation-state, even though it retains the citizens' basic loyalty; and they look at the UN with greater misgivings, both because they have been out-voted so often in the UN on colonial issues, and because they contest the wisdom of spreading all over the world the disease of nationalism which they, too, contracted once, and from which they have suffered grievously.

       ❊ ❊ ❊ ❊ ❊ ❊ ❊

The following considerations on what the role of international organization *should be* in the present world are based on the following postulates. *a)* The nation-state, conceived as a legally sovereign unit in a tenuous net of breakable obligations, is not the framework in which the ideals we have defined at the outset can *all* be realized or approximated. It can hardly be maintained that it affords the greatest possibilities of economic advance, and even, in many areas, of orderly political and social change. *b)* Experience to date has shown that political organization on a world scale cannot, by itself, advance beyond the stage of the nation-state: its fate is linked to the nation-state. Three consequences flow from these postulates.

The first consequence concerns the role of the political organs of the UN. If they cannot shape new forces, they should at least prevent the nation-states from getting even further away from the distant objectives which the UN proclaims. The two tests—rather negative ones, one may fear—which each decision or recommendation should meet are, first, a test of responsibility: will it decrease, increase, or leave unchanged the state of tension with which it is supposed to deal? If it will not contribute to decreasing tensions, it should not be made, except if inaction is clearly bound to produce even worse consequences than intervention. This test is particularly necessary in colonial affairs. . . . Secondly, a test of efficiency: is the measure advocated, sound as it may be, backed by a sufficient combination of interests and forces? Otherwise, it will be an empty gesture.

The second consequence suggests the need for building new institutions which will help the nation to go beyond the stage of the nation-state. A case can be made—and has often been made—against excessive and premature attempts at establishing "rigid legal norms" and institutions; it has been said that the process of integrating nations must be left to the free interplay of political, economic and social forces within them. Undoubtedly, no organization can be effective if there are no such favorable forces; it can not create them. But where they do exist, a network of legal obligations and institutions can consolidate the common interests at the expense of the divergent ones, and act as the indispensable catalyst of an emergent community; otherwise there would be no opportunity to select, seize, save and stress the unifying forces. The reason why the nations tend to organize themselves as states and why the highest allegiance of the citizens usually belongs to the state is that this form of political organization affords them protection, security, justice, gratifications and services. Therefore, the only way to transfer loyalty to another set of institutions is to create new agencies which will provide the citizens with some of these advantages and help in gradually building communities larger than nations.

But these new agencies will be solid and effective only if they are accepted freely by the peoples they are supposed to link. This means, in the first place, that the peoples will have to reach the "national stage" first. Recognition of the insufficiency of the nation as framework of social organization can only come *after* the nation has achieved a large measure of self-government. Consequently, in areas where no nation-state has yet been established, the national stage cannot, in all probability, be skipped. However, independence might be accompanied by an agreement on "interdependence" with other countries for clearly defined and accepted functions.

In the second place, wherever the nations, new or old, have all the attributes, blessings and curses of the sovereign state, a difficult task of incitement and negotiations will have to be performed. Political federation is probably ruled out in the early stages. Except perhaps in the limited European area where disillusionment with the nation-state is strongest (but how far does it go?) one cannot expect, even under the stress created by necessities of defense or economic development, that nation-states will agree to the kind of wholesale transfer of powers which political federation requires. Suicide, so to speak, if it takes place at all, will have to be piecemeal. Political power cannot be expected to be abandoned first. Nor is it sure that political federation is always a desirable goal. The main enemy of international stability and individual liberty, in those countries where the nation-state has ceased to be a refuge and become a prison, is not the nation, but the state; it is the concentration of political, economic, military power, etc. . . . in one set of institutions. The creation, by amalgamation of existing nation-states, of a new state similar in its essence to the previous ones and even larger in area can hardly be called an improvement. A federation strong enough to survive the strains of birth and youth might soon develop into a super-nation; the trend toward centralization, observed in all federations, could lead to such a result. A decrease in the number of leviathans is no gain if it is compensated by an increase in their respective power. Thus, the only practical way to reach the aim—a decentralization of allegiance— seems to be the establishment of functional institutions based on transnational interests. In order to be effective, these agencies would have to be geographically limited. Or, if in certain cases a regional limitation makes little sense economically,[1] they should possess some ideological, historical or technical justification. They would therefore, as a rule, not be universal

[1] See the case against regionalism in economic organizations in Raymond F. Mikesell, "Barriers to the Expansion of UN Economic Functions," *Annals of the American Academy of Political and Social Science*, November 1954 (Vol. 302), pp. 39–40.

institutions like the UN and its specialized agencies, but, for instance, organizations in which certain underdeveloped countries sharing one common economic problem would cooperate with more advanced nations which have solved or faced the same problem at home or in their colonies. The nation-state would thus be caught in a variety of nets. Gradually, unobtrusively perhaps, a large measure of economic power would be transferred to the new agencies. They would for a long time to come leave to the state a kind of negative power to destroy the net; nevertheless, they could reach and provide the individuals with tangible services.[2] They would not constitute an immediate rival for the states and would therefore expect more consent or at least less violent resistance. The most effective attack on sovereignty is not a frontal one—it is one which slowly but clearly deprives sovereignty of its substance, and consequently of its prestige. The build-up of interlocking functional communities is required both by the presently strong attachment to formal sovereignty and by the actual interlocking interests which can become a positive force in world politics only if they are institutionalized.

As a third consequence of our two postulates, the UN should concentrate on and develop its role as a "center for harmonizing the actions of nations in the attainment of (the) common ends," which these joint interests suggest. Indeed the UN should either take the initiative or at least assume responsibility for the establishment and coordination of the regional or functional communities we have advocated. Two reasons militate for such a policy. In the first place, it is necessary to provide the UN, checkmated on political issues, with a new area of activities in its own interest. Secondly, the west, increasingly unable in political matters to get its views accepted by others through a process of "collectivization of interests," but unable also to discard the world body, must find constructive ways of seizing the initiative. In the inevitable clash of ideas between east and west, the west cannot merely offer to the nations the ideal of internal democracy; it must also present the image of a more satisfactory world order. The Soviet Union, which wants to prevent a consolidation of the non-communist world, plays upon the strong attachment which is still felt to the nation-state and to nationalism, sovereignty and independence. The west cannot fight back on this ground; it would mean giving up the objectives we have mentioned. Nor can the west propose such revolutionary changes that the Soviets might successfully exploit this continuing attachment to the shelter of sovereignty, as well as charge the west with hypocrisy, since none of the leading western states is ready to sacrifice large areas of its own sovereignty.

Again, a progressive middle road seems to be the right one. This is precisely where the UN can operate. Militarily, the role of the UN, as we indicated, can only be a very limited one; it is therefore normal that initia-

[2] See I. L. Claude, "Individuals and World Law," *Harvard Studies in International Relations*, 1952.

tives for collective defense be taken outside of it. But initiatives for economic action should be made within the UN. This would be politically advantageous. The suggested regional or functional institutions can hardly function without western economic assistance. Now, the new nations have shown a distrust of purely western initiatives, interpreted as cold war moves, and a respect for the UN, which suggest that the UN should be selected as the channel for such assistance. It is also wise technically; there is a need for coordination of the present and future technical institutions, which can best be exercised by the UN.[3] As the French Foreign Minister, M. Christian Pineau, has recently suggested, an agency for world economic development should be created within the framework of the UN. This agency would coordinate and control specialized agencies such as the International Monetary Fund and the International Bank for Reconstruction and Development, as well as the UN technical assistance activities and more recently created or proposed UN institutions such as the International Finance Corporation and the Special United Nations Fund for Economic Development. It should give its aid, gifts, loans, technical assistance, raw materials or energy, etc., to the regional or functional organizations we have recommended, rather than to states directly. These organizations would be sponsored by the UN agency and established among the under-developed nations (with or without direct participation of the industrialized ones). They would be the pioneers of supra-national development. The UN agency, being international by virtue of the Charter, would play the more modest but essential role of an instigator.

*   *   *   *   *   *   *

If we state, then, what can be done, and compare it with what should be done, the prospects appear both modest and not at all hopeless. Far less can be done than the most ardent internationalists desire or sometimes expect. But somewhat more can be done than the spokesmen for reliance on "wise statesmanship" or on the manifestation of "perennial forces" seem to believe, and certainly quite a lot more should be tried.

The defenders and promoters of international organizations would have a much stronger case if they recognized frankly the two following limitations. First, there is no sudden mutation in world politics, and the forces that may some day break the crust of the nation-state can only be helped, not created, by international organization. This is why the basis of action remains the state, why the chances of truly supranational institutions, even limited to certain functions, are far smaller, in most parts of the world, than those of organs of international cooperation, why even ambitious supra-national schemes might not operate very differently from these, and finally why in

[3] See Edgar S. Furniss, Jr., "A Re-examination of Regional Arrangements," *Journal of International Affairs*, May 1955 (Vol. 9, No. 2), pp. 79–89.

the new bodies "power politics" will continue. But this is not what matters. Power politics also survive in the internal affairs of any nation. What counts is the framework and the general direction of the process.

Secondly, the mushrooming of international institutions will not solve the fundamental issue of security. They can be created on all sides of the big abysses that separate the nations and threaten world peace—the cold war, the colonial revolution; they cannot bridge the gaps. Here the balance of power between the superpowers, and between the crumbling empires and the rising new nations, are the decisive factors. The most international organization can do is to provide restraints on the superpowers and centers of cooperation between old and new nations after the colonial issue has been decided by force or by local agreements.

Once these limitations are accepted, the role of international organization should appear in its true light. Even if it were not much more than that of an "amiable civilizer," it would still be a far bigger one than many challengers seem to suggest. They usually leave this role to traditional diplomacy. International organization as a fragile but still badly explored diplomatic method can, within its own limits, help the nations to transcend the limits of the nation-state.

CHAPTER 4

THE CONTRAST OF REGIONAL AND FUNCTIONAL APPROACHES

J. W. Burton's article on regionalism and functionalism in this chapter puts greater stress on the former and analyzes international organization in terms of "associative" and "dissociative" characteristics, that is, the tendencies to encourage or impede interaction between states. He notes that the UN Charter provides for both characteristics, the former in Chapter VIII and the latter in Chapter VII, more particularly in Article 51. He points out that the effect of bringing disputes into an enlarged UN arena tends to internationalize even local disputes, and that then the dissociative effects harm the organization's own efforts in associative endeavors. Regionalism, Burton suggests, is a way of overcoming the undesirable results of dissociation. The same benefits accrue from the decentralization of economic and social affairs.

One must raise a few questions regarding the assumptions of Burton's arguments. If association and integration of conflict have positive effects, there ought to be evidence available to substantiate this. And yet one may question whether functionalism is not more influenced by the cold war than the reverse. One needs to question further whether nuclear weapons have provided integration of conflict or merely forced the conflict into more traditional forms. Hoffmann and Burton both hold that the need to shift loyalties is critical and that this is more likely to come gradually, as important benefits can be seen in functional services and activities. (Hoffmann, it should be noted, is sympathetic to this end in part as a way to offset increasing Soviet encroachments upon non-communist societies, a position Burton does not reflect.) Both play down the role of the Security Council as an associative agency.

Burton is undoubtedly correct when he stresses the strong associative characteristics of regional organizations, although it is hard to comprehend why the British Commonwealth should be considered under that rubric. It has been noted by a number of authorities that the "new" Commonwealth does provide the opportunity for exploration and agreement on many issues in international politics which are not as readily available to other states outside that group. But in each example Burton lists there was, and in some cases still is, a strong dissociative flavor. Even the British Commonwealth, with its trade-preference system, had, not too long ago, not an integrative but an invidiously discriminating characteristic. And certainly so did and does the Arab League, first against Britain and then against Israel. One may even question the extent to which the Organization of American States is associative, particularly in the light of the Guatemalan, Cuban, and Dominican crises. Perhaps, therefore, the necessary factor for an associative organization is interests which cannot have undesirable effects on member states, rather than interests which make possible harmonious relationships among the member states. Even here, if the purpose is to make possible such benefits among the members, but if little operational impact is felt—as in the OAS—it is questionable whether these examples are worthy of note. In fact, in terms of all-round effectiveness, the British Commonwealth today seems to meet the tests the best.

One gets a somewhat different perspective in the Eighth Report of the Commission to Study the Organization of the Peace. Here it is agreed that although the right of self-defense is upheld in the Charter and may take several different forms, for example, bilateral, multilateral (Articles 51, 53, and, until the Security Council is able to function as expected, Article 106) and regional (Article 52), all of these are subservient, either initially or immediately thereafter, to the overarching jurisdiction in such matters of the Security Council. In cases of self-defense the Council likewise is expected to play an associative role, and if it does not, it is because of the way it has been used and not because of the functions it has been assigned. Of course, one may raise the question of whether an organ whose function is in large measure expected to be negative, that is, an organ which is expected to oppose undesirable behavior, is likely ever to take on the image of an associative agency. And yet despite the Council's poor record in this regard, we know that many states, whatever their ulterior motives, have continued to bring their "threats to the peace" to the Council as was intended.

FURTHER READINGS

Haas, Ernest B., *Beyond the Nation-State*. Stanford: Stanford University Press, 1964.

———, "International Integration, the European and Universal Process," *International Organization*, Vol. 15, 1961, pp. 366–392.

———, "Regionalism, Functionalism and Universal International Organization," *World Politics*, Vol. 8, January 1956, pp. 238–263.

Lerche, Charles O., "Regional Security and the United Nations." Washington, D.C.: The Brookings Institution, 1965.

Mitrany, David, *A Working Peace System*. London and New York: Royal Institute of International Affairs, 1946.

REGIONALISM, FUNCTIONALISM, AND THE UNITED NATIONS

J. W. Burton*

Regionalism has been widely used to describe a form of international organisation limited in membership, and with functions and objectives which may be unlimited. *Functionalism*, on the other hand, has been employed to designate those international organisations which may be universal, but which are limited as to function and to purpose. For instance, the Economic and Social Council has several regional organisations, and it also has associated with it a number of specialised or functional agencies.

Regionalism, strictly, would seem to refer to international organisation on a geographical basis, and this is the normal usage. As such, however, the term has a limited application, and may be misleading. Geographical proximity may be the geatest single factor in the evolution of sub-systems; but the reason is not this proximity so much as the common language, cultural, economic, defence and other ties which tend to bind together peoples within a region. Exploration, conquest, and trade carry these ties to points outside the original regions, lessening the importance of proximity as the main integrative factor. An example of strictly geographical regionalism is the Pan-American Union, or Organisation of American States established in 1948. However, this association is no more integrated [than], and is little different in kind, from that of the (British) Commonwealth, members of which are scattered throughout the world. In between these two extremes there are a number of organisations usually described as regional; but the geographical influences are not the most important. SEATO includes nations outside the region, but not all of those within it. The Arab League is within a region; but more importantly it has a linguistic and cultural basis. The Communist countries have a certain geographical propinquity; but this is secondary to an ideological basis of association. It is appropriate, therefore, for the term *regionalism* to connote all forms of association amongst limited numbers of nations, whether the association has developed out of strictly

* J. W. Burton, "Regionalism, Functionalism, and the United Nations," *Australian Outlook*, Vol. 15, 1961, pp. 73–87. By permission of *Australian Outlook* and J. W. Burton.

J. W. Burton is a senior lecturer in International Relations at the University College, London. He is the author of *Peace Theory* and *International Relations, a General Theory*.

geographical circumstances, or out of common linguistic, cultural, traditional, ideological, and other common features which tend to bind nations together.

Both Regionalism and Functionalism may each be either associative or dissociative, that is, they may each tend to bring nations together into an international community, or they may tend to create barriers between groups of them. The 1953 proposals for a political union of six Western states could be regarded as integrative or associative: they were intended to draw the six nations together without at the same time increasing barriers to co-operation with nations outside the group, or provoking their hostile and retaliatory responses. The (British) Commonwealth cannot be regarded as dissociative now that Imperial Preference is no longer a feature. The Pan-American Union, the Arab League, and the Afro-Asian community each has strong associative features, but also some dissociative ones. NATO, SEATO, ANZUS and the Warsaw Pact, being exclusive military alliances directed against some outside groups of powers, are strongly dissociative regional arrangements.

Specialised organisations dealing with Civil Aviation (ICAO), Education (UNESCO), Health (WHO), Postal Services (UPU), Tele-communications (ITU), and others of this nature are non-discriminatory, universal, and integrative functional arrangements. The operation of sugar, steel, and oil combines, which seek to control markets in the interests of particular nations, are predominantly dissociative. There are a number of private organisations, some of which are formally registered with the United Nations, such as the International Chamber of Commerce, the International Federation of Christian Trade Unions, and others which can have no universal application, and these probably tend to be dissociative.

It is the purpose of this article to suggest that the further promotion of Regionalism and Functionalism in their associative forms, and their discouragement in their dissociative forms, may be a means of overcoming some of the problems which currently seem to be threatening the successful operation of the United Nations. More particularly, the purpose is to suggest that the decentralisation of international organisation by these means will not merely remove an administrative burden too great for any central organisation to carry; but will in addition make a contribution directly to the removal of conflict situations, and to the settlement of disputes.

The intention of the United Nations Charter was to promote associative, and to discourage dissociative forms of regionalism. Chapter VIII of the Charter deals with "Regional Arrangements" and it is wholly associative in intention: its purpose is co-operation regionally amongst nations in the promotion of their security and welfare, and in the settlement of disputes at an early stage by those with direct knowledge. . . . These would seem expressly to exclude dissociative forms of regionalism, such as NATO and the Warsaw Pact. For instance, it is intended that all nations in a particular area, friendly or otherwise, should take part in an endeavour "to achieve pacific settlement of local disputes." Secondly, all the activities and contemplated activities of the regional organisation are to be reported to the Security Council. Both provisions would seem to rule against exclusive military pacts and alliances.

Dissociative military alliances may be justified under Article 51 of Chapter VII dealing with "Action with respect to threats to the peace, breaches of the peace, and acts of aggression." In this article there is a provision that "Nothing in the present Charter shall impair right of individual or collective self-defence. . . ."

Professor Stone and others have argued that Chapter VIII must be read in the light of the over-riding provisions of Article 51, and that regional military arrangements are sanctioned by the Charter. The reasons given are that individual and collective self-defence in modern conditions cannot wait upon attack, and must include planning in advance, and therefore defensive regional organisations. Plans for self-defence, moreover, cannot be communicated to the Security Council, for the probable enemy would then become acquainted with the defence secrets of the members of the defensive organisation.

On this argument, governments do not need to defend their military alliances by rationalisations regarding Chapter VIII (as in fact Western governments have done), for they have separate and over-riding rights under Chapter VII. However, even under Article 51, the right of self-defence is not an absolute one. The Article reads, "Nothing in the present Charter shall impair the inherent right of individual or collective self-defence *if an armed attack occurs* [presumably the right exists only when attack occurs] until the Security Council has taken the measures necessary to maintain international peace and security." Again, as in Chapter VIII "Measures taken shall be immediately reported to the Security Council. . . ." It is difficult to see how this article sanctions preparations in advance, such as military alliances. Reading Chapter VIII and Chapter VII together, the right of self-defence given in the Charter would seem to be no more than the right to employ national forces if attacked.

The fact is, however, that the major policy decisions have been taken, and dissociative alliances do exist, whether or not intended by those who drafted the Charter. Let us assume, for the sake of exposition, that Article 51 justifies exclusive and secret military alliances and preparations, and that Chapter VIII was intended not to prevent them, but to provide alongside them, broad regional arrangements of a non-military character.

The position is that while Article 51 has been implemented, advantage has not been taken of Chapter VIII: there does not exist any net-work of regional arrangements which are designed to settle disputes as they develop, and before reference to the Security Council is made necessary. The consequence of the existence, on the one hand, of dissociative regional arrangements, and of the absence, on the other, of associative ones, is that the whole burden of peaceful settlement of disputes, together with the consequences of competitive arming arising out of dissociative alliances, is placed upon the one central international organisation—the United Nations. The burden is carried in particular by the Security Council and the Secretary General. Every dispute, no matter how trivial, how local, must come before the central organisation. By the time it has been referred to the Security Council it is at an advanced stage, frequently one of open conflict.

Evidence that this burden is too great for a centralised United Nations to carry is in several developments which now threaten, not merely the future strength of the United Nations, but even its present level of operations. There is, primarily, an administrative burden. The proceedings of the United Nations, and in particular of the Security Council, could originally be followed in detail by responsible political leaders: adequate reponsible attention and direction could be given. It is now an organisation which meets almost continuously, dealing with many minor disputes which arise out of local circumstances, not understood by most nations. It is impossible for national leaders to follow proceedings, and delegates frequently act without responsible instruction. This in turn encourages bloc voting—the following uncritically of the leadership of a friendly Great Power which, it is assumed, knows the facts. In these circumstances it is not surprising that the United Nations has become a forum at which national and improvised view-points are expressed in propaganda terms.

The central staff of the United Nations has become immersed in the details of world affairs, and tied to a routine which effectively prevents the imaginative leadership and advice which should be expected of an international secretariat. The routine of the United Nations, the day-by-day work and responsibilities, place a burden on the Secretary-General, probably greater than that carried by the political head of any government. He has no responsible Cabinet with whom to share the burden.

Furthermore, the advantages of decentralisation, now widely appreciated in the field of domestic administration, are wholly lacking. The Secretary-General and his staff in the Congo instance—and this is merely one of very many—were required at a moment's notice to make recommendations to, and to carry out the decisions of, the Security Council, on matters about which they could not be informed fully, and which more appropriately would have been dealt with, in the first instance at least, by a regional body acquainted with local circumstances. In dealing with the complex subject-matter of international political relations, it is impossible for a central organisation to be fully advised, and to act with the necessary wisdom.

These two administrative difficulties, the enormous quantity of business which prevents responsible national supervision, and the complexity of the subject-matter on which the Secretariat cannot adequately be informed, both have been increased by addition to an original fifty [members and have] rendered the body ineffective as a deliberative, fact-finding, conflict-resolving organisation.

Administratively, then, the United Nations, by reason of its wholly centralised nature (we are at the moment concerned with political relations), now faces problems which could lead to its break-down.

In addition to the administrative problems, and arising out of this centralised administrative structure, there are grave political difficulties. Local disputes in their origin frequently do not concern other powers. They would more easily be resolved by local argument, or local argument could define the issues for Security Council decision. But in the centralised organisation, local disputes become extended and confused, and reflect and aggravate the already existing Great Power rivalries.

The centralised international organisation of the United Nations, operating in the absence of associative regional bodies, and in a world environment dominated by dissociative military alliances, has thus itself become a dissociative influence. The United Nations (in its political work) is contributing to the extension of conflicts, and its dissociative influences are threatening even its own existence.

The progressive development of regional organisations of the Chapter VIII type (even though the military arrangements assumed to be sanctioned by Article 51 were still to remain in existence), could help to solve some of these pressing problems of the United Nations. Chapter VIII implies, as we have seen, that all nations, regardless of their power bloc affiliations, should be members of the regional group. It also implies that conflict should be resolved within these organisations. (See Article 52[2].) Furthermore, the Security Council is obliged to rely upon these regional organisations for the settlement of disputes. (See Article 52[3].) Chapter VIII provides, in effect, a plan for decentralisation of international organisation.

Decentralisation also helps directly to prevent the development of conflict situations, and in the settlement of disputes. Firstly, the various regions of the world tend toward a cultural homogeneity within themselves. The countries of Africa, Europe, South East Asia, for example, comprise groupings which have faced common problems, and have had many common experiences. Debate, discussion, procedures, and negotiations are likely to be more fruitful in these circumstances. The New Delhi Conference of 1949 on Indonesia comprising Asian, African, and Middle East governments, was a regional meeting in the sense that those attending had common policies in respect [to] independence, and all had experienced subjection. Being interested in issues of independence they were all well informed on Indonesian affairs, and quickly arrived at a recommendation to the Security Council which contributed to a final settlement.

Secondly, the discussion of local conflict situations within a regional group tends to confine the issues to those immediately relevant, and to exclude strategic and other considerations of interest only to outside powers. If the recent Congo situation had in the first instance been dealt with by an established regional organisation of independent African states, less opportunity would have been given to Great Powers to pursue their conflicting interests in relation to Africa, and in relation also to the central organisation of the United Nations.

Thirdly, conflict-integration is given greatest scope in regionalism. . . . Clearly "some measure of integration exists in any overt conflict situation by virtue of the very fact that an overt conflict implies some contact between the parties." But there is more involved than mere contact. The first step in any integration, as with compromise is to uncover the conflict. When the demands of both sides are broken up, then it is possible for the parties to evaluate the issues. "It is assumed, under such circumstances, that neither side ever 'gives in' but that there often comes a moment when interests on both sides are suddenly perceived in a new perspective, and unity precipitates itself. So it frequently comes about, once an integration is effected, that the compatible, even co-operative, effort compels a change in the whole motivation of the two parties, and a new relationship emerges."[1] Centralised organisation in international relations does not take advantage of these behaviourist possibilities of conflict integration.

At the present stage of development of political science, it is not necessary to argue either the advantages of decentralisation in administration, or the benefits of conflict integration. The problem of form and structure which would incorporate these advantages is the one which requires acceptable solution.

We have so far confined comments to international political organisation. There is in the economic field a high degree of decentralisation under the central direction of the Economic and Social Council. This decentralisation has taken two forms, firstly in the creation of a number of specialised agencies, Food and Agriculture, Health, UNESCO, UNICEF, and others, and secondly, in regional organisations, such as ECAFE, and the European, African, and Latin American regional organisations of the Council. It would be difficult to estimate the associative influence of this quite vast net-work of economic organisation. The sessions of the Economic and Social Council and of the specialised agencies are not news—they have few administrative problems with political implications to justify head-lines. There may be inefficiencies, arguments about contributions and priorities; but the work of the agencies and of the regional bodies is smooth, and the sessions of the Council place no undue burden on the central administration. Indeed, if it were not for this associative work, the standing of the United Nations would

---

[1] Robert North, "The Integrative Functions of Conflict." Article in *Conflict Resolution*, Vol. IV, No. 3, September, 1960, pp. 355–384.

probably not command as much popular support [as it does] in the majority of countries which now take a special interest in the United Nations.

Two questions arise. Why was this Economic and Social Council decentralisation possible, and why was there no similar Security Council development? Secondly, and a related question, are the conditions which mitigated against decentralisation in the political field still operative?

Post-war reconstruction planning commenced on an international basis even before the end of hostilities, and in the context of pre-war analyses of the causes of war, which were economic in emphasis. By the time the Charter conference was convened at San Francisco in 1945, there was in existence a number of specialised agencies, and it was a matter for easy agreement that they should be brought into relationship with the United Nations. The [Economic and Social] Council had a co-ordinating function from the outset. The development of regional consultation on economic matters was, from a political and practical point of view, an easy operation, welcomed by all governments despite political differences. On the political side, there was no such body of agreement and organisation to be incorporated into the United Nations. Chapter VIII merely provided for its future development, and there was no world public opinion which saw its need. The Security Council was conceived as a body with the negative function of stopping conflict, unlike the Economic and Social Council which had a positive function of creating conditions in which conflict would not arise. In 1945 it was not appreciated that ideology and political rivalry could, quite apart from economic conditions, create conditions of hostility, and nowhere in the Charter was provision made for the study of fundamental political problems in international relations. Furthermore, the distrust and suspicion amongst the Great Powers of the pre-war and war-time periods continues, and a certain degree of informal military alliance existed amongst them. If the Security Council inherited any decentralised political organisation it was of this dissociative type which finally took the form of military pacts. These added to the burden of the Council, and did nothing to relieve it of the responsibilities of conflict resolution.

It is interesting to note that at San Francisco the Latin American States pressed hard for the recognition of regional organisations, pointing to the achievements of the inter-American system. Supported by the USA, they managed to have inserted into the Charter the present Article 51. However, the agreement which constituted the Organisation of American States made three years later was not inconsistent with Chapter VIII. The intention was the regional settlement of disputes, and the general co-operation envisaged in Chapter VIII. There were regional defence objectives also, but none which would not reasonably fall within the purposes of Chapter VIII. Unfortunately, and probably because they were never consulted over the Dumbarton Oaks draft, the Latin Americans failed to grasp the opportunity of giving the United Nations a model for Chapter VIII, and they provided, by introducing Article 51, the justification for regional military pacts which were at that stage not intended by any delegation.

Has the world environment changed in any way which would make possible even now the developments intended under Chapter VIII?

There have been since 1945 a great many developments conducive to associative trends. No estimate of the practical significance of any is possible: all that can be said is that they are in practice associative, and to this extent helpful to regionalism and integration. The possession by Great Powers of nuclear devices has altered the political situation, and in some respects assisted in resolving conflict. East and West seem now to be more inclined to accept neutralist governments and compromise solutions in areas of undetermined political allegiance. Laos and Congo both lend support to this view. An extension of neutralism to the most troublesome of political situations, Germany and Korea, is in the nuclear age at least conceivable. Once there is an acceptance by Great Powers of neutralism as a possible means of avoiding nuclear conflict, the way is open for conflict resolution on a regional basis, on the basis of local facts and circumstances, and without reference to great power rivalries.

Secondly, there have been very great sociological and political changes in the two main rival systems. The virtual end of colonialism, the development of the welfare state in the West, and the acceptance by the West of Communism as a system, and the ideological and practical changes which have emerged in the communist states, and the recognition of the viability of capitalism, together with common fear of nuclear warfare, seem to be leading to an international political environment in which compromise and integration will be possible.

There have been other environmental changes which now make possible regional integration. For instance, before the war, with unemployment and competition from low-cost countries a constant fear, each nation was defensive in its policies, and regionalism where it did exist was dissociative. For example, the British Commonwealth clung to Imperial Preference. Now that there is confidence in the ability of financial policy to maintain high levels of employment, now that there is an accepted stability in domestic economies in the advanced countries, associative trends are likely to strengthen. Australia can import large quantities of Japanese goods with the minimum of political reaction. Integration of developed and underdeveloped countries, even customs unions and joint developmental planning, can now be contemplated. More Australian integration with Asia is likely to develop in this way.

The independence of states is in itself an associative factor. Colonial areas were usually administered in the interests of the colonial power, and underdeveloped states in the same region so administered had little opportunity for co-operation. Independence removes this dissociative factor, and future development could easily be the closer association or even unification of neighbouring states previously under separate colonial control.

There are in addition many other associative trends, including improved communications and education, which help to create an environment less favourable to dissociative regionalism, and more conducive to integration and regional co-operation in political relations.

Assuming that the environment is, or is likely to be ripe for regionalism in political relations, what form is possible?

NATO, SEATO, Warsaw and other alliances are so much based on military arrangements, and so discredited amongst those against whom they are aimed, that it is unreasonable to expect them to function in accord with Chapter VIII of the United Nations Charter. Certain steps have been taken in SEATO to broaden its objectives, but it remains a discriminatory, dissociative pact. A separate organisational development has to be postulated.

There already exist regional arrangements which are essentially associative. The (British) Commonwealth, the Pan-American Union and the Afro-Asian community, are strongly associative. The Arab group, and the Communist countries both have important regional functions in relation to the settlement of disputes. The (British) Commonwealth in particular, now that its members contain many nations of different stages of development, and of different culture, must be regarded as having an important associative influence in the world community. These are organisations outside the United Nations; but each makes a contribution to the objectives of the United Nations, and relieves the United Nations of some of its burden, in so far as each avoids dissociative policies and actions.

Most nations are within some group of this character. However, regional arrangements of this kind touch only the fringe of the problem of conflict, for it is not within these groups that the conflict is most likely to arise. Formal regional arrangements of the Chapter VIII type, superimposed on these more natural associations, are required in order to reduce their dissociative features, and to encourage associative activities amongst members of different groups.

Regional groups of small powers are possible, and in a sense the Afro-Asian community constitutes one. There would be some advantages in the formation of regional groups which excluded all Permanent Members of the Security Council, so that regional disputes could be resolved in their absence. This would also solve difficulties which would occur whenever a region happened to contain opposing Great Powers. It would avoid also the danger of nations being dominated in a regional organisation by one Great Power. However, in order to obtain the maximum benefit of conflict integration, and the maximum influence of small powers on world affairs, strictly geographical regions would seem to be beneficial. This would mean that

Great Powers would be represented only in those regions in which they had their metropolitan territories, and would have no claim to interests outside their own region. This is a reversal of traditional procedures: even ECAFE includes all Great Powers. It is, however, a procedure more in accord with a world structure of independent nations, and more likely to result in peaceful settlement of local disputes. The pattern of international political relations which would develop would be, say, six regional organisations, Europe (including Russia), Asia, Oceania, Africa, the Levant, and America, each a little United Nations in itself. The main function of the Assembly and of the Security Council would be to hear reports from these organisations, to deal with issues referred to it, and to refer issues for advice. Disputes which could not be dealt with by this simple system of decentralisation would include those between countries in two different regional organisations, and disputes over territories controlled by a power not in the region. The United Nations central administration would have in these cases the additional function of arranging or directing consultation between regional organisations.

These are purely speculative considerations designed to raise the general problems of the United Nations, and to point to the advantages of regionalism. Their realism is a matter of judgment. New Guinea is an interesting and topical case on which to test these proposals. Here is a dispute which affects countries in a particular region (primarily Indonesia and Australia), and one outside the region (the Dutch). There are others interested, for instance, New Zealand and Malaya. The parties to the dispute, and others which have shown an interest, all declare their support of the principle of self-determination. Rival claims are legal ones, based on interpretations of agreements, and on past administrative structures. Clearly, the motivations are endeavours to pre-determine self-determination. If this situation becomes acute, the Security Council will be required to settle it. The issues will be wider, a great power rivalry will enter into it. Settlement will then be unlikely. A regional organisation would probaly not arrive at any firm agreements. Nevertheless, there would be a clarification of issues, and probably some suggestions which would change the nature of the dispute. For instance, conflict integration could take place, and suggestions of customs unions, mutual development-planning, joint defence and common use of bases and other such regional proposals would be thrown up, which could wholly change the background against which the dispute was taking place. Out of the New Guinea dispute there could develop a lasting enmity between Australia and Indonesia, especially if the dispute went to New York and became a part of Great Power rivalries. It could, on the other hand, lead to conflict integration, and many regional developments, of mutual benefit.

Other test cases are Formosa, Korea, Germany, Congo, Laos, and Israel. An interesting exercise would be to speculate on the type of conflict resolution or opposing recommendations which would emerge from discussions in the relevant regional organisation dealing with each of these issues.

Functionalism can have a similar integrative effect, and equally could take some of the burden from the United Nations. Indeed, it is already doing this. Agreements which were operative before the creation of the United Nations, covering navigation, post and telegraph, health controls, and hosts of other matters, have had added to their number since the Second World War, many of far-reaching importance. GATT, the Antarctic neutral zone, and agreements which have resulted from the operation of the Economic and Social Council and its agencies, have taken politics out of international commercial relations.

So far functionalism has not penetrated far into international political life. Nuclear test bans, control on export of arms, the control of intelligence agencies, are amongst a long list of subject matters which would lend themselves to a functional approach to peaceful relations. Disputes arising out of these matters would be dealt with by the specialised organisation, and not argued in the Security Council, or on the propaganda platform of the Assembly.

One important functional agency required is an international centre of political research. At no point within the United Nations is there a centre of political research to which reference can be made by the Secretary-General, or any of the organs of the United Nations. There are research agencies in the economic and social fields. It is at this point in the organisation that the three-power representation suggested by the Soviet could be introduced. If there were unanimity at a research level, the Secretary-General could be expected to accept the facts presented. If not, he could be forgiven for using his discretion. Pugwash[2] experience is that agreement is possible internationally on a scientific or academic level.

Another functional agency which still seems to be required is one to deal with all economic and technical assistance on a non-discriminatory and co-ordinated basis. UNRRA was of this kind, but Cold War developments led to its cessation. In the new circumstances of the current political situation, a specialised agency to carry out the technically complex problem of under-development might be possible.

A United Nations, resting on developed regionalism, and on ever-extending functionalism, could become an effective instrument of international policy co-ordination. The withering away of the United Nations, and the building up of these two integrative systems, might provide a surer foundation of peaceful international relations.

What has been suggested is no more than was intended in 1945. The

2 'Pugwash' is a meeting of scientists, originally convened in 1957 by Lord Russell, and which has met six times. Strong Western and Communist teams of scientists usually attend.

Charter as it stands contains the provisions necessary for the evolution of a decentralised United Nations. An unfortunate turning was taken as a result of Cold War circumstances. Now the nuclear stalemate is forcing reconsideration of their policies by all larger powers. The time might be ripe to pursue the objective originally intended. The United States may now have the leadership capable of applying the lessons of Inter-American organisation to other regions.

The initiative still has to be taken. This is a matter of national policy. Few countries have more to gain by a Chapter VIII approach to international organisation than Australia. "Support for the United Nations" is not in itself a policy, especially at a time at which the structure of the United Nations itself is in question. Support for a decentralised United Nations, and for the development of associative Regionalism and Functionalism both within and without the United Nations, is a positive policy touching upon economic, social, and political relations. For Australia it could lead to associative relations with countries in the region in which Australia is placed, on which alone, in the final analysis, rests Australian security.

REGIONAL ARRANGEMENTS FOR SECURITY*

Examination of the Charter indicates that it recognizes three distinct types of arrangements of political importance apart from the institutions of the members and of the United Nations itself. These types have been confused in the actual political arrangements which exist but it is believed that understanding of the proper scope and functions of regional arrangements will be facilitated by distinguishing them.

First is the type of arrangement referred to as "regional arrangements or agencies" in Chapter VIII of the Charter. They are intended primarily to keep peace among the members of the arrangement, or, as stated, "to deal with such matters relating to the maintenance of international peace and security as are appropriate for regional action" and "to achieve pacific settlement of local disputes." The members are encouraged to seek settlement of their disputes through such regional arrangements and agencies

* Commission to Study the Organization of Peace, "Regional Arrangements for Security Recommendations," Eighth Report, Sec. II (New York, United Nations Association, 1953), pp. 9–35. By permission of the Commission to Study the Organization of Peace.

before appealing to the Security Council, but the arrangements must be consistent with the Charter and must not impair the authority of the Security Council under the Charter. Enforcement action cannot normally be taken under such arrangements without the authorization of the Security Council but the latter may utilize them "for enforcement action." These provisions make it clear that regional arrangements and agencies of this type are intended to be subordinate to the Security Council. It was, in fact, the fear of too great limitation upon the autonomy of regional arrangements and alliances that led to the provisions for the other types of political arrangements.

It was suggested that these regional arrangements should be established only among states which constitute a "natural geographic, cultural or historic group." The Egyptian delegation at San Francisco proposed an amendment in the following terms:

There should be considered as regional arrangements, organizations of a permanent nature, grouping in a given geographical area several countries which, by reason of their proximity, community of interests or cultural, linguistic, historical or spiritual affinities, make themselves jointly responsible for the peaceful settlement of any dispute which may arise between them and for the maintenance of peace and security in their region, as well as for the safeguarding of their interests and the development of their economic and cultural relations.

This amendment was rejected because many states desired to include as regional arrangements groups of a purely political or military character and also perhaps groups like the British Commonwealth which were not concentrated geographically. It seems to have been thought, however, that the typical regional arrangement would have the general character described in this proposed amendment.

Article 53 of the Charter, however, recognizes a second type of "regional arrangements." These include the arrangements among the Allies recognized in Article 107 of the Charter and also "regional arrangements directed against renewal of aggressive policy on the part of any such [enemy] state." These arrangements which were excepted from the normal control of the Security Council were not in fact regional arrangements at all but bi-lateral political alliances between states which were in most cases separated geographically. Thus they included the alliances of the Soviet Union with France, Great Britain and the satellite countries and of France with Great Britain.

* * * * * * *

A third type of political arrangement is implied by the terms of Article 51 of the Charter which permits members of the United Nations to engage in "collective self-defense." Such arrangements may or may not be regional in character and the provisions concerning them do not in fact occur in the chapter of the Charter dealing with "regional arrangement." Article 51 was, however, inserted at San Francisco, as were the provisions concerning the second type of regional arrangement, in order to permit exceptions from the extensive control exercised by the Security Council over regional arrangements of the normal type.

It was obvious that "collective self-defense" arrangements might appear to be a menace to neighboring states not included within them. Yet the provisions permitting "collective self-defense" were designed to be a permanent feature of the United Nations and not a response to a temporary situation as was the case with the second type of regional arrangement. Efforts were, therefore, made to prevent aggression in the name of defense. This was done by permitting action in pursuance of the "inherent right of individual or collective self-defense" only "if an armed attack occurs against a Member of the United Nations." Furthermore such action was permitted only "until the Security Council has taken the measures necessary to maintain international peace and security," and any measures taken were to be immediately reported to the Security Council. Finally it was provided that such measures "shall not in any way affect the authority and responsibility of the Security Council under the present Charter to take at any time such action as it deems necessary in order to maintain or restore international peace and security." This provision implies that the Security Council is the final judge of whether action in alleged self-defense really is of that character and that it is competent to initiate action against the alleged defender if it concludes that in fact its action constitutes aggression.

Self-defense, whether individual or collective, although described as an inherent right is, therefore, taken out of the realm of domestic questions. It belongs to international authority to give the final judgment on the legitimacy of the exercise of the right in given circumstances although the state exercising the right is, of course, free to take action on the basis of its initial judgment. The Security Council can only function after the act and not before it, as it can in the case of the first type of regional arrangement.

It appears that the second type of regional arrangement is identical in principle with this type. Both are in law collective self-defense arrangements though the bi-lateral alliances which were in the minds of the drafters of the exceptions made at San Francisco in Article 53 are in other respects very different from the Inter-American system in the mind of the drafters of Article 51. Since the American system was not designed for defense against Germany or any other enemy power of World War II it could not come under the exception which had already been inserted in Article 53 at the insistence of France and the Soviet Union. Consequently Article 51 was drafted with the object of preventing a veto vote in the Security Council from frustrating action by the Inter-American system or other collective self-defense arrangements not directed against enemies in the Second World War. Article 51 is, however, broad enough in terms to include the World War II alliances insofar as they became operative only in case of armed attack and were designed only for collective self-defense.

The exception in Article 53 seems to have been retained even after Article 51 was drafted because the action authorized by these arrangements might in some instances have gone beyond "collective self-defense if an armed attack occurs against a Member of the United Nations" and also because the parties to the World War II alliances may have wished to escape the ultimate control of the Security Council provided for collective self-defense arrangements under Article 51. From the point of view of international peace and security such control seems desirable. Consequently it would appear as was indeed the intention, that the special exception in Article 53 should in course of time be eliminated, and that the "regional arrangements" which it protected should continue to be recognized only insofar as they conform to Article 51.

The intention of the Charter is in general to coordinate collective self-defense and regional arrangements with the United Nations system by providing for their control by the United Nations through prior authorization or subsequent action by assuring the formal consistency of their terms with the purposes and principles of the Charter, by continuous reporting of action under them to the United Nations, and by utilization of them by the United Nations for pacific settlement or enforcement purposes. In all of these matters, however, the United Nations was to function through the Security Council acting with the veto vote. The inoperability of this system led the General Assembly in the Uniting for Peace Resolution of November, 1950 to establish a Collective Measures Committee to report to it in 1951 on methods "which might be used to maintain and strengthen international peace and security in accordance with the Purposes and Principles of the Charter, taking account of collective self-defense and regional arrangements." The report of this Committee noted that many Member States "have alluded to the possibility that all or some of their national forces committed under such (collective self-defense or regional) arrangements might under appropriate circumstances be made available to the United Nations in implementation of the Uniting for Peace Resolution" and recommended that when the United Nations is engaged in collective military measures "there should be a mutually supporting relationship between the activities of such arrangements or agencies and the collective measures taken by the United Nations." . . . This clearly implied that the General Assembly might make recommendations to regional agencies. While such recommendations would not have the binding character attached to decisions of the Security Council, they might nevertheless be effective and can be made by a two-thirds vote of the General Assembly thus avoiding the veto. There is no doubt but that the general powers of recommendation conferred upon the General Assembly by the Charter make such recommendations permissible.

PART III

THE UNITED NATIONS AS A CONSTITUTIONAL AND POLITICAL SYSTEM

CHAPTER **5**

CHANGING CONCEPTIONS OF RIGHTS AND OBLIGA- TIONS

Quincy Wright's interpretation of the UN Charter is built on historic and effective bases. His approach is to examine the various views on major provisions of the Charter and to ask which view lends itself to achieving the primary purposes of the Charter. Many authorities have argued that the document is ambiguous in many places and lends itself to the charge of being inconsistent; for example, Article 2.7 prohibits the Organization from intervening "in matters which are essentially within the domestic jurisdiction of any state . . ." and Article 55 provides that "the United Nations shall promote higher standards of living, full employment, and conditions of economic and social progress and development, . . . universal respect for, and observance of, human rights and fundamental freedoms. . . ." In Article 56 all members pledge themselves to take joint and separate action in cooperation with the Organization for the achievement of the purpose set forth in Article 55.

Of course, this is not expected to restrict either the United Nations from proferring its good offices or the Security Council from carrying out enforcement measures. And this applies as much to resolutions expressing a viewpoint as to those authorizing action. One of the effects of these ambiguities is to make it possible for states to argue vigorously the question of which are the correct interpretations, and this condition, plus the differences among the great powers, provides increased maneuverability, especially for the small states.

Is the cause of a stable world order enhanced by this condition or would increased certainty of the obligations of members be preferable? If greater predictability is a characteristic of a more stabilized society, is the need more likely to be met by attempts at legal clarification, or are these uncertainties simply a reflection of political differences which do not lend themselves to a juridical approach?

Every institution goes through a process of change and therefore a constitution must be flexible enough to permit change. This has perhaps become most notable regarding certain procedures in the Security Council and certain practices in the General Assembly. Suppose, for example, that one of the major powers on the Security Council abstains from voting. Ruth Russell indicates that the practice of not considering such an abstention as a failure to meet the voting requirements of Article 27.3 has allowed for increased flexibility. A second move toward flexibility, she relates, has been the increased use of the General Assembly in matters of "peace and security," starting with the Polish effort to have the Spanish government defined as a source of "international friction" in 1946, continuing at an increasing rate thereafter, and eventually requiring the creation of ad hoc commissions to investigate matters associated with security issues. Perhaps the best example of this practice comes with the Uniting for Peace Resolution which authorized the Assembly to continue to try to meet the threat to the peace in Korea in 1950, the resolution being reintroduced in the Middle East crisis and other crises during that decade.

Some have considered that even greater, more significant results have occurred with the stepped-up tempo in economic and social activities by the UN. And while this may constitute more a change of degree than of kind, one must see this change in connection with the increasing importance of the UN for the developing states, as well as the UN's relationship to the movement for independence or improved well-being by peoples in colonial and non-self-governing territories. There is, of course, the one other development which is noted in the article, although not discussed, the effects of which remain unclear at this time: the expanded role of the Secretary-General.

In each of the above examples expansion did not develop through formal amendment but took place as a by-product of a consensus which emerged when certain problems or conditions appeared intolerable. Necessity is apparently the mother of modification as well as invention.

Does change by a slow process of accretion always provide a more reliable, more solid, and more liberal revision than formal amendment would? Accepting the fact that a formal process may not always be feasible, and will always be slower, is it not just as possible for the informal method to be retrogressive? Do we not have such a case in the refusal to support peace-keeping costs that are not approved by the Council? Is there not also a potential danger that future members, especially powerful ones, who must accept a formal document and its obligations upon joining, will feel no constraints to accept also formerly established informal agreements when they are employed at crucial moments? In any case, informal change will undoubtedly proceed regardless. The main issue to consider is: When is it wise to approach such change on a formal, in contrast to an informal, basis?

FURTHER READINGS

Bowett, D. W., *The Law of International Institutions.* New York: Frederick A. Praeger, Inc., 1963.

Calvocoressi, Peter, *World Order and New States.* New York: Frederick A. Praeger, Inc., 1962.

Corbett, Percy L., *Law and Society in the Relations of States.* New York: Harcourt, Brace & World, Inc., 1951.

Jessup, Philip C., *A Modern Law of Nations.* New York: The Macmillan Company, 1950.

ANALYSIS OF THE CHARTER

Quincy Wright*

The provisions of the Charter fall into five classes dealing respectively and successively with *purposes, principles, members, organs,* and *procedures.* The first four of these matters are dealt with in the preamble and chapters one, two and three. The remaining sixteen chapters deal largely with procedures. Six chapters describe the procedures available to each of the principal organs along with details of their structure and powers, and ten describe procedures for accomplishing major purposes of the United Nations.

The Soviet Union has declared that the unanimity of the great powers is the "fundamental principle" of the Charter, but scrutiny of the text and of the history of that instrument suggests that this unanimity is merely a procedure of limited applicability. The concurrence of all the permanent members is required explicitly only for non-procedural "decisions" of the Security Council and amendments of the Charter. The line between procedural and non-procedural matters is not defined and it is not clear from the text whether "recommendations" on such matters as pacific settlement of disputes, admission of new members, and appointment of a Secretary-General are to be regarded as "decisions," although practice has, up to date, so regarded them. The provisions concerning the unanimity of the great powers is not included among the "principles" of the Charter, the organs other than the Security Council are not affected by them, and the members have by overwhelming majorities sustained the use of alternative methods, permitted by the Charter and not involving the great power veto, when the Security Council veto stood in the way of achieving the purposes and maintaining the principles set forth in the Charter. Judging by the activity of its organs, the policies of most of its members, and the attitudes of most of its peoples, the provisions concerning purposes and principles are more fundamental and persistent aspects of the Charter than those concerning organs and procedures.

* Quincy Wright, excerpts from *International Law and the United Nations* (New Delhi, Asia Publishing House, 1960), Chaps. 2 and 3. © Indian School of International Studies, New Delhi, 1960. By permission of Asia Publishing House and Quincy Wright.

Quincy Wright is Professor Emeritus of International Relations at the University of Chicago and presently Professor of Political Science at Rice University, Houston, Texas. He is the author of numerous books and articles including *A Study of War* and *The Study of International Relations.*

The same conclusion can be drawn from the history of the Charter. Secretary of State Stettinius, chairman of the United States delegation at the San Francisco Conference, said of the Charter in his official report to the President:

Its outstanding characteristic and the key to its construction is its dual quality as declaration and as constitution. As declaration it constitutes a binding agreement by the signatory nations to work together for peaceful ends and to adhere to certain standards of international morality. As constitution it creates four over-all instruments by which these ends may be achieved in practice and these standards actually maintained.

He then states the commitments of the members by the "declaration" mainly found in the first chapter and says:

The Charter in its capacity as constitution creates, in addition to its Secretariat and the Trusteeship Council with its specialized but vital functions, four principal over-all instruments to arm its purposes and to accomplish its ends: an enforcement agency; a forum for discussion and debate; a social and economic institute through which the learning and the knowledge of the world may be brought to bear upon its common problems; and an international court in which justiciable cases may be heard.[1]

It is to be noticed that this description of the functions respectively of the Security Council, the General Assembly, the Economic and Social Council and the International Court of Justice does not accurately conform to the functions they are actually performing today. The purposes and principles have remained the same but the functions and procedures of the organs have changed.

The fundamental character of the purposes and principles of the Charter can best be indicated by reciting them. The "purposes" include: (i) the "saving of future generations from the scourge of war" by "practising tolerance" and "uniting strength to maintain international peace and security"; (ii) the "reaffirmation of faith in the dignity and worth of the human person" by "promoting and encouraging respect for human rights and fundamental freedoms for all without distinction as to race, sex, language or religion"; (iii) the "reaffirmation of faith in the general rights of nations, large and small" by "respecting the equal rights and self-determination of peoples"; (iv) "the establishment of conditions under which justice and respect for the obligations arising from treaties and other sources of international law can be maintained"; and (v) "the promotion of social progress and better standards of life in larger freedom" by "employing international machinery for the promotion of the economic and social advancement of all peoples." Purposes are also stated in later articles of the Charter but they appear to

[1] Charter of the United Nations, Report to the President on the Results of the San Francisco Conference by the Chairman of the United States Delegation, the Secretary of State, June 26, 1945, pp. 12, 13.

be consistent with and subordinate to these major purposes which may be designated as *peace, human rights, self-determination of nations, international justice,* and *social progress.* "We the peoples of the United Nations" expressed in the Charter our "determination" to accomplish these purposes.

The "principles" of the Charter assert: (1) the *right of members* to "sovereign equality," and independence from United Nations "intervention" in matters of "domestic jurisdiction"; (2) the *duty of members* to "fulfil in good faith the obligations assumed by them in accordance with the Charter," to settle international disputes "by peaceful means," to "refrain in their international relations from the threat or use of force" except as permitted by the Charter, "to give the United Nations every assistance in any action it takes in accordance with" the Chapter, and "to refrain from giving assistance to any state against which the United Nations is taking preventive or enforcement action"; and (3) the *duty of the United Nations* to respect the rights of its members and to ensure that non-members "act in accordance with these principles so far as may be necessary for the maintenance of international peace and security." Other principles are stated in later articles of the Charter but these appear to be intended either as subordinate to, or explanatory of, the general principles of *sovereignty, good faith, pacific settlement, non-aggression* and *collective security* applicable to both members and non-members. The Charter states that "the organization and its members, in pursuit of the Purposes" shall act in accordance with these principles. The "principles" seem, therefore, to have been considered second only to the "purposes" in importance and permanence.

The provisions of the Charter concerning membership have been controversial. When the permanent organization of the United Nations was being considered during the war many believed that this organization should, in principle, be universal. Thus in 1943 a group of American jurists, educators, and statesmen, under the leadership of Judge Manley O. Hudson published a statement on "The International Law of the Future" which proposed that "the community of states should be organized on a universal basis. All states which exist or which may come into existence in the future should be included. No provision should be made for the expulsion or withdrawal of any state." It was argued that the purpose of preventing war and maintaining law could not be achieved unless every state was subject to the obligations and control of the United Nations. This point of view was vigorously urged by some states at San Francisco and was accepted as an ideal goal by most of the others. Universality of Membership was also urged in the Twenty Year Programme for Peace presented by the Secretary-General in June 1950 as a result of extensive consultations with the major governments. This programme was commended by the Fifth Session of the General Assembly and referred for study to the relevant agencies of the United Nations by a vote which was unanimous except for the Soviet Bloc.

Others wished the United Nations to be confined to states who could be relied upon to maintain its purposes. They were thinking of the responsibilities of the members to enforce the Charter rather than of their obligations to observe it. This view appeared to be accepted by the provisions of Article 4 limiting original membership to the Allies in the war, that is to those who had signed the Declaration by United Nations of January 1, 1942; and confining eligibility to subsequent membership to "peace-loving states" which accepted the obligations of the Charter and were "able and willing" to carry them out. The provisions interpreted as giving each of the great powers a veto on new members and the provisions for expulsion of members which "persistently violated the principles" of the Charter seemed also to support this point of view.

On the other hand, the universal principle was recognized in the provision authorizing the organization to ensure that non-members observe the principles of the Charter necessary for the maintenance of international peace and security. Furthermore, the General Assembly was given authority to "decide" on admissions to membership and the Security Council was given power only to "recommend" on this subject. If this were construed, as has been urged by the Argentine and other members of the United Nations, to permit the General Assembly to admit new members after examining the Security Council's recommendation, the United Nations would have approached universality much more rapidly. Such a construction was clearly supported by the committee that prepared the text at the San Francisco Conference. The interpretation accepted in an advisory opinion by the International Court of Justice, with two Latin American judges dissenting, required a favourable recommendation by the Security Council. In practice such recommendation has been considered subject to veto by the permanent members. This procedure resulted in a long deadlock on the admission of new members, happily broken by the tenth General Assembly which admitted sixteen of the twenty-two states, most of which had been applicants for several years. Others have subsequently been admitted. A dozen states remain non-members but half of these are politically unimportant. The non-members include several very small states (Monaco, San Marino, Liechtenstein, Andorra and Vatican City), Switzerland which has not applied because of fear that its traditional neutrality might be impaired, Mongolia which has limited international relations and three states divided between Communist and non-Communist governments, Germany, Korea and Viet Nam. China, though a member, is represented by the Nationalist government with no control of China's 650 million people on the Mainland under a Communist government.

Thus 800 million people, nearly a third of the world's people, remain outside the United Nations. The more nearly universal the United Nations becomes, the more reluctant would members be to withdraw and consequently the greater the influence it can exert. If many important states are not members, they may form powerful blocs outside the United Nations and seek to induce some members to withdraw from the United Nations and join them. Before he became Secretary of State but after he had had much experience in the American delegation to the United Nations, Secretary of State Dulles wrote:

I have come to believe that the United Nations will best serve the cause of peace if its Assembly is representative of what the world actually is, and not merely representative of the parts which we like. Therefore, we ought to be willing that all the nations should be members without attempting to appraise closely those which are "good" and those which are "bad." Already that distinction is obliterated by the present membership of the United Nations.

Some of the present member nations, and others that might become members, have governments that are not representative of the people. But if in fact they are "governments"—that is, if they "govern"—then they have a power which should be represented in any organization that purports to mirror world reality.

In his statement to the Wiley Sub-committee on January 18, 1954, Mr. Dulles, then Secretary of State, presented the same argument and favoured "approximate universality."

Universality of membership, thus making the United Nations an organization of the world, should be regarded as a fundamental objective and purpose toward which the United Nations should move as rapidly as possible.

During the period of deadlock most of the non-member states actually became associated with the United Nations through membership in one of the organs such as the International Court of Justice, the Trusteeship Council or a regional commission under the Economic and Social Council, or through membership in one of the specialized agencies, or regional arrangements.

Other provisions of the Charter, concerning organs and procedures, have been interpreted flexibly to facilitate achievement of the purposes and principles. Most of the members have accepted the opinion that if existing procedures prove inadequate to realize the purposes and principles, other methods within the spirit of the Charter and not forbidden by its letter, should be devised. In fact interpretations, practices and supplementary agreements have resulted in much adaptation of these provisions. The liberal principle of Constitutional construction, practised by Chief Justice John Marshall, has been generally accepted by organs of the United Nations as applicable to construction of the Charter.

The Soviet Union, as noted, has insisted that the great power veto is the fundamental principle of the Charter and has shown no disposition to eliminate it, with the result that the Security Council has proved much less useful than anticipated in forwarding the purposes for which it was designed. Other great powers, while ready to regard the veto as inapplicable in respect to recommendations on membership and pacific settlement, cling to it in regard to collective security action. The result is that efforts to eliminate the veto are not likely to be successful so long as the amending procedure, in which the veto exists, is respected. If this procedure were ignored the principle of universality would probably be frustrated through withdrawal of the Communist and perhaps other states.

It appears to be the predominant opinion that the principle of universality should be regarded as fundamental and, therefore, amendments to the Charter should not be pressed to the point of eliminating the participation of the Soviet and satellite states. This conclusion recognizes that progress toward adapting the organs and procedures of the United Nations, better to achieve its purposes and to maintain its principles, will probably be a slow process which will proceed more by interpretation, practice and supplementary agreements than by formal amendments.

The opinion, entertained by some unofficial groups, that it would be better to develop a strong United Nations even if the Soviet group of states withdrew, appears, therefore, to be incompatible with the basic purposes of the United Nations. It is generally believed that such a policy would tend toward war rather than peace. A United Nations thus truncated would not be an organization of the world to achieve the purposes and to maintain the principles of the Charter but would be regarded by the Soviet Union as an alliance against it. It would tend to accelerate the arms race and to eliminate the one general institution offering a promise of co-operation across the Iron Curtain.

This opinion does not deny the value of regional and collective self-defence arrangements provided they are kept within the conception of such special political arrangements set forth in the Charter itself. In this connection the recommendation of the Commission to Study the Organization of Peace in June 1953 deserves attention:

Every effort should be made to strengthen the United Nations so that no regional or collective defence arrangement can be more powerful in any situation. To this end the United Nations and the governments of the nations through diplomatic action should seek to stop a trend toward a bipolarized world by fostering various centers of power and committing each to United Nations' responsibilities.

AMBIGUITIES OF THE CHARTER

Classification of the provisions of the Charter and identification of its general objectives is not adequate to guide the agencies and governments that have to apply it in their day-to-day work. Such guidance is important because it is through the continuous and proper application of the Charter that the United Nations develops as an institution.

The Charter, as has often been pointed out, is not a model of precise drafting. It is full of ambiguities and even inconsistencies, making possible wide divergencies of interpretation and development. Some vagueness is inevitable in an instrument like the Charter. A precise document would probably never have been adopted by the governments, and if by a miracle it had been adopted, it would have proved incapable of functioning for any length of time in a changing world. Fortunately absolute precision is beyond the capacities of the ordinary language in which international instruments are drafted. There is always room for different interpretations and, as Professor Kelsen has pointed out, no interpretation can often be regarded as absolutely right. Even if some of the operational clauses appear precise in their terms, the symbolic preamble and the broad assertions of purposes and principles provide ample opportunity for supplementing, complementing, or modifying their apparent meaning. The Charter, however, because of the political circumstances of its birth, may suffer from an excess of poor drafting and consequent ambiguity. It has in fact within its terms potentialities of at least five quite different types of organization.

The first lines of the preamble (We the peoples) and the repeated emphasis upon individual rights looks toward a *world federation* in which the central agencies act directly upon individuals.

The theory expressed during the war of a nuclear alliance of the great powers to maintain peace, the dominant position given the great powers in the Security Council, the broad discretionary powers given that body, and the obligation which its decisions impose on all members, opens the door for a five-headed *world empire* if the Big Five should ever be able to unite. It has been pointed out, especially by citizens of the smaller states, that the continued liberties of the small states is dependent upon the continued division of the great powers, in spite of their asserted nuclear alliance. The fear of a development in this direction seems to have contributed to the unwillingness of Switzerland to join.

The improbability of such unity, the limited power given the General Assembly, and the broad reservations of equal sovereignty, domestic jurisdiction, and self-defence by the members suggest a continuance of *balance of power politics* in which the Great Powers will play a major role both within and without the United Nations. The present emphasis upon this interpretation in the practice of the great powers is obvious.

Sceptics who emphasize the veto vote in the Security Council, the limitation of the powers of other organs to study and recommendation, the consequent lack, in any of the organs of the United Nations, of powers which are both authoritative and operative, look upon the Charter as primarily an affirmation of *moral principles* and a forum for their discussion.

Most writers, however, look upon the United Nations as an *international organization* within which states have undertaken definite obligations and responsibilities, and which provides agencies for co-operation to stated ends and procedure for the assumption of further obligations in the future. This interpretation is at present formally accepted by governments and applied by United Nations organs.

As the United States constitution had within it up to the Civil War potentialities both of a United Nation and of an alliance among sovereign states with powers of nullification reserved by each, so the United Nations Charter has within it potentialities of world federation, world empire, power politics, unsanctioned moral commitment, and international organization. The latter concept, most widely accepted, represents a position of unstable equilibrium among the other possibilities.

These extraordinary ambiguities and possibilities of divergent development, render the problem of Charter interpretation of the greatest importance. The future of the United Nations is not determined by the Charter but by what is made of it as history progresses.

INTERPRETATION OF THE CHARTER

. . . According to international law, "intervention" means dictatorial interference by a state in the internal affairs of another state or in the relations between other states. Tenders of good offices, representations seeking information or co-operation, and protests against breaches of international law do not constitute intervention. Intervention may, however, be diplomatic as well as military. A diplomatic communication of peremptory or threatening tone, implying possible use of military or other coercive measures, may constitute intervention.

The United Nations as such is authorized to intervene in this sense only if the Security Council decides upon enforcement measures under Chapter VII of the Charter, but such intervention, even though affecting the domestic jurisdiction of the state against which the measures are taken, is expressly permitted by the last clause in Article 2 (7).

The Charter permits the Security Council to "call upon" members or to "utilize" regional agencies to preserve international peace and security; permits the General Assembly and the Security Council to "recommend" action by members to carry out the purposes and principles of the Charter and permits the Economic and Social Council and the Trusteeship Council, within the scope of their functions, to make "recommendations" to members. Such resolutions, while they might in some instances urge "intervention" in the affairs of a state by members or regional agencies, would not usually constitute intervention by the United Nations itself. To place a matter on the agenda, to discuss it, to study it, or to pass a general resolution on principles would clearly not be to intervene. It thus appears that few otherwise permissible activities of United Nations organs are subject to the limitations of Article 2 (7). In practice, however, United Nations organs have hesitated, perhaps with excess of caution, to address a recommendation to a particular state unless the recommendation involved that state's international obligations and, therefore, was not within its domestic jurisdiction. They have usually preferred to address recommendations not involving such obligations to all members, letting each decide whom the cap fits.

Thus the issue of whether a resolution constitutes an "intervention" has been treated as a matter of form, rather than of substance. Some members of the General Assembly, for example, thought a resolution addressed to the South African government, criticizing it for its *apartheid* policy, would constitute "intervention" in that country's domestic jurisdiction, but approved a substitute resolution which, though referring in the preamble to racial conflict in South Africa resulting from the policy of *apartheid* of the government of the Union of South Africa, in its operative part condemned all governmental policies designed to perpetuate or increase discriminations as inconsistent with Article 56 of the Charter and "solemnly called upon all member states to bring their policies into conformity with their obligations under the Charter to promote the observance of human rights and fundamental freedoms." The resolution was addressed to all, but the General Assembly made it clear in the preamble whom it intended the cap to fit.

United Nations organs have felt free to pass resolutions dealing with matters which are essentially within the domestic jurisdiction of a state so long as the resolution applies a principle and is formally addressed to all members or to all members of a particular class, such as members administering non-self-governing territories, and does not propose action against, or in the territory of a particular state. Such resolutions are generally conceded not to constitute "intervention" by the United Nations. "Action" by the Security Council against a state or within its territory and, therefore, constituting "intervention" in its domestic jurisdiction is expressly permitted if it constitutes an "enforcement measure under Chapter VII."

Other resolutions of the General Assembly have been addressed to a particular state, but in these cases the resolution has dealt with a definite international obligation of the state addressed and so has not been a matter within its domestic jurisdiction. This was true of resolutions concerning the refusal of the Soviet Union to permit departure from its territory of the Soviet wives of aliens, including the wife of the Chilean Ambassador's son; concerning the suppression of civil and religious liberties guaranteed by the peace treaties in Bulgaria and Hungary; and concerning the treatment of Indians in South Africa contrary to the requirements of agreements between that country and India.

To summarize, Article 2 (7) does not prevent the organs of the United Nations from passing a resolution on matters within the domestic jurisdiction of a member provided the resolution is not in a form constituting "intervention," or from passing a resolution in a form constituting "intervention" provided it deals with international obligations of the state involved and so does not concern its domestic jurisdiction. The prohibition of Article 2 (7) applies, therefore, only to a resolution of a United Nations organ which is both an "intervention" and on a matter within the domestic jurisdiction of a state. It may be added that since protests against breaches of international law are usually excluded from the concept of "intervention," a United Nations resolution of this character would be neither an intervention nor a matter of domestic jurisdiction.

THE MAINTENANCE OF INTERNATIONAL PEACE AND SECURITY

In the political and military field members of the United Nations have assumed obligations concerning collective security and pacific settlement. As Security Council action under Chapter VII is expressly excepted from Article 2 (7) . . . and as the subject of collective security will be considered fully in the next chapter, the matter will here be considered very briefly. Members assume explicit obligations to settle international disputes peacefully, to permit investigation by the Security Council of any dispute not so settled and, if continuance of the dispute or situation is found to endanger the maintenance of international peace and security, to refer it to the Security Council or the General Assembly. It would appear that the line determining whether a dispute or situation is within the competence of a United Nations organ depends on whether international peace and security is endangered. Hostilities between two factions within a state, as in Korea, or between a colony and a mother country, as in Dutch Indonesia, were considered threats to international peace and security if not actual breaches of international peace and therefore not within the domestic jurisdiction of these countries. Reference in Articles 2 (3) and 33 to "international peace and security" and in Article 2 (4) to "international relations" does not prevent the United Nations organs from dealing with insurrections or hostilities within a state, if of such magnitude and so disturbing to surrounding states that international peace is actually threatened. Such disturbance can be assumed if an internationally accepted military or juridical boundary is violated, as was the case in Korea, or as would be the case if Formosa were attacked from mainland China. In the case of civil strife, therefore, the international obligations of states, and, conversely, their domestic jurisdiction, depend upon the magnitude and probable effects of internal disturbances. Under the Charter, states accept the obligation to prevent disturbance or other conditions from developing within their territory threatening the peace and security of neighbouring states, or threatening the continuance of international settlements. Decision on whether a state is fulfilling the obligation is clearly an international function but it depends necessarily on a political judgment and should, therefore, be made by a political organ of the United Nations rather than by the Court and request for advisory opinion would not usually be in order.

CHANGING PATTERNS OF
CONSTITUTIONAL DEVELOPMENT

Ruth B. Russell*

At the end of its twentieth year the United Nations is in the midst of a constitutional crisis the outcome of which is still in doubt. During its lifetime it has survived other profound changes, some no less constitution shaking than the present one. Other developments were absorbed chiefly through a process of informal Charter interpretation and institutional adaptation; whereas the current financial crisis was allowed to reach the stage where formal confrontation of conflicting Charter interpretations could be avoided only by adopting a procedural device to evade decision that, unfortunately, also brought the Assembly to a halt.

❊ ❊ ❊ ❊ ❊ ❊ ❊

The tie between political context and constitutional issue is always present in some degree. It is exceptionally strong in the UN which, as a voluntary international agency, is not an independent center of political power. It rather reflects the confluence of power factors in other political arenas of the world it seeks to organize. The constitutional development of the UN has consequently been shaped by political disputes outside the Organization as well as by the nature of its Charter.

Controversial issues at San Francisco were often resolved not in favor of one extreme or the other but by "fuzzing over" the controversy at the lowest common denominator of agreement and in language that was inevitably vague if not confusing. Strictly speaking, all that the Conference decided was the form of words that went into the Charter's provisions and into certain official interpretations.

The linguistic puzzle was further complicated by the lack of provision for authoritative interpretation. This left matters to the daily decisions necessary in the work of each organ and to procedures for resolving differences within or between organs. But if such interpretations were not "generally

* Ruth B. Russell, "Changing Patterns of Constitutional Development," *International Organization*, Vol. 19, 1965, pp. 410–425. Copyright 1965, World Peace Foundation. By permission of *International Organization*.

Ruth B. Russell is a senior staff member of the Foreign Policy Studies Division of The Brookings Institution and author of *A History of the United Nations Charter*.

acceptable," the Conference considered that they would not be binding and that Charter amendment might be required.

A proposed amendment can be blocked by any permanent member of the Security Council failing to ratify it (Article 108), leaving matters quite inflexible when there is a serious difference among the major powers—as in the present crisis. The difficult amendment procedure has meant that, despite numerous constitutional disputes since 1945, the first amendments were officially proposed only in December 1963 to enlarge both the Security Council and the Economic and Social Council (ECOSOC)—changes widely desired for many years but never voted because of Soviet opposition to any structural change while Peking did not occupy China's seat in the Organization.[1] A special "review conference," callable any time after ten years, was also provided for (Article 109) to mollify delegations that were dissatisfied with various provisions. No strong sentiment for convening such a conference has ever arisen, however, due to the continuing differences among the powers.

Had the UN achieved effective consensus on either a "strict" or a "liberal" construction of the Charter, it could have developed peacefully as either the "static conference machinery" or the "dynamic instrument of governments" which Secretary-General Dag Hammarskjöld described as its future alternatives in his final *Annual Report*. The kind of Charter interpretation that would have become customary under the second alternative was shown early in 1946 when the Soviet representative announced he was abstaining from voting on, but not vetoing, a Security Council resolution. This became accepted practice in spite of the literal meaning of the requirement in Article 27(3) that decisions must receive "the concurring votes" of all permanent Council members. A more recent pragmatic adaptation, also generally accepted, has been to split the two-year terms of elected Council members between two contestants when neither could command the requisite majority. That device not only resolved certain election difficulties but it also permitted more states to participate as Security Council members, which partly compensated for the inability to enlarge that organ after the UN's membership had increased so greatly.

In the years since 1945 the UN, without such consensus, has in practice had to "flesh out" the Charter skeleton of authority and principle, of machinery and procedures, for the attainment of its declared objectives. The record, while not consistent and steady, has on balance been "dynamic." Constitutional developments have also displayed a variety of patterns in the areas symbolized by the three Councils which reflect partly the changing

[1] Under General Assembly Resolution 1991 A and B (XVIII), December 17, 1963, the Security Council would be increased to fifteen members (all new members to be elected ones) and ECOSOC to 27.

world outside the UN, partly the inconsistency of Members within it, and partly the continuation of fundamental conflicts of interest that made it difficult to negotiate the Charter in the first place.

ACTION, REACTION, AND STALEMATE IN THE SECURITY FIELD

At Dumbarton Oaks the Soviet Union initially favored a postwar organization limited to security functions; even when it accepted the broader institution proposed by the United States and the United Kingdom, it wanted the Assembly confined to discussing only those matters referred from the Security Council. At San Francisco, a deadlock over this question of the Assembly's competence was only broken by an appeal to Moscow. The Assembly ultimately received the broad authority contained in Articles 10–12 and 14, which have always been interpreted by the vast majority of Members so as to allow them to discuss and recommend on practically anything they consider "international."

Although the Soviet Union has protested that any recommendatory "action" by the Assembly in matters of peace and security is illegal (thus interpreting Article 12 to fit its original desire), it has often gone along, on the basis of abstention, with the majority view; and it has sometimes promoted the use of the Assembly when the Security Council was prevented by a veto from acting. The first such shift to the Assembly was in fact initiated by Poland, in 1946, on the Spanish question. This practice was extended in 1947, on Western initiative, after a Soviet veto of further Council action in the Greek border case. In 1956 the Soviet Union voted in favor of invoking an emergency session of the Assembly after Anglo-French vetoes in the Security Council had prevented decision there on the Suez invasion.

The Assembly early established the use of subsidiary organs for field operations. Thus in 1947 it set up a UN Special Committee on the Balkans (UNSCOB) to observe and report on Greek border violations, a UN Temporary Commission on Korea (UNTCOK) to observe proposed elections intended to unify the country; a UN Special Committee on Palestine (UNSCOP) to investigate the situation and make recommendations concerning its future government and subsequently the UN Palestine Commission to implement the Assembly's plan for partition.

The utilization of military officers as field observers also began with the early operations by UNSCOB in Greece and by the Security Council's Consular Committee in Indonesia (1947) to report on a cease-fire; by a similar consular Truce Commission for Palestine (1948); and by more elaborate and continuing truce observation machinery set up in Kashmir (1948) and Palestine (1949). A significant change also occurred in the composition of such groups. Initially made up of government representatives, with minimum services by the Secretariat, their personnel gradually came under the Secretary-General's authority, either as part of the regular Secretariat (e.g., the

UN Field Service) or as seconded national officials, including military officers.

There was thus a considerable body of experience with field operations authorized on a recommendatory basis by the time Korea exploded while the Soviet representative was boycotting the Security Council. Abstention was already accepted as not equivalent to a veto, and now the other Council members extended the doctrine to cover absence as well. Since Soviet–United States differences had prevented conclusion of any agreements to make armed forces available to the Council (Article 43), that body simply recommended that all Members come to the aid of South Korea. It improvised a UN Unified Command, asking the United States to take charge as the only practical method in the circumstances.

When the Soviet representative returned to his seat and vetoed further action on Korea, the question was shifted to the Assembly, then opening in September 1950.[2] It passed the Uniting for Peace Resolution in an effort to rectify Council inability to act by providing formally for Assembly supervision of enforcement action under its recommendatory authority. It included a procedural change to speed the transfer of a question from Council to Assembly and established a standing Peace Observation Commission, thus seeking to institutionalize that recognized type of field machinery. It also recommended that Members earmark units of their armed forces to be maintained in readiness for future use under either Council or Assembly resolutions (equivalent to Article 43 obligations); authorized a panel of military experts (equivalent to the Military Staff Committee) to advise governments on the technical aspects of doing that; and a Collective Measures Committee to recommend further steps to improve UN ability to meet future aggression. This attempt to provide the elements of a sanctions force in readiness was destined to have no more success in practice than the Charter provisions for achieving the same end. Thus, the constitutional changes often attributed to the Uniting for Peace Resolution seem much overrated; although the objective may have been to enhance the Assembly's powers—"showing the way to an enforceable rule of law," as United States Secretary of State Dean Acheson put it at the time—it did not in fact result in any such institutionalization of earlier practice beyond the procedural change. The former view has nonetheless persisted so strongly that the current crisis has been widely and erroneously described as in effect nullifying the Uniting for Peace Resolution.

[2] Had action been so vetoed in June, with the Assembly not in session, convening an emergency session might have seemed too slow in the circumstances, and the United States might have sought to rally collective support for Korea under Article 51. In effect, the Korean operation was a collective self-defense action but carried on within the UN framework rather than outside it, as originally anticipated. See, for example, the explanation of the United Kingdom representative in Security Council *Official Records* (2nd year), 140th meeting, June 10, 1947, pp. 994–995.

Similar jumping to conclusions was indulged in when the Suez case in 1956 was shifted from a vetoed Security Council to the Assembly, which authorized the establishment of the UN Emergency Force (UNEF) by the Secretary-General. The sheer novelty of seeing an international armed force, in the name and under the flag of the UN and commanded by Secretariat officials under Assembly direction, was so great that its relationship to the earlier and smaller—but politically and functionally similar—field operations noted above was largely overlooked, although General Burns (its first Commander) and his initial staff were drawn directly from the Palestine armistice team. As with the earlier groups, UNEF's functions were essentially the same nonfighting type of impartial, pacific-settlement activity, carried out with the consent of the parties in conflict and for the purpose of assisting them to comply with their undertakings to suspend violence. Those basic characteristics have applied to all subsequent peacekeeping operations in spite of their varying sizes, mandates, and details of organization. Even the highly contentious Congo operation got into trouble primarily because in rapidly changing and often chaotic circumstances it was unable to make effective those same guidelines as laid down by the Secretary-General and accepted by the Security Council.

*   *   *   *   *   *   *

REVOLUTIONARY CHANGE IN DEVELOPING LANDS

Radical change has likewise marked the expanding relationships of the UN to dependent territories and peoples, but it has been accompanied by continuous conflict over the Organization's jurisdiction, in contrast to the economic and social field, and has resulted in clear victory for one side rather than the stalemate that prevails in the security field. The nature of the substantive conflict underlying the constitutional developments has, moreover, brought about another, and wholly unexpected, revolution in the nature of the human rights problems in the UN.

The viewpoints in conflict since 1945 were already in evidence before then. President Franklin D. Roosevelt and other United States leaders were convinced that the emerging nationalist demands of colonial peoples would be a major political factor in the postwar world. Their somewhat vague vision of an international trusteeship system was a projection of United States policy in the Philippines, the theme of which was training for self-government with target dates for independence. But neither during nor after the war were they successful in persuading the chief European imperial powers to "go and do likewise" in the interests of peaceful, evolutionary decolonization. By the time of San Francisco, the United States' position was somewhat ambivalent as a result of military insistence on retaining the Japanese-mandated islands for security reasons. At the Conference, the other major powers divided on this issue along lines that later became so familiar: The United Kingdom and France opposed any significant extension in the UN role beyond that of the League in the mandate system, while the Soviet Union and China favored much stronger international activity.

* * * * * * *

In 1945, however, since the provisions of the Charter had to be voluntarily accepted, the colonial powers by threatening to reject *any* trusteeship provisions successfully opposed proposals to put all colonies in trust if not to declare their imminent independence. To forestall more drastic provisions, they accepted the Declaration Regarding Non-Self-Governing Territories (Chapter XI of the Charter). They praised its uniqueness as a joint statement of colonial policy principles but insisted on its form as a "Declaration" supposedly not binding them beyond responsibility to promote the well-being of dependent peoples and voluntarily to transmit technical data ("for information purposes" only) on dependencies of their own choosing. That eight states promptly listed 74 territories as in this class indicated their evident self-confidence that the Charter contained adequate safeguards from their point of view.

The trusteeship provisions were even more permissive. This system depended on the sovereign states voluntarily placing territories under UN trusteeship on their terms although it was understood that former mandates and any "detached" enemy territories would be included. The membership of the Trusteeship Council, moreover, was evenly divided between "administering" and "nonadministering" governments, thereby compensating for the former's numerical inferiority in the UN even in 1945 by practically guaranteeing a deadlock over contentious issues. The potentials of the Charter for the development of a wide-ranging trusteeship system along Rooseveltian lines could only be realized through the initiative of the imperial powers—which was not forthcoming. In fact, only ten of the former mandates (all but South West Africa) and the former Italian colony of Somaliland were made trust territories. By 1965 the Trusteeship Council had about "withered away," as eight of its territories, all but New Guinea and Nauru (Australia) and the Pacific Islands Trust Territory (United States), had become independent. This left a curious situation. The Council can only be constituted in nominal accord with the terms of Article 86 by including New Zealand and the United Kingdom as "administering authorities" although Australia alone administers Nauru on their behalf.

The Charter also contained a time bomb, little recognized in 1945, in the "principle of equal rights and self-determination of peoples" as the basis of "friendly relations among nations." (Article 1[2].) No one was prepared to oppose the principle which was first suggested by the Soviet Union but neither was there agreement on its meaning; the rights of revolution and secession were both debated but the result was one of the fuzziest terms in the Charter. By 1960, however, it had been "defined" in practice and embodied in an Assembly resolution as the right of colonial peoples to be freed from imperial rule. As newly independent states, however, they adopted the almost universal view of governments of whatever age in refusing a right of secession to any domestic group.

These developments were more the result than the cause of the historical decolonization movement. But the world spotlight on the UN stage has misled many to credit the Organization with more authority than it can in fact exert. However, the Assembly early established its right to set up a Committee on Information to consider the "technical data" transmitted on the non-self-governing territories, and it pressed increasingly into the political field as well. One committee has succeeded another until the present Special Committee on the Situation with Regard to the Implementation of the Declaration on the Granting of Independence to Colonial Countries and Peoples (Special Committee of Twenty-Four).

Every step increasing the Assembly's area of concern has been resisted by the colonial powers under the claim that the subject was *ultra vires*—a position still adhered to by Portugal and South Africa. Even today, the Assembly's actions may be pragmatically accepted by the more liberal colonial states while its competence is formally denied, as when a UN representative was authorized to supervise elections in the Cook Islands at New Zealand's request. The Assembly has nonetheless established its right to determine which territories fall under Article 73 (Portugal's resistance notwithstanding), and the Special Committee of Twenty-Four now receives petitions, hears individuals, makes field investigations in relation to dependent areas, and somewhat resembles liberal hopes of 1945 for the Trusteeship Council.

In the course of this transformation the issue of national self-determination became inextricably mixed with that of racial discrimination, a prevalent characteristic of colonialism. The legal approach to human rights as a field of UN activity began with the relatively rapid achievement of the Universal Declaration of Human Rights of 1948, but then the intended development of covenants specifying those rights in detail and making them binding never passed the drafting stage. However, a political approach to the issue also appeared in 1946 when India complained against discriminatory treatment of Indians by South Africa. In 1952 the general problem of *apartheid* was added to the particular case with the charge that race conflict also threatened the peace. The idea that racism could be such a threat, even though an internal issue, was recognized in 1945, as the horrors of Nazi concentration camps were being revealed. At San Francisco, for example, France proposed that the domestic jurisdiction reservation should not apply if serious violation of human rights became a threat to the peace. Article 2(7) was phrased so as to make that or any other internal source of international disorder subject to the enforcement authority of the Security Council.

By 1960 the Declaration on the Granting of Independence to Colonial

Countries and Peoples pronounced colonialism a "denial of fundamental human rights," incorporated the right of self-determination as defined in the pending human rights covenants, and admonished all states also to observe the Human Rights Declaration and the Charter.[3] Since then the denial of both self-determination and racial equality have been ever more strongly condemned as threats to the peace. The Assembly and the Security Council have even recommended that Members apply diplomatic and economic sanctions and an arms embargo against South Africa. Pressures mount for even stronger mandatory sanctions but no general consensus has yet developed on the criteria for determining when, in the French terms of 1945, "the clear violation of essential liberties and human rights constitutes in itself a threat capable of compromising the peace."[4]

As long as these two group rights—self-determination and racial equality—remain far from universal realization, pressures for their achievement will certainly continue to take priority over any significant expansion of UN activity in other human rights areas. Indeed, the end of both colonialism and racism might not mean much greater UN concern with the rights of individuals. For those touch upon sensitive domestic policies of *all* countries, not just of a small minority of the Assembly—and few governments are yet prepared to be as liberal about their own policies as about others', as the Soviet Union demonstrates when pressing for UN intervention in other dependent areas generally while remaining silent on its own policies in the Kuriles.

CONCLUSION

The foregoing sketch of developments since 1945, incomplete as it is, demonstrates how constitutional adaptation to change in the international scene in a period of serious political conflict tends to be made through informal interpretation and usage rather than through formal interpretation and amendment. The political conflict itself reflects the fact that we live in a transitional world where old norms of international law are no longer so widely accepted while new ones are still being painfully forged on the anvil of contemporary political experience. The International Court of Justice has consequently been less utilized than was the Permanent Court of International Justice under the League of Nations. Given the flexible terms of the

[3] In view of the stubborn adherence to domestic jurisdiction claims by the colonial states generally, it is curious that not one of them voted against the Declaration, which was passed by 90 in favor, none opposed, with 9 abstentions (Australia, Belgium, Dominican Republic, France, Portugal, Spain, South Africa, United Kingdom, United States). A similar reluctance to declare public opposition was seen in 1948 when the Communist Bloc states abstained in the vote on the Universal Declaration of Human Rights.

[4] *Documents of the United Nations Conference on International Organization, San Francisco, 1945* (New York: United Nations Information Organization, 1945), Vol. 3, p. 386.

Charter and effective consensus of the Members, however, the doctrine of implied powers has provided adequate rationale for rather liberal constitutional adaptation. The controlling factor in the future will continue to be the "effectiveness" of that consensus which must include, in the positive consent of the required majority, those states with means to implement the decision in question and, additionally, at least the "negative consent" of abstinence on the part of those in the minority with power to prevent implementing action. The current crisis demonstrates that such power—either to prevent or to implement—may be psychological and political as well as financial or military.

The lack of common accord on the standards of peace to be enforced through Security Council action continues to prevent the constructive use of that body as originally planned in the Charter. It has been partially compensated for in times of crisis by the development of enough consensus to support action through the Organization to contain outbreaks of violence. In such circumstances, operations by the Secretariat have expanded into the vacuum left by the Security Council's inability to act through its own machinery. The role of the Secretary-General has developed in answer to the demand created by the difficulties of operating under the original division of constitutional functions. In the field of economic and social development, the role of the Secretariat has likewise expanded beyond the 1945 concepts to fit the changing nature of the problem as perceived in the Organization and to the extent of the willingness of Members to support its operations. Since the near future promises no rapid change for the better in the degree of international cooperation likely to be practiced, there is also little reason to anticipate much change either in the prevalent mode of constitutional development in the foreseeable future.

The degree of national commitment to action through international organization is still weak, especially when it involves giving rather than getting on the part of Member States. This is true in specific instances even of states that are generally strong supporters of the United Nations. In part, this results from the relative novelty of multilateral activity; for governments, like individuals, tend to be suspicious of the new. Even when willing to engage in collective action, moreover, they are novices in utilizing the potentialities of the permanent organizations. Yet the League was only a pale foreshadowing of what the United Nations has become under far from optimum conditions of growth; given the normal slowness of social evolution, the range of concern of the Organization has expanded remarkably in the past twenty years. In that perspective, we may look to the next twenty years with more optimism than the immediate situation seems to warrant.

CHAPTER **6**

THE DIVISION OF LABOR

The construction of a bicameral legislature seems almost a natural law of politics. It is found in almost all countries of the world and has become a standard feature in multipurpose international organizations. Why do we have it in the United Nations and what functions do the two houses serve? In the first place, it is perfectly clear that there was no intent on the part of the major victorious powers after either World War I or World War II to establish an imperium, although it is doubtful that they could have done so even had they wanted to, especially after World War I. The victorious powers wanted to create a democratic organization that would have a wide membership base and a separation of powers, and the question was on what grounds some kind of executive authority could be established. The solution was that which had become most common since the rise of independent states in the seventeenth century: the

97

more powerful states simply assumed both the responsibility and privilege. Hence one small organ, the Security Council, was given the primary, but not exclusive, authority for dealing with issues that posed an immediate threat to the peace; the other organ, containing all the members, the General Assembly, was given a special authority in all other matters whose bearing upon peace was real but less immediate.

Two things should be noted. First, this careful division soon became clouded, especially with regard to the Assembly's jurisdiction. Second, this emphasis on action, which has frequently led many commentators to characterize the two organs as political, ignores the fact that law is made by political means and that both organs are law-making bodies for the organization as well as for the international community in general (see Article 2.6).

The Council, originally composed of 11 states (and since 1966 of 15), is presumably able to operate faster, because of its small size, and more authoritatively, because of the power of its members than the General Assembly. Both of these assumptions were predicated upon a more basic one: that a large measure of harmony of views would prevail among the Council's most powerful members. The latter assumption having not proved true, the Council's ability to reach decisions has been weakened by internal divisions and protracted because the divisions allow for intensive lobbying for support among the other members.

Leland M. Goodrich surveys the early expectations and he contrasts these with the actual results up to the latter part of the 1950's. He indicates what the various attitudes of the larger states have been toward the use of the Council, examines in detail the effect of the veto, and argues that the Council still provides many advantages which would be lost if efforts were made to consider the Assembly as an oppropriate substitute.

Muhammad Zafrulla Khan, a former delegate from Pakistan to the United Nations and a president of the Seventeenth General Assembly notes the great importance of UN membership to many of the new states. In his view, one of the most significant objectives of the Assembly is to achieve consensus whether the issue be political, economic, or social. While the reader might assume this to be natural, the observer will note the effect of this on the interplay of roles between an individual as a national delegate and that same individual as a UN representative. This integration takes place not only when the Assembly undertakes to achieve majority support for a resolution, but also whenever delegates are appointed or elected to serve on ad hoc bodies which are expected to bring forth reports of investigations or solutions of problems. Zafrulla Khan's article on the Assembly does not attempt to analyze how the Assembly functions, but rather stresses the ends it serves. The question remains: Can these ends include a common set of values, deeply enough felt to act as a restraining influence on states as well as on the Security Council? A further question is: Can the Assembly's debates, resolutions, and decisions have any great sinificance as a source of pressure on governments unless the Assembly becomes newsworthy in most countries at times other than crises? And, finally, one may ask even if it is not possible—nor indeed necessary—for delegates to overlook the opportunity to expound their viewpoints in a propagandistic fashion: can debates be so managed that members engage more in dialogues than monologues? This is not to say that debate cannot serve the ends of creating a stable world order, but only to indicate that the procedures and results of the Assembly suffer the flaws of any large parliamentary body when dispatch and responsible performance are absent.

There are many questions the student can consider regarding the place of debate in both organs. The most obvious is the purpose of debate. Is it designed to bring issues to a formal vote, to act as a forum to arouse public opinion, or to persuade participants to a point of view? It would seem that much of the latter takes place elsewhere. One might also ask, considering the way they are often used, are the General Assembly and the Security Council in competition with each other? If the answer is yes, what is the impact that this is likely to have on the effective operation of the system? Of course, we should not be misled into assuming that if such competition exists it is peculiar to the UN, for we are likely to find this situation in all two-chamber legislatures.

This chapter, which is concerned with the division of labor, does not contain any articles on the other two principle organs, the Trusteeship Council and the Economic and Social Council, both of which are dealt with elsewhere. It may be charged that this is an arbitrary division, but it could be answered that both of these councils are responsible to the Assembly and hence are organizationally and juridically not on a par with those which are discussed. We turn next, therefore, to the third organ, the Court. Max Sorensen's article, "The International Court of Justice: Its Role in Contemporary International Relations," is really a description of the Court's procedures, organization, and jurisdiction. Despite the Court's care to make sure that the major legal systems of the world are represented on the Court, that the judges while performing their duties are not unduly influenced by their own countries nor by the broad base of jurisdiction allowed the Court, it is still true that the Court's lack of enforcement powers and its inability to compel parties to appear before it restricts its performance to a degree not to be found in any other agency. Thus the Court's record is only a very modest one in terms of its impact on international politics. Although it is clear that judicial integrity and a representative character are necessary for the Court in order that it have the confidence of all the states, yet it is also clear that its lack of influence on major world problems is not a reflection of its structures or composition. Its jurisdiction, stated in Article 36.2, could have been more significant if a great many of the signatories had not attached reservations to that jurisdiction.

Furthermore, the whole issue of when a dispute is legal and when polit-

ical, has still not been definitively answered. And we do not have any more reason to assume that it can be answered on the basis of the facts in the case than on the basis of the attitudes of the disputants. It is clear, however, that reluctance to make the Court a significant actor in the international political game reduces its stature and potency. One need not conclude that the Court must receive all legal disputes any more than one needs to accept the argument that disputes phrased in judicial terms are easier to resolve in order to appreciate its minor status. The record alone or by comparison with the "Old" Court (PCIJ) will support this viewpoint.

FURTHER READINGS

Alker, Hayward R., Jr., and Russett, Bruce M., *World Politics in the General Assembly*. New Haven: Yale University Press, 1965.

Claude, Inis L., "The Management of Power in the Changing UN," *International Organization*, Vol. 15, Spring 1961, pp. 219–236.

Gordenker, Leon, "The Political Process in International Organization," *World Politics*, Vol. XIV, 1962, pp. 519–531.

Lissitzyn, Oliver J., "The International Court," *Virginia Law Weekly*, Vol. XIV, No. 24, April 27, 1962.

Schachter, Oscar, "Enforcement of International Judicial and Arbitral Decisions," *American Journal of International Law*, Vol. 54, 1960, pp. 1–24.

de Visscher, Charles, *Theory and Reality in Public International Law*. Princeton: Princeton University Press, 1957.

THE UNITED NATIONS SECURITY COUNCIL

Leland M. Goodrich[*]

It has been the unfortunate fate of the United Nations to have been most conspicuously unsuccessful in performing that task which was to be its major responsibility and for which it was supposed to be best equipped. Naturally this has also been the fate of the Security Council upon which the Members of the Organization, by the terms of Article 24, conferred "primary responsibility for the maintenance of international peace and security." Against this background of failure and consequent dissatisfaction, many have been asking whether the Security Council is fated to become like the human appendix, an atrophied organ with no useful function to perform, or whether the present condition is not one that can and should be remedied or that perhaps will be changed in any case by an improvement in the state of international relations. To form a judgment on these possibilities it is necessary to recall the original conception of the Security Council, to review its record, and to analyze the causes of its decline and the likelihood of their elimination or counterbalancing by other forces.

The peace and security provisions of the Charter appear to have been based in part on conclusions that were drawn by their authors with respect to the causes of the failure of the League system. First of all, it was rightly believed that a major cause of the failure of the League system was its lack of universality, and particularly the absence of the United States. Consequently, the first concern of the Charter-makers was to have as members all the major powers in the Organization, and above all the Soviet Union and the United States. Secondly, it was believed that a weakness of the League system was its provision that sanctions should be applied against every aggressor, irrespective of whether or not it was a major power, and whether or not all the major powers joined in applying them. Consequently the authors of the Charter stressed the need of agreement among the permanent members of the Security Council as a condition of enforcement action, thus

* Leland M. Goodrich, "The United Nations Security Council," *International Organization*, Vol. 12, 1958, pp. 273-287. Copyright 1958, World Peace Foundation. By permission of *International Organization*.

Leland M. Goodrich is Professor of International Organization and Administration at Columbia University and a member of the Board of Editors of *International Organization*. He is coauthor with Edward Hambro of *Charter of the United Nations: Commentary and Documents*.

returning to the principle underlying the European Concert in the nineteenth century. Thirdly, it was believed that an important reason for the failure of the League system was the absence of any effective provision for the use of military force and the unwillingness of states under a voluntary system to take such extreme measures for defeating aggression. Therefore, the authors of the Charter were concerned with placing effective military force at the disposal of the Organization and making certain that it would be used when necessary. Finally, it was apparently believed, by some at least, that the League system was weakened by the failure of the Covenant clearly to delimit the respective responsibilities of Council and Assembly. Therefore the Charter-makers sought to define the limits of the responsibilities of the UN counterparts of these two organs.

As written at San Francisco, after a lengthy process of elaboration in which the United States government played a leading role, the Charter set the maintenance of international peace and security as the first purpose of the Organization. It prescribed two principal approaches to the achievement of this purpose: collective measures for preventing or removing threats to the peace and suppressing acts of aggression or breaches of the peace, and adjustment or settlement of international disputes or situations by peaceful means. The regulation of armaments was made a subsidiary approach with emphasis upon agreements to make armed forces and facilities available to the Security Council and upon achieving "the least diversion for armaments of the world's human and economic resources"[1] consistent with the assured maintenance of international peace and security.

The primary responsibility for doing these things was placed on the Security Council, an organ so constructed and with voting procedures so defined that no decision other than a procedural one could be taken except with the concurrence of the five permanent members.[2] This gave assurance that no action could be taken against a permanent member or without its consent. The powers given to the Security Council were such as to give assurance that once the permanent members were in agreement and had the support of two other members—which would in all likelihood not be difficult to achieve—effective action could be taken to maintain peace and security. The requirement of unanimity, moreover, was regarded as assurance that the coercive power vested in the Council would not be abused. Thus, in effect, the maintenance of international peace and security was to be made the responsibility of a "concert of the permanent members."

It was assumed that the members of this concert would each have an interest in the maintenance of peace and security, following a war which had imperiled them all. Furthermore, the members of the Council were required to act in accordance with the Purposes and Principles of the Or-

[1] Article 26 of the Charter.
[2] The one qualification was that a permanent member must abstain from voting when a decision was being taken under Chapter VI or Article 52, par. 3.

ganization, as set forth in Chapter I, in discharging their responsibilities. But it was also recognized that the concert might not always materialize in fact.

The underlying theory, however, was that if one of the major powers were to prove recalcitrant, or were to refuse to abide by the rules of international behaviour that were being inscribed in the Charter, a situation would be created in which the recalcitrant nation might have to be coerced; and it was apparent that no major nation could be coerced except by the combined forces of the other major nations. This would be the equivalent of a world war, and a decision to embark upon such a war would necessarily have to be made by each of the other major nations for itself and not by any international organization.[3]

There was no disagreement among the major powers at San Francisco or in previous discussions on the principle that unanimity of the major powers should be required. There was disagreement as to how far the principle should be applied in disputes involving one or more of the major powers. The view of the United Kingdom was that no one, even a permanent member of the Council, should be allowed to vote in its own case. The Soviet view was that the unity of the major powers was the important consideration and no provision should be included in the Charter which would tend to encourage disagreement. At Yalta, however, Stalin accepted President Roosevelt's proposal that a member of the Council, party to a dispute, even though a permanent member, should not be allowed to veto a decision which the Council might take in the performance of its function of peaceful settlement or adjustment. The agreement reached at Yalta did not fully hold at San Francisco, however, when it became evident that it was not interpreted in like manner by all the parties to it. Extensive further discussions among the four sponsoring governments were necessary before final agreement was reached on the scope of the unanimity requirement.[4] By the San Francisco agreement, accepted by France, it was made clear that the requirement of unanimity of the permanent members did not apply to Council decisions to consider and discuss matters brought to its attention, or to decisions inviting parties to disputes to be heard. On the other hand, the "chain of events" theory as elaborated in the Statement was interpreted as preventing the Security Council from deciding to conduct an investigation or take any subsequent non-procedural decisions save with the concurrence of the permanent members, the one exception to the rule being that above

[3] Leo Pasvolsky, "The United Nations in Action," *Edmund J. James Lectures on Government*, Fifth Series, Urbana, University of Illinois Press, 1951, pp. 80–81.

[4] See Dwight E. Lee, "The Genesis of the Veto," *International Organization*, February 1947 (Vol. 1, No. 1), pp. 33–42. For text of Statement by the Delegations of the Four Sponsoring Governments on Voting Procedure in the Security Council, see United Nations Conference on International Organization, *Documents*, XI, pp. 710–714, and Goodrich and Hambro, *Charter of the United Nations: Commentary and Documents*, rev. ed., Boston, World Peace Foundation, 1949, pp. 216–218.

indicated. Furthermore, the Statement asserted that the question whether or not a particular matter was procedural was itself non-procedural. While the Statement contained no commitment not to use the right of veto excessively or unreasonably, it did contain the statement that it was

not to be assumed . . . that the permanent members, any more than the non-permanent members, would use their "veto" power wilfully to obstruct the operation of the Council,

and representatives of the permanent members reaffirmed their sense of responsibility in Conference discussions.

With respect to the division of powers between the Security Council and the General Assembly, there was even less disagreement among the permanent members up to the time of the San Francisco Conference. The Tentative Proposals of July 18, 1944, which the United States submitted to the other participants in the Dumbarton Oaks Conversations gave the executive council (Security Council) the "primary responsibility for the peaceful settlement of international disputes, for the prevention of threats to the peace and breaches of the peace, and for such other activities as may be necessary for the maintenance of international peace and security." They empowered the General Assembly "to take action in matters of concern to the international organization which are not allocated to other organs by the basic instrument," and specifically

a. to make on its own initiative or on request of a member state, reports on and recommendations for the peaceful adjustment of any situation or controversy, the continuance of which it deems likely to impair the general welfare;
b. to assist the executive council, upon its request, in enlisting the cooperation of all states toward giving effect to action under consideration in or decided upon by the council with respect to:
   1) the settlement of a dispute the continuance of which is likely to endanger security or to lead to a breach of the peace;
   2) the maintenance or restoration of peace; and
   3) any other matters within the jurisdiction of the Council.

This proposed delimitation of the respective responsibilities of the two organs was substantially accepted at Dumbarton Oaks and incorporated into the Dumbarton Oaks Proposals. This not only represented Department of State thinking, but it was in line with Soviet reluctance to permit extensive participation by the lesser powers in the activities of the Organization in the maintenance of international peace and security.

At San Francisco, a variety of pressures—the insistence of the lesser powers on a larger measure of participation, growing skepticism regarding the likelihood of cooperation among the major powers, and the insistence of Republican leaders and Congressional members of the United States delegation—led to the broadening of the powers of the General Assembly, particularly by the inclusion of Articles 10 and 14, and the consequent blurring of the line dividing Security Council and General Assembly responsibilities and powers. Thus the Charter foundation was laid for the subsequent development of the role of the General Assembly in the field of action originally reserved to the Security Council. The primary role of the Security Council was further jeopardized by the inclusion of Article 51 recognizing explicitly "the inherent right of individual or collective self-defense" in case of an armed attack upon a Member, until such time as the Security Council has taken measures necessary to the maintenance of international peace and security.

The most striking trend in the practice of the UN since its establishment has been the increasing inability of the Security Council to serve the purposes for which it was intended and the growing preference of Members to make use of the General Assembly. This trend has been accompanied by the gradual breakdown of the lines of functional separation between the Security Council and the General Assembly, drawn up at Dumbarton Oaks and preserved, though with important modifications, at San Francisco, and by the gradual assumption by the General Assembly of an active role in the maintenance of international peace and security.

A quantitative measurement of the trend, though obviously inadequate, provides us with an indication of the changing role of the Security Council within the UN machinery. The declining frequency of the meetings of the Security Council in a world beset with conflicts, together with the increasing number of political questions considered by the Council, underscores the diminishing role of the Council. The figures are extremely illuminating:

| | | SUBSTANTIVE POLITICAL QUESTIONS CONSIDERED BY THE | |
| | MEETINGS OF THE SECURITY | SECURITY | GENERAL |
PERIOD	COUNCIL	COUNCIL	ASSEMBLY
Jan. 17, 1946–July 15, 1946	50	5	2
July 16, 1946–July 15, 1947	108	8	4
1947–1948	180	8	5
1948–1949	92	8	11
1949–1950	46	6	10
1950–1951	72	7	19
1951–1952	43	6	12
1952–1953	26	1	14
1953–1954	59	4	11
1954–1955	22	3	15
1955–1956	32	1	11
1956–1957	52	6	13

Since the peak reached in the period from July 1947 to July 1948, there has been a general decline in the number of meetings. Even in the period comprising the crises which simultaneously arose in the Middle East and Hungary in the fall of 1956, the frequency of Council meetings registered merely a moderate reversal of the trend. The provision of Rule I of the Provisional Rules of Procedure of the Security Council that "the interval between meetings shall not exceed fourteen days" was fairly well observed during the first three years, when there were only three instances in which the interval between meetings exceeded fourteen days. The situation began to deteriorate in 1949, and has not been remedied since.

Although the decline in the number of meetings of the Security Council and the number of new questions submitted to it would appear to be indicative of a decline in the importance attached to the work of the organ, one would not be justified in drawing conclusions regarding the effectiveness of the Council from these figures alone. Before passing final judgment upon the degree to which the Council has been effective in performing its Charter responsibilities, it is necessary to examine in some detail the Council's actual record of performance in the principal fields of its activity. These can be roughly defined as four in number: 1) the taking of collective measures to keep or restore international peace and security in case of threat or actual violation; 2) the peaceful settlement or adjustment of disputes and situations; 3) the regulation of armaments; and 4) the performance of certain organizational functions, including the recommendation of new members and the recommendation of a Secretary-General.

In the performance of the first function, the Council has achieved a considerable measure of success in dealing with those situations where its permanent members, for whatever reasons, have had a sufficient interest in the maintenance of restoration of international peace and security to agree on a common course of action. Thus in dealing with the situation in Indonesia created by Dutch "police" action to re-establish the authority of the Netherlands in Indonesia, the Security Council was able eventually to get the parties to agree to the cessation of hostilities leading to an acceptable political settlement. It must be recognized, however, that Security Council action alone might not have been effective without strong supporting action of an economic nature by the United States and certain Asian states. The major powers were unwilling, however, to use military force to achieve their purpose.

In dealing with the Palestine question during the initial period of crisis, the Security Council achieved considerable success. Although it was not willing to undertake the enforcement of the partition plan recommended by the General Assembly in its resolution of November 29, 1947, it did exercise steady and increasing pressure on the parties to the hostilities which broke out after the Israeli declaration of independence of May 14, 1948, to cease fighting and agree to permanent armistice arrangements. Largely as a result of this pressure, the armistice agreements were concluded, and a system of international supervision under the general oversight of the

Council was established. Until the Israeli attack of late October 1956, this system was effective in preventing a resumption of general hostilities, notwithstanding the failure of the UN to achieve a peaceful settlement of outstanding issues, occasional incidents of violence, and the deterioration of relations between the Soviet Union and the western powers.

The Security Council also achieved a considerable measure of success in dealing with hostilities involving India and Pakistan over Kashmir. The parties acceded to the proposal made by the Council's commission that a ceasefire be concluded under a system of international observation established with the consent of the parties, and a condition of non-fighting has since been maintained, even though efforts to settle the dispute have failed.

Only under exceptional conditions, has the Council been at all effective in dealing with threats to or breaches of the peace where the vital interests of permanent members have been directly in conflict. When, following the Communist *coup* in Czechoslovakia in February 1948, the complaint of Soviet intervention in that country was brought before the Council, any action, even the appointment of a committee to study the situation, was prevented by Soviet vetoes. It is difficult to see how any effective action could have been taken in any case, even if the right of veto had not existed, unless the western powers were willing to risk the unleashing of a general war.

In September 1948, the Council was asked to consider the situation resulting from the Soviet blockade of Berlin. The Soviet Union, by its veto, prevented any action from being taken. Again it is difficult to see what the Council could have done, even without the veto, without risking a general war, other than provide, as it did, the occasion for representatives of the interested parties to meet and negotiate.

When North Korean forces attacked the Republic of Korea on June 25, 1950, the Security Council was presented with a unique opportunity to take action in a situation involving the conflicting vital interests of permanent members, since the Soviet representative was absent in protest against the seating of the Chinese representative appointed by the Nationalist government. This condition of affairs proved to be temporary, and when the Soviet representative returned to the Council at the beginning of August, the possibility of making further use of the Council to guide and determine UN action ceased.

It was this situation which led to the adoption by the Assembly of the "Uniting for Peace" resolution of November 3, 1950, by which the Assembly asserted for itself, under a liberal interpretation of Charter provisions, the right to consider any threat to the peace, breach of the peace, or act of aggression, if the Council, because of lack of unanimity of its permanent members, had failed to discharge its primary responsibility, and to make appropriate recommendations, "including in the case of a breach of the peace or act of aggression the use of armed force when necessary." While the

General Assembly was to exercise this "residual responsibility" only after the Council had failed to take action and had removed the item from its agenda, the fact that this could be done by a procedural vote made it impossible for a permanent member by its veto to prevent Assembly consideration. Thus, the relationship between Council and Assembly which had been spelled out in the Department of State proposal of July 18, 1944, and in the Dumbarton Oaks Proposals and maintained in principle in the Charter was explicitly redefined to permit a majority of seven in the Council, in the face of opposition by as many as four of the permanent members, to transfer the consideration of an alleged threat to or breach of the peace to the General Assembly. Thus the way was prepared for making the Council's "primary responsibility" largely nominal, unless the permanent members were in full accord, and for making the Assembly's "residual responsibility"—based on extremely liberal Charter interpretation—major in fact, at least for as long as the cold war continued.

The Hungarian and Middle East crises in October 1956 again demonstrated that the Council was incapable of acting in a situation involving the conflicting vital interests of the major powers, though in the latter case it was not the cold war that was mainly responsible. In both cases, action was taken by the General Assembly, in the first case with no visible effect on the actual course of events and in the second case effectively. This experience tended to show that even when the General Assembly acts, the chances of successful action are small unless the United States and the Soviet Union are on the same side.

In discharging its second function, the peaceful settlement or adjustment of international disputes and situations, the Security Council has had very limited effectiveness. The disputes and situations that have been brought to its attention have, almost without exception, fallen into one or the other of two main categories: 1) disputes and situations resulting from the cold war —the ideological power conflict between the communist powers and the western powers; and 2) disputes and situations resulting from the conflict of interests between the more advanced western powers, including particularly the colonial powers, and the states, mainly of Asia and Africa, which had recently emerged from colonial domination or have strong attachments to the cause of Asian-African nationalism.

In dealing with disputes and situations in the first category, the Council has only exceptionally had some measure of success. Pressure brought to bear through the Council appears to have influenced the Soviet Union to withdraw its military forces from Iran in 1946 after that country had complained of their illegal presence. Following a Council recommendation, the dispute between the United Kingdom and Albania over damage to United Kingdom ships in the Corfu Channel was submitted to the International Court of Justice for decision. However, Albania did not accept the award of damages. The Council was not able to agree on the appointment of a governor of the Free Territory of Trieste. It was unable by its own action to bring about a settlement of the dispute leading to the Berlin blockade. It was unable to take decision on various complaints submitted to it at the time of the Korean conflict. For the most part, the parties initiating UN consideration of cold war questions have considered the General Assembly better suited to their purposes.

In handling disputes and situations in the second category, the Council has not been much more effective. Only in the Indonesian case did it play a major part in bringing about an agreed settlement. The fact that the Soviet Union has generally aligned itself with the Asian and African states in their differences with the West and that some of the other permanent members have taken a rigid stand in opposition has largely eliminated the possibility of agreement among the permanent members of the Council on any course of action. Even the major western powers themselves have often been in disagreement, largely due to the unwillingness of the United States to go as far as the United Kingdom and France in opposing Asian and African claims. Generally speaking, the Asian and African Members have preferred to bring the questions involving claims against the West before the General Assembly where their voting strength is proportionately greater. When the western powers find it in their interest to bring a question before the Security Council, as in the case of the Anglo-Iranian oil dispute or the Suez Canal dispute, any effective Council action is likely to be prevented by a Soviet opposition or by disagreement among the western powers themselves.

The disputes between the Arab states and Israel and between India and Pakistan over Kashmir do not completely fit into either of the above categories. Here, too, the Council has failed as an organ of peaceful settlement. And one of the decisive factors in these cases, as in the ones previously considered has been the failure of the permanent members to agree, as the result of their conflicting interests in the cold war. Without his agreement, not only may the Council be prevented from taking a decision, but even if it is able to take a decision as the result of one or more abstentions by a permanent member, the authority of the Council is greatly weakened.

In the performance of its third function, the achievement of agreement on the regulation of armaments, the Council has a record of complete failure. In the first place, it has been unable to conclude any agreement with Members by which they would undertake to place military forces and facilities at the disposal of the Council. This has been due to the inability of the permanent members, the members of the Military Staff Committee, to agree on the principles to be applied in the conclusion of these agreements. As a result, the Council has not had available to it the military forces essential to the full discharge of its responsibility for the maintenance of peace. Without these forces it can only recommend military measures, as it did in the Korean case. Secondly, all efforts that the Security Council has made to prepare proposals for the regulation of national armaments, whether atomic or conventional, have ended in complete deadlock due to the inability of the major powers to agree. Nor has the Assembly, which has taken the leading initiative in disarmament discussions, been more successful.

In discharging its functions relating to membership and the internal organization of the UN, the Security Council has had a mixed record. Because of vetoes cast by the Soviet Union, a deadlock developed over the admission of new members with the result that from 1950 to 1955 not a single new member was admitted. Indicative of the seriousness of the situation was the fact that in 1953, 21 applications for membership were listed by the UN as not having been favorably acted upon by the Council. Down to December 14, 1955, the UN admitted only nine new members. The log-jam was broken in December 1955 when, under the terms of a "package deal," sixteen new members were admitted. . . .

In performing its recommending function in connection with the appointment of a Secretary-General, the Council has probably contributed to strengthening the role of that official in the work of the Organization. The requirement of agreement of the major powers increases the likelihood that the Secretary-General will have their confidence, which in turn is helpful, if not essential, to the full and most effective use of his powers. While the Council, due to the Soviet veto, did prevent the reappointment of Trygve Lie in 1950, the use of the General Assembly to break the deadlock did not produce very satisfactory results. In 1953, the Council recommended, and the Assembly appointed, Dag Hammarskjöld as Lie's successor. Experience since then has demonstrated the advantage of having a Secretary-General who commands the confidence of the major powers.[5]

Clearly the Security Council has failed to discharge its Charter responsibilities in the manner and with the degree of effectiveness which the authors of the Charter envisaged. Furthermore, there can be little doubt that the Council has declined greatly in prestige and has seemed to most Members of the UN less useful than in the beginning. This decline has been accompanied by a corresponding increase in the prestige and use of the General Assembly. What have been the reasons for the Council's decline?

The one reason upon which most people would seem to agree is the "veto." It is common to cite the number of vetoes cast and to draw the conclusion that the excessive use of the veto has been the cause of the Council's failure. Eighty-nine vetoes were cast in the Security Council up to May 2, 1958. The number of vetoes cast, however, does not tell the whole story regarding the influence of the veto on the work of the Council. It is necessary, first of all, to consider the nature of the proposals that have been vetoed. Of the total number, 48 vetoes were cast on proposals to admit new members,

[5] The repudiation of Hammarskjöld by the Soviet Union in the 15th General Assembly supports this observation [ed.].

and in some instances the same country was "vetoed" four times. Thirty-nine were used to defeat proposals made in connection with the discharge by the Council of its responsibility for the maintenance of international peace and security. Two vetoes have been cast in connection with the appointment of the Secretary-General.

If we consider only the vetoes that fall into this second category, we find a number of cases where the majority of the Council's members appear to have maneuvered to force the minority permanent member to repeat its veto on substantially the same issue for the record. For example, during the consideration of the Greek complaint against its northern neighbors in August 1947, the Soviet Union cast two vetoes consecutively, first on the Australian draft resolution and then on the United States draft resolution. The second veto must have been anticipated since the United States resolution was stronger than the Australian and therefore more objectionable to the Soviet Union.

The veto of a proposal has not necessarily prevented its substance from being put into effect. In the Syrian and Lebanese case, for example, the United States draft resolution expressing the confidence of the Security Council that the United Kingdom and French troops would be withdrawn "as soon as practicable" was not adopted due to the negative vote of the Soviet Union, which wanted a stronger resolution urging the immediate withdrawal of foreign forces. Nevertheless, the representatives of France and the United Kingdom declared that their governments were willing to give effect to the majority opinion, and the withdrawal of forces was carried out to the satisfaction of all concerned.

On the other hand, in those situations where the cooperation of the vetoing power is necessary to the carrying out of the proposal, the veto simply registers a factual situation. Even if the right of veto did not exist and the proposal were adopted by the required majority, there would be little likelihood that the dissenting major power would back down, if a vital interest was at stake, except under compulsion that might risk general war. Thus, if the Security Council had been able to take a decision in the Czechoslovak and Hungarian cases notwithstanding Soviet opposition, there is little reason to believe that the results would have been different since the majority members were not prepared to take those measures of coercion which alone had any chance of influencing Soviet action.

Concentration of attention upon the voting procedure of the Council as an explanation of Council weakness seems somewhat misplaced, since the real cause lies deeper than a mere organizational or procedural defect. The veto, when used, reflects the schism in the relations among the permanent members of the Council. It is a symptom, rather than the cause, of a disunited world.

The primary cause of the decline of the Security Council and especially of its role in relation to the General Assembly must be sought in the breakdown since 1945 of the wartime alliance of the Soviet Union, the United Kingdom, and the United States—the alliance whose continuation was the assumption upon which the idea of the Security Council as the guarantor of peace was constructed. The rivalry among the major powers induced them in many cases to use the Security Council as a tool for propaganda purposes to advance their divergent political objectives rather than to harmonize the action of nations in the attainment of common purposes, as intended by the authors of the Charter. Furthermore, these same powers discovered that for purposes of appealing to world opinion, and gaining support for their respective policies and programs in the cold war the General Assembly provided a more effective forum than the Security Council.

The work of the Security Council has been hampered by the conflicts among former Allied powers over the peace settlements. The authors of the Charter had remembered the onus attached to the Covenant of the League because of its close association with the settlements after the First World War. Accordingly, they provided a separate machinery for the making of the peace treaties with the Axis powers after the Second World War. Contrary to their hopes, however, the Allied unity broke down soon after the disappearance of the common enemies, and from the outset the Security Council had to carry burdens beyond its capacity [and] to deal with questions arising from the differences among the major powers concerning the peace settlements, such as the questions of Greece, Iran, and Czechoslovakia, the status of the Free Territory of Trieste, and the Berlin and the Korean questions. Deadlocks over the terms of the major peace settlements, moreover, were bound to make agreement on other issues more difficult to achieve.

Another cause contributing to the diminishing role of the Security Council has been the post-war emergence of numerous new nations in Asia and Africa, their crucial role in the world's balance of power, and their general preference for the Assembly rather than the Council for bringing their influence to bear in connection with the issues of colonialism, human rights, and disarmament. The anxiety of the major powers to win resounding political victories by the support of these newly independent states has helped the Assembly to gain further importance.

In addition, the advance in the use of mass media of communications and the increasing role of public opinion in the governmental process have tended to revolutionize traditional views on the relative merits of public discussion and participation in foreign policy making on the one hand, and quiet diplomacy and private negotiations on the other. The result has been that the attention of the strategists of national policy has turned to the manipulation and exploitation of the General Assembly as a world forum. Doubtless the Assembly provides a more spectacular arena to wage the "war of ideas" than a small body like the Council.

It would seem likely that any amelioration of the relations among the major powers would bring about an improvement in the effectiveness of the Security Council; it would also reduce the desire of the major powers to turn to the General Assembly for political propaganda reasons. Amelioration of the major power relations does not, however, appear to be a sufficient condition to bring about the complete revival of the Security Council as the predominant organ for the maintenance of international peace and security as envisaged by the authors of the Charter, because the newly independent, non-western nations would be most reluctant to relinquish their power of effectively influencing political developments in the world through the General Assembly rather than through the Security Council, unless the composition of the Security Council is revised to meet their objections to its west-slanted membership. With the world situation as it is, it seems probable that the major questions of political adjustment, of the cold war as well as of the liquidation of colonialism, will remain the primary concern of the General Assembly rather than of the Council.[6] The Security Council is more likely to confine itself to dealing with specific disputes or situations related to the maintenance of peace and security, which require swiftness of action and continuity of study and surveillance by the international organization, and about which the permanent members are able to achieve some measure of agreement.

The inclination of the western states to clarify and bring to the fore the residual responsibility of the Assembly in matters related to peace and security, as exemplified by their support for the "Uniting for Peace" resolution, appears to have been checked as a result of their realization of the new situation brought about by the increase in the voting power of the Asian and African states, often unsympathetic to the West. In fact, the Asian and African states have come to possess a potential veto over Assembly decisions. In consequence, the passage of west-sponsored resolutions through the Assembly can no longer be taken for granted. It was noteworthy that when the Syrian-Turkish question (1957) was brought before the Assembly, the representatives of Australia, France, the Netherlands, the United Kingdom, and the United States raised the constitutional issue that the proper place to deal with a threat to the peace under the Charter was the Security Council, not the Assembly. This was in marked contrast to the Soviet silence regarding the competence of the Assembly in connection with the question. The seeming reversal of the positions of the western and communist states on the respective roles of the Security Council and the General Assembly on questions of peace and security is indicative of the fluidity of Members' preferences for one organ over another, stemming from the changing political configuration of these organs, caused partly by the addition to the Asian and African group of recently admitted states and partly by the trend of some members of this group of nations toward neutralism.

6 This has in fact proved to be the case [ed.].

Setting aside broad political considerations which would ultimately determine the relative roles for peacemaking of the Security Council and the General Assembly, several advantages which the Council possesses over the Assembly, from an organizational point of view, are worth noting. The Security Council is an executive committee of small size in a state of constant alertness. Its members, even non-permanent members chosen for two-year periods, can accumulate considerable knowledge and skill with respect to disputes and situations brought to its attention. It is able to act at a moment's notice, continue its supervisory functions without intermission, and serve as an effective negotiating body. In comparison, the size and lack of continuity of the General Assembly, together with the publicity attendant on its consideration of questions and the deficiency of experience of some of the delegates to the Assembly, suggest that it is primarily a forum of the nations for the discussion of questions of a general character, rather than an organ suited to perform intricate diplomatic functions of negotiation and conciliation. The establishment of subsidiary organs like the Interim Committee, the United Nations Commission on Korea, and the Advisory Committee on the United Nations Emergency Force, may overcome some of the organizational deficiencies of the Assembly. But an effective use of the Security Council would have several advantages not possessed by the subsidiary organs of the Assembly. It would also avoid an unnecessary duplication of functions.

THE GENERAL ASSEMBLY IN UNITED NATIONS AND WORLD AFFAIRS

Muhammad Zafrulla Khan*

As a parliamentary body the Assembly bears only a rough resemblance to the average legislature. National parliamentarians serving for the first time in the Assembly sense a lack of the normal attributes of legislative action. There is no party representation in the normal sense, although there

* Muhammad Zafrulla Khan, "The General Assembly in United Nations and World Affairs," in A. W. Cordier and W. Foote, eds., The Quest for Peace (New York: Columbia University Press, 1965), pp. 167–182. Copyright © 1965 Columbia University Press. By permission of Columbia University Press.

Muhammad Zafrulla Khan is a judge on the International Court of Justice. He has served as Foreign Minister of Pakistan and permanent representative of Pakistan to the United Nations.

are blocs that sometimes vote uniformly. There are no visible floor leaders; there is no party whip; there are no majorities or minorities so characteristic of most national parliaments. Thus to the novice there appears to be a lack of discipline, a lack of the pressures producing a sense of direction in a debate. The Assembly debates; it differs; it disagrees and agrees; but almost always it reaches a conclusion on the matter under discussion.

While many of the accepted attributes of a democratic national legislature are lacking in the General Assembly, their very absence throws some light upon the real characteristics of the Assembly. Each delegation sitting in the Assembly represents a sovereign nation, a Member of the United Nations.

Here it might not be inappropriate to digress briefly and indicate the importance assumed by this attribute of membership in such a world body in the minds of the many newly created and newly admitted states. For these newcomers, who have hitherto played little part in traditional diplomacy and who were simply dominated by its results, to take their seats in the General Assembly is to join the world. To come, as of right, to the Headquarters of the United Nations, which in many cases itself helped former colonial territories to achieve statehood, is a symbol of sovereignty; this provides, incidentally, a unique opportunity, among many other things, for the rapid assimilation of the conduct of diplomatic business and, equally important perhaps, access to a forum where all views may be aired and heard.

Indeed, what Woodrow Wilson said of the Assembly of the League of Nations may well be thought to be largely true of the General Assembly of the United Nations:

> The underlying conception of the assembly . . . is that it is the forum of opinion. . . . It is the debating body; it is the body where the thought of the little nation along with the thought of the big nation is brought to bear upon . . . those matters which affect the good understanding between nations upon which the peace of the world depends; where the stifled voice of humanity is at last to be heard, where nations that have borne the unspeakable sufferings of the ages that must have seemed to them like aeons will find voice and expression, where the moral judgment of mankind can sway the opinion of the world. . . .
>
> The assembly was created in order that anybody that purposed anything wrong should be subjected to the awkward circumstance that everybody could talk about it.

. . . each state in the General Assembly has one vote: old states or new states, rich or poor, strong or weak.

Critics of this system of one vote for one nation have pointed to the effects on voting of the achievement of sovereignty by newly independent states and the crystallization of regional or underdeveloped blocs or groups, arguing that the preponderance of votes by the middle and smaller Powers damages the usefulness of the United Nations. Be that as it may, it is difficult to devise an alternative system of weighted voting (based on such factors as population area, or financial contribution to the budget of the United Nations) that would be practicable and would not have even greater defects.

. . . It is the Charter that provides not only the framework of action but the compelling sense of direction for delegations sitting in the Assembly. . . . [It] is a safe and sure compass that provides a sense of direction for the action of the Assembly.

. . . in the field of procedure, the Assembly operates in accordance with a set of rules which in the main serve it well. . . . The rules are intended not to slow down work but to expedite it, not to be warped in the interest of one group against another but to provide opportunity for free and full debate leading to a decision which is generally taken in the form of a resolution. It is the function of the President to apply and to interpret the rules judiciously in the interest of the whole membership and with a view to achieving timely results. Fairness, equity, and at times a reasonable degree of firmness are qualities expected of the Chair in the application of the rules.

A third factor having the effect of channeling debate into consensus reflected in a resolution is the practice whereby delegations concert their efforts actively to reach such solutions. There are two general classes of such action by delegations. One is operative in the field of political disputes or situations involving clashes between two or more Members of the United Nations. In such a setting it has long since become the practice of other Members acting as third parties to coordinate their efforts in seeking a solution. Such groups in the Assembly have sometimes been known as "fire brigades." They were actively at work and made a decisive contribution in the Suez crisis, in the Lebanon-Jordan crisis, and, although the character of the problem was different, in the case of the Congo. Third-party action was also of great importance in the development of lines of policy in that situation.

Another area in which widespread joint participation by delegations is common relates to such programs as technical assistance and economic development. The original technical assistance program was presented in its general form by the United States delegation some fifteen years ago. It was discussed at length by the Assembly and the great program that emerged was the product of the thinking of the total membership. It therefore started as a program that belonged to everybody, and the continued strength of the program as represented both by technical assistance and by the Special Fund arises in part from this very broad-based initial support.

It is well known that Resolution 1514, adopted during the fifteenth session, embodying the declaration on the granting of independence to colonial countries and peoples, furnished an impetus for the process of decolonization which is still being pursued vigorously through the activities of what has come to be known as the Committee of Twenty-four.

Third-party action in the first category of problems and the almost universal, if not universal, participation in the second category of problems arise from the obligation (indeed the opportunity) that devolves upon individual governments and their delegations. As one delegate put it upon leaving the United Nations:

I regard my experience at the United Nations as the richest in my diplomatic career. Here as Ambassador I wore two hats: one as the representative of my country, expressing and championing its views as necessary in matters of direct concern to it, but also I valued highly the opportunity of wearing the second hat, which was made possible by the ratification by my country of the Charter of the United Nations, placing it under obligations of great importance to the welfare of humanity generally, which I have regarded as my privilege to assist in carrying out.

Most delegates, indeed, have the consciousness of this dual responsibility, this dual opportunity, and it is in this capacity that the embryonic forms of world community can be seen and that the excesses of effervescent nationalism can be moderated.

In contrast with the Councils, the General Assembly consists of representatives of the entire membership, a fact which tends to increase the importance of its role and the frequency of its use. These facts, and in particular the tendency of Members to refer matters to the General Assembly, do not, however, affect, nor have they altered, the constitutional position of the Assembly in relation to other organs.

Even the Uniting for Peace resolution, adopted by the Assembly soon after the beginning of the Korean crisis, kept strictly within the provisions of the Charter with regard to the respective functions of the General Assembly and the Security Council. That resolution provided a mechanism whereby a serious dispute or situation or a threat to the peace could, if the Security Council failed to act, be brought speedily to the attention of the General Assembly. In the 1956 Suez crisis Dag Hammarskjöld was very careful to avoid the pressures which would have given the General Assembly something more of a recommendatory authority in the field of Egyptian acceptance of conditions which were thought necessary for the stationing of the United Nations Emergency Force (UNEF) on its soil. In fact, the very effectiveness of the Assembly flows largely from the respect that its Members and the Secretary-General have for its constitutional limitations and authority, as set forth in the Charter.

This authority is not inconsiderable. At San Francisco the smaller Powers engaged in various and successful efforts to extend the competence of the General Assembly beyond the terms contained in the Dumbarton Oaks Proposals. The competence of the General Assembly was widened particularly in Articles 11, 13, and 14. The last article states that the General Assembly

may recommend measures for the peaceful adjustment of any situation, regardless of origin, which it deems likely to impair the general welfare or friendly relations among nations, including situations resulting from a violation of the provisions of the present Charter setting forth the Purposes and Principles of the United Nations.

Article 13 empowers the General Assembly to

initiate studies and make recommendations for the purpose of: (a) promoting international cooperation in the political field and encouraging the progressive development of international law and its codification; (b) promoting international cooperation in the economic, social, cultural, educational, and health fields, and assisting in the realization of human rights and fundamental freedoms for all without distinction as to race, sex, language, or religion.

The vastly important field of human rights was thus brought within the realm of discussion and of the recommendatory authority of the General Assembly. This power of the Assembly has often been challenged because of its possible conflict with the domestic jurisdiction clause of the Charter, Article 2 (7), but the Assembly has uniformly asserted its right to proceed with its debates and to act in accordance with Article 13.

. . . Fortunately, for the peace of the world, procedures exist for the referring of disputes from one body to the other and for the making of recommendations by the General Assembly to the Security Council. Article 12 provides that

while the Security Council is exercising in respect of any dispute or situation the functions assigned to it in the present Charter, the General Assembly shall not make any recommendation with regard to that dispute or situation unless the Security Council so requests.

The spirit of this article has been preserved but not always its letter. Since 1955, in the Palestine dispute, items have been placed on the agenda of the General Assembly, sometimes with a somewhat different wording, while the same general item remains on the agenda of the Security Council.

The Trusteeship Council operates under the authority of the General Assembly and assists the Assembly in carrying out the functions attributed to the Council. Responsibilities in the field of international economic and social cooperation, which belong in the first instance to the General Assembly, are delegated under the authority of the General Assembly to the Economic and Social Council.

The powers of the General Assembly are sometimes also exercised through the establishment of subsidiary organs, a power vested in the Assembly by Article 22 of the Charter. The Assembly has established some fifty subsidiary organs, most of which are *ad hoc* in character.

✧   ✧   ✧   ✧   ✧   ✧   ✧

As already stated, the effectiveness of the Assembly flows in no small part from the respect which its Members and the Secretariat have for its constitutional authority. The conclusion of the deliberative process is generally the passage of a resolution. Since the beginning the Assembly has approved nearly 1,900 resolutions. Many of these are routine in character and some deal with administrative detail, but many are of great importance to the effective impact of the United Nations upon world affairs. One need only refer to the resolutions relating to Korea, to Suez, and to the Congo as demonstrating the importance of policy and executive action aimed at bringing these crises under control.

It has been argued that the United Nations has been bypassed too often by member nations and in particular by the great Powers. There may be some measure of truth in this but it is also true that the Members of the United Nations have used its organs and in particular the General Assembly in so many emergencies as almost to overwhelm it. The new nations have looked upon the United Nations as their best protection in a world saturated with Cold War issues and other threats to security. Perhaps some problems that are now brought to the United Nations could be settled by direct action of the parties concerned, but experience shows that the resources for handling problems in the General Assembly and through the Secretariat are such as to foster the practical use of settlement through these channels.

*   *   *   *   *   *   *

The setting and character of the General Assembly lend themselves to public diplomacy as opposed to private diplomacy. Public diplomacy has its merits, but when delicate issues need to be resolved it is also important that it operate in conjunction with private diplomacy. There is a place for quiet corridor or office consultations, the results of which do not see the light of day until they become part of the ultimate solution. Lester B. Pearson, a former President of the United Nations General Assembly, put the matter this way:

The United Nations is a place where we can meet either to settle problems or to make settlement more difficult. It is a place where we can try to find collective solutions, or one which we can use to get support and publicity for purely national solutions. It is a place where we can talk to each other with a view to securing general agreement, or to television and radio audiences in order to explain that disagreement is the fault of somebody else. . . .

But the United Nations has, or it should have, a private as well as a public face. There should be opportunities here for other than public appearances. . . .

It is, of course, essential that all free peoples should know and understand the great issues of policy which may mean life or death to them. But it is not essential, as I see it—indeed it is often harmful—for the negotiation of policy always to be conducted in glass houses.

Before we deal with the ever-present need for strictly private negotiation, it should be noted that in and around the General Assembly is practiced a modern and very special form of diplomacy which has been called "parliamentary diplomacy."

. . . Parliamentary or conference diplomacy conducted in or around the General Assembly may usefully be supplemented by more quiet diplomacy within the United Nations, and it is one of Dag Hammarskjöld's outstanding contributions to have insisted as he did that the one should not exclude the other. In his words:

The legislative process in the United Nations is not a substitute for diplomacy. It serves its purpose only when it helps diplomacy to arrive at agreements. . . .

It is diplomacy, not speeches and votes, that continues to have the last word in the process of peace-making.

Indeed, public diplomacy without private diplomacy can easily become frozen diplomacy, limiting the capacity of the parties directly concerned to maneuver freely toward a solution.

❋   ❋   ❋   ❋   ❋   ❋   ❋

Reference has been made to the General Assembly as a magnet drawing many questions to its attention on the initiative of its Members. There is another aspect of the work of the Assembly which represents a contribution to peace that was hardly anticipated at the time of the San Francisco Conference. An increasing number of top governmental representatives attend the annual session of the General Assembly, particularly in its early stages. Apart from frequent visits by heads of state and government, the opening weeks of the General Assembly session are now marked by the presence of more than seventy foreign ministers out of its total membership of one hundred and thirteen. Many of these foreign ministers participate in the general debate and play an active role in major questions on the agenda of the Assembly. The existence of the Assembly also provides an opportunity, seized by many foreign ministers, to carry on an exchange of views with other foreign ministers on matters outside the agenda. Some of the foreign ministers have stated that as much as 25 to 50 percent of their time is spent on the furthering of interests not related to the agenda but of importance to the direct relationship between their own and other counrties. This "extracurricular" activity would not be possible if it were not for the annual sessions of the Assembly, and while the Assembly benefits from their presence, the world generally benefits from this exceptional opportunity that foreign ministers have of exchanging views with each other.

The role of the General Assembly can hardly be understood without reference to the existence at the United Nations of the permanent missions.

It is natural that the permanent and other members of the Security Council, which, under the Charter, "shall be so organized as to be able to function continuously," should be required to be represented at all times at the seat of the Organization. However, the variety of roles assumed by the

General Assembly and the multiplicity of the activities conducted in and about it has led all other Member States as well to establish permanent missions in New York, the head of which usually has ambassadorial rank and is assisted by a number of foreign service officers and other civil servants.

The functions of the permanent missions have developed considerably; some of the newer nations find it more convenient to keep in touch with many governments through their permanent missions at United Nations Headquarters. In the absence of diplomatic relations between states and indeed even where such relations may have been severed, these states can engage in informal discussions through their representatives in New York.

Between sessions the permanent missions do much to help implement resolutions of the preceding session and to engage in thorough preparation for the next session. In general they carry the main burden of representation in the sessions of the General Assembly. Without them, sessions of the General Assembly would be much more *ad hoc* in character, far less well prepared, and more lacking in substance and thoroughness than we know them to be. The heads of the missions make up practically all of the personnel participating in the so-called fire brigades in times of crises. They also do more of the sustained and other tedious work in the long-range planning for the launching of major programs of the United Nations.

All in all, over six hundred members of the various diplomatic corps are permanently in New York, thus constituting what Dag Hammarskjöld has called a "standing diplomatic conference."

This results in continuous negotiation on a variety of questions, quite apart from the importance of personal intimacy and understanding among the staffs of these missions, even across substantial political barriers. In the words of Lord Hankey, "Perhaps the most important result of conducting diplomacy by conference is the knowledge responsible statesmen acquire of one another." The close personal contacts and the understandings that develop among the permanent missions facilitate negotiation and the arrival at conclusions on matters under debate.

. . . In 1960 there was a large influx of new Members; at this time some of the delegates representing the older national communities said in reference to the new African nations: "They will have much to learn from us." This observation at the time seemed quite natural and justified. Representatives of older communities with strong governments and established parliamentary institutions, with well-observed traditions and efficient administrations, would seem to be in a position to transmit much knowledge to representatives of the new nations. Yet in 1964 these same delegates put their experience of contact with the representatives of new governments in a strikingly different form: "We are learning much from each other." This new phrase is as logical and meaningful in 1964 as the other seemed to be in 1960. It demonstrates one of the great values of the United Nations and particularly of the General Assembly. It proves that the General Assembly is a most valuable school for top-level polticial education in the world today. Each group is learning much from the other.

THE INTERNATIONAL COURT OF JUSTICE

Max Sørensen[*]

In his concluding volume in the Carnegie Endowment's series of National Studies on International Organization, Professor MacIver observes that the International Court of Justice, as set up in 1945, was not so much a new institution as a new promise. It was closely modelled on its predecessor, the Permanent Court of International Justice, and Article 92 of the UN Charter expressly recognized the continuity with the past in affirming that the Statute of the new Court was based upon that of the old one. The promise lay in the fact that the new Court was declared to be "the principal judicial organ of the United Nations" and thus called upon to play a more significant role than the old Court, which had never been an organic part of the League of Nations structure. Professor MacIver concludes, however, that the promise remains in important respects unfulfilled.

In analyzing the nature and possible causes of this discrepancy between expectations and fulfillment it may be useful to consider separately two sets of problems: those relating, on the one hand, to the institutional aspects of the Court, and, on the other hand, to the place and scope of the judicial function in international relations. The two sets of problems are, of course, intimately connected in the sense that adequate institutional arrangements are a prerequisite for the proper exercise of the judicial function. They are distinct, however, insofar as several factors other than the institutional determine the place and scope of the judicial function.

JUDICIAL INDEPENDENCE AND ELECTION OF JUDGES

Judicial independence is the essence of any court of law, whether national or international. The Statute of the International Court of Justice in various ways conforms to this standard. It prescribes that the Court shall be a

[*] Max Sørensen, "The International Court of Justice: Its Role in Contemporary International Relations," *International Organization*, Vol. 14, 1960, pp. 261–276. Copyright 1960, World Peace Foundation. By permission of *International Organization*.

Max Sørensen is Professor of International, Constitutional, and Administrative Law at the University of Aarkus, Denmark. He and Hiels J. Haagerup are coauthors of *Denmark and the United Nations*.

"body of independent judges, elected regardless of their nationality from among persons of high moral character, who possess the qualifications required in their respective countries for appointment to the highest judicial offices, or are jurisconsults of recognized competence in international law." During their terms of office they are not allowed to exercise any political or administrative function, or engage in any other occupation of a professional nature, and they cannot be dismissed except by unanimous decision of the other members of the Court. It has never been seriously alleged that this standard of independence has not been effectively attained. On the contrary, examples may be cited of judges who have pronounced themselves against the arguments and submissions of their own governments in cases before the Court. Although the judges in question have come from countries where judicial independence is firmly entrenched, there is nothing to indicate that judges from countries without such firm traditions have ever been exposed to undue political influence.

On the other hand, the election procedure has been criticized as favoring political considerations in the choice of judges. According to the Statute, judges are elected by the General Assembly and the Security Council, the two bodies voting separately and an absolute majority of votes being required in each of them for the election of any candidate. Current practice tends to disregard the provision of the Statute which requires that judges shall be elected regardless of their nationality, and to consider the candidates more or less as representatives of their countries. This was strikingly illustrated when elections were held in 1956 to fill the vacancy caused by the death of Judge Hsu Mo. One of the candidates nominated, Ambassador Wellington Koo, was generally considered to be the nominee of the Nationalist government of China. The disagreement over the representation of China was reflected in the election procedure. In the Security Council Mr. Wellington Koo obtained an absolute majority in three successive meetings. In the General Assembly majorities were repeatedly cast for a Japanese candidate, and it was only at a fourth meeting, and after 18 ballots, that Mr. Wellington Koo obtained a majority in the General Assembly also.

Nor can it be ruled out that election of a candidate to the Court, or withdrawal of support for a candidate, becomes part of a bargain concerning election of a country to another organ, such as the Security Council. In this connection it may not be irrelevant to recall what happened in 1957, when elections of non-permanent members of the Security Council were held at the same meeting as the election of five members of the Court. Japan was elected a member of the Security Council for the years 1958 and 1959, after it had been announced that a Japanese candidate for the Court, Mr. Shigeru Kuriyama, had withdrawn his candidature.

The Institute of International Law has expressed its concern over practices of this kind and has recommended that elections of judges should be clearly separated from elections to other bodies and held as early as possible during the session of the Assembly. No account seems to have been taken of this recommendation, and it appears doubtful, moreover, whether any such administrative or technical expedient would affect the attitudes of delegates to the Security Council and General Assembly. The roots of the difficulty go deeper and are, in particular, embedded in the problem of geographical distribution.

COMPOSITION OF THE COURT

The principle of equitable geographical distribution is well established in UN practice, and may, indeed, be said to permeate the whole organizational structure. Article 23 of the Charter expressly recognizes this principle as one of the factors to which regard shall be given in the election of non-permanent members of the Security Council. It is not, however, recognized by the Statute of the Court as applicable to the election of judges, as Article 9 provides rather that in the Court as a whole the main forms of civilization and the principal legal systems shall be represented. This is a different principle. One might, for instance, argue that the four seats on the bench actually held by Latin American judges are more than the number required to represent the Latin American form of civilization and legal system, although this is a fair number on the basis of proportional geographical distribution, or that the common law system and British form of civilization have had more than their due with a British as well as an Australian judge.

On the other hand, it is beyond doubt that the Statute does not exclude the possibility that one legal system may have more than one representative in the Court. What really matters, therefore, is whether any main form of civilization or principal legal system is left out. These concepts are too vague to allow a clearcut answer, but it may be pointed out that Islamic law and Soviet law are now represented in the Court, which was not the case in the old Court. A comparison between the present composition of the Court and the composition of the Permanent Court reveals a striking evolution. Out of the 15 judges and deputy-judges who took office in 1922 after the first election, there were ten Europeans (including Eastern Europe, but not the Soviet Union), two Latin Americans, two nationals of Far Eastern countries (Japan and China) and one United States citizen. As composed at present, the Court has four judges who are nationals of countries in Europe outside the Communist group, two belonging to Communist countries, four Latin Americans, three Afro-Asians (Egypt, Pakistan, and China), one North American, and one Australian. It is common practice, although not a statutory obligation, to assure that there is always a national of each of the five permanent members of the Security Council, and the above figures include these judges.

❋   ❋   ❋   ❋   ❋   ❋   ❋

In other UN bodies the geographical distribution is a means to secure a certain spread of political influence, or to counteract the predominance of the few major powers. Considerations of this kind ought to be irrelevant to the composition of the Court. . . . International law, however, is not a closed system. Among the sources of law which the Court shall apply, Article 38 of the Statute lists the general principles of law recognized by civilized nations. The authors seem to have intended that general principles recognized in national legal systems for relations between subjects of national law might find corresponding application in relations between states as subjects of international law. In its jurisprudence, the Court has consistently drawn on this source.[1] Only a Court which is truly representative of the various legal trends and systems in the world can crystallize those general principles which, as a common denominator, must hold the national legal systems together in a coherent system of world law.

These rational grounds for a balanced composition of the Court in actual practice have to compete with traditional concepts of geographical distribution.

✻   ✻   ✻   ✻   ✻   ✻   ✻

As to the substance of the proposals [in the Assembly] the debate has indicated general agreement on the desirablity of enlarging ECOSOC, a more cautious attitude toward an increase of membership of the Security Council, and clearly divided opinions as to the advisability of enlarging the Court. Against the argument concerning geographical distribution it has been stated that what the Statute requires, namely, the representation of main forms of civilization and legal systems, is perfectly feasible without an increase in the number of judges. Furthermore, it has been adduced that any such increase would seriously hamper the efficient working of the Court and, in particular, make its internal deliberations and the drafting of its decisions extremely cumbersome.[2] . . .

JURISDICTION OF THE COURT

The organic link between the UN and the Court is reflected by Article 93 of the Charter, under which all members of the UN are automatically parties to the Statute of the Court. Non-member states may become parties to the Statute on conditions to be determined in each case by the General Assembly upon the recommendation of the Security Council. At present, Switzerland, Liechtenstein, and San Marino have thus become parties to the Statute. Furthermore, according to Article 35 of the Statute, the Court is open not only to states parties to the Statute, but also, on conditions to be laid

[1] Sir Hersch Lauterpacht, *The Development of International Law by the International Court*, London, Stevens and Sons Ltd., 1958, Chapter 9.

[2] General Assembly *Official Records* (13th session), Special Political Committee, 114th and 115th meetings, November 27 and 28, 1958, and *ibid.* (14th session), Special Political Committee, 127th–139th meetings, October 13–30, 1959.

down by the Security Council, to other states. A resolution of the Council of October 15, 1946, requires such states to recognize the jurisdiction of the Court by a special declaration. Declarations to that effect have been made by Vietnam in connection with the Japanese Peace Treaty and by the Federal Republic of Germany in connection with certain European treaties.

The Court is thus a true world court in the sense that it is open to all states of the world. Access to the Court and submission to its jurisdiction, however, are different matters. In 1920 proposals for the compulsory jurisdiction of the Permanent Court foundered on the objections of several states, in particular the great powers. In 1945 sentiments were somewhat stronger in favor of making the new Court's jurisdiction compulsory. At the San Francisco Conference, as well as in the Committee of Jurists, which, meeting in Washington before the Conference, had prepared a draft statute for the new Court, there was a considerable majority in favor of compulsory jurisdiction. It is well known, however, how the Conference bowed to the objections of the United States and the Soviet Union and accepted what to the majority was only the next best solution, namely, the maintenance of the system under which the old Court had been functioning.[3]

The basic principle of that system is that jurisdiction over a state can only be exercised with its consent. Such consent, however, may be given in a number of different ways:[4]

1. The classical method of referring a particular dispute to international arbitration or adjudication, namely, by special agreement, or *compromis*, after the dispute has arisen, is applicable also for bringing a case before the Court . . . between 1946 and July 1959, only three were submitted by special agreement.

2. The consent of the parties may also be expressed more generally in a treaty or convention with respect to future disputes of certain categories. . . . Since 1945, however, few treaties of this type have been concluded, and rarely, if ever, has a case been submitted to the Court under such a treaty.

More important are the clauses inserted in treaties and conventions on other subjects providing for reference to the Court of any dispute which might arise with respect to the interpretation and application of that particular treaty or convention. A very great number of such treaty clauses exists, including a number of bilateral treaties to which the United States is a party. In particular such clauses are found in many multilateral conventions concluded under the auspices of the UN. The genocide convention of 1948 contains such a clause, and it was with respect to this clause that the Soviet Union made a reservation when ratifying the convention. The practice of inserting such clauses in UN conventions has recently suffered certain set-

[3] Ruth B. Russell and Jeannette E. Merther, *A History of the United Nations Charter*, Washington, Brookings Institution, 1958, pp. 884–890.
Académie de Droit International, *Recueil des Cours*, 1950 (Vol. 76, No. 1), p. 125 ff.
[4] See Edvard Hambro, "The Jurisdiction of the International Court of Justice," in

backs. Most conspicuous is the rejection by the UN Conference on the Law of the Sea in 1958 of provisions which, as integral parts of the conventions adopted by the conference, would have established the competence of the Court to decide all disputes concerning the interpretation and application of these conventions. The optional protocol which the conference adopted for the settlement of such disputes was only a meager substitute for the proposals rejected, because of its very optional character. It is significant that the opposition to the compulsory clauses came not only from the states of the Soviet group, but also from leading Asian countries and certain Latin American countries.

3. A third method of expressing consent to the jurisdiction of the Court is to make a declaration under the so-called optional clause of the Statute. Article 36, paragraph 2, of the Statute provides that a state party to the Statute may at any time declare that it recognizes as compulsory, *ipso facto* and without special agreement in relation to any other state accepting the same obligation, the jurisdiction of the Court in all legal disputes. This clause was taken over from the Statute of the old Court. In 1945, as in 1920, it was found to be a reasonable compromise between those who favored and those who were opposed to compulsory jurisdiction. It allowed the states who were ready to accept compulsory jurisdiction to do so in their mutual relations without excluding the opponents of such jurisdiction from becoming parties to the Statute. As a compromise, it was, in fact, fairly successful in the inter-war period. By the end of 1934 not less than 42 states were bound by declarations under the optional clause.

* * * * * * *

Developments since 1945 have followed a different trend. In spite of the increased number of states, only 38 declarations are now in force. . . . Broken down according to geographical distribution, the figures include 13 states in western Europe, 10 Latin American states, and 10 states of the Afro-Asian group. In addition, declarations have been made by the United States and the four "old" British Dominions. Conspicuous by their absence are the states of the Soviet group.

Furthermore, there has been a marked tendency to weaken and narrow the scope even of the declarations made. Many are made without time limit, which in practice is understood to mean that they are subject to denunciation without prior notice. Reservations are often attached to the declarations.

* * * * * * *

Much has been said about the reservation made by the United States, and copied by a considerable number of other countries, to the effect that the Court shall not have jurisdiction over "disputes with regard to matters which are essentially within the domestic jurisdiction of the United States of America as determined by the United States of America." It has been argued that a reservation which in this manner leaves it to the subjective appreciation of a government to decide in any particular case whether or not it shall submit to the jurisdiction of the Court invalidates the declaration as a whole. The line of reasoning is that an undertaking in which the party reserves for itself the exclusive right to determine the extent or the very existence of its obligation cannot be considered to be a legal undertaking. It is a declaration of political principle or purpose, not a legal instrument. Furthermore, it is considered to be incompatible with Article 36, paragraph 6, of the Statute, according to which the Court, and not a party, decides in case of doubt whether it has jurisdiction or not. . . .

The Court, however, reached a conclusion which clearly shows how a reservation intended to protect the interests of the state which makes it may be turned against the state through the effects of the principle of reciprocity. The case was brought before the Court by France, relying upon the declarations made under the optional clause by itself as well as by Norway. France had made a reservation as indicated, but Norway had accepted the jurisdiction without reservation. Norway objected to the jurisdiction of the Court on various grounds, one of them being that, by virtue of the principle of reciprocity, Norway could be bound to no greater extent than France, and that the Norwegian government considered the subject-matter of the dispute—whether service of coupons and redemption of bonds relating to certain Norwegian loans should be made at gold value—to be essentially within Norwegian national jurisdiction as understood by the government of Norway. The Court accepted this argument and concluded that it was without jurisdiction in the matter.

* * * * * * *

4. Finally, the consent of a state to submit to the jurisdiction of the Court may be expressed simply by a positive response to a unilateral summons. This is the principle of *forum prorogatum* on which the Court based its jurisdiction in the Corfu Channel case. Even under this doctrine, however, it is unquestionable that the failure of a state to recognize, expressly or tacitly, the jurisdiction of the Court leaves the Court without any authority to proceed with a case which has been submitted to it by unilateral application.

* * * * * * *

DISPUTES INVOLVING INTERNATIONAL ORGANIZATIONS

In one particular respect, the Statute of the Court contains an anachronistic element. Characteristic of recent development of international law has been the emergence of international organizations as subjects of legal rights and duties in their relationship to states, whether members or nonmembers, to individuals, and between themselves. As experience shows, controversial issues are likely to arise in these new legal relationships, and the need for a procedure of judicial settlement is apparent. The Statute of the Court, however, does not authorize the parties to take such issues before the Court for judicial decision. On the contrary, Article 34 provides that only states may be parties in cases before the Court.

*   *   *   *   *   *   *

Nevertheless, questions of law arising in connection with the activities of international organizations have to some extent been brought before the Court. The possibility under the Charter and the Statute for different UN organs to ask the Court for advisory opinions has been utilized for that purpose. Whereas the Permanent Court in the League of Nations period was often requested to give advisory opinions on points of law which related to the substance of a dispute between two or more states which had been brought before the League, the new Court has on only one occasion been asked for an advisory opinion in such circumstances.

Most of the legal questions submitted to the Court for advisory opinions have related to the powers and functions of the UN bodies or to disputes in which the UN or another international organization was a party as an independent subject of international law. Most outstanding is the Reparations case in which the Court expressed the opinion that the UN could bring a claim against a state with a view to obtaining reparations in respect of damage caused to the UN because of an injury suffered by one of its agents in the performance of his duties.[5]

With respect to various groups of cases involving an international organization as one of the parties the use of advisory opinions has been carried one step further. By appropriate provisions it has been accepted in advance that the advisory opinion of the Court shall be considered as binding upon the parties. A prominent example is Article VIII, section 30, of the 1946 Convention on Privileges and Immunities of the United Nations, which provides that any difference concerning the interpretation or application of the convention arising between the UN on the one hand and a Member State on the other hand shall be submitted to the Court for an advisory opinion, and the opinion given by the Court shall be accepted as decisive by the parties.

*   *   *   *   *   *   *

It should also be kept in mind that an advisory opinion can only be requested by the competent organs, but never by a government or an individual. The party which believes its rights to have been violated by an international organization cannot directly institute proceedings before the Court.

---

[5] See also the Stoessinger selection, "The World Court Advisory Opinion," for a more recent example of a request for an advisory opinion, Chap. 9 [ed.].

Consequently, there is no judicial review of decisions by international organizations comparable to the judicial review instituted within the framework of the European Communities (Coal and Steel Community, Economic Community and Atomic Energy Community).[6]

However inadequate the procedure of advisory opinions has been for the purpose, it has, nevertheless, in the words of an eminent member of the Court, enabled the Court to contribute to disciplining the activity of international organizations.

THE JUDICIAL FUNCTION IN INTERNATIONAL RELATIONS

Although minor shortcomings or flaws, from one point of view or another, may be found to exist in the Statute of the Court, they are not of such proportions as to explain the relatively insignificant part of the Court in world affairs. It is true that the absence of a compulsory jurisdiction clause may be pointed to as a reason for the small number of cases submitted to and decided by the Court. It is reasonable to assume, however, that a general obligation for all States Members of the UN to accept the jurisdiction of the Court would not have been readily honored by each and all of them, and that the authority of the Court, if not its very existence, would have been in a constant state of crisis if any such provision had been inserted in the Statute.

The question to be answered, therefore, is that of why states are reluctant to recognize the jurisdiction of the Court, whether in general or for the purpose of a particular dispute. As the answer to this question depends upon an analysis of the motives of governments in deciding concrete matters of high policy, political or legal science is not able to afford a definite answer, because sources of information on such motives do not flow freely. The answer must be in the nature of certain hypotheses, based on whatever observable facts may be available, but constantly subject to verification or correction in the light of new data.

One factor which immediately comes to mind is the ambivalent attitude of many governments to international law as a coherent system of binding norms. In the international debate, even of highly political matters, legal argument has a prominent place. Before political bodies such as the UN General Assembly or Security Council, parties to a dispute very often rely on legal considerations to justify their respective attitudes. Nevertheless, important groups of states do not hesitate to question the authority of the traditional system of international law. The communist states consider traditional international law as an instrument designed to serve the interests of capitalist-imperialist powers. They are disposed to consider themselves

[6] See D. G. Valentine, The Court of Justice of the European Coal and Steel Community, The Hague, 1955.

bound only by such rules as they have recognized, explicitly or implicitly. The Soviet member of the Court, Judge S. Krylov, declared in an academic lecture given in 1947: "It goes without saying that the Soviet Union only accepts those international customary rules which conform to the principles of democracy, the requirements of humanity, etc."

Many new states which have recently gained independence likewise reserve their attitude toward rules and principles whose origin antedate their appearance on the international scene. Even states which gained independence at an earlier date question the authority of certain elements of contemporary international law which they consider to reflect the particular interests of great powers. When the International Law Commission in 1957 discussed the law of state responsibility, the Mexican member, Mr. Padilla Nervo, expressed the opinion that:

the vast majority of new States had taken no part in the creation of many institutions of international law which were consolidated and systematized in the nineteenth century. In the case of the law of the sea, for example, though the future needs and interests of newly established small countries were not taken into account, at least the body of principles thus created was not directly inimical to them. With State responsibility, however, international rules were established not merely without reference to small States, but against them, and were based almost entirely on the unequal relations between great Powers and small States.

*   *   *   *   *   *   *

Coupled with such views of traditional international law goes an unreserved affirmation of the principle of sovereignty and non-interference with domestic jurisdiction, amounting to a repudiation of international legal regulation. When the governments of Denmark and Sweden in 1950 objected to the extension of Soviet territorial waters in the Baltic to twelve miles and proposed to submit the dispute to the International Court, the Soviet government argued that the determination of maritime territorial limits was a matter falling within the exclusive competence of each state, and that consequently no basis existed for bringing the question before the Court.

A second factor is the very nature of most international disputes. Very rarely, if ever, is a controversy between two governments merely a matter of divergent views on abstract points of law. The political element in the sense that the solution affects national interests is always present . . . the great majority of controversial international issues arises, not over differences as to what the law is, but over claims involving modifications of established rights and duties, and changes of the existing legal order.

The judicial process is an unsuitable instrument for the solution of such disputes. Although it is clear that the International Court of Justice has not taken an extreme conservative view of the law and rigidly adhered to old concepts, but has, on the contrary, contributed to the adjustment of traditional principles to the requirement of present-day international relations,[7] the Court cannot disregard unambiguous legal positions. The process of adjustment between such established legal positions and the national aspirations of new and smaller states is essentially a political process. The states whose interests lie in the orderly and moderate course of that adjustment may in certain circumstances find the judicial process suitable for their purposes, but those states who see their interests in an accelerated development must, for the very same reasons, refuse to submit to the jurisdiction of international judicial organs.

But even disputes which do not ride astride any of the major political cleavages of our time may be unsuitable for judicial settlement because of the political factors involved. The possibilities offered by traditional bilateral diplomacy, and perhaps even more so by modern multilateral diplomacy, of exercising political pressure, of mobilizing support by third parties, of compromising and negotiating, are categorically excluded from the judicial process. "No one who has taken part in contentious litigation before the Court," writes Professor Waldock, "can have failed to sense the radical transformation which the handling of a dispute undergoes on its transfer from the political sphere of diplomacy to the judicial sphere of the Court."[8] Once the Court has spoken, its decision stands with such authority that the losing party cannot usually revert to the political sphere in order to take advantage of any superiority over its opponent in that sphere. "The decision to seek the solution of a dispute by judicial settlement is as much a political decision as one to seek a solution by some other method," writes Rosenne. It is a decision which narrows down the gamut of arguments and range of moves which a government can play, and many a government will think twice before imposing such restraint upon itself. While international law and the judicial process were considered, at the beginning of this century, to be the best safeguard of small states' interests, modern methods of multilateral diplomacy have brought about a change in this respect. In a political forum like the UN General Assembly small states may today, by sheer weight of number and by cunning evocation of bloc-solidarity, promote their particular interests more efficaciously than by any other method.

If factors such as these explain the modest part that the International Court has been called upon to play in contemporary international affairs, it may be argued that they do not justify the prevailing reluctance of governments to use the Court. Whatever short-term advantages may be gained by one state or another through reliance upon political factors cannot outweigh the benefits which an effective legal order administered by a far-seeing tribunal offers to mankind. It is therefore a source of hope that influential governments seem to be revising their policies in the matter.

[7] See Sir Hersch Lauterpacht, *The Development of International Law by the International Court*, in particular Part III, "Judicial Legislation."

[8] *British Yearbook of International Law*, 1958 (Vol. 34), p. 446.

PART IV

INTERNAL ASPECTS OF ORGANIZATION

7

THE
SECRETARIAT

The chapters of Part IV are presented as a means of identifying the loci and parameters of leadership. As the titles of the officials indicate, one can identify the leaders in the Secretariat, in the two major organs of the United Nations (although the chairman's position in the Security Council rotates monthly, which obviates the likelihood of any formal leadership developing there) and among the delegations. A study of this subject has not been undertaken yet in any thorough and comprehensive fashion. These chapters do not attempt to compare the various positions of leadership, but the reader is encouraged to draw some generalizations about them from the individual descriptions and analyses presented.

In studies of international organization in the past no attention has ever been paid to the role and functions of the secretariats and, in particular, to the office of the Secretary-General. In the literature of the past ten to fifteen years more and more interest has been shown in this subject.

Perhaps this interest may be traced to the much more active role the UN Secretary-General, and in particular Dag Hammarskjöld, has felt called upon to play. Perhaps it may be attributed to the political pressures which have built up in the Organization and which in turn have opened (or forced) the door of the Secretary-General. Much remains to be investigated by scholars, but contemporary writing tends to compare the League of Nations with the United Nations and to indicate the greater responsibility and scope the latter permits its chief administrative officer. As T. A. Pyman notes in "The United Nations Secretary-Generalship: A Review of its Status, Functions and Role," Articles 98 and 99 of the Charter were bound to provide this increased stature of the office. Hammarskjöld's interpretation of Article 98 added to that possibility, particularly in connection with the peacekeeping operation. But it is also important to note that both he and his successor have used the obligations established by this article to submit, in the annual report, a statement of their views regarding major policy problems. This opportunity to communicate to all members on a broad and comprehensive basis gives him an opportunity available to none other.

Pyman's discussion makes it clear that the deadlock in the Security Council forced the Assembly to face up to a range of problems probably not originally anticipated, and thus encouraged a greater responsibility on the part of the Secretary-General because of the lack of executive leadership in the Assembly. So, likewise, did the office of Secretary-General change dramatically just as the organization itself changed after 1955. From then on both the large increase in members and the similarity of their economic problems and historical experiences added to and altered his status.

One of the major headaches of such an officer, and one that was tied to the attack on Hammarskjöld by the Russians, pertains to the staffing of the Secretariat. Charles Winchmore reminds us that not only is the Secretary-General superordinate to the rest of the Secretariat, but, because he is the chief administrative officer of the Organization, he in fact acts as the tie between the two. He is, as the author quotes Hammarskjöld, "the only elected officer in principle representing all members."

Winchmore provides a brief history of the development of the organ and the major reasons for the centrifugal effect which characterizes the pressures the Secretary-General must overcome. This undoubtedly best manifests itself in the tug between the demands for competence and integrity on the one hand and those for geographical representation on the other.

But the tugging on the Secretary-General is likewise a result of endemic differences in the concepts of civil service among the members. These differences are built upon national conceptions where qualifications, training, and frames of reference often depart considerably from that expected of staff members at Turtle Bay. And Winchmore also provides an excellent account of how the increasing demands of newer members have greatly expanded the function of the Secretariat in the economic, social, military, and political spheres.

Perhaps the two biggest problems confronting the Secretary-General are (1) maintenance of a sensible balance between members' demands that their staff quotas be increased, and at the highest ranks, and the appointment of competent men whose integrity and dedication to the Organization are unquestioned; and (2) the need to sustain a forward thrust in the effort to solve the tremendous problems which are brought to the United Nations, while at the same time maintaining the confidence of the major powers. The latter may not only block his reappointment but, even more serious, may declare him persona non grata, as the Russians did to two Secretaries-General.

Both of these problems are highlighted in the exchange between Nikita Khrushchev and Dag Hammarskjöld, and, although almost all who witnessed that interchange would probably conclude that Hammarskjöld won the prize, it was the Russians who held the trump card in the shape of a powerful political position in the Organization. Although the Secretary-General's sudden death ended that controversy, the debate presented here reveals the heart of a dilemma likely to remain throughout the history of international organization. Are there any steps, institutional devices, or policies that might be adopted to reduce this difficulty? And must they be mutually undertaken or can future Secretaries-General employ them unilaterally with a reasonable expectation of success?

There is one other question which must be raised. Despite the unfairness which many believe characterizes the criticism of Lie and Hammarskjöld by Soviet as well as some French leaders, the criticism did point up one factor which may become the critical one in the choice of future Secretaries-General: the fact that not only must this civil servant remain scrupulously unbiased in the fulfillment of his office, but he must also appear to be so as well. That is, the question of bias in the future will not only hinge on what he does, but who he is. If this is so, it seems quite probable that future Secretaries-General will have to come not only from small states but also from among the non-aligned newer states.

Given that consideration, one may ask if there are guidelines which can be employed in the recruiting of civil servants so that an international organization is truly international in staff, as well as competent. Has the organization the responsibility for emphasizing the first in its recruitment while providing training programs to develop the second? And can the Secretary-General himself find ways of bestowing upon his office both dignity and vigor while minimizing its vulnerability to partisan criticism?

FURTHER READINGS

Bailey, Sidney D., *The Secretariat of the United Nations*, rev. ed. New York: Frederick A. Praeger, Inc. 1962. Chap. IV.

Korovin, Y., "Ways of Reorganizing the UN Executive Organs," *International Affairs* (Moscow), vol. 12, Dec. 1960, pp. 7–9. (Published in English in Moscow.)

Langrod, G., *The International Civil Service*. Dobbs Ferry, N.Y.: Oceana Publications, Inc., 1964.

THE STATUS OF THE SECRETARY-GENERAL

T. A. Pyman*

I t should be realised that . . . the "static" concept [of the Secretary-General's office] as it is now described, tends to throw great stress on the need for Secretariat officers to be chosen in a way that ensures representation of all major national interests in the key executive posts of the Secretariat. But this insistence in itself does not ensure that the [other] approach, the "dynamic" concept, becomes impracticable because the critical issue is the determination of the point at which the responsibility for decisions is re-posed. Clearly the power of ultimate decision in relation to any matter requiring Secretariat determination has been vested exclusively in the Secretary-General. His colleagues in the senior executive posts grouped around him are patently sub-ordinated to his direction.

A number of these key posts have been distributed amongst the major powers—at their insistence. Indeed, the U.N. Charter in Article 101 requires that, in the employment of staff, "due regard shall be paid to the importance of recruiting the staff on as wide a geographical basis as possible." Neither of the first two Secretaries-General appears to have resented the practice of distributing staff appointments on a global basis and giving major power nominees senior executive posts. It may well be that they rather welcomed the opportunity of having staff who were drawn from diverse backgrounds and of being able to gauge the possible attitudes of the major groups in the U.N. through the reactions of some of their senior executive officials.

❈ ❈ ❈ ❈ ❈ ❈ ❈

POWERS AND FUNCTIONS OF THE SECRETARY-GENERAL

Whilst the U.N. Charter derived a great deal of guidance from the League of Nations Covenant in the matter of the independence of the Secretariat from national pressures, re-affirming principles already accepted in the Covenant, it introduced new elements in connection with the powers and functions of the Secretary-General.

* T. A. Pyman, "The United Nations Secretary-Generalship: A Review of its Status, Functions and Role," *Australian Outlook*, Vol. 15, 1961, pp. 240–259. By permission of Australia to the United Nations for several years.

T. A. Pyman was a member of the Australian Embassy staff and a delegate from *Australian Outlook* and T. A. Pyman.

First, it affirmed that the Secretary-General "shall be the chief administrative officer of the Organisation" (Article 97) thus underlining his administrative preeminence. The League Covenant did not contain such an affirmation though probably the role was implicit in the position of the Secretary-General of the League. Its inclusion in the Charter made incontrovertible the administrative supremacy of the Secretary-General and denied the right of any U.N. organ to interfere in the process of administering the Secretariat. There was a slight "political" element involved in this exclusive administrative authority of the Secretary-General. The preparation of documents (working papers, summaries, draft reports—all the documents that sap the energy of the junior officials in each national delegation if not [the energy of] their senior colleagues) carries with it a limited capacity to influence decisions through guiding the course of discussion. This ability to influence decisions was frankly recognized by the U.N. Preparatory Commission which met in December, 1946 after the San Francisco Conference and before the first General Assembly when it stated that "while the responsibility for the framing and adoption of agreed international policies rests with the organs representative of the members . . . the essential tasks of preparing the ground for those decisions and of executing them in co-operation with the Members will devolve largely upon the Secretariat."

It is not, however, merely by inference from the wording of Article 97 of the Charter that the root concept of the Secretary-General as an international statesman is established. The most specific indication of this concept is to be found in Article 99 under the provisions of which the Secretary-General is entitled to bring to the attention of the Security Council any matter which, in his opinion, may threaten the maintenance of international peace and security. This provision clearly reflects the general desire of virtually all the member Governments, including the most influential of those Governments, namely, the major powers, that the head of the new organisation should be endowed with specific political prerogatives. There was even a tendency in some quarters (e.g., the United States) at an early stage of the planning for the organisation to consider whether there should be a President, for political and executive matters, and a Secretary-General who would attend to administration as in the International Civil Aviation Organisation. This plan was dropped before the major powers produced the Dumbarton Oaks proposals in which they proposed the creation of a single permanent officer combining each of these functions on the assumption that the Secretary-General (as the officer was rather modestly dubbed) would be more than the U.N.'s highest administrative functionary.

Elements of political discretion of almost equal significance are to be found in Article 98 which, first, provides for his right of attendance at the meetings of the Assembly, Security Council, Economic and Social Council, and the Trusteeship Council. His precise capacity at such meetings was left to be filled out by rules of procedure. The provisional rules of procedure of the General Assembly, for instance, provide that the Secretary-General may, at any time, upon the invitation of the President, make oral or written statements concerning any question under consideration. Similarly, he is given the privilege of placing items on the General Assembly agenda, and such items could, of course, be political issues (this is analogous to his power to bring questions before the Security Council under Article 99). The powers mentioned provide a means of leverage, the value of which to the Secretary-General should not be measured in terms of actual usage (in fact the latter power has been exercised rarely), but by the fact that their existence exerts pressure on governments to place matters on the agenda of the Assembly, or to raise issues in the Security Council, in the belief that if this is not done the Secretary-General can himself bring these matters before these bodies.

Secondly, Article 98 directs the Secretary-General to perform such other functions as are entrusted to him by the Assembly and the Security Council. This article has been interpreted by the Secretary-General in recent years, with some justification at least from a legal point of view, as entrusting him with tasks involving the execution of political decisions. It constitutes one of the principal foundations of Secretariat organisation and supervision of such "instruments" as the United Nations Emergency Force in the Middle East and the United Nations Congo Force.

Thirdly, the Secretary-General was required by the Charter (Article 98) to make an annual report to the General Assembly on the work of the Organisation. This duty again presented the Secretary-General with an opportunity to give direction to the annual debates in the U.N. Assembly. The annual report has in fact been consistently used as a vehicle for dis· cussion of major policy issues in the context of the relationship of Charter principles and objectives to such issues; in particular, it has become traditional for the Secretary-General to discuss important general issues affecting the functioning and status of the Organisation in the Introduction to his Annual Report.

✻   ✻   ✻   ✻   ✻   ✻   ✻

ELECTION OF THE SECRETARY-GENERAL

The role of the Secretary-General was not a central issue at San Francisco in 1945, and agreement was reached with comparatively little discussion on the principal features of his powers and functions. The major powers' effort to undermine these through creating a guiding board or committee of elected deputies was, as has been recalled above, easily defeated. Only the Soviet showed any lasting reluctance to abandon this plan for elected deputies. Major power influence was, however, retained in relation to the election of the Secretary-General. The major powers insisted on maintaining electoral control through the procedure under which a recommendation for appointment must come from the Security Council (subject to the veto, as it was not regarded as a procedural matter) to the Assembly. The existence of the veto has meant that, in practice, the major powers must agree on the person recommended to the Assembly. A protracted wrangle is therefore almost inevitable under the circumstances of present day ideological and great power conflict.

* * * * * * *

THE ROLE OF THE FIRST TWO SECRETARIES-GENERAL

The terms of the Charter and the resolutions and rules of procedure of the principal U.N. organs, as has been seen, have provided "a legal spring-board" (in Schwebel's words) for the activity of the Secretary-General. The crucial test was not whether the Secretary-General, in practice, would be a sound administrator (in the tradition of Sir Eric Drummond's Secretary-Generalship of the League of Nations) but rather whether he would utilise fully the political powers bestowed on him by the Charter and thus assume the role of international "statesman" (paradoxical though the term may sound) contemplated for him. The first two Secretaries-General have clearly done so though each has followed a different method, the choice being partly determined by the political circumstances prevalent during their respective terms of office and partly by their differing temperaments and training. A study of the principal features of their respective periods of leadership throws light on the validity of proposals for basic changes in the Secretariat system and, in particular, the role of the Secretary-General. It should be stated by way of explanation at the outset that there has been no suggestion that the purely administrative tasks of supervising the performance of the Secretariat's "house-keeping" work (and this covers such important operations as the preparation of the Budget) should be done by anyone other than the Secretary-General.

* * * * * * *

Whilst the differences in method of the first two Secretaries-General reflected undoubted differences in temperament, outlook, and training it is essential for an understanding of the development of Secretariat activity during the two periods of office to appreciate that a most significant change occurred in the composition and, subsequently, in the functioning of Organisation after 1955.

Up to 1955, and therefore through the whole period of Trygve Lie's office, the Security Council and, to a less extent (nevertheless quite effectually), the Assembly were very much under the influence of the Western Powers group led by the United States. Their policy on major international security issues had an appeal on most occasions to a large number of Latin-American countries whose numerical representation at that time constituted the largest group interest in the U.N. . . .

At the same time from 1950 onwards Western power influence was increasingly exerted through General Assembly action. The Security Council being frequently paralysed by the Soviet veto, resort was had to a General Assembly resolution (the "Uniting for Peace" Resolution of 1950), the principal long-term effect of which was to enable the Assembly to be seized with a situation threatening international peace and security immediately after the Security Council had failed to take action because of the exercise of the veto. . . .

The situation of strong Western influence in the Assembly underwent a considerable change after 1955 early in the Hammarskjöld period of office. New members were admitted in a fairly large group in that year. In the succeeding years large numbers of new members, particularly from Africa, have doubled the total membership, and ended the Western dominance of major Assembly decisions, reducing, in the process, the high proportion of Latin American states to the total membership. The natural consequence was that a far greater diversity of opinion on international political issues was introduced into Assembly discussions. But the most important effect was that it became exceedingly difficult for any group of governments to win approval in detail for any particular course of action which it believed the U.N. should take in relation to a specific situation threatening international peace and security. On important issues of this kind, a two-thirds majority vote is required.

It was precisely this situation which enabled Dag Hammarskjöld to advance the cause of the Secretariat as a detached international medium, the sole purpose of which was to achieve a settlement on the basis of the purposes and principles of the U.N. through the method of "reconciliation" as he described it, of clashing interests. His success with the conciliation technique in the Suez affair, combined with the willingness of the vast majority of member governments, especially the new members, to vest in him the responsibility for this activity, produced in 1956–60 the direct involvement of the U.N. in a number of major political crises to which reference has been made earlier.

What are the conclusions to be drawn [regarding the Office] of the Secretary-General in the first fifteen years of existence of that institution? First, it is clear that the effectiveness of the U.N. has become increasingly dependent on the Secretary-General. The Security Council and the General Assembly have not possessed throughout this period sufficient flexibility or displayed a capacity to attain such a basic consensus as would enable either one of them to direct international conciliation processes. As the Western powers lost effective control over the recommendations of the main U.N. organs the tendency to use the executive powers of the U.N. organs as a weapon in the "cold war" diminished, and in its place appeared the endeavour to use the powers of these organs as a means of bringing conciliation processes into operation and thus reducing to a minimum the likelihood of intervention by either side in the "cold war."

The chosen instrument for this purpose, the Secretary-General, could recall that a similar approach had achieved some useful results in the League of Nations era when distinguished individuals known as "rapporteurs" were appointed for the specific purpose of acting as conciliators, working privately with the parties in dispute, to reconcile conflicts of view and report progress to the League organs. The United Nations extension of this concept involved the use of a permanently available conciliation machinery in the shape of the Secretariat to act as a concilation and reporting medium backed by the vast majority of member Governments, many of them "neutrals," refusing to be aligned with one or the other power bloc. Because of this widespread support the decisions taken by the Secretary-General, in carrying out the extremely general directives of the U.N. organs, have been upheld although strenuously challenged at times by minority groups of members.

It is not suggested, of course, that in a matter affecting the basic security interests of a great power (as assessed by that power) the U.N. is able to exert a decisive influence in the face of a display of superior military and other force. The nature of the pressure applied in such cases can only be that of moral suasion whether the issue be Hungary, cessation of nuclear tests, or Algerian independence. When physical and military resources cannot be concentrated easily or the risks of global conflict, compared with apparent immediate benefits, are too great, and also the main participants to a dispute are prepared to accept conciliation techniques, then the scope for U.N. action is wider. The Secretariat (as in the Congo) then assumes a responsible and definite role within an area from which the two major power blocs have, in effect, eliminated one another through a process of balancing of power and, in effect, neutralization of each other's influence.

The second conclusion to be derived from U.N. experience is that the assertion of the ability of the international body to play an appropriate role in international conciliation efforts required determined and skilful efforts by the Secretary-General to demonstrate positively the contribution such a medium could make. That such a "political" role had been envisaged for the Secretary-General by the "planners" in pre-charter days seems to have been forgotten in the general stress produced by the development of the cold war. When the Secretary-General first essayed an intervention his efforts were greeted (principally by non-Communist powers) with some anxiety and even distaste and the suggestion that the Secretariat was beginning to exceed its proper role. It was Hammarskjöld's achievement that this criticism became far less frequent. He was unable, however, to convince the Communist powers of his impartiality, and this fact clearly became his greatest problem in the last two years of his Secretary-Generalship.

Hammarskjöld, however, had to accept the risk of alienating the opinions of some governments. To have refused to reach decisions because it was feared that they would antagonise one group of powers (however powerful) in the U.N. would have caused the U.N. conciliation process to wither because it would then have almost certainly lacked the strength afforded by the support of the vast majority of member governments.

Thirdly, the very nature of the situations in which Secretariat intervention was requested by the U.N. Assembly or Security Council required the personal supervision of the Secretary-General. The circumstances were new and problems of some complexity, insofar as the application of Charter principles was concerned, presented themselves; moreover, the Secretary-General was obliged to take personal responsibility for all important decisions, knowing full well that his actions would be subjected to intensive scrutiny from points of view that reflected basic differences of approach and objective. As each situation arose there was an assumption that the personal efforts of the Secretary-General should be concentrated upon the problem. His prestige and success intensified this demand for his services by the principal participants. Whenever possible, sub-ordinates were used, but if critical situations arose the presence of the Secretary-General himself appeared to be regarded as imperative and the tireless Hammarskjöld appeared at the scene of operation to smooth out differences and work for conciliation and peaceful adjustment of differences.

Fourthly, it became quite clear in all this activity at the international level that decisions had to be made positively and often at short notice. This requirement became a commonplace almost in the handling of the activities of the Congo Force. Whilst maintaining constant consultation with his staff and with the representatives of governments in New York, the Secretary-General had to determine the disposition and general objectives of the U.N. Force. There was no room for equivocation or even hesitation. In short, the U.N. executive had to have a capacity for quick and vital decisions. Inability to reach them could mean disaster and almost certain chaos in the international operation.

. . . There is perhaps a need for a spreading of responsibility more widely amongst senior international officials if only to relieve the burden of the Secretary-General. Perhaps even an official "panel of conciliators" may become a feasible arrangement provided that it is on the basis that, when a deputy of the Secretary-General is acting in such a capacity, he is doing so as an agent of the Secretary-General through whom he is responsible to the U.N. organ concerned with the matter.

. . . the fact should not be obscured . . . that conciliation by the international body may only be possible if the parties in dispute are prepared to accept such international intervention. Hammarskjöld himself always made it clear that direct U.N. involvement, for instance, in the Berlin situation, to take a leading example, was dependent entirely upon Soviet-Western Power agreement that U.N. agencies could be usefully employed. U.N. executive activity under the guidance of the Secretary-General can only become effective on the basis of the consent and co-operation of the governments in dispute. It is, in short, a method of international adjustment predicated on the willingness of governments to accept it. The pressure it exerts on member governments is primarily that of moral suasion, namely the attitude of the members of the international body that processes of international conciliation deserve support and acceptance. Although the effects of such pressure may be regarded as doubtful in the face of the sovereign will of a major power, sufficient [success] has been achieved to suggest that even when major powers come into direct conflict with the processes of international conciliation they are unlikely to be able to reverse them and may suffer some loss of prestige and influence when they attempt to do so. The real test, still to be decided, is, of course, whether the major powers will be prepared to accept international conciliation processes directed by the U.N. Secretary-General when their own interests, especially their security interests, are regarded by them as directly involved.

THE SECRETARIAT: RETROSPECT AND PROSPECT

Charles Winchmore*

B y the Charter of the United Nations the Secretariat is established as one of the six principal organs of the United Nations. The Secretary-General is designated "the chief administrative officer," not—be it noted—of the Secretariat but of the Organization. The Secretariat comprises the Secretary-General together with the staff appointed by him. The two institutions, the Secretariat and the Secretary-General, may well be regarded as distinct but inseparable—distinct in that the Charter confers in Articles 98 and 99 certain functions and powers specifically on the Secretary-General; inseparable in that the Secretariat is a unitary institution, organized on a functional basis, the members of which are "subject to the authority of the Secretary-General" and "responsible to him in the exercise of their functions."

Perhaps the experience of two decades has served to accentuate rather

* Charles Winchmore, "The Secretariat: Retrospect and Prospect," *International Organization*, Vol. 19, 1965, pp. 622–639. Copyright 1965, World Peace Foundation. By permission of *International Organization*.

Charles Winchmore is a former Research Scholar at the Royal Institute of International Affairs.

than to diminish the distinctiveness of the two institutions. In particular, the office of Secretary-General has been shaped by the character of its three successive incumbents, and more especially by the outstanding achievements of the second Secretary-General, Dag Hammarskjöld. His own description of the post as a "one-man 'executive' " (the term employed by him in his address at Chicago in May 1960) marked a climax in the mounting prestige of the office. On many occasions it is the office of Secretary-General, rather than the Secretariat, which has been referred to as the sixth principal organ of the United Nations and with considerable justification since, to use again Dag Hammarskjöld's words, "he is the only elected officer in principle representing all members," and since his authority extends over the Secretariat as a whole. Nevertheless, it is not without significance that the Charter ascribed the quality of "principal organ" to the Secretariat rather than exclusively to its chief administrative officer.

EVOLVING ROLES OF THE SECRETARIAT AND SECRETARY-GENERAL

The functions of the Secretariat have a less dramatic quality than the role of the Secretary-General and, though this is perhaps debatable, have shown a lesser capacity of dynamic development. Yet undoubtedly the scope of the Secretariat's work has also undergone a remarkable expansion, partly as a reflection of the activities of the Secretary-General but also as a response to the need of the nations of the world to pursue through international institutions certain common social and economic, and even political, objectives. It is timely to reflect on this experience and to seek to ascertain to what extent the achievements of the two decades are merely eccentricities of history, destined to leave no permanent mark on the world's political development, or to what extent they have laid a basis which affords further opportunities of constructive growth.

It may be regarded as to some extent inherent in the circumstances of the Organization in the first decades of its development that the distance between the two institutions, the Secretariat and the Secretary-General, has tended to increase with the passage of the years. It necessarily fell to Trygve Lie to grapple with the initial administrative problems of the Secretariat—the financial structure, terms of employment, and similar questions. In large measure these initial administrative problems had been successfully dealt with by the end of the first Secretary-General's tenure of office. On assuming his position as Secretary-General, Mr. Hammarskjöld envisaged perhaps that his contribution would be primarily administrative, more especially in the social and economic field, and he undertook at the outset an overhaul of the structure of the Secretariat. Nevertheless, the main problems of personnel and finance had been largely settled by 1953. The post of Assistant Secretary-General for Administration and Finance was allowed to lapse with the retirement of Byron Price, partly on the grounds that only a residuum of administrative problems remained to be dealt with, problems which should not demand more than about an hour a day on the part of the Secretary-General and which involved decisions which he should be and would be in a position to take himself. But in the second decade of the life of the United Nations, the office of Secretary-General became with remarkable rapidity the focal point of international activities of a relatively novel character. The crisis of October 1956 gave rise to the circumstances in which political forces needed the Secretary-General as their catalytic agent, and the experience he then gained proved applicable also in later crises. The new political duties of the office necessarily had a primary claim on the attention of the Secretary-General, and to some extent his increasingly close relations with governments and delegations were achieved at the price of greater remoteness from the generality of the Secretariat. He himself realized that this was so, and it is significant that his last speech, on September 8, 1961, was a speech to his own staff. Undoubtedly, if the Secretariat is to maintain a lively sense of unity, it is essential for any Secretary-General to ensure that his office functions as a center from which the sense of purpose and dedication permeates the entire staff.

This consideration is the more important in that the fissiparous tendencies in an international secretariat are undoubtedly more marked than in any national civil service. Within a national civil service, men and women are brought together as public officials who have been reared in a common cultural background and who, by reason of their experience, pay homage to institutions which symbolize the unity of their political community. An international civil service has no such "natural" basis on which to operate. It is essentially an institution derived from an exclusively rational recognition of the need for its existence. Within it men and women work together who, brought from the four quarters of the globe, are of the most diverse cultures and are bound together by little but their common humanity and their commitment to the ideals of the institution which they serve. For these reasons the administrative structure of an international secretariat is necessarily somewhat fragile. In many respects the relationships within an international secretariat are diplomatic rather than administrative—diplomatic in that cooperation depends rather on persistent recourse to the arts of persuasion than on continuous exercise of the power of command. This generalization holds perhaps with regard to any administrative structure, but most of all with respect to an international secretariat.

Moreover, many of the members of the international secretariat who joined in the early years became civil servants at a time when they had already mapped out for themselves a quite different professional career. The international civil service is still too recent an innovation for many men and women to have engaged in it as the vocation of a lifetime and so to have become wholly molded to its quite special exigencies. Those who join it become for the most part exiles, living in circumstances alien to them. Hence the disintegrative tendencies in an international secretariat are strong. Conscious effort is required to develop the corporate spirit capable of absorbing into itself the energies of the individual members of the Secretariat and of imparting to them a sense of "belonging" in order to compensate in some measure for their alienation from their own natural background. This infusion of a common sense of purpose requires a conscious and tireless effort, and in the development of this common purpose the leadership of the Secretary-General is vital. In the absence of such leadership each department, even each division or section, may tend to become a segregated area in itself, taking its character to only too great an extent from the qualities of its head. So too the secretariat of each agency remains largely particularized, its character deriving in part from its special sphere of work but reflecting also the qualities of its first principal administrator. The unification of the international secretariats—and even coordination between agencies within a common system—remains largely a task of the future. The obstacles which lie in the path of any such achievement are formidable. Perhaps what is remarkable about international secretariats is not that at times they may display some inefficiency in the utilization of their resources of manpower; what is remarkable is that this artificial structure works at all. It is indeed a testimony to the adaptability of the human mind.

CONCEPTIONS OF AN INTERNATIONAL SECRETARIAT

For these reasons it would seem crucial that the Charter itself stipulated that the necessity of securing the highest standards of efficiency, competence, and integrity was to be the paramount consideration in the employment of the staff and in the determination of the conditions of service; and that the Charter designated the responsibilities of the Secretary-General and his staff to be of an "exclusively international character," which the Members of the United Nations are committed to respect. The Staff Regulations approved by the Assembly and the Staff Rules promulgated by the Secretary-General represent the effort over two decades to translate into detailed terms these general stipulations of the Charter. They are not and cannot be rules of a trade union nature devised to protect the vested interests of the employees of the United Nations; they constitute rather a deliberate judgment, developed over two decades of experience, as to the essential conditions required for the maintenance of a secretariat characterized by "efficiency, competence, and integrity." Protection of the interests of the members of the Secretariat finds a place in those rules insofar as such protection is essential to ensure that those members may devote themselves wholeheartedly and exclusively to the service of the Organization. At a time when the very character of the international secretariat is under attack by those who would in effect replace it by seconded governmental officials, the anchorage of the existing system in the stipulations of the Charter itself should be kept prominently in mind.

The Preparatory Commission of the United Nations reported that it was essential that the bulk of the staff should consist of persons who would make their career in the Secretariat since insofar as members of the staff remained dependent on national administrations for their future, they could not be expected to subordinate the national interests of their countries to the international interest. The principle of a career staff is therefore embedded in the detailed stipulations of the Staff Regulations and Rules: the conditions of appointment providing for probationary appointments leading to "indefinite appointment," the arrangements for affording reasonable prospects of promotion within the service, and the safeguards against wrongful termination. Emphasis on the career character of the staff necessarily leads to a certain rigidity in its composition, inseparable from the expectation that the normal staff member will devote some 35 years to the service. The necessity to adapt the composition of the staff to the expanding membership of the United Nations has led since 1960 on the one hand to greater emphasis on nationality in matters of recruitment and on the other hand to the more extensive use of the fixed-term contract as a means of ensuring greater flexibility in composition. The problem of recent years has been whether efficiency, in the sense of the recruitment of the best man for the post, can be reconciled with the requirement of recruitment with a view to the improvement of geographic distribution and whether greater recourse to the fixed-term contract might detract from the career character of the staff and tend to erode the sense of exclusive devotion to the interests of the Organization. The General Assembly has asserted that no incompatibility arises between the obligations of efficiency, competence, and integrity on the one hand and the requirements of geographic distribution on the other. Undoubtedly, in the long run, these dual objectives can be served and an efficient secretariat of appropriate national composition achieved.

At the same time the temptation must be withstood to regard the international character of the Secretariat as synonymous with its multinational character. The wide distribution of nationalities within the Secretariat may contribute to its international character, but it is not and cannot be the decisive factor. The Secretariat must remain international in the sense in which science is international—not by reason of the diffusion of scientists among the many nationalities of the world but by reason of their commitment to purposes of universal validity.

In fact, the concept of the international civil servant would seem not only to have withstood with considerable success the strains placed upon it during the two decades which have elapsed but also to have been given sharper definition and embodied in more precise institutional form as the years have passed. The tensions which resulted from the engagement of a high proportion of the UN staff on temporary indefinite contracts in the first years were surmounted in 1952 when, as a result of the survey of the staff by the Walters Selection Committee for the Review of Staff Members on Temporary Appointments, the proportion of staff on permanent contracts was raised to 70 percent. Though concessions were made to the United States government in 1953 in relation to Secretariat members of United States nationality, concessions such as the introduction of a procedure for clearance of United States nationals on recruitment, the permission of United States governmental agencies to conduct their inquiries within the premises of the UN itself, and the dismissal of staff members who refused to testify before a United States Federal Grand Jury, the more extreme pressures of the United States government were in the end successfully resisted. Staff members were enabled to test the legality of their dismissal before the Administrative Tribunal, and the independence of the Tribunal in the award of damages was vindicated by the International Court of Justice. So too the pressures arising from the increase of membership since 1960 and from advocacy of a changed basis for the Secretariat have not been permitted to subvert the fundamental character of the Secretariat. The adjustment of the composition of the Secretariat in response to the demands for more equitable geographic distribution has proceeded gradually as vacancies have arisen to permit the new recruitment to take place. It is true that greater use has come to be made of the fixed-term contract, notably as a basis for the engagement of officials seconded from government service or as a means of recruiting for a defined period persons with qualifications and experience not to be found within the staff itself. Yet while the recruitment of outsiders on fixed-term contract at the higher levels may have lessened somewhat the prospects of promotion of the career staff, the principle of promotion, as distinct from recruitment, has not been allowed to be affected by considerations of geographic distribution, and the prospects of promotion appear in fact to have remained reasonably good. The International Civil Service Advisory Board (ICSAB) has established a standard definition of the obligations of the international civil servant; and the Board itself has recently been reorganized and strengthened in order that it may make further contributions to the reinforcement of the concept of the service.

If the international civil service has thus resisted the strains placed upon it, some credit for this performance may be attributed to the efforts of the staff itself and to the means which have been established to enable the staff to make its own constructive contribution to the shaping of the service. The Staff Council of the UN Staff Association, which was established through the spontaneous action of the staff in the first instance, was duly recognized by the General Assembly in 1952 as the means of ensuring continuous contact between the staff and the Secretary-General. The Council is entitled to be consulted on questions relating to staff welfare, including policy on such matters as appointments and promotions, and to make proposals to the Secretary-General on such questions. The position taken by the UN Staff

Council was undoubtedly a factor in checking the degree to which the pressures exercised by the United States government upon the UN Secretariat in 1950–1953 were permitted to give rise to deviations from established Secretariat practices. The staff associations of the various international organizations are linked together in the Federation of International Civil Servants, which brings together the principal staff representatives for consultation on common problems. While consultation between the Secretary-General and the Staff Council is confined to general problems of policy, considerable progress has also been made in the second decade in associating staff representatives in the work of both administrative and semi-judicial bodies within the Secretariat. These provisions with regard to staff participation in problems of administration have served to ensure greater harmony between the Secretary-General and his staff in the second decade of the Secretariat's history than in the first decade, though opinions may vary as to whether the staff has seized the opportunity to make as continuous and constructive a contribution to the shaping of an international secretariat as these provisions make possible.

It has seemed desirable to draw attention, no matter how summarily, to the progress made in the past two decades in the formulation of rules and the establishment of institutions to govern the effective functioning of the international civil service. For the significance of advances in the realm of international administration can only too readily be minimized or even overlooked. The contentious political problems which come before international institutions, whether problems of long standing, such as disarmament or the control of nuclear weapons, or evanescent problems such as the Congo (Leopoldville), tend to overshadow in public attention the far less dramatic developments in international administration. Yet, in the long run, the world's success in dealing with its major political problems is likely to depend on the establishment and maintenance of sound and effective practices of an administrative character on an international scale. Political agreements may come to be concluded to deal with problems of armaments and nuclear weapons and other matters which need to be regulated on a global scale; but the smooth implementation of such agreements must depend in no small measure on the establishment of conditions which enable international officials to work smoothly, effectively, and loyally together.

Compared with national institutions, international institutions still remain fragile and inchoate. The arena of world politics is for the most part concerned with the clash of national purposes. Yet the concept of an international civil service has proved to be a concept of increasingly expanded application in the past twenty years. Indeed, it may be held that, in the transference of the concept from the framework of the League of Nations to that of the United Nations, the concept imperceptibly underwent a revolutionary transformation. For the League was, by the terms of the Covenant, essentially an instrument in the hands of its members. The United Nations is, by the terms of the Charter, committed to the pursuit of certain "Purposes and Principles." These principles are not static; they have been developed in Assembly declarations. Whereas the essential quality of the League Secretariat might well be regarded as neutrality between the policies of its members, the international character of the United Nations Secretariat must depend in large measure on its positive commitment to the Purposes and Principles which govern the Organization itself.

Such considerations warrant the conclusion that the concept of the international civil service has been given more precise expression in the last two decades. The justification of the international secretariat must depend in the long run on its ability to serve purposes which can be discharged neither by any national civil service nor by a service composed of civil servants seconded from their national governments. The international civil servant is called upon to display qualities of mind and character, and indeed of intellect, which are inseparable from his calling and which are likely to be developed only as a result of long acclimatization to the service of an international organization. The national civil servant is likely to be conscious of a defined framework of policy within which he works and to be committed to pursue that policy with a certain rigor and insistence. The intellectual qualities and outlook which he is expected to display are likely to be those developed within the university in his own country at which he has been trained. The international civil servant on the other hand is likely to find that even his professional training needs to be readapted to the special requirements of the international organization in whose employ he finds himself. Rarely will he find himself working within a clearly defined framework of policy, and his concern must be to serve the interests of the Organization while avoiding offense to the susceptibilities of Member States. While caution and discretion necessarily mark his approach to any problem, he must be ever alert to detect these opportunities for advancing the common aims which arise, often in seemingly adverse circumstances, and he must display resourcefulness in working toward the achievement of desired objectives.

THE EXPANDING ROLE OF THE SECRETARIAT

In appraising the role of the international secretariat, the generalization might be advanced that the effective contribution of the Secretariat to the work of the United Nations in any sphere of activity will very directly with the degree to which a common purpose can be developed between the Member States. It is indeed a function of the Secretariat to translate into precise form the often inchoate elements of cooperation which can be discerned between the Members of the Organization. Secondly, the greater the degree to which agreement exists as to appropriate technical means for pursuing the common purpose, the greater will be the degree to which work is delegated to the Secretariat. Because these two conditions are to some degree fulfilled in the sphere of social and economic activity, the role of the Secretariat in social and economic matters is greater and more firmly based than in the political sphere. But perhaps the most novel extension of the concept of the international secretariat in the past decade has been the involvement of the military profession in peacekeeping activities under the direction of the Secretary-General.

These three aspects—social and economic, military, and political—may be briefly reviewed to illustrate the expanding application of the concept of the international civil service.

THE SOCIAL AND ECONOMIC SPHERE. In a statement to the Economic and Social Council (ECOSOC) meeting at ministerial level on July 11, 1960, Secretary-General Hammarskjöld made the following brief summation of the development of the United Nations: "Born as an instrument for multilateral diplomacy, the United Nations has grown into an operational agency of significant dimensions." This growth took place in the first instance with regard to the work of the Organization in social and economic matters and in technical assistance, for in these areas of activity the preconditions for the expansion of Secretariat activities, viz., community of purpose among governments and widespread agreement on techniques, were found to exist.

The common objective has been provided by the general acceptance of responsibility for the economic development of underdeveloped countries. Throughout the two decades, the economic activities of the United Nations and of the specialized agencies have tended to focus increasingly on this aspect, and the United Nations and its agencies have provided a ready instrument in the service of this end. They have constituted the only universal agency in which countries with widely differing political institutions and at different stages of economic development could discuss and initiate collective action. Such collective action has been made possible through the broadness of the provisions of the Charter on the subject of the promotion of economic and social cooperation.

*   *   *   *   *   *   *

This development has been facilitated insofar as issues that were initially regarded as primarily political have been transformed into activities of a predominantly technical character, accepted by governments as appropriate functions for international civil servants. Officials of the Secretariat have been called upon more and more to assist in the formulation of programs, the determination of priorities, and the most effective types of aid to be given. Activities of this character are a far cry from research and servicing activities in the narrow sense. It remains true, nevertheless, that the influence of the Secretariat in these matters has been mainly indirect, taking the form of recommendations to governments. At the same time it is significant that heads of agencies themselves have, in their addresses to organs of the United Nations, taken a lead in recommending policies or warning against certain courses of action.

In matters of technical assistance the Secretariat has exercised its influence in the form of recommendations to governments. But the record of twenty years would be incomplete without at least passing reference to those instances in which international civil servants have assumed more direct responsibility for governmental processes. That responsibility was most complete in the case of the United Nations Temporary Executive Authority (UNTEA) for West Irian, which was provisionally placed under the authority of an Administrator appointed by and responsible to Secretary-General U Thant for the purpose of effecting the transfer of the area from Netherlands to Indonesian sovereignty. Such a venture in international administration in the fullest sense of the term may well prove to be unique—the product of special political circumstances in which the transient control of the territory by the United Nations averted the menace of conflict between the two states directly involved. As in all such situations of crisis, expedition in the recruitment of the necessary corps of administrators was essential to the success of the operation; and such expedition was in large measure made possible by the experience gained earlier in the recruitment of experts for purposes of technical assistance. A venture of hardly less political significance but more directly the outcome of previous United Nations efforts in the area of technical assistance was the civilian operations for the United Nations Operation in the Congo (ONUC) within which the United Nations and the specialized agencies joined in a unified administrative structure for the purpose of maintaining in working order the social, economic, and administrative structure of the new state.

THE MILITARY SPHERE. It is hardly to be expected that this expansion in the realm of the economist could be or would be matched in the sphere of activity normally falling within the purview of the military profession. The precaution with which the drafters of the Charter approached the problem of the involvement of the military profession in the activities of international political organization is exemplified by the text of the Charter itself. It was realized that the collaboration of the military profession in the working of the Organization might well be a condition of its success. This line of reasoning was one factor in the inclusion in the Charter itself of provisions relating to the Military Staff Committee. Yet the Military Staff Committee has remained a somewhat anomalous body among United Nations organs. The Charter specified in Article 47 that it should be composed "of the Chiefs of Staff" of the permanent members of the Security Council or their representatives. Its peculiar status is reflected in the organization of its secretariat which functions under the direction of the Principal Secretary of the Committee, a post which is held in successive months in rotation by a member of the constituent delegations. It is significant also that no solution was arrived at in the Charter as to the command of armed forces to be placed at the disposal of the Security Council; the provision was simply included that this question was to be worked out subsequently. Since the agreements called for by Article 43 have not been concluded, the question of command has necessarily remained in abeyance.

The failure to implement Chapter VII of the Charter has made it necessary for the United Nations to supplement its resources for the maintenance of peace by the establishment, on the one hand, of the United Nations Field Service on a permanent basis and, on the other hand, of special peacekeeping forces such as the UN Emergency Force (UNEF) and ONUC on an *ad hoc* basis.

. . . The Special Committee on a United Nations Guard, set up by the General Assembly in 1949 to examine the Secretary-General's proposal for a United Nations Guard, reported that his revised proposal for a Field Service "was not an international military force" but "would in fact amount to a systematization of the regular functions of the Secretariat." The Field Service has since played a supremely important role in the provision of technical services for United Nations missions. The Special Committee concluded that Article 97 of the Charter provided the Secretary-General with full authority for the establishment of such a unit.

The relation of United Nations peacekeeping forces to the institution of the Secretariat cannot be stated in any such clear-cut manner as in the case of the Field Service. Yet there is good reason to consider to what degree these forces constitute an outgrowth of the Secretariat.

. . . The regulations for the forces which defined their international character have been derived, *mutatis mutandis*, from the Staff Regulations which govern the Secretariat—the obligation imposed on members to discharge their functions and to regulate their conduct with the interest of the United Nations only in view; to receive instructions only from the UN commander and the chain of command designated by him; and to exercise the utmost discretion in all matters relating to their duties and functions. Directives to the United Nations forces have been derived from the "Principles and Purposes" of the United Nations and from the texts of the relevant resolutions of the principal organs. In such respects the position of the United Nations forces may be considered as at least analogous to that of the Secretariat. Soldiers from the armed forces of Member States, serving under the UN flag, though still subject to national discipline, have thus gained experience in applying "the arts of war to the infinitely subtle and difficult problem of maintaining the peace."

THE POLITICAL SPHERE . . . . It is particularly in the realm of political activity that the distinction between the Secretary-General and the Secretariat, alluded to at the outset, has become most marked. It is a matter of common knowledge that in national governments the office of the prime minister, under the direction of the prime minister himself, not infrequently assumes the predominant role in the formulation and conduct of foreign policy, especially in circumstances of national crisis, with the consequence of relegating the foreign office to a quite secondary role. In an international secretariat, within which it is far more difficult to maintain coherence of views than in a national government, the tendency of the Secretary-General to retain the direction of political matters in his own hands and to discharge his obligations through collaborators well known to him and especially chosen by him is necessarily even more marked. In large measure it is a condition of his personal ability to retain the confidence of governments in his conduct of policy. One consequence has been that the Secretary-General has discharged the political duties entrusted to him to a far less degree through the oridinary machinery of the Secretariat in political matters than in other matters. . . .

Attention may be drawn to another factor which has vitally affected the role of the Secretariat in political matters—the establishment of the permanent delegations of the Member States in New York. The permanent delegations constitute in effect an institution of the United Nations which was not provided for by the Charter but which has grown up as a byproduct of the General Assembly and of the continuity of conference arrangements at Headquarters.

*   *   *   *   *   *   *

The special relationship of the Secretary-General to the delegations is perhaps most clearly evidenced by the establishment of the Advisory Committee on UNEF and the later Advisory Committee on the Congo. They constitute the most defined institutional response to a problem of which the late Secretary-General was acutely conscious—the need to "find constitutional means and techniques to assist him insofar as possible in reducing the elements of purely personal judgment." The Secretary-General strove to ensure that his personal judgment should to the utmost degree be of a constitutional character; and, as many writers have pointed out, to this end he excelled in deriving lines of political action from the Principles and Purposes of the Charter. Even so, he urgently needed a means of testing his own conclusions as the responsible executive against the advice and judgment of those who were in a position to build up and maintain a consensus of support for his activities within the political organs of the United Nations. For this purpose he needed an institutionalized mode of consultation, which he found in the Advisory Committees. They were in a sense anomalous bodies: composed of the representatives of delegations, external to the Secretariat, yet sitting under the chairmanship of the Secretary-General who sought to formulate the conclusions to be derived from the discussion.

The establishment of permanent delegations has exercised considerable influence on the role of the highest officials of the Secretariat. In 1946 it was envisaged that the Assistant Secretaries-General would have, as one of their functions, the maintenance of liaison with governments of the areas from which they originated. This function, though still of some importance, has declined in significance. Changes have in consequence been effected, though these changes have also been motivated by reasons arising from the administration of the Secretariat itself. The designation of Assistant Secretary-General for the heads of Departments was dropped at the outset of Dag Hammarskjöld's term of office and was replaced by that of Undersecretary to emphasize the essentially administrative responsibilities of these officials. The Departments were reduced to three in number—Political and Security Council Affairs, Trusteeship, and Social and Economic Affairs; other major units came to be designated as "Offices." The question of the political significance of the senior posts has, however, remained a recurring theme throughout the discussion of the higher organization of the Secretariat. The Secretary-General pointed out in his 1953 report on the structure of the Secretariat that it was the original intention that the Assistant Secretaries-General should constitute a group of officials

broadly representative of the Member nations, on the highest responsible level, who, in addition to being heads of departments, would serve the Secretary-General in a representative capacity with individual Member countries and groups of countries.

The reorganization of 1954 might be regarded as having brought this position to an end; but from time to time the question of the specifically political responsibilities of the Secretary-General's senior advisers has recurred. It assumed special prominence at the time of the election of the present Secretary-General who, on assuming office, undertook to consult with certain principal advisers "individually, collectively, or otherwise" as the occasion should demand.

One enduring modification introduced by Dag Hammarskjöld has proved to be the creation of the posts of Undersecretary for Special Political Affairs. The broader suggestion made by him in June 1961, in response to the recommendations of the Committee of Experts, for the appointment of five Assistant Secretaries-General to advise the Secretary-General on political problems was not in the end implemented, though the post of Undersecretary-General for General Assembly Affairs was established as an outcome of those suggestions.

The question as to what extent the Secretary-General can develop within the normal structure of the Secretariat the facilities for policy advice in the discharge of his political responsibilities will doubtless continue to be explored. Experienced political advisers within the Secretariat should be in a position to remain broadly familiar with the policies of Member States. They should be in a position to convey to the Secretary-General a knowledge of the political preoccupations, which are not infrequently of a domestic character, emotionally charged attitudes, and the calculated political interests which

sway governments in the conduct of their policies. Because of their habitua-
tion to the work of an international organization, they are more likely to be
in a position to advise the Secretary-General in these respects with clarity
and in a disciplined manner than are the members of permanent delegations.
Their advice should be the more usable by the Secretary-General in being
free from the elements of pressure and urgency which necessarily attend the
presentation of representatives of governments. These means of advice
should be developed to the utmost. But there are inbuilt limitations to the
advice received by the Secretary-General from within his own staff. As
international civil servants, they cannot be in constant communication with
governments, as are permanent representatives. They are unacquainted with
the more confidential considerations which enter into the formulation of
government policy. They may be precluded from assessing the varying degrees of urgency in the different elements of government policy. They will
remain largely unaware of those points on which governmental policy is
adamant and of those areas where some elements of flexibility remain. In
short, their quality as international civil servants is achieved at the cost of
ceasing to act as the tentacles of Member governments, and it is precisely
with these tentacles that the Secretary-General must remain in touch. The
conclusion would seem to follow that one important line of advance within
the United Nations will continue to the institutionalization of the channels
of communication between the Secretary-General and the permanent delegations. What may be contemplated, if the United Nations is to consolidate its
strength as an organization, is that the permanent delegations will be increasingly integrated within the framework of the United Nations.

*   *   *   *   *   *   *

Such developments mainly concern the Headquarters staff. But perhaps
even greater emphasis should be laid on the vital contribution made by the
career officers sent out from Headquarters to undertake political responsibilities "in the field," whether in connection with committees of investigation or
mediation or with representative duties on behalf of the Secretary-General,
as in the Congo (Leopoldville). The success of United Nations activities
in such circumstances depends in rather greater measure on the skill and
wisdom of the Secretariat members assigned to such tasks than it does in
the case of functions exercised at Headquarters. Especially with regard to the
Congo it would be difficult to overestimate the contribution made by career
staff members of all ranks sent out to perform functions of a relatively unprecedented character. Such situations can be seen to have called for a
combination of resourcefulness and self-restraint linked with a deep knowledge of and dedication to the special purposes of the Organization, qualities
which are most likely to be displayed by those who have committed themselves fully to the international service. The view may perhaps be advanced

that the progress of the international secretariat can be measured by the degree to which the higher—and even the highest posts—in a representative capacity under the Secretary-General come to be filled from within the service rather than by the *ad hoc* appointment of eminent persons from outside the Secretariat. The possibility of rising to posts involving the discharge of public international responsibilities of the highest order is likely to be an essential condition of the recruitment and retention within the career service of men and women of outstanding ability.

NIKITA KHRUSHCHEV AND DAG HAMMARSKJÖLD INTERCHANGE*

MR. KHRUSHCHEV, CHAIRMAN OF THE COUNCIL OF MINISTERS OF THE UNION OF SOVIET SOCIALIST REPUBLICS

The executive machinery of the Organization is constructed in a one-sided manner. It often approaches the solution of questions from the standpoint of a particular group of countries. This is particularly true of the activities of the United Nations Secretary-General. The Western countries which are members of the military blocs of the Western Powers usually exploit that office in their own interests by nominating for the post of United Nations Secretary-General a candidate acceptable to them. The result is that in many cases the practical, routine work of the United Nations and of its Secretariat is carried out in a one-sided manner. The staffing of the Organization is also one-sided.

The bias in the implementation of practical measures on the part of the United Nations Secretariat was particularly glaring in the case of the events which have taken place in the Congo. In implementing the Security Council's decisions, the Secretary-General in effect adopted the position of the colonialists and of the countries that support the colonialists. That is a very dangerous thing.

We are now firmly convinced that the time has come to take steps to create conditions for an improved functioning both of the United Nations as a whole and of the Organization's executive, working organ. I repeat, the matter relates primarily to the Secretary-General and his staff. We must particularly bear in mind the necessity for certain changes and improvements, with a view to the immediate future.

* General Assembly Plenary Meetings, 15th Session: 869th (September 23, 1960); 871st (September 26, 1960); 882nd (October 3, 1960); 883rd (October 3, 1960).

*   *   *   *   *   *   *

An identical point of view has emerged in our proposals and in those of the countries making up the NATO military alliance regarding the necessity of following up an agreement on disarmament with the establishment of armed forces of all countries, under international control, to be used by the United Nations in accordance with the decision of the Security Council.

The Soviet Government considers that if a correct approach is taken to the utilization of these international armed forces, they may indeed be useful. But the experience of the Congo puts us on our guard. That experience indicates that the United Nations forces are being used exactly in the way against which we warned, a way we emphatically oppose. Mr. Hammarskjöld, the Secretary-General, has taken a position of purely formal condemnation of the colonialists. In actual practice, however, he is following the colonialists' line, opposing the lawful Government of the Congo and the Congolese people and supporting the renegades who, under the guise of fighting for the independence of the Republic of the Congo, are actually continuing the policy of the colonialists and are evidently receiving some reward from them for their treachery.

*   *   *   *   *   *   *

The Soviet Government has come to a definite conclusion on this matter and wishes to expound its point of view before the United Nations General Assembly. Conditions have clearly matured to the point where the post of Secretary-General, who alone directs the staff and alone interprets and executes the decisions of the Security Council and the sessions of the General Assembly, should be abolished. It would be expedient to abandon the system under which all practical work in the intervals between General Assembly sessions and Security Council meetings is determined by the Secretary-General alone.

*   *   *   *   *   *   *

In brief, we consider it advisable to set up, in the place of a Secretary-General who is at present the interpreter and executor of the decisions of the General Assembly and the Security Council, a collective executive organ of the United Nations consisting of three persons each of whom would represent a certain group of States. That would provide a definite guarantee that the work of the United Nations executive organ would not be carried on to the detriment of any one of these groups of States. The United Nations executive organ would then be a genuinely democratic organ; it would really guard the interests of all States [who are] Members of the United Nations irrespective of the social and political system of any particular Member States. This is particularly necessary at the present time, and it will be even more so in the future.

THE SECRETARY-GENERAL

[T]his is a question not of a man but of an institution. Use whatever words you like, independence, impartiality, objectivity—they all describe essential aspects of what, without exception, must be the attitude of the Secretary-General. Such an attitude, which has found its clear and decisive expression in Article 100 of the Charter, may at any stage become an obstacle for those who work for certain political aims which would be better served or more easily achieved if the Secretary-General compromised with this attitude. But if he did, how gravely he would then betray the trust of all those for whom the strict maintenance of such an attitude is their best protection in the world-wide fight for power and influence. Thus, if the office of the Secretary-General becomes a stumbling block for anyone, be it an individual, a group or a government, because the incumbent stands by the basic principle which must guide his whole activity, and if, for that reason, he comes under criticism, such criticism strikes at the very office and the concepts on which it is based. I would rather see that office break on strict adherence to the principle of independence, impartiality and objectivity than drift on the basis of compromise. That is the choice daily facing the Secretary-General. It is also the choice now openly facing the General Assembly, both in substance and in form. I believe that all those whose interests are safeguarded by the United Nations will realize that the choice is not one of the convenience of the moment but one which is decisive for the future, their future.

One last word. Sometimes one gets the impression that the Congo operation is looked at as being in the hands of the Secretary-General, as somehow distinct from the United Nations. No: this is your operation, gentlemen. And this is true whether you represent the African and Asian Member countries, which carry the main burden for the Force and for its Command, or speak and act for other parts of the world. There is nothing in the Charter which puts responsibility of this kind on the shoulders of the Secretary-General or makes him the independent master of such an operation. It was the Security Council which, without any dissenting vote, gave this mandate to the Secretary-General, on 14 July. It was the Security Council which, on 22 July, commended his report on the principles that should be applied. It was the Security Council, on 9 August which again, without dissenting vote, confirmed the authority given to the Secretary-General. Again, just a week ago, the General Assembly, without any dissenting vote, requested the Secretary-General to continue to take vigorous action. . . . Indeed, as I said, this is your operation, gentlemen. It is for you to indicate what you want to have done. As the agent of the Organization I am grateful for any positive advice, but if no such positive advice is forthcoming—as happened in the Security Council on 21 August (887th meeting), when my line of implementation had been challenged from outside—then I have no choice but to follow my own conviction, guided by the principles to which I have just referred.

MR. KHRUSHCHEV

In reply to the statements of certain speakers, I should like once again to make clear the attitude of the Soviet delegation toward one of the important questions placed before the United Nations General Assembly, at its present session, for consideration. I refer to the role and position of the executive organ of the United Nations which we propose should replace the post of Secretary-General.

I do this in order to refute those who have been misinterpreting our position, and also to clarify it for the benefit of those who have not yet fully comprehended the significance of our proposal, but would like to study it and understand it aright.

* * * * * * *

The responsibility for interpreting and executing all the decisions of the General Assembly and the Security Council at present falls upon one man. But there is an old saying that there are not, and never were, any saints on earth. Let those who believe in saints hold to their opinion; we do not credit such tales.

So this one man—at the present time, Mr. Hammarskjöld—has to interpret and execute the decisions of the General Assembly and the Security Council, bearing in mind the interests of the monopoly-capitalist countries as well as those of the socialist countries and of the neutral countries. But this is not possible. Everyone has heard how vigorously the imperialist countries defend Mr. Hammarskjöld's position. Is it not clear then, in whose interest he interprets and executes those decisions whose "saint" he is?

Mr. Hammarskjöld has always been prejudiced in his attitude towards the socialist countries; he has always upheld the interests of the United States of America and the other monopoly-capitalist countries. The events in the Congo (Leopoldville), where he played a simply deplorable role, were merely the last drop which filled the cup of our patience to overflowing.

* * * * * * *

In order to prevent any misinterpretation, I should like to repeat: we do not, and cannot, place confidence in Mr. Hammarskjöld. If he himself cannot muster the courage to resign, in, let us say, a chivalrous way, we shall draw the inevitable conclusions from the situation. There is no room for a man who has violated the elementary principles of justice in such an important post as that of Secretary-General.

Some say that we should, perhaps, replace Mr. Hammarskjöld by another, more worthy man. They reason as follows: let us admit that Mr. Hammar-skjöld made a great mistake; could we not correct it by substituting for him someone else? Of course we could do that. But should we thereby be guaranteeing the United Nations against a repetition of such mistakes in the future? I do not think so. We cannot expect any Secretary-General to be the impartial representative of three different groups of States.

. . . The post of Secretary-General is occupied by a representative of the Western Powers; not once in all these fifteen years has a representative of the socialist countries been allowed to act as President of the General Assembly. But this is a situation which requires no great explanation!

*   *   *   *   *   *   *

In the present circumstances, then, how can we find one man for the post of Secretary-General of the United Nations who can take into consideration the interests of all three groups of States? In our view, this is impossible. Of course, if we are thinking in terms of devotion to the ideas of peace and love of mankind, we could find for the post of Secretary-General a man from the socialist countries, and such a man would truly reflect the most progressive ideas of mankind today, ideas for the preservation of peace. But we can say in advance that the Western Powers would have no faith in such a man, and that would be understandable.

But if we ourselves are prepared to admit that the appointment, to the post of Secretary-General, of a representative of the socialist countries would not create proper conditions for the functioning of the United Nations, how can the Western Powers ask us to believe in the impartiality of their candidate—in the present case, Mr. Hammarskjöld? The neutral countries, too, wish to play their part in the United Nations; they want their interests to be protected; and these legitimate demands of theirs must be taken into account.

*   *   *   *   *   *   *

THE SECRETARY-GENERAL

The head of the Soviet delegation to the General Assembly this morning, in exercising his right of reply, said . . . among other things, that the present Secretary-General has always been biased against the socialist countries, that he has used the United Nations to support the colonial forces fighting the Congolese Government and Parliament in order to impose "a new yoke on the Congo"; and, finally, that if I myself cannot muster the courage to resign, in, let us say, a chivalrous way, we (the Soviet Union) shall draw the inevitable conclusions from the situation." In support of his challenge the representative of the Soviet Union said that there is no room for a man who has "violated the elementary principles of justice in such an important post as that of Secretary-General."

❋   ❋   ❋   ❋   ❋   ❋   ❋

The Assembly has witnessed over the last weeks how historical truth is established. Once an allegation has been repeated a few times it is no longer an allegation, it is an established fact even if no evidence has been brought out to support it. However, facts are facts and the true facts are there for whomsoever cares for truth. Those who invoke history will certainly be heard by history. And they will have to accept its verdict as it will be pronounced on the basis of the facts by men free of mind and firm in their conviction that only on a scrutiny of truth can a future of peace be built.

I have no reason to defend myself or my colleagues against the accusations and judgments to which you have listened. Let me say only this: that you, all of you, are the judges. No single party can claim that authority. I am sure that you will be guided by truth and justice. In particular, let those who know what the United Nations has done and is doing in the Congo, and those who are not pursuing aims proper only to themselves, pass judgment on our actions there. Let the countries which have liberated themselves in the last fifteen years speak for themselves.

I regret that the intervention to which I found it necessary to reply has again tended to personalize an issue which, as I have said, in my view is not a question of a man but of an institution. The man does not count; the institution does. A weak or non-existent executive would mean that the United Nations would no longer be able to serve as an effective instrument for active protection of the interests of those many Members who need such protection. The man holding the responsibility as Chief Executive should leave if he weakens the executive. He should stay if this is necessary for its maintenance. This and only this seems to me to be the substantive criterion that has to be applied.

I said the other day that I would not wish to continue to serve as Secretary-General one day longer than such continued service was considered to be in the best interests of the Organization. The statement this morning seems to indicate that the Soviet Union finds it impossible to work with the present Secretary-General. This may seem to provide a strong reason why I should resign. However, the Soviet Union has also made it clear that if the present Secretary-General were to resign now, it would not wish to elect a new incumbent but insist on an arrangement which—and this is my firm conviction based on broad experience—would make it impossible to maintain an effective executive. By resigning I would, therefore, at the present difficult and dangerous juncture throw the Organization to the winds. I have no right to do so because I have a responsibility to all those Member States for which the Organization is of decisive importance—a responsibility which over-rides all other considerations.

It is not the Soviet Union or indeed any other big Powers which need the United Nations for their protection. It is all the others. In this sense, the

Organization is first of all their Organization and I deeply believe in the wisdom with which they will be able to use it and guide it. I shall remain in my post during the term of office as a servant of the Organization in the interest of all those other nations as long as they wish me to do so.

In this context the representative of the Soviet Union spoke of courage. It is very easy to resign. It is not so easy to stay on. It is very easy to bow to the wish of a big Power. It is another matter to resist. As is well known to all Members of this Assembly I have done so before on many occasions and in many directions. If it is the wish of those nations who see in the Organization their best protection in the present world, I shall now do so again.

CHAPTER **8**

LEADERSHIP

The Introduction to the Secretary-General's Annual Report has been provided as a means of helping the student discern the responsibilities of that office by approaching it through the functions performed. No careful study of it yet exists despite the many articles and a few books that have been published on the topic, especially since most of these fit into the biographical category, and many are highly impressionistic. Therefore, it has seemed the better part of wisdom to permit the student to examine the office by studying a message which deals with the problems confronting the Organization and which reveals the Secretary-General's sense of responsibility in terms of those problems. His Introduction nicely illustrates the various political nuances of issues which the Secretary-General must keep in mind in order not to antagonize any state and at the same time to present a reasoned assessment of the facts as they appear to him. It further reveals the need, and how he meets it, of reminding the members of their unfulfilled commitments and his skill in pointing out the difficulties created by their omissions. And, finally, it discloses the obligation of the administrator-statesman to express confidence in his staff, in particular those assigned delicate and difficult tasks, and to show a seasoned optimism that important objectives will be attained.

To do all this and to oversee a multitude of very complex and often emotionally and ideologically highly charged programs takes an exceptional talent and unusual perseverance. To do it all without incurring the ill-will of any major power presumably exhausts the store of good luck that any mortal is entitled to, and hence two chief UN officers have fallen into the bramble. But at least one of these fell from grace because he had a firm notion of what the office of Secretary-General entailed and because his convictions were so strong he would not sacrifice them before the winds of expediency. Dag Hammarskjöld's Oxford speech is a classic description of the office of Secretary-General and reveals how one occupant viewed it. It is an answer to the challenge thrown down by the then Premier Khrushchev. It is also an answer to the charge of bias in the fulfillment of his duties. And finally it is an expression of what one school of thought believes international civil service means.

In his address the late Secretary-General traces the historical development of that office from the League to the UN, and indicates why he believes that that transition permits one to draw a conclusion that the Drummond interpretation of the office was not appropriate to the present-day operation of the Organization. It is also clear in this statement that Hammarskjöld placed great reliance on the belief that a man in a responsible position must and can exercise restraint over his own behavior and concluded that these decisions can be both sound and right. His guidelines would be drawn from general principles of international law, past decisions of the UN, and, especially, from the Charter itself. And all of these he must interpret as best he can. Such a belief clearly enhances the status of the occupant of the office of Secretary-General and is bound, it would seem, to provoke hostility from some quarter.

One of the most serious questions which needs to be considered regarding the office of the Secretary-General is whether it is being wisely used. And it should be examined not only from the perspectives of the incumbents, but also with a view to the demands made of it by the members. The phrase "let Dag do it" reveals not only the desire by the members to have certain things done, but also their willingness to "pass the buck" to the Secretary-General when the going got rough rather than to work on the problem until the solution was finally forthcoming.

The President of the General Assembly also has an opportunity to exert leadership. The Office has received almost no attention from scholars, and the editor's own research on the role of leaders at the UN revealed the extent to which there is disagreement and even misunderstanding about the potentiali-

ties of this office among the delegates. It is extremely useful, therefore, to have an interpretation of that office by a former President of the General Assembly and a man who now sits on the International Court of Justice. He not only defines the tradition which has established the prerequisites of the office, but also looks at the presidency within the framework of the functions and demands of the Assembly, the Secretariat, and his own delegation. Although the article reveals some of the limitations upon the President it does not attempt to raise the question of whether it is desirable to increase the nature and authority of the Presidency, or what, if any, changes ought to be considered. The reader will want to consider this question himself as a possible means of enhancing the prestige and importance of the Organization in its efforts to help build a peaceful international society.

Diplomacy has probably been an important factor in international relations since men first organized themselves into sovereign political units. And essays, books, and treatises have been written to describe the basis of good diplomacy for almost that long. Not until the twentieth century was there any serious change in the rules or practice of diplomacy. With the belief that foreign policy should reflect democratic values—for example, Woodrow Wilson's doctrine of self-determination of peoples—and the assumption that international organization would be one manifestation of this reflection, classic or traditional diplomacy began to give way to open and conference diplomacy. Thomas Hovet in "United Nations Diplomacy" compares the older with the newer forms and in particular tries to clarify the process followed at the UN, where a mixture of both is displayed. In addition to focusing on the general characteristics of diplomacy, Hovet adds an additional dimension by discussing the diplomatic function as revealed by the performance of the individual delegate. Because the author has had long and continued observation of this phenomenon his judgments are particularly worthy of note.

The last sources of leadership to be considered are the national representatives. The constitutional bases for the composition and functions of national missions and delegations, as described by Richard Pedersen, Counselor of the United States Mission, are important to comprehend, for it is their actions which formally establish the policies of the Organization. In his article "National Representation in the United Nations," Pedersen discusses the question of influence by the delegates on their countries' foreign policies and although his emphasis in the article is on the United States delegation, he indicates that for some of the other delegations there exists an even greater opportunity to be influential. But of particular importance is his analysis of how this influence can make itself felt, both in terms of a state's foreign policy as well as in terms of public opinion. The article ends with a discussion of the importance of the personal impact delegates can make in their day-to-day contacts inside as well as outside the Headquarters Building.

Because of the role that he plays does the delegate tend to have a divided personality? Because of his assignment and his ego-involvement as an officer of his government as well as an organizational participant, does he act in a way that reflects his dual function, and, if so, in what way? For him the United Nations is a primary institution in a way that it cannot be for the average outside observer. The delegate is therefore a link between two agencies, and a fascinating one to study.

We dare not draw conclusions without careful investigation, but in order to know how to proceed with such an inquiry it would be desirable to know more about the internal activity of the delegations. For enlightenment on this subject we have articles by members of two delegations, John Hadwen of the Canadian delegation and Johan Kaufmann of the Netherlands delegation. They discuss the importance of mutual accommodation as well as the strategies involved in preparing these objectives and in seeking accord on the introduction of resolutions. Further, the authors take us to look at the tactics employed in voting, the uses of debating, and the objectives in socializing. The intricacies of behavior can be assumed to match the complexity of the Organization itself. Whether all of these efforts in formulating and carrying out strategy pay off are questions always in the minds of delegates and scholars, but there is no easy, objective test one can apply to answer them. Nor can one put a monetary price tag on the results of these efforts. If, however, one is to judge from the opinions of delegates, there can be no doubt that the rewards are considered to be high.

FURTHER READINGS

Alger, Chadwick F., "United Nations Participation as a Learning Experience," *Public Opinion Quarterly*, Vol. XXVII, 1963, pp. 411–426.

Alexandrowicz, Charles H., "The Secretary-General of the United Nations," *International and Comparative Law Quarterly*, Vol. XI, 1962, pp. 1109–1130.

Bailey, Sydney D., "The Troika and the Future of the UN," *International Conciliation*, No. 538, May, 1962.

Kerley, Ernest L., "Voting on Important Issues in the UN," *American Journal of International Law*, Vol. LIII, April 1959, pp. 324–340.

Rusk, Dean, "Parliamentary Diplomacy—Debate v. Negotiation," *World Affairs Interpreter*, Vol. 26, No. 2, Summer 1955, pp. 121–122.

THE SECRETARY-GENERAL'S
ADMINISTRATIVE ROLE*

. . . The desire of the members to resolve the [financial and voting] crisis in which the Organization had found itself was reflected in the decision of the General Assembly, before it recessed in February, to establish the Special Committee on Peace-keeping Operations with the task of conducting a comprehensive review of the question of peace-keeping operations in all their aspects, including ways of overcoming the financial difficulties of the Organization. During the subsequent months, strenuous efforts were made in the Special Committee to find at least an interim solution to the constitutional and financial problems covered by its terms of reference.

* * * * * * *

Tribute is due to the patient and constructive work of the Committee and to the co-operation of all delegations, which made this result possible. Much, of course, remains to be done. The actual financial situation of the Organization, to which I refer elsewhere in this introduction, remains precarious at the time of writing. In addition, I wish to address an appeal to all member states to co-operate with the Special Committee in completing its work and finalizing its recommendations on all points covered by its terms of reference. In my view it is essential for the successful conduct of peace-keeping operations in the future that we should have well-established ground rules and guidelines to govern them. . . .

CONSTRUCTIVE WORK

The difficulties of the Organization proper were overshadowed through this period by adverse developments in international relationships, to which I shall make further reference in the pages that follow. Yet, although a review of the last ten months may leave behind it a general feeling of lack of achievement, much constructive work, in the whole range of activities from peace-keeping operations to technical assistance, has been carried out during the period. For example, the United Nations Force in Cyprus has made a significant contribution to the maintenance of peace in the area and to bringing quiet to Cyprus, even though the political problems remain unsolved.

* Excerpts from the Introduction to the Annual Report (covering the period from June 16, 1964, to June 15, 1965) of the Secretary-General on the Work of the Organization (including developments up to September, 1965), UN Monthly Chronicle, Vol. 2, No. 9, October, 1965, pp. 92–117.

❖   ❖   ❖   ❖   ❖   ❖   ❖

I must add that it is the feeling of the executive heads of all the organizations that a pre-condition for the continued success of economic, social and cultural co-operation on an international plane is the preservation to the greatest possible extent of the essentially technical character of such action. I have previously had occasion to observe that it would be a matter for regret on the part of the entire international community if important meetings dealing with these questions, and depending for their success on the vital element of international co-operation, were to fail to yield solid results because of the introduction of highly contentious political issues into the discussions and deliberations. The admitted difficulty of drawing a clear line between what is political and what is not must not be allowed to distract the member states from their specific duty to respect the Charter, the conventions and the constitutional procedures of the agency concerned and from their general obligation to safeguard, in the common interests, the future of international order itself.

❖   ❖   ❖   ❖   ❖   ❖

DISARMAMENT

The deterioration in the international situation generally, as well as the inability of the nineteenth session of the General Assembly to function normally, have made an adverse impact in the field of disarmament. No substantial progress has been achieved since my last report, and the high hopes engendered by the agreements reached in 1963 have been greatly diminished.

❖   ❖   ❖   ❖   ❖   ❖   ❖

A recognition of the sheer necessity of finding some way to cope with the dangers of the arms race and of nuclear proliferation has at last led to a renewal of disarmament discussions and negotiations. The Disarmament Commission, composed of all the members of the United Nations, undertook a comprehensive review of the whole range of disarmament problems and reached some significant decisions. One resolution welcomed the proposal for a world disarmament conference and recommended that the General Assembly should consider the proposal at its next session. A second resolution specifically recommended that the Conference of the Eighteen-Nation Committee on Disarmament should give priority to agreement on preventing the proliferation of nuclear weapons and extending the partial test-ban treaty to underground tests. The Commission indicated that in seeking new approaches to disarmament, all states, large and small, nuclear and non-nuclear, could make a contribution. It also recognized that partial measures and limited steps offered the best prospects for early agreement.

* * * * * * *

PEACEFUL USES OF OUTER SPACE

There has been some further progress in the area of international co-operation in the peaceful uses of outer space. Several international programmes, such as the International Year of the Quiet Sun, the International Indian Ocean Expedition, the World Magnetic Survey and others, have developed successfully during the period.

On the basis of unanimous opinion within the Committee on the Peaceful Uses of Outer Space, it was decided that the Scientific and Technical Sub-Committee need not meet in 1965, but that the Committee, with the assistance of the Secretariat, should continue to fulfil the objectives in the field of science and technology which were outlined in its previous report. In response to the Committee's request, the Secretariat has been compiling information for a report on the possibility of establishing a civil world-wide navigational satellite system. The Secretariat has also continued to compile information on facilities for education and training in basic subjects related to the peaceful uses of outer space, as well as to compile reviews of national and co-operative international space activities on the basis of information voluntarily submitted by member states. These compilations are to be published every other year.

The Secretariat has continued to receive from member states literature on the goals, tools, applications and results of space technology. The member states have been given information on various space conferences and symposia open to their scientists. Consultations have proceeded with the specialized agencies and the Committee on Space Research on the question of the possible need for material which would enhance popular understanding of space activities and also on the question of the distribution of technical literature.

* * * * * * *

TRADE AND DEVELOPMENT BOARD

Some consolation may be drawn from the fact that neither the sharpening of international political problems nor the financial crisis within the United Nations seriously affected the momentum of existing international action in the economic and social fields. Yet here, too, a disturbing shadow has been cast, in the form of a worsening of the relative economic position of the developing countries. . . .

This situation gives added significance to the results of the first United Nations Conference on Trade and Development and to the action which has followed it. The work started by the Geneva Conference was carried an important step further when the General Assembly gave its unanimous approval to the establishment of the new institutional machinery of the Conference. The machinery is endowed with an instrument that is new to the United Nations system—a mechanism consisting of special procedures with which to formularize conciliation between various interests before voting takes place. The primary objective of these procedures is to maintain the fundamental principle of equality of vote while at the same time taking into account the fact that specific recommendations for action may substantially affect the economic and financial interests of particular countries. . . .

The main objective during the past year has been the administrative and organizational consolidation of the new institutional machinery. A solid foundation for future work has now been established. The first session of the Trade and Development Board established four specific committees, all of which will bear important responsibilities and will become centres for the formulation of policies in their respective fields, with an appropriate institutional basis. They will thus be capable of contributing efficiently and expeditiously to the implementation of the work programme of the Conference.

* * * * * * *

INTENSIFIED ACTIVITY IN ECONOMIC AND SOCIAL FIELDS

Aside from trade, this year of political and financial difficulties has been one of intensified activity in all sectors of the economic and social field. The fact that twenty years after the signing of the Charter we find ourselves at the midpoint of the United Nations Development Decade, as well as the realization that, so far, progress towards the objectives of the Decade has been disappointingly slow, has led member states to look to the United Nations for greater assistance in their efforts to achieve more rapid progress and to sharpen and multiply the tools available to the Organization for this purpose. This is clear from the recent records of the Economic and Social Council and its subsidiary bodies.

* * * * * * *

The Economic and Social Council has reaffirmed the objectives of the United Nations Development Decade and stressed the importance of increasing the quantity and quality of international aid and co-operation. It is to be hoped that the interest shown in better planning at the national level will lead to those objectives being translated into a coherent set of interrelated goals and targets providing a framework for the development efforts of the world community over the next five or ten years, as well as a better means of measuring the progress achieved. This should enhance our ability, in the years to come, to improve upon the performance in the first half of the United Nations Development Decade, during which shock-ing disparities in conditions and levels of living have continued to persist.

DEVELOPMENT ASSISTANCE PROGRAMMES

In the current Expanded Programme, field operations are continuing at the record level of $101 million for the biennium 1965–1966. A new element in the Programme is the use of its funds to assign to several countries a small number of experts with formally defined operational and executive respon-sibilities, pursuant to a decision made by the Economic and Social Council in 1964. The greater part of the Programme, however, consists as before of the supply of advisory experts, consultants, instructors and fellowships.

✻   ✻   ✻   ✻   ✻   ✻   ✻

Increased resources are needed by both the Expanded Programme and the Special Fund if they are to meet a larger proportion of the rising requests for their services. That is why I have urged that the General Assembly raise to $200 million the annual target for the two programmes together. . . . I have expressed the view on other occasions that this consolidation has now become a matter of some urgency; it should help to rationalize the efforts and considerably to strengthen the capacity of the United Nations family of organizations to help meet the urgent needs of the developing countries for accelerated economic and social advance in the second half of the United Nations Development Decade.

✻   ✻   ✻   ✻   ✻   ✻   ✻

PEACE-KEEPING OPERATIONS

The repeated extension of the [peace-keeping] Force by the Security Council, involving the agreement of the parties directly concerned in the Cyprus problem, attests abundantly to the helpful if not indispensable role of the Force.

✻   ✻   ✻   ✻   ✻   ✻   ✻

The need . . . becomes all the more urgent to achieve a political solution to the Cyprus problem. To help the parties find this solution, the United Nations Mediator on Cyprus, Mr. Galo Plaza, devoted his best efforts from September 1964 to March 1965. On March 26, he submitted to me a report on the mediation activities, which I found encouraging because it envisaged a reasonable basis for a settlement of the problem. In view of the importance which I attach to the Mediator's report, I decided to transmit it immediately to the parties concerned as well as to the members of the Security Council.

Unfortunately, two of the parties reacted negatively to the report, to such an extent that the Mediator has been unable actively to continue his endeavours since the publication of the report. . . . At my request, the Mediator remains available to the parties for the continuation of the mediation effort, in accordance with the provisions of [the March 4, 1964 Security Council] resolution.

✿   ✿   ✿   ✿   ✿   ✿   ✿

SITUATION IN THE DOMINICAN REPUBLIC

The situation in the Dominican Republic arising from the civil strife which broke out in Santo Domingo at the end of April 1965 was of unusual complexity. It had considerable international repercussions, reflected in numerous Security Council meetings, particularly with regard to the unilateral military involvement of the United States in the initial stage and, later, to the actions of the Organization of American States, including the establishment and deployment in Santo Domingo of a force designated as the Inter-American Peace Force. . . .

While the mandate of my Representative in the Dominican Republic is a limited one, the effect of his role has been significant. When he arrived in Santo Domingo on May 17, fighting between the two Dominican contending parties had flared up despite a cease-fire agreement reached on May 5 under the auspices of the Organization of American States. My Representative played a major role in bringing about a cessation of hostilities on May 21. Since then the situation has remained generally quiet, although there have been a number of isolated incidents. My Representative, assisted by a small but efficient staff, has kept me informed as to the situation both in Santo Domingo and in the interior of the country, regarding not only the observance of the cease-fire but also serious cases of violations of human rights and the prevailing economic conditions. I have transmitted this information to the Security Council at frequent intervals, thus keeping the Council informed of all important events and developments.

✿   ✿   ✿   ✿   ✿   ✿   ✿

STUDY OF LONG-TERM SOLUTIONS

The newer peace-keeping efforts of the United Nations in Cyprus and in the Dominican Republic have naturally tended to overshadow those of much longer standing: the United Nations Truce Supervision Organization in Palestine, the United Nations Emergency Force and, until the recent renewal of conflict over Kashmir, the United Nations Military Observer Group in India and Pakistan. To the extent that any generalization can be valid, these three operations, like the United Nations Force in Cyprus, have often seemed to possess the limitations of their own success, namely, that they have helped over long periods to contain and isolate explosive situations without really affecting the basic causes of conflict. Two of the three have lasted for sixteen years and one for nearly nine years; all have been indispensable for most of that time to relative peace and order in the areas in which they operate, and their withdrawal would without question have had far-reaching consequences.

* * * * * * *

I have been taking steps, in consultation with the appropriate specialized agencies, to establish a programme for the education and training of South Africans abroad. A limited number of fellowships and grants have been awarded for the academic year 1965–1966, and the full programme is expected to come into operation next year. I hope that this programme will receive the generous support of member states.

FINANCIAL CRISIS OF ORGANIZATION

I feel bound to emphasize that the actual financial crisis, in which the Organization has for too long found itself placed, has by no means been dispelled by the consensus reached by the Special Committee on Peace-keeping Operations and, in effect, accepted by the General Assembly on September 1, 1965. As I write these words, our financial difficulties remain serious. . . .

* * * * * * *

It has been agreed, in the terms of the consensus referred to earlier, that these financial difficulties should be solved through voluntary contributions by member states. At the time of writing, such contributions paid or pledged total somewhat less than one-fifth of the amount required. I have already made an urgent appeal to all who have not yet done so to come forward with contributions. I should like to reiterate this appeal; and I do so with some confidence that, on reflection, governments will see the clear and pressing need to enable the Organization to solve its financial difficulties, in view of the stake they have in its survival and the value they attach to its present and potential usefulness.

* * * * * * *

THE CONFLICT IN VIET NAM

It is because of the profound effect that the Viet-Nam situation is having on problems of global as well as regional importance, and the shadow it casts on almost every area of international co-operation, that I have devoted considerable personal effort in the realm of quiet diplomacy to getting the parties concerned to stop the fighting and to start the discussions which alone, in my view, can lead to a solution. I remain as fully convinced as ever that total victory or total defeat for one side or the other is out of the question and that military action cannot bring peace and restore stability to the area. The only way to those goals is the way of discussions; and it is clear, as I have stated previously, that those discussions can yield fruitful results only if there is a willingness by all sides to make major concessions.

* * * * * * *

I also venture to hope that at its twentieth session the General Assembly will approve the recommendations of the Disarmament Commission to hold a world disarmament conference. In this connection, I cannot help observing that progress in disarmament, whether general or nuclear, can hardly be made if all the major military powers of the world, both in terms of conventional and nuclear weapons, are not enabled to participate in the deliberations. I would regard it as essential, therefore, that the world disarmament conference should be held under conditions which would make it possible for all countries, if they so wished, to participate in it.

UNIVERSALITY OF MEMBERSHIP

. . . I should like to renew the suggestion which I made in the introduction to my last annual report to the effect that, in the meantime, the countries not at present represented in New York should be enabled to maintain contact with the world body and listen to its deliberations, and thus be more directly exposed to the views of the rest of mankind. I feel, indeed, that the experience of the last ten months has reinforced the view I expressed on this matter last November. I have no doubt that the true interests of peace would be better served if non-member states were to be encouraged to maintain observers at United Nations Headquarters so that they may be in a position to sense the currents and cross-currents of world opinion which are so uniquely concentrated in the Organization.

* * * * * * *

In addition to making progress toward universality of membership, we have also striven very hard to achieve the participation of nationals of all member states in the Secretariat of the United Nations. Special efforts have been made to secure an adequate place in the Secretariat for nationals of those countries which, for one reason or another, have continued to be underrepresented during recent years. These special efforts have included the dispatch of special missions for the recruitment of suitable candidates from countries of Africa and Eastern Europe. I hope that, thanks to their efforts, we shall be able to obtain a larger number of qualified candidates for service not only at Headquarters but also with the economic commissions and in the field offices.

THE SECRETARY-GENERAL'S POLITICAL ROLE

Dag Hammarskjöld*

In a recent article Mr. Walter Lippmann tells about an interview in Moscow with Mr. Khrushchev. According to the article, Chairman Khrushchev stated that "while there are neutral countries, there are no neutral men," and the author draws the conclusion that it is now the view of the Soviet Government "that there can be no such thing as an impartial civil servant in this deeply divided world, and that the kind of political celibacy which the British theory of the civil servant calls for, is in international affairs a fiction."

Whether this accurately sums up the views held by the Soviet Government, as reflected in the interview, or not, one thing is certain: The attitude which the article reflects is one which we find nowadays in many political quarters, communist and non-communist alike, and it raises a problem which cannot be treated lightly. In fact, it challenges basic tenets in the philosophy of both the League of Nations and the United Nations, as one of the essential points on which these experiments in international cooperation represent an advance beyond traditional "conference diplomacy" is the introduction on the international arena of joint permanent organs, employing a neutral civil service, and the use of such organs for executive purposes on behalf of all the members of the organizations. Were it to be considered that the experience shows that this radical innovation in international life rests on a false assumption, because "no man can be neutral," then we would be thrown back to 1919, and a searching re-appraisal would become necessary.

The international civil service had its genesis in the League of Nations but it did not spring full-blown in the Treaty of Versailles and the Covenant. The Covenant was in fact silent on the international character of the Secretariat. It contained no provisions comparable to those of Article 100 of the Charter and simply stated:

The permanent Secretariat shall be established at the Seat of the League. The Secretariat shall comprise a Secretary-General and such secretaries and staff as may be required.

* Dag Hammarskjöld, "The International Civil Servant in Law and in Fact," United Nations Press Release SG–1035, May 29, 1961.

Dag Hammarskjöld was Secretary-General of the United Nations from 1953 until his death in 1961.

In the earliest proposals for the Secretariat of the League, it was apparently taken for granted that there could not be a truly international secretariat but that there would have to be nine national secretaries, each assisted by a national staff and performing, in turn, the duties of Secretary to the Council, under the supervision of the Secretary-General. This plan, which had been drawn up by Sir Maurice Hankey, who had been offered the post of Secretary-General of the League by the Allied Powers, was in keeping with the precedents set by the various international bureaux established before the war which were staffed by officials seconded by Member countries on a temporary basis.

It was Sir Eric Drummond, first Secretary-General of the League, who is generally regarded as mainly responsible for building upon the vague language of the Covenant a truly international secretariat. The classic statement of the principles he first espoused is found in the report submitted to the Council of the League by its British member, Arthur Balfour:

By the terms of the Treaty, the duty of selecting the staff falls upon the Secretary-General, just as the duty of approving it falls upon the Council. In making his appointments, he had primarily to secure the best available men and women for the particular duties which had to be performed; but in doing so, it was necessary to have regard to the great importance of selecting the officials from various nations. Evidently, no one nation or group of nations ought to have a monopoly in providing the material for this international institution. I emphasize the word "international," because the members of the Secretariat once appointed are no longer the servants of the country of which they are citizens, but become for the time being the servants only of the League of Nations. Their duties are not national but international.

Thus, in this statement, we have two of the essential principles of an international civil service: (1) its international composition and (2) its international responsibilities. The latter principle found its legal expression in the Regulations subsequently adopted which enjoined all officials "to discharge their functions and to regulate their conduct with the interests of the League alone in view" and prohibited them from seeking or receiving "instructions from any Government or other authority external to the Secretariat of the League of Nations."

Along with the conception of an independent, internationally responsible staff, another major idea was to be found: the international Secretariat was to be solely an administrative organ, eschewing political judgments and actions. It is not at all surprising that this third principle should have originated with a British Secretary-General. In the United Kingdom, as in certain other European countries, a system of patronage, political or personal, had been gradually replaced in the course of the nineteenth century by the principle of a permanent civil service based on efficiency and competence and owing allegiance only to the State which it served. It followed that a civil service so organized and dedicated would be non-political. The civil servant could not be expected to serve two masters and consequently he could not, in his official duties, display any political allegiance to a political party or ideology. Those decisions which involved a political choice were left to the Government and to Parliament; the civil servant was the non-partisan administrator of those decisions. His discretion was a limited one, bound by the framework of national law and authority and by rules and instructions issued by his political superiors. True, there were choices for him, since neither legal rules nor policy decisions can wholly eliminate the discretion of the administrative official, but the choices to be made were confined to relatively narrow limits by legislative enactment, Government decision and the great body of precedent and tradition. The necessary condition was that there should exist at all times a higher political authority with the capacity to take the political decisions. With that condition it seemed almost axiomatic that the civil service had to be "politically celibate" (though not perhaps politically virgin). It could not take sides in any political controversy and, accordingly, it could not be given tasks which required it to do so. This was reflected in the basic statements laying down the policy to govern the international Secretariat.

* * * * * * *

The fact that the Secretary-General is an official with political power as well as administrative functions had direct implications for the method of his selection. Proposals at San Francisco to eliminate the participation of the Security Council in the election process were rejected precisely because it was recognized that the role of the Secretary-General in the field of political and security matters properly involved the Security Council and made it logical that the unanimity rule of the permanent Members should apply. At the same time, it was recognized that the necessity of such unanimous agreement would have to be limited only to the selection of the Secretary-General and that it was equally essential that he be protected against the pressure of a Member during his term in office. Thus a proposal for a three-year term was rejected on the ground that so short a term might impair his independent role.

The concern with the independence of the Secretary-General from national pressures was also reflected at San Francisco in the decision of the Conference to reject proposals for Deputies Secretary-General appointed in the same manner as the Secretary-General. The opponents of this provision maintain that a proposal of this kind would result in a group of high officials who would not be responsible to the Secretary-General but to the bodies which elected them. This would inevitably mean a dilution of the responsibility of the Secretary-General for the conduct of the Organization and would be conducive neither to the efficient functioning of the Secretariat nor to its independent position. In this action and other related decisions, the drafters of the Charter laid emphasis on the personal responsibility of the Secretary-General; it is he who is solely responsible for performing the functions entrusted to him for the appointment of all members of the Secretariat and for assuring the organ that the Secretariat will carry out their tasks under his exclusive authority. The idea of a "Cabinet system" in which responsibility for administration and political functions would be distributed among several individuals was squarely rejected.

It is also relevant in this connection that the provision for "due regard to geographical representation" in the recruitment of the Secretariat was never treated as calling for political or ideological representation. It was rather an affirmation of the idea accepted since the beginning of the League Secretariat that the staff of the Organization was to have an international composition and that its basis would be as "geographically" broad as possible. Moreover, as clearly indicated in the language of Article 101, the "paramount consideration in the employment of the staff" should be the necessity of securing the highest standards of efficiency, competence and integrity. This terminology is evidence of the intention of the drafters to accord priority to considerations of efficiency and competence over those of geographical representation, important though the latter be.

To sum up, the Charter laid down these essential legal principles for an international civil service:

It was to be an international body, recruited primarily for efficiency, competence and integrity, but on as wide a geographical basis as possible;

It was to be headed by a Secretary-General who carried constitutionally the responsibility to the other principal organs for the Secretariat's work;

And finally, Article 98 entitled the General Assembly and the Security Council to entrust the Secretary-General with tasks going beyond the *verba formalia* of Article 97—with its emphasis on the administrative function— thus opening the door to a measure of political responsibility which is distinct from the authority explicity accorded to the Secretary-General under Article 99 but in keeping with the spirit of that article.

This last-mentioned development concerning the Secretary-General, with its obvious consequences for the Secretariat as such, takes us beyond the concept of a non-political civil service into an area where the official, in the exercise of his functions, may be forced to take stands of a politically controversial nature. It does this, however, on an international basis and, thus, without departing from the basic concept of "neutrality"; in fact, Article 98, as well as Article 99, would be unthinkable without the complement of Article 100 strictly observed both in letter and spirit.

Reverting for a moment to our initial question, I have tried to emphasize the distinction just made. If a demand for neutrality is made, by present critics of the international civil service, with the intent that the international civil servant should not be permitted to take a stand on political issues, in response to requests of the General Assembly or the Security Council, then the demand is in conflict with the Charter itself. If, however, "neutrality" means that the international civil servant, also in executive tasks with political implications, must remain wholly uninfluenced by national or group interests or ideologies, then the obligation to observe such neutrality is just as basic to the Charter concept of the international civil service as it was to the concept once found in the Covenant of the League. Due to the circumstances then prevailing the distinction to which I have just drawn attention probably never was clearly made in the League, but it has become fundamental for the interpretation of the actions of the Secretariat as established by the Charter.

The criticism to which I referred at the beginning of this lecture can be directed against the very Charter concept of the Secretariat and imply a demand for a reduction of the functions of the Secretariat to the role assigned to it in the League and explicitly mentioned in Article 97 of the Charter; this would be a retrograde development in sharp conflict with the way in which the functions of the international Secretariat over the years have been extended by the main organs of the United Nations, in response to arising needs. Another possibility would be that the actual developments under Articles 98 and 99 are accepted but that a lack of confidence in the possibility of personal "neutrality" is considered to render necessary administrative arrangements putting the persons in question under special constitutional controls, either built into the structure of the Secretariat or established through organs outside the Secretariat.

. . . recent examples demonstrate the extent to which the Member States have entrusted the Secretary-General with tasks that have required him to take action which unavoidably may have to run counter to the views of at least some of these Member States. The agreement reached in the general terms of a resolution, as we have seen, no longer need obtain when more specific issues are presented. Even when the original resolution is fairly precise, subsequent developments, previously unforeseen, may render highly controversial the action called for under the resolution. Thus, for example, the unanimous resolution authorizing assistance to the Central Government of the Congo offered little guidance to the Secretary-General when that Government split into competing centers of authority, each claiming to be the Central Government and each supported by different groups of Member States within and outside the Security Council.

A simple solution for the dilemmas thus posed for the Secretary-General might seem to be for him to refer the problem to the political organ for it to resolve the question. Under a national parliamentary regime, this would often be the obvious course of action for the executive to take. Indeed, this is what the Secretary-General must also do whenever it is feasible. But the organs themselves to resolve the controversial issue faced by the Secretary-General. When brought down to specific cases involving a clash of interests serious problems arise precisely because it is so often not possible for the and positions, the required majority in the Security Council or General Assembly may not be available for any particular solution. This will frequently be evident in advance of a meeting and the Member States will conclude that it would be futile for the organs to attempt to reach a decision and consequently that the problem has to be left to the Secretary-General to solve on one basis or another, on his own risk but with as faithful an interpretation of the instructions, rights and obligations of the Organization as possible in view of international law and the decisions already taken.

It might be said that in this situation the Secretary-General should refuse to implement the resolution, since implementation would offend one or another group of Member States and open him to the charge that he has abandoned the political neutrality and impartiality essential to his office. The only way to avoid such criticism, it is said, is for the Secretary-General to refrain from execution of the original resolution until the organs have decided the issue by the required majority (and, in the case of the Security Council, with the unanimous concurrence of the permanent members) or he, maybe, has found another way to pass responsibility over on to governments.

For the Secretary-General this course of action—or more precisely, non-action—may be tempting; it enables him to avoid criticism by refusing to act until other political organs resolve the dilemma. An easy refuge may thus appear to be available. But would such refuge be compatible with the responsibility placed upon the Secretary-General by the Charter? Is he entitled to refuse to carry out the decision properly reached by the organs, on the ground that the specific implementation would be opposed to positions some Member States might wish to take, as indicated, perhaps, by an earlier minority vote? Of course the political organs may always instruct him to discontinue the implementation of a resolution, but when they do not so instruct him and the resolution remains in effect, is the Secretary-General legally and morally free to take no action, particularly in a matter considered to affect international peace and security? Should he, for example, have abandoned the operation in the Congo because almost any decision he made as to the composition of the Force or its role would have been contrary to the attitudes of some Members as reflected in debates, and maybe even in votes, although not in decisions?

The answers seem clear enough in law; the responsibilities of the Secretary-General under the Charter cannot be laid aside merely because the execution of decisions by him is likely to be politically controversial. The Secretary-General remains under the obligation to carry out the policies as adopted by the organs; the essential requirement is that he does this on the basis of his exclusively international responsibility and not in the interest of any particular State or groups of States.

This presents us with the crucial issue: is it possible for the Secretary-General to resolve controversial questions on a truly international basis without obtaining the formal decision of the organs? In my opinion and on the basis of my experience, the answer is in the affirmative; it is possible for the Secretary-General to carry out his tasks in controversial political situations with full regard to his exclusively international obligation under the Charter and without subservience to a particular national or ideological attitude. This is not to say that the Secretary-General is a kind of delphic oracle who alone speaks for the international community. He has available for his task varied means and resources.

Of primary importance in this respect are the principles and purposes of the Charter which are the fundamental law accepted by and binding on all States. Necessarily general and comprehensive, these principles and purposes still are specific enough to have practical significance in concrete cases.

The principles of the Charter are, moreover, supplemented by the body of legal doctrine and precepts that have been accepted by States generally, and particularly as manifested in the resolutions of United Nations organs. In this body of law there are rules and precedents that appropriately furnish guidance to the Secretary-General when he is faced with the duty of applying a general mandate in circumstances that had not been envisaged by the resolution.

* * * * * * *

Experience has thus indicated that the international civil servant may take steps to reduce the sphere within which he has to take stands on politically controversial issues. In summary, it may be said that he will carefully seek guidance in the decisions of the main organs, in statements relevant for the interpretation of those decisions, in the Charter and in generally recognized principles of law, remembering that by his actions he may set important precedents. Further, he will submit as complete reporting to the main organs as circumstances permit, seeking their guidance whenever such guidance seems to be possible to obtain. Even if all of these steps are taken, it will still remain, as has been amply demonstrated in practice, that the reduced area of discretion will be large enough to expose the international Secretariat to heated political controversy and to accusations of a lack of neutrality.

I have already drawn attention to the ambiguity of the word "neutrality" in such a context. It is obvious from what I have said that the international civil servant cannot be accused of lack of neutrality simply for taking a stand on a controversial issue when this is his duty and cannot be avoided. But there remains a serious intellectual and moral problem as we move within an area inside which personal judgment must come into play. Finally, we have to deal here with a question of integrity or with, if you please, a question of conscience.

The international civil servant must keep himself under the strictest observation. He is not requested to be a neuter in the sense that he has to have no sympathies or antipathies, that there are to be no interests which are close to him in his personal capacity or that he is to have no ideas or ideals that matter for him. However, he is requested to be fully aware of those human reactions and meticulously check himself so that they are not permitted to influence his actions. This is nothing unique. Is not every judge professionally under the same obligation?

If the international civil servant knows himself to be free from such personal influences in his actions and guided solely by the common aims and rules laid down for, and by the Organization he serves and by recognized legal principles, then he has done his duty, and then he can face the criticism which, even so, will be unavoidable. As I said, at the final last, this is a question of integrity, and if integrity in the sense of respect for law and respect for truth were to drive him into positions of conflict with this or that interest, then that conflict is a sign of his neutrality and not of his failure to observe neutrality—then it is in line, not in conflict, with his duties as an international civil servant.

Recently, it has been said, this time in Western circles, that as the international Secretariat is going forward on the road of international thought and action, while Member States depart from it, a gap develops between them and they are growing into being mutually hostile elements; and this is said to increase the tension in the world which it was the purpose of the United Nations to diminish. From this view the conclusion has been drawn that we may have to switch from an international Secretariat, ruled by the principles described in this lecture, to an intergovernmental Secretariat, the members of which obviously would not be supposed to work in the direction of an internationalism considered unpalatable to their governments. Such a passive acceptance of a nationalism rendering it necessary to abandon present efforts in the direction of internationalism symbolized by the international civil service—somewhat surprisingly regarded as a cause of tension—might, if accepted by the Member nations, well prove to be the Munich of international cooperation as conceived after the first World War and further developed under the impression of the tragedy of the second World War. To abandon or to compromise with principles on which such cooperation is built may be no less dangerous than to compromise with principles regarding the rights of a nation. In both cases the price to be paid may be peace.

THE PRESIDENT OF THE GENERAL ASSEMBLY

Muhammad Zafrulla Khan*

Article 21 of the Charter of the United Nations provides that the General Assembly shall adopt its own rules of procedure and shall elect its President for each session. No other mention of the President of the General Assembly is to be found in the Charter and, as in the British fashion, his role is more a reflection of evolution than definition in the rules of procedure. It is perhaps for this reason that the highest office of the General Assembly has not been described at any length in the literature about the United Nations.

ELECTION PROCEDURE

An unwritten convention excludes the five permanent members of the Security Council from the Presidency, and the post has in practice often been held by the representative of a smaller Member State. This procedure has become traditional although, as the membership of the Organization has expanded, the roster of Presidents has reflected an increasingly wider geographical distribution. Indeed, with the rising importance of geographic groups in the Assembly, the Presidency now passes from group to group on the basis, once again, of an unwritten understanding among Member States. In a resolution on the composition of the General Committee, adopted at the eighteenth session of the General Assembly, a reference was made to this practice, thereby giving it some formal recognition. However, the precise manner in which the Presidency would rotate among various regional groups was not specified in the resolution, on the ground that to do so would detract from the prestige attaching to the office and the personal qualities of impartiality, experience, and eminence required of the President. In point of fact, as the Afro-Asian group now constitutes more than half the membership, it seems likely that every other year the President will be chosen from these nations and that in alternate years the office will be held by representatives of countries of Latin America, western Europe, and also eastern Europe.

* Muhammad Zafrulla Khan, "The President of the General Assembly of the United Nations," *International Organization*, Vol. 18, 1964, pp. 231–240. Copyright 1964, World Peace Foundation. By permission of *International Organization*.

Muhammad Zafrulla Khan is a judge on the International Court of Justice. He has served as foreign minister of Pakistan and permanent representative of Pakistan to the United Nations.

The choice of a particular candidate from within a regional grouping depends on many factors including the standing in the world community of the country to which he belongs, but his personal qualities and qualifications are usually the most important considerations.

Normally, a past chairman of the First Committee, provided that he has handled the business well, is considered a prime candidate if he comes from the proper group. The training in procedure and leadership which the chairman receives is an excellent preparation for the President's post. I had not had such experience prior to my election in the seventeenth General Assembly and I was initially somewhat concerned.

There are qualities other than the experience of chairmanship which establish an individual as a possible choice, but they tend to be highly personal. Since group alternation is almost a governing principle, outstanding figures within the geographic groups can often claim candidacy. The general bearing, deportment, and contacts of UN representatives are judged, and over a period of service in the United Nations certain persons are recognized as capable leaders. My own experience in the United Nations began in 1947 and for the following seven years I represented Pakistan in the General Assembly. I left the UN, however, in 1954 and returned only in 1961 when practically the whole representation had been changed.

By the early spring of 1962 people were beginning to discuss the Presidency of the seventeenth General Assembly. When asked if I would stand for election, I expressed the view that the Presidency should rotate among area representatives and that an Afro-Asian, Mr. Mongi Slim, should not be followed immediately by another Afro-Asian. There grew a consensus that perhaps Latin America should provide a candidate and that Ambassador Amadeo (Argentina), who had been an excellent chairman of the First Committee, should stand. Unfortunately, a shift of government in Argentina led to his resignation as UN representative, and the candidacy of an Asian once more seemed probable.

At that point my candidacy was circulated and a contest developed between Ambassador Malalesekera (Ceylon) and myself. The Assembly therefore had the opportunity to choose between personalities since both candidates were Asians. One important point is that the President of the General Assembly stands by name, and not by country, while the Vice Presidents stand by country, not by name.

THE ORGANIZATION OF THE ASSEMBLY

The President has considerable help in handling the business of the chamber. The most important group in this respect is the General Committee which includes, besides the President, the sixteen Vice Presidents and the seven Committee chairmen. It was my experience that the Committee chairmen have a more difficult task than the President because there is more rough and tumble and dispute in committee life than in the plenary meetings where the vigorous cut and thrust of debate are somewhat restrained by the necessity to walk up to the rostrum in order to participate in the discussion.

Chairmen of Committees are expected to maintain their pace if the work is to be finished by the closing date of the Assembly session set by the General Committee. In the past, the last few weeks of the session found delegates working throughout the day and sometimes a good part of the night to finish up, and this was not always conducive to clarity or businesslike results.

During the seventeenth Assembly the chairmen were asked to establish schedules of business, and if a Committee began to fall behind in its work, late sittings would be instituted at that point. This was found to be a useful procedure and will probably become the common practice within the Organization.

THE ROLE OF THE PRESIDENT

In a formal sense, the President of the General Assembly has only one function—the conduct of the Assembly's business—and in performing this task, he must serve the will of the Assembly. Any ruling which he makes can be upset by a simple majority vote; cases have occurred in which a ruling given by the President has made him a figure of controversy. The President cannot, of course, and should not shirk from giving a ruling in order merely to avoid controversy.

Assembly resolutions carry the full weight of world opinion only when they are backed by the broad consensus of the Members of the Organization. The President is in a position to help the Assembly develop this consensus and, in doing so, he not only expedites its business but serves to further the true purposes of the United Nations. In working thus as a servant of the Assembly with an interest in smoothing the path of its debates and facilitating the adoption of resolutions, the President has very little actual power. What he can do depends a great deal on his own tact, his ability to elicit the confidence of others, and his skill in bringing together divergent points of view and personalities.

In certain cases of controversy the President can voice his concern that the matter be settled. This is an invitation to use the President's good offices in the interest of general business. In other cases a tentative expression of views by the President may help to remove a hindrance to cooperation. If the Members feel that the President is not a partisan to the case and that his only concern is to serve them with a view to their broader interests, he is in a position to smooth over minor disagreements which sometimes delay business.

The same general point might be made concerning rulings made from the chair. In the seventeenth session of the General Assembly there were for the first time in my memory no requests for rulings from the chair. This is a reflection of mutual tolerance among delegates and also an indication of accommodation having been reached outside the Assembly hall on points of procedure, discussion of which on the floor of the Assembly can be so time-consuming and sometimes acrimonious. My experience was that the delegates treated me very cordially and were willing to accept my advice on procedural matters, even though they might have disagreed with some of my suggestions.

There was considerable interest in the fourth special session of May 1963 in how I would rule on the application of Article 19 in the case of a Member being in arrears for two years or more in payment of its contributions. When the General Assembly met, the Secretary-General, in a letter to me dated May 19, reported that Haiti was in arrears in the payment of its financial contribution "within the terms of Article 19." In my reply of May 15, I stated that as President I "could have made an announcement drawing the attention of the Assembly to the loss of voting rights in the Assembly [of Haiti and] had a formal count of votes taken place in the presence of a representative of that State at the opening plenary session." I also stated that I was transmitting a copy of the Secretary-General's letter to the chairman of the Fifth Committee so that he might be informed of the situation which would give rise to the loss of voting rights in the Fifth Committee. Subsequently a payment was made, making Article 19 inapplicable.

It should be the President's care to ensure that he does not project his views over those of the membership. Although he remains a member of a national delegation, he is asked to serve as an individual and his service is subject to nearly complete control by the Assembly. In the interests of a general consensus he is pledged to serve the need for common understanding throughout the Assembly.

In the day-to-day conduct of the Assembly's work the President can do much in making it more effective by being punctual. His first duty is to conduct the business in an orderly manner and with dispatch. Most delegates are in the UN building on time but tend to cluster in the Delegates' Lounge and elsewhere, and their early morning resolve is dissipated in discussions in the lobby. My own resolve was to set an example in the matter of punctuality, the need for which had been emphasized by my distinguished predecessor, H. E. Mongi Slim of Tunisia, in his report as President of the sixteenth session. A reporter asked me shortly before my election, "What is it that you intend to do if you become President?" I said, "For one thing, I intend to follow the British system with regard to meetings rather than what has become normal in the United Nations." When asked to explain, I added, "I mean that the second stroke of Big Ben has scarcely ceased its reverberations by the time the speaker calls the House of Commons to order." My success in following this example is a tribute above all to the seriousness with which delegates approached their task in the Assembly and the cooperation they were willing to extend to the President in this matter. Punctuality added to the time available for business at the seventeenth session. It also helped to lend to the proceedings a brisker and more businesslike air.

Another way of expediting business, and one which I found very useful, is to take the Assembly into confidence on matters relating to the arrangement of the day's business. The general practice during the earlier sessions of the General Assembly was that the daily agenda was more or less settled by the Secretariat and announced in the Journal. At the seventeenth session of the General Assembly the practice was introduced of giving as much advance notice of the agenda as possible so that, if objections were raised to the inclusion of any item, the matter could be effectively handled; advance notification of the agenda also allowed a longer time for preparation on the part of the delegates.

The accessibility of the President is equally important. A beautiful suite on the 38th floor of the Secretariat building at the other end of the corridor from the Secretary-General's office is provided for the President, but its use would make the President more remote and less able to establish the constant contact with the delegates which the President must have if he is to know their mind. There is a small room behind the podium on the same level as the floor, and it gives the easy access to the President which delegates welcome. In the middle of the morning or afternoon, the President can turn the chair over to a Vice President and carry on any exchanges that delegates might desire. I often did this and found it very helpful.

THE PRESIDENT OF THE ASSEMBLY AND THE SECRETARIAT

The President in his tasks has not only the support of the Committees, and especially the General Committee, but of the Secretariat staff as well. Previous Presidents learned to lean on the advice of Dr. Andrew Cordier, who from long experience had become a real expert on every technical aspect of the General Assembly. Furthermore, he had a canny sense of developing problems and would forewarn Presidents of their consequences. Dr. Cordier left the UN before the seventeenth Assembly, and consequently I did not have the pleasure of the benefit of working with him. His place was taken by Mr. Narasimhan, an able administrator, whom I knew when he was a civil servant in India. The entire Secretariat staff, from top to bottom, does everything possible for the President: every facility is provided, every assistance is furnished. During my term Mr. Malania, the principal assistant to the President in Assembly affairs, worked a six-day week from nine a.m. until midnight, greatly helping in a wide range of affairs.

The Secretary-General, of course, does not in any way participate in the proceedings of the Assembly—although he considers it important to be present as often as possible. During the seventeenth Assembly, in the interests of his very busy schedule, the practice was to release the Secretary-General from prolonged attendance. He can, after all, tune into any of the debates on his office intercommunication system, and his presence in the Hall is mostly symbolic.

THE PRESIDENT OF THE ASSEMBLY AND HIS NATIONAL DELEGATION

The relationship between the national delegation and the President of the Assembly is generally a highly personal one. In my case I continued to lead the delegation and attended my office in Pakistan House for two or two and one-half hours before proceeding to the Assembly. The delegation, however, had a natural and very proper feeling of restraint in discussing matters that fell within the purview of the Presidency. At various times members of my delegation told me of developments arising in the Assembly, but so did members of other delegations. It is perfectly legitimate for delegations to seek out the views of the President and keep him informed of the various national interests. He cannot be effective if he is partial either to one country or to a group of countries, and he violates the trust of the Assembly if he does other than serve the general interest.

THE PROBLEMS OF THE PRESIDENT

There are several areas in the working of the Assembly which are taxing on its President. Of these, the most important is the process of nominating members of *ad hoc* committees set up by the Assembly for one purpose or another. I might mention the Special Committee on Implementation of the Declaration on the Granting of Independence to Colonial Peoples, as one of the most important of these and certainly the one whose membership appears to be the most coveted. During the seventeenth General Assembly many nations were interested in being appointed to this Committee, membership of which was to be expanded from seventeen to 24. In an organization as varied as the General Assembly, the process of balancing regional and bloc interests and the selection of able men to carry on the business are complicated undertakings. The President's task is facilitated through consultation with the chairman of the main committee concerned and with the chairmen of the various regional groups. The President has the responsibility, however, and he takes [sic] the decisions.

The President often encounters difficulty in fixing the dates for the elections to the Security Council, the Economic and Social Council, the Trusteeship Council, etc. Although the countries elected do not take up their new positions until the new year, Members are naturally eager to have the elections early in the session so that they can concentrate their efforts on business other than electioneering and canvassing. On the other hand, those who feel their chances might improve as the session progresses, will seek a delay in the election. During the seventeenth Assembly these views were reconciled behind the scenes, and the entire balloting for all three Councils was completed in 55 minutes. No seat in the Security Council was split, the three candidates being elected for a full term, and for the other Councils a second ballot was not even necessary. But this was unusual and the timing of the elections remains somewhat of a problem for the President.

❋ ❋ ❋ ❋ ❋ ❋ ❋

It is sometimes supposed that Cold War issues or perennial problems like the seating of the People's Republic of China weigh heavily on the President of the Assembly. They are certainly important, but their resolution lies largely outside the determination of the General Assembly. Even where a decision has to be reached in the Assembly as, for instance, on the seating of the People's Republic of China, the Assembly would in all probability only provide the forum for registering an accord arrived at behind the scenes. The Assembly remains primarily a chamber of the small states whose sole power is one of investigation, recommendation, and exhortation. To carry force, its recommendations must be nearly unanimous. This pattern ill accords with the so-called great-power struggles, and the Assembly President is not therefore intimately concerned with their specifics.

❋ ❋ ❋ ❋ ❋ ❋ ❋

THE PRESIDENT AS EX-PRESIDENT

It is a great honor to have been elected as the President of the General Assembly. The position elicits high trust and warm appreciation. The President is frequently invited to visit various Member States; during my term I went to Africa, the Soviet Union, and Scandinavia. During these trips the President's views on various questions are sought by host governments, but almost everyone knows that the President of the General Assembly has little actual power. The President does, however, symbolize in his person the existence of the world community but he does so in a rather different way than does the Secretary-General. The Secretary-General, as chief executive officer of the Organization, exercises a great deal of power of action and initiative but, for that very reason, often finds himself at the hub of a controversy. The President being detached from the actual exercise of power is perhaps better able to fulfill the representative function.

The end of the term of the President is marked by the Chief of Protocol escorting the President-elect to the podium and the ex-President to his seat. If the President has remained a member of the delegation, there is no break or dramatic shift in status. Of course, a certain prestige attaches to former

Presidents and they have an unrivaled opportunity to make new friendships throughout the Organization. The experience becomes part of one's personality.

* * * * * * *

THE PRESIDENT OF THE GENERAL ASSEMBLY AS A PRESIDING OFFICER

A useful concluding statement might be to contrast the position of the President of the General Assembly with the role of the presiding officers of two other great chambers, the House of Commons and the United States House of Representatives. In the Commons the Speaker is a symbol of dignity and neutrality and holds the honor of the House. His latitude is limited by the canons of the past as well as his concern for the general good of the House. The Speaker of the House of Representatives, however, is not entirely dissociated from his party's interests. On a continuum between the two poles, I would consider the "Speaker" of the General Assembly closer to the House of Commons model.

It should be remembered, however, that the conventions and practices of the United Nations are still being shaped. The control of the agenda is by no means settled, and the President has a considerable say in the matter as he does with certain appointments. He is therefore more powerful and less symbolic than the Speaker in the House of Commons, but his authority is in no way commensurate with that of the Speaker of the House of Representatives, nor indeed is it desirable that it should be.

UNITED NATIONS DIPLOMACY

Thomas Hovet, Jr.[*]

Diplomacy in the United Nations has been characterized in many ways. Traditionally it has been called multilateral diplomacy, public diplomacy, conference diplomacy, or parliamentary diplomacy. On occasion it has been

[*] Thomas Hovet, Jr., "United Nations Diplomacy," *Journal of International Affairs*, Vol. 17, No. 1, 1963, pp. 29–41. Copyright 1963 by the board of editors of the *Journal of International Affairs*. By permission of the *Journal of International Affairs*.

Thomas Hovet is Professor of Political Science at the University of Oregon and author of *Bloc Politics in the United Nations* and *Africa in the United Nations*.

termed bloc diplomacy, diplomacy by groups, and even diplomacy by majorities. When the diplomatic processes in the United Nations have been more comparable to the classical methods of diplomacy, the methods there have been referred to as private or quiet diplomacy. When the features of public and quiet diplomatic methods were combined, the diplomatic process in the United Nations has been characterized as preventive diplomacy or the diplomacy of reconciliation.

The key to any understanding of United Nations diplomacy is a recognition of the role the organization plays as an instrument of diplomacy. As a diplomatic instrument the United Nations is, in some senses, a permanent international conference. Representatives . . . are in almost continual attendance at the headquarters in Manhattan of the Organization, and their very presence provides a ready atmosphere for constant diplomatic negotiations. As a center for harmonizing the actions of states the United Nations provides a formal framework for diplomatic operations. In the thirteenth Annual Report of the Secretary-General, the late Dag Hammarskjöld wrote that "as an instrument for reconciliation and for worldwide cooperation the United Nations represents a necessary addition to the traditional methods of diplomacy as exercised on a bilateral or regional basis." Within the framework of its formal organization and agreed procedures the United Nations provides a diplomatic instrument that can be used at a moment's notice. While the preliminary negotiations for an *ad hoc* multilateral international conference may require months or even years to agree upon the procedures for the conference, the United Nations provides a framework already established to which states can bring their problems without delay. Because most states have established permanent missions at United Nations headquarters, a state that does not want to avail itself of the formal procedures of the United Nations can have easy contact with the diplomats of other states and carry on negotiations in the traditions of the more classical forms of diplomacy. To the newer and smaller states which may not be able to afford diplomatic representation in a wide variety of countries, this center of diplomatic activity at the United Nations may provide their primary area of contact with other states. Thus the United Nations is not only a diplomatic instrument itself, but it is also a center of diplomatic activity constantly available to states in their negotiations with other states.

[As one surveys] the evolution of the diplomatic method in the United Nations it appears that the process has evolved from one which stressed public or conference diplomacy to one which stresses private or quiet diplomacy. The use of "evolution" may be an oversimplification because diplomacy in the United Nations has not really been of one type or the other. The development of the diplomatic method in the United Nations has seen an increasing recognition of the possibilities of supplementing conference diplomacy with quiet diplomacy. Secretary-General Hammarskjöld constantly argued for a greater awareness of the variety of diplomatic techniques that could be realized within the setting of the United Nations. In his tenth Annual Report, the Secretary-General explained that

Within the framework of the Charter there are many possibilities, as yet largely unexplored, for variation of practices. The United Nations is at a very early stage in that development. . . . It is my hope that solid progress can be made in the coming years in developing new forms of contact, new methods of deliberation and new techniques of reconciliation.

The problem of diplomacy in the United Nations has been a question of evolving an adjustment between the processes of conference and quiet diplomacy. Diplomatic methods are in a constant state of evolution. A process applied in one situation may or may not be used in other situations. The problem for the diplomat in the United Nations is to recognize the strengths and weaknesses of particular diplomatic techniques and to adjust to new diplomatic methods that may or may not require the particular type of skills generally associated with diplomacy in its classical sense. Diplomatic techniques in the United Nations can be called successful if they provide an atmosphere which allows negotiations to continue, and unsuccessful if the method or combination of methods inhibits the process of negotiation.

PUBLIC DIPLOMACY

The emphasis on conference or public diplomacy in the United Nations is not only related to the adjustment of the diplomatic method to the growth of representative government, the impact of scientific developments, especially in the area of communications, and the experiences of the League of Nations; it also reflects concepts inherent in the minds of the drafters of the United Nations Charter. Basic to this type of diplomacy is a belief in the importance of public discussion and in the importance of world public opinion. By focusing the spotlight of public opinion on a situation it is felt that this public exposure can freeze a situation and prevent a chain of events that might lead to conflict. At the same time there is a feeling that public discussion of an issue provides an opportunity for states not directly involved in the situation to make their influence felt in resolving the issue. The focus of publicity on the actions of a particular state threatening the peace may place that state not in an offensive but rather in a defensive position in which it must justify and explain its action. In many instances the use of this type of public diplomacy in the United Nations has had a bearing on the adjustment of a problem. The public discussions in the Security Council and the General Assembly in 1960 undoubtedly had an influence in minimizing the actions of the United States and the Soviet Union in the Congo. The Security Council considerations of the situation in Iran in 1946 had an influence on the withdrawal of Soviet troops from that country. The actions in 1956 of Great Britain and France in the Suez were curtailed by exposure to the spotlight of public discussion in the United Nations. The public consideration in the General Assembly in 1953 and 1954 of the Burmese complaint over the presence of Chinese Nationalist troops within its borders was a determining factor in the withdrawal of those forces. The public discussion in the Security Council in 1962 was a factor in the easing of tensions between the United States and the Soviet Union over the presence of Soviet missiles in Cuba. The states administering Trust Territories and Non-Self-Governing Territories have continually been forced to justify their policies publicly in the Trusteeship Council and the General Assembly, and there can be little doubt that their policies in these territories have been modified as a result. The continual discussions in conference of economic and social questions have served to isolate fundamental problems and to make all states aware of the variety of attitudes on these crucial issues.

While it is apparent that conference or public diplomacy in the United Nations has been a factor in preventing many particular situations from getting out of hand, it is just as clear that adjustment of a situation often cannot be resolved by public discussion. Public diplomacy may expose the issue, but its resolution is generally the result of quiet diplomacy. Too often, policy positions taken in the public eye of conference diplomacy prevent states from adjusting their attitudes on an issue. Public diplomacy places stress not on negotiation but on "success" or "failure." Having once taken a strong public position a state cannot easily adjust its position without having it interpreted as a concession; a public shift of policy is often interpreted as a diplomatic defeat. With its emphasis on formal voting and other procedures, public diplomacy in the United Nations often results in competition between states. The spotlight of publicity places undue pressure on a state, not on its ability to adjust to a situation, but on its ability to preserve its position. Delegates are tempted to play to the public arena instead of concentrating on negotiations that will resolve the problem; they may ridicule the representatives of other states because it is pleasing to their fellow countrymen, but it does not help the process of negotiation. They are constantly motivated to prove to the public in their own countries that they are defending national policy. In a sense they are placed in a position of acting as if they were representatives in a parliament, their constituents being the people in their own country. But they are not parliamentary representatives, because the United Nations is not a parliament.

The fact that resolutions are adopted in the United Nations by majority vote means that the diplomats are often tempted to negotiate for votes, not to negotiate for the adjustment of problems. The public spotlight emphasizes votes, not the resolution of international problems. The public spotlight de-emphasizes the fact that resolutions are not law, but merely recommendations. The public spotlight inclines the representatives of states to take stands on issues which may not be of vital interest to their own countries. In the resumed Thirteenth Session, for example, the Indian ambassador took a public stand on a question of the nature of elections in the Trust Territory of the Camerouns under French Administration. By his public stand he found himself in a position of being at odds with the representatives from all the African states. His motive may have been to seek what he thought was a proper action, but the result of taking this position in public meant that he openly antagonized a number of states on an issue that was of vital concern to them but of little concern to his country. Had his suggestions been made in private the ensuring animosity would have been negligible, because he could have reversed his position without any loss of prestige for India. Having taken the position in public, he could not reverse himself. Thus on an issue of no major importance to India he found himself creating not only conflict between India and the African states, but an atmosphere of animosity that would transfer to other issues at other times.

The ability to win votes and to pass resolutions, however, may not resolve issues. Between 1946 and 1962, fifty-six resolutions have been passed by the General Assembly, for example, on the question of South West Africa, more resolutions than have been passed on any other issue before the United Nations. Yet none of these resolutions has had any major impact upon the policies of South Africa toward South West Africa. Even if South Africa might want to adjust its policies toward South West Africa, it would be difficult to do so because it would appear to the South African public as if the Government were not defending its national interest. Any adjustment of its policy in the face of these resolutions would be interpreted as a defeat for the South African Government. Thus, in the face of these resolutions, the South African Government has become more adamant. Rather than reducing the conflict between South Africa and the other states, [public diplomacy has increased the tension].

QUIET DIPLOMACY

While public diplomacy has an important role, especially in certain types of situations, it is apparent that the success of diplomacy in the United Nations depends upon the use of public diplomatic methods in conjunction with more quiet forms of diplomacy. If there has been the development of a distinctive diplomatic method in the United Nations, it has been the development of a wide variety of techniques that provide an opportunity to intermingle and balance public and private procedures of diplomacy.

This blending of public and quiet diplomacy gives a uniqueness to the diplomatic method of the United Nations that has been influenced by at least three factors: the growth of the role of the Secretary-General, the establishment of permanent missions, and the development of caucusing groups and blocs. Each of these three elements is, in a sense, an outgrowth of the nature of public diplomacy in the United Nations, but the significance of these elements has really been felt in the environment they have created for the development of quiet diplomacy.

As the United Nations developed and the agenda of each organ expanded, the Headquarters became the location for a continual round of meetings. The General Assembly hardly finishes its sessions before the Trusteeship Council and the Economic and Social Council, together with their commissions and committees, are in session. Moreover, the Security Council is organized so as to be able to meet at any moment. Even if a state is not a member of one or another of these organs, its ability to keep abreast of the issues demands that it have some sort of permanent representation at United Nations Headquarters. By 1962 almost all of the members of the United Nations had permanent missions located at the seat of the Organization. It is natural that the existence of these permanent missions provides a basis for continual contact between nations. States are thus provided with another area of diplomatic contact in addition to the normal exchange of ambassadors. In some respects, contact between states at the United Nations has the advantage of being more informal than contact between ambassadors at a national capital. The existence of these permanent missions, therefore, provides a convenient framework for quiet diplomacy.

*   *   *   *   *   *   *

In addition to the permanent missions, . . . the very nature of the composition of the General Assembly also provide[s] a bridge between public and quiet diplomacy that is unique. The fact that in session after session more and more foreign ministers, prime ministers, and chiefs of state attend General Assembly meetings means that there is an opportunity for contact between states that is unparalleled. While foreign ministers participate in the public debates, especially in the initial stages of the Assembly, they also use the opportunity to meet informally with their counterparts from other countries. Even their participation in the General Assembly is significant. The foreign ministers usually participate in the so-called general debate at the beginning of each General Assembly session. The general debate provides these foreign policy leaders with an opportunity to assess the current nature of international problems from a new perspective. It also provides all members with an awareness of the general philosophical approach of each state to significant problems. The Charter provides for the Security Council to serve on occasion as a meeting ground of heads of state. While this development has been encouraged by the Secretary-General, it has not come into operation.

As the United Nations evolves, these various developments create a bridge between techniques of public and quiet diplomacy. It is not easy, however, to develop the proper balance between the areas in which quiet diplomacy is most useful and those areas in which public diplomacy is most useful.

One problem lies in the nature of the diplomatic skills that are required. It is an unusual delegate who is skilled in the techniques of both public and quiet diplomacy. A diplomat used to more traditional forms of diplomacy may be shocked at his first experience in the General Assembly where the procedure is more similar to that of a parliament or a state legislature. Skills may be needed in coping with the rules of procedure. In this situation the member of a delegation who may have come up through the ranks of a political party will find himself more at home. He is familiar with parliamentary give and take. Such an individual, however, may become so concerned with manipulating the procedure that he will lose sight of the fact that the United Nations is not a parliament, that success is measured not in passing resolutions but in providing means through which negotiations can continue. There is a temptation to insult other delegations, a temptation to consider resolutions passed as victories, and a temptation to demonstrate proficiency in the use of procedural rules. Such temptations, if not curbed, can create more disharmony than advance the cause of peace.

The delegate accustomed to more traditional forms of diplomacy may be inclined to overlook elements in United Nations diplomatic method that are necessary for the achievement of his tasks. For example, he may confine his contacts with delegations to the ambassadorial level. But within the United Nations, the interplay is as much between delegations as between leaders of delegations. With each delegation individuals are assigned particular tasks, and to some extent they develop areas of speciality upon which their delegation leaders place considerable reliance. Depending upon the category of issue that is being considered, there are, sometimes, informal leaders within a delegation whose influence is substantial in determining the policy attitudes of a delegation. Successful negotiation may depend, therefore, upon discerning the identity of these leaders. The delegation that confines its contacts to the ambassadorial level may, as a result, find its negotiations fruitless. Successful negotiations between delegations should involve contact at every level so as to provide useful intelligence on the latitude of instructions given to delegations, and therefore the areas within which an accommodation of viewpoints can be negotiated.

Most of the major powers have a problem in this process of the interplay of public and private diplomacy precisely because they are major powers, with wide interests in virtually all issues before the United Nations. Their latitude for give and take may be limited because of the universality of interests. Conversely, smaller states must be constantly aware that, though they may build voting majorities, no resolutions in the United Nations can be realistic unless concessions are made to the power relationships among the larger states.

The United Nations has only begun to explore the variety of techniques of diplomacy that are at its disposal to facilitate negotiations between states. While all of its attempts have not been successful, it has nonetheless achieved success in a variety of cases. One of its most notable developments has been in the area of what Mr. Hammarskjöld called preventive diplomacy—that which combines . . . elements of [both] public and quiet diplomacy. In the Introduction to the fifteenth Annual Report, the late Secretary-General explained that

preventive diplomacy . . . is of special significance in cases where the original conflict may be said to be either the result of, or to imply risks for, the creation of a power vacuum between the main blocs. Preventive action in such cases must, in the first place, aim at filling the vacuum so that it will not provoke action from any of the major parties, the initiative for which might be taken for preventive purposes but might in turn lead to a counter action from the other sides. The ways in which a vacuum can be filled by the United Nations so as to forestall such initiatives differ from case to case, but they have this in common: temporarily, and pending the filling of the vacuum by normal means, the United Nations enters the picture on the basis of its non-commitment to any power blocs, so as to provide to the extent possible a guarantee in relation to all parties against initiatives from others.

This type of preventive diplomacy has been exercised by the United Nations in different circumstances and with different techniques. In Greece, the Special Committee on the Balkans focused attention upon foreign sources of subversion. The United Nations Observation Group in Lebanon checked reports of foreign intervention. In Laos, a Security Council subcommittee verified whether a crisis existed. In the Congo, the United Nations prevented intervention by outside powers by providing assistance in the maintenance of law and order when the established government there collapsed. These cases illustrate the fact that although the diplomatic method evolving in the United Nations has the ability to achieve concrete results, its full potential has not been reached. Progress is nevertheless being made, for the ability to produce conditions in which negotiations can proceed is a mark of good diplomacy.

At the same time that a distinctive diplomatic method is gradually evolving, the expansion in United Nations membership is creating problems for diplomacy. The procedures and the structure of the General Assembly are being strained by the size of its membership. There are more issues on the agenda, more delegates desiring to speak, more draft resolutions submitted, more amendments introduced, more votes requested, more meetings to attend, and more delegates to be consulted. As the sessions become longer, it is more difficult for foreign ministers and heads of states to participate, except for brief periods. Delegations, especially small ones, are severely taxed in providing representatives to attend the increased number of meetings. States cannot afford to allow key individuals in their foreign offices to spend one third or one half of [their] time at the United Nations. They must either rotate personnel attending sessions there or else send less qualified officials, [. . . an unsatisfactory alternative because,] to be effective, public diplomacy needs persons experienced in its procedures and qualified to deal with the issues being considered.

Up to the present the evolution of diplomatic method in the United Nations has been concerned with an expansion of opportunities for quiet diplomacy. In the future the adjustment of procedures of public diplomacy to the enlarged membership will probably be the more serious problem faced by the world body. The ability of the United Nations to balance techniques of public and quiet diplomacy will depend on the successful development of workable procedures integrating the two diplomatic methods.

NATIONAL REPRESENTATION IN THE UNITED NATIONS

Richard F. Pedersen*

The traditional concept of embassies and missions abroad as custodians of the national interest is a familiar one which applies also in the context of United Nations diplomacy. The responsibility for advancing national policy through the United Nations is borne by permanent missions and special delegations—representatives who, like their counterparts in bilateral diplomacy, act in close coordination with a state department or foreign office and under the instructions of their home governments. Because of the multilateral and "parliamentary" nature of United Nations diplomacy, however, the task of UN missions and delegations is in many ways more exacting than that of their traditional counterparts.

Most Member States maintain staffs known as permanent missions on a year-round basis in New York. In addition to carrying out day-to-day functions on behalf of the state, the permanent missions serve as a body of experts on the uses of parliamentary diplomacy by advising the home government on: 1) the advantages and disadvantages of utilizing the UN as a diplomatic instrument; 2) the criteria determining whether and how specific issues might be raised; and 3) the manner in which the state can maximize its gains from UN participation.

* Richard F. Pedersen, "National Representation in the United Nations," *International Organization,* Vol. 15, 1961, pp. 256–266. Copyright 1961, World Peace Foundation. By permission of *International Organization.*

Richard F. Pedersen is chief of the political section of the United States Mission to the United Nations.

The chief representative of a state in the United Nations is its permanent representative, usually a person with the rank of ambassador. He is customarily assisted by one or two deputies and a staff of political, economic, and social advisors. Some permanent missions also have on their permanent staffs representatives accredited to special UN bodies such as the Economic and Social Council and the Trusteeship Council. Other countries send special representatives to such Council meetings, or accredit the permanent representative himself. The permanent missions range in size from the one-man Icelandic mission to the 43 members of the Soviet mission, all with diplomatic rank, listed in the UN Bluebook.

Except on unusual occasions, the Security Council is staffed by members of the permanent missions, and the Permanent Representative to the United Nations represents his state in the Council. By provision of the Charter every member of the Security Council must keep a permanent representative in New York since the Security Council is organized to meet on 24-hour notice or less at the call of any UN Member. Foreign ministers and heads of government are authorized, without special credentials, to represent their [countries] in the Security Council, and they have occasionally done so on key issues.

✻   ✻   ✻   ✻   ✻   ✻   ✻

During sessions of the General Assembly, states are represented by specially appointed delegations. Each state may have five representatives and five alternates (who are in fact not substitute representatives but have responsibilities and authority equivalent to those of the representatives) plus supporting staff. By virtue of Rule 27 of the Rules of Procedure, credentials for General Assembly sessions must be issued either by the head of the state or government or by the minister for foreign affairs, and they must be presented separately for each session. The permanent representative may or may not be the chief of this delegation. Frequently, in fact, he is not, as the foreign minister or political representative of a country may be appointed for this purpose.

The composition of such delegations varies considerably according to the state concerned. Some states appoint not only their permanent representatives but also other members of the diplomatic service; others appoint prominent representatives of the government at ministerial level, members of parliament, and well-known persons from private life. The United States delegation has customarily included the Permanent Representative to the United Nations as chairman of the delegation (except when the Secretary of State is in attendance), the Deputy Representative (or Representatives), two members of Congress (in alternate years from the House and Senate), and six delegates typifying various segments of American life, including, *inter alia,* economic, regional, religious, and racial groups; there is usually at least one woman delegate (traditionally the United States representative on the Human Rights Commission).

Supporting staffs are customarily composed both of the personnel of permanent missions and of specialists and officials from respective foreign offices, regular diplomatic posts, or other government agencies. This staff also, including personnel of permanent missions, is issued credentials for each session. A similar process applies to other meetings of UN bodies such as the Trusteeship Council and the Economic and Social Council and its subsidiary organs. Meetings of the Security Council which take place during a session of the General Assembly, however, are customarily handled by the permanent representative and the permanent mission; a dual situation then arises in which the mission is functioning separately in the Council but only as part of the larger delegation in the Assembly.

THE PRACTICE OF UN DIPLOMACY

The functions entrusted to UN missions and delegations[1] include: 1) negotiation and parliamentary action; 2) the formulation of policy and tactics; 3) influencing opinion; 4) information gathering; 5) representation; and 6) public relations.

* * * * * * *

THE FORMULATION OF POLICY AND TACTICS. Perhaps equivalent in importance to the negotiating and parliamentary responsibilities of a delegation are its responsibilities to participate in the formulation both of the policy and of the tactics to be followed by the government. Because this is an "internal" role carried on within the privacy and secrecy of particular governments, it is difficult to make any clear estimates of the amount of control delegations have over policies and tactics. In general, however, it is apparent that they have a large measure of discretion in tactics and considerable, although less, influence on policies.

On policy questions the role of delegations is mainly advisory. There are exceptional cases when issues must be decided immediately and UN delegations are compelled to vote without instructions from their governments; such votes may establish governmental policy. It is essential, however, in UN diplomacy as well as in traditional international negotiations, that the responsibility for establishing policy reside in the government and that the role of the delegation be advisory. Nevertheless, the functioning of a UN delegation in its advisory capacity may exert significant influence on na-

1 The functions subsequently described are substantially the same for "delegations" and "missions." The term "delegation" is therefore employed except where an activity primarily limited to a mission is discussed, as in practice "delegation" is the term commonly used to embrace both groups.

tional policy, as evidenced in numerous reports of Senators and Congress-
men following their participation as delegates to the General Assembly. Reporting on their participation at the 13th General Assembly, for example,
Senators Hickenlooper and Mansfield noted that "suggestions for changes
in position are made by the delegation and frequently approved by Washington." [2] Although UN delegations have varied degrees of influence on
their countries' foreign policies, it may be assumed that every delegation
exerts some pressure on policy. Some delegations, in fact, receive only general instructions, allowing them the latitude to make many decisions themselves.

The influence of a delegation on policy may be exerted from the time
when an issue first arises, but it is strongest after actual consideration of an
issue has begun. If a delegation reports, on the basis of its negotiations,
that an objective cannot be achieved without modification, or if it recommends that the objective would be too high to justify pursuing it, its judgments necessarily carry considerable weight, as it is the only authority in
a position at that moment to evaluate most of the available facts. Missions
and foreign offices naturally seek to anticipate such a situation in preparing
their policy positions, and missions to the United Nations customarily advise their foreign offices on the feasibility or desirability of varying courses
in advance. However, anticipation is not fact, and when anticipated difficulties actually arise, the influence of the negotiators is much greater than
beforehand. As a source of information on the attitudes of other governments and delegations, as an agency of the government professionally concerned with effective use of the United Nations in foreign policy, and as a
tactically minded unit which may be able to predict whether certain lines of
policy may or may not be successfully carried out, a delegation is likely to
exert substantial influence on policy formulation throughout the consideration of any individual issue.

Some of the circumstances of policy formulation in the United States
government have been described by James N. Hyde. Noting that a position
paper (the government's policy instruction to the delegation) may deal
clearly and precisely with the issue at hand, he continues:

However, it may contain vague language to hide rather than reveal differences of
opinion. It may have intentional gaps because the critical decision cannot be made
so far in advance or because the Secretary prefers to keep it to himself. Also, it
may purposely not indicate positions to which US representatives can retreat because some delegate may retreat too readily. In this case the paper may state that
if a certain situation develops, the State Department should be consulted for further guidance.

---

[2] *Observations on the United Nations,* Report of Senators Bourke B. Hickenlooper
and Mike Mansfield (Members of the U.S. Delegation to the 13th General Assembly of
the United Nations), Government Printing Office, 1959, p. 7.

Concerning the participation of officers of the US Mission to the United Nations in conferences preparing position papers he comments:

One role of these officers has been to make suggestions on substantive and procedural aspects of the policy problems as well as to supply factual intelligence drawn from conferences with representatives of other UN members at New York. These suggestions, often in the form of telegrams, receive wide and immediate distribution at higher levels in the State Department and bring to attention alternatives which are the basis of possible decisions. There have been cases in which it has been easier for the departmental hierarchy to accept or reject a suggestion of the mission than to clear the thing suggested in the form of an instruction.

And he concludes:

In sum, the formulation of policy cannot be considered as at an end when the delegation is instructed and sent to the conference or meeting. There are inevitable changes and readjustments that occur during all the stages of implementation.

If policy determination is the final prerogative of governments, and delegations must work on the basis of instructions from their foreign offices, questions of tactics are frequently left to the discretion of the delegation. Since policy and tactics constantly interact, however, there is often a feeling, among major delegations at least, that although their discretion on tactics is broader than that on policy, foreign offices exert too much influence on questions of tactics also.[3] Nevertheless, a delegation's role in the formulation of tactics and in the precise manner of implementing policy

[3] In commenting further on the 13th session of the General Assembly, Senators Hickenlooper and Mansfield in their afore-mentioned report to the Congress stated: "Certainly it is true that central guidance of policy is necessary. However, if policy is to be pursued effectively in the General Assembly, which includes over 80 other nations— nations whose differing views as well as idiosyncrasies of their representatives must be reckoned with—the ambassadors and the members of the permanent mission must have a measure of freedom for parliamentary maneuver.

"We are not, on the basis of our limited experience, in a position to suggest precisely where the line ought to be drawn between firm central control over policy and flexibility in its pursuit at the United Nations. However, many of those who work day in and day out with other delegations over the years feel that the line that is now drawn errs on the side of excessive central control. As a result, it is contended, other delegations are often unnecessarily antagonized or alienated on particular issues and US representatives are frequently handicapped in their efforts to win support for undertakings in which we are interested.

"Our experience at the United Nations suggests that there is some validity in this contention. It is certainly the case that the official position on almost any issue is spelled out by Washington in very minute detail. The delegation is guided very closely not only on questions of substance but often even on matters of procedure. Against this is also the practice insofar as many other member nations are concerned.

"Nevertheless, during the course of a General Assembly, unanticipated developments often create a need for changes—frequently minor changes—in positions of procedure. These changes almost invariably require prior clearance from Washington. The requirement would not be so burdensome, perhaps, if only one bureau of the Department of State were involved in sanctioning them. Not infrequently, however, even a slight change

is usually decisive. The tactical situation varies so rapidly from day to day, and the calculation of probable voting and of the attitudes of other countries is so crucial in achieving a successful result, that tactics must be left reasonably flexible. Even such a question as when to inform other delegations of a country's policy can be a critical decision. Such factors as the order in which various people are approached, the concessions which a delegation can make within the limits of its authorization, and the level and timing of moves are best judged as closely to the necessary action as possible, both in time and in distance.

Tactical considerations can thus be crucial in determining whether an issue should be taken to the United Nations, when and how it should be presented, and the precise action which should be sought. What may be desirable must be tempered by what is possible. The possible is affected not only by the basic political attitudes of other states but also by prevailing rules, practices, and attitudes within the UN structure. In fact, a nation's whole policy position in the United Nations may be determined by tactical considerations to the extent that such considerations tailor its policies and attitudes toward realistic expectations.

It must also be said for the sake of balance that, while a delegation to the United Nations, like any diplomatic mission, tends to resist instructions the execution of which it believes will be costly in good will and attended by high risks, such instructions are sometimes reaffirmed on broader considerations than the delegation itself can judge. The government (including its delegation) may at times prefer to pursue a policy to defeat rather than modify it to the point of general acceptance. When such policies have been established or reaffirmed, they are naturally carried out fully.

INFLUENCING OPINION. Another principal characteristic of diplomacy in the United Nations is the widespread and powerful influence UN proceedings have on world opinion—domestic and foreign, governmental and private. A considerable portion of the planning of every delegation must therefore be directed to the question of how it can most effectively use the United Nations to persuade the world of the validity of its government's policies. The chief instrument of persuasion is the UN speech. Since in most cases a delegation is seeking to achieve a number of objectives at the same time, and since most UN speeches must be directed to more than one audience, drafting a speech is more complex than it might seem at the outset.

One problem is to decide on the audience or audiences to which a speech

---

in the phrase of a statement of an official position at the UN may call for clearance by any number of bureaus and offices scattered throughout various executive agencies and departments.

"Apart from the enormous cost in salaries and time which must be involved in these clearance practices, a desirable change may be so long delayed or so watered-down before it is sanctioned by Washington that it loses all or most of its value in New York." (Senators Hickenlooper and Mansfield, *op. cit.*, p. 7.)

is to be directed. A speech on a major political issue in the General Assembly is usually addressed first of all to the members of an Assembly Committee, where it is intended to guide debate in a certain direction, to discourage undesirable courses of action, and to influence both the negotiating process and the voting. Since this is the audience and function for which speeches in the United Nations ostensibly are designed, the speeches must have a UN "cast" and must be responsive to tactical considerations.

Any important speech, however, is also aimed at governments, and addressing governments is not necessarily the same as speaking to their representatives. What may be a helpful speech in producing tactical advances in a UN debate can easily cause difficulties in bilateral relations with an offended government. UN speeches are often scrutinized carefully by key governmental officials in the countries concerned, and they can affect relations for a long period to come. In some circumstances, skillful diplomacy calls for stating a policy so precisely and in so limited a context that it produces tactical results without creating commitments or revealing positions on larger issues. In some cases, circumlocution and ambiguity may be equally advantageous or necessary.

A major UN speech also has direct access to public opinion in many foreign countries, a circumstance leading both to peculiar opportunities and to difficult problems. The advantages of using the United Nations as a major platform for policy speeches are clearly recognized, and strenuous efforts are made by press officers, governmental radio facilities, and the information media of various states to assure that what is said is widely reported throughout the world. Many speeches, especially general debate statements and leading policy statements both in the General Assembly and in the Security Council, are drafted primarily with a view to appealing to foreign public opinion. However, when a speech must be prepared both for relatively sophisticated and possibly cynical delegates in the General Assembly, to whom at least theoretically it is addressed, and for relatively unsophisticated popular opinion abroad, obvious problems of conflict arise.

Still another large and important audience to which UN speeches are addressed is the domestic public opinion of the state which is speaking. Numerable speeches in the United Nations are in fact addressed primarily to this audience. Some of them are intended to reflect popular opinion; others are intended to inform and to shape domestic public opinion. As is natural and normal in public affairs, but sometimes tedious and vexing to delegates of other countries, speeches are sometimes made not just for their general domestic impact but also for their influence on immediate internal political developments.

It is rare that all of these various audiences can be addressed effectively in one speech. There are no rules by which to determine the proper course. Careful judgments have to be made in each case, and the negative as well as the positive consequences of any choice must be accepted. One of the difficulties of speaking both for domestic and for world public opinion, for example, is that those elements of policy and tactics which may be most persuasive to domestic opinion may produce negative reactions in the international sphere. Denunciation of an antagonist may receive enthusiastic endorsement by the home audience, but it may at the same time cause adverse reaction among the other audiences—Committee delegates, other governments, and foreign public opinion.

*   *   *   *   *   *   *

INFORMATION GATHERING AND EXCHANGE. The traditional information-gathering function of diplomatic missions is also a significant element in the work of UN delegations. As the United Nations provides ready contact among the representatives of almost every nation in the world on a continuous informal basis, it is a unique center for obtaining quick and reasonably authoritative answers on all kinds of questions, even on short notice when delegates may be without instructions from their governments. Information and the consequent assessment of it by delegations often are crucial elements in final governmental policy decisions.

First in importance is knowledge of the plans of other delegations and of their policies on current issues. The acquisition and exchange of information involves a large percentage of the time of UN delegations. Information on the probable course of action of another delegation obtained reasonably far in advance not only assists materially in the preparation of policies and attitudes to meet it but also facilitates the reaching of agreement.

Quick reactions on world events can also be obtained in the UN. Since casual conversation in the corridors and in UN assembly halls can produce a remarkably large number of well-informed opinions, contacts among delegations are important sources of information on developments, political and non-political, in various countries. The normal course of conversation produces informed assessments of the political and economic climate within a country and other data, including information about governmental personnel and attitudes.

REPRESENTATION. Inseparable from every issue of the moment and from every function of a diplomatic mission is the role of the individual representative as the symbol of his country. Foreign policy is made up not only of isolated issues, stated conferences, or the problems and events of the moment, but also of long-term impressions and attitudes which can be affected to some extent by the personal experiences officials have had with representatives of other countries. One of the responsibilities of a diplomat at the United Nations, as elsewhere, therefore, is to leave as good an impression as possible of his own country. He must be an ambassador for his country in a general as well as in a specific sense.

Personal contacts and relationships may, over long periods of time, have a significant impact on the attitudes of other officials and ultimately on governments. Especially in newly sovereign and underdeveloped countries where the number of educated people is proportionately small, many men with diplomatic experience become important political leaders; their previous experience with foreign representatives obviously colors their attitudes. Many diplomatic officials, from ambassadors down, exert considerable influence on their countries' foreign policies; their judgments likewise inevitably are affected by their impressions of the representatives of other countries with whom they are in contact. The ability and friendly attitude of Yugoslav diplomats in the United Nations, to cite one example, have undoubtedly influenced the views of many other delegates about Yugoslavia.

In a more immediate sense, the creation of friendly contacts is indispensable to the effective conduct of business. The members of missions and delegations share common professional aims and experiences; they spend much of their time seeking to reach agreement and understanding on individual issues. Yet, they come from diverse national and cultural backgrounds and serve different national interests, and they are moved frequently from post to post. Under these circumstances, more or less institutional means for establishing face-to-face contacts and harmonious personal and working relationships must be relied upon to an unusual degree. Hence, as in other arenas of international affairs, the United Nations is the scene of a steady succession of receptions, dinners, luncheons, parties, entertainment, and other opportunities for social contacts, the great majority of which have no ostensible political or diplomatic objective. Whether such social gatherings have any immediate effect on international relations is difficult to say, but that they are necessary to facilitate its conduct there is no doubt. To the extent that most national representatives in the United Nations want to create a peaceful world, even though not on the same terms, the constant rubbing of elbows is of some help in encouraging greater mutual understanding and a common desire to reach agreements that will foster a more peaceful and mutually satisfactory international community. The long-term impact of personal contacts may be intangible, but it is nevertheless real. As the Secretary-General said in Copenhagen on May 2, 1959:

Over the years, the diplomatic representatives accredited to the United Nations have developed a cooperation and built mutual contacts in dealing with problems they have in common, which in reality make them members of a kind of continuous diplomatic conference, in which they are informally following and able to discuss, on a personal basis, all political questions which are important for the work of the Organization. . . . Public debate in the United Nations is dominated by the same differences among the parties as international political life as a whole. But behind closed doors these differences are diluted. The human factor carries more weight there, and confidential exchanges are possible even across frontiers which otherwise appear impassable.

PUBLIC RELATIONS. As a consequence of their participation in the diplomatic activities discussed above, delegations become involved in direct contact with the public, both on UN matters and in behalf of their country generally. Because United Nations Headquarters is in the United States, public relations is particularly important for the United States delegation. Direct contact with the public is a not insignificant part of the functions of other delegations, however, since they are constantly being approached for information on their policies, both by their own nationals and by United States citizens and groups.

Many of the nongovernmental organizations represented at the United Nations send observers to, consult with, and even speak in various United Nations bodies on matters within their competence. Some of the nongovernmental organizations are of international scope; others, over 100, are United States organizations, the majority of which are nation-wide. Most of them maintain part-time observers in New York who seek the views of Secretariat officials and of various delegations and frequently ask to be briefed on issues before the UN or to discuss them with delegations. Since it is through such organizations that considerable information reaches public opinion and that reactions can be measured, the United States delegation briefs these observers about once a month.

THE ORGANIZATION AND METHODS OF DELEGATIONS

John G. Hadwen and Johan Kaufmann*

. . . There are great differences in the amount and nature of instructions which delegations receive. Some are given lengthy and detailed instructions which severely limit their freedom of manoeuvre. Some governments appear to instruct their delegation in terms of the position of other governments, i.e., "Vote more or less like . . ." or "If . . . votes 'no' you can abstain." Some

* John G. Hadwen and Johan Kaufmann, "The Organization and Methods of Delegations," in *How United Nations Decisions Are Made* (New York: Oceana Publications, 1962), Chap. 2, pp. 26–55. © Copyright A. W. Sijthoff, 1961. By permission of A. W. Sijthoff.

John Hadwen has been a special assistant to the Secretary of State for External Affairs of Canada since 1964. He was Chargé d'Affaires at the Canadian Embassy in Washington from 1961 to 1964. From 1956 to 1959 he was the First Secretary of the Canadian Mission to the United Nations.

Johan Kaufmann is now Minister Plenipotentiary and Permanent Representative of the Netherlands to the United Nations office in Geneva. Prior to that he was a counsellor to the Permanent Mission of the Netherlands to the United Nations from 1956 to 1961. He was on the staff of the Netherlands Ministry of Economic Affairs and served in Washington, D.C., from 1945 to 1953 and in Mexico from 1953 to 1956.

governments provide no instructions at all, leaving matters to the discretion of the delegation. The ideal instructions would result from careful study by the officials of the interested departments in the national capital and subsequent approval by the highest political authorities of the general positions to be adopted. Such ideal instructions would be specific as to objectives and the degree of activity required but would leave considerable freedom of action to the delegation if events took an unexpected turn. The precise drafting of the language of a resolution cannot usually be done in instructions prepared in advance.

The effectiveness of the U.N. would be seriously damaged if in many cases delegations did not receive instructions. This would mean that the government concerned did not find the U.N. discussions important enough to warrant serious consideration. In order to ensure that as many delegations as possible do have instructions, major proposals are generally widely discussed before they are made. Surprise has its value but the balance in the U.N. is generally on the side of advance notice.

No matter how close or how continuous contact may be between delegations in New York and the authorities in their national capitals, much of necessity remains the responsibility of the local representatives. At the U.N. events often move so quickly and their development is so complicated that it is virtually impossible to report all relevant factors and have them taken into account before a decision is taken and instructions despatched from headquarters. Of course, on decisions of great importance there is often a "strategic postponement" to give time for delegations to obtain instructions from home. The distance from New York to the national capital and the efficiency of the confidential communications facilities available also influence the type of instructions possible for each delegation.

Finally, the instruction pattern of a government is influenced by domestic or other issues which may overshadow U.N. discussions. In that case officials who should be involved in the preparation of instructions for a delegation to the U.N., may only be able to give little attention to U.N. matters.

In New York delegations are generally free to interpret within limits the positions of their governments but cannot take major policy decisions on the spot unless the Foreign Minister or another competent authority is present and able to assume responsibility. If therefore a delegation wishes to influence the policy of another delegation on some major specific issue it must generally do so through diplomatic channels. The first approach having been made through U.N. delegations, others may be made elsewhere.

. . . Delegations naturally try to influence others to adopt their views but in many cases the issue is discussed on its merits. The U.N. is no better and no worse in this respect than, for example, the national parliaments of member governments.

In the U.N. *do ut des,* "I will help you to achieve your objective but you must help me to achieve mine," is to be expected. This process of mutual accommodation is generally implemented by gentlemen's agreements. Nothing is committed to writing. Naturally an arrangement of mutual advantage occurs most often between individual delegations. Sometimes, however, it assumes a regional or group character, with say the Asian-African group supporting some proposal of the Latin-American group, because it is tacitly or explicitly understood that at some later occasion the Asian-African group can count on reciprocal support. [Note the similarity of behavior in national Parliaments, ed.]

Because of differences of language and of culture many consultations in New York take the form of an exchange of a "piece of paper." It is then possible, even for delegations speaking different languages and without bilingual personnel to help them, to co-operate quite closely provided each knows in writing what the other intends. Most negotiations take place privately in order to protect national prestige and to give the participants greater freedom of manoeuvre. In such meetings personal relations are paramount. If a delegate is to be effective it is necessary for him to know and approach the right person in the right delegation at the right time. If this approach is made under conditions of pressure and decisions are urgent, close personal understanding between the individuals concerned is of special importance.

INITIATING ACTION

After a delegation has taken a preliminary decision to present a proposal to the U.N. great activity is required. This action may depend on the expected reaction to the proposal, i.e., "we will present this resolution only if it appears that we can get a majority." It may therefore be necessary to sound out key delegations even before the proposal is drafted in specific language. Sometimes a delegation's viewpoint is pressed regardless of whether it expects to get a majority and sometimes with the express purpose of being defeated. A delegation may even invite defeat in order to prepare a position for use at a later meeting or to reflect some aspect of domestic public opinion. Generally however, delegations tend to put forward proposals which they hope may be finally adopted. There are, however, situations in which a delegation may ask for more than it expects to get so as to leave room for manoeuvre.

RESOLUTIONS

Most U.N. decisions are in the form of resolutions. They generally consist of two parts, a preamble and an operative section. The preamble is designed to explain the purpose of the resolution. In it an effort is made to rally as much support as possible for the operative paragraphs which follow. . . . The preamble often refers to earlier decisions, thus establishing some measure of continuity with previous U.N. action. If there are no previous U.N. decisions bearing directly on this subject, reference is often made to some appropriate article in the U.N. Charter.

The operative sections take the form of a request for action, an endorsement of a situation or a statement of opinion. Few United Nations decisions are mandatory. United Nations bodies come closest to mandatory decisions when requesting reports or studies to be undertaken by the U.N. Secretariat. When the resolution concerns governmental policies it is generally framed in language calculated to avoid giving offence even to those governments which are not expected to comply. The strenuous measures delegations pursue in order to amend, defeat or avoid such resolutions, even when these contain very vague language, indicates the importance attached to these texts. The concern of a delegation may arise from direct instructions, or be dictated by what it believes, on the basis of general policy statements, its government's reaction might be.

Drafts of resolutions are usually prepared in New York on the basis of general instructions from the national capitals, although from time to time on matters of great importance drafts of resolutions may be sent from the national capital concerned. If the draft originates in New York it generally takes the form of a preliminary working document, subject to correction from the national government to which the text will be referred. At this stage the Secretariat may be consulted on legal or other aspects of the text and on its drafting.

If the delegation intends to gain approval for a particular proposal, the first step must be to obtain the support of the delegation's close friends. At this stage perhaps not more than two or three other delegations are concerned. The proposal is presented in preliminary form and may frequently be altered to ensure the necessary basic support.

Without Great Power support of some kind a resolution is in difficulties. In almost every case a Great Power will be amongst those first consulted. Most delegations would consider that it would be irresponsible to press a draft resolution without taking into account Great Power attitudes. Action *can* be taken over their protests but it probably would not *mean* very much or, in the economic field, be supported financially. For many middle and small powers it is an important consideration that the appropriate Great Powers have assumed their fair share of responsibility on each issue. Otherwise many delegations will say: "Why should we assume the responsibilities, both financial and political, for decisions which have little chance of being implemented, for lack of Great Power support?" This is one of the reasons why some Great Power support is necessary at an early stage for any resolution, except in those cases where a majority decides deliberately to exercise pressure on one or more Great Powers by adopting a resolution against their wishes.

The next step, if there is time, is to approach either directly, or in conjunction with the close friends, a larger representative group and then through this group as many delegations as possible from amongst potential supporters. There is no point in these early discussions in approaching enemies or delegations which, for historical, personal or political reasons will clearly oppose the proposal. There is no use helping the opposition to prepare its tactics. Nevertheless the opposition, and there is always an opposition of some kind arising from one of a wide variety of possible motives, will almost certainly obtain a copy of the text once it gets wide circulation. Therefore it is sometimes desirable—before formal presentation in Committee—to explain to the opposition what a proposed text means so as to avoid unnecessary difficulty.

❖   ❖   ❖   ❖   ❖   ❖   ❖

Eventually a text of a draft resolution is given to the Secretariat for translation, editing and official circulation. Before that time, of course, a delegation will have endeavoured to meet as many as possible of the points which have been made by those it has consulted so that the text submitted has the best possible chance of being adopted.

❖   ❖   ❖   ❖   ❖   ❖   ❖

In this process it is frequently considered desirable to obtain a representative group of co-sponsors. The names of these countries are printed on draft resolutions. The names of the sponsors are not retained on the texts of resolutions after adoption. If the delegations of a number of representative countries from, for example, Latin America, Europe, the Middle East and Asia, agree to co-sponsor a resolution it has a better chance of easy adoption than a resolution sponsored only by European countries. On the other hand sometimes it is preferable for a delegation to submit a resolution without co-sponsors. The delegation originally responsible for the basic text of a proposal is normally among the co-sponsors, but this is not an invariable rule. Sometimes a country does not sponsor a resolution which it favours because to do so might arouse unnecessary opposition.

If a resolution has only a small number of co-sponsors, they will find it easier to take any necessary quick decisions on suggested modifications of the text and to co-ordinate tactics. If a resolution has a large number of co-sponsors, the difficulties involved in discussing and negotiating amendments are sometimes very great, although the committed support may be worth the trouble. Therefore the list of co-sponsors on a resolution is usually long only if it is non-controversial or if there has been fairly general advance agreement and the text is unlikely to be drastically amended. In some cases a long list of sponsors is used as a means of bringing pressure to bear on other delegations and to impress them with its probable support in the voting. Perhaps the best group of co-sponsors for a difficult resolution would be five or six representative countries whose delegates were on friendly terms. However, opposition is sometimes created if too few delegations are included amongst the co-sponsors. Countries represented by "difficult" delegates are often sought as co-sponsors to prevent them, so far as possible, from proposing changes. Choosing and getting a good list of co-sponsors requires tact and diplomacy of a high order and a detailed knowledge of the current international political situation.

Once a resolution has been formally submitted to the Secretariat, it is circulated in the working languages (French, Spanish and English to which Russian is usually added) to all participants. At this stage further co-sponsors may be added. When the subject is reached on the agenda with or without (usually with) a formal presentation speech by one of the sponsors, oral and formal written amendments, also sponsored by one or more delegations, may be introduced. The sponsors of the original text may accept some of these amendments. Usually a revised draft will be circulated before the actual vote.

Resolutions are seldom adopted in the exact phrasing in which they are presented. The late John Foster Dulles noted that "every major debate in the United Nations Assembly has brought about changes of opinion so that there was a larger measure of agreement. Seldom has a major proposal emerged without undergoing substantial changes, so that it better reflected world opinion."

❖   ❖   ❖   ❖   ❖   ❖   ❖

VOTING

The final stage in this process is that of voting. At this point a statement in private or in public of its intention to vote for or against a particular paragraph or text by an influential delegation will influence the votes of others. If the voting pattern is not clear, there may be hurried and more or less obvious consultations, between possibly likeminded delegations. Efforts may also be made at this stage to persuade some delegations to change their votes from a negative or positive vote to an abstention or vice-versa. In general it would be hard to change voting patterns on a major issue at the last minute and therefore efforts to do so are usually not worth the time and trouble. The voting reflects positions already developed in the debate and in informal discussions. There may, however, be surprises and sometimes there are mistakes. A delegate may have missed a key point in the debate or have failed to assess the situation correctly before the vote is taken. He is in particular danger if the vote is a roll call vote (in which each delegation is asked to indicate its vote orally) and his delegation is required to vote early on the list as it is called out in alphabetical order by the Committee secretary. (The order of voting in a roll call vote is determined by chance: the chairman picks a slip of paper with a country's name out of a box containing the names of all member countries.) If, however, the more usual procedure of voting by a show of hands is followed, a delegate may have difficulty seeing how others are voting. At the U.N. not all hands rise at the same time when a vote is called. Some delegates more or less conspicuously try to see how their friends or enemies are voting or how the majority is voting before casting their vote. These problems are less obvious but equally real in roll call votes and in the secret ballots held for elections. Sometimes the confident raising of an early and obvious hand can influence votes, particularly on procedural issues where the lines of division are not too clear. A delegation will request the type of voting most favourable to its purposes. A roll call vote will be sought if a detailed record showing each country's vote is required. This might embarrass some delegations. A vote by a show of hands goes into the record merely as total numbers for, against and abstaining.

❀   ❀   ❀   ❀   ❀   ❀   ❀

NEGOTIATING

Some negotiation takes place on the telephone. This is effective only when delegations understand each other's language perfectly and when security considerations do not interfere. If there is a possibility of misunderstanding, discussions are conducted face to face. This is to a large extent because the U.N. is a body in which national attitudes and political considerations not easily expressed have a considerable importance. At the U.N. *the why* and *the how* is often much more important than *the what*, and the atmosphere in which agreement is reached is frequently more significant than the nature of the agreement itself.

Most U.N. talks take place between small groups of delegations. As Dean Rusk concludes: "important policy decisions must include the diplomatic procedures to carry them out, for the availability of promising procedures and the political profits and losses involved in the use of such procedures have to be considered as a part of the policy decision itself." Dean Rusk was recognizing that the existence of an informal U.N. machinery for consultations affects the willingness of governments to discuss problems at the U.N. He goes on, "debate without full advance preparation by negotiation is likely to be unproductive and disconcerting, and it can be dangerous."

Some of these negotiations take place outside the U.N. building, at informal luncheons or at more formal meetings in delegation offices. However, there is a tendency for the greater part of these discussions to take place in the U.N. building itself, firstly because it is easier for all concerned to meet there in a non-partisan atmosphere and secondly, because, particularly during the General Assembly, officials like to meet on the U.N. premises to save time. The U.N. setting is also comfortable for those delegations who feel inhibited in other locations. In the U.N. building all delegations are on the same social and political level and all are and feel part owners of the building.

The U.N. building in Geneva, the famous "Palais des Nations," is used as much as possible for meetings of organs other than the General Assembly, particularly in the summer when New York is unattractive. Countries in or convenient to Europe can also be represented more easily and economically at Geneva than at New York. U.N. meetings have been held elsewhere than in New York or Geneva. While the same pattern of behaviour is followed wherever meetings are convened, it is true that a meeting in Latin America or Asia or Africa will have a different character and perhaps slightly different results than one held in Europe or North America.

Within the U.N. building most delegates practise what has been called "the fine art of corridor sitting." Many delegates go to the United Nations, its lounges and its bars, without any specific purpose in mind other than that of keeping in touch.

. . . Consequently there is a more relaxed social atmosphere than at perhaps any other diplomatic centre.

CHAPTER **9**

FINANCING

Until the United Nations undertook extensive peace-keeping operations, the budget never really became an issue in the Organization's debates. The League of Nations went through several years of strenuous discussion regarding the allocation of budget authority, but in the United Nations this power was determined in the Charter and hence the only early arguments that arose were with regard to assessments. This relative calm did not continue as more and more states established membership and made demands upon the Organization for assistance. The assumption that increased membership assessments would keep up with increased costs was tempting but erroneous, primarily because the increase was in poorer states rather than in wealthy ones.

The major problem, of course, arose over the issue of peace-keeping, for the special account that was established in 1956 to pay for it soon exceeded the size of the regular budget. Furthermore, the insistence by the Soviet and Arab blocs that the aggressors should pay and not the victim meant that many states would not in fact contribute. And when the Congo crisis erupted four years later in 1960 and mushroomed into a UN operation that in cost and size rapidly eclipsed that of the Middle East, the Organization's stability as well as its utility was seriously challenged. This condition was aggravated when the number resisting payment increased to approximately one third of the members.

The three selections on the finances of the UN by John Stoessinger clearly describe the nature of the budget from the perspective of the total Organization and the individual members. He also delves, in the second article, into the problems of assessments, comparing the UNEF and ONUC operations. And, finally, because those needs became so onerous that the question of the nature of the obligation to pay the special assessments was taken to the Court, Stoessinger presents the various arguments and the Court's judgment on the matter.

This chapter closes with a challenging viewpoint to the American position forcefully presented by two Soviet writers, G. Morozov and Y. Pchelintsev. Theirs is both a constitutional and historical argument, which, in its attack on the Uniting for Peace Resolution, overlooks the fact that the Soviet Union supported the use of the resolution against the British and French in the Suez crisis. However, the argument, based largely on debates regarding Article 50 and the Court's role vis-à-vis the other UN organs, is a well-reasoned one in terms of the meaning and the status of advisory opinions.

A number of critical questions have to be raised regarding the financial question. Perhaps first and foremost one must ask whether, on major issues, a refusal to pay the costs is tantamount to a veto, as many commentators claimed it was. A Security Council veto declares a substantive resolution null and void. Refusal to pay for a program means that a country stays out on the issue, leaving for the rest who approve the program the way to meet the costs. Confusing a refusal to pay with a veto by assigning them an identical classification would seem to do no service to statesmanship or scholarship. In fact, would the term veto *be appropriate if only small states refused to pay or is the term to be reserved for the refusal by large contibutors? One must also consider—as does Professor Gross in his article in Chapter 17— whether the Assembly has enforcement powers or can only make recommendations with regard to programs. While it is true that the payment of dues was expected to be obligatory, is it correct to assign the same obligation to a special budget?*

Another question that is relevant is the legality of trying to transform an advisory opinion into a legal decision. Why was the Court given two kinds of mandates, one to try cases and the other to give advice? Do more benefits than dangers accrue when an attempt is made to transform the latter into the former? Can one, any more in the art of politics than in the manufacture of pocketbooks, change a sow's ear into a silk purse?

One sees in this issue another serious problem regarding the allocation of authority in the United Nations. Since authority to maintain peace and security lies in one organ and the financial powers in another, have we not a built-in arrangement that can be counted on to create deadlocks? We cannot expect these deadlocks to be resolved through legal legerdemain but only through conciliation.

FURTHER READINGS

Claude, Inis L., "The Political Framework of the United Nations' Financial Problems," *International Organization*, Vol. 17, Autumn 1963, pp. 831–860.

Singer, David J., *Financing International Organization*: The United Nations Budget Process. The Hague: Martinus Nijhoff, 1961.

BUDGET ALLOCATIONS AND ASSESSMENTS

John G. Stoessinger*

The regular budget . . . comprises three broad categories. First, administrative expenses, accounting for about 60 per cent of the total, include the costs of providing the services essential for the work of the Organization, such as personnel, conference servicing, public information, and over-all "housekeeping" activities. Second, basic non-operational programs comprising the work of the Departments of Political and Security Council Affairs, Economic and Social Affairs, Trusteeship, and Legal Affairs, account for roughly 20 per cent of the total. The final 20 per cent is earmarked for operational activities in member states, such as the regular technical assistance program, and for special missions, such as the United Nations Truce Supervision Organization in Palestine and the Committee on South West Africa.

The Charter provisions with regard to the budget are embodied in Articles 17, 18, and 19. Article 17 reads as follows:

1. The General Assembly shall consider and approve the budget of the Organization.
2. The expenses of the Organization shall be borne by the Members as apportioned by the General Assembly.
3. The General Assembly shall consider and approve any financial and budgetary arrangements with specialized agencies referred to in Article 57 and shall examine the administrative budgets of such specialized agencies with a view to making recommendations to the agencies concerned.

Several observations are pertinent. In the first place, the Charter makes it quite clear that ultimate budgetary authority lies with the General Assembly. The League of Nations Covenant omitted this stipulation and thus precipitated a tug of war of several years' duration between the League Council and Assembly before the latter finally gained fiscal control. In the United Nations system, this power of the purse placed the General Assembly in a strategic position. Second, the General Assembly was to apportion the budget among the member states. In this connection, the framers at San

* John G. Stoessinger, "Budget Allocations and Assessments," *Financing the United Nations,* November, 1961, *International Conciliation,* No. 535, pp. 4–32. By permission of the Carnegie Endowment for International Peace.

John G. Stoessinger is Professor of Political Science at Hunter College of the City University of New York, and Visiting Professor of International Relations at the School of International Affairs, Columbia University. He is the author of *The United Nations and the Super Powers* and *The Might of Nations.*

Francisco decided to give the Assembly as much flexibility as possible, refusing to tie it down to any detailed method of budgetary procedure.

Finally, Article 17 recognizes the autonomous character of the specialized agencies within the United Nations system. Whereas in the League all technical programs were subsumed under the League budget, the United Nations system includes twelve specialized agencies and the International Atomic Energy Agency, each with a budget and financial system of its own. Based on the powers written into Article 17, the United Nations has signed agreements with specialized agencies and IAEA which vary somewhat but in most cases provide for consultation by the agencies with the United Nations in preparing their budgets and possible recommendations by the General Assembly; the agencies in general agree to "conform as far as may be practicable to standard forms and practices recommended by the United Nations." Two important exceptions are the agreements with the International Bank for Reconstruction and Development and the International Monetary Fund: these agencies, which finance their own operations from earnings and merely furnish annual reports to the Assembly, are exempt even from this perfunctory degree of supervision. In practice, the budgetary processes of most of the specialized agencies follow the United Nations pattern, with fiscal power vested in the deliberative body. This means that the United Nations system comprises a mutiplicity of assessed budgets, with the General Assembly in clear control of the United Nations budget but with little more than a foot in the door of the specialized agencies.

Article 18, which deals with voting procedure in the General Assembly, is relevant to finance in the sense that it specifically provides that budgetary questions are to be decided by a two-thirds majority. The League of Nations required unanimity on budgetary matters and was often almost paralyzed as a result.

Article 19 incorporates one more lesson that the framers learned from precedent. Nothing in the League Covenant had provided for action in case of failure by a member state to pay its assessed contributions. As a result, League members had accumulated arrears without inhibitions. The San Francisco Conference, after weighing several possible penalties, decided on the loss of voting privileges in the General Assembly. As stated in Article 19:

A Member of the United Nations which is in arrears in the payment of its financial contributions to the Organization shall have no vote in the General Assembly if the amount of its arrears equals or exceeds the amount of the contributions due from it for the preceding two full years. The General Assembly may, nevertheless, permit such a Member to vote if it is satisfied that the failure to pay is due to conditions beyond the control of the Member.

*   *   *   *   *   *   *

ASSESSMENTS

The assessment principle was implied but not spelled out in detail in Article 17. The Committee on Financial Arrangements recommended in late 1945 that the task of preparing a detailed scheme be entrusted by the General Assembly to an expert Committee on Contributions whose members were to serve for "relatively long terms," be selected on the basis of "broad geographical representation and experience," and be nationals of different states. This Committee, in preparing the assessment scale, was to take into account member states' capacity to pay as determined by four criteria: total national income, per-capita income, war-caused economic dislocation, and ability to acquire foreign currency.

The ten-member Committee on Contributions has a broad mandate and hence a very delicate job. Its history has been quite stormy. When first confronted in 1946 with its important task—the preparation of a scale of assessments—its difficulties were compounded by the absence of complete and reliable statistical information with regard to the four criteria that were to serve as guidelines. To help the Committee's evalution of "capacity to pay," the United Nations Statistical Office was instructed to gather the relevant information as quickly as possible. Although the Committee found "some lacunae" in the figures submitted to the Statistical Office, it nevertheless proposed a scale for the first three years of United Nations operations.

The proposed United States assessment—almost half the total budget—was most controversial. That country's delegation objected strenuously on two grounds. Senator Arthur H. Vandenberg pointed out that the 49.89 per cent figure was not an accurate reflection of the United States' capacity to pay. Moreover, even if the figures were accurate, it would be unwise to make the Organization so dependent upon the financial contribution of one member. Instead, he proposed that no state should be assessed more than one-third of the total budget. Nevertheless, the United States agreed to a temporary assessment of 39.89 per cent for 1946.

During the next ten years the United States gradually succeeded in having its assessment reduced to the one-third ceiling. At the same time it waged a vigorous campaign to raise the Soviet share, which then amounted to 6.34 per cent. A 1954 Senate Foreign Relations Committee study noted:

Senator Alexander Wiley reports that on one day in 1952, for example, he listened to a member of the Ukrainian delegation in one committee of the General Assembly speak with great pride of the remarkable economic progress his country had made since the war. The Senator then went to another committee where he heard a second member of the Ukrainian delegation explain with equal fervor why his Government was unable to increase its contribution to the U.N. budget.

During the ten-year battle in the Committee on Contributions, statistical information gradually improved, war damages were repaired, the European economies recovered, and momentous changes occurred in the international balance of payments. All these developments were reflected in the annual alterations made by the Committee in the assessment scale. By 1956 a formula could for the first time be codified for a three-year period. The United States was reduced to the one-third limit, the Soviet share increased to nearly 14 per cent, and the United Kingdom assessment lowered to less than 10 per cent.

The battle in the Contributions Committee, however, was not merely a reflection of the East-West struggle. The one-third ceiling suggested by the United States elicited in 1954 a Canadian demand for a ceiling on any member state's per-capita assessment, in addition to the ceiling on its total assessment. The net effect would have been that countries with high national incomes and small populations would not be assessed more per capita than the United States. The Canadian plan was vigorously opposed by the delegates from the small developing nations on the ground that it would lead to a greater financial burden for the poorer countries. As a result, a compromise resolution was adopted in which those countries whose per-capita assessment exceeded that of the United States (Canada, New Zealand, Sweden, and Iceland) were promised that the difference between their per-capita assessment and that of the United States would not increase.[1]

Since 1956 the Committee on Contributions has had little more than routine responsibilities. The basic pattern of assessment has been set and the changes in each subsequent evaluation have been minor. Contrary to expectations, the admission of new states has made little difference in total revenues. Most of the new African nations have been assessed the minimum of 0.04 per cent. Not only has the increase in membership not resulted in an appreciable reduction in the share of member states already in the Organization, but the cost of alterations at United Nations Headquarters to accommodate the increased membership has required an increase in the older members' contributions.

Surveying the present pattern of assessment, one conclusion is striking: a large portion of the United Nations regular budget is dependent upon a very small minority of the membership. Fifty countries constituting 50 per cent of the membership are assessed only a little over 3 per cent of the budget. Twenty countries constituting 20 per cent of the membership contribute almost 90 per cent of the total. The Big Five are responsible for almost two-thirds, the United States for almost one-third.

THE REGULAR BUDGET

In the case of the regular budget the collection of contributions has not posed a serious problem. Every year a number of states lag behind, but the total of arrears has never exceeded 15 per cent of the entire budget. Some members fall almost two years behind but always manage to complete their

---

[1] By 1961 the U.S. per-capita assessment was exceeded only by Canada's.

contributions before the question of invoking Article 19 arises. China has been the largest single debtor and has usually been responsible for over three-quarters of the total arrears. This is not surprising, since that country continues to pay the fifth largest assessment, calculated on the basis of mainland China although its resources are limited to the island of Formosa. . . .

Conscious of the potential problem of arrears, the General Assembly in 1946 established a Working Capital Fund from which the Secretary-General is authorized to advance "such funds as may be necessary to finance budgetary appropriations pending receipt of contributions." The Fund has fluctuated between $20,000,000 and $25,000,000. Until the Congo crisis of 1960 threatened the entire financial structure of the United Nations, the Working Capital Fund was a fairly successful device for meeting emergencies.

In its attempts to close the gap between assessment and actual payment, the General Assembly has also empowered the Secretary-General to accept funds in currencies other than United States dollars. Although originally contributions were to be assessed and paid in the currency of the host country, in practice the Secretary-General has found it possible each year to accept a certain sum in other currencies. The total thus payable has fluctuated over the years between 5 per cent and 35 per cent of the Total budget. On several occasions it has resulted in prompt payment by states which otherwise might have accumulated arrears.

In the search for revenue, the size and nature of the appropriations must always be kept in mind. As the Organization's revenue problems have grown, so, too, have demands for economy in expenditures. Authorizing and approving expenditures under the United Nations regular budget is a lengthy and cumbersome process. In the words of the Senate Foreign Relations Committee study:

The U.N. budget probably is given as careful a scrutiny as any budget of a similar size anywhere in the world. Representatives from member states in the General Assembly often spend days debating relatively modest sums which would be considered by some national legislative bodies in a matter of hours or even minutes.[2]

The United Nations budget process somewhat resembles that of the federal government of the United States. Budget estimates for each fiscal year are prepared by the Secretariat and approved by the Secretary-General. These estimates are then studied by a specially constituted body, the General Assembly's advisory Committee on Administrative and Budgetary Questions. This nine-member committee is supposed to be a body of individual experts, but in fact it has become a political body, little more than a Fifth Committee in microcosm. Its comments and recommendations are submitted to the Fifth

    [2] *Budgetary and Financial Problems of the United Nations*, Staff Study No. 6, Dec. 1954, in *Review of the United Nations Charter: Compilation of Studies Prepared . . . Pursuant to S. Res. 126*, Subcommittee on the United Nations Charter, Cmtte. on For. Rel., U.S. Senate, 83rd Cong., 2nd Sess. (Washington, GPO, 1955), p. 160.

along with the original budget estimates of the Secretary-General. In practice, this very often gives the Advisory Committee members, now wearing different hats as Assembly delegates, the chance to recommend further cuts in appropriations. Although the Secretary-General usually participates in the debates of the Fifth Committee to defend his figures, the General Assembly in most cases adopts the Advisory Committee's recommendations as modified by the Fifth Committee. The entire process is characterized by such a strong emphasis on economy that one expert sees "national miserliness" showing through everywhere, and wistfully suggests that delegates "give at least as much attention to the *policy* implications of *financial* decisions as they do to *financial* implications of *policy* decisions."

The United Nations regular budget has risen over the years in a gentle upward curve. This has also been true of the assessed budgets of the specialized agencies, whose combined total is a third more than that of the United Nations. The pattern of raising revenue and appropriating expenditures in the agencies resembles the budgetary process of the parent organization, although there are two minor variations worthy of note. First, the wide variations in membership (from 45 in the case of the Inter-Governmental Maritime Consultative Organization to 102 in the Universal Postal Union) has resulted in different scales of assessment; and second, the Soviet bloc's erratic membership pattern has skewed assessments in some agencies.

UNEF

It is generally accepted today that the United Nations Emergency Force was a political and military milestone for the United Nations. For the first time an international force was constituted, one not dominated by any single power. What is less well known is the fact that it also represented a fiscal milestone in the life of the world organization. For the first time an international body decided that the costs of such an international force should be shared by the nations of the world community. This decision was to have far-reaching consequences.

The father of UNEF was Lester B. Pearson of Canada. When, on 2 November 1956, the General Assembly was locked in acrimonious debate over the British-French-Israeli action in Suez, Mr. Pearson proposed that peace and security be restored through a United Nations Force. The Canadian resolution passed without a negative vote and the Secretary-General set about improvising the Force. After a great deal of delicate maneuvering, 6,000 troops—contingents from ten countries (Brazil, Canada, Colombia, Denmark, Finland, India, Indonesia, Norway, Sweden, and Yugoslavia)— were ready for action.[3] But it was clear that unless the question of financing

---

[3] For a complete analysis of the political and military implications of UNEF, see William R. Frye, *A United Nations Peace Force* (New York, Oceana for the Carnegie Endowment for International Peace, 1957).

was solved, the Force would not get beyond the paper stage. And unless it was solved reasonably well, UNEF would be short-lived indeed. Hence the Secretary-General, in his proposals to the General Assembly, gave the matter of financing the Force his most careful attention.

On 21 November 1956, the Secretary-General recommended that a Special Account outside the regular budget be set up for UNEF and that the costs of the Force be shared by the member states on the basis of the scale of assessments to be adopted for the 1957 budget. In addition, he suggested an initial assessment of $10,000,000 to meet the immediate cash needs of the Force. As will be seen, the Special Account device was a crucial decision. The Secretary-General preferred it to inclusion of UNEF expenditures in the regular budget because he wanted funds for the Force immediately, while the latter course would almost certainly have resulted in serious delay. This technique was successful and the General Assembly established the Special Account of $10,000,000 on 26 November as an interim measure.

On 3 December the Secretary-General faced the central problem—that of allocating the balance of the expenses of the Force—and indicated to the Assembly that the only equitable way of meeting the costs henceforth was to share them in accordance with the 1957 scale of assessments. Although financed under a Special Account, the Secretary-General nevertheless considered UNEF costs as "United Nations expenditures within the general scope and intent of Article 17 of the Charter."[4] This proposal touched off a storm of controversy and profoundly divided the Fifth Committee of the Assembly.

The United States delegate agreed with the Secretary-General and pointed out that the Committee's decision would be of crucial importance for the future of the Organization. He was supported by most of the Western nations. The statement of the delegate from New Zealand was typical: "Such responsibilities must be borne not by a fifth or a quarter of the Members or by one or two countries, but by all." This view was sharply challenged by the delegates from the Soviet bloc, who insisted that the entire cost of the operation should be borne by those countries which had precipitated the crisis—Britain, France, and Israel. The New Zealand delegation retorted that not even in the case of Korea had it been considered that the country named as aggressor by the Assembly should pay the costs of the Korean action. The Arab states supported the Soviet view and suggested that it was "morally and logically unfounded" to expect Egypt, a victim of aggression, to contribute to the costs of the Force.

Several delegations expressed points of view which fell along a fairly wide spectrum between the two extremes of the Western and Soviet positions. The Brazilian delegate suggested that countries contributing troops should have their assessments reduced accordingly. The Spanish representative proposed

---

[4] United Nations General Assembly, *Official Records* (GAOR): 11th Sess., 5th Cmtte., 541st Mtg., 3 Dec. 1956, para. 79.

a formula whereby the major part of the cost would be borne by the Big Five, and the remaining portion by all member states including the Big Five. The Latin American countries, in a joint statement, disputed the Secretary-General's position. The suggestion that the costs of UNEF should be considered under Article 17 was, they asserted, "at the very least, open to question" and offered the added disadvantage that Article 19 might thereby be invoked: "the principle of collective responsibility was established. . . . The assessment pattern was now set [along the general lines of assessment to the regular budget]."

✽   ✽   ✽   ✽   ✽   ✽   ✽

The decision to assess the member states has not solved the problem of financing UNEF. The heart of this problem has been to close the gap between assessment and collection. Each year arrears and defaults have amounted to roughly one-third of the total assessment. Since voluntary contributions have rarely exceeded 20 per cent of the annual cost of operations, UNEF has been running a serious annual deficit and has had to draw heavily on the Working Capital Fund. . . .

Over one-third of the member states of the United Nations have defaulted in part or in full on their assessment. Some of the members in arrears, notably the newly admitted nations, have conceded their legal responsibility to pay but have claimed financial hardship. Theirs is primarily a practical problem and poses the least difficulty. Others, however, such as most of the Latin American countries, have regarded each Assembly resolution solely as a recommendation, not as a legal obligation. They pose the problem of legal principle. Finally, and most radically, the Soviet bloc and the Arab countries, by stressing that "the aggressors must pay," have raised the problem of legal obligation under the Charter in its starkest form.

TABLE I
ASSESSMENTS FOR UNITED NATIONS FORCES IN 1961
($US in thousands)

MEMBER	UNEF (1 Jan.-31 Dec.)			ONUC (1 Jan.-31 Oct.)		
	GROSS ASSESSMENT	NET ASSESSMENT[1]	PAYMENTS	GROSS ASSESSMENT	NET ASSESSMENT[2]	PAYMENTS
Afghanistan	11.3	5.6	—*	59.4	11.9	—*
Albania	7.5	7.5	—*	39.6	7.9	—*
Argentina	208.8	103.3	—*	1,099.6	219.9	—*

*In full arrears after 1957.   *In full arrears, 1960 net assessment.

†In partial arrears after 1957.   †In partial arrears, 1960 assessments.

[1] After reductions requested and received under General Assembly Res. 1575 (XV).
[2] After reductions pursuant to General Assembly Res. 1619 (XV).

TABLE I *(Cont'd)*

MEMBER	UNEF (1 Jan.-31 Dec.)			ONUC (1 Jan.-31 Oct.)		
	GROSS ASSESS-MENT	NET ASSESS-MENT[1]	PAY-MENTS	GROSS ASSESS-MENT	NET ASSESS-MENT[2]	PAY-MENTS
Australia	336.7	334.9	in full	1,773.2	1,773.2	1,422.0
Austria	80.9	80.5	–	426.0	426.0	–°
Belgium	244.5	243.2	200.0	1,287.8	1,287.8	–°
Bolivia	7.5	7.5	–°	39.6	7.9	–°
Brazil	191.9	94.9	–	1,010.4	202.1	–°
Bulgaria	30.1	29.9	–°	158.5	31.7	–°
Burma	15.0	7.4	in full	79.2	15.8	–
Byelorussia	88.4	87.9	–°	465.6	465.6	–°
Cambodia	7.5	3.7	–	39.6	7.9	–°
Cameroun	7.5	7.5	–	39.6	7.9	5.8
Canada	585.0	581.9	in full	3,080.7	3,080.7	2,650.0
Cent. Afr. Rep.	7.5	3.8	in full	39.6	7.9	–
Ceylon	18.8	9.3	in full	99.1	19.8	–
Chad	7.5	3.8	–	39.6	7.9	–°
Chile	50.8	25.1	–†	267.5	53.5	–°
China	942.4	466.2	–°	4,962.9	2,481.4	–°
Colombia	58.3	28.8	–†	307.1	61.4	–°
Congo (Brazza.)	7.5	7.5	–	39.6	7.9	–°
Congo (Leo.)	7.5	3.8	–	39.6	7.9	–°
Costa Rica	7.5	3.7	–†	39.6	7.9	–°
Cuba	47.0	46.8	–°	247.6	49.5	–°
Cyprus	7.5	3.8	–	39.6	7.9	–°
Czechoslovakia	163.7	162.8	–°	861.8	861.8	–°
Dahomey	7.5	3.8	3.4	39.6	7.9	7.0
Denmark	112.9	112.3	in full	594.4	594.4	in full
Dominican Rep.	9.4	9.4	–	49.5	9.9	–°
Ecuador	11.3	5.6	in full	59.4	11.9	–°
El Salvador	9.4	4.7	–°	49.5	9.9	–°
Ethiopia	11.3	5.6	–°	59.4	11.9	–°
Fed. of Malaya	32.0	15.8	in full	168.4	33.7	–
Finland	67.7	67.4	in full	356.6	356.6	–
France	1,203.9	1,197.5	in full	6,339.8	6,339.8	–°
Gabon	7.5	3.8	in full	39.6	7.9	–
Ghana	13.2	6.5	–	69.3	13.9	–°
Greece	43.3	21.4	–°	227.8	45.6	–°
Guatemala	9.4	4.7	–†	49.5	9.9	–°
Guinea	7.5	7.5	–	39.6	7.9	–°
Haiti	7.5	3.7	–†	39.6	7.9	–°
Honduras	7.5	3.7	–†	39.6	7.9	–°

°*In full arrears after 1957.*   °*In full arrears, 1960 net assessment.*

†*In partial arrears after 1957.*   †*In partial arrears, 1960 assessments.*

[1] *After reductions requested and received under General Assembly Res. 1575 (XV).*
[2] *After reductions pursuant to General Assembly Res. 1619 (XV).*

TABLE I *(Cont'd)*

MEMBER	UNEF (1 Jan.-31 Dec.)			ONUC (1 Jan.-31 Oct.)		
	GROSS ASSESS-MENT	NET ASSESS-MENT[1]	PAY-MENTS	GROSS ASSESS-MENT	NET ASSESS-MENT[2]	PAY-MENTS
Hungary	79.0	78.6	—°	416.0	83.2	—°
Iceland	7.5	3.7	—	39.6	7.9	—
India	462.8	228.9	—†	2,436.9	1,218.4	in full
Indonesia	88.4	43.7	—	465.6	93.1	—°
Iran	39.5	19.5	—	208.0	41.6	—°
Iraq	16.9	16.8	—°	89.2	17.8	—°
Ireland	30.1	29.9	in full	158.5	31.7	in full
Israel	26.3	26.2	—	138.7	27.7	—°
Italy	423.3	421.0	—	2,228.8	2,228.8	—°
Ivory Coast	11.3	5.6	—	59.4	11.9	10.3
Japan	412.0	203.7	in full	2,169.4	1,084.7	—
Jordan	7.5	7.5	—°	39.6	7.9	—°
Laos	7.5	3.7	—	39.6	7.9	—°
Lebanon	9.4	4.7	—†	49.5	9.9	—°
Liberia	7.5	3.7	—†	39.6	7.9	in full
Libya	7.5	7.5	—°	39.6	7.9	—°
Luxembourg	11.3	11.2	in full	59.4	11.9	—†
Madagascar	11.3	5.6	2.5	59.4	11.9	—†
Mali	7.5	7.5	—°	39.6	7.9	—°
Mexico	133.6	132.8	—°	703.3	140.7	—°
Morocco	26.3	13.0	—†	138.7	27.7	—°
Nepal	7.5	3.7	—°	39.6	7.9	—°
Netherlands	190.0	189.0	in full	1,000.5	1,000.5	in full
New Zealand	79.0	78.6	in full	416.0	416.0	in full
Nicaragua	7.5	3.7	—†	39.6	7.9	—°
Niger	7.5	3.8	—	39.6	7.9	—°
Nigeria	39.5	19.8	—	208.0	41.6	—
Norway	92.2	91.7	in full	485.4	485.4	in full
Pakistan	75.2	37.2	—	396.2	79.2	—
Panama	7.5	3.7	—°	39.6	7.9	—°
Paraguay	7.5	3.7	—°	39.6	7.9	—°
Peru	20.7	20.6	—°	109.0	21.8	—°
Philippines	80.9	40.0	—†	426.0	85.2	—°
Poland	257.7	256.3	—°	1,357.1	678.6	—°
Portugal	37.6	37.4	in full	198.1	39.6	—°
Romania	64.0	63.6	—°	336.8	336.8	—°
Saudi Arabia	11.3	11.2	—°	59.4	11.9	—°
Senegal	11.3	5.6	—	59.4	11.9	—°
Somalia	7.5	7.5	—	39.6	7.9	—°

°*In full arrears after 1957.* °*In full arrears, 1960 net assessment.*

†*In partial arrears after 1957.* †*In partial arrears, 1960 assessments.*

[1] *After reductions requested and received under General Assembly Res. 1575 (XV).*
[2] *After reductions pursuant to General Assembly Res. 1619 (XV).*

TABLE I *(Con'td)*

MEMBER	UNEF (1 Jan.-31 Dec.)			ONUC (1 Jan.-31 Oct.)		
	GROSS ASSESS-MENT	NET ASSESS-MENT[1]	PAY-MENTS	GROSS ASSESS-MENT	NET ASSESS-MENT[2]	PAY-MENTS
South Africa	105.3	104.8	in full	554.7	554.7	—*
Spain	174.9	174.0	—*	921.2	184.3	—*
Sudan	11.3	11.2	—*	59.4	11.9	—*
Sweden	261.5	260.1	—	1,376.9	1,376.9	—*
Thailand	30.1	14.9	in full	158.5	31.7	—
Togo	7.5	3.8	—	39.6	7.9	—*
Tunisia	9.4	4.7	in full	49.5	9.9	—
Turkey	111.0	54.9	in full	584.4	116.9	in full
Ukraine	338.6	336.8	—*	1,783.1	1,783.1	—*
USSR	2,562.1	2,548.5	—*	13,491.8	13,491.8	—*
UAR	60.2	59.9	—*	317.0	63.4	—*
United Kingdom	1,462.5	1,453.9	in full	7,706.8	7,706.8	5,780.1
United States	6,115.5	6,115.5	in full	32,204.1	32,204.1	in full
Upper Volta	7.5	7.5	—	39.6	7.9	—*
Uruguay	22.6	11.2	—†	118.9	23.8	—*
Venezuela	94.1	46.5	—	495.3	99.1	—*
Yemen	7.5	7.5	—*	39.6	7.9	—*
Yugoslavia	65.8	32.6	in full	346.7	69.3	—*
Total	$18,989.9	$17,234.9	$4,852.7	$100,000.0	$84,694.4	$45,950.4

*In full arrears after 1957.

†In partial arrears after 1957.

*In full arrears, 1960 net assessment.

†In partial arrears, 1960 assessments.

[1] After reductions requested and received under General Assembly Res. 1575 (XV).
[2] After reductions pursuant to General Assembly Res. 1619 (XV).

Sources: United Nations Docs. ST/ADM/Ser. B/150, 4 Oct. 1961, and A/C.5/879, 28 Sept. 1961.

The Secretary-General's position was clear: all member states have a legal obligation to pay under Article 17 of the Charter. This view has been supported by a majority of the membership. It is a view that may be buttressed by several arguments. First, UNEF's status is that of a subsidiary organ of the General Assembly under Article 22 of the Charter. Such an organ comes within the meaning of Article 17. Second, the language of Articles 17, 18, and 19 is imperative and clearly implies that even those voting against a financial resolution are bound by the principle expressed in the statement that "the expenses of the Organization shall be borne by the Members as apportioned by the General Assembly.". . .

On the other hand, the majority position is open to reasonable doubt. The finances of all United Nations organs are subsumed under the regular budget. UNEF, however, is financed through a Special Account separate from the regular budget. While the Secretary-General preferred this technique because at a time of acute emergency it probably would not have been possible to persuade the Assembly to include UNEF in the regular budget, this procedure opened the door to a good deal of ambiguity and may well have set an unfortunate precedent for the future financing of United Nations peace and security operations.[5] By thus isolating the finances of the Force, the Secretary-General implied that the costs of UNEF were of an extraordinary nature. Thus the question may be raised whether Articles 17 and 19 are indeed applicable in this case.

❋   ❋   ❋   ❋   ❋   ❋   ❋

ONUC

Historians may differ with Mr. Hammarskjöld's view that the United Nations' task in the Congo was the most important responsibility that the world organization had to shoulder in the first fifteen years of its lifetime. Few, however, will disagree that the Congo problem required every diplomatic and military resource that the United Nations could possibly muster.

❋   ❋   ❋   ❋   ❋   ❋   ❋

On 24 October 1960, the Secretary-General estimated the cost of the Congo Force for 1960 at $66,625,000. This estimate was considered by the Advisory Committee on Administrative and Budgetary Questions, which recommended that the total costs of ONUC for 1960 be held to $60,000,000, and echoed a hope expressed by the Secretary-General that nations would forgo reimbursement for troop transport. Both the United States and the Soviet governments informed the Committee that they would waive their claims of $10,000,000 and $1,500,000 respectively. Hence, the crucial question to be decided by the Fifth Committee was how to apportion the remaining $48,500,000 among the member states.

The debate in the Fifth Committee began in a relatively mild tone. Ireland, Liberia, and Sweden suggested that ONUC's 1960 expenses be included in the regular budget and apportioned in accordance with the 1960 scale of assessments. This, the three powers maintained, would be the simplest solution and would avoid the ambiguity of the UNEF precedent. It would clearly bring ONUC within the scope of Articles 17 and 19 of the Charter.

Pakistan, Senegal, and Tunisia instead proposed a resolution creating an *ad hoc* account for financing ONUC operations, but clearly stipulating that the 1960 costs of the Congo Force were to "constitute 'expenses of the Organization' within the meaning of Article 17" and that assessments for it

[5] For a detailed study of UNEF financing, see Gabriella Rosner, *The United Nations Emergency Force*, Chap. 7 (unpub. doctoral dissertation, Columbia Univ., New York, 1961).

were to create "binding legal obligations." This procedure, too, would make the enterprise a collective responsibility but would keep it separate from the regular budget for accounting purposes. In addition, the three powers suggested the solicitation of voluntary contributions to be applied to reduce assessments of member states with the least capacity to pay. This view was supported by the United States and most of the newly admitted nations.

The Communist nations stated their intention not to contribute to any part of ONUC's expenses since, in their opinion, "the main burden . . . should be borne by the chief culprits—the Belgian colonizers." The rest of the money should be raised through voluntary contributions. The Latin American countries . . . suggested that the expenses be paid largely by the permanent members of the Security Council.

※　※　※　※　※　※　※

Finally the Fifth Committee, by a vote of 45 to 15, with 25 abstentions, approved the draft resolution proposed by Pakistan, Tunisia, and Senegal. It recommended an *ad hoc* account for the expenses of ONUC in the amount of $48,500,000 to be assessed on the basis of the 1960 scale. It stressed that these assessments would be "binding legal obligations" on member states with the meaning of Article 17 of the Charter. It called on the government of Belgium to make a substantial contribution and recommended that voluntary contributions be applied to reduce by up to 50 per cent the assessment of those states with the least capacity to pay. On 20 December, this recommendation was adopted by the General Assembly by 46 to 17, with 24 abstentions.

THE COSTS OF UNITED NATIONS MEMBERSHIP

John G. Stoessinger*

TRENDS IN OVERALL COSTS

The rising cost of the United Nations system to the member states can be simply stated: starting from an initial budget level of $50 million in 1946, the overall annual cost of the United Nations system has risen to almost $500 million in 1963. These costs comprise four categories: the regular

* John G. Stoessinger, "The Costs of United Nations Membership," in *Financing the United Nations System* (Washington, D.C.: The Brookings Institution, 1964), Chap. 3, pp. 63–78. © 1964 by The Brookings Institution. By permission of The Brookings Institution.

budget, the peace-keeping operations, the special voluntary programs, and the specialized agencies. To these expenses must be added the many "hidden costs" of membership such as the maintenance of missions in New York, Geneva, and other major centers, and the backstopping staff at home plus communication, information, and transportation costs.

The normal operating expenses of the Organization covered by the regular budget have risen gradually from $19 million in 1946 to $93 million in 1963. There has been no precipitous rise nor any abrupt cutback at any time. The period may be divided into three parts: an initial growth period from 1946 to 1949, a fairly sustained stabilization from 1949 to 1956 in which the overall rise was less than $10 million; and a persistent upward trend since 1957 as many new states have entered the Organization and new demands have been continually pressed on it. In this last period the budget has risen by 65 percent over the 1956 level.

The increase in the administrative and running costs of the Organization since 1946 is understandable when it is considered that the membership has more than doubled, costs have risen, the institution has been confronted with an almost continuous succession of international crises, and there has been an unremitting demand that it concern itself with an ever-growing circle of problems and activities.

The upward curve of the United Nations regular budget would have been much steeper if the costs of some of the more expensive special programs cared for by voluntary contributions or of the large emergency peace and security operations had been absorbed. The separate financing of these activities has saved the regular budget from a much larger multiplication.

The most significant feature in the growth of costs of the United Nations is, of course, the upsurge in expenditures for peace and security operations since 1956. There is no more impressive change in the overall pattern than the sharp upward turn of expenditures occasioned by the establishment and maintenance of the United Nations Emergency Force in the Middle East (UNEF) and the United Nations Military Operation in the Congo (ONUC).

For the period from November 1956 to the end of 1963, the United Nations costs for UNEF amounted to approximately $150 million. These expenditures ran initially over $20 million a year, but since 1958 have been reduced to the $18-$19 million level.

The United Nations commitments for the military operation in the Congo amounted to approximately $400 million by the end of 1963, with $60 million expended between July and December 1960, $120 million from January to December 1961, roughly $120 million in 1962, and $100 million in 1963.

Another prominent feature of the rising cost of these operations has been the large and steadily mounting expenditure for the special programs financed by voluntary contributions. From a figure of $67 million in 1952, these had risen to $203 million by 1963. Taken as a whole, the special voluntary programs accounted for 40 percent of total United Nations expenditures in 1963.

While the portion of costs of the Organization covered by government voluntary contributions is less than one-half of total expenses of the United Nations system, it is clear that this means of support has been providing an average of more than twice the income provided by the regular budget since 1956. The amounts raised in this manner have fluctuated widely, but, on the whole, the trend has clearly been upward. The rise has been especially steep since 1959 due to the expansion of economic development activities financed by the Expanded Programme for Technical Assistance (EPTA) and the Special Fund. By 1963, government voluntary contributions provided the largest single item in the four categories outlined above.

Finally, the budgets of the specialized agencies have risen in a gentle upward curve. The rise has been strikingly similar to that of the regular budget. From $28 million in 1949, the budgets of the agencies, not including the brief life span of the International Refugee Organization, had risen to $98 million by the end of 1963.

COSTS OF MEMBERSHIP

The second question, how much it costs nations to be members of the United Nations, may be answered in two ways: first, in terms of actual amounts contributed either in dollars and cents and percentages of the total cost of the United Nations system; and second, in terms of the member's national income.

In 1962 and 1963, costs of the United Nations including assessments for the regular budget, peace-keeping operations, and specialized agencies plus voluntary contributions amounted to about $500 million. Table 1 shows the states in order of their payments expressed in percentages of the $500 million

TABLE I

PERCENT OF TOTAL UNITED NATIONS CONTRIBUTIONS 1961, AND REGULAR BUDGET ASSESSMENT SCALE 1962-63

MEMBERS IN ORDER OF THEIR PAYMENTS TO THE U.N. SYSTEM	PERCENT OF CONTRIBUTIONS	ASSESSMENT SCALE
1. United States	46.910	32.02
2. United Kingdom	8.778	7.58
3. Union of Soviet Socialist Republics	8.249	14.97
4. France	4.943	5.94
5. Canada	3.844	3.12
6. Sweden	2.012	1.30
7. China	1.939	4.57
8. The Netherlands	1.916	1.01
9. India	1.908	2.03
10. Italy	1.862	2.24

TABLE I *(Cont'd)*

MEMBERS IN ORDER OF THEIR PAYMENTS TO THE U.N. SYSTEM	PERCENT OF CONTRIBUTIONS	ASSESSMENT SCALE
11. Australia	1.587	1.66
12. Japan	1.474	2.27
13. Ukrainian Soviet Socialist Republic	1.087	1.98
14. Denmark	.970	.58
15. Belgium	.969	1.20
16. Brazil	.752	1.03
17. Norway	.750	.45
18. Poland	.710	1.28
19. Czechoslovakia	.534	1.17
20. Argentina	.518	1.01
21. New Zealand	.477	.41
22. Mexico	.457	.74
23. Turkey	.425	.40
24. Spain	.416	.86
25. United Arab Republic	.368	.30
26. Austria	.365	.45
27. Venezuela	.349	.52
28. South Africa	.347	.53
29. Byelorussian Soviet Socialist Republic	.308	.52
30. Pakistan	.275	.42
31. Yugoslavia	.268	.38
32. Finland	.262	.37
33. Indonesia	.227	.45
34. Philippines	.225	.40
35. Rumania	.207	.32
36. Iran	.202	.20
37. Chile	.201	.26
38. Colombia	.194	.26
39. Hungary	.180	.56
40. Cuba	.144	.22
41. Thailand	.142	.16
42. Greece	.118	.23
43. Nigeria	.105	.21
44. Israel	.098	.15
45. Liberia	.095	.04
46. Peru	.090	.10
47. Portugal	.088	.16
48. Ireland	.087	.14
49. Morocco	.082	.14
50. Uruguay	.076	.11
51. Bulgaria	.070	.20
52. Iraq	.066	.09
53. Burma	.064	.07
54. Sudan	.062	.07

TABLE I *(Cont'd)*

MEMBERS IN ORDER OF THEIR PAYMENTS TO THE U.N. SYSTEM	PERCENT OF CONTRIBUTIONS	ASSESSMENT SCALE
55. Ghana	.057	.09
56. Ceylon	.053	.09
57. Jordan	.052	.04
58. Ecuador	.044	.06
59. Ethiopia	.043	.05
60. Lebanon	.042	.05
61. Malaya	.039	.13
62. Tunisia	.036	.05
63. Saudi Arabia	.035	.07
64. Afghanistan	.034	.05
65. El Salvador	.033	.04
66. Guatemala	.033	.05
67. Luxembourg	.032	.05
68. Libya	.032	.04
69. Costa Rica	.031	.04
70. Honduras	.029	.04
71. Dominican Republic	.028	.05
72. Haiti	.028	.04
73. Bolivia	.027	.04
74. Senegal	.026	.05
75. Panama	.025	.04
76. Laos	.025	.04
77. Guinea	.024	.04
78. Iceland	.024	.04
79. Nicaragua	.023	.04
80. Paraguay	.022	.04
81. Cambodia	.021	.04
82. Albania	.019	.04
83. Cameroon	.018	.04
84. Madagascar	.017	.04
85. Ivory Coast	.017	.04
86. Togo	.015	.04
87. Nepal	.015	.04
88. Congo (Leopoldville)	.014	.07
89. Yemen	.014	.04
90. Central African Republic	.014	.04
91. Mali	.013	.04
92. Cyprus	.013	.04
93. Congo (Brazzaville)	.013	.04
94. Upper Volta	.013	.04
95. Somalia	.013	.04
96. Chad	.012	.04
97. Gabon	.012	.04
98. Niger	.011	.04

TABLE I *(Cont'd)*

MEMBERS IN ORDER OF THEIR PAYMENTS TO THE U.N. SYSTEM	PERCENT OF CONTRIBUTIONS	ASSESSMENT SCALE
99. Dahomey	.011	.04
100. Syria	.011	.05
101. Mauritania	.010	.04
102. Mongolia	.010	.04
103. Sierra Leone	.010	.04
104. Tanganyika	.010	.04

Source: Norman J. Padelford. *"Financial Crisis and the Future of the United Nations,"* World Politics *(July 1963), pp. 538–539.*

total. The figures do not indicate what every state paid since a number were in arrears or in default on their peace-keeping assessments in 1962. They do represent what membership would have cost if each state had paid what was assigned to it after rebates, plus the voluntary contributions that it made. This way of expressing contributions as a percentage of the total received and due to the United Nations reveals a range of 46.91 percent for the highest contributor, the United States, to .01 percent for the smallest contributors. It further reveals that 13 states bore a higher percentage of the overall support than their ratios under the regular budget scale while 97 had a lower percentage. The "over-and-above" states included only two permanent members of the Security Council—the United States and the United Kingdom. The others were Canada, Sweden, the Netherlands, Turkey, Iran, Denmark, Norway, New Zealand, Liberia, the United Arab Republic, and Jordan. These 13 states were relatively large contributors to the voluntary programs. The Soviet bloc countries stood far below their assessment levels. Their failure to pay UNEF and ONUC assessments brought their payments down by a considerable margin even below these levels. France, China, and many of the newly admitted nations were also on the low side of the normal scale. In most instances, these meager contributions can be explained not so much by reasons of economic incapacity as by the political unwillingness of states to support the highly controversial peace-keeping operations in the Middle East and in the Congo.

❀   ❀   ❀   ❀   ❀   ❀   ❀

HIDDEN COSTS AND HIDDEN SAVINGS

To complete the overall picture of the costs of membership in the United Nations, two additional factors must be taken into account: first, the cost to member governments of maintaining missions in New York City and at the headquarters of some or all of the specialized agencies, and second, the financial implications for the United States of being host country to the United Nations as an illustration of benefits that accrue to host states.

Expenditures of member governments for their missions range from the costly establishments of the United States and the Soviet Union to the modest quarters of several small nations, some of which are unable to afford United Nations missions separate from their consular offices. In all cases, expenses include office rentals, residences for top personnel, equipment, communications, transportation, and entertainment. The average cost per member state for these items is approximately $100,000 a year, bringing the total amount to something over $10 million. In addition, there are staff salaries to be paid to roughly 700 permanent delegation members of diplomatic status, and to roughly 1,000 professional personnel. These salaries come to approximately another $10 million a year. To these items must be added the costs of several hundred governmental delegates and staff who come to New York City each year for the sessions of the General Assembly. Most member states also maintain small missions or liaison offices in Geneva and the host cities of the specialized agencies. All told, the overall "hidden costs" of membership in the United Nations may amount to roughly $25 million.

The largest expenses are, of course, incurred by the United States, the United Kingdom, and the Soviet Union. The costs of their missions and staff range between $1.5 million and $2 million a year. This, however, is only a small fraction of what these nations contribute to the regular budget of the Organization. As absolute amounts go down, relative costs in terms of regular budget assessments tend to increase, however. India's annual cost of $360,000 amounts to more than 25 percent; Mexico's expense of $270,000 is the equivalent of half of its regular assessment; in the case of Indonesia, the annual cost of its representation is the same as Mexico's, but that figure is equal to its entire regular budget contribution. A number of states pay more for their missions and staff than their contributions to the regular budget. Iraq, for example, pays five times the amount. Many of the new nations from Africa run expenses that are multiples of their assessments. Extreme cases are Liberia and the Congo (Brazzaville) whose "hidden expenses" run to ten times those under the regular budget.[1] Prestige factors and costs of public relations are chiefly responsible for this. It must also be remembered that, for certain of the newer nations, a United Nations mission may obviate the need for representation in some capitals where those nations might otherwise have to be represented.

Turning to the special case of the United States in order to evaluate the financial impact of United Nations Headquarters on that country, three different but related questions must be answered: What is the impact of United Nations Headquarters on the economy of New York City? What is its impact on the New York City budget? What is its impact on the American economy as a whole?

[1] The figures presented here are estimates conveyed by the missions to the author.

IMPACT OF PRESENCE OF UNITED NATIONS HEADQUARTERS ON NEW YORK CITY

It has often been said that the presence of the United Nations has made New York City the "capital of the world." This prestige has not remained altogether intangible. Indeed, a substantial amount of money flows into the economy of New York City every year as a direct result of the presence there of the United Nations. An estimate of specific items follows for the year 1962.

First, during 1962, the United Nations paid $40 million in salaries and wages to its staff. Of the 4,500 recipients, 3,000 were stationed at Headquarters. Their share was 64 percent, or $26 million. Assuming that approximately 5 percent or $1.3 million was spent abroad, the amount that flowed into the city was about $25 million. Second, UNICEF paid $1.4 million in salaries and wages. Allowing for a similar deduction, the city gained $1.3 million. Third, staff allowances of $2.3 million were paid. Allowing the same ratios as for salaries and the same deduction, the amount is $2.2 million. Fourth, the United Nations spent $2.5 million for travel of staff including appointments, transfers, and separations. Of this sum, 40 percent, or $1 million, may have been spent in New York. Fifth, the overhead expenses of the United Nations, including equipment, maintenance, operation, rentals, utilities, supplies, and services came to $9 million. The cost for Headquarters was about $7 million. Sixth, the maintenance of missions and staff discussed above comes to $25 million. Eighty percent of this amount, or roughly $20 million, flows into the city. Seventh, New York profits from the presence of journalists and representatives of nongovernmental organizations who are accredited to the United Nations. An estimate of $5,000 for each of the 250 permanently accredited journalists and of $1,000 for each transient journalist amounts to $2 million. In addition, 150 nongovernmental organization representatives are permanently residing in New York City. Their salaries plus those of several hundred transients add another $2 million.

Hence, if the above approximations are reasonable, an amount of more than $60 million flows into the economy of New York City as a result of the presence there of the United Nations.

The impact of the Organization on the New York City budget involves items on the plus and on the minus side. The city's obligation to provide added police protection is an example of the latter. During the Fifteenth Session of the General Assembly, an extraordinarily large number of heads-of-states, prime ministers, and other dignitaries congregated in New York City. This posed great problems for the police. The costs involved led to requests for a federal subsidy, which, in turn, led to a congressional hearing and a subsequent report from the city's Budget Director.

During the congressional hearings in 1961, several bills were introduced to reimburse the city for the extraordinary expenses involved. A second item that came up during the hearings was the question of tax loss as a result of the Headquarters agreement exempting the United Nations from taxation by the city. The Budget Director estimated this amount at $3.4 million. On the other hand, a spokesman for the United States Department of State pointed out that the property values in the United Nations area had increased enormously as a result of the presence of the Organization, thus providing the city with substantial additional sources of revenue.

* * * * * * *

IMPACT OF PRESENCE OF U.N. HEADQUARTERS ON THE UNITED STATES

The total picture shows that an annual amount of roughly $82 million accrues to the American economy primarily as a direct result of United Nations Headquarters location in New York. This "hidden saving" is slightly more than the combined United States assessments for the regular budget, UNEF, and ONUC in 1962. The presence of the International Bank for Reconstruction and Development and the International Monetary Fund in Washington, D.C., increases the above "saving."

It may be safely asserted that modest increments flow into the national economies of Switzerland, Italy, France, Canada, Great Britain, and Austria as a result of the location there of specialized and affiliated agency headquarters.

THE WORLD COURT ADVISORY OPINION

John G. Stoessinger[*]

The problem of financing peace-keeping operations did not remain confined to the political and fiscal realms of the United Nations. . . . [I]t also came before the world's highest judicial tribunal, the International Court of Justice. The judicial phase of the Organization's financial crisis is of sufficient importance to merit separate treatment. . . . [Now we] will analyze the majority and minority opinions on the main issues with which the Court had to deal, and explore the implications of the advisory opinion for the future of the United Nations.

When the General Assembly, on December 20, 1961, requested the World

[*] John G. Stoessinger, "The World Court Advisory Opinion," *Financing the United Nations System* (Washington, D.C.: The Brookings Institution, 1964), Chap. 6, pp. 140–156. © 1964 The Brookings Institution.

Court to give an advisory opinion, it asked for guidance on the following question:

Do the expenditures authorized in General Assembly resolutions . . . relating to the United Nations operations in the Congo . . . and to the operations of the United Nations Emergency Force . . . constitute expenses of the Organization within the meaning of Article 17, paragraph 2 of the Charter of the United Nations?

The World Court asked for written statements from the members of the United Nations, and received twenty-one such statements, as well as three letters whose authors referred to their governments' views previously expressed in discussions in the General Assembly. In May 1962, oral proceedings were held before the Court; nine states, whose views had already been communicated to the Court in the written statements, were represented in the oral proceedings. On July 20, 1962, the opinion of the Court was announced: by a vote of 9 to 5, the Court stated that the expenditures authorized in the General Assembly resolutions dealing with the financing of UNEF and ONUC "constituted 'expenses of the Organization' within the meaning of article 17, paragraph 2 of the Charter." Of the nine judges in the majority, three, Sir Percy Spender, Sir Gerald Fitzmaurice, and Gaetano Morelli, wrote separate opinions, and one, Judge Spiropoulos, made a separate declaration. Each of the five dissenting judges, President Winiarski, Jules Basdevant, V. Koretsky, Lucio M. Moreno Quintana, and J. L. Bustamante, wrote his own dissenting opinion.

THE DIALOGUE ON THE COURT

If the advisory opinion handed down on July 20, 1962, was one of the most significant in the history of the World Court, it was also one of the most fractured. There was disunity within the ranks of the majority as well as within the minority; the judges differed not only on their answers, but also on the way in which they felt the question should have been phrased by the General Assembly. All this gives an air of great complexity to the opinion. The arguments and conclusions of the five judges who spoke for the majority opinion, Vice-President Alfaro and Judges Badawi, Wellington Koo, Tanaka, and Jessup, will be considered first; then the four concurring and five dissenting opinions will be discussed.

The five majority judges at the outset rejected the contention that the alleged political character of the problem precluded a juridical opinion; they maintained that the request made of the Court was in keeping with the role of the Court: the interpretation of a treaty provision in the United Nations Charter. Next, the majority turned its attention to a French draft amendment that had been rejected by the Assembly during the debates in December 1961 on the question whether the Court ought to be asked for an advisory opinion. The French amendment would have asked a "previous" question: Were the Assembly resolutions themselves in conformity with the

Charter? In other words, France would have had the Court pronounce on the legality of the basic resolutions before deciding whether the costs incurred as a result of these resolutions were "expenses of the Organization." This draft amendment had been rejected because most delegations believed this distinction to be too blurred, or agreed with the delegate of Canada who maintained that it would be "invidious for . . . [the] Assembly to go to the Court and put into question a large number of its own decisions taken over a number of years."[1]

The majority opinion, in reference to the proposed French amendment, declared that the Assembly's rejection of it should not preclude an investigation of the resolutions themselves if the Court should find such an investigation relevant: "The Court must have full liberty to consider all relevant data available to it in forming an opinion in a question posed to it for an advisory opinion."[2]

The majority then turned to an examination of Article 17, paragraph 2 of the Charter in an attempt to identify "expenses of the Organization." Did these expenses imply "regular" and "administrative" expenses only? The majority noted that Article 17 (1) of the Charter spoke of the "budget" of the United Nations, while paragraph 3 of the same article spoke of the "administrative budgets" of the specialized agencies. Hence, the Court concluded that the framers of the Charter, recognizing a distinction between "administrative" and "operational" budgets, would have inserted the word "administrative" before "budget" in Article 17 (1) had they intended the budget to be limited to administrative expenses. Actually, the United Nations had from the beginning included operational items in the regular budget, such as the annual appropriations for "special missions and related activities," "unforeseen and extraordinary expenses" relating to the maintenance of peace and security, as well as a variety of expenses for technical assistance, programs of economic and social development, human rights activities, public administration, and narcotics drug control. There was therefore no basis for interpreting the term budget in its narrowest sense.

The five judges then examined Article 17 in relation to the general structure and intent of the Charter. They noted that Article 17 placed control over the finances of the United Nations in the General Assembly, and that the Assembly was not precluded from dealing with expenses relating to the maintenance of peace and security. They observed that, while the Security Council had primary responsibility for operations in this realm, its responsibility was not exclusive. When expenditures related to this end were not

[1] U.N. General Assembly, Sixteenth Session, *Official Records*, Annexes, Agenda Item No. 62 (1961); and U.N. Doc. A/PV.1086 (Dec. 20, 1961).

[2] International Court of Justice, *Certain Expenses of the United Nations (Article 17, paragraph 2, of the Charter), Advisory Opinion of 20 July 1962: I.C.J. Reports, 1962*, p. 157. (Cited hereinafter as *Opinion.*)

otherwise provided for, the Assembly had the authority to apportion them among member governments. The provision of Article 11, paragraph 2, whereby "any such question [relating to the maintenance of international peace and security] on which action is necessary shall be referred to the Security Council by the General Assembly either before or after discussion," did not restrict the Assembly's authority in all matters concerning peace and security. This article, declared the Court, referred to action of a coercive or enforcement character. But if the "action" was not of an enforcement nature, the last sentence of Article 11 (2) did not apply.

Article 43 of the Charter was also found inapplicable to the question at hand. The majority found that, while expenditures for enforcement action were within the sole authority of the Security Council, those of other actions relating to peace and security constituted "expenses of the Organization within the meaning of Article 17, paragraph 2."

The Court then passed on to an examination of the peace-keeping expenditures in terms of the overall purposes of the United Nations. It noted that an expenditure that was not made for one of the purposes of the Organization could not be viewed as an "expense of the Organization," but went on to say that if an expense was in harmony with the overall purpose of the United Nations, but was made "by the wrong organ, [this] was irregular as a matter of internal structure, but would not necessarily mean that the expense incurred was not an expense of the Organization." Cases in which the body corporate or politic might be bound by an *ultra vires* act of an agent were not unfamiliar to national and international law. Having said this, the Court proceeded to the two central questions: First, were UNEF and ONUC related to the purposes of the United Nations? Second, were these two peace-keeping operations the type of noncoercive, nonenforcement action that came under the jurisdiction of the General Assembly?

UNEF, the Court declared, had been created by the General Assembly without a single dissenting vote in order to promote and maintain peace and security in the Middle East. It had been established with the consent of the states most intimately concerned, including that of the host state, Egypt, and its duties had clearly been envisaged as noncoercive in character. Hence, the Emergency Force was obviously not an enforcement measure. The Court dismissed the view that the establishment of a separate account for UNEF's expenses implied that the funds were not to be derived from contributions assessed on the members of the General Assembly. The majority thus concluded that, since the inception of UNEF, its costs were to be regarded as expenses of the Organization within the meaning of Article 17 (2).

Turning to the operation in the Congo, the Court pointed out that ONUC had been initially authorized by the Security Council without a dissenting vote, and that it had been invited by the government of the Congo in order to maintain international peace and security. The Court rejected the argument that the resolution establishing ONUC violated fundamental Charter provisions, which endowed the Security Council rather than the Secretary-General with the authority to carry out decisions involving the maintenance of peace and security. After reviewing the various resolutions pertaining to the operation, the majority concluded:

In the light of such a record of reiterated consideration, confirmation, approval and ratification by the Security Council and by the General Assembly of the actions of the Secretary-General . . . it is impossible to reach the conclusion that the operations in question usurped or impinged upon the prerogatives conferred by the Charter on the Security Council. The Charter does not forbid the Security Council to act through instruments of its own choice: under Article 29 it may establish such subsidiary organs as it deems necessary for the performance of its functions; under Article 98 it may entrust "other functions" to the Secretary-General.[3]

Moreover, since ONUC's operations did not entail the use of armed force against a state that the Security Council, under Article 39, had defined as an aggressor or peace-breaker, and since ONUC did not take military action against a state, its actions, like those of UNEF, did not involve "enforcement measures." Hence, the Security Council did not have exclusive jurisdiction in the matter.

Thus, as in the case of UNEF, the majority came to the conclusion that the costs of ONUC were to be regarded as "expenses of the Organization." The Court was not deterred by the fact that the Assembly had twice decided "that the extraordinary expenses for the United Nations in the Congo [were] essentially different in nature from the expenses of the Organization under the regular budget and that therefore a procedure different from that applied in the case of the regular budget [was] required for meeting these extraordinary expenses." The majority felt that its conclusions were supported by the two Assembly resolutions themselves, which had stated that the decision to use the regular scale of assessment had been made "pending the establishment of a different scale of assessment to defray the extraordinary expenditure: The only alternative—and that means the 'different procedure'— contemplated was another *scale* of assessment and not some method other than assessment. 'Apportionment' and 'assessment' are terms which relate only to the General Assembly's authority under Article 17."

An examination of the text of Article 17 (2) of the Charter thus led the majority to the conclusions that UNEF and ONUC were in keeping with the purposes of the Organization, that they were noncoercive in character, and that, therefore, the expenditures incurred by them were to be regarded as "expenses" within the meaning of Article 17 of the Charter.

The majority opinion was supported by four concurring opinions. Judge Spiropoulos, in an explanatory "declaration," answered the Assembly's ques-

[3] *Ibid.*, pp. 176–177.

tion in the affirmative on the ground that the expenditures had been incurred by a two-thirds vote of the Assembly for what were clearly legitimate purposes of the United Nations. He felt that the Assembly's rejection of the proposed French amendment indicated that it did not wish that the Court concern itself with the "prior" question of the legal validity of the resolutions themselves. Similarly, Judges Spender and Morelli declared that the validity of the resolutions themselves was not relevant since the expenditures they authorized clearly came within the meaning of Article 17. Judge Fitzmaurice, while concurring with the majority, indicated that "although given expenditures [were] expenses of the Organization, there may not necessarily or always be an obligation for every Member State to contribute to them." He suggested that "expenses of the United Nations" could broadly be divided into obligatory and permissive ones, the former being of a peace-keeping nature and the latter economic and social in character. The former type of expense should be shared by all members, but dissenters should not be bound to contribute to the latter. He warned that unless Article 17 were interpreted in this more restricted sense, "the Assembly could vote enormous expenditures, and thereby place a heavy financial burden even on dissenting States, and as a matter of obligation even in the case of non-essential activities. This would be reading a lot into such a provision as Article 17, paragraph 2."

Of the dissenting justices, Judge Koretsky expressed the most radical opposition to the majority and concurring opinions. To him, the entire issue appeared fundamentally as a political, rather than a legal one. The resolutions authorizing the UNEF and ONUC expenditures were invalid and themselves based on prior resolutions that had been carried out illegally. He considered UNEF and ONUC as enforcement actions falling within the meaning of Article 39 since there had been breaches of the peace and acts of aggression involved. He rejected the majority's narrower interpretation of enforcement action and saw the two operations as destructive to the balance established by the Charter between the Security Council and the Assembly, a balance that gave the primary role in peace and security operations to the former. Hence, since the operations had been conceived and carried out in direct violation of the Charter, there existed no obligation to pay for them.

President Winiarski also denied the legality of the UNEF and ONUC resolutions. He pointed out that not only had many members refused to pay because they thought the operations to be illegal, but the resolutions themselves had preserved a separation "between the normal administrative expenses of the Organization and those called for by exceptional circumstances." And even if the expenditures in question were "expenses of the Organization," no legal obligation to pay necessarily followed, since resolutions of the Assembly had the status of recommendations only.

Judges Moreno Quintana and Bustamante felt that the "previous" question of the validity of the Assembly resolutions themselves was at the heart of the matter and deplored the fact that the proposed French amendment, which would have clarified the issue, had been rejected by the Assembly. Judge Quintana indicated that the resolutions had been illegal for "any use of armed force intended for whatever purpose implie[d] by definition enforcement action." According to Judge Basdevant, the Assembly's failure to ask this more basic "previous" question had led to inexactness in the way in which the request for an advisory opinion had been framed. This failure of the Assembly to comply with Article 65, paragraph 2, of the Statute of the Court requiring "an exact statement of the question upon which an opinion is required," made it impossible for Judge Basdevant to concur with the majority.

THE ADVISORY OPINION AND THE CHARTER

An analysis of the advisory opinion suggests three fundamental constitutional issues on which the arguments of the fourteen judges hinged. An attempt to cull these basic principles from the legal labyrinth of the arguments may make it easier to assess the opinion's contribution. These basic issues seem to be: first, the legal role of the General Assembly in the realm of peace and security operations; second, the nature of the Assembly's fiscal powers; and third, the role of the Court itself in interpreting the Charter.

On the first issue, the Court clearly affirmed the right of the Assembly to establish subsidiary organs for the purpose of maintaining international peace and security. The "primary" responsibility of the Security Council in this realm was admitted but limited to the kind of "action" that was "indicated by the title of Chapter VII of the Charter, namely 'Action with respect to threats to the peace, breaches of the peace, and acts of aggression.'" Recommendations made by the Assembly or the Council establishing subsidiary organs for peace and security purposes were not enforcement actions. Both UNEF and ONUC had been established on the basis of such recommendations. The Court implied that when the nature of the action in question was somewhat obscure, the decision should be governed by the fundamental and overriding purpose of the Organization, the maintenance of peace and security. It rejected the concept of a rigid separation of functions between the Security Council and the General Assembly.

As mentioned above, two judges in the minority rejected, and the three others seriously questioned, the competence of the Assembly in matters of peace and security. They felt that the separation of powers between the General Assembly and the Security Council should be maintained.

An analysis of the opposing positions on this issue reveals striking similarities to the debates preceding the "Uniting for Peace" Resolution in 1950. During these discussions, the majority of the member states had asserted the competence of the Assembly to consider any case in which "there appear[ed] to be a threat to the peace, breach, or act of aggression," with respect to which the Council, "because of the lack of unanimity of the permanent members, fail[ed] to exercise its primary responsibility." Indeed, the "Uniting for Peace" Resolution had formalized this view over the objections of the Soviet Union.

     ❉   ❉   ❉   ❉   ❉   ❉   ❉

The arguments of the majority judges and the objections of Judges Koretsky and Winiarski were in fact a repetition of the arguments over the "Uniting for Peace" Resolution. The majority opinion in effect reaffirmed the principles of that resolution, and the minority with equal determination wished to prevent any such extension of the General Assembly's mandate.

It may well be that the most significant contribution of the opinion was in the second fundamental problem area: the Assembly's fiscal powers. The Court found no limitation on the Assembly's authority in the financing of peace-keeping operations that did not constitute enforcement action:

The provisions of the Charter which distribute functions and powers to the Security Council and to the General Assembly give no support to the view that such distribution excludes from the powers of the General Assembly the power for the financing of measures designed to maintain peace and security.

The financial powers of the Assembly, declared the Court, extended to all financial requirements of the organization, as long as these requirements were consonant with the purposes of the United Nations and outside the purview of Chapter VII.

In its reasoning on this matter, the Court relied heavily on the principle of ultimate effectiveness, determined in this instance by the overall purposes of the United Nations. This was not without precedent in the history of the Court. For example, the real basis of the Court's Advisory Opinion in 1949 on *Reparation for Injuries Suffered in the Service of the United Nations* was the assumption that certain powers must be implied in the Charter as being essential to the purposes of the Organization: "Under international law, the Organization must be deemed to have those powers which, though not expressly provided in the Charter, are conferred upon it by necessary implication as being essential to the performance of its duties."

The Court broadened this interpretation even further in 1962 by asserting, as noted above, that even if the financial action had been taken by the wrong organ, this did not necessarily mean that the expense incurred was not an expense of the Organization. Both national and international law contemplated cases in which the body corporate or politic may be bound, as to third parties, by the *ultra vires* act of an agent.

A survey of the literature on the doctrine of *ultra vires* reveals considerable conflict of opinion. On the one hand, a distinguished group of international lawyers—Anzilotti, Cavagliori, Bittner, Verdross, Basdevant, and Willoughby—maintain that the *ultra vires* act of an agent does not legally bind the body corporate. On the other hand, an equally distinguished group of writers—Strupp, Schücking, Politis, de Visscher, Challey, Hyde, and Kosters—hold the opposite view. The advisory opinion clearly aligned the Court with the latter group.

In view of the great financial powers which the majority opinion saw fit to vest in the General Assembly, it followed quite logically that the Court should regard the assessments imposed by the Assembly for UNEF and ONUC as legally binding obligations on the entire membership. In this connection, the Court noted carefully that:

> . . . The functions and powers conferred by the Charter on the General Assembly [were] not confined to discussion, consideration, the initiation of studies and the making of recommendations; they [were] not merely hortatory. Article 18 dealing with *"decisions"* [did] indeed include certain recommendations, but others [had] dispositive force and effect. Among these latter decisions, Article 18 include[d] suspension of rights and privileges of membership, expulsion of Members, and "budgetary question."[4]

The Court noted further that the "decision" to approve the budget had a close connection with paragraph 2 of Article 17,

> . . . since thereunder the General Assembly [was] also given the power to apportion the expenses among the Members and the exercise of the power of apportionment creates the obligation, specifically stated in Article 17, paragraph 2, of each Member to bear that part of the expenses which is apportioned to it by the General Assembly. When these expenses include expenditures for the maintenance of peace and security, which are not otherwise provided for, it is the General Assembly which has the authority to apportion the latter amounts among the Members.[5]

The majority was especially careful in presenting its case for the legally binding effect of the UNEF and ONUC assessments, and the minority was especially bent on disproving that assertion. The Court was not alone in its disagreement on this matter. This is readily demonstrated by a survey of the literature on the subject.

In Sir Hersch Lauterpacht's view, there are two kinds of legal obligation: some are "rudimentary, elastic and imperfect . . . intangible and almost nominal," such as the obligation of member states to give due consideration in good faith to resolutions of the Assembly. Others are "automatic" and require that "full effect" be given to them. He stressed that "in some matters,

---

[4] *Opinion,* p. 163.
[5] *Ibid.,* p. 164.

such as the . . . *approval of the budget and the apportionment of expenses,* the full legal effects of the Resolutions of the General Assembly are undeniable."[6] James L. Brierly writes that *"apart from its control over the budget,* all that the General Assembly can do is to discuss and recommend and initiate studies and consider reports from other bodies."[7] Francis O. Wilcox and Carl M. Marcy agree with this dictum, but Hans Kelsen goes further: the term "recommendation" in the Charter may have several meanings. A recommendation of the General Assembly in the field of the maintenance of international peace and security may possibly be binding. Leland M. Goodrich and Edvard Hambro declare that Article 17(2) "empowers the General Assembly to apportion the expenses of the United Nations among the Members and places the members *under the obligation* to bear these expenses." Finally, Daniel S. Cheever and H. Field Haviland express a practical view on Assembly resolutions: "It is not so much their legal character as 'recommendations' which determines their effectiveness but rather the quality, quantity and intensity of community support behind them."[8]

It is fairly clear from the above cross-section of opinion, that a majority of jurists and scholars seem to feel that, while there are definite limits to the Assembly's authority, its resolutions pertaining to financing and apportionment of expenses are legally binding in character. The advisory opinion further strengthens this interpretation.

The third contribution of the opinion may be found in its relevance to the evolving body of international constitutional law on the United Nations Charter. The Court was asked by the General Assembly to interpret a treaty provision. This had occurred several times in the past. In that sense, the advisory opinion of 1962 was not unorthodox and "seemed to fit comfortably within the scope of accepted judicial interpretation."[9] But the Court has never been the sole interpreter of the Charter. No agreement had been reached at San Francisco on the question: By whom is the Charter to be

[6] *Voting Procedure on Questions Relating to Reports and Petitions Concerning the Territory of South-West Africa,* I.C.J. *Reports,* 1955, p. 115. Italics added. F. Blaine Sloane, "The Binding Force of a 'Recommendation' of the General Assembly of the United Nations," *British Yearbook of International Law,* Vol. XXV (1948), pp. 1–33, agrees with Lauterpacht's view.

[7] *The Law of Nations: An Introduction to the International Law of Peace* (5th ed., Oxford University Press, 1955), p. 107. Italics added.

[8] D. S. Cheever and H. F. Haviland, *Organizing for Peace: International Organization in World Affairs* (Houghton, 1954), p. 89. The Court in its opinion also seemed to be aware of the importance of community support behind a resolution by stressing the fact that UNEF and ONUC were created without dissenting votes and financed time and again by two-thirds majorities.

[9] James Fergusson Hogg, "Peace-Keeping Costs and Charter Obligations—Implications of the International Court of Justice Decision on Certain Expenses of the United Nations," *Columbia Law Review,* Vol. LXII (November 1962), p. 1246.

interpreted authoritatively? This power was not bestowed unequivocally on any one organ of the United Nations. In this connection, one authority has written:

The easiest, the most primitive, and the most unsatisfactory solution is to say that each individual Member has the right to decide for itself how to interpret the Charter. . . . The next solution is that each organ of the United Nations should decide its own competence. This is in practice what happens in the Constitution of many individual State.[10]

The latter course of action is in effect what has happened in practice at the United Nations. The 1962 advisory opinion contributed further to the evolving trend of interpreting the Charter through combined action of the Assembly and the Court. One seems to be on sound legal grounds when maintaining that interpretation of the Charter has been achieved when the Court adds its support to the position taken on repeated occasions by a two-thirds vote of the General Assembly, and the Assembly in turn accepts the Court's opinion. Whether the Assembly's request for an advisory opinion in 1962 and the Court's subsequent role were politically wise in addition to being legally sound is a question that is far more difficult to answer.

THE ADVISORY OPINION AND THE FINANCIAL CRISIS

It is not easy to evaluate the impact of the advisory opinion on the financial structure of the United Nations. The Court has confirmed the Assembly's role in peace-keeping activities and has also underwritten its authority to impose legally binding assessments on the member states. This means that, in financing peace-keeping activities, a two-thirds majority of the General Assembly may bind the entire membership, including those states that vote against. In that sense, the opinion signifies a tentative step toward the principle of international taxation of states by the world community. More broadly, it lends support to the principle of majority rule in international relations. The Court also gave the Assembly or the Security Council free reign to establish other noncoercive forces in the future and to arrange for their financial support, provided they are in accord with the purposes of the United Nations. On the whole, therefore, the Court gave its approval to Dag Hammarskjöld's conception of the United Nations as a "dynamic instrument" capable of "executive action" toward "increasingly effective forms of active international cooperation," as against the notion of the Organization as a mere "static conference machinery."

The practical effect of the opinion on the treasury of the United Nations is not likely to be too significant. Although the seventeenth General Assem-

---

[10] Pollex, "The Interpretation of the Charter of the United Nations," *British Yearbook of International Law, 1946*, pp. 50–57.

bly decided to "accept" the opinion by a large majority of 76 in favor, 17 against, with 8 abstentions, while the sixteenth had requested it by a vote of only 52 in favor, 11 against, with 32 abstentions, the politically motivated delinquents have not been eager to abide by the opinion. A considerable number of other nations in arrears, on the other hand, were guided by the opinion and cleared their accounts. . . . But their payments amounted to only a small part of the unpaid assessments.

The opinion also makes it possible for the Assembly to invoke sanctions if it chooses to do so. The Court has not pronounced on this matter, and there is no precedent for sanctions in the United Nations. As noted in the preceding chapter, the heart of the problem of sanctions is not legal, but political. To ignore the possibility of invoking Article 19 altogether would be to ignore the implications of the advisory opinion; but to insist on sanctions might lead to an exodus of disgruntled states from the United Nations. On balance, if Article 19 has to be invoked, it should be made clear that the thrust of the sanction is not against a given state, but for the law of the Charter.

The political import of the opinion was reflected in each of the ten different statements. All the judges labored under the difficulty of applying legal tools to what was also a controversial political issue. It is true that the Assembly asked the Court a legal question; but it is equally true that its request for an advisory opinion was also an attempt to exert pressure on a stubborn minority. It is probably not an accident that all the judges save one —Judge Badawi of the United Arab Republic—took voting positions that were congruent with those of their national governments.

In its broadest form, the issue at stake may be described as that of majority rule versus state sovereignty. The advisory opinion advanced the cause of the former and, by so doing, affirmed the power of the General Assembly. It in effect reversed the stand taken by the Permanent Court of International Justice in 1927 in the Lotus case, which had asserted the principle that limitations on the sovereignty of states cannot be presumed, with its implication that what is not explicitly surrendered by states is retained. This great power of the Assembly may be used constructively and with a sense of fiscal responsibility; but, as Judge Fitzmaurice warned, it could also be used by impatient majorities eager to push vast economic and social programs to impose large assessments on a reluctant minority by deciding that such expenditures were "expenses of the Organization appropriate for the fulfillment of one of the stated purposes of the UN." Majority rule per se does not guarantee progress toward order in the relations of states. Nor will the advisory opinion clear the way for a definitive solution of the financial crisis. But it may be an important building block if the Assembly chooses to build on it with wisdom, prudence, and imagination.

BEHIND THE U.N. FINANCIAL CRISIS

G. Morozov and Y. Pchelintsev*

. . . In contrast to the League of Nations Covenant, the U.N. Charter delineates the powers of the General Assembly and the Security Council in the maintenance of international peace and security, it empowers the General Assembly to consider the general principles of co-operation in the maintenance of international peace and security (Article 11, Paragraph 1), to *discuss* any questions relating to the maintenance of international peace and security, and to *make recommendations* with regard to any such question to the state or states concerned or to the Security Council or to both (Article 11 [2]).

But no powers are conferred on the Assembly to take decisions concerning *any action* for the maintenance of international peace and security. Article 11, Paragraph 2, is absolutely specific on this point and contains a provision ruling out the possibility of any other reading. It says: "Any such question on which action is necessary shall be referred to the Security Council by the General Assembly either before or after discussion."

This provision, together with the provisions of Articles 24 and 39, vest *exclusive powers* in the Security Council in determining the existence of any threat to the peace, breach of the peace, or any act of aggression and in deciding on the measures to be applied (whether or not involving action by air, sea or land forces) to maintain or restore international peace and security. The Security Council's sole competence in these matters means that such measures may not be taken by any other U.N. organ, including the General Assembly.

The Western Powers have tried to prove that the General Assembly decision setting up the U.N. Emergency Force in the Middle East was legal and legitimate by references to the notorious General Assembly Resolution 377 (V) of November 3, 1950, which bears the demagogic title of United Actions for Peace and which was pushed through by the imperialist Powers at the Fifth General Assembly with the aid of their voting machine. They now say it has empowered the General Assembly—in the event of a breach of the peace or act of aggression—to adopt decisions on measures involving the use of armed force to maintain or restore international peace and secu-

* G. Morozov and Y. Pchelintsev, "Behind the U.N. 'Financial Crisis,'" *International Affairs* (Moscow), June 1964, pp. 23–29.

G. Morozov is a member of the Soviet delegation to the United Nations.

Y. Pchelintsev has been a member of the Soviet delegation to the United Nations.

rity, should the Security Council fail to apply the necessary measures because of disagreement among its permanent members.

However, the Soviet Union has always said that Resolution 377 (V) violates the basic principles of the U.N. Charter, and therefore cannot be regarded as valid or as having any juridical consequences. No clause of the Charter can be amended by any General Assembly resolution (least of all by the clause adopted in contravention of the Charter and in face of the objections of a whole group of states). The only way to amend the Charter is to follow the procedures laid down by its Chapter XVIII.

It follows that the General Assembly decision setting up the U.N. Emergency Force in the Middle East was taken in violation of the U.N. Charter and in circumvention of the Security Council. In virtue of this it cannot be accepted as legitimate or as imposing any obligations on U.N. members to contribute to the cost of maintaining the U.N. Emergency Force in the Middle East.

* * * * * * *

Western spokesmen have been making a similar effort to confuse the issue of dispatching U.N. troops to the Congo. They say these troops were sent to help resolve the Congo's internal difficulties and establish law and order. Nothing could be farther from the truth.

* * * * * * *

The Security Council set the U.N. armed force an absolutely clear-cut task, that of helping the Congo to fight aggression on the part of Belgium, and safeguard the independence and territorial integrity of the young republic.

There was no abuse in that case of the Security Council's exclusive powers to decide on the measures to be taken to maintain or restore international peace and security, but the Charter was observed only in the adoption of the resolution by the Security Council. All the subsequent acts in fulfilment of the resolution entailed gross violations of the Charter and the U.N. task in the Congo.

Article 48 of the U.N. Charter says: "The action required to carry out the decisions of the Security Council for the maintenance of international peace and security shall be taken by all the members of the United Nations, or by some of them, as the Security Council may determine." This means that the Security Council, and it alone, has the power to decide which U.N. members are to take part in the action in pursuance of the Council's decisions. The Charter does not confer such powers on any other U.N. organ.

The Charter also places on the Security Council primary responsibility for the employment and command of any U.N. Armed Forces.

This flows directly from its Article 46, which says: "Plans for the application of armed force shall be made by the Security Council with the assistance of the Military Staff Committee." The fact that the Charter mentions assistance by the Military Staff Committee in the exercise of these functions merely goes to accentuate the Council's primary responsibility, because, according to the Charter, the Military Staff Committee is a consultative organ and is in all matters subordinate to the Security Council.

The Security Council's primary responsibility for the employment and command of armed forces was reaffirmed in a number of agreed points contained in a report by the Military Staff Committee, entitled General Principles Governing the Organisation of the Armed Forces Made Available to the Security Council by Member Nations of the United Nations.

* * * * * * *

One conclusion follows from what has been said. Since the formation of the U.N. Emergency Force and its operations in the Middle East and the Congo entailed violations of imperative provisions of the Charter, there can be no question at all of U.N. members bearing the expense of such operations.

In effect, for quite a long time this question did not even arise but since the expense of maintaining the U.N. Armed Forces grew so much, the Western Powers tried to make all U.N. members share the burden and suggested that the General Assembly was the only U.N. organ possessing powers in financial matters.

What followed is a matter of common knowledge. When the Secretary-General, ignoring the Security Council, asked the Assembly for appropriations to cover the cost of the U.N. operations, it went well beyond its powers and adopted the unlawful resolution imposed on it by the Western Powers. At the 17th General Assembly the Western Powers made use of an advisory opinion handed down by simple majority of the International Court of Justice and secured a resolution to the effect that the expenditures on the Congo and Middle East operations were deemed to be expenses within the meaning of Article 17, Paragraph 2, of the Charter. At the Fourth Special General Assembly, held in the summer of 1963, the imperialist Powers pushed through another series of unlawful decisions, including the far-reaching resolution 1874 (S-IV) entitled General Principles To Serve As Guidelines for the Sharing of the Costs of Future Peace-keeping Operations Involving Heavy Expenditures.

In their efforts to make out a case for the General Assembly's right to apportion expenses on U.N. operations in the maintenance of peace in general, and operations in the Middle East and the Congo in particular, the Western Powers argued that the General Assembly had exclusive—and virtually unlimited—powers in financial matters. The Netherland's delegate told the International Court of Justice that, "no limitation whatsoever of this [Assembly's—Ed.] fiscal power is provided for in the text of the Charter itself."

But this thesis will not bear scrutiny. The powers of each U.N. organ are strictly defined by the Charter and the only way to enlarge them is to employ the procedure stated in Articles 108 and 109 of the Charter itself. The idea that the Assembly's financial powers are unlimited has only one meaning: it is an attempt to confer on the Assembly supranational powers in financial matters which it does not possess.

Nor will the idea of the Assembly's exclusive financial powers hold any water. The Western Powers refer to Article 17, Paragraph 2, of the Charter in their efforts to prove that the General Assembly alone is empowered to apportion expenses on U.N. operations in the maintenance of peace.

Article 17, Paragraph 2, deals with the Assembly's power to apportion expenses between U.N. members, but what kind of expenses? Do they include expenses on operations in the maintenance or restoration of international peace? Both the documents connected with the framing of the relevant provisions of the Charter, and U.N. practices until quite recently offer convincing evidence that the expenses dealt with in Article 17, Paragraph 2, are the Organisation's ordinary administrative expenses, whereas the expenses on operations of the U.N. Armed Forces come under the head of extraordinary expenses.

Back in 1945, the First Committee of the Second Commission of the San Francisco Conference rejected Australia's amendment to Article 19 proposing that this article should be extended to cover expenses connected with the fulfilment of obligations by U.N. members in implementing practical measures in the maintenance of peace.[1]

This means that the framers of the Charter did not regard the expenses on U.N. operations in the maintenance of peace as expenses within the meaning of Article 17, Paragraph 2. This is confirmed, among others, by the well-known commentators of the Charter, Goodrich and Hambro (both of whom attended the San Francisco Conference). They say the expenses referred to in Article 17, Paragraph 2, "do not include the cost of enforcement action."[2]

Article 43, together with other relevant articles of the Charter, in particular, Article 24, Paragraph 1, Articles 39 and 42, Article 48, Paragraph 1, and Article 50, is the legal basis of the Security Council's powers to apportion expenses for operations in the maintenance of peace.

Article 50 calls for a special analysis. It says that every state has the right to consult the Security Council about any special economic problems arising from the carrying out of preventive or enforcement measures against any state by the United Nations. These problems may naturally be extremely various but the text does not, at any rate, rule out the possibility of the article applying to the cost of operations by U.N. Armed Forces, since sharing in such cost may well confront many states with special economic problems.

---

[1] *Documents of the United Nations Conference on International Organization*. San Francisco, 1945, Vol. XII, p. 513; see also Vol. VIII, pp. 453, 470–471 and 476.

[2] L. M. Goodrich, E. Hambro, *Charter of the United Nations. Commentary and Documents*. Second and Revised Ed., Boston, 1949, p. 184.

Some of the circumstances in which Article 50 was adopted in San Francisco are worth recalling here. An amendment was made to Chapter VIII, Section B, Paragraph 11 of the Dumbarton Oaks Draft (the paragraph now appears as Article 50 of the U.N. Charter) laying down that the cost of carrying out enforcement measures should be borne by the guilty state.[3]

This proposal was supported by a number of other states, with the U.S. delegate alone objecting to the amendment. He sought to prove that if this principle were accepted to the exclusion of all others it might create obstacles for the normal implementation of enforcement measures by the Council, and added that Article 50 "already provided for the relief of economic hardship which might be incurred by some states as a result of their participation in enforcement measures." While all the conferees agreed with this interpretation of Article 50, they did not regard the U.S. objection to the amendment as constituting an objection to imposing the burden of material responsibility on the guilty state. Additional evidence of this is the fact that the principle was included in the report of the relevant committee.[4]

* * * * * * *

How much weight should be attached to the Court's advisory opinions, including the one in question? The U.N. Charter allows the General Assembly and the Security Council, and any of the U.N. organs and specialised agencies which may be so authorised by the General Assembly, to request advisory opinions of the Court of *legal* questions. This should be especially emphasised because the question of financing the U.N. operations in the Middle East and the Congo, as several members of the International Court showed, was not a legal question but a political one.

But . . . what needs to be stressed here is that the U.N. Charter does not confer on the International Court any powers to dictate its will to the other principal organs and member states of the United Nations. The Court's advisory opinions are not legally binding on the states. If this were otherwise, it would clash with the principle of sovereign equality on which the United Nations rests, and would turn the Court into a supranational seat of judgement.

What it all amounts to is that the Court's advisory opinions are simply advice tendered by expert legal counsel which is not binding. Be it noted, incidentally, that the advisory opinion in question was adopted by nine votes to five, with the President of the Court, Winiarski, voting against. The U.N. Charter, which is an international covenant of a special type and significance is subject to a special procedure of interpretation. The majority of the International Court were forced to admit this highly important fact, although they did not say it in so many words. What they said was: "Pro-

---

[3] *Documents of the United Nations Conference on International Organization*, San Francisco, 1945, Vol. III, p. 478.

[4] *Ibid.*, Vol. XII, pp. 393, 513.

posals made during the drafting of the Charter to place the ultimate authority to interpret the Charter in the International Court of Justice were not
accepted; the opinion which the Court is in course of rendering is an
advisory opinion."[5]

Quite apart from the fact that references to this advisory opinion as
juridical ground binding the states to pay for U.N. operations are invalid
for general reasons of principle, the opinion itself needs analysing in substance.

In this case the Court went beyond its powers by taking cognisance of a
patently political question, and this predetermined the erroneous and ground-
less assertions and conclusions set forth in its advisory opinion. This aspect
of the matter was noted by several members of the Court, above all the
prominent Soviet jurist, member of the Academy of Sciences of the Ukrainian Republic, V. M. Koretsky, who wrote a detailed and well-argumented
dissenting opinion, and also by Bustamante of Peru.[6]

In taking cognisance of this question, the Court ignored other essential
circumstances. When the Plenary Meeting of the General Assembly on
December 20, 1961, debated the matter of requesting the International Court
for the advisory opinion in question, the French delegation motioned an
amendment to the draft resolution requesting the Court to examine whether
or not the expenses for U.N. operations in the Middle East and the Congo
were in line with the U.N. Charter. Without going into the French motives
for tabling such an amendment, it should be said that the question was in-
disputably a legitimate one. The Assembly rejected the amendment, while
the Court, although mentioning it briefly in the opening lines of its advisory
opinion, in effect skipped this important point.

As President of the Court Winiarski said, the General Assembly's resolutions sanctioned expenses for U.N. operations without referring to the
Articles of the Charter on which these resolutions were based. This is a
tell-tale fact. Can a law be applied without any specific references being
made to it? If it can, then this leaves the way open for arbitrary acts. However, the majority of the Court failed to give a proper assessment of this.

Another essential thing the Court ignored was that the Assembly made
its request *post factum*, that is, after it had passed a number of illegal
resolutions sanctioning the said expenses. By ignoring this fact, the majority
of the International Court took the attitude of encouraging such inadmissible
General Assembly practices.

[5] *Certain Expenses of the United Nations (Article 17, Paragraph 2, of the Charter).
Advisory Opinion of 20 July 1962: I.C.J. Reports 1962*, p. 168. The Second Committee
of the Fourth Commission at San Francisco said in its report: "It is to be understood,
of course, that if an interpretation made by any organ of the Organisation or by a Committee of Jurists is not generally acceptable it will be without binding force." (*Documents
of the United Nations Conference on International Organisation*. Vol. XIII, p. 710).

[6] *Certain Expenses of the United Nations (Article 17, Paragraph 2, of the Charter).
Advisory Opinion of 20 July 1962: I.C.J. Reports 1962*, pp. 254, 283, 307.

The positive answer given by the advisory opinion, handed down at the General Assembly's request, was designed to legalise the unlawful practice of expending funds on U.N. operations in the Middle East and the Congo. The main line of reasoning, the whole grounds for this opinion, has an absolutely unlawful premise and is based on equally unfounded arguments. The advisory opinion is in effect an attack on the constitutional structure of the United Nations, and tries to destroy the system of the U.N. principal organs and break down division of their powers.

In order to legalise the General Assembly's unlawful acts, the authors of the advisory opinion put a highly biased interpretation on the meaning of "the expenses of the Organisation," as provided for by Article 17 of the U.N. Charter; they make a play on the term "administrative budgets," used in Paragraph 3 of Article 17 in relation to specialised agencies, and set it in opposition to the term "the budget of the Organisation," which occurs in Paragraph 1 of the same Article.[7] They deduce that the Charter implies that the expenses on operations by the U.N. Emergency Force are to be included in the Organisation's regular budget.

But this conclusion is far-fetched, to say the least, for if the framers of the Charter had anything of the sort in mind they would undoubtedly have said as much, since expenses arising from emergencies are unquestionably of greater importance than the expenses of specialised agencies. The whole point is that the Charter contains the special Chapter VII dealing with all matters connected with U.N. action with respect to threats to the peace, breaches of the peace and acts of aggression, and its Article 43 provides all the grounds for making a special examination, approving and apportioning the appropriate expenses.

In other words, the International Court's advisory opinion gives an absolutely unacceptable interpretation of U.N. expenses, and its authors seem to realise that they are on shaky ground. There can be no other meaning to the following statement which appears in the advisory opinion: "If the action was taken by the wrong organ, it was irregular as a matter of that internal structure, but this would not necessarily mean that the expense incurred was not an expense of the Organisation."[8]

The above is probably the most glaring evidence of the groundlessness of the Court's advisory opinion, for it flouts generally accepted rules and common sense itself by openly sanctioning arbitrary acts and breaches of the U.N. Charter.

[7] Ibid., p. 159.
[8] Ibid., p. 168.

CHAPTER 10

THE POLITICAL PROCESS

"Authorship and sponsorship are
. . . key factors in the politics of
legislation." This is the conclusion
of A. Glenn Mower, Jr., in his
study, "The Sponsorship of Pro-
posals in the United Nations Gen-
eral Assembly." Mower discusses
the process whereby proposals are
formulated and sponsored and
identifies the various types of
sponsors as to their meanings and
roles. No student will have a
thorough grasp of the dynamics
of international organization un-
less he is familiar with the general
diplomatic strategies employed by
the permanent delegates. He will
miss the propaganda potential
proposals provide, the policy in-
terests that can be advanced, and
the initiative and maneuver which
are all a part of the UN political
game. A careful observer of the
art of sponsorship will not only
learn much about international
organizations but also will develop
understanding of what could be
called the personality of delega-
tions.

262   INTERNAL ASPECTS OF ORGANIZATION

Another important aspect of international organization is revealed in the study by Yash Tandon, "The Peaceful Settlement of International Disputes." Tandon notes that much of the UN procedure has developed in a highly pragmatic fashion and that, as usual in such a circumstance, those techniques which have been successful have been continued. Yet where peace keeping has been involved, it has been necessary to avoid behavior inappropriately borrowed from inapposite circumstances, and to recognize the importance of flexibility. This requirement was revealed in the use of good offices in the Indonesian, Palestine, and India-Pakistan disputes, as well as in others.

The author classifies different kinds of disputes (for example, cold-war, colonial, and internal with international effects) and suggests improvements which can be made in the settlement of each. He does not suggest any significant changes that would measurably improve the performance of the General Assembly. Hence we have omitted the portion of his discussion that deals with the General Assembly and included only his observations on the Security Council and the office of the Secretary-General. Tandon's emphasis on changing the Secretary-General's office may be questioned. Since all changes require a political consensus, is there any reason why formal proposals for changes in that office are more likely to be acceptable than in others?

Changes come when they are widely desired and have among their supporters those with maximum influence. Of course, in an organization in which there are deep splits among those with such influence, the opportunities for change are limited and successes therefore few. Every proposal for change is bound to be looked at in terms of who will benefit and who will not. Perhaps because of this, change sometimes comes through the back door, so to speak, and in the UN that back door for a period was the Secretary-General's office. Because of deadlocks in the Council this office began to be looked to in a modest way as a means of overcoming certain dilemmas. And, as this proved to be a successful device, it grew into practice, because the major nations involved did not lose face and solutions which they did not object to but did not want to support openly could be provided. Perhaps these same major nations also permitted this practice because the Secretary-General was the least independent person and therefore the most susceptible to pressure in the UN.

With regard to the whole question of peaceful settlement, we may ask what guidelines can be established to help determine how the UN's facilities can be made most useful. Should states be encouraged to bring their difficulties to the UN at an early stage? The practice has generally been just the opposite, for members have been expected to work matters out on their own and to come to the organization only when they cannot. This is expected to enhance the sovereign independence of the states and reduce the burdens on the Organization. But by the same token it means that the United Nations gets problems that have become too hot for the states to *handle and thus its chances of aiding the disputants and adding to its own prestige are greatly diminished.*

Another proposal that Tandon discusses and that has been referred to earlier is to increase the use of regional organizations. But what ought to be considered a wise relationship between regional associations and the UN? Can a common mold for these relationships be established, or must each be worked out ad hoc? And should the option of using the UN always be left open to any disputant who prefers not to use a regional organization? If not, what will this do to the prestige of the UN when members are blocked from taking problems they want to take to it?

FURTHER READINGS

Bloomfield, Lincoln P., "Law, Politics and International Disputes," *International Conciliation*, No. 516, January 1958.

Gordenker, Leon, *The United Nations and the Peaceful Unification of Korea: The Politics of Field Operations, 1947–1950*. The Hague: Martinus Nijhoff, 1959.

Stone, Julius, "The International Court and World Crises," *International Conciliation*, No. 536, January 1962.

THE SPONSORSHIP OF PROPOSALS IN THE
UNITED NATIONS GENERAL ASSEMBLY

A. Glenn Mower, Jr.*

When George Hoar opined in his *Autobiography of Seventy Years* that "in 1890 a bill was passed which was called the Sherman Act for no other reason that I can think of except that Mr. Sherman had nothing to do with the framing of it whatever," he called attention to one of the intriguing facets of the legislative process: the source of the proposals that eventually become law. The origin of proposals is a question of more than academic interest, for the legislative fate of an idea may well depend on whose idea it is and who introduces it for official consideration. Authorship and sponsorship are thus key factors in the politics of legislation and are recognized as such both by observers of the legislative process and by those who seek to use this process to advance their interests. The author and the sponsor are by no means necessarily identical; and because of the powers and responsibilities devolving upon the introducer of a bill,[1] sponsorship in particular becomes a focal point of interest to those who follow the workings of deliberative bodies on all levels.

"All levels" includes the international, where a quasi-legislative process goes on in the General Assembly of the United Nations. This process centers in the Assembly's main committees, responsible for producing recommendations on the various agenda items confronting the Assembly. Here, in the committee phase, member states employ standard political techniques in the attempt to ensure that the recommendations adopted either reflect their interests or at least do not go seriously counter to them; and one of the techniques resorted to is the adroit use of the sponsorship-of-resolutions phase of committee action. Thus delegations measure the relative values of direct or indirect sponsorship and critically appraise the various purposes to which the sponsorship process can be put, as well as the political ground that

* A. Glenn Mower, Jr., "The Sponsorship of Proposals in the United Nations General Assembly," *Western Political Quarterly*, Vol. 15, 1962, pp. 661–666. Reprinted by permission of the University of Utah, copyright owners.

A. Glenn Mower, Jr. is Professor of Political Science at Hanover College. He is the author of "You Can't Trust the Russians" and "Observer Countries: Quasi Members of United Nations Organizations."

[1] These include the duty to defend the proposal, answer questions about it, line up support for it, accept or reject amendments to it, and generally steer it through the legislative jungle.

may be lost by injudicious entry into the list of sponsors. These and other aspects of sponsorship of proposals in General Assembly committees will be explored in the following pages.

DIRECT SPONSORSHIP

Proposals are sometimes made openly by delegations, either individually or jointly. In some cases it may be strategically desirable for a delegation to make a clear statement of its policy preference concerning an issue by presenting a draft resolution in its own name, either alone or jointly with others. A delegation will play a lone hand in sponsoring a resolution when it wants to declare itself in relation to an issue and the solution it wants to see adopted. Open, individual sponsorship has the advantage of providing a strong lead for those delegations whom it hopes either to influence, warn, or simply harass. There are other advantages to this approach: (1) it avoids compromise with other sponsors, in the drafting stage, in matters a delegation does not want to compromise; (2) it may reflect more credit on the sponsoring state; and (3) it permits a delegation to use draft resolutions for propaganda purposes.

Joint sponsorship is used when several delegations have a common interest in an issue that will be served through a particular solution. Typical of this are the various resolutions proposed by Afro-Asian delegations during the discussions of North African issues in the First (Political) Committee over a number of years. All these resolutions expressed this bloc's interest in promoting the cause of anti-colonialism, since they called for self-government for the peoples of this part of the French Empire.

Co-sponsorship registers agreement on a proposal; therefore, the longer the list of co-sponsors the greater is the political impact of the proposal. This is one reason why delegations sometimes seek additional sponsors for a measure. Perfection at this point was attained during the fourteenth session, when all eighty-two nations joined in co-sponsoring a resolution on "General and complete disarmament." At other times a delegation may operate selectively in seeking co-sponsors. Thus Canada, interested in proposing a resolution on radiation at the same session, wanted countries like India, Yugoslavia, Ghana, Japan, and New Zealand associated with the proposal because it was felt that these countries were responsible, respected, moderate, and interested in the question.

INDIRECT SPONSORSHIP

Proposals are not always made openly and directly by countries favoring a certain approach to an issue. There are times when a government may choose to work through other delegations in getting its policies before a committee in the form of a draft resolution.

The Soviet Union claimed to have detected this strategy of one power using others as a front during a phase of the debate on the question of the relations of United Nations Members with Franco Spain. Speaking of a resolution introduced into the First Committee by Latin-American states, the Soviet delegate asserted that this resolution repeated, almost word for word, the policy expressed by the United States Secretary of State, Dean Acheson, in a letter of January 18, 1950. According to the Russian spokesman, this proved that the United States was using the Latin-American states "merely as a front for its own sinister purposes." On the same point the *New York Times*, in its issue of October 28, 1950, reported that the United States had contributed materially to the Latin-American proposal to rescind portions of the 1946 General Assembly resolution on Spain.

Another example of the fact that a sponsor of a resolution may not be the prime mover of that proposal was supplied by India, also in the First Committee, during one session's discussion of the question of the treatment of Indians in the Union of South Africa. Here India was the instigator but the resolution was in the name of Arab and Asian states and Yugoslavia. This action can be explained by the fact that India was dependent on the moral support of the Arab and Asian states and did not want the issue to be strictly one of India versus South Africa. The strategy was therefore one of making the treatment of Indians in South Africa appear to be a concern of delegations other than India, and the tactic was a resolution in the names of other states.

Sometimes the indirect sponsor may not even be a member of the United Nations. An example of this occurred in the fourteenth session, when the Provisional Government of Algeria presented a draft resolution on the Algerian question through a group of Afro-Asian states. This was the Provisional Government's way of trying to get itself established as the only Algerian political group authorized to deal with the French Government. An Argentinian amendment sought to block this objective by deleting "two" from the part of the resolution urging "the two parties concerned to enter into *pourparlers*. . . ." The amendment would have had the effect of opening the way to another Algerian political element to participate in the conversations.

Indirect sponsorship is a tactic employed for a number of reasons, in addition to those suggested in the preceding examples. In some cases a resolution has a better chance of being well received if it is not directly identified with a particular country. For example, there was some conjecture that the United States was the indirect sponsor of a proposal to reactivate the Palestinian Conciliation Commission at the fourteenth session, when there seemed to be no satisfactory approach available to the question of the Palestinian refugees. The Commission had previously been denounced as an agent of imperialism; therefore political wisdom dictated that the idea of reactivating it be put forth by a country that could not be accused of seeking to further some imperialistic interest. Ceylon accordingly became the sponsor of this proposal, which was then supported by the United States as a compromise approach to the problem.

The desire, then, to avoid handicapping a resolution by attaching it to an unpopular or hostility-provoking sponsor may lead to indirect sponsorship.[2] So may the desire to retain freedom of action. A delegation may not want to make a formal commitment on an issue facing the committee, preferring to maneuver in the process of diplomatic bargaining. By having others sponsor its ideas through a proposal, a delegation gets these ideas before the committee and yet is not committed, on the record, to any particular solution to the problem. Negotiations can then be engaged in without the danger of losing face.

Delegations at times prefer this tactic rather than run the risk of finding themselves in the position of the Afro-Asian states whose stiff resolution on Algeria in the fourteenth session failed to gain a two-thirds majority in committee. To avoid complete loss of face, these countries then toned down the resolution and had one delegation offer the milder form as a proposal for which all could vote, and which might command the necessary two-thirds support in plenary meeting. This maneuver is most effective when the formal sponsor of the substitute proposal is not from the same interest bloc as those who presented the original resolution.

The use of indirect sponsors is not always a face-saving device: sometimes it is part of the bargaining process in which a country pitches its original offer high with the anticipation that it may have to settle for something lower. Thus country A may introduce a resolution that embodies 100 per cent of its policy position on an issue. Then, when reactions to this have so dictated, A may have B come in with a proposal that modifies the original measure to 75 per cent of A's position. This is particularly likely to happen when pressure for modification is exerted by friends of the sponsor of the original proposal, as concessions through a third party will sometimes be made to friendly delegations that would not be made to others.

Finally, indirect sponsorship may be resorted to because having others make the proposal brings increased support for a delegation's policies. This added support results not only from the appearance of certain names as sponsors of a measure, but from the fact that these sponsors must defend the measure in committee.

In considering indirect sponsorship, two final points should be noted concerning this tactical device. First, such subterfuge as using others to sponsor a desired proposal is not easily concealed. In the case of the Indian-motivated proposal cited above, for example, India's role was an "open secret." Generally the content of speeches during the opening committee debate provides a clue to whose interests are reflected in a given resolution, and there are other formal and informal means available to governments to discover who is really behind a given recommendation. Secondly, indirect sponsorship does not necessarily mean that the formal sponsor is merely acting on behalf

2 When political lines are firmly drawn, as in the East-West conflict, a resolution sponsored by one faction and having political implications is almost certain to be rejected by the opposite party on the simple grounds of identity of the sponsor.

of others and that the measure does not embody its own interests. Behind the use of others as sponsors there may lie no little informal consultation and negotiation based on the realization that the interests of prime mover and official sponsor must coincide to some degree. Both parties to indirect sponsorship must be satisfied with the proposal that eventually enters committee discussion.

OTHER FACTORS IN SPONSORSHIP

The introduction of proposals is sometimes a device to grind a propaganda axe or to embarrass another faction within the committee. This motivation would explain a proposal such as Romania's, to the Second (Economic and Financial) Committee, in the fourteenth session, asking for international cooperation in the development of the petroleum industry in underdeveloped countries. If carried through, this suggestion would have served the positive purposes of getting Soviet technicians into oil-producing countries and disposing of some Communist-bloc machinery. There was little likelihood, though, that this proposal would be adopted by the Committee; therefore the real purpose behind it seemed to be to embarrass the colonial powers. The proposal evoked statements by the United Kingdom, the United States, and the Netherlands that could be interpreted as expressing opposition to the discussion of oil in the United Nations. This, rather than the fate of the resolution itself, was in all probability the major concern of the resolution's sponsor, for objection to the multilateral approach to economic issues is not likely to win friends among the underdeveloped countries.

Policy interests can thus be served by advancing proposals in committee even when those proposals have little chance of adoption. They can also be served by not introducing measures. Thus it is seldom that Administering Powers will introduce amendments or proposals in the Fourth (Trusteeship) Committee. These powers proceed on the premise that there is no international responsibility, for example, in cases such as the non-self-governing territories and that they have done their part by transmitting such information as they choose. Therefore they will not take the initiative by introducing resolutions that would tacitly concede the principle of international organizational competence in this field.

While Administering Powers tend to avoid making proposals directly in the Fourth Committee, they will frequently engage in preproposal consultations with other delegations and thereby have a hand in shaping the resolutions that enter committee discussion. These consultations may take the form of the caucuses held during the fourteenth session on the question of a plebiscite for the South Cameroons. Representatives of African states, the Cameroons, and the Administering Power, England, met for a number of days until they had worked out a resolution that was agreeable to all of them. The same procedure was followed in order to fix the date for the independence of Italian Somaliland. Prior to submitting their draft resolu-

---

tion on this question, the countries serving as co-sponsors met with the Administering Power, Italy; and when the resolution was presented to the Committee, it was with Italy's agreement.

An administering Power may not only meet with others and assist in the preparation of proposals formally sponsored by others, but it may take the initiative in calling such caucuses. The United Kingdom followed this procedure in the fourteenth session in the attempt to meet a situation arising from the pending independence of Nigeria. The North Cameroons, a territory under British administration, had been administered as a part of Nigeria, a British dependency. With Nigeria due to become independent in 1960, the British wanted to avoid having to set up a new administrative establishment solely for the Northern Cameroons; therefore they favored a new plebiscite on the status of the territory. After some initial failures, the British were able to get sponsorship for a resolution calling for another plebiscite on the alternatives of joining an independent Republic of the Cameroons or the Federation of Nigeria.

Thus Administering Powers find, as do others in relation to other types of questions, that when a national interest in an issue is strong enough, some form of sponsorship of proposals must be resorted to. As the foregoing discussion has demonstrated, there is a variety of choices open to a delegation when it perceives the political desirability of taking some initiative in an Assembly committee's proceedings. How to maneuver in the face of such choices is one of those tests of skill that determines the success with which governments play the game of international politics at the United Nations.[3]

THE PEACEFUL SETTLEMENT OF INTERNATIONAL DISPUTES

Yash Tandon[*]

Many prescriptions are offered for improving the functioning of the UN: this or that procedure is good for settling international disputes, and therefore the UN should adopt it as a matter of course. Eric Stein, for instance,

[3] Much of the discussion in this article is based on personal interviews with United Nations personnel, delegation members, press correspondents, and other observers during visits to the United Nations in 1955, 1957, and 1959.

[*] Yash Tandon, "The Peaceful Settlement of International Disputes," *Internationl Relations*, Vol. 2, April 1964, pp. 555–587. By permission of The David Davies Memorial Institute of International Studies.

Yash Tandon submitted the winning essay for the Cecil Peace Prize in 1963.

recommends one: "In the early years of the Organisation, whenever an important matter came before the Security Council or the General Assembly, these bodies, *almost as a matter of standard practice*,[1] appointed committees from among their members which would investigate the problem and proceed if necessary to the scene of the controversy, and report with proper recommendations to the proper body. This practice might well be resumed."[2] How far do such prescriptions help to foster a greater use of the United Nations? How far do the existence of procedural arrangements govern the functioning of the Organisation? Did the UN in the past institute investigation into a dispute as a matter of course, and should it do so in [the] future?

It is pointless to quarrel with the technique of international investigation *per se*. It could be convincingly argued that members of the UN should refuse to deal with a problem until they are fully informed of the facts relevant to the dispute in question. But it is incorrect to say that the UN has in the past adopted the practice of instituting investigation as a matter of standard procedure; further, it is unwise to suggest that it should continue, or resume, the practice as a matter of course.

Investigation is only one of several weapons to deal with an international problem in the arsenal of the United Nations and it is not in all circumstances the best one. Instead of setting up an investigation commission, it could decide, for instance, to set up a conciliation commission, or if circumstances demanded, a cease-fire commission or a truce-supervision commission.

❊   ❊   ❊   ❊   ❊   ❊   ❊

Another example of a procedural device prescribed for the United Nations is that suggested by Sydney D. Bailey, in his excellent book, *The Secretariat of the United Nations:* "The use of special rapporteurs, both to elucidate the issues and to make proposals for a solution, was one of the more successful practices of the League of Nations, and it is a pity that United Nations organs have not followed the practice." As a matter of fact, the UN has used this practice when necessary.

. . . just as the rôle of the United Nations depends very much on the political circumstances in which it has to function, so does the manner in which it functions, and the procedure it adopts in assisting the settlement of international disputes. . . . Thus even where it was decided that further consideration of a dispute should not be carried on by the UN but should be left to the parties themselves (as with Algeria in December 1960, and with Cuba in April 1961), the decisive factors behind such decisions were political and practical, rather than legal or procedural. Political differences between States

---

[1] Italics mine.

[2] "Mr. Hammarskjöld, the Charter Law and the Future Role of the United Nations Secretary-General," *American Journal of International Law*, vol. 56, no. 1 (January 1962), p. 28.

cannot be transformed into procedural questions and be resolved through procedural devices.

What is true of the *ad hoc* manner in which the United Nations has customarily chosen its procedural devices or modes of settlement (whether it is to institute investigation or set up a good-offices commission, whether it is to employ the services of a rapporteur or ask the Court's advisory opinion), is also true of the *ad hoc* way the Organisation has set up new institutions and tailored its machinery to suit the needs of each situation. The UN has discarded institutions which are no longer applicable to the needs of international life, and has created new ones where none existed. In all the talk about reforming the procedural or institutional aspects of the UN, it is customary to overlook or to underrate the adjustments made by the UN itself in response to changing conditions and changing needs.

One such institution within the system of the United Nations that failed to materialise, for instance, was the idea of a United Nations armed force provided in Article 43 of the Charter. The Charter, it must be admitted, is a remarkable document—a product not only of a compromise between the interests of the States responsible for drafting it, but also a compromise between the hard facts of international life and ideological aspirations. It is no wonder therefore that not everything in it has relevance to the existing social realities of international politics.

In the context of the cold war that bedevilled the world in the aftermath of the Second World War, the idea of a UN armed force did not mature. Who was to command this force? What sorts of troops were to be contributed to it, by whom, and in what proportions? Were there to be UN bases all over the world, with the forces of the UN permanently stationed there, ready to quell all rebellion and smother all potential or actual disturbances to international peace? As the United States and the Soviet Union arrayed themselves on opposite sides of each controversial question, and as long and protracted negotiations failed to produce more than a mouse of an agreement, it became obvious that the Charter was dead on that issue.

But while there was no room for a UN force of the type envisaged in the Charter, there was a definite need for some sort of a functional international force. The best examples of such a "force" are, of course, the United Nations Emergency Force created in 1956 during the Suez Crisis, and the ONUC set up in July 1960 during the Congo upheaval.

Both the UNEF and the ONUC were initiated *ad hoc* in response to emergency situations, their structure and the principles of their operation were shaped by the political circumstances under which they had to function. Had somebody proposed barely two months before the Suez crisis that a force of 6,000 soldiers should be recruited from "neutral" States, and be stationed in the troubled areas of the world, including the Palestine and the Suez Canal area, the proposal would have certainly encountered overwhelming opposition. In the absence of a concrete situation, answers to a thousand and one questions such as, which States are "neutral" States, and whether and in what conditions the force can employ its arms, assume only abstract importance. Besides, States have been chary of committing their forces to a permanent international force which might later be deployed against the interests of themselves or their allies. The situation, however, is different when viewed in the light of an international crisis. One knows who one's friends and foes are in respect to that particular dispute; and faced with an emergency situation, one is prepared to agree to emergency measures to help avert the crisis, provided, of course, that the measures taken deal only with that specific crisis.

It is, of course, true that once a technique has been used during one crisis, it becomes easier to re-employ it during another. But whether it will be employed or not depends on what other alternatives are open to statesmen at that time, and on the political circumstances of the new crisis. The decision to use a particular procedure or technique is, as noted above, a political not a technical or procedural decision. Besides, even if the UN decided to use the same technique to resolve a dispute (e.g., induction of a UN force), the old formula may not fit the new conditions. Thus in the Lebanon and Jordan Dag Hammarskjöld found that a UNEF-type force was not suitable, for it would have inevitably got itself involved in internal Arab politics. The 500 Observers sent to the Lebanon did not have the quasi-military functions assigned to the UNEF; and in Jordan, where many expected the UN to send such a quasi-military force, it was decided to station a purely civilian body of men of a very limited size, headed by the personal representative of the Secretary-General, and this filled the need extremely well. The UN force sent to the Congo turned out to be yet quite a different type of force. The duties assigned to ONUC were infinitely more complex than those assigned to UNEF, and the circumstances under which ONUC functioned were very different to those under which UNEF operated. To cite only one such difference: while UNEF could operate in an environment physically unhampered by complicated interests or by inhabitants, ONUC could not avoid contact with Congolese life at every point, and sometimes, even failure to take some action involved interference in domestic affairs. Although this does not mean that efforts to think in terms of building up a UN force should be abandoned, the experience of the UN does underline the futility of trying to perfect in abstraction and in the absence of a concrete political crisis, procedures or machinery for the settlement of international disputes—for such a perfect system does not exist.

. . . The experience of the United Nations seems to have vindicated the advantages of keeping its good-offices machinery flexible enough to enable it to adopt the machinery to the needs of each situation. Thus the Security Council Committee of Good Offices on the Indonesian dispute consisted of three members: two appointed separately by each of the parties (the Netherlands and Indonesia), and the third designated by the previous two. The

UN Commission for India and Pakistan followed a similar pattern, but the third "neutral" member of the Commission was appointed by the Council itself. Often, however, an individual has advantages as a mediator over a commission, especially if he is a person of distinction: for example, Count Bernadotte and later Ralph Bunche in the Palestine dispute, and Owen Dixon and Frank Graham in the Kashmir dispute. Frequently, the Secretary-General has acted in the capacity of a mediator, as in the dispute between Cambodia and Thailand in 1958.

In concluding this section it should be pointed out that the way the UN itself selects and creates its own procedures and techniques in relation to the concrete needs of each situation is indeed a far better and more effective method of building up machinery for the settlement of international disputes, than the planned, deliberate, and *a priori* method of doing it. The UN, in this, has at least two major advantages on its side. Firstly, as we observed above, in the heat of an international crisis, particularly if there is a danger that the crisis may escalate into a major war, the UN is better able to exploit the willingness of States to agree to novel devices and procedures which would help to restore the situation. Proposed in the abstract, these methods are looked upon as suspect by the members of the international society, and therefore they rarely strike deep roots. Secondly, it is easier to build a machinery in the context of a particular international dispute than in a political vacuum. Experience has shown that since what is built today has to relate to future needs, the procedural devices and techniques proposed in a political vacuum have to cater for an infinite number of hypothetical possibilities, often with contradictory probabilities, so that discussions almost invariably degenerate into vague generalities.

Nonetheless, while recognising the merits of instituting procedures and machinery *ad hoc* and in response to changing needs, as against an *a priori* method of doing it, it is still possible to think that there is room for some constructive advance planning. And to this I now turn.

❋ ❋ ❋ ❋ ❋ ❋ ❋

FUTURE DEMANDS LIKELY TO [BE] MADE ON THE UNITED NATIONS

There are four types of disputes in the settlement of which the United Nations is likely to be of assistance in the near future: cold war disputes; colonial disputes or what are left of them, *viz.* disputes between a colonial power and its dependency striving for self-determination; post-independence internal disorders within a newly-emerged State, with possible international repercussions (e.g., the Congo); and disputes among States of Africa, Asia, and the Middle East.

COLD WAR DISPUTES. These disputes are a product of the post-Second World War confrontation between the Soviet Union (and satellites) and the

United States (and allies), and constitute the biggest festering sore on the body politic of international society. They are particularly menacing for three reasons: first, the cold war disputes tend to be extremely difficult to resolve, with neither party willing to yield an inch of substantive ground for fear of upsetting the world balance of power (for example, in Germany and in Korea); the result, of course, is a perpetuation of mutual ill-feeling, distrust, and for those who are directly involved (e.g., Germans and Koreans), a sense of frustration. Second, these disputes potentially contain seeds of a possible nuclear explosion. The slightest miscalculation on the part of either of the contestants, or an escalation of a local war, can, if not checked in time, trigger a world war. Third, like a contagious disease, the cold war has a tendency to infect all other types of disputes, local as well as international (for example, in Greece from 1948 to 1953, in the Middle East particularly since 1956, and presently in Laos and Vietnam); therefore, if not contained, the cold war could exacerbate in difficulties of reaching a settlement on all international disputes.

How are the cold war disputes likely to be handled in [the] future, and how much assistance can the UN render either in resolving them or in containing their aggravation or dissemination? It is to be expected that, as in the past, so in the immediate future, they will be handled in four ways: (a) *Through unilateral action* by either the United States or the Soviet Union: this is particularly true of those disputes which fall within the respective "spheres of influence" of the two Great Powers—Eastern Europe in the case of the Soviet Union (*passim*, Hungary, 1956–57), and Latin America in the case of the United States (*passim*, Cuba, 1960–63). It is further safe to assume that disputes within the Communist bloc (China-Soviet Union, Albania-Yugoslavia) are not likely to come into the ambit of the United Nations; nor are possible disputes between the members of the North Atlantic Alliance. . . . (b) *Through reciprocal diplomatic bargaining between West and the Soviet Union;* . . . (c) *Through the good-offices of the "neutral" States*: a method which could be of particular relevance to the settlement of disputes which fall outside the immediate "spheres of influence" of the two Powers, as in Laos. (d) *Through the United Nations*: although the settlement of the cold war disputes must be left to negotiations between the parties concerned, the UN can be of assistance in a number of ways. In the first place the UN can provide a readily available diplomatic meeting place for Soviet and Western negotiators. . . . Secondly, while the nonaligned or neutral nations can mediate between the US and the USSR in cold war disputes outside the United Nations (as in Laos), they can also do so through the agency of the UN. Of particular importance is their role in counselling restraint to the USA and the USSR in an international crisis, when unwise action could be taken by the parties either in the heat of excitement or excess zeal. During the Korean crisis, the neutrals, led by India, played a significant role as mediators, both when hostilities were in progress, and when the armistice agreements were being negotiated. Thirdly, while it is not the task here to suggest possible lines of settlement of say the German question, yet if ever the parties concerned agreed to some form of disengagement in Europe (and it would be unwise to rule it out completely) then the availability of a UN force consisting of troops from the "neutral" States, could provide valuable, if only marginal, assistance. In the final analysis, the usefulness of such a "buffer force" would be not in the moral weight of the force (although that could be an important consideration in the mind of a potential aggressor), but in the traditional doctrine of mutual sanctions, namely, whoever chose to break the agreement and march against or fly over the UN buffer force would incur the onus of inviting retaliatory action by the opposite side. Incidentally, a UN force could be useful not only in assisting political settlement of a dispute, but also in negotiating and maintaining arms control agreements. Fourthly, the United Nations can play a significant part in preventing the spread of the cold war into regions where the interest of the two Super-Powers are not directly involved; but this aspect will be considered later.

COLONIAL DISPUTES. The colonial era of the European Powers in Asia and Africa is quickly receding into history: since the war, more than forty-odd new nations have gained their independence from colonial rule. For the most part, therefore, the colonial disputes have more or less been settled. The most notable problems that are still left in this category and that are likely to remain with us for some time to come, are: Southern Rhodesia, the Portuguese territories of Angola and Mozambique, South-West Africa and South Africa—and these are by far the most difficult nuts to crack.

How are these disputes likely to be tackled and what demands are likely to be made on the resources of the United Nations with regard to these problems? Of the three ways in which these disputes may be handled—through the efforts of the dependent peoples themselves, either by negotiation with the authorities currently administering these territories or by insurrection; through a collective action (possibly military) by the African States, joined perhaps, by some Asian and Middle Eastern States; and through the United Nations—it is the last which is likely to feature most in the near future. The resources of the African States for launching a military campaign against South Africa are rather limited at least for some years to come; and insurrection or attempts at negotiation by the dependent peoples themselves will not persuade a determined South African or Portuguese Government to yield the sort of concessions they demanded, although the Government in Southern Rhodesia might do so.

What sort of demands are likely to be made on the United Nations in settling these disputes? Firstly, the Afro-Asian states will probably continue to use the UN (and the International Court of Justice, where appropriate) to exert pressure on the South African and Portuguese Governments (even if South Africa were expelled from the Organisation), and, but much more, perhaps, to influence the other members of the UN, particularly Britain, France, and the United States, to impose sanctions—diplomatic, economic and military—on these governments. Secondly, if the Afro-Asians manage to convince the Great Powers of the desirability and practicability of imposing sanctions on South Africa, the UN will have to create, for the first time, a true sanctions machinery, with the task of supervising an economic boycott or an arms embargo. Thirdly, if the plan for imposing sanctions on South Africa fails to materialize, and attempts to negotiate a mutually acceptable settlement to the problem also fail, then collective military action by the independent States of Africa is a possibility, even if they have to "go else-where" to purchase arms. In such an eventuality, the UN might have to step in to effect and supervise a cease-fire.

POST-INDEPENDENCE INTERNAL DISORDERS WITH INTERNATIONAL EFFECTS. This type of dispute is typified by the Congo upheaval of the last three years. That a similar situation is likely to occur again in other parts of Africa and Asia is difficult to predict, but such a possibility cannot be ruled out. Angola contains all the characteristics for erupting into a similar crisis: lack of suffi-cient skill and experience among the indigenous people to take over the administration, conflicting local and tribal loyalties, and a possibility of an emergency exit by the Portuguese administration in a fit of political desper-ation, either as the result of a domestic crisis in Portugal or of external pres-sure exerted by members of the United Nations. A breakdown of law and order is possible even among the other independent States of Africa, vulner-able to a political crisis caused by a military coup or by tribal dissension, especially where the civil service and the army have divided loyalties as well. The dangers of such outbreaks should not, of course, be overdramatised or exaggerated. A real threat, however, exists where a possible power vac-uum leaves an opening for Great Power intervention either directly, or indirectly through the sale of arms and ammunition to opposite factions, as has, in fact, happened in the Far East (Laos and Vietnam).

Apart from the measures that can be taken to avert such a crisis in the first place, either by the States themselves (for example, by creating institu-tions of law and order based on the common consent of the people), or by the international community (for example, by economic and technical aid to stabilise their economy and administration), what can be done when such a situation does arise? How is the United Nations likely to be of assistance in a situation of this sort? There are three alternatives to intrusion by the cold war contestants: (a) *Attempts to remedy the situation internally*: that is, without external help. When all is said and done, the ultimate method by which a lasting settlement can be arrived at is by negotiation between the leaders of the various factions. This is bound to be difficult at the start, for, unless the political leaders restrain themselves voluntarily, they are likely to seek outside help, perhaps even indiscriminately. Some amount of interven-tion is bound to take place, if only from the State across the borders. (b)

Insulation of the conflict by a regional organisation: one of the ways in which a future Congo-like situation can be insulated from the cold war is through a partial or complete take-over by an African regional organisation. A feeling prevails in Africa that this should be so, exemplified, for instance, by Nkrumah's one-time suggestion of creating an African High Command to take over the Congo problem from the United Nations.

Where regional organisations can resolve a dispute, they must be encouraged, for apart from other things, they can shoulder some of the burdens of the UN. In any case, it is safe to assume that in a future Congo-like situation in Africa, the African States will first attempt to settle the problem themselves. They are likely to go to the UN only as a last resort, under one of the following eventualities: (1) an effective regional machinery may not exist; (2) where it does exist, it may not be able to mobilise itself because of internal dissension; (3) there may be rival organisations seeking to control the situation; (4) a regional organisation may be unable to prevent intervention by a Great Power determined to take advantage of the situation; (5) inability of a regional organisation to sustain itself for a long period (as the UN was able to do in the Congo for more than three years): in the context of Africa in the throes of a political revolution and constant flux, regional groups are likely to be extremely frail; (6) a regional organisation may lack enough administrative and technical skill "to go it entirely alone," and therefore may require aid and personnel channelled through the UN. (c) *Insulation of the conflict by the United Nations*: as observed above, although the UN is more likely to be used as a last resort, it may have to intervene for one reason or another, even if it be for the purpose of insulating the conflict not only from the cold war, but probably also from interference by rival States within the region. In Yemen, for instance, the UN had to intervene to isolate the civil war from interference by the UAR and Saudi Arabia.

* * * * * * *

IMPROVEMENTS THAT CAN BE MADE IN THE EXISTING MACHINERY FOR THE SETTLEMENT OF INTERNATIONAL DISPUTES

Improvements in the United Nations Organisation can be made at three levels: at the level of its peace-keeping machinery; at the level of its good-offices machinery; and at the level of its decision-making machinery.

THE UNITED NATIONS PEACE-KEEPING MACHINERY. An international standing army is out of the question. It is not the problem of finance that is the deterring factor, but questions of control, of permanent bases and above all the problem of political will. It must be admitted that however desirable it may be to create an international army to, for instance, enforce the decisions of the International Court of Justice or of the Security Council, in the context of the present international society, it is impracticable.

The difficulties of creating even a stand-by force are not inconsiderable. There are so many possible combinations of variable factors that it is impossible to draw up models of an international force. But, after all the difficulties have been enumerated, the fact remains that the UN is likely to be called upon to perform similar, if not identical, tasks in the settlement of international disputes. The question is: why should not the UN be left to set up its peace forces *ad hoc*? Although it is true that it is impossible to eliminate all improvisations since every dispute is in some sense *sui generis*, yet the answer is not to despair and build from scratch at every fresh international crisis, but to lay down certain procedures and machinery which are flexible enough to be used in varying situations. Some advance planning can be carried out to reduce the hazards of improvisation, to make a future UN operation more systematic and less haphazard.

* * * * * * *

THE UNITED NATIONS GOOD-OFFICES MACHINERY. The tendering of good offices is in one sense the most important function of the United Nations, and the least advertised. But while some amount of advance planning is both desirable and practicable as regard the peace-keeping machinery of the United Nations, both experience and reason vindicate the desirability of keeping the conciliation machinery of the United Nations extremely flexible. It is not, for instance, as difficult to set up a conciliation commission or choose a mediator, as it is to launch a truce or an investigation commission. A permanent good-offices commission is not likely to improve this aspect of the United Nations functions. The most that could be done is for the Secretary-General to keep a list of mediators skilled in the arts of diplomacy and persuasion, especially in view of the fact that of late years greater use has been made of the good-offices services of the Secretary-General and his personal representatives. It is possible that he already has such a list, which could be extended by the inclusion of diplomats who have played a valuable role as negotiators in the United Nations, provided they have retired from national politics.

* * * * * * *

THE UNITED NATIONS POLICY-MAKING MACHINERY. The inadequacy of the General Assembly and the Security Council as policy-making organs has been best exemplified by the growth of the power of the Secretary-General in recent years.

* * * * * * *

How far is the growth of the powers of the Secretary-General an undesirable development? Insofar as he can genuinely help in the settlement of disputes when the parties concerned prefer to use him as a mediator rather than the other organs of the UN (as in the Cambodia-Thailand dispute of 1958), the role of the Secretary-General, and his representatives, should certainly be recognised as desirable. But there are at least two dangers inherent in this development. Firstly, the office of the Secretary-General becomes vulnerable to political attack by States who cannot reconcile themselves to the outcome of certain political settlements (for example, the Soviet Union on the Congo question). Secondly, there is a growing belief that the Secretary-General can act not only independently of the General Assembly and the Security Council, but also independently of the overall diplomatic context in which he has to function. This is a highly dangerous doctrine, for even if the Secretary-General were a perfect sensitive barometer gauging the consensus of diplomatic opinion in the Assembly, sooner or later, he has to look over his shoulder to the Assembly or the Council to see if, when the circumstances of the situation warranted, he could count on sufficient diplomatic (and, if necessary, military) backing among the members of the Organisation. He cannot go on justifying his actions on the basis of the high principles of the Charter. Even Hammarskjöld realised this when, exasperated by a lack of sufficient direction from the Council during the Congo operation, he remarked: "It cannot shirk its responsibility by expecting from the Secretariat action on which it is not prepared to take decisions itself."

The problem of improving the policy-making mechanism of the United Nations is therefore a genuine one. What can be done about it?

THE SECURITY COUNCIL. The suitability of the Council as a policy-making organ is undeniable. It is small enough to sit in continuous session and review its political operations constantly in the light of changing situations. Furthermore, it is the seat of the Great Powers without whose acquiescence or influence it might be difficult to settle international disputes. How can the Council be mobilised?

The first problem is the veto. Although it is true that without the veto probably the UN might not have been created in the first place, yet it must be admitted that it has become a slight anachronism. In its impact, the veto in the Council has absolute power, that is, if one of the Permanent Members considers a certain measure proposed in the Council inimical to its interests, then it can paralyse the Council by its veto. The exercise of the veto by a power does not measure the intensity of the hostility felt by that power against the action proposed, that is, the veto does not indicate to what extent the State concerned is prepared to go to prevent the proposed action from being put into effect if it came to a show-down. Would the Soviet Union be prepared to risk war if the United Nations should decide to support anti-Communist revolution in Hungary? She probably would. Would she be prepared to risk war if the UN should give authority to its force in the Congo to carry out a certain measure disapproved by the Soviet Union?

Under the circumstances, she most likely would not. And yet in both cases, the Soviet Union *can* block action in the Council by an exercise of her veto right, even if in one case she genuinely felt her very being threatened, while in the other case the measure proposed only aroused her displeasure. The veto thus simplifies reality to the level of distorting it, and thus is indiscriminating in its effect.

The General Assembly is a different sort of organ with no formal provision of the veto. The word formal is used advisedly because an informal veto does operate. A veto in the Assembly operates on a realistic assessment of the relative power of the recalcitrant State or States and the power or pressure that could be mustered in the UN to put a proposed action into effect. For example, the Assembly passed two Resolutions in its two Emergency Special Sessions of 1956–57, one on Suez and the other on Hungary. The one on Suez was carried into effect, and the one on Hungary was not. Why?—because while Britain and France were neither prepared nor able to resist the tremendous pressure exerted against them at the United Nations, the Soviet Union was both able and, if the need arose, prepared to resist any such pressure on the question of Hungary. The Great Power veto was an effective veto in the latter case, but not in the former. And yet, in the Security Council the veto could inhibit further action in both cases. Against the abolition of the veto it is usually argued that it must stay because it is a symbol of power reality that exists behind it; this is a rationalisation: to say this of the exercise of the British and French veto on the question of Suez is a serious distortion of the facts of power.

Power is a matter not only of capability but also of the will to exercise it. The veto in the Security Council, while recognising the strength of the Permanent Members, also assumes their willingness to exercise all power in every issue that they veto. The so-called veto-free General Assembly carries out, however precariously, an assessment of both the capability of the big States to exercise power and their willingness to do so. If politics is the art of the possible, then the General Assembly is more of a political animal than the Security Council. Thus while action by the Council is stopped through a mere show of strength by one of the Permanent Members, in the General Assembly, the State concerned has not only to demonstrate its strength but has to give the delegates reason enough to believe that it has every intention of using all strength available to prevent action by the United Nations when the final chips are down. In assuming positive co-operation between the Soviet Union and the United States as a basis of its action, the Security Council therefore cannot do anything where such positive co-operation is not present. The General Assembly recognises that in the context of the cold war, a pledge of positive co-operation between the two great contestants is not easy to get, but it is nevertheless prepared to act if they eventually keep each other out of a dispute.

THE OFFICE OF THE SECRETARY-GENERAL. The proposals that have so far been made to reform the office of the Secretary-General have not been well received.

＊　＊　＊　＊　＊　＊　＊

The most that can be done under the circumstances is [to see] that the office of the Secretary-General should be kept independent of political pressures, and efforts should be directed toward both reducing the burden laid on the Secretary-General and providing him with buffers against political criticism. While there is no ideal solution to the problem, attempts should be made to reduce the ill-effects of the less than ideal solution. Firstly, the General Assembly and the Security Council should, wherever possible, use their own commissions and committees to resolve differences between parties to a dispute, rather than "leave it to the Secretary-General.". . . Secondly, where the Secretary-General's services are deemed to be indispensable, as when a high degree of co-ordination is required between a UN field operation (such as ONUC), the principal organs of the United Nations and the Secretariat, then the Assembly or the Council should consider setting up a committee among its own ranks to act in the capacity of a consultative or an advisory body to the Secretary-General (as in the case of UNEF or ONUC). It is not possible to say how useful such a committee is likely to be (it might even prove a hindrance to quick action by the Secretary-General), or whether the Council or the Assembly should invariably set up such a committee. It can nevertheless play a significant role as a two-way liaison between the Secretary-General and the principal organs of the UN.

CONCLUSIONS

Surveying the ground covered in this paper, three points can be made in conclusion. Firstly, major developments in the task of building international institutions for settling disputes between States must, in the final analysis, proceed in step with developments in the other aspects of the evolution of human relations, mainly in the growth of common interests between the family of nations. The mutual fear of nuclear weapons has created some common interest in the maintenance of peace at the universal level, but smaller wars may yet take place, and it would require the best ingenuity of diplomats to avert such wars, and more importantly, to resolve the causes that spark them. Secondly, the inability to reach perfection on earth does not justify a disregard for the less ambitious steps that can be taken to minimise the ill-effects of an imperfect world. Thirdly, while imaginative thinking should go on and new ideas which are capable of application as circumstances arise be made available, all channels—UN and extra-UN—must be kept open to allow of constant negotiations between diplomats over the settlement of international disputes.

CHAPTER **11**

BLOCS AND GROUPS: THEIR HISTORY AND FUNCTION

In every parliamentary assemblage in which the principle of freedom of speech prevails, members tend to coalesce on a basis of party, region, or project. Not only is this true of national legislatures, but it is also true of the General Assembly of the United Nations. And although little evidence of the active functioning of these coalitions was revealed in the first half-decade of the Assembly's existence, by the end of that decade one of the most noted and commented-upon developments in the Assembly was the formation and function of blocs. The manifestation of this political behavior can be explained in part by the great increase in members between the years 1955 and 1960, and in part by the change in background and outlook of many of the newer states. Finally, it should be noted, the breakdown of the rigid bifurcation defined as the East-West split has changed the once satellite-like behavior of many states associated with the two chief antagonists in the split.

The chapter that follows provides an attempt to define the meaning of the terms groups *and* blocs, *and to identify some of the major ideological and behavioral characteristics of these factions. Thomas Hovet, Jr. is one of the outstanding scholars of the subject. In his work,* Bloc Politics in the United Nations, *Chapter II of which is reprinted here, he indicates the various alignments one finds at the UN. Distinguishing between blocs and groups, he notes that the latter is a broad classification under which can be subsumed such combinations of major significance as caucusing groups, geographical groups, regional groups, and common-interest groups. Some of these are as old as the Organization itself, but some have been of more recent origin and may prove to be but temporary alignments in the passing parade.*

Robert Owen Keohane's study, Political Influence in the General Assembly, *from which we have selected his first chapter, "The Framework of Influence," supplements the observations of Hovet and then proceeds to examine how these groups function. He points to the difficulty of the delegates' coming up with meaningful and useful conclusions while maintaining national interests. The result is reflected in votes which reveal greater agreement between states in different groups than is often found among states in the same group. Except for the Eastern European bloc the groups are not unified actors within the Assembly. Coalitions form outside of groups as well as within. Nevertheless, as Keohane points out, average scores of unity on voting behavior are higher within groups than they are within the Assembly taken as a whole.*

In these voting studies certain states are found to play an especially important role because their votes, which are very often with the majority, indicate they help tip the balance of voting power. These are not the states one would normally have guessed would be in such a position, indicating again the value of these newer studies in adding to our understanding of international organizational behavior.

Following the general analysis of these political groups we turn to a more detailed study of certain major ones. Because it has seemed desirable to present equally sympathetic articles on each group we have selected only those studies whose authors are nationals of one of the states of the group they describe. Although the four groups selected are by no means the only ones of significance in the United Nations, nevertheless the reader should be able to appreciate and compare the primary objectives and concerns of each individual group, to discern the areas of disagreement, and to comprehend the operating procedures followed.

Thomas B. Millar, in his article, "The Commonwealth and the United Nations," discusses the changes in membership and interests in the British Commonwealth, one of the oldest groups in the United Nations and one whose history can be traced back to the League of Nations. He discusses the formal and informal evidences of its UN existence and one of its most unique characteristics, the ubiquitousness of its membership: "at least one

Commonwealth country in, or with close contact in, most of the United Nations groups or blocs." We perceive likewise not only how the group's role becomes manifest in the total organization, but also what benefits accrue by virtue of membership in the group. Because this is such a heterogeneous combination it is clear that its members' national policies are not likely to be greatly altered by virtue of their association. But the combination is a "harmonizer," Millar argues, breeding understanding.

Africa, the newest continent to "join" the United Nations represents perhaps its greatest paradox. It has within its borders a state which was instrumental in helping to found the League of Nations, but this same state represents a viewpoint most heatedly denounced today by its African colleagues. The fact that so many of the newer UN members come from this continent and that two of the Presidents of the General Assembly since 1960 have come from Africa helps to explain two of the most salient features of the United Nations: its dramatic change from an essentially white, Western European-dominated organization in 1945, and the noticeable African impact on many of the programs and debates of the institution in the middle of the 1960's. But despite the common recent heritage of so much of the African continent it is no more homogeneous than the British Commonwealth—to which a number of these states belong. John Karefa-Smart, who has held a high government position in one of the African states, discusses this rising tide of African influence in the UN, but also notes the impact of the Organization on the group. It is because of the latter—the belief of many African leaders that the UN has helped to establish their independence and to sustain them—that the Organization has more meaning for them than perhaps for any other group. This helps to explain their strong attachment to non-alignment, although the meaning of that concept is not identical among all of its advocates.

The Latin American states came to the United Nations with memories of the League, memories which were not too pleasant for a number of them. Bryce Wood[1] and Minerva Morales M. trace the Latin American states' unsatisfactory relationship with the League and compare this with the highly favorable attitude almost all of these states had toward the UN at the outset of their participation in it. The new association must be seen not only in terms of this past experience but also in connection with the establishment of a regional organization, the Organization of American States, and the question of its relationship to the UN. This question has been unresolved since 1948, when the Charter of the OAS was adopted. The debates over the latter issue parallel the periods of tension and hostility between one or more of the Latin American states and the United States. Hence this voting group, like those discussed prior to it, is also divided and meets more often

[1] Wood is the one exception to the statement made earlier that all of the authors of these articles are natives of the regions about which they have written.

as a group to work out questions of candidacies for office than questions of substantive policies. As a matter of fact, the more the United States, which is not a member of the Latin group but is of the OAS, attempts to force controversial continental issues into the OAS forum, because its influence is greater there than in the UN, the more some of the Latin states divide and disagree strongly among themselves about the utility of the OAS.

The Asian states, although similar in some historical and economic respects to the African states, and in a more limited extent, to the Latin American states, nevertheless confront the UN with a predicament not comparable to that presented by any other region. Their natural leader, China, plays no role among them within the UN because those who rule Mainland China have not been seated as delegates. At the same time the Nationalists, who are seated, are not recognized by many of the Asian states, and the Chinese Communists are outside the Organization and are extremely critical of it. As long as this condition prevails it will continue to have a distorting effect not only upon foreign relations in Asia but also in the UN.

Arthur Lall has had a very notable career in government and in academic circles. In his discussion, "The Asian Nations and the United Nations," he points to India as a second source of natural leadership. This leadership, however, did not make itself manifest in the founding days of the Organization's history. Of course, as he acknowledges, the Indian delegates at San Francisco were picked by the British and thus not truly representative of nationalist sentiments in India. These sentiments, which within a half-dozen years were to become of paramount importance in world affairs, had not yet come to make a noticeable stir anywhere. The result was that the Charter took on a different cast in 1945 than it undoubtedly would have later.

The Korean War not only created a felt need for a closer association of the African and Asian members, but in at least one respect provided for a forerunner of the role they were to fill later in the Suez crisis and in the Congo eruption. For in all of these affairs the African and Asian members played an increasingly important role as non-aligned intermediaries and peace-keepers. Perhaps because their individual strengths cannot provide much impact on the world balance of power, and because relations of a hostile nature tend to reduce the efforts and funds for economic and social welfare badly needed by these states, the non-aligned nations, almost one half of the present UN membership, have adopted what is for them the wisest position. This is a far cry from the cool reception the position received when put forth by statesmen such as Prime Minister Nehru in the early 1950's. In addition to their many other important roles the Asian states have maintained a steady pressure to move the disarmament discussions along both within and outside the UN.

It becomes clear from these selections that the decisive effects of the formation of groups and blocs, which was originally feared and often commented upon adversely, has had a positive influence more often than not in maintaining fluidity between the major poles of power. It has aided in an effort to probe for solutions rather than to accept positions on a take-it-or-leave-it basis.

Do bloc members tend to vote so as to maintain bloc solidarity rather than to support positions which have been individually thought out? In other words, do the merits of issues get lost sight of because of a preference to be in the good graces of the bloc? And, even if the evidence supports such a conclusion, does this distinguish the General Assembly from other parliamentary forums? We might also ask whether national policies become distorted in the search for votes, as some observers contend. The student will need to think about and investigate these questions with care if he wishes to improve his comprehension of the foreign politics of his day.

FURTHER READINGS

Bailey, Sydney D., *The General Assembly of the United Nations*, rev. ed. New York: Frederick A. Praeger. Inc., 1964.

Fawcett, J. E. S., "The Commonwealth in the United Nations," *Journal of Commonwealth Political Studies*, May 1962.

National Studies on International Organization. Prepared for Carnegie Endowment Series, New York: Manhattan Publishing Company.

Risselbach, L. N., "Quantitative Techniques for Studying Voting Behavior in the UN General Assembly," *International Organization*, Vol. 14, Spring 1960, pp. 291–306.

AN OVER-ALL VIEW OF BLOCS AND GROUPS

Thomas Hovet, Jr.*

. . . There has been little or no attempt at systematic examination of [bloc politics]. As a result there is still much vagueness as to exactly what blocs and groups do exist in the General Assembly. Since many of them have similar names, they are often assumed to be one and the same when actually they are not. For example, it appears that the "Soviet bloc" and the "Eastern European group" are generally considered synonymous and identical although in fact they have slightly different memberships and roles in the Assembly. Moreover, as a result of the fact that the groups are flexible and many have overlapping memberships, one encounters not only confusion as to bloc and group identities but also only partial awareness of the full extent of the bloc and group structure in the General Assembly and the United Nations.

Thus the first step in any attempt to relate the operation of bloc politics in the United Nations to the effective participation of the United States in that world body must be to clarify the nature and extent of the bloc and group development in general.

Compared with the early years, the General Assembly of 1959 presents a fairly complicated structure of blocs and groups, the identities and extent of which can be best considered in terms of the following categories based on the roles they play and the degree to which they are organized—or unorganized, as might be the case: blocs, caucusing groups, geographical distribution groups, regional organization groups, common interest groups, and temporary groups.

BLOCS

A *bloc* might best be defined as a group of states which meets regularly in caucus and the members of which are bound in their votes in the General Assembly by the caucus decision. Using this definition, there is present only one true *bloc*—the Soviet bloc, which to all intents and purposes operates as a single unit with nine votes, the number of its members. The members of the Soviet bloc at the present time are: Albania, Bulgaria, Byelorussia,

* Reprinted by permission of the publishers from Thomas Hovet, Jr., *Bloc Politics in the United Nations* (Cambridge, Mass.: Harvard University Press), Chap. 2, pp. 29–46. Copyright 1960, by the Massachusetts Institute of Technology.

Thomas Hovet, Jr. is Professor of Political Science at the University of Oregon and author of *Bloc Politics in the United Nations* and *Africa in the United Nations*.

Czechoslovakia, Hungary, Poland, Rumania, Ukraine, and the Soviet Union. In contrast to a *bloc*, the other "informal" political organizations in the Assembly are generally termed *groups*. There are several types of groups but all are distinguished from blocs by the fact that, although they share a common basis for consultation on issues, such consultation does not result in a decision which binds their members as to how they vote in the Assembly.

CAUCUSING GROUPS

The term *caucusing group* may be applied to any group of member states in the Assembly which has some degree of formal organization, holds fairly regular meetings, and is concerned with substantive issues and related procedural matters before the sessions of the General Assembly. (Thus the list below does not include such groups as the "old Commonwealth" and NATO which function on an *ad hoc* basis only.) As of 1959, there were eight caucusing groups in the General Assembly:

ASIAN-AFRICAN GROUPS. 29 members—Afghanistan, Burma, Cambodia, Ceylon, Ethiopia, Ghana, Guinea, India, Indonesia, Iran, Iraq, Japan, Jordan, Laos, Lebanon, Liberia, Libya, Malaya, Morocco, Nepal, Pakistan, Philippines, Saudi Arabia, Sudan, Thailand, Tunisia, Turkey, United Arab Republic (Syria and Egypt), and Yemen

ARAB GROUP. 10 members—Iraq, Jordan, Lebanon, Libya, Morocco, Sudan, Saudi Arabia, Tunisia, United Arab Republic (Syria and Egypt), and Yemen

AFRICAN GROUP. 9 members—Egypt, Ethiopia, Ghana, Guinea, Liberia, Libya, Morocco, Sudan, and Tunisia

BENELUX GROUP. 3 members—Belgium, Luxembourg, and the Netherlands

COMMONWEALTH GROUP. 9 members—Australia, Canada, Ceylon, Ghana, India, Malaya, New Zealand, Pakistan, Union of South Africa, and the United Kingdom

LATIN AMERICAN GROUP. 20 members—Argentina, Bolivia, Brazil, Chile, Colombia, Costa Rica, Cuba, Dominican Republic, Ecuador, El Salvador, Guatemala, Haiti, Honduras, Mexico, Nicaragua, Panama, Paraguay, Peru, Uruguay, and Venezuela

SCANDINAVIAN GROUP. 4 members—Denmark, Iceland, Norway, and Sweden

WESTERN EUROPEAN GROUP. 5 members—Belgium, France, Italy, Luxembourg, and the Netherlands.

The newly organized African group began operating within the framework of the Thirteenth Session. The Scandinavian group might be placed in a separate category since, although it holds meetings, these meetings are generally held before the Assembly comes into session and not as often during the sessions as are those of the other caucusing groups. It is apparent that there is an overlapping of membership between the Asian-African, Arab, African, and Commonwealth groups, and between the Benelux and Western European groups.

The caucusing groups are the main political-interest groups that operate in the Assembly and are involved in behind-the-scene negotiation on most of the crucial issues. Ten members of the Assembly—Finland, Yugoslavia, China, Austria, Greece, Ireland, Portugal, Spain, Israel, and the United States—do not belong to any caucusing group.

GEOGRAPHICAL DISTRIBUTION GROUPS

Geographical distribution groups exist by virtue of informal "gentleman's agreements," consensus, or formal agreements[1] for the purpose of allocating seats on the General Committee, the three councils, the International Court of Justice, and other less-than-full membership committees.

The term "geographical distribution" as applied to this category of political factions is really a misnomer. They are the result of a working political interpretation developed from the phraseology of Article 23 of the Charter, and any true geographical distribution in the groups is coincidental. They are generally referred to as geographical distribution groups because diplomatic tact prevents them from being called, more rationally, political compromise groups with some reflection of geographical areas. In essence, they consult only to agree upon which of their members are to be "nominated" so as to give a geographical distribution to the composition of the smaller bodies in the United Nations in accord with the number of seats allocated to the particular group.

There are five distinct geographical groups in which there is no overlap of membership:

EASTERN EUROPEAN GROUP. 10 members—Albania, Bulgaria, Byelorussia, Czechoslovakia, Finland, Hungary, Poland, Rumania, Ukraine, and Yugoslavia

ASIAN AND AFRICAN GROUP. 29 members—Afghanistan, Burma, Cambodia, Ceylon, Ethiopia, Ghana, Guinea, India, Indonesia, Iran, Iraq, Japan, Jordan, Laos, Lebanon, Liberia, Libya, Malaya, Morocco, Nepal, Pakistan, Philippines, Saudi Arabia, Sudan, Thailand, Tunisia, Turkey, United Arab Republic (Egypt and Syria), and Yemen

LATIN AMERICAN GROUP. 20 members—Argentina, Bolivia, Brazil, Chile, Colombia, Costa Rica, Cuba, Dominican Republic, Ecuador, El Salvador, Guatemala, Haiti, Honduras, Mexico, Nicaragua, Panama, Paraguay, Peru, Uruguay, and Venezuela

WESTERN EUROPEAN AND OTHER STATES GROUP. 18 members—Australia, Austria, Belgium, Canada, Denmark, Greece, Iceland, Ireland, Israel, Italy, Luxembourg, the Netherlands, New Zealand, Norway, Portugal, Spain, Sweden, and the Union of South Africa

PERMANENT MEMBERS OF THE SECURITY COUNCIL GROUP. 5 members—China, France, the Soviet Union, the United Kingdom, and the United States.

[1] The only formal agreement is contained in General Assembly Res. 1192 (XII).

In addition to these five geographical distribution groups, which are exclusive in membership, there is one other which has widely overlapping membership but which is also acknowledged in the distribution of elective seats.

COMMONWEALTH GROUP. 9 members—Australia, Canada, Ceylon, Ghana, India, Malaya, New Zealand, Pakistan, and the Union of South Africa.

The members of the Commonwealth geographical distribution group are also either members of the Asian and African geographical distribution group or the Western European and Other States geographical distribution groups. Most of the election voting "agreements" provide that at least one of the members elected should be from the Commonwealth. Whichever Commonwealth member seat is secured will also count as a seat for the other geographical distribution group to which that Commonwealth member belongs.

It is fairly apparent from a glance at the memberships of the geographical distribution groups and the caucusing groups that these are in several instances identical groupings of states, and that in the other groupings there is considerable similarity of membership. Chart 1, which shows the interrelations of membership between these two general categories of interest groups in the General Assembly, demonstrates the reason for much of the confusion about blocs and groups. It shows that the Soviet bloc and the Eastern European group are not identical in membership. It should also be noted that, although the Soviet Union is not actually a member of the Eastern European group from which the geographical distribution seats are chosen, the Soviet Union does participate in the meetings of the group to agree upon the group's candidates for an election. This situation is also true of the United Kingdom in the case of the Commonwealth geographical distribution group and of France in the Western European geographical distribution group.

Chart 1 also illustrates the fact that "geographical" distribution groups do not represent true geographical divisions of states but are essentially efforts to arrive at a working division of major political interest subdivisions in the General Assembly. Any truly geographical division would: include China, the Union of South Africa, and Israel in the Asian and African Group instead of putting them elsewhere; somehow include Canada and the United States with the other Western Hemisphere states; include Austria with Eastern Europe; possibly include Greece with Eastern Europe. (Actually, in earlier sessions, Greece was given an "Eastern European" seat over the united protests of the other Eastern European Members.) Finland might just as well be with the other Scandinavian states in Western Europe as in Eastern Europe; and Australia and New Zealand might be in a separate category or with the Asian and African states. If geographical distribution were actually

CHART 1*

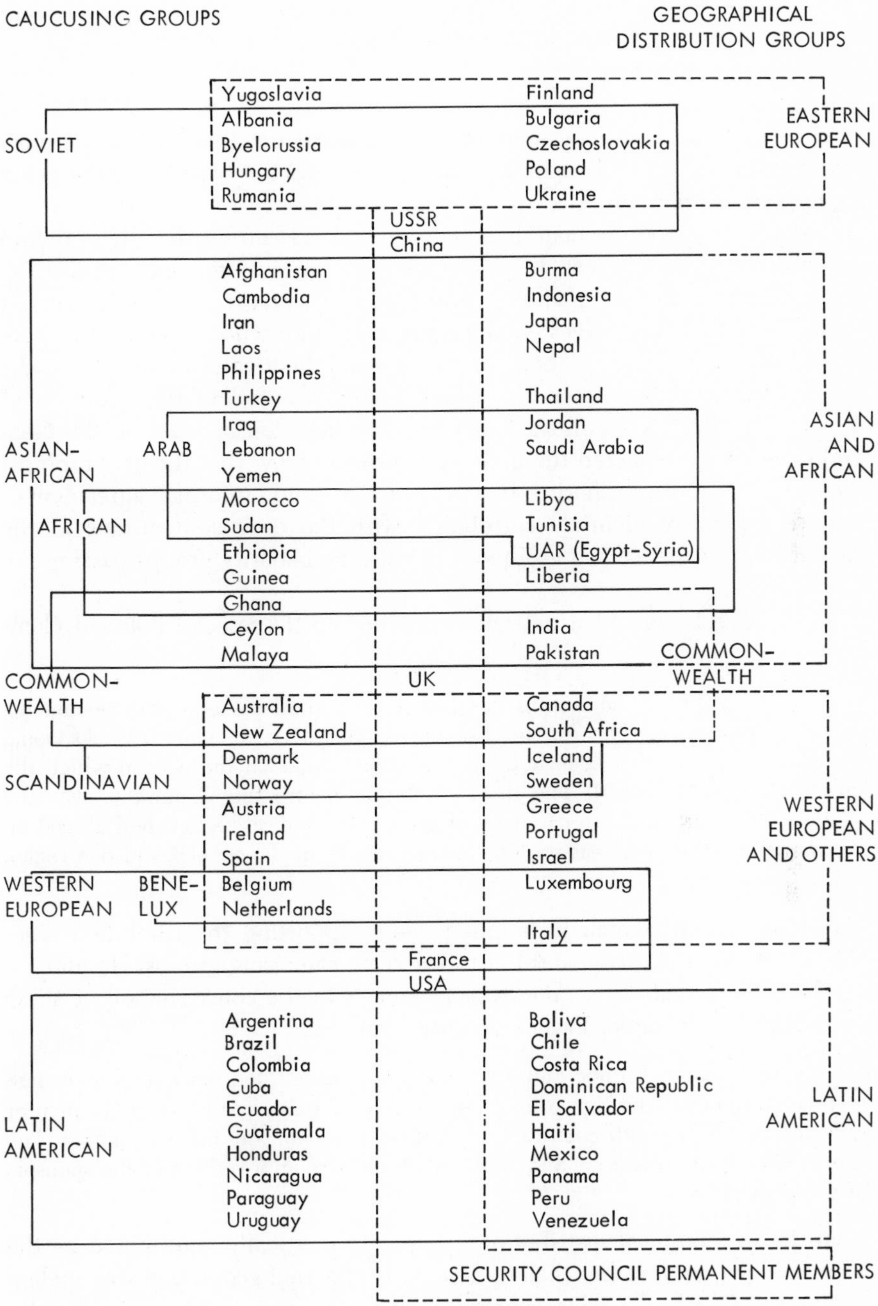

CAUCUSING GROUPS

GEOGRAPHICAL
DISTRIBUTION GROUPS

	Yugoslavia	Finland
	Albania	Bulgaria
SOVIET	Byelorussia	Czechoslovakia
	Hungary	Poland
	Rumania	Ukraine

EASTERN
EUROPEAN

USSR
China

	Afghanistan	Burma
	Cambodia	Indonesia
	Iran	Japan
	Laos	Nepal
	Philippines	
	Turkey	Thailand
	Iraq	Jordan
ASIAN– ARAB	Lebanon	Saudi Arabia
AFRICAN	Yemen	
	Morocco	Libya
AFRICAN	Sudan	Tunisia
	Ethiopia	UAR (Egypt–Syria)
	Guinea	Liberia
	Ghana	
	Ceylon	India
	Malaya	Pakistan

ASIAN
AND
AFRICAN

COMMON-
WEALTH

COMMON-
WEALTH   UK

	Australia	Canada
	New Zealand	South Africa
	Denmark	Iceland
SCANDINAVIAN	Norway	Sweden
	Austria	Greece
	Ireland	Portugal
	Spain	Israel
WESTERN BENE-	Belgium	Luxembourg
EUROPEAN LUX	Netherlands	
		Italy

WESTERN
EUROPEAN
AND OTHERS

France
USA

	Argentina	Boliva
	Brazil	Chile
	Colombia	Costa Rica
	Cuba	Dominican Republic
	Ecuador	El Salvador
LATIN	Guatemala	Haiti
AMERICAN	Honduras	Mexico
	Nicaragua	Panama
	Paraguay	Peru
	Uruguay	Venezuela

LATIN
AMERICAN

SECURITY COUNCIL PERMANENT MEMBERS

*Members of the United Nations arranged according to their membership in caucusing and
geographical distribution groups operating in the General Assembly at the start of the XIVth
Session in 1959.

on a basis of geography, logic might make it much more appropriate to separate the African states from the Asian states.

* * * * * * *

The use of such a geographical formula as in the International Atomic Energy Agency depends upon a desire to elect upon a basis of actual geography rather than on a basis of political alliance. In an organ with a majority voting requirement like the General Assembly, the division into "geographical regions" can be determined on any criteria that satisfies the groups making up the majority, and the minority groups which are not united may find themselves "lumped together" in a wholly unrealistic "geographical region." The debate in the Special Political Committee in the XIIth Session of the Assembly, which finally resulted in the adoption of Resolution 1192 (XII) on the basis for the allocation of seats on the General Committee, reflected the dominant majority view that the geographical distribution groups, adhering to past practices and "informal agreements," represent a fairly identical correlation with the caucusing groups in the cases where the caucusing groups were with the majority groups passing the resolution.

As the Czechoslovakian delegate explained to the Special Political Committee:

Delegations had had two months in which to obtain all the necessary documents and to prepare themselves for the discussions. Moreover, for several weeks, some groups of countries had been holding preliminary talks on the way in which the problem could be solved. The draft resolution before the Committee was the result of those negotiations; countries of three geographical regions had agreed on a common position, whereas the objections came from the countries of one region only. . . .

The three groups which he implied were supporting the resolution were the Soviet, Asian-African, and Latin American caucusing groups. He lumped all the other members as "one region"—much to the consternation of these members. For example, France [pointed out that]

the group "Western Europe and other countries" in . . . the draft resolution bore no relation to facts. The European group, which did exist, had never held caucuses with the Commonwealth countries, the United States or any other countries. The expression "Western Europe and other countries" was an invention of the sponsors of the joint draft.

That the geographical distribution groups are politically determined by the Assembly majority, rather than on any basis of actual geography was spelled out by the Czechoslovakian sponsor of this only formal distribution resolution, when he stated:

The specification of geographical regions was equally the result of informal negotiations among groups of countries. Those regions correspond to the political realities which have been reflected for years in all United Nations bodies. . . .

In spite of the protests on the character of the geographical distribution groups, there is considerable correlation between them and the caucusing groups, as indicated on Chart 1. Certainly any efforts to alter the geographical distribution groups recognized by the majority of the United Nations must recognize that those who disagree with the present formal and informal agreements need to alter the present caucusing group coalitions if they are to build a majority supporting some other basis of geographical distribution groups. Such action, therefore, would have to be directed either to forming new caucusing groups or to winning over other caucusing groups so as to build the necessary majority.

Chart 1 also indicates that, by virtue of membership in several of the groups, some states possess pivotal positions making them key states from the standpoint of political tactics. For example, the fact that the United Arab Republic and Libya belong to the Arab, African, and Asian-African groups means that they are members which if cultivated by interested parties would offer access to at least three fairly large caucusing groups. Similarly, Ghana as a member of the African, Asian-African, and Commonwealth caucusing groups, is also in a key position. To a lesser degree, this is also true of Ceylon, India, Malaya, and Pakistan, which belong to both the Commonwealth and Asian-African caucusing groups.

REGIONAL GROUPS

In addition to the one bloc, eight caucusing groups, and six geographical distribution groups which provide a basis for group coalitions, there are two other categories of groupings which are factors in the political situation in the general Assembly. These might be termed *regional groups* and *common interest groups*. They are primarily distinguished by the fact that for the most part they do not have any regular procedural or organizational features operating behind the scenes of the General Assembly but are groups of states bound together by certain factors present and operating independently of the framework of the United Nations.

The *regional groups* which might be distinguished are groups of UN members "bound" together either by common membership in a regional organization not connected directly with the United Nations, such as regional collective-security organizations, regional alliances, or regional economic organizations, or by common participation in important regional conferences which, while not establishing any permanent organization, nevertheless draw the participating countries together in establishing an agreement on principles of mutual consultation.

None of these regional groups caucuses in the General Assembly. However, since regional cooperation yields mutual agreement on certain areas of concern, there is good probability that such agreement is carried over into the General Assembly. This is certainly true if the regional agreements take the form of binding commitments. Although even in the case of binding commitments the issues reflected in the Assembly may not be precisely the same, it has been implied that these groups operate as a caucus in the Assembly, a point which is often denied. Following such implications, Mr. Lloyd of the United Kingdom explained to the Assembly that,

Mr. Gromyko (USSR) referred to them as "blocs." The countries of NATO do not vote as a bloc in this Assembly. We do not even hold meetings to discuss Assembly matters together, and we rarely, all of us, vote the same way. Exactly the same applies to the countries in the Baghdad Pact and the countries of SEATO. . . .

The degree to which any regional organization, arrangement, or conference has a behind-the-scenes influence on the group politics of the General Assembly is difficult to determine because the specific concerns of the regional interest may bear on only one aspect of the Assembly's areas of concern. For example, such regional arrangements as the Baghdad Pact, the North Atlantic Treaty Organization, and the South East Asia Treaty Organization, which are to a great part concerned with collective defense against the Soviet Union, may have an influence primarily in the area of issues before the General Assembly which are concerned with aspects of East-West tension. Similarly, it might be argued that a regional arrangement like the Colombo Plan, concerned with uniting efforts for economic development, might reflect this joint concern in Assembly debates concerned with economic development. Certainly, one of the easiest ways of determining the possible effect of a regional arrangement in the Assembly is to examine the voting records of the regional arrangement's members. If they evidence a greater degree of cohesion in the General Assembly after the conclusion of the regional "agreement" than before the "agreement," it may be a good indication that the regional arrangement operates as a group in the General Assembly—even though it may not hold any caucus meetings or consultations during the session.

For the purposes of this study 21 possible regional groups will be examined for evidence of cohesive voting in the Assembly. These might be termed the more "important" regional arrangements since they are the ones most often encountered in "corridor conversations" with members of delegations in the General Assembly. The twenty-one regional groups are:[2]

ANZUS COUNCIL. 3 members—Australia, New Zealand, and the United States

ARAB LEAGUE. 10 members—Iraq, Jordan, Lebanon, Libya, Morocco, Saudi Arabia, Sudan, Tunisia, United Arab Republic (Egypt and Syria), and Yemen

[2] The number of members listed in each group include only those members of the group who are also members of the United Nations.

BAGHDAD PACT. 5 members—Iraq, Iran, Pakistan, Turkey, and the United Kingdom

BALKAN ALLIANCE. 3 members—Greece, Turkey, and Yugoslavia

BANDUNG CONFERENCE. 25 members—Afghanistan, Burma, Cambodia, Ceylon, Ethiopia, Ghana, India, Indonesia, Iran, Iraq, Japan, Jordan, Laos, Lebanon, Liberia, Libya, Nepal, Pakistan, Philippines, Saudi Arabia, Sudan, Thailand, Turkey, United Arab Republic (Egypt and Syria), and Yemen

COLOMBO PLAN. 17 members—Australia, Burma, Cambodia, Canada, Ceylon, India, Indonesia, Japan, Laos, Malaya, Nepal, New Zealand, Pakistan, Philippines, Thailand, United Kingdom, and the United States

COMMONWEALTH. 9 members—Australia, Canada, Ceylon, Ghana, India, Malaya, New Zealand, Pakistan, and the Union of South Africa

CONFERENCE OF INDEPENDENT AFRICAN STATES. 8 members—Ethiopia, Ghana, Liberia, Libya, Morocco, Sudan, Tunisia, and the United Arab Republic

COUNCIL OF EUROPE. 14 members—Austria, Belgium, Denmark, France, Greece, Iceland, Ireland, Italy, Luxembourg, the Netherlands, Norway, Sweden, Turkey, and the United Kingdom

EUROPEAN ATOMIC ENERGY COMMUNITY. 5 members—Belgium, France, Italy, Luxembourg, and the Netherlands

EUROPEAN COAL AND STEEL COMMUNITY. 5 members—Belgium, France, Italy, Luxembourg, and the Netherlands

EUROPEAN COMMON MARKET. 5 members—Belgium, France, Italy, Luxembourg, and the Netherlands

EUROPEAN PAYMENTS UNION. 15 members—Austria, Belgium, Denmark, France, Greece, Iceland, Ireland, Italy, the Netherlands, Luxembourg, Norway, Portugal, Sweden, Turkey, and the United Kingdom

NORDIC COUNCIL. 4 members—Denmark, Iceland, Norway, and Sweden

NORTH ATLANTIC TREATY ORGANIZATION. 14 members—Belgium, Canada, Denmark, France, Greece, Iceland, Italy, Luxembourg, the Netherlands, Norway, Portugal, Turkey, United Kingdom, and the United States

ORGANIZATION FOR EUROPEAN ECONOMIC COOPERATION. 15 members—Austria, Belgium, Denmark, France, Greece, Iceland, Ireland, Italy, Luxembourg, the Netherlands, Norway, Portugal, Sweden, Turkey, and the United Kingdom

ORGANIZATION OF AMERICAN STATES. 21 members—Argentina, Bolivia, Brazil, Chile, Colombia, Costa Rica, Cuba, Dominican Republic, Ecuador, El Salvador, Guatemala, Haiti, Honduras, Mexico, Nicaragua, Panama, Paraguay, Peru, Uruguay, Venezuela, and the United States

ORGANIZATION OF CENTRAL AMERICAN STATES. 5 members—Costa Rica, El Salvador, Guatemala, Honduras, and Nicaragua

SOUTH EAST ASIA TREATY ORGANIZATION. 8 members—Australia, France, New Zealand, Pakistan, Philippines, Thailand, United Kingdom, and the United States

WARSAW PACT. 7 members—Albania, Bulgaria, Czechoslovokia, Hungary, Poland, Rumania, and the Soviet Union

WESTERN EUROPEAN UNION. 6 members—Belgium, France, Italy, Luxembourg, the Netherlands, and the United Kingdom.

A glance at the membership of these regional groups makes it apparent that there is a great deal of similarity, if not identity, between the regional groups and the caucusing groups, and that in most instances there is also a considerable overlap of membership between the various regional groups.

Probably the best way to make evident the extent of similarity and overlap of membership between the regional groups themselves and the caucusing groups is to examine them region by region. Chart 2 compares the "Western European" countries as to their membership in various regional groups with the caucusing groups. Several points became fairly obvious. The memberships of the Western European caucusing group, the European Atomic Energy Community, the European Common Market, and the European Coal and Steel Community are identical. The memberships of the Nordic Council and the Scandinavian caucusing group are also identical. The Benelux caucusing group is identical with the Benelux Customs Union. Although this latter regional body was not listed as a regional group, it might well have been included. The high degree of overlapping membership between the other "Western European" regional groups indicates that, although they may not be identical with any caucusing groups, nonetheless these countries have, through their membership in these regional bodies, many elements of common interest. Further, all of the members of these "Western European" regional groups are also members of the Western European geographical distribution group.

Chart 3 illustrates the overlapping memberships between the "Asian and African" regional groups and caucusing groups. The African caucusing group is identical to the Conference of African States, the Arab League is identical to the Arab caucusing group, and all of the members of the Bandung Conference are members of the Asian-African caucusing group. If the Commonwealth were included in this list of regional groups, it would be apparent that its membership is identical with that of the Commonwealth caucusing group.

Chart 4 illustrates the membership in the "American" regional bodies in relationship to the Latin American caucusing group, and Chart 5 shows the "Eastern European" regional groups in relation to the membership of the Soviet caucusing group.

These four charts suggest that certain members are in rather key positions. Turkey is a member of the Asian-African caucusing group, the Baghdad Pact, and the North Atlantic Treaty Organization as well as the Council of Europe, the European Payments Union, and the Organization of European Economic Cooperation. Iraq is a member of both the Arab and Asian-African

CHART 2*

REGIONAL GROUPS

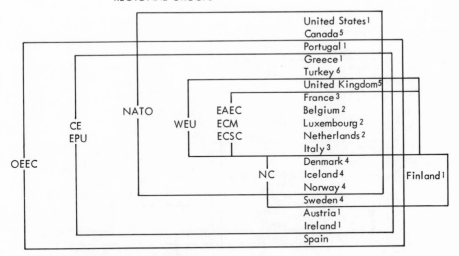

Symbol key to regional groups:
   CE: Council of Europe
   EAEC: European Atomic Energy Community
   ECM: European Common Market
   ECSC: European Coal and Steel Community
   EPU   European Payments Union
   NATO: North Atlantic Treaty Organization
   NC: Nordic Council
   OEEC: Organization for European Economic Cooperation
   WEU: Western European Union (formerly Brussels Treaty Organization)

1. Does not belong to a caucusing group
2. Belongs to Benelux and Western European caucusing groups
3. Belongs to Western European caucusing group
4. Belongs to Scandinavian caucusing group
5. Belongs to Commonwealth caucusing group
6. Belongs to Asian-African caucusing group

*Comparison of the membership in "Western European" regional groups and the membership in caucusing groups.

CHART 3*

MEMBERSHIP IN
CAUCUSING GROUPS

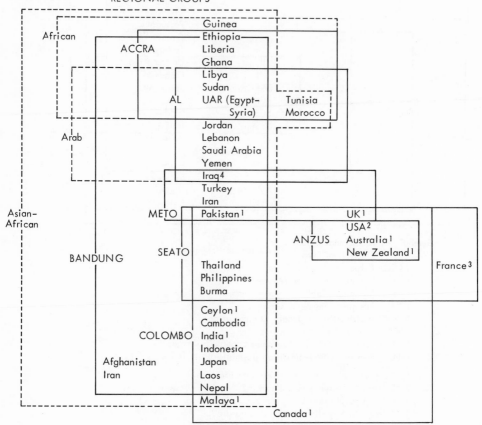

Symbol key to regional groups:

ACCRA: Conference of Independent African States
AL: Arab League
ANZUS: Anzus Council
BANDUNG: Asian-African Conference
COLOMBO: Colombo Plan
METO: Baghdad Pact
SEATO: Southeast Asian Treaty Organization

1. Member of the Commonwealth caucusing group
2. Does not belong to a caucusing group
3. Member of Western European caucusing group
4. Member of Baghdad Pact until 1959

*Comparison of the membership in "Asian and African" regional groups and the membership in caucusing groups, at the end of the XIIIth Session.

CHART 4*

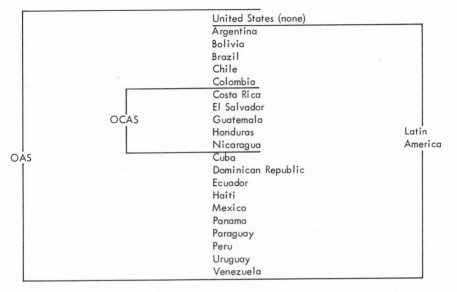

REGIONAL GROUPS   MEMBERSHIP IN CAUCUSING GROUPS

United States (none)
Argentina
Bolivia
Brazil
Chile
Colombia
Costa Rica
El Salvador
OCAS   Guatemala
Honduras   Latin
Nicaragua   America
OAS   Cuba
Dominican Republic
Ecuador
Haiti
Mexico
Panama
Paraguay
Peru
Uruguay
Venezuela

Symbol key to regional groups:
    OAS: Organization of American States
    OCAS: Organization of Central American States

*Comparison of the membership in "American" regional groups and the membership in caucusing groups.

CHART 5*

REGIONAL GROUPS   MEMBERSHIP IN CAUCUSING GROUPS

WARSAW   Albania
PACT   Bulgaria
                Czechoslovakia
                Hungary   Soviet
                Poland
                Rumania
                Soviet Union
                Byelorussia
                Ukraine
BALKAN   Yugoslavia (none)
ALLIANCE   Turkey (Asian–African)
                Greece (none)

*Comparison of the membership in "Eastern European" regional groups and the membership in caucusing groups.

caucusing groups and of the Arab League, and the Bandung Conference. France, Belgium, Luxembourg, the Netherlands, and Italy as well as Norway, Denmark, and Iceland belong both to caucusing groups and to most of the European regional groups. Many other such pertinent relationships are obvious from a close study of these charts and suggest possible political roles for the members.

It should be pointed out that many of the regional groups have been formed for specific purposes and that their reflection of regional group consensus in the General Assembly is generally limited to the particular issues upon which they have developed common points of view. Their real importance might well be viewed as indicating certain common interests which might provide a basis for forming new caucusing groups as the General Assembly develops. Obviously, many of the regional groups may espouse concepts which are not wholly in accord with other regional groups and particularly with other regional groups that belong to the same caucusing groups. For example, there certainly are many divisive forces in the Asian-African caucusing group when it is made of such "conflicting" regional groups as the Arab League, the Baghdad Pact, and SEATO, to give but one illustration. This fact will become even more apparent when these groups are considered individually.

COMMON INTEREST GROUPS

Common interest groups might be defined as groups of states which, although not bound together by any sort of formal arrangement or membership in a regional body, nevertheless have some elements in common which tend to provide a common outlook on certain types of issues before the General Assembly. Whether these common interest groups actually exist may be a moot question; some observers indicate that they do exist and have an influence. At least seven might be distinguished:

MOSLEM STATES. 15 members—Afghanistan, Indonesia, Iran, Iraq, Jordan, Lebanon, Libya, Morocco, Pakistan, Saudi Arabia, Sudan, Tunisia, Turkey, United Arab Republic (Egypt and Syria), and Yemen

ARAB STATES. 10 members—Iraq, Jordan, Lebanon, Libya, Morocco, Saudi Arabia, Sudan, Tunisia, United Arab Republic (Egypt and Syria), and Yemen

BIG THREE. 3 members—France, United Kingdom, and the United States

TRUST ADMINISTRATORS. 7 members—Australia, Belgium, France, Italy, New Zealand, United Kingdom, and the United States

COLONIAL POWERS.[3] 10 members—Australia, Belgium, France, Italy, the Netherlands, New Zealand, Portugal, Spain, United Kingdom, and the United States

ANTI-COLONIAL STATES. 37 members—Afghanistan, Albania, Bulgaria,

[3] "Colonial" and "anti-colonial" are terms used in referring to these groups of members and in no way imply an application of the actual definition of these terms.

Burma, Byelorussia, Cambodia, Ceylon, Czechoslovakia, Ethiopia, Ghana, Guinea, Hungary, India, Indonesia, Iran, Iraq, Jordan, Laos, Lebanon, Liberia, Libya, Malaya, Morocco, Nepal, Pakistan, Philippines, Poland, Rumania, Saudi Arabia, Sudan, Thailand, Tunisia, Ukraine, USSR, United Arab Republic, Yemen, and Yugoslavia

UNDERDEVELOPED COUNTRIES. 57 members—Afghanistan, Argentina, Austria, Bolivia, Brazil, Burma, Cambodia, Ceylon, Chile, China, Colombia, Costa Rica, Cuba, Dominican Republic, Ecuador, El Salvador, Ethiopia, Finland, Ghana, Greece, Guatamala, Guinea, Haiti, Honduras, Iceland, India, Indonesia, Iran, Iraq, Israel, Japan, Jordan, Laos, Lebanon, Liberia, Libya, Malaya, Mexico, Morocco, Nepal, Nicaragua, Pakistan, Panama, Paraguay, Peru, Philippines, Saudi Arabia, Spain, Sudan, Thailand, Tunisia, Turkey, United Arab Republic, Uruguay, Venezuela, Yemen, and Yugoslavia.

These groupings are not derived from abstract reasoning but are based on discussion with members of delegations. There is considerable correlation between the membership in these common interest groups and the caucusing groups. In essence, the so-called anti-colonial states as a group consist of the Soviet and Asian-African caucusing groups, excluding Japan and Turkey. Logic might exclude Austria and Finland from the "underdeveloped countries," but most individuals consulted indicated that they are generally included in this common interest group. These groups do not, of course, have any formal organization, but they have obvious common ties which doubtless provide a sense of cohesion in particular issues. For the most part they are actually either coalitions of caucusing groups or coalitions of the majority of members from the various caucusing groups.

TEMPORARY GROUPS

There seem to have been at least three temporary groups which have materialized on particular issues before the Assembly in certain sessions:

SPANISH LANGUAGE GROUP. The Spanish speaking countries of Latin America plus the Philippines, which exerted an influence in several sessions on questions pertaining to Spanish language documents and Spanish as a working language of the United Nations

THE SIXTEEN. The sixteen members of the United Nations, that sent combat troops to Korea, and seem to have maintained regular consultations with respect to matters of joint concern

SOUTH EAST ASIAN PRIME MINISTERS. India, Indonesia, Ceylon, and Pakistan have held meetings outside the United Nations which have been reflected in the Assembly, especially in the Suez situation in 1956.

Other temporary groups may well have existed since it is only natural that special consultations or coalitions are worked out on certain specific issues in certain sessions; but it would be difficult if not impossible to determine all the special temporary groupings that have developed on particular issues before the United Nations.

The bloc and group patterns in the United Nations have been a gradual but steady development. Some of the caucusing groups, such as the Latin American, Commonwealth, and Arab groups, were in existence at the San Francisco Conference; others have gradually emerged. The geographical distribution groups have been in existence in one form or another since the First Part of the First Session. The regional groups have emerged as particular regional organizations have come into being over the twelve-year history of the organization. The common interest groups have been inherent in the Assembly from the outset. The growth of the bloc and group pattern is to a considerable extent a reflection of the expanding membership of the organization. As the United Nations has grown in size, like interests, cohesive factors, and joint participation in other international organizations have drawn members into group relations in order to have a more effective vote bargaining power.

THE FRAMEWORK OF INFLUENCE

Robert Owen Keohane[*]

The diversity of the United Nations is obvious. The size of the Organization makes some form of regularized cooperation among states necessary, yet its diversity insures that such cooperation will remain essentially limited in nature. Although most states in the General Assembly are members of regional groups, their first loyalties are to their own national interests, which may differ considerably from those of other states in the same region. Thus the most striking feature of the regional groups is their weakness. Not only do the groups fail to make authoritative policy, but often they do not even reflect the real patterns of political coalition in the organization. Therefore, while they are undoubtedly important, their significance can easily be over-emphasized.

[*] Robert Owen Keohane, "The Framework of Influence," *Political Influence in the General Assembly*, March 1966 issue of *International Conciliation*, No. 557, Chap. 1, pp. 5–16. By permission of the Carnegie Endowment for International Peace.

Robert Owen Keohane, Instructor of Political Science at Swarthmore College, presently has a grant from the Social Science Research Council to complete a more elaborate study of the General Assembly.

The major regional groups may be defined as those that nominate candidates (states or individuals, as the case may be) for offices of the General Assembly. There are six such groups: Western European, Latin American, East European,[1] African, Asian, and African-Asian. Africa and Asia are included separately as well as together; states in these regions belong to their respective groups as well as to the broader one. Since these six groups are functioning entities rather than mere geographic expressions, certain discrepancies exist between group membership and geography. China, Cuba, Israel, and South Africa, for example, do not attend meetings of the caucusing groups for their geographic regions.

These six major groups do not exhaust the group structure of the Assembly. On the contrary, within and across group lines there are more or less well-organized subgroups arranged along political, historical, ethnic, or special-interest lines. For example, the thirteen Arab states and the five Nordic countries are merely the most cohesive examples of subregional groups operating in the Assembly. A large array of developing states (known as the Seventy-Five) acts as an intra-Assembly interest group working for favorable trade and development policies. Even the Commonwealth states meet occasionally, although they are politically divided and no longer have a significant joint role in nominating candidates for Assembly offices.

Little is known about the actual operations of the East European group, which will therefore be excluded from this analysis. It is difficult to determine in what ways interaction and consultation take place within this group. Nevertheless, its high degree of voting cohesion should be noted. One may assume that there are more discussions and fewer commands in the group now than ten or fifteen years ago.

The scope of group action for the other five associations varies considerably. The Asian and Western European groups function almost exclusively as mechanisms for decisions on candidacy and related problems. Neither group, however, plays a significant role in the process by which substantive resolutions are adopted. Both are too divided politically to discuss effectively important issues in group meetings. In addition, the Western European group suffers under the handicap of having France and the United Kingdom as co-chairmen; the French and British delegations do not depend as heavily on group consultation and common action as their smaller colleagues.

The African, African-Asian, and Latin American groups meet regularly and often while the Assembly is in session to discuss a large variety of issues. Even in these groups, however, the scope of decision-making is limited. The African group has so far primarily discussed questions directly related to

[1] As a regional group in the General Assembly, it includes the following states: Albania, Byelorussia, Bulgaria, Czechoslovakia, Hungary, Poland, Romania, Ukraine, and USSR. Cuba and Mongolia now also form part of the group. See Sydney D. Bailey, *The General Assembly of The United Nations* (rev. ed.; New York: Frederick A. Praeger, 1964), p. 32.

Africa, leaving broader issues to the joint African-Asian group. Yet the latter group also does not discuss the entire range of issues before the Assembly. According to one Asian representative, "The African-Asian group does not discuss such matters as nuclear tests and disarmament. It only discusses matters on which there is a common interest—such as colonial questions, *apartheid,* and economic matters."[2]

Whether or not this statement is literally true, it illustrates an important point. Controversial issues that would raise or exacerbate conflicts within the diverse African-Asian group are usually considered in informal consultations or in nonregional associations of states with similar viewpoints. Thus a number of African and Asian states, along with Yugoslavia, have formed a "non-aligned" group in which they can work together within a framework of common interests and attitudes. Diversity is particularly great within the African-Asian group; in the Latin American group—Cuba being excluded—political outlooks are more similar on non-hemispheric issues, and the scope of discussion therefore is broader.

Even within their areas of effective operation, the regional groups by no means act as nascent political parties or real decision-making units. On the contrary, they are principally means of consultation and communication among states with certain similarities of aims and attitudes, tenuous though these affinities may be. They provide a continuing forum for discussion and an organizational structure within which occasional common action may be planned.[3] The reasons for regional group weakness are not hard to discern. Composed of states with independent decision-making processes rather than —as in national legislatures—of politicians dependent to some extent on their political parties for re-election, the groups possess little power vis à vis recalcitrant members. If a unamimously accepted compromise cannot be reached, no official group action is taken. None of the groups makes decisions by majority vote that are binding on all members. Even an overwhelming majority is relatively powerless to impose its will on one or a few dissenters; it is limited to exhortation, persuasion, and appeals to group solidarity.

The chief business of the groups is, therefore, to create a consensus within the limitations imposed by independent sovereignties and intra-regional diversity. Thus drafting committees may be appointed to formulate compromise resolutions that will be generally acceptable, but their recommendations remain subject to the approval of each member of the group. In some instances, negotiating committees will be formed to deal with other groups. However, there is no assurance that agreements reached will be acceptable to the group as a whole. The process is often frustrating and its results frequently vapid.

[2] Quotations without sources are from the author's interviews with delegates, whose comments specifically were not for attribution.

[3] For a historical and procedural discussion of groups, see especially Bailey, *op. cit.,* Chapter 2.

These difficulties reach their quintessence in the African-Asian group. Its members number more than sixty and range geographically, culturally, economically, and politically from Japan to Guinea, from the Philippines to Ethiopia. This array of states is so diverse that it may even be questioned whether the African and Asian states can act effectively as a group on significant as opposed to ritualistic issues. The recent movement among African delegations to emphasize the importance of the African group rather than the joint one indicates that perhaps it cannot. Size may confer more the semblance than the reality of political power.

TABLE I

AGREEMENT SCORES FOR REGIONAL GROUPS IN THE 15TH AND 18TH GENERAL ASSEMBLY SESSIONS

	15TH SESSION			18TH SESSION		
	MEAN	LOW	HIGH	MEAN	LOW	HIGH
Eastern Europe	99.4	98.8	100.0	98.9	95.8	100.0
Latin America	83.7	68.4	95.4	91.1	78.9	100.0
Western Europe	79.2	57.8	98.4	83.5	60.9	98.6
Africa	78.9	55.1	97.9	88.1	68.8	100.0
Asia	77.6	52.6	96.2	82.4	55.0	97.6
Africa-Asia	76.5	48.1	98.1	85.2	54.1	100.0

With this background, it is not surprising that the regional groups, excluding the East European one, do not act as voting blocs in the sense of rigidly disciplined units. Table 1 provides evidence for this conclusion by presenting agreement scores for the fifteenth and eighteenth sessions, 1960–61 and 1963, respectively. These agreement scores measure the frequency of voting similarities between any two states according to a formula that takes into account abstentions and absences. Complete disagreement would be represented by a score of zero; complete agreement by a score of 100. The first column shows the mean agreement scores of all states in each group with all others of the group; the second column gives the lowest intra-group score; and the third indicates the highest score between two group members.

This table points to a dual conclusion. The occurrence of low intra-group scores indicates that there is considerable dissension within most of the regional groups. On the whole, however, the regional groups maintained greater cohesion than the mean for the Assembly, although the differential was not strikingly large.

To some extent the improvement in group unity in the eighteenth session —indicated by higher agreement scores both within and between regions—is the result of diminished controversy in the Assembly that year. It may also be significant that the African and Latin American groups increased their cohesion about twice as much as did the Asian and Western European groups; furthermore, the lowest scores in the African and Latin American groups rose by at least ten points each compared with minimal gains for the two other regions. Since it was in the African and Latin American groups that members tried hardest to increase group unity between 1960 and 1963, these differences may indicate that their efforts met with some success.

When voting patterns in the eighteenth session are analyzed independently of regional affiliations, however, it becomes clear that cross-regional cooperation and cleavage remained important in 1963. Specifically, cross-group coalitions of African, Asian, and Latin American states are evident. A number of states in each of these groups agreed more often with certain states in the two other groups than with members of their own group. As will be shown below, many of the Assembly's voting patterns have regularly been based on intra-regional and inter-regional coalitions rather than strict adherence to regional group boundaries. The use of the term "bloc voting" should not obscure an awareness of this reality.

VOTING ALIGNMENTS

If a clear understanding of actual voting patterns in the General Assembly is to be gained, the voting data must be analyzed not only in regional group terms, but also without reference to the regional groups. An analysis focusing on regional groups and their cohesion cannot determine to what extent significant cross-regional coalitions exist and is therefore likely to obscure rather than illuminate many important features of voting in the Assembly.[4] Thus the analyst who merely studies the cohesion of caucusing groups cannot detect the presence, on a given issue, of a high degree of agreement among such geographically diverse but politically congenial states as Austria, Brazil, Denmark, Iceland, Iran, Malaysia, Norway, Pakistan, the Philippines, Sweden, and Thailand; yet such a coalition did exist in the fifteenth and sixteenth sessions on the issue of disarmament.

To determine voting patterns by using actual voting data, Assembly votes for either a session or a particular issue can be evaluated in terms of agreement scores. In one such analysis, agreement scores were calculated separately for the fifteenth, sixteenth, and eighteenth sessions, and for six issue-areas of the fifteenth and sixteenth sessions taken together. The six issue-areas were: disarmament, peacekeeping, colonialism, other political issues, economic and social issues, and legal issues. This analysis indicated that regional groups in the Assembly do not necessarily act as unified and disciplined blocs.

In all six issue-areas and in the three Assembly sessions, significant divisions were apparent within the major regional groups except for the East European one. The African-Asian group was divided on all occasions into a number of subgroups: usually, the anti-Western states, the moderate African

---

[4] See Thomas Hovet, Jr., *Bloc Politics in the United Nations* (Cambridge: Harvard Univ. Press, 1960); see also the critique by Lijphart, *op. cit.*

states, the Western-allied Asian states, and the French-speaking African states. The Western European group was often split between the Nordic states and neutrals on the one hand, and the NATO-allied continental countries, frequently joined by the United States, on the other. Divisions among Latin American states were also omnipresent, although the lines of cleavage were not as consistent as they were for the other regions.

Moreover, cross-regional coalitions were very much in evidence on a number of issues. This was particularly true of those relating to disarmament, but was also true of votes on peacekeeping, colonialism, other political issues, and social and economic questions. The composition of cross-regional coalitions varied, but participating states were usually more moderate (closer to the political center of the Assembly) than most other members of their regional groups. Thus Nordic states and other European nations with neutralist inclinations, such as Austria and Ireland, often voted with pro-Western Asian and African states, such as Iran, Japan, Liberia, Malaysia, Nigeria, Pakistan, Thailand, and Tunisia. At the eighteenth session, voting agreement was quite pronounced between Latin American states, such as Bolivia, Costa Rica, Haiti, Mexico, and Uruguay, and moderate African and Asian states, such as Gabon, Liberia, Madagascar, Malaysia, and Thailand.

This evidence for cross-regional cooperation should not be taken as a suggestion that rigid cross-regional cleavages exist in the Assembly. The "voting coalitions" that can be defined are far from being distinct blocs sharply set apart from one another, and often include states having very high agreement scores with states in other voting clusters. Such interrelationships are symptoms of a fluid political process characterized by *ad hoc* coalitions, independent decision-making by states, and the absence of any effective system to coordinate voting among large numbers of countries.

Quite a variegated pattern thus presents itself to the observer of voting in the General Assembly. Allies on one issue may be opponents on another. Yet coalitions do operate within certain fairly well-defined political boundaries. Although Thailand may find itself in sympathy on peacekeeping issues with the United States, on disarmament with Sweden, and on decolonization with Ecuador, it is hardly likely to be allied on a major group of issues with Guinea, Mali, or the Soviet Union.

POLITICAL POSITION AND THE BALANCE OF POWER

The General Assembly is faced most frequently with two types of questions: those concerning relationships between the two great-power blocs (cold war issues) and those primarily affecting the relations between established, economically developed states and economically less-developed states, many of which have attained sovereignty only recently. On both sets of issues, the United States and the Soviet Union have usually found themselves in opposition to one another. In the eighteenth session, for example, the lowest over-all agreement-scores in the Assembly occurred between the Warsaw Pact states and NATO members.

With the framework set by frequent East-West opposition, however, a good deal of variation has occurred; different issues produce different voting coalitions. Instead of viewing political positions as distributed along an East-West line, it is useful therefore, to consider separately positions on issues related to the cold war and on those of concern to the developing nations. Thus the United States and its European allies are pro-Western and relatively unsympathetic to African and Asian demands, whereas the USSR and some African and Asian states take the opposite stand. Other African and Asian states are more pro-Western but remain sympathetic to the aspirations of the developing states, whereas certain European states, such as the Scandinavian countries, are less pro-Western on cold war issues, but also less sympathetic to African and Asian proposals.[5]

Within this context, which states most often hold the balance of voting power in the Assembly? States that frequently vote in the majority tend to be in the majority so often because it is their weight on either side of the scale that tips the balance. Thus an investigation of which states vote most frequently with the majority of the Assembly will indicate those delegations whose support is usually essential to the passage of major Assembly resolutions.

The states most often found in the majority for the fifteenth, sixteenth, and eighteenth sessions were moderate African and Asian states and other countries not firmly members of any one regional group. They tended to be slightly more pro-Western than pro-Soviet Union in cold war attitudes, but sympathetic to aspirations for self-determination and economic development. Listing particular states, Liberia and Malaysia were among the ten states with highest majority-agreement scores for all three sessions; Cyprus, Haiti, and Iran were the only other states in this category more than once. Iran, Liberia, and Malaysia are all African-Asian group members with powerful cross-pressures pulling them toward the West. Cyprus and Haiti, on the other hand, both have ties to more than one group: Cyprus to Africa-Asia and Western Europe (it is a member of both caucuses); Haiti to Latin America geographically and to Africa ethnically. By contrast, the United States and the USSR, along with Western European and communist states in general, had relatively low majority-agreement scores for the sessions under consideration.

No regional or voting group can succeed in dominating the Assembly consistently on the whole spectrum of issues before it. Therefore the attitudes of those African, Asian, and Latin American states that take independent and moderate courses in General Assembly politics are crucial. Moreover, the balance of power shifts somewhat with the issues being considered, even

[5] See Hayward R. Alker, Jr., and Bruce M. Russett, *World Politics in the General Assembly* (New Haven: Yale Univ. Press, 1965), Chapter 6.

though certain states, such as those mentioned above, tend to have high majority-agreement scores in every area of Assembly activity. This dual pattern can be seen more clearly by examining majority-agreement results for a number of separate issues in the fifteenth and sixteenth sessions taken together.

Moderate Western predominance characterized the patterns for peace-keeping questions concerning United Nations forces and their financing. Malaya, New Zealand, Nigeria, Pakistan, Sweden, and the United States were among those most often in the majority, whereas the communist states were consistently in opposition, and many non-aligned states occupied a middle position on the scale of majority agreement. This Western predominance in part reflected the inability of non-aligned African and Asian states to collaborate on a common position. With respect to colonialism, the more anti-Western African and Asian states did better, and the Soviet Union was in the majority more often than the United States. In this situation, states such as Iran, Lebanon, Malaya, Nigeria, the Philippines, and Tunisia were also all near the top of the list. On disarmament issues, the great powers and their allies were quite strikingly isolated from the mainstream, which was occupied by a coalition of moderate states including Brazil, Malaya, Norway, and Sweden. Clearly no "mechanical majority" currently exists, except possibly on questions of colonialism and *apartheid*. It is the small and moderate states rather than the large and purposeful ones that most often succeed in identifying themselves with the decisions of the Assembly as a whole.

Therefore, "winning" in the General Assembly requires not merely the solid support of one's own regular allies and supporters, but the assistance of other members as well. This has meant that African and Asian states with moderately but not slavishly pro-Western governments have generally held the balance of power. However, when a two-thirds majority has been required to pass a resolution, the Soviet Union and the African and Asian states particularly opposed to the status quo must attract support from states even less sympathetic to their general outlook, especially from the liberal European states and Latin American countries; the Western allies must gain adherents among non-aligned and anti-colonial African and Asian states in order to accomplish similar objectives. States in the political center will attempt to attract support for their proposals from both sides. Since no group can be assured of victory on a consistent basis, except on a few particularly favorable and often ritualistic issues, compromise and bargaining must be engaged in continually by all sides to obtain the best possible terms. This lack of control over the Assembly by any group of states, as well as the absence of large and cohesive groups, means that a powerful force for compromise—the necessity to acquire uncommitted votes—is added to whatever self-restraint may be practiced by representatives for other reasons.

THE COMMONWEALTH AND THE UNITED NATIONS

Thomas B. Millar*

At the beginning of the seventeenth session of the General Assembly, there were thirteen[1] Commonwealth countries at the United Nations, constituting one-eighth of the total membership. Jamaica and Trinidad-Tobago (which both became independent during August 1962) and Uganda (which received its independence in October) became Members of the UN during the seventeenth session. Kenya and British Guiana are two other Commonwealth countries approaching independence.[2] If there are no other new United Nations Members in the meantime, and if these five remain in the Commonwealth, as they are expected to do, their addition would mean that one-sixth of the Members of the UN were also Commonwealth members.

This is important only if their being members of the Commonwealth is significant. Are they influenced by the Commonwealth connection? Does it affect their policies or their actions? Can the Commonwealth be said to exist as a cohesive group at the United Nations?

Formal recognition that the Commonwealth exists and is a group to be taken into account for certain purposes is contained in the annex to Resolution 1192 (XII) of the General Assembly, adopted at the 728th plenary meeting on the "Composition of the General Committee of the General Assembly." Paragraph 3 of the annex states:

At least one of the Vice-Presidents in categories (a) two representatives from Asian and African states or (d) [two representatives from Western European and other states] . . . or the President or one of the Chairmen of the Main Committees, will be from a Commonwealth country, without altering the geographic distribution of seats in the General Committee, as defined. . . .

In practice there have usually been two Commonwealth countries, in

* Thomas B. Millar, "The Commonwealth and the United Nations," *International Organization*, Vol. 16, 1962, pp. 736–757. Copyright 1962, World Peace Foundation. By permission of *International Organization*.

Thomas B. Millar is a research fellow in International Relations at the Australian National University in Canberra. He was a visiting research fellow in International Organization of Columbia University.

[1] United Kingdom, Canada, Australia, New Zealand, India, Pakistan, Ceylon, Ghana, Federation of Malaya, Nigeria, Cyprus, Sierre Leone, Tanganyika.

[2] Kenya received independence on Dec. 12, 1963, and British Guiana as Guyana on May 25, 1966 [ed.].

addition to the United Kingdom, represented on the General Committee, and sometimes three. The balloting may not continue to yield these results, and there is no guarantee that it will even provide one Commonwealth member. But the fact that the General Assembly has passed this resolution is an indication that the Commonwealth countries have felt a desire to be recognized formally as a group, and have managed to convince a majority of the Assembly that they should. . . .

Informal recognition of the Commonwealth as an electoral group is found in the fact that there has always been one Commonwealth country as a nonpermanent member of the Security Council. This stems from the private negotiations (sometimes referred to, especially by Soviet delegates, as a "gentleman's agreement") during the first part of the first session in London in 1946, on the distribution of the nonpermanent seats[3]—the other five being allotted to Latin America (2), eastern Europe, western Europe, and the Middle East. The allocation of one nonpermanent seat to the Commonwealth is partly attributable to its significant contribution toward winning the war.[4] It is also a reflection of the fact that none of the Commonwealth countries in 1946 fitted into a regional grouping, and they were almost the only Member States who did not. Only India and the Philippines in Asia, and Liberia and South Africa among the independent African nations, could not be included within the middle east group. Canada, Australia, and New Zealand were the only other UN Members not in a regional group. To provide a "Commonwealth seat" was thus not unreasonable.

As the character of the General Assembly changed, and the number of Members from Asia and Africa increased, the Commonwealth helped provide a means for having these areas represented in the Security Council: India (1950–1951), Pakistan (1952–1953), and Ghana (1962–1963) [which] have all held Security Council seats since 1950. When the "Commonwealth seat" has been held by a European Commonwealth member, attempts have been made to place an Asian in the east European seat.[5] Commonwealth representation has thus not been incompatible with the changing character

---

[3] The nature of this "agreement" is not easily determined, and has been variously reported. Trygve Lie speaks only of an agreed "slate" negotiated in advance (*In the Cause of Peace: Seven Years in the United Nations* [New York: Macmillan, 1954], p. 27). The results for the first few years followed the pattern given above. See also p. 6, note 1, and Sydney D. Bailey, *The General Assembly of the United Nations* (London: Stevens, 1960), pp. 165–167.

[4] Article 23 (1) of the Charter states that in the election of nonpermament members, due regard shall be "specially paid, in the first instance to the contribution of Members of the United Nations to the maintenance of international peace and security and to the other purposes of the Organization, and also to equitable geographical distribution."

[5] For example, the Philippines shared a seat with Yugoslavia in the 1956–1957 period, and Japan did so in 1958–1959. The Philippines will share with Romania in the 1962–1963 period.

of United Nations membership. Certainly the Commonwealth has always been over-represented in the Security Council in proportion to the total membership of that body. This is doubtless one reason why Commonwealth members want to keep the "Commonwealth seat" on the Council, as most are much more likely to be elected as a Commonwealth representative than as the representative of a regional group.

The Economic and Social Council (ECOSOC) has regularly included, in addition to the United Kingdom, at least one "older" Commonwealth member and (except in 1960–1961, due apparently to a disagreement between India and Pakistan) at least one "newer" member. These are not specifically "Commonwealth vacancies," although in practice the election of the "older" Commonwealth representative comes almost into that category. The Commonwealth is also a factor in the election, in that members usually support one another and will try to organize matters so that they are not competing.

        ✿   ✿   ✿   ✿   ✿   ✿   ✿

It is of interest that delegates from Commonwealth countries have been used disproportionately in important Assembly and committee positions. The Commonwealth has provided five Presidents of the General Assembly,[6] fourteen chairmen of main Assembly committees, and many more vice-chairmen or rapporteurs. These important posts have not been restricted to "old" Commonwealth members: India, Pakistan, and Ceylon have each provided two main committee chairmen, and India has provided a President of the General Assembly. One reason for this may be that practice in parliamentary processes has enabled these countries to provide people with the right type of experience. Also, it could be that the Commonwealth connection has helped to make them better informed and perhaps given them a slightly greater stature than they would otherwise have had. It is not unlikely that the proportions will fall as the Commonwealth expands. The more recent Commonwealth members appear to have much smaller cadres (even relatively) of trained officials or experienced parliamentarians.

At least once every two weeks during the session of the General Assembly —generally on Thursday mornings—and irregularly at other times, there is a meeting of Commonwealth delegates, usually the senior representative and one or two others from each delegation. The agenda consists of whatever the members wish to discuss. The secretary of the meeting, who circulates the agenda in advance of the meeting after contacting each delegation, is the senior Commonwealth Relations Office representative on the British delega-

[6] One ex-Commonwealth country, Ireland, has also provided a President, while another, Burma, has contributed the Acting [now regularly elected] Secretary-General. [Since that time Mr. Alex Quaison-Sackey of Ghana has served as President of the 19th session of the General Assembly, bringing the number of Commonwealth Presidents to six.]

tion. He takes minutes of the meeting for the benefit of his own delegation and the British Foreign Office, but he may also (at his discretion) send a summary of the proceedings to any delegation not represented at the meeting. The chairman is usually the leader of the British delegation, although sometimes another delegate will call a meeting and may then take the chair. Meetings are almost invariably friendly, even if discussion becomes brisk. The purpose of the meetings is not to arrive at a consensus, although that may occur, but to present views on current important topics and to state in advance what actions are contemplated by member governments, so that other members can give their reactions and can also prepare accordingly. Members obviously value these meetings. Delegates have observed that Commonwealth meetings are more intimate and more friendly than those of other groups, especially than those of the Afro-Asian group. Commonwealth members have a broadly common outlook and set of values. There is no posturing, no maneuvering at these meetings; there is a wide spectrum of discussion, and discussion is on the whole mature. Delegates are not asked to commit themselves. The fact that all delegates speak English is a great advantage.

Part of the value of the meetings is that there is at least one Commonwealth country in, or with close contacts in, most of the United Nations groups or blocs.[7] Thus, reports are made at the Commonwealth meetings on actions being considered by, or trends developing within, the various groupings. This is of considerable benefit to all the Commonwealth delegates and to their home governments.

In addition to the formal meetings, there are a number of informal meetings held at the United Nations during the session. Perhaps after a committee meeting, the Commonwealth delegates will get together for a few minutes to explain some initiative, attempt to iron out a misunderstanding, or confer on the working of a resolution.

The advantages of the Commonwealth meetings will vary from situation to situation and from member to member. Some delegates are under such close instruction from their governments that they have little or no room for flexibility or maneuver, and are sometimes also prevented from revealing their position. One delegate remarked that he would have appreciated receiving much more information of a confidential nature, and felt that this lack limited the value of the meetings.

To the new Commonwealth country joining the United Nations, the Commonwealth is of special value. Consider the case of Tanganyika. Its first

[7] Cyprus is in the unusual position of being a member of both the western European group and the Afro-Asian group, and in the sixteenth session it received a Vice-Presidency as a representative of the latter and became a member of the Committee of Seventeen (on decolonialization) as a representative of the former. Ceylon, also rather curiously, attends meetings of the "Casablanca" powers—Ghana, Guinea, Mali, Morocco, and the United Arab Republic.

permanent representative, Dr. V. K. Kyaruzi, received diplomatic training with the New Zealand Department of External Affairs and was then attached for some months to that country's delegation to the United Nations as a "special adviser." When his country became independent in December 1961, he was already on close and friendly terms with the delegates from other Commonwealth countries, was familiar with United Nations procedures and diplomacy, had attended Commonwealth meetings, and knew and was known to many non-Commonwealth delegates. His country, and thus he as its ambassador, had access to the confidential information that circulates among Commonwealth countries. Tanganyika's experience is representative of that of most of the new Commonwealth countries.

Common membership of the Commonwealth means that many of the delegates came to be on much better terms with one another than they would otherwise expect to be. Without the Commonwealth, for example, it is unlikely that the delegates of Sierra Leone and Australia, Canada and Nigeria, or India and New Zealand would have very much contact. The Commonwealth connection provides this contact, and more than contact. It is a link, an association, a sense of "belonging"—a feeling of being, if less than kin, still much more than strangers.

Such being the milieu, what is the effect on attitudes in debates or votes on resolution? In every issue discussed at the United Nations, there is a host of factors that each Commonwealth country will have considered in arriving at its position. The opinions of other Commonwealth members will be among those factors, since the particular issues will, almost invariably, have been discussed by Commonwealth delegates at a regular or special meeting or informally. But the views of Commonwealth members will vary and may not—frequently do not—carry any weight in the individual government's decision-making process. Commonwealth delegates may alter the presentation of a case, the loudness of voice, or the choice of adjectives as a result of these meetings, but only rarely will they alter the direction of policy or its substance. The most that members seem to hope for, in a controversial matter, is to be able to persuade other members to abstain rather than vote against.

The reasons for this situation are not all equally apparent. Firstly, of course, the Commonwealth as a whole is not the main consideration in the decisions of any member, except perhaps, in certain circumstances, the United Kingdom. The national objectives of members are such that the role of the Commonwealth may sometimes be helpful but is almost always marginal. National security is believed to result from either the American defense umbrella or from neutrality, not as a benefit of Commonwealth membership. In the case of economic assistance—and eight of the thirteen Commonwealth countries are underdeveloped—the United States has long ago, for most of them, replaced the United Kingdom as principal benefactor (though not principal investor), and the neutral nations also may seek aid from the communist bloc. Social status is found in a geographic or racial grouping. Other objectives, not ostensibly tied to security or to economic well-being, may also determine national policy. Thus Mr. Nehru, on the side of the angels, at least until his Goan adventure, saw himself as a man of peace with a role to play in moderating between the two giants. For this purpose he had to keep roughly equidistant between them. Mr. Nkrumah, picturing himself . . . as Africa's man of destiny, . . . put the destiny of Africa before anything else. There may also be resentments demanding expression, old humiliations to be revenged, new roles to be loudly asserted in case the world should not be aware of them. The Commonwealth, as an organization, cannot satisfy these desires. There is, quite obviously, a somewhat different approach on the part of the new African and Asian members of the Commonwealth and, especially, the United Kingdom, with respect to matters which have or can be construed to have anti-colonialist implications. In private, most Asian and African Commonwealth delegates will agree that British policy is directed toward the same goal as they wish to achieve. The *pace* of change is the main issue between Great Britain and its former colonies, and even here, many accept that Britain cannot simply abdicate its responsibilities and leave its former subjects to fight out a solution. One Congo at a time is enough.

But *in public*, there are other matters to be considered, not the least of which is home opinion. As with other nations, Commonwealth delegates make many of their UN speeches to the folks at home, and domestic politics frequently determines their actions. The home opinion of new nations is understandably anti-colonialist in principle.

Secondly, the formation of groups and blocs, resulting in bargaining between them and a certain solidarity within each, are the inevitable adjuncts of the United Nations' role as a public forum. The fact that the Commonwealth embraces nations from all continents and most groups means that members will often be committed to their own regional bloc or group, as a matter of self-interest. There are many advantages in this factionalizing, as there are in the parliamentary party system, but one of the most frequent casualties is independence of action.

✻   ✻   ✻   ✻   ✻   ✻   ✻

If anti-colonialist nationalism has buffeted Britain and shaken the Commonwealth, it is also, of course, one of the main reasons for the existence of the Commonwealth in its present form. That present form, with its diversity of size and location, of background, experience, culture, interests, and ambitions, is a challenge to each member. For here is the one voluntary association of nations at the United Nations which transcends blocs, transcends

QUESTION OF THE REPRESENTATION OF CHINA
VOTING OF THE COMMONWEALTH COUNTRIES IN THE GENERAL ASSEMBLY
DECEMBER 15, 1961

COUNTRY	QUESTION OF PRIORITY[a]			DRAFT RESOLUTION CONTAINED IN DOCUMENT A/L.372[b]			DRAFT RESOLUTION CONTAINED IN DOCUMENT A/L.375[c] (FIRST PART)			DRAFT RESOLUTION CONTAINED IN DOCUMENT A/L.375[d] (SECOND PART)			DRAFT RESOLUTION CONTAINED IN DOCUMENT A/L.360[e]		
	YES	NO	ABST.	YES	NO	ABST.	YES	NO	ABST.	YES	NO	ABST.	YES	NO	ABST.
Australia	X			X				X			X			X	
Canada	X			X				X			X			X	
Ceylon		X			X		X			X			X		
Cyprus			X			X			X			X			X
Fed. of Malaya	X			X				X			X			X	
Ghana			X			X	X			X			X		
India		X			X		X			X			X		
New Zealand	X			X				X			X			X	
Nigeria			X			X			X	X			X		
Pakistan			X			X	X			X			X		
Sierra Leone			X			X			X	X					X
Tanganyika			X			X			X	X				X	
United Kingdom	X			X					X	X			X		
Commonwealth	5	2	6	5	2	6	4	4	5	8	4	1	6	5	2
Total UN	61	21	20	61	34	7	23	40	39	30	45	29	36	48	20

[a] This vote was on the proposal by the Australian delegation that the draft resolution it sponsored (Document A/L.372) should have priority in voting over the other draft resolutions being considered (Documents A/L.375 and A/L.360).

[b] The draft resolution (Document A/L.372) submitted by the delegations of Australia, Colombia, Italy, Japan, and the United States proposed that the Soviet's draft resolution contained in Document A/L.360 (see footnote e below) should be considered an "important" question, and thus require a two-thirds majority (under Article 18 of the Charter).

[c] The draft resolution (Document A/L.375) submitted by the delegations of Cambodia, Ceylon, and Indonesia, as an amendment to the Soviet draft resolution (Document A/L.360), proposed to delete the operative paragraphs in the Soviet draft resolution and substitute the following: "Decides in accordance with the above declaration that the representatives of the Government of the People's Republic of China be seated in

the United Nations and all its organs." The first vote was on the inclusion of the words "in accordance with the above declaration [i.e., the two preambular paragraphs of the Soviet draft resolution]."

ᵈ The second vote on the draft resolution contained in Document A/L.375 was on the remainder of the amendment.

ᵉ The draft resolution submitted by the Soviet delegation (Document A/L.360) was as follows:

The General Assembly,

Considering it necessary to restore the lawful rights of the People's Republic of China in the United Nations,

Bearing in mind that only representatives of the Government of the People's Republic of China are competent to occupy China's place in the United Nations and all its organs,

Resolves to remove immediately from all United Nations organs the representatives of the Chiang Kai-shek clique who are unlawfully occupying the place of China in the United Nations,

Invites the Government of the People's Republic of China to send its representatives to participate in the work of the United Nations and of all its organs.

race, includes East and West on equal terms, and demands no commitments. At the Commonwealth meetings, the . . . [African] delegate does not have to say rude things about the imperialists, for they would ring hollow; he does not have to assert his equality with the white man, for he is among white friends; he does not need to explain his political conceptual framework, because it is broadly the same as that of everyone else there. His stature depends on his intellectual capacity. He has no audience except a few people who know him well.

The impression that most Commonwealth delegates give is that, whereas the Commonwealth association is not a vote changer, it is a harmonizer. It breeds understanding and respect even amid disagreement. It helps blur the lines and blunt the edges of blocs.

✿   ✿   ✿   ✿   ✿   ✿   ✿

Does the Commonwealth then exist as an international political entity? Yes, but not in the same way—or, rather, not in the same degree—that the United Nations exists as an international political entity. The United Nations has forces in the Congo and in the middle east. It has a "presence" in various places; it has agencies throughout the world and a headquarters in New York to which you can write and get an answer. It has a written constitution. The Commonwealth has no forces, no overseas presence, no headquarters. It has a few coordinating agencies in London, and various semi-official and unofficial bodies. But if you wrote to the Commonwealth you would never get an answer. And nobody says, "We must ask the Commonwealth what it thinks about this or what it can do about that." For the Commonwealth has no mind, no voice of its own, no secretary-general, no executive, no flag, no glass building, least of all a written constitution. It is still more than the sum, or the arrangement of its parts, but not too much more. It has never had a common foreign policy nor a common economic policy. It is not—is not conceived by its members to be—that kind of a body. Actually, only the Soviet bloc, in any significant degree, is that kind of a body. The Commonwealth is a surprisingly representative piece of the world, and the tensions that tug at and divide the world tug at and divide the Commonwealth.

. . . the Commonwealth contributed very little toward a settlement [of the India-Pakistan dispute]. Despite repeated proddings from Pakistan, the Commonwealth countries have refused to consider arbitrating the matter for the simple reason that India would never agree to such arbitration; and there is virtually no support in the Commonwealth for the creation of a court of arbitration, even from those members usually considered much more pro-Commonwealth than Pakistan. The Commonwealth has, of course, brought extensive pressure to bear, officially and unofficially, on both disputants. There was not full-scale war between the two armies in the early stages partly because both were commanded by British generals. When the dispute was referred to the United Nations, the other Commonwealth countries were put in the invidious position of being pressured to take sides. This did not improve Commonwealth relations. The only time when Mr. Nehru publicly asserted the possibility of India's leaving the Commonwealth was when it appeared that Britain was openly siding with Pakistan at the United Nations.

The only other intra-Commonwealth dispute aired at the United Nations has concerned the rights of approximately 400,000 persons of Indian origin resident in the Union of South Africa. The matter first came before the General Assembly in 1946 at the request of the interim government of India.

❋   ❋   ❋   ❋   ❋   ❋   ❋

As with Kashmir, it cannot be said that the Commonwealth has been any more successful in the India-South Africa problem than the United Nations. The matter was raised at an Imperial Conference in London in 1921, and the South African government was criticized but felt unable to change its position at that time. With the evolution to independence within the Commonwealth of Asian and African nations since the Second World War, South African racial policies have come in for increasing strictures, including in some cases the severance of trade relations, withdrawal of high commissioners, and unofficial boycotts in some Commonwealth countries (including Britain) of goods of South African origin. Finally, at the March 1961 prime ministers' meetings, the other members—or the majority of them—made it clear to South Africa that it would have to choose between modifying its racial policies and leaving the Commonwealth. It chose the latter.

There are grounds for claiming that the United Nations has been a safety valve for intra-Commonwealth disputes, but it has also operated as a fire beneath the pot.

AFRICA AND THE UNITED NATIONS

John Karefa-Smart[*]

At the beginning of its nineteenth session the General Assembly of the United Nations decided by acclamation that Alex Quaison-Sackey, the permanent representative of Ghana, should preside over the session. This

❋ John Karefa-Smart, "Africa and the United Nations," *International Organization*, Vol. 19, 1965, pp. 764–773. Copyright 1965, World Peace Foundation. By permission of *International Organization*.

John Karefa-Smart is former Foreign Minister of Sierra Leone and Associate Director of International Health at Columbia University.

was only the second time in eighteen years that this, the highest honor in the Organization, was accorded to a representative of an African state, and the first time that a Negro African was thus chosen.

In 1945, at the San Francisco Conference, the only African states that were independent and therefore could become Members of the new international body were—not counting South Africa—Egypt, Ethiopia, and Liberia. It was not until ten years later at the tenth session of the General Assembly that these three original African Members were joined by Libya. During the eleventh session Ghana, Morocco, the Sudan, and Tunisia were admitted to the UN, and almost two years later Guinea joined the small group of African countries. By the time Sierra Leone became the 100th Member of the United Nations in September 1961, there were already 24 African Member States,[1] and with the expected admission of Gambia before the close of the nineteenth session, the African states will number 35[2] out of a total membership of 115. This enormous increase in the African membership has been a result of the unprecedented dissolution of the French and British colonial empires—a process which was fully supported through various resolutions and through the pressure of debate by the United Nations. It is not surprising to find that the majority, if not all, of the African countries regard representation at the United Nations as their most important diplomatic assignment.

During the first fifteen years of the Organization, the twenty Latin American countries formed the largest single bloc in the UN. As a result, they were able to play an important role in mediating between the Great Powers and at the same time to win for themselves valuable concessions in elections to the major UN bodies' important posts within the Organization. The African states during this same period had no such influence as a separate group. They, however, eventually joined forces with the Asian countries which, they felt, shared their interests in economic development, human rights, and the struggle against colonialism. Thus, especially after the first Asian-African Conference in Bandung, the African and Asian delegations began to meet together regularly at the United Nations. Whenever questions of "due regard to geographical distribution" arose at the UN, the Afro-Asian group was viewed unofficially as a unit.

THE RISING TIDE OF AFRICAN INFLUENCE

It was not long, however, until their rapidly increasing numbers led the African nations to seek to express themselves as a separate entity. Therefore, after the admission of the first large aggregation of newly independent countries, the African delegations began to meet together monthly at the UN. The

[1] South Africa is not included in this figure.
[2] South Africa is not included in this figure.

group thus formed, which followed the familiar UN practice of having a rotating chairmanship, could not make binding decisions but met for the purposes of consultation and informal exchanges of views. It was given a formal identity by the Organization of African Unity (OAU) when, at the May 1963 Addis Ababa Conference, the heads of African states and governments adopted a resolution according it official status. At this Conference the African UN delegations were authorized to establish a secretariat and to cooperate with any other group that shared its objectives.

The African group has already begun to make its presence recognized and felt. In the past those African countries which were represented on the Security Council have occupied seats allocated by the San Francisco "gentleman's agreement" to the Middle East and the British Commonwealth. Now the African group is making a claim for representation on the Security Council in its own right, pointing out that the twenty Latin American countries have always had two seats, while the African group, now numbering more than 30, must compete for a single seat allocated to a non-African group or region. This African demand, of course, creates a problem that can only be resolved either by a change in the gentleman's agreement or a revision of the Charter to enlarge the Security Council. We will return to both of these possibilities later.

IMPORTANCE OF THE UN TO THE AFRICAN STATES

As has been noted above, each newly independent African country has immediately taken steps to be admitted to the United Nations. Membership in this Organization has come to be regarded in Africa, along with a new flag and a national anthem, as one of the visible signs of independence. But this is not all that the United Nations means to the new African states.

First, although they believe that certain provisions of the Charter should be revised to provide for the adequate representation of Africans on the principal UN bodies and even though the Charter was written and adopted while most of the African states were still colonial territories, the Africans nonetheless hold the Charter of the United Nations in the highest esteem. They feel that the Charter embodies their hopes for a world in which all nations, large and small, rich and poor, powerful and weak, will work together in peace and security and contribute, each according to its means, to the development of the whole world's resources and to the economic, social, and cultural betterment of all people and the preservation of freedom and human dignity.

Secondly, many African states owe their very independence to the emphasis which the United Nations has placed on the obligation of Members administering colonial or trust territories to develop self-government within them. In this sense the United Nations is the foster mother of all the former dependencies which have now attained independence and been admitted to the Organization.

Thirdly, the United Nations has met the needs of the African states in some quite definite ways. Without the United Nations, it would have been difficult for new nations, especially when they were at the same time weak and impoverished, to break into the closely knit diplomatic circles of the older states. In the same way as the League of Nations allowed the Emperor of Ethiopia to appeal to the community of nations against the Italian assault on his country's territorial integrity, so the United Nations has provided a forum in which African leaders, both heads of state and their accredited permanent representatives, could express their views on world problems and seek support in matters of special interest to their countries. The privilege of using this forum derives solely from membership in the Organization and does not depend on the size or power of the nation or of its diplomatic mission.

✿   ✿   ✿   ✿   ✿   ✿   ✿

It is not only from its function as a forum, however, that the African states have derived great benefit from the United Nations. Concrete results have been achieved otherwise, to the benefit of Member States, by special United Nations bodies and the specialized agencies.

✿   ✿   ✿   ✿   ✿   ✿   ✿

AFRICA AND THE GREAT POWERS

. . . The African states found that practically every question which appeared on the agenda of the General Assembly or of the various committees was discussed in terms of [the] East versus West alignment. When the African countries showed a particular interest in economic and social questions, in human rights, and in the work of the Trusteeship Council, they found that the East and the West vied with each other for the role of champion of the causes in which the Africans were interested. The realization that the United Nations was far from "united" and that the East and the West constituted two separate power blocs, each one competing to obtain the votes of the new Members, led to the early assumption by the African states—following the lead given by India—of a position of nonalignment with respect to the two contending groups.

Nonalignment as the African states use the term simply means a refusal to be committed in advance to giving support to one group or the other in discussions of international problems. It is not intended to mean neutrality. Once the opportunity has been given to listen to both sides of any given controversy and to examine the facts and the arguments, the African countries expect to, and nearly always do, decide on which side to cast their votes or to whom they will lend support. Such support, however, is *ad hoc;* it is intended to be limited to the matter in hand and does not imply support in other future controversies or disputes. Since this position of nonalignment is intended to safeguard freedom of action at all times, it requires the avoidance of bilateral treaties or other agreements by which the African states would bind themselves to one of the Great Powers.

An important reason for adhering to a policy of nonalignment, although it has not been explicitly expressed in formal declarations, is that the African states are generally not impressed with ideological considerations. Their problems of economic development and social welfare are so urgent that they prefer to put all their resources into efforts to solve these problems and to receive assistance from any source. They suspect that to become too deeply involved in ideological disputes and to commit their support to any one side would restrict their freedom to receive assistance wherever it can be found or is offered.

DISILLUSIONMENT WITH THE UNITED NATIONS

In spite of all the positive aspects of their membership in the United Nations, the African countries have also experienced a certain disillusionment with the United Nations in the following areas.

First, the continuation of the Cold War and the huge sums of money spent by the Great Powers in defense and armaments cause concern among the African countries. In general, they regard the Great Powers' refusal to conclude peace treaties with East and West Germany and the related question of self-determination and reunification for the German people as constant potential threats to the free exercise by all small countries of their rights. Even more alarming is the extension of the Cold War to the internal struggles in the Middle East, in the Congo (Leopoldville), and, with almost catastrophic results, in Cuba in 1962.

Secondly, the African nations have been distressed by the refusal of the Western powers to support in the Security Council strong economic measures against South Africa. This failure to back up with positive action the nearly 40 resolutions of the General Assembly against *apartheid* has led the African countries to lose faith in the UN's ability to bring about a just solution of questions which do not primarily affect the Great Powers. In the same way they view Portugal's intransigence, despite adverse world opinion, in refusing to grant self-determination to its African colonies as being sustained by the unwillingness of Portugal's NATO allies to offend that government.

A third perennial question in the United Nations, on which, despite disagreement as to the solution, there is universal concern, is the question of the participation of Communist China in the Organization. Most African governments seem to realize that the obvious solution of granting membership to both the "exile" government in Formosa and the *de facto* government on the Chinese mainland is equally unacceptable to both Chinas. Nevertheless, they wish to remove the feeling of impotence that has resulted from inconclusive struggles over procedural aspects of the subject rather than a direct confrontation. The need to bring a population of some 700 million people into the family of nations seems more important to most African countries than the question of which China should occupy the present seats in the United Nations and its committees and agencies.

Fourthly, there is the present deadlock over payments for the peacekeeping operations in the Middle East and the Congo (Leopoldville). . . . The African countries are principally concerned over the stubborn refusal of both the United States on the one hand and France and the Soviet Union on the other to accept compromise solutions to the problem. According to the Africans, compromise requires a willingness not to insist on constitutional arguments and specific interpretations of the Charter. The important question for the African nations is not which interpretation of the Charter is the correct one, but what can be done now to provide funds to meet current deficits and to guarantee adequate financial support for future peacekeeping operations. . . .

HOPE FOR ASSISTANCE ON MODERNIZATION

Generally speaking, the African countries place great hope in the UN as a channel through which the economic and social development which is necessary in order to accelerate progress toward modernization will take place. It was with this in mind that they hailed the declaration of a Development Decade by the UN with enthusiasm.

The three main categories into which African interest in the UN role development falls are: increased and more mutually advantageous trade; technical assistance for the development of education, health, and other social services; and the provision of capital for development purposes.

           *   *   *   *   *   *   *

LOOKING TO THE FUTURE

The African countries have not lost confidence in the United Nations. Whether or not the great faith they have in the Organization will be maintained depends, of course, on whether effective solutions are found to some of the questions already raised.

LATIN AMERICA AND THE UNITED NATIONS

Bryce Wood and Minerva Morales M.[*]

When the governments of the Latin American states were taking part in the negotiations leading to the founding of the UN, they could hardly have done so with nostalgic memories of the League of Nations. The League had provided no protection to the Caribbean countries from interventions by the United States, and, largely because of United States protests, it did not consider the Tacna-Arica and Costa Rica–Panama disputes in the early 1920's. Furthermore, Mexico had not been invited to join; Brazil withdrew in 1926; and Argentina and Peru took little part in League affairs. The organization was regarded as being run mainly for the benefit of European states with the aid of what Latin Americans called an "international bureaucracy," in which citizens from the southern hemisphere played minor roles. The United States was, of course, not a member, and both the reference to the Monroe Doctrine by name in Article 21 of the Covenant and the organization's practice of shunning any attempt to interfere in inter-American affairs against the wishes of the United States made the League in its first decade a remote and inefficacious institution to countries that were seriously concerned about domination by Washington.

Although two disputes that the American states found intractable were the subjects of action by the League of Nations in the 1930's, its interposition did not improve its reputation in the Americas. In these cases Latin American countries were the embarrassed recipients of two reprehensible "firsts" in the history of the League. Paraguay during the Chaco War was the first state to be regarded as an aggressor by the League and to be the object of sanctions. It withdrew from the League in 1935 at this affront to its national honor. In the Leticia conflict the prestige of Peru was barely saved when in 1933 the League's Administrative Commission for the Territory of Leticia, carrying out the first "police action" in the history of general international organizations, masked the reoccupation of Leticia by Colombian troops.

[*] Bryce Wood and Minerva Morales M., "Latin America and the United Nations," *International Organization*, Vol. 19, 1965, pp. 714–727. Copyright 1965, World Peace Foundation. By permission of *International Organization*.

Bryce Wood is Executive Associate of the Social Science Research Council and a member of the board of editors of *International Organization*. He was a Visiting Professor of Public Law and Government at Columbia University.

Minerva Morales M. is a professor at the Centro de Estudios Internacionales, El Colegio de Mexico, and has been a visiting scholar at the Institute of Latin American Studies at Columbia University.

The services of the League were unappreciated, however, and in the protocol terminating the dispute the League was ignored, while the two countries congratulated themselves on their "agreeable duty" to prevent conflicts because of their "historical, social and sentimental ties" as states of the "American community."

If Latin America's retrospective view of the League was aloof and even unfriendly, its view of the inter-American "system" as a device for maintaining peace, rhetoric apart, was that it was nearly useless. In the Chaco, at Leticia, and in the Marañón conflict between Ecuador and Peru in 1941–1942, the nonbelligerent American republics had neither prevented nor shortened open hostilities, and their long and painful attempts to achieve enduring peace settlements resulted, in the main, in the ratification of positions won by the military victors—Paraguay, Columbia, and Peru, respectively. The Latin American states, on the basis of their own recent diplomatic and military history, were therefore ready in 1945 to contemplate more efficient methods for the pacific settlement of their quarrels.

The policy of the United States in these three conflicts, which were the first serious breaches of intra-Latin American amity in half a century, exemplified both neutrality and objectivity. Thus, the Latin American governments had good reason to believe that the great influence of the United States would be exerted only to prevent conflicts or, as in the Leticia affair, to maintain the validity of established treaties and not to gain any advantage for itself. Further, in the decade of the 1930's the United States government developed and demonstrated a conscious and principled adherence to a new policy known as that of the "good neighbor." This policy, in practice and in formal legal statement, renounced "intervention" in the domestic and foreign affairs of other American states, and for several years Washington ceased trying to implement its preferences among presidential aspirants and governmental policies in the Caribbean states by its previously customary methods of influence and diplomatic pressures. In whatever way the term "intervention" may be construed in the inter-American protocols and declarations of this period, the fact was evident to all in 1945 that since January 1933 the United States government had not put troops ashore in any Latin American country for other than mutually acceptable measures of hemispheric defense. In addition, the protection given in this decade to North American enterprise in Latin American countries in cases of actual or threatened expropriation had been sufficiently moderate in manner to permit satisfactory intergovernmental or other arrangements to be achieved.

Finally, the generally effective wartime collaboration of the American states except Argentina had created a new warmth of sympathy and a new sense of confidence and ease of relationships. The financial and technical assistance provided by the United States to Latin American countries during World War II helped to enhance this modern "era of good feeling," which reached a high point in 1945.

With this background the Latin American governments were strongly disposed in 1945 both to establish new ways of keeping peace among themselves and to strengthen ties with the United States, whose "hegemony" was no longer feared as it had been in the 1920's. In addition, they were concerned about the great and growing power of the Soviet Union and the consequently anticipated stimulus to activities of Communist parties in America.

LATIN AMERICAN CONTRIBUTIONS TO SHAPING THE UN

These factors and a reaction against "great-power domination" on the part of the Latin American countries combined to evoke intense opposition in 1944 when the Dumbarton Oaks Proposals were unveiled by the United States, the United Kingdom, the Soviet Union, and China. The intensity of the Latin American response to the Proposals appears to have surprised the United States Department of State, which agreed to Latin American demands for an Inter-American Conference on Problems of War and Peace, which was held in Mexico City in February–March 1945. In the Act of Chapultepec resulting from the Conference the parties recommended the negotiation of an inter-American treaty to meet acts or threats of aggression as a

regional arrangement for dealing with such matters relating to the maintenance of international peace and security as are appropriate for regional action in this Hemisphere.

Consequently, at the United Nations Conference on International Organization in the spring of 1945, the Latin American states were unanimous in demanding recognition in the Charter for a special jurisdiction for regional organizations in matters of peace and security. This was achieved principally through Article 51 of the Charter, but also through some changes in Chapter VIII, Section C, of the Dumbarton Oaks Proposals.

The Latin American countries were not alone in the campaign to give regional agencies more scope under the Charter. Nevertheless, they played such a prominent role in promoting the amendments to the Proposals that they should be credited at least with sharing responsibility as principal agents in the framing of Article 51 and the final form of Chapter VIII of the Charter. Expressing their interests as minor powers, Latin American governments played leading parts, but with much less success, in efforts to broaden the role of the General Assembly, to extend the jurisdiction of the International Court of Justice by way of the optional clause in Article 36 of its Statute, and restrict the scope of the exception to "intervention" by the United Nations contained in Article 2, paragraph 7, of the Charter.

At Rio in 1947 and Bogotá in 1948 the American states equipped themselves in the Inter-American Treaty of Reciprocal Assistance (Rio Treaty) and in the Charter of the Organization of American States (OAS) with institutions and procedures for maintaining peace among themselves. The OAS has had a remarkably successful record among the Latin American states. Brief fighting has occurred in a number of cases, but it has been limited in duration by the application of collective peacekeeping efforts which had never been utilized before 1948 in American conflicts. For example, the prompt arrival of neutral observers at scenes of violence has been effective in quickly bringing to a stop fighting in the more than half-dozen armed clashes occurring around the Caribbean since the 1948 Costa Rica–Nicaragua affair. These actions have been taken quite apart from the United Nations, except for *pro forma* reporting under Article 54 of the Charter of measures adopted by the OAS. It may therefore be said that the Latin American objective expressed at Chapultepec has been attained through the operation of the American system for dealing with questions of peace that "are appropriate for regional action in this Hemisphere."

REGIONAL VERSUS UNIVERSAL PROCEDURES

The fencing off of an area of regional jurisdiction from that of the United Nations did not mean that the Latin American countries intended to limit their international activities to inter-American affairs. The fence they had built was a barrier only to outsiders, and even then, only when appropriate. Latin American governments soon demonstrated their determination to make the most of their membership in both the world and the regional organizations, not only in peace and security issues but even more notably in the economic and cultural spheres.

With respect to peace and security, Latin American countries have aired quarrels among themselves in the United Nations; taken disputes with the United States to the Security Council and General Assembly; and appealed decisions by OAS organs to the United Nations.

✻   ✻   ✻   ✻   ✻   ✻   ✻

UNITED STATES–LATIN AMERICAN DISPUTES. Disputes with the United States have been appealed to the United Nations by Guatemala in 1953 and 1954 and by Cuba in 1960, 1961, and later. In neither case were military forces of the United States directly involved, but it was generally considered that the United States government had, in the first instance, provided equipment to the successful invading forces of Colonel Carlos Castillo Armas and, in the second, had trained and equipped Cuban exiles for their unsuccessful invasion of Cuba in April 1961. These appeals demonstrated that Latin American countries did not regard the OAS as providing the most effective source of restraint on the exercise of military power by the United States, and they were the occasions for important declarations affecting the relations between regional agencies and the United Nations. Indeed, the question of regional-global relationships with respect to the use of force is the most important

feature of Latin American contacts with the United Nations, and it is therefore given detailed consideration in this discussion.

The results of the appeals of Guatemala and Cuba to the United Nations
were not satisfactory either to the appellants or to other Latin American
governments. In the Guatemalan case, the Security Council first refused to
refer the matter to the OAS and then declined to place a second Guatemalan
complaint on its own agenda. Before further action could be taken by the
United Nations or the OAS, Colonel Castillo Armas was in control of the
country. The failure of the Security Council to act gave rise to serious
criticisms by Latin American governments, which were repeated in the
Cuban crises in 1961 and 1962. For example, the delegate of Ecuador stated
in the General Assembly on October 1, 1954:

We are members and staunch supporters of the Organization of American States,
but we cannot by any means agree that it has exclusive jurisdiction in a dispute
such as the one I have just mentioned [Guatemala's appeal]. . . . We hope that
there will be no more such negative decisions by the Council, lest the prestige of
the Organization suffer and one of the fundamental objects of the Charter—
protection against attack—become illusory or come too late.[1]

Similarly, the delegate of Uruguay stated on September 28, 1954, that his
government considered that

the principles of the regional system and the safeguards which it offers cannot be
invoked in order to prevent States from having direct and immediate access to
the jurisdiction of the United Nations or to deprive them, no matter how temporarily, of the protection of the agencies of the world community. The legal
protection afforded by both systems should be combined, never substituted for
one another. . . . The delegation of Uruguay considers that any protest to the
United Nations against aggression is entitled at least to a hearing.[2]

Finally, the representative of Argentina stated in the General Assembly on
October 4, 1954:

The existence of regional agreements does not mean that they or the agencies
created under them take precedence over the United Nations, or that the United
Nations should refrain from discussing or endeavouring to settle problems submitted to it by a government representing a Member State. . . . To hold that
the regional organization has exclusive jurisdiction would in our view lead to the
absurd position that a State Member of the United Nations which was a party
to a regional agreement would be at a disadvantage as compared with other
States which for some reasons were not members of regional agencies. We cannot accept a legal argument that would involve a discriminatory situation in regard
to the United Nations Charter, and which would make the security of a country
depend on the special political characteristics and circumstances of regional arrangements.

[1] General Assembly *Official Records* (9th session), p. 148.
[2] General Assembly *Official Records* (9th session), p. 98.

The Argentine Republic cannot accept a view that might deprive it of the right, as a Member of the United Nations, to request the United Nations to consider or settle any international problems affecting it.[3]

❋   ❋   ❋   ❋   ❋   ❋   ❋

When Cuba appealed to the United Nations in April 1961 on the occasion of the Bay of Pigs invasion, the General Assembly was in session. Previous Cuban complaints, made as early as October 1960, that the United States was planning an invasion of Cuba, had been referred to the Assembly's First (Political and Security) Committee, and the new appeal was considered there.

Draft resolutions more or less condemnatory of the United States were presented by Rumania, by Mexico, by Venezuela on behalf of six other Latin American states, and by the Soviet Union.

❋   ❋   ❋   ❋   ❋   ❋   ❋

In [the] voting it was clear that the Latin American delegations were significantly divided. The existence of a "bloc" or "caucusing group" among the Latin American delegations to the United Nations has been examined elsewhere, and no more than brief consideration is possible here. There are various ways of defining "blocs," and for some purposes it is sufficient to say that they are sets of states that show certain common voting patterns. For other purposes, the issue of policy may be relevant to the definition of a "bloc." Whether or not the delegations of states with common voting patterns hold meetings to concert policy does not necessarily determine whether the states form a bloc, as the usefulness of such meetings would depend primarily on the amount of discretion which the participant nations' foreign offices allow to their UN delegations. At any rate, in recent years the delegations of Latin American governments have rarely held meetings for the working out of common voting tactics on questions other than those related to personnel. When such matters are at stake as chairmanships of committees, seats on the International Court of Justice, and officerships of the General Assembly, delegations of Latin American countries, presumably provided with lists of names by their foreign offices, meet to agree upon candidates who will be solidly supported by the group. Otherwise, delegations usually vote without formal "Latin American" gatherings, although a substantial amount of informal, pre-voting communication undoubtedly takes place. Similarly, it appears that the United States delegation does not hold meetings with Latin American delegates as a group but handles its problems of persuasion or dissuasion on a bilateral rather than a multilateral basis.

❋   ❋   ❋   ❋   ❋   ❋   ❋

The Guatemalan and Cuban cases showed that the United States government, which had had to be convinced at San Francisco of the merits of

[3] General Assembly *Official Records* (9th session), p. 174.

Article 51 and the amendments to Chapter VIII, had become more regional than the original regionalists. As a result of the OAS, the United States government has been able to increase its influence in conflicts among Latin American states. The regional organization permits the United States to remind disputants of a relatively firm set of obligations, and it can successfully press for a quick, impartial investigation of a military situation. In cases where its own conduct is protested, the United States appears to consider that its interests will be better served if the forum for complaints is the Council of the OAS rather than either the Security Council or the General Assembly, where it would be exposed to the criticism of the Soviet Union and other unfriendly countries. In the OAS, its opponents do not have the support of non-American allies, and they probably are less bold in censuring the United States in the more direct confrontation of the regional body, where diplomatic pressures exerted by the United States can effectively influence a large proportion of the total voting group. For example, it is questionable whether the Mexican government would have taken as strong a leadership initiative in the OAS at the time of the Bay of Pigs affair as it did in the General Assembly.

APPEALS TO THE UN FROM OAS DECISIONS. Latin American states have occasionally appealed decisions by OAS agencies to the Security Council. As a preface, it may be noted that the Soviet Union asked the Security Council in September 1960 to deny the validity of diplomatic and economic sanctions adopted against the Dominican Republic by a vote of 19-0 (with the Dominican Republic and Venezuela abstaining) by the Sixth Meeting of Consultation of Ministers of Foreign Affairs of the OAS at San José, Costa Rica. The request was based on the claim that the sanctions were "enforcement action," which, under Article 53 of the United Nations Charter, was not to be taken "by regional agencies without the authorization of the Security Council." The Soviet Union was supported in the discussions by other members, but the decision by the Council was to "take note" of the OAS action without making any judgment on its legitimacy.

Presumably aware of this unpromising precedent, Cuba on March 19, 1962, asked that the Security Council request from the International Court of Justice an advisory opinion clarifying the competence of regional agencies to deal with pacific settlement of disputes and, particularly, to adopt "enforcement action." The Cuban draft resolution was aimed at the measures adopted against it at the Eighth Meeting of Consultation of the OAS held in January 1962 at Punta del Este, Uruguay. The only support for Cuba in the Security Council came from the Soviet Union and Rumania; Chile and Venezuela voted with the United States in a 7-2 majority; the United Arab Republic abstained; and Ghana was absent.

It should be noted that, despite significant but by no means unanimous Latin American opposition to the policy of the United States in the Guatemalan and Cuban cases, there was unanimous support for President John F.

Kennedy in his "quarantine" of Cuba in October 1962. During the missile crisis the United States requested support for its policy from the Council of the OAS. The members of the regional organization did not on this occasion ask that the great-power dispute be taken to the United Nations, and their support strengthened the position of the United States. The circumstances were regarded as entirely appropriate for the application of regional procedures—in this case, the Inter-American Treaty of Reciprocal Assistance of 1947.

In summary then, in cases of disputes between Latin American republics the nations involved, except Ecuador, have preferred the OAS over the UN as the agency of settlement. In cases where the United States has been accused of giving aid or encouragement to invasions of Latin American states, however, the attacked governments have preferred to take their appeals to the United Nations and not to the regional body. When these circumstances have occurred, the aggrieved government has received substantial support from several other Latin American states including Mexico. This type of situation was unforeseen in 1945, possibly because Latin America may well have hoped that the policy of nonintervention would be continued by the successors of Presidents Franklin D. Roosevelt and Harry S Truman. In addition, Cuba has appealed to the United Nations against the sanctionative judgments of its fellow Americans assembled in the OAS; and, finally, during the principal great-power crisis in the history of the Americas, the Cuban missile affair of 1962, the Latin American countries, operating through the OAS, expressed solid support for the United States, and they also endorsed its policy in the United Nations.

There is thus little that is doctrinaire about the policies of the Latin American countries with respect to their regional ties and institutions. The word "regionalism" has not been in this discussion since the evidence does not suggest that there is, on the part of the Latin American countries, a principled commitment to handling American disputes at home despite the obligation to do so in Article 2 of the Rio Treaty and Article 39 of the UN Charter. Changing moods and interests, rather than treaty or theory, seem to inspire their policies.

THE ISSUE OF COLLECTIVE INTERVENTION

One of the most controversial issues in inter-American affairs at the present time is that of "collective intervention." As early as 1958 Mr. Castañeda claimed for a group of influential Mexicans that the aims of the Rio Treaty were being deformed. He said that enforcement measures were being used

not for their fundamental purpose—which is to repel armed aggression or to serve as an instrument of collective security of the United Nations under the authority of the Security Council—but as a means to judge, condemn, and eventually overthrow the internal regimes of the states, to the extent that they do not meet with the approval of the majority of the American republics.[4]

In contrast, the United States Deparment of State as recently as September 1964 has declared that it favors the broadening of the scope of "collective action" in cases where

repression, tyranny and brutality outrage the conscience of mankind. . . . The United States has never believed that collective action for such purposes is proscribed by the Charter of the Organization of American States; but if the majority of the member states are of a contrary opinion, then let us amend the Charter.[5]

Mr. Castañeda, however, has said that if the Rio Treaty were to be used "for intervention in the domestic affairs of the American States," Mexico should seriously consider the denunciation of the Treaty.

The problem of the proper treatment of internal tyranny is a source of tension not only between Mexico, as representative of some Latin American countries on the one hand, and the United States and certain Latin American countries on the other, but also between the OAS and the United Nations. On this issue Mexico and its supporters insistently oppose "collective action" by the American republics and would consistently appeal to the United Nations in all cases that might undermine what Mr. Castañeda has called the "cornerstone of the inter-American system . . . intransigent non-intervention."

The Mexican government has refused to accept as binding on it the decision, approved by a 15–4 vote, of the Ninth Meeting of Consultation of Ministers of Foreign Affairs of the OAS in July 1964 that diplomatic and economic ties with Cuba should be broken. Bolivia, Chile, and Uruguay, the other states in the minority, decided later to act in accordance with the resolution, leaving Mexico as the only member country of the OAS that maintains relations with Cuba. Mexican sources have suggested that this difference of views about interpretation of the OAS Charter, the Rio Treaty, and Chapter VIII of the UN Charter might be referred to the International Court of Justice. The United States has not wished to take this question to the Court, any more than it desired to accept the similar Cuban proposal which has been mentioned earlier, apparently because it does not want any non-American body to issue authoritative interpretations of inter-American treaties. The Mexican government is alone among the American states in desiring a Court opinion on this issue, but the action itself is evidence of an enduring Latin American view that the United Nations is the principal and perhaps the only,

[4] Jorge Castañeda, *Mexico and the United Nations* (New York: Manhattan Publishing Co., 1958), p. 187.

[5] *Foreign Affairs Outline No. 8—Democracy vs. Dictators in Latin America—How Can We Help?* (Department of State Publication 7729, Inter-American Series 90) (Washington, D.C.: U.S. Government Printing Office, 1964).

albeit dim, hope for rectification of an unacceptable decision by the Organization of American States.

IMPORTANCE OF UN AGENCIES IN DEVELOPMENT

In the economic field the principal Latin American achievement in the United Nations was the establishment in 1948 of the Economic Commission for Latin America (ECLA). At that time the Pan American Union maintained a section on economic affairs, but it was under the direction of a United States citizen, and the plans of Latin American economists could be carried out neither in that setting nor through the Economic and Social Council of the OAS.

The United Nations afforded to Latin America through ECLA the opportunity to escape from the constraining influence exerted by the United States in all of the American regional agencies. At the same time, the Latin American governments did not place themselves under a form of restraint by working in a body established under the United Nations. The formation of ECLA, which they effectively controlled, liberated them from United States domination, and they found it possible to operate within a heady atmosphere of collaboration in a freedom which they had never known before.

THE ASIAN NATIONS AND THE UNITED NATIONS

Arthur Lall*

In terms of the opening phrase of the Charter of the United Nations—"We the peoples of the United Nations"—the dominant image which comes to mind is that of Asia. Though not all the countries of Asia are Members of the United Nations—notably Korea, Vietnam, and now Indonesia—the Asian peoples of the United Nations (including the Chinese) not only greatly exceed in numbers those from any of the other major areas of the world but considerably outnumber all the peoples from these areas taken together.

Twenty-three Asian states are Members of the United Nations.[1] This nu-

* Arthur Lall, "The Asian Nations and the United Nations," *International Organization*, Vol. 19, 1965, pp. 728–748. Copyright 1965, World Peace Foundation. By permission of *International Organization*.

Arthur Lall is a lecturer in international law at Cornell University and former permanent representative of India to the United Nations.

[1] This figure includes Cyprus and Turkey, states which sit in the Afro-Asian group at the United Nations, and excludes Israel although that state is geographically in Asia.

merical figure exceeds that of any other regional grouping except Africa, which now contributes 35 Member nations (including South Africa) and very soon will add a 36th state (Gambia). However, in terms of population, Asians outnumber Africans in the proportion of six to one.

The foregoing facts are relevant to an appreciation of the role of Asia in the United Nations over the last twenty years and the current feelings of Asian states and peoples regarding the Organization. Moreover, they have their place in any assessment of the universalist aspirations of the United Nations.

ASIA AND THE MAKING OF THE UNITED NATIONS

Asia did not play a large role on the international scene during the formative years of the United Nations. Of the 26 countries which originally signed the Declaration by United Nations at Washington, D.C., on January 1, 1942, only two were from Asia—China and India. By the spring of 1945 the number of Asian signatories was swelled by the modest addition of six states—Iran, the Philippines, and the four Arab states of Lebanon, Iraq, Saudi Arabia, and Syria. Consequently, no more than these eight states made up the Asian contingent at the San Francisco United Nations Conference on International Organization at which 50 states met in April 1945 to draw up the Charter of the United Nations. On the other hand, all twenty states from Latin America were present at the Conference; and of the fourteen Western European Members, eight were represented at San Francisco.

Nor is it irrelevant to observe that although, as a result of President Franklin D. Roosevelt's efforts, China was among the powers that sponsored the San Francisco Conference, only the United States, the United Kingdom, and the Soviet Union took part in the first, and by far the more important, of the two rounds of discussions at Dumbarton Oaks in 1944 prior to the convening of the San Francisco Conference. Moreover, China at that time was not only struggling against Japan but was not united internally. It was further along toward the cataclysmic changes which were to be completed before the end of the fifth decade of the twentieth century than was generally realized. In short, for a number of reasons China was not able to play its full potential role either in the preparatory phases or at the Charter Conference, although it did make a number of substantive contributions.

What of the other seven Asian participants at San Francisco? India was not yet independent. Indeed, India's national leaders, who were to come into *de facto* power about a year and a half later, were strongly opposed to the policies of the then British government of India. The Indian delegates to the San Francisco Conference and their British-appointed advisers neither had the support of nationalist India nor did they voice the opinions of that India. It was to these kinds of representatives that Winston Churchill referred when, justifying to his own government the case for the admission of the Ukrainian and Byelorussian Soviet Socialist Republics as separate Members of the United Nations, he wrote: "For us to have four or five members, six if India is included, when Russia has only one is asking a great deal of an Assembly of this kind." Little wonder then that India's role at the San Francisco Conference turned out to be a minor one.

❊   ❊   ❊   ❊   ❊   ❊   ❊

The nature of the Asian situation in 1945 was by and large not such as to ensure an adequate expression of the attitudes of the by far most populous area of the world in the profoundly important task of the making of the law of the world Organization. Had Asia been in a state of quiescence, this fact might not have been of great consequence. But the fact was that Asia was in the throes of a great reawakening which would inevitably bring into focus its major problems, political as well as economic and social. If this increased realization of Asian problems had occurred before the calling of the Charter Conference instead of in the next four or five years, the concepts on which the UN was based and its structural makeup might have been more appropriate to the world as presently constituted. It might, moreover, have somewhat enhanced the capacity of the United Nations to engage itself successfully in the problems which were to arise in subsequent decades in Africa.

❊   ❊   ❊   ❊   ❊   ❊   ❊

THE EARLY YEARS OF THE UNITED NATIONS

In spite of the very slight impact that Asia had on the making of the United Nations, membership in the Organization was a strong stimulus to the growth in international stature of some of the Asian states which became Members. . . . [The results of the complaint by Iran against the Soviet Union, January 19, 1946, provided a] lesson for the Asian states: While the crux of the growing dispute between the "European powers"—the Asians included both the United States and the Soviet Union in this grouping—was foreign to the Asians, nevertheless, this dispute could be used in order to further their own (Asian or national) ends. In other words, if the United Nations did not bring into being a wholly effective system of international security and peace, it did offer the services of great-power champions and in this way provided to the small powers a degree of international protection which they had hitherto lacked.

If the arrangements envisaged in Chapters VI and VII of the Charter had worked smoothly, it is possible that the fiats handed down by the Great Powers acting in concert might on occasion have been not only onerous but, in terms of Asian situations, arbitrary. Suppose, for example, great-power unanimity had resulted in the Security Council's taking the view that the Soviets had a right to maintain troops in Iranian Azerbaijan. This would have been very much to be detriment of an Asian state. Or, in the Syrian-Lebanese complaint, we might envisage great-power unanimity permitting British and French troops to remain in the Levant for an indeterminate period in the interests of international security—which would not have been incompatible with a Franco-British agreement of December 13, 1945. In replying to the charges of the Syrian and Lebanese delegations in the Security Council, the representatives of the United Kingdom and France both explained that the agreement implied no intention on the part of their governments to keep troops in the Levant indefinitely and *in the absence of a discussion in the Security Council.* It is easy to see that this formulation might raise apprehensions among the Asian states concerned that the Great Powers desired to direct the discussions in the Security Council so as to provide sanction for the continuance of British and French forces in their territories. It was in this view of the matter that the representatives of Syria and Lebanon requested that the phrase in the United States draft resolution which expressed "confidence . . . that negotiations to that end [the withdrawal of foreign troops from Syria and Lebanon] will be undertaken by the parties without delay . . . " should be amended to read "technical negotiations exclusively to that end will be undertaken by the parties without delay." The statement of the representative of the United Kingdom that he would not accept this amendment could not have relieved the fears of the two countries concerned.

The Soviets came to the assistance of the Asian parties by introducing three amendments to the United States draft resolution, including one in the sense of the amendment requested by Syria and Lebanon and refused by the United Kingdom. These amendments were defeated, and in response the Soviets voted against the United States proposal.

The final outcome was not unpleasing to the Arab states involved. The United Kingdom and France kept their word to the Security Council that, though the United States resolution had been vetoed, they would abide by its terms. Within the next three months they reported to the Security Council that evacuation of their troops from Syrian and Lebanese territories was being completed. The evacuation was, in fact, completed as reported. Thus, the Asian states achieved the objective which they had sought in going to the Security Council. In addition, the wrangle in the Council between the Great Powers had given them the feeling that they had found a champion. Statements to this effect will, of course, not be found on the Security Council records, but they were voiced in private to friendly delegates.

This feeling, we should note, has been a continuing aspect in the attitudes of Asian and other countries toward the United Nations. In an unanticipated way the Security Council has become the guarantor of what a state might deem to be rights which an unfriendly neighbor was trying to wrest from it. Students and writers tend to allude to the vetoes of the Soviet Union as if they were merely expressions of selfish Soviet interests in the world. While it is, of course, clear that the Soviets would not call the veto into play unless they felt it furthered their own international position or interests, it is well to remember that the Soviet veto has not always been cast directly to safeguard a Soviet position. The Soviets have used their veto power also in defense of the interests of other states, generally Asian or African states, when it has appeared that the other party to the dispute or situation before the Security Council could count on the support of other Great Powers in the Council. It is well to bear in mind that this is how many Asian states have viewed the exercise of the Soviet veto power. In short, to them the use of the veto has been not a manifestation of a Machiavellian Soviet policy aimed at frustrating efforts to bring order into a specific dangerous international situation but rather an insistence by the Soviets that the parties concerned must find the ways and means of agreeing in direct negotiations to resolve, or at any rate alleviate, the threatening situation in which they find themselves.

Of course, it was not only the Soviet veto which was available for this purpose. The Western side too could champion the states of Asia, and often did.

*   *   *   *   *   *   *

A discussion of the lessons learned by the Asian countries during the early years of the United Nations does not, however, provide a complete view of the significance of those years in terms of Asian participation in the work of the Organization. We must further note a preoccupation with themselves to the exclusion of an interest in world problems, except insofar as those problems concerned the question of colonialism. It is true that from the very beginning the Indian and the Philippine delegations played a noteworthy role in the Fourth (Trusteeship) Committee of the General Assembly and had much to do with the setting up by the Assembly of the Committee on Information from Non-Self-Governing Territories. Futhermore, the Indian delegation at the first session of the General Assembly raised the matter of the treatment of people of Indian origin in the Union of South Africa and thereby sparked the most extended debate in United Nations history on the meaning and applicability of Article 2, paragraph 7, of the Charter. But this discussion of a most important Charter provision was incidental as far as India was concerned—India was raising a matter of direct interest to itself.

*   *   *   *   *   *   *

It is, of course, relevant that the natural leader of Asia had during these very years suffered a total eclipse as far as the United Nations was concerned. From the very beginning it was clear that China was not pulling its weight in the councils of the United Nations. Then came the revolutionary change in regime, and, whatever might have been their views as to which kind of government they would like to see in China, many of the Asian Members of the United Nations believed that the small group of Chinese on the island of Taiwan could not possibly speak effectively for China. The one Great Power in Asia, in terms of the United Nations Charter, became totally ineffective at Lake Success and thereafter on the East River. This fact left the Asian cause in the United Nations without its natural helmsman and must not be overlooked in assessing the part played by the Asian countries and their effectiveness.

THE EXPRESSION OF THE ASIAN VIEW AT THE UNITED NATIONS

As the fifth decade of this century turned into the sixth a combination of events and circumstances tended to broaden the Asian view at the United Nations. These included the Korean War, increasing awareness of the nature of the Cold War, an increase in the number of Asian UN Members, a degree of realization that the new technological age made it unrealistic to focus attention solely on national or regional issues, and an increased concern about economic well-being and the relevance of international action in this regard.

The Korean War directly involved Asia in the first major post-World War II armed struggle and brought the realization that some of the problems of the Asian continent were such that the Great Powers of other continents would get involved in them. The new situation thus differed from the inter-war years when the advance of Japan into Manchuria and other parts of China did not lead non-Asian powers into the military involvement on the Asian continent. Now, however, it became clear that even "civil" wars might tend to become global. The fact that the United Nations had much to do with the articulation of this development meant that the states of Asia, like other states, had to realize that the terms of their membership in the Organi-zation were not really compatible with a narrow view of international life, a confining of attention to questions of parochial interest.

At the United Nations itself we must take note of two important occur-rences related to the Korean War. First, it led to the formation of the Afro-Asian group, and secondly, it was finally an Indian proposal in the General Assembly which solved the prisoners-of-war tangle which had been holding up the signing of an effective armistice to end the fighting in Korea.

✻   ✻   ✻   ✻   ✻   ✻   ✻

ROLE OF THE NONALIGNED

A most important development flowed from these meetings. This was that many of the leading countries in the group began to tend toward an inde-pendent or nonaligned foreign policy—or neutralism as some writers, in-accurately, in the Asian-African view, have termed it. The showing of the Afro-Asian countries in the United Nations, particularly the leading part they played in supporting Egypt during the 1956 Suez crisis and their robust opposition to colonialism, impressed the new Members of the United Nations and was a factor in spreading the view that nonalignment was a policy that could best represent their own interests and predilections in international affairs. New countries launched upon the sea of international responsibility generally have tended to seek a course which they could chart without yielding, or seeming to yield, their recently achieved independence. The two sides to the Cold War could offer these new countries certain obvious inducements which could not be matched by the largely indigent nonaligned world. It was also common knowledge that, on the whole, those countries which had joined one bloc or the other in the Cold War had received more per capita aid than those that had remained nonaligned. But there were strong countervailing factors: The nonaligned countries had not been refused economic aid by either side; they had pressed hard in the United Nations on all issues connected with human rights, economic programs, and colonialism; and, finally, they had maintained an independence of the Great Powers. Whereas such autonomy seemed to be an appropriate fulfillment of national political independence, to join one side or the other appeared to be the acceptance of leadership from without.

It has been largely an Asian initiative at the United Nations, strongly supported by the United Arab Republic, that has spurred the spread of nonalignment. In the early fifties the nonaligned at the United Nations numbered a bare half-dozen states, but with the passage of time many states which appeared at first to be more disposed to one side or the other have joined the ranks of the nonaligned on most world issues. This has happened over the years in the cases of Ethiopia, Mexico, the Sudan, Ceylon, Laos, Cambodia, and some of the Latin American states; and it appears to be happening on a widening scale. According to *The New York Times* of March 14, 1965, when President Muhammad Ayub Khan returned earlier in the month from his trip to Communist China, this hitherto staunch and committed ally of the West "was hailed as the leading neutralist of Asia." There are press reports that Turkey is considering a neutral policy, and similar reports emanate from Thailand. Though reports are not easily available regarding the mood of Hanoi, it is sometimes reported, notably via France, that North Vietnam would be disposed to adopt a nonaligned position not unlike that of Yugoslavia. In any event, we have the fact that the mere half-dozen nonaligned countries of the early fifties became 25 states by September 1961 when the first Conference of Nonaligned Nations met at Belgrade and rose spectacularly to some 47 states when the second Conference was held at Cairo in October 1964.

The significance of the United Nations as a world forum has been great in influencing countries toward nonalignment. It is here, for example, that the Member States have heard the nonaligned delegations press for the banning of nuclear tests—a move made yearly by India since Prime Minister Jawaharlal Nehru first turned the attention of the United Nations to this issue in April 1954. This sort of move has caught the imagination of a growing number of countries and has won from them support and a consequent growth of the nonaligned approach. This particular nonaligned initiative reached its logical climax when, at the seventeenth session of the General Assembly, the nonaligned countries—with a strong Asian infusion—submitted a draft resolution which flatly condemned all nuclear-weapons tests and suggested ways of securing an agreement to end them. It was a measure of the matured strength of nonalignment that the resolution was adopted by a vote of 75 in favor, none opposed, with 21 abstentions, in spite of the fact that both the Soviet Union, on the one hand, and the United States, the United Kingdom, and France, on the other, did not support it. The inclusion of non-Asian delegations among the sponsors of this resolution meant that what had been an Asian initiative had been espoused by an ever increasing number of states from practically all regions of the world.

. . . Ambassador Burudi Nabwera, the permanent representative of Kenya, in a speech on May 1, 1964, said:

It was not until after India had achieved independence, and this was after the second World War, that the policies of nonalignment or positive neutrality began to take shape. The credit for this radically new policy goes to Premier Nehru of India and his compatriots who thought it out carefully and gave it practical expression on an international plane. Hitherto, neutrality had meant a withdrawal from the conflict. That is to say, those countries which regarded themselves as neutral were not prepared to make public pronouncements on the burning issues of the day. But since the advent of positive neutrality the situation has changed. Nehru argued, and this is the very core of positive neutralism as we know it today, that when there is an issue or a conflict we should examine its pros and cons. . . . [Today] practically all the African countries, under the Addis Ababa agreement, have declared themselves nonaligned. Many countries in Asia and some countries in Europe, the Caribbean and Latin America also belong to this group.[2]

To grasp how this happened we must go back to the starting point already indicated—the decade which opened with the Korean War. War had come to Asia, a war which seemed to contain the seeds of a possible global conflict to be fought out on the soil of Asia. Moreover, this was a United Nations war. These factors combined to create an attitude of vigilance on the part of the Asian states, particularly those at the United Nations, and they felt it to be their duty to try to explore all possible avenues of diplomatic effort. It is not possible in this brief study to trace the course of the efforts launched through Delhi, largely at the urging of the then permanent representative of India to the United Nations, Sir Benegal N. Rau, but it is worthwhile recollecting that the purpose of these efforts was so patently to try to bring about

[2] Text of statement obtained from the permanent mission of Kenya to the United Nations.

a cessation of the fighting that they gained a certain measure of support both in the West and in Communist China.

❄   ❄   ❄   ❄   ❄   ❄   ❄

India, through V. K. Krishna Menon, presented its plan for a solution of the seemingly unbridgeable gap [between the Western Powers and Communist China]. The scheme presented took into account Communist China's susceptibilities as India saw them, and, of course, it also sought to meet the Western position. The Indian plan seemed to furnish some of the magic which the moment demanded. Dean Acheson and Anthony Eden immediately signified their interest and agreed that the Indian draft resolution should have priority over their own text in the voting. Unfortunately, at that stage of the Cold War the clear support of one side meant the almost automatic opposition of the other. Mr. Vishinsky would have no part of the Indian plan, and he suggested that Peking would not either. The Soviet Union voted against the Indian proposal, but the West, the Asian states, and other nonaligned delegations supported it, and it was handsomely carried. What is more, the Indian reading of Communist Chinese attitudes turned out to be more correct than that of the Soviet Union: The Chinese eventually signified their interest in the Indian formula which became the basis of the accepted plan for the settlement of the prisoners-of-war issue and brought about an end to the fighting in Korea. This whole incident was of profound significance. It marked the first fruits of Asian nonalignment at the United Nations, one might almost say of "Asianism" at the United Nations because this was a move which neither those committed to the West nor those devoted to the Communist cause would have conceived. It came out of synthesizing attitudes which, at that time, one could hardly expect of two great opposing champions.

MOUNTING PARTICIPATION IN DISARMAMENT DISCUSSIONS

It was this success and the world factors which prompted the effort toward it that brought the Asians out of their parochialism at the United Nations and led to the focusing of part of their attention on world issues. Up to that time the debates on such subjects as disarmament had been debates between the two sides in the Cold War with minimal participation by other countries and the proposals put before the Assembly almost always were presented by the Cold War adversaries. From the eighth session of the General Assembly (1953) onward, however, this ceased to be the case. At its ninth session the Assembly, for the first time since 1946, reached unanimity on a resolution on the crucial subject of disarmament.[3] That resolution included ideas suggested by the Asian countries, and, furthermore, it transmitted to the Disarmament Commission a draft resolution on the subject which had

[3] General Assembly Resolution 808 (IX), November 4, 1954.

been proposed by India and another draft which had been introduced by the delegations of Australia and the Philippines jointly.

Thereafter the Asian countries and some of their nonaligned friends came increasingly into the foreground of disarmament discussions at the United Nations.

. . . Thus, the Eighteen-Nation Disarmament Committee, which has been longer in near continuous session than any other disarmament negotiating body and which, unlike its predecessors, has to its credit some tangible successes in the field, represents in a sense the flowering from an Asian seed.

CONTRIBUTIONS TO PEACEKEEPING

We should take note of another flowering from the same Asian seed. This is the significant role of the nonaligned countries in many of the peacekeeping operations which the United Nations has conducted in recent years. Indeed, nonalignment in considerable measure facilitated the earliest major peacekeeping operations by providing sources which could ensure prima facie nonpartisan contingents for the situations concerned.

When the United Nations Emergency Force (UNEF) was assembled in 1956 following the Suez crisis, India furnished the largest national unit for service on the perimeter of the Gaza Strip. Indonesia was another Asian country which contributed forces to this operation. When peacekeeping operations had to be mounted in the Congo (Leopoldville), the Asian states of Ceylon, the then Federation of Malaya, India, Indonesia, and Pakistan all contributed forces. The Indian contingent was once again the largest, and Indonesia's was at one stage among the largest. Finally, it was a large Pakistani force which kept the peace in West Irian during the short interim period of United Nations control before the territory was handed over to the administration of Indonesia.

If we do no more in this study than to note rather than discuss extensively the role of the Asian states at the United Nations in the movement to terminate colonialism and to advance to independence the states in the trusteeship system, it is because this role is widely acknowledged. We have already drawn attention to the early efforts of the Philippines and India in these matters. Thereafter, and notably until the large influx of African Member States in 1960, the Asian states constituted the vanguard of opposition to the continuance of colonialism within the Fourth Committee of the General Assembly and the Trusteeship Council.

* * * * * * *

DIVERSITY WITHIN ASIA

The impression must not be given by what has been said that all the Asian states are of one mind in the Assembly. On the contrary, the differences between them remain sharper than those in other regions such as Latin

America or even Africa. There are cleavages between India and Pakistan, Malaysia and Indonesia, Thailand and Cambodia, and some Asian states, such as the Philippines, continue to oppose strongly the alteration of the representation of China. Furthermore, unlike Latin America and Africa, there is no regional organization where Asian states come together to discuss their affairs. Though Africa has many problems, the Organization of African Unity (OAU) might be able to deal with some of them and alleviate the circumstances created by others. Of the vitality of the inter-American system there can be no doubt. Asia is without any comparable arrangements, and its divisions are clearly apparent at the United Nations. Furthermore, though some viable adjustments of inter-Asian problems are undoubtedly possible, Asia is probably further away from any form of unity than all the other areas of the world. This being so, while one can discern certain largely Asian contributions to the United Nations, as we have been engaged in doing, it would be unrealistic to expect the emergence of a single Asian voice at the UN. This is not necessarily a disadvantage. Asia is historically a zone of much exchange of culture and mixing of races. It is natural that at the United Nations as elsewhere it should speak with many voices. This diversity is the wealth of Asia.

12

ECONOMIC
AND SOCIAL
AFFAIRS

There are really only two broad categories of international organizations: one based on membership qualifications, and the other based on program. In the former, membership may be restricted to certain states within a particular regional area, or it may be open to all states on virtually an unrestricted membership basis. Under the program category, membership will be open to those with similar problems or positions on a problem. Of course, the two categories are not mutually exclusive and it is possible to have membership on a universal basis among states who have a limited purpose just as it is possible to restrict the membership but have very broad objectives. In effect one could establish a traditional 2×2 chart to express this (It will be seen that such a classification does not conform to the thinking of J. W. Burton, who in Chapter 4 speaks of the functionalism in universal terms only, but this is a questionable and unnecessarily restricted interpretation of the term.)

	PROGRAM	
NUMBER OF MEMBERS:	BROAD	NARROW
Open	1 UN	2 FAO
Restricted	3 OAS	4 ECLA

Organizations such as those found in Box 1 are often referred to as universal multipurpose organizations, those in Box 2 as universal functional organizations, those in Box 3 as regional multipurpose organizations, and those in Box 4 as regional functional organizations.

Functionalism was a much-discussed form of international organization after World War I, and a school of supporters developed around David Mitrany, the outstanding exponent of the belief that peace was more likely to be achieved on a lasting basis through the functional approach than by any other. Since the demise of the League and since the emphasis given to the role of functionalism during its dying days in the Bruce Commission Report, functionalism has come back stronger than ever, in practice if not in literature. The United Nations not only embraces functionalism but has established a special council for its coordination. Have the results of functional organizations supported the belief that they help provide those conditions upon which international peace and security are built? Obviously no definitive answer to such a question can be provided. But Professor Stephen S. Goodspeed does examine these questions generally in his contribution, "Political Considerations in the United Nations Economic and Social Council." Goodspeed describes the organizational structure and particularly the methods by which recommendations and policies are worked out. He relates the examination to various struggles—East-West, North-South and those of a special nature. Because the Council is a political organization the disagreements associated with these struggles have led to many criticisms and charges of inadequacy. One appreciates from this study the reasons why functionalism can probably never be divorced from politics, and the impact that this has on the goals sought by functional organizations.

Lest one conclude, however, that progress in the sphere of economic and social affairs has been either missing or too limited to warrant comment, we have included excerpts from a report of EPTA, the Expanded Technical Assistance Program. This report, "15 Years and 150,000 Skills" is not a dry statistical account of accomplishments but an imaginative presentation of a hypothetical documentary based on real reports on file with the Technical Assistance Board. Revealed here are not only the procedures used once the "country target" has been established, but also the role of the Resident Representative, who acts as liaison, stimulator, encourager, and adviser from the UN and its agencies to local government, and in particular to its Coordinator. In addition the article identifies the relative degree of involvement of the different agencies in the Expanded Program and the changes in the missions over the years.

The next two articles in the chapter deal with rarely discussed subjects: the role of leadership in the specialized agencies and the issue of centralization and decentralization in the supervision of their programs. The first selection, Part III of the Fourteenth Report of the Commission to Study the Organization of Peace, stresses the fact that although there are some similarities between the institutional patterns of the specialized agencies and those of the UN, there are also some striking differences. These pertain to the voting rules in the election of the chief executive officers, the powers of these officers—none of the agency executives can compare with the Secretary-General of the UN in this regard—and the staffs, which tend to consist to a greater extent of government officials and less of international civil servants than in the parent body. As for the relationships of the various executive directors to their boards, in the main the Specialized Agencies seem to have struck a good balance and one that the Secretary-General in the parent body might do well to study.

Malinowski, in his selection, "Centralization and Decentralization in the United Nations Economic and Social Activities" reminds us of one of the significant changes that has developed in the functioning of the UN family. Although, as he notes, the Charter seems to envisage "a centralized organization," it is clear that decentralization has in fact become the mode. The establishment and successful operation of the regional commissions have helped assure this. And although these are subordinate to ECOSOC and the General Assembly, and in theory could be abolished by them, in fact the regional commissions have become so well entrenched because of their popularity that there is little likelihood that such an abolition would be made or seriously considered. One of the reasons the commissions succeed may well be the closer sense of identification with regional organs for many members than they feel toward a larger, more remote universal organization. Another may be the greater sense of pride that comes from close identification when programs are carried out successfully. And still a third reason may be the desire to show the more advanced countries the capabilities these countries have to manage (and manage well) their own research and operational programs. Why should the larger states, those who contribute the most to those undertakings, insist on a greater emphasis on centralization? Perhaps because to so many of them efficiency (and control?) is increased by this arrangement. But it is also clear that the regional agencies have won their spurs, so to speak, and are likely to agitate for increased autonomy despite their financial dependence.

Difficulties in organizing these functional programs stem from three problems: (1) the cost of the programs, which no country, especially the wealthier ones, seems willing to provide in truly generous amounts on a sustained basis; (2) the uncertainty as to whether greater efficiency and more beneficial results (are these objectives always compatible?) will derive from more centralized operation or from decentralized operation which allows maximum freedom for all decisions on a regional and agency basis; and (3) the question of the proper relationship with the host government. By what standards ought one judge how much each state should contribute? Or ought attention not be paid to the issue of assessment but rather to that of stimulating contributions? And what weight should be given to the issue of efficiency of operation and how much to the feeling of local pride and satisfaction that comes when programs are mapped out and results achieved without the close supervision of the larger powers? Here we might ask whether the methodology and skills of more advanced powers are always useful to the less advanced and whether styles of operation may perhaps have to be carefully tailored to the needs of those concerned. Connected with this, of course, is the overriding problem of how to reduce the impact of the cold-war hostility on the recruiting of staffs, the operation of programs, and the nature of the projects themselves.

Considering all of these difficulties would it be wiser to distinguish between the economic and human-rights types of programs, and then to attempt to coordinate those divisions rather than to encourage ECOSOC to improve its over-all coordination?

FURTHER READINGS

Asher, Robert E., *et al.*, *The United Nations and the Promotions of the General Welfare.* Washington, D.C.: The Brookings Institution, 1957.

Sharp, Walter R., *Field Administration in the United Nations System.* New York: Frederick A. Praeger, Inc., 1961.

POLITICAL CONSIDERATIONS IN THE UNITED NATIONS ECONOMIC AND SOCIAL COUNCIL

Stephen S. Goodspeed*

. . . There is a strong belief that social discontent in one country may have a very marked effect upon other States, inasmuch as people who believe that they suffer from economic injustices or who endure a reduction in their standard of living or join a growing mass of unemployed may become easy prey for those who would use them for their own purposes. Severe economic and social dislocation may encourage a government to risk war in an effort to divert attention away from misery to the honour and glory of aggressive pursuits.

However, economic and social stability will not alone guarantee peace and security. Unstable economic and social conditions may very likely be the consequence of war and not its cause. In the final analysis, power, prestige and national interests among the major Powers will dictate the course of peace or war. The peace failure of 1919–39 cannot be attributed directly to economic factors since political and psychological considerations were of greater significance. It is virtually impossible to prevent the intrusion of political factors into fields which traditionally have been considered non-political. Indeed, political tensions actually retard the effective functioning of agencies devoted solely to welfare purposes.

That hunger, poverty, economic dislocation and disease can be alleviated by the combined efforts of States has been proved. The record of the League of Nations in the welfare field has been obscured by political questions and the failure to answer them, yet it is a record in which the League could take considerable pride. Similarly, the money and effort spent through the United Nations in furtherance of technical assistance and other social and economic programmes have been worthwhile in terms of the immediate objectives of these programmes.

At the same time, it is extremely difficult to prove that the economic and social activities, say, of the United Nations' system, have contributed, in a tangible fashion, to an atmosphere of co-operation in the world. It is prob-

* Stephen S. Goodspeed, "Political Considerations in the United Nations Economic and Social Council," *The Year Book of World Affairs, 1961* (London: Stevens & Sons Ltd., 1961), pp. 135–161. By permission of Stevens and Sons Ltd.

Stephen S. Goodspeed is Vice Chancellor and Professor of Political Science at the University of California at Santa Barbara. He is author of *The Nature and Function of International Organization*.

ably true that the individuals who work for international agencies in these fields, coming from different countries and working in foreign areas, have come to know and understand each other's national problems and the way of life in the lands where they may be stationed. More concretely, governments have learned to work with international agencies on a give and take basis, recognising the basic truth that these agencies are devoted to assisting them in the solution of specific problems. A spirit of co-operation inevitably will arise among those who labour on joint projects, and governments themselves learn to co-operate with each other through the medium of the international agency. By directing attention to fields of common interest, the agencies may condition certain responsible individuals to a system of international intercourse based upon positive, constructive collaboration. Beyond this, however, the measure of co-operation which is developed is highly debatable. International agencies themselves do not touch directly upon the lives of many individuals and ordinarily are concerned with matters which do not arouse interest to any degree comparable to that of the activity engaged in by national governments. Loyalty to national institutions is very real, associated as it is with national myths, symbols and beliefs. People are interested in the practical aspects of life, such as a better standard of living, improved educational and sanitary facilities, and agricultural development; but projects such as these cannot compare in emotional impact with national symbols. By and large, then, much of the contact fostered by these agencies is intergovernmental and, while it is important as far as it goes, such contact represents only a small beginning toward a goal of universal contact and understanding among all peoples.

It is only in this setting that one can understand fully the nature of the economic and social activities of a universal international organisation and, more particularly, of the Economic and Social Council of the United Nations. ECOSOC is rooted in a political framework and its achievements and failures are directly linked to the attitudes of the members of the United Nations, attitudes which are motivated primarily by political considerations.

PURPOSES AND GENERAL FUNCTIONS OF THE COUNCIL

. . . The framers of the United Nations Charter at San Francisco . . . recognised the importance of economic and social stability. Consequently, in Article 1:3 of the Charter, one of the purposes of the United Nations is "to achieve international co-operation in solving international problems of an economic, social, cultural or humanitarian character. . . ." Later, in Article 55, the Charter gives full recognition to this purpose. Exclusive final authority over economic and social matters rests with the General Assembly since, according to Article 60 of the Charter, ECOSOC functions "under the authority of the General Assembly." At the same time, Article 7:1 establishes the General Assembly and ECOSOC as "principal organs" of the United

Nations. Any ambiguity in this arrangement has been resolved in favour of Article 60, since ECOSOC must obtain Assembly approval for much of its work, including such matters as concluding agreements with the specialised agencies, calling international conferences, submitting draft resolutions for consideration by member States, and the performance of services requested by members and specialised agencies.

As a major organ of the United Nations, ECOSOC makes studies and reports on international economic, social, cultural, educational, health and related matters. International conferences are called on matters which lie within its competence. In addition, ECOSOC makes recommendations on such matters to members of the United Nations and the specialised agencies. By no means the least of its functions is the act of co-ordinating the activities of the specialised agencies through consultation with and recommendations to such agencies and through recommendations to the General Assembly and to the members of the United Nations.[1]

The General Assembly elects the eighteen[2] members of ECOSOC from the ranks of the United Nations to serve three-year terms. There is no prohibition with regard to re-election. The permanent members of the Security Council have no privileged position but have served continuously as members of ECOSOC. Some attempt has been made to grant membership to different economic and cultural systems and allow geographical representation where possible. Any member of the United Nations may be invited to participate, without a vote, in its deliberations "on any matter of particular concern to that member."[3] Arrangements are also made for representatives of the specialised agencies to participate in its deliberations on the same basis. Various non-governmental organisations consult with ECOSOC when matters of mutual concern are before it.

As might be expected from its broad terms of reference, ECOSOC has developed a complex organisational structure. Several types of subsidiary organs report to it: functional commissions such as the Commission on Human Rights; regional economic commissions for Europe, Africa, Latin America and Asia and the Far East; special bodies such as the Permanent Central Opium Board; and standing and *ad hoc* committees. In addition, ECOSOC supervises a number of special funds such as the United Nations Korean Reconstruction Agency.

The experience of the League showed that when it began its work in economic and social fields, there was a glaring shortage of information available on a world-wide basis. One of the great contributions made by the League was the compilation of statistical and other data which proved to be of inestimable value when any of its organs or members was confronted with questions which were related to such matters as population,

[1] Article 63, 2, of the Charter.
[2] Twenty-seven as of 1966 [ed.].
[3] Article 69 of the Charter.

migration, water resources, employment indices and levels of industrial and agricultural productivity. By no means did all countries compile information on items such as these. Either they could not afford to do so or lacked the trained researchers required. Certainly many countries are not able to collect this type of information about other nations. Making available studies and reports to all States is a service which can be provided only by an international agency. ECOSOC has continued the work begun by the League and, as a result of greater financial support, has expanded it to a remarkable degree.

✻   ✻   ✻   ✻   ✻   ✻   ✻

Many of the studies and reports which have been prepared are discussed at length before being acted on by ECOSOC. They are then quite frequently adopted by a resolution which contains a recommendation that the members of the United Nations heed the findings and subscribe to a particular course of action. Other recommendations are directed to the various organs and agencies of the Organisation. In no case does a resolution have any binding effect on the member States or on other organs of the United Nations. Possibly the best known plan worked out in an ECOSOC resolution was that which resulted in the United Nations' Expanded Programme of Technical Assistance. The discussion which precedes the adoption of resolutions, despite digressions and propagandising intended for home consumption, frequently serves to clarify issues and bring home to the peoples of the world the many problems confronting them and the possible means of solution. Undoubtedly, public discussion is most effective when ECOSOC is examining specific action programmes such as that developed for technical assistance.

Two additional methods of discussion and recommendation are the prerogatives of ECOSOC. One is the preparation of draft conventions which are submitted to individual members, and sometimes to non-members, for adherence. The Charter wisely made this provision in the belief that nations may be more receptive to signing an international agreement if they are offered the opportunity on an equal basis without the necessity of engaging in lengthy negotiations. The rough draft invariably originates in one of ECOSOC's subsidiary organs. The initial suggestion for such a draft may come from such an organ, from ECOSOC, from the Secretariat, or from the General Assembly. ECOSOC has submitted more than a dozen draft conventions of a substantive nature to the General Assembly, covering such matters as prostitution, genocide, narcotic drugs, political rights of women, and fundamental human rights. The Council also began the work on the constitutions of the International Refugee Organisation, World Health Organisation, the abortive International Trade Organisation, and the Intergovernmental Maritime Consultative Organisation.

The other method is the calling of international conferences on items falling within its own competence. ECOSOC does this either on its own initiative or on instructions from the General Assembly. Certain rules were prescribed in 1949 for ECOSOC by the General Assembly, which define its authority in the latter case. Care must be taken that the work to be done by the conference is not performed by some other organ or specialised agency. The terms of reference for the conference, the provisional agenda, the States to be invited, the date and place, the provisional rules of procedure, and the selection of an executive secretary all are matters taken care of by ECOSOC with the assistance of the Secretariat.

CO-ORDINATING ACTIVITIES

One of the most difficult yet extremely important functions of ECOSOC is that of co-ordinating "the activities of the specialised agencies through consultation with and recommendations to such agencies and through recommendations to the General Assembly and to the members of the United Nations." Each of the agencies, with their various organs and subsidiary bodies, committees and commissions, is essentially an autonomous international organisation. The possibility of duplication of effort and needless financial expenditures is very real. Under the guidance of the General Assembly, ECOSOC has constantly struggled to co-ordinate many policies and activities with those of the United Nations.

The specialised agencies are brought into relationship with the United Nations through agreements negotiated by ECOSOC which are subject to approval by the Assembly. They reveal the relationships between the agencies and the Organisation and thereby exist as the basis for co-ordinating their activities and policies with the United Nations. It is important to note that none of the agreements provide the United Nations with controlling or coercive powers. Using the agreement signed June 10, 1946, between the United Nations and the Food and Agriculture Organisation as an example, the following points are typical of the agreements concluded with most of the agencies:

1. Reciprocal representation and participation, without vote, in all meetings.

2. Reciprocal proposal of agenda items. However, the specialised agencies may propose items only for ECOSOC, its commissions, and the Trusteeship Council.

3. Recommendations from the United Nations to the agencies, "consultation with the United Nations upon request with respect to such recommendations," and the obligation of the agencies to report the action taken "to give effect to such recommendations."

4. "Subject to such arrangements as may be necessary for the safeguarding of confidential material," provision is made for "the fullest and promptest exchange of information and documents."

5. Assistance as requested to the Security and Trusteeship Councils.

6. Information to the International Court of Justice and the right of the

agencies to request advisory opinions from the Court on legal questions arising within the scope of their activities other than questions concerning the mutual relationships of the agencies and the United Nations.

7. Development of "common personnel standards with the recognition that the eventual development of a single unified civil service is desirable from the stand-point of effective administrative co-ordination. . . ."

8. Maximum co-operation in statistical, administrative and technical services with a concerted attempt to avoid duplication of effort.

9. Recognition of the need for close budgetary and financial relationships with consultation concerning appropriate arrangements for the inclusion of the budgets of the agencies within the general budget of the United Nations.

10. Implementation of the agreements by mutual decision of the Secretary-General and the executive directors of the agencies.

11. Revision of the agreements through negotiation between the agencies and ECOSOC.

The International Bank for Reconstruction and Development and the International Monetary Fund have unique functions which require a special type of arrangement with the United Nations. This type of agreement permits the greatest autonomy enjoyed by any of the agencies. Reciprocal representation is limited by the fact that representatives of the United Nations may only attend meetings of the respective Board of Governors. Greater emphasis is placed on the need for the safeguarding of confidential information. Only "due consideration" need be given by the Bank and the Fund to agenda items proposed by the United Nations instead of reciprocal proposals. Recommendations from the United Nations cannot be made "without reasonable prior consultation with regard thereto." Furthermore, the United Nations agrees that it is "sound policy to refrain from making recommendations to the Bank with respect to particular loans or with respect to terms or conditions of financing by the Bank." Limited exchange of information is provided and there is agreement on the need for the co-ordination of statistical, administrative, and technical services. Assistance is to be provided to the Security and Trusteeship Councils and both the Bank and the Fund may request advisory opinions from the Court. But the appropriate authorities of the Bank and the Fund "enjoy full autonomy in deciding the form and the content" of their budgets and need not transmit them to the United Nations.

The essential features of these agreements indicate that the specialised agencies need do little more than co-operate with the United Nations in some matters through certain procedures. The agencies submit their reports to ECOSOC and other appropriate organs. All except the Bank and the Fund freely agree to consider the recommendations of the Organisation and report the action taken. Beyond this point, the burden of implementing co-ordination falls to ECOSOC and the General Assembly.

The Council has been fully aware of its responsibilities, and as a result of its request the Secretary-General created the Administrative Committee on Co-ordination composed of the heads of the agencies and chaired by the Secretary-General. The Committee has advised ECOSOC on matters of budgetary and programme co-ordination and priorities for international action. Despite continuing attempts to establish a common approach to planning economic and social programmes with definite priorities, ECOSOC still continues to struggle with co-ordination processes with modest success. At the heart of the problem lies "the concept of functional decentralisation that inspires the United Nations system.[4]

❊   ❊   ❊   ❊   ❊   ❊   ❊

THE COUNCIL IN ACTION: CHARACTERISTICS AND UNDERLYING FORCES

A glance at the organisational chart of ECOSOC reveals at once its sprawling and complex structure and machinery. An examination of the multiplicity of [ECOSOC's] functions first indicates that it has some of the characteristics of a specialised agency. That is to say, ECOSOC has broad responsibilities through its commissions in various fields which resemble the activities of such bodies. The Commission on Human Rights and the regional economic commissions are good examples of this. Secondly, ECOSOC must co-ordinate the programmes of the specialised agencies, certainly an important and continuing duty. Thirdly, it functions as a group of diplomatic negotiators on important social and economic questions and, in addition, offers advice and information on these political and economic matters with its debaters fully cognisant of the propaganda value of their remarks.

This is indeed an awesome array of responsibilities and the conclusion is inescapable that undoubtedly ECOSOC is overburdened. Ineffective action certainly can be the result of such a multiplicity of functions. There has been the tendency to try to undertake too much, a fact which can be seen from a perusal of the agendas of ECOSOC and its various commissions. An inability to perform one of its basic functions, that of co-ordination of social and economic programmes, invariably is the result. Some of the recommendations of ECOSOC can be carried out by the specialised agencies. But there has developed the tendency to forget that behind those agencies and behind the United Nations itself are the individual member nations upon whom the Organisation must depend, in the final analysis, for implementation of policies and decisions.

❊   ❊   ❊   ❊   ❊   ❊   ❊

Probably the most abiding force in shaping the programmes of economic and social co-operation has been the conflict between the Soviet world and the leaders of the Western bloc. No greater, more fundamental barrier to

---

[4] See W. R. Malinowski, *infra* pp. 554–572 [ed.].

effective action by ECOSOC in implementing the objectives of the Charter can be found than in the East-West struggle itself and in the lack of any political basis for co-operative action on economic and social matters between the great-power blocs. A foundation of political security and trust is essential for international social and economic co-operation. Furthermore, multilateral programmes, especially in the economic field, demand common political objectives, since action at a governmental level cannot be divorced from political aims.

* * * * * * *

Further complicating [the] situation has been the development of divergent political attitudes among the States of the non-Soviet in relation to the Soviet world, even extending to the most adequate means of restraining Soviet ambitions. Frequently one discovers a division, especially in economic matters, between wealthy and poor nations, with Afro-Asian, Middle Eastern and Latin American countries in disagreement with Britain, France and the United States. The smaller nations of Western Europe can be found on both sides, depending upon the issues and the national interests involved. There has generally been less enthusiasm on the part of these middle Powers for the creation of subsidiary bodies and for taking the lead in challenging enterprises. In world economics, as in matters of security, there is the realisation that the ability to implement major programmes rests with a small number of large States and there is a natural inclination to wait for their initiative before making any commitment. Since most of the poorer nations are not represented on ECOSOC, due to its comparatively small size, they have been unwilling to accept ECOSOC recommendations as final and take matters to the General Assembly where, in concert, they can muster a majority. They are convinced that their opinions will receive more understanding in the larger body. . . .

As a consequence of employing the General Assembly to accomplish objectives not obtained in ECOSOC, the Council has had imposed upon it, programmes which it originally was unwilling to recommend or not ready to propose or has been reversed in its policy decisions. Although this has occurred in a number of fields, most conspicuous has been the refusal of the Assembly to accept ECOSOC's efforts in the area of human rights, primarily because again the issues involved are highly political and ECOSOC is not truly representative of the United Nations.

* * * * * * *

Sharp political divisions have also arisen in the regional economic commission. This has been especially true in the Economic Commission for Latin America, due primarily to differences in economic interest and structure and the absence of a common political orientation. Geographical propinquity alone cannot replace political cohesion and agreement on basic goals.

REFLECTIONS AND CONCLUSIONS

The Economic and Social Council, as preceding pages have revealed, is intimately concerned with virtually every facet of the work of the United Nations in the general welfare field. Consequently, ECOSOC has been involved with the problems of the underdeveloped countries, attempts to improve standards of living, transportation and communications matters, questions of full employment and economic stability, general items of welfare and social defence, problems of international trade and payments and production and development, plus action to relieve emergency situations. Such an impressive listing cannot begin to tell the story of the infinite variety of problems with which the Council has had to deal. It follows, inevitably, that the performance of ECOSOC since its inception has not been satisfactory to all the members of the organisation. Its work is being criticised with continued severity. It has been claimed that its sessions are too long, that it has failed to co-ordinate the activities of the specialised agencies, that it is not representative of the total membership of the Organisation, that there is too much duplication of work between it and the General Assembly, that it tries to do too much and that there are too few experts appointed as representatives of the individual members. To correct these deficiencies, it has been suggested that ECOSOC be divorced from its functions in the field of human rights, that its role should be made into a professional instead of a policy-making body, that it should be abolished, that it should be given more power and detached from the General Assembly.

*   *   *   *   *   *   *

There is no point in criticising the sessions of ECOSOC for resembling those of the Assembly in terms of its being an arena devoted frequently to political debate. There still persists the belief that somehow ECOSOC can divorce itself from political considerations. Behind this thinking lies what has been called the "functionalist" approach to international relations.[5] Briefly stated, there is the belief that war can be traced to a large number of causes deeply rooted in social and economic maladjustments. Misery, poverty and injustice create fear, hatred and suspicion, which are the breeding places of war. The most appropriate way to eliminate these causes is to encourage the development of functional organisations that presumably serve the highest common measure of interests among peoples. Such interests are not represented alone by national sovereignty and political authority. They can be stated only in terms of individual well-being, social security, and human welfare. Therefore, it follows that only organisations effectively serving such ends can satisfy these needs. Fundamental to this approach is the assumption that technical or welfare activities are separate

[5] For the best expression of this position, see D. Mitrany, *A Working Peace System*, 1946.

from the realm of politics, that technical matters are non-political and non-controversial. In accepting this thesis, it is held that such non-political activity can be made the foundation for international organisation because nations will not protest against the granting of non-controversial authority to institutions that will work to satisfy the basic needs and demands of all peoples.

The inherent weakness in the "functionalist" approach is the assumption that it is possible to prevent the intrusion of political influences into the realm of technical and welfare activities. There is no clear dividing line. It can be said that only with respect to certain specific technical functions, such as postal rates, that political considerations remain unimportant.

✻ ✻ ✻ ✻ ✻ ✻ ✻

Stated another way, the basic argument for international programmes in the welfare field as opposed to unilateral ones is that assistance to the less fortunate peoples can be divorced from the political dictation of the Great Powers, that international agencies can offer help free from the motivations of special economic and political interests of national states. This means that the nations which contribute most to international development programmes, for example, are expected to employ a non-political agency for accomplishing what they may consider to be long-range security or political objectives. Since the decision by a Great Power to support financially an international welfare programme is made in political terms, that country will inevitably expect that it be given a commanding position in the allocation and use of the funds involved so that its primary interests will not be compromised. But the policies of any international agency dominated, say, by the United States and its powerful allies, very possibly will not develop fundamental criteria of an objective nature that will satisfy those in the less-developed category. It follows that economic and social co-operation will not increase to any degree until the political climate of international relations becomes more benevolent.

PROCEDURES IN THE EPTA PROGRAM*

HOW THE PROGRAMME TAKES SHAPE

An idea that becomes a project, that qualifies technically as such for assistance and that secures the necessary priority to become part of a country's

* "The Program in Action" in *15 Years and 150,000 Skills, An Anniversary Review of the United Nations Expanded Programme of Technical Assistance*, United Nations, pp. 34–40.

EPTA programme, can be born and take shape in one of several different ways and at almost any point of time in a continuous process. In most cases, it either originates spontaneously within a ministry of the Government concerned, obtains endorsement from the Government's co-ordinating unit and is referred, preferably through the Resident Representative, to the international agency most likely to be able to carry it out; or else it arises from "pre-programming" discussions between a field or headquarters representative of the agency and officials of the ministry and other institutions concerned about specific problems of action or development which confront the latter and about the possible ways in which technical assistance could help to meet those problems. That this process is in fact continuous, allowing urgently-needed new projects to be added at almost any time to a country's programme either through substitution or the use of contingency financing, is a measure of the flexibility of the Expanded Programme, although the scale of such changes has important financial and other practical limitations.

The point in time and space at which to start a brief account of the practical working of the Expanded Programme must therefore be somewhat arbitrarily selected. For present purposes the place chosen is an office building thousands of miles removed from any Headquarters, carrying the blue and white flag of the United Nations against most likely, a tropical sky. The building houses the office of the Resident Representative of the Technical Assistance Board: it is a fairly modest place, wholly or partly paid for by the Government of the country in whose capital it lies, and the Representative shares it not only with his own small staff of internationally and locally recruited assistants, secretaries and clerks but also with some of the country representatives, where these exist, and specialist staff of the major Participating Organizations, of whom others may be found by preference of the Government, attached to the Ministries with which they are most directly concerned. The building may house also a United Nations information centre, perhaps an area office of the United Nations Children's Fund (UNICEF) and a sub-office of the regional United Nations economic commission, and thus be the centre of United Nations activities in the country, and possibly for neighbouring countries and territories as well.

The moment equally arbitrarily chosen for the start of this account is that at which the Resident Representative draws from his daily flow of official mail a letter by which TAB Headquarters informs him of the "country target." This is the notional total of EPTA funds which, on best existing estimates, are likely to be available to help meet the country's basic assistance requirements in the two-year programme period starting twelve months in the future. A target of this kind will have been established simultaneously for almost all of the 120 countries served by the Expanded Programme, and communicated also to the Participating Organizations and through them to their own field offices. It will have been fixed partly on the basis of assistance projects already under way and likely to continue; partly in the light of indications from the Resident Representative and the Participating Organizations of the country's general needs and capacity and its particular requirements for new kinds of assistance; and partly according to the concern of the Executive Chairman for considerations of equity, as well as efficiency, in the proposed allocation of funds. But the target is not in itself an allocation, and, since the resources available can only be intelligently guessed at rather than known in advance, it is not even a sure promise. On the other hand, it is not necessarily a ceiling, either, for unless the future resources fall disastrously short of expectations, there will be scope in the Chairman's planning reserve to allow some properly justified increase in the country's total, and scope also within his contingency authority to meet urgent additional requests that may arise in the course of the Programme period.

With these reservations clearly indicated, and with a further comparing of notes with the agency representatives, the Resident Representative communicates the notional figure to the Government: usually directly to the Minister concerned, but in any case to his point of day-to-day contact in the administration. This may be the director of the planning organization, or the secretary of the treasury, or some other senior official responsible for the co-ordination of the country's technical assistance requests and activities. The Resident Representative must tell the Government, too, as precisely as he can how much assistance the money can buy if and when it does become available. For this purpose he will be armed with the "standard costs" established by the Participating Organizations, the normal average amount in dollars required to provide an expert or a fellowship by the year and by the month. This information may not surprisingly give rise to a rueful exchange of remarks on how quickly the country's target figure of, say, one million dollars worth of assistance can be made to disappear: at the current averages, which take into account not only the salary to be offered to a competent expert but also the costs of his fares, his dependents, his leave and his allowances, that figure would provide for the continuous services over the biennium of only 25 to 50 experts. It would pay for several times that number of fellowship years, but experience has shown, as mentioned earlier, that most developing countries call upon the Expanded Programme far more heavily for expert services than for fellowships.

The Resident Representative will also remind the Government, and the agency mission chiefs will remind the ministries, that in preparing a programme-request up to the level of the target figure it will need to allow first for the cost of projects which it wishes to be continued either from the existing programme or from contingency allocations authorized or pending. This factor, in the typical country, means that usually much more than one half of the potential resources will have been, in effect, committed in advance. This presents an opportunity for the Government—as the Resident

Representative now encourages it to do—to review the ongoing projects in the light of their results and their importance as compared with that of new needs which may have arisen and which may call for changes in the programme.

It is likely that the Government coordinator's files, if not his head, already contain a long list of projects for which external assistance needs to be sought or continued. Ideally, they will be related to aspects or phases of the country's development plan existing or projected, and accordingly designed to achieve one or more of a number of things that must be done to facilitate a particular form of development or, frequently, to help the Government determine whether substantial resources should be committed to such development: for example, a survey to prove the extent and quality of a mineral deposit, or a study of the feasibility of a certain type of manufacturing industry, or a review of the economic viability of a proposed social security scheme, or the training of local staff in techniques not previously used, or even the setting up of a completely new service. The need for and priorities of the projects, and the assurance of local support for them, will have been established by the country's economic planners and technical ministries and approved at the political level. That approach to technical assistance programming, it must be emphasized, is the ideal; in fact, it still represents a degree of co-ordination and a level of planning that only a few receiving countries have yet achieved. In any event, it is now the co-ordinator's task to obtain the skilled assistance needed to carry out the projects which his Government wants undertaken. His country may have access to technical assistance from a number of different sources, including other individual Governments, but experience as well as guidance from the ministries will have given him some sense as to which projects are likely to secure assistance more promptly and effectively from the Expanded Programme than elsewhere, or at least are better suited to assistance from the United Nations system in general because of its international character and its access to a world-wide range of disciplines and experience.

Most of the Organizations, moreover, will already have prepared and sent to the Resident Representative and the Government their own lists of projects to be continued or undertaken as their components of the country's EPTA programme. These are suggestions which do not in themselves bind the Government, but most of them will in fact have been prepared in close consultation with the ministries and already will have been virtually assured of a place in the Expanded Programme. The agency representatives stationed in the field or sent from their headquarters for the purpose (except where they request the Resident Representative to act on their behalf) will, given the measure of co-operation agreed upon by all of the partners in the Expanded Programme, have been in frequent contact with the Resident Representative for this purpose. In this, as in their subsequent help to the Governments in the actual programming, including the writing of project and job descriptions, as well as in the eventual delivery of the assistance requested, they have at their disposal the resources of the technical divisions of their central and regional headquarters, a vital element in the operation of the Expanded Programme. In the best of circumstances they will have kept and will continue to keep the Resident Representative closely informed of and to some extent involved in this pre-programming activity, for it is his responsibility to obtain, through his wider and usually higher-level contacts with the Government, a broader view of needs and priorities over the whole field covered by the Expanded Programme, and some knowledge of the limits which the central authority of the Government will need to impose on the claims of one ministry as compared with another. In the worst of circumstances—now rarely encountered as the priority-making machinery of Governments has improved—visitors from the agencies will have operated with insufficient knowledge of or regard for the country's over-all priorities and for the accepted co-ordinating function of the Resident Representative. Thus they may have stimulated ministries to ask for the continuation or institution of projects whose importance or urgency would seem doubtful in any systematic assessment of the country's real needs. This kind of thing happens without ulterior motives: technical assistance is so largely an enterprise of as well as for human beings that if it continues to sustain some doubtful undertakings and even some "pet projects" this seems more often than not the result of well-meant enthusiasm and idealism. In the last resort, the responsibility for the composition of the Expanded Programme rests with the Government concerned, more clearly than ever since the automatic allocation of funds to the Organizations came to an end.

Having at his hand his Government's own considered list of requirements in their order of priority, the Participating Organizations' suggested projects, and the limited flexibility left to him by the EPTA target figure for his country, the co-ordinating officer and his staff gradually bring the country programme submission into final shape over the next few weeks, compiling "Category I" programme whose cost matches the target figure and a "Category II" list (about half the value) of additional projects, in their order of priority, which may be drawn upon should additional funds become available. During this process there is continuous two- and three-way consultation, as appropriate, with the Resident Representative and with representatives on the spot or in the regional or home offices of the agencies, whose views on the technical soundness of the projects are essential, on a variety of matters: defining and sometimes changing the specifications of a project, the writing of job descriptions, queries on the availability of experts of particular disciplines or experience, discussing with an organization the possibility of providing for a project in its regular programme instead of EPTA, determining the extent of the Government's interest in proposed regional projects, and the like. A good eight months before the start of the programme period, the submission is completed, approved at the ministerial level and transmitted through the Resident Representative to the Technical Assistance Board and simultaneously to the headquarters of the Participating Organizations. There it is examined and checked, to some extent for its balance but especially for the accuracy of its costing and for the attribution of particular projects to the appropriate agencies, and it becomes part of the global Expanded Programme to be approved by the Board and by the Technical Assistance Committee of the United Nations Economic and Social Council.

IMPLEMENTING THE PROGRAMME

Implementation begins formally on the first day of the programme period: the first day of January in the first year of the biennium. By this time—if all has gone well, particularly at the annual Conference at which Governments pledge their contributions—the necessary allocation of funds will have been made to the Participating Organizations. The large proportion of each new biennial Programme represented by continuing projects means that much existing work simply carries on; but the new or amended projects still leave considerable recruiting of experts to be done. The Organizations, which will have started preliminary work on this task even before funds have been allocated, can draw on a number of sources. They will tend to look for suitable candidates in the first instance among experts known to them from previous assignments or through Governments, institutions and private firms with which they frequently deal. Or they may need, in order to secure the necessary professional and language qualifications as well as the desirable personal attributes, and also in order to make the fullest use of the many currencies allocated to them, to cast their nets more broadly through worldwide recruiting systems in which agencies of many Governments and national committees in many countries play an invaluable part. In each case a detailed personal history of the candidate, or possibly a series of candidates, is submitted to the recipient Government: just as the selection of the project for assistance is the prerogative of the Government, so also is the final choice of the man or woman for the job.

It would be a rare country where, in the meantime, the EPTA operations stood still and waited for the new experts to arrive. Developing countries are dynamic places. The months elapsing between the compilation of the programme and the start of its implementation may well have seen ideas and priorities change, project and job descriptions need adjustment, and new demands arise to require modifications in the programme. This process of adjustment and substitution continues and indeed grows in volume in the programme period itself, and is most marked in countries feeling their way through the early years of independence or adjusting to radical new turns of economic policy. It has always been relatively easy to make such changes within each Participating Organization's sector of the programme;

in very recent years it has also become feasible for a Government to request that a project in one Organization's sphere of competence should be replaced by one in another realm. This rule was designed to reassert the Government's right to determine its own priorities over the whole range of EPTA assistance. It is a principle more easy to state than to apply; an Organization's willingness to transfer resources to another must be tempered by such factors as contractual commitments, currency utilization and the need for stable planning and management in general.

Nominations of experts arrive—seldom without some delay, which may reach acute proportions in the case of economic planners, statisticians, engineering instructors and a few other kinds of specialists—and are shepherded through the Government's processes of selection and acceptance usually with the help of the Resident Representative, who is also often called upon to press for the nomination of candidates for fellowships. Once accepted, the expert is placed under contract by the Participating Organization concerned and enters a short briefing period which seeks not only to make him more familiar with the nature and cirumstances of his assignment but also to sharpen his sensibilities to the demands that will be placed on his personal attributes: the need to temper zeal with tact and patience, the ability to translate sophisticated experience into assimilable instruction and demonstration, the capacity for integrity and impartiality that befits an international servant. Eventually he arrives in his country of assignment; and from the Resident Representative and from his own agency's representative, if there is one, he will absorb more such advice, focused down to the local level, as well as receive help in finding a place to live, in making himself known to the people with whom he will work, in collecting his pay and his mail and, above all, in going about the tasks assigned to him.

The implementation of the country programme is a never-ending and an ever-changing affair. Many and disparate factors exert their influence on it, from the disability (or more rarely the unsuitability) of an expert and the consequent need to replace him, to the emergence of new requirements and new policies on the part of the Government. The Resident Representative is on constant call. A general practitioner ministering to every kind of need that affects the programme, he divides his attention and time as impartially as he can between economic problems of the Government and professional and personal troubles of experts; between discreetly pressing the local treasury for the payment of local cost contributions and pledges and less discreetly urging upon the Executive Chairman of the Technical Assistance Board the allocation of contingency funds for unexpectedly needed new projects or emergency assistance in natural disasters; between negotiating standard agreements with the Government and badgering the agencies for belated expert nominations and final reports; between balancing his office accounts and meeting obligations to make public speeches; and between the whole gamut of his responsibilities toward the Expanded Programme and those which he owes also to the Special Fund, the World Food Programme, always to one (the United Nations proper) and often to more of the Participating Organizations not otherwise represented in his country and, sometimes, to the United Nations Secretary-General in matters of public information and special tasks of representation. His colleagues representing individual Participating Organizations—although there are few countries where all or even most of these are directly represented—have kindred responsibilities and duties, sometimes in a whole group of countries, and including their functions as technical negotiators with the Governments and advisers to the Resident Representatives in their special fields.

Meanwhile, the experts are at work with the people of the country in which they serve. Depending upon their tasks, they may be in the capital of the country; or they may be found miles away from it, wherever what amounts to a direct battle against poverty, disease and ignorance has to be fought. An expert may be down a dangerous mine, demonstrating the use of new safety equipment, or in the heart of a forest training men at a logging camp. He may be in a swamp showing a team of men and women how to fight malaria; or 15,000 feet high in the mountains, enlisting the support of a whole community to build a simple school where children will be taught new trades. He will be writing from time to time to the Resident Representative, asking his support, for example, in obtaining from the Government an essential part of the equipment that is needed for the project; or he may be making the necessary tools with the help of his trainees. An expert may be, as the chief of a team, smoothing differences of opinion between experts recruited from several countries. Or he will be discussing with his counterparts the next steps to be taken for the success of the project and the suggestions to be made to his agency's headquarters or to the Government for further action.

Such is the manner of the delivery of EPTA assistance to countries and territories around the world. Mostly out of sight of the recipient country, many other parts of the large and complex machinery of the Expanded Programme are in motion, producing or sustaining the other ingredients that have been found essential to its operation: among them, inter-governmental policy-making decision and supervision; the lines of communication and co-ordination among the Participating Organizations; headquarters administrative and financial controls and accounting; the management of currencies; the processes of recruitment of experts and placement of fellowship-holders; the technical back-stopping by the Participating Organizations of their experts in the field; the organization of regional training institutions, seminars, accelerated courses and study tours; the standardization of conditions of service; the evaluation of results.

Of these activities, back-stopping and evaluation have an ever-increasing importance. The close technical supervision and servicing of field projects are deemed essential for a variety of reasons, among them the need to ensure that operational work is consistent with international standards, and the desirability of bringing about the most fruitful possible inter-action between operational and non-operational activities to the benefit of both. Evaluation of the progress and the results of technical assistance, while difficult in many cases to carry out with certainty, is no less essential both for ensuring that the assistance is effective and for providing lessons in improved methods and guidelines for future programming.

THE SCOPE AND KINDS OF ASSISTANCE

The fact that any project judged capable of contributing to the economic and related social development of a country is eligible for technical assistance under the Expanded Programme means that the subjects in which help can be given are limited only by the competences of the eleven Participating Organizations. These limits are broad indeed. Ten of the agencies specialize in particular fields, but in the cases of a number of them the fields themselves are wide. The eleventh—the United Nations—provides services which for the time being fill the most crucial gaps between the fields of the other agencies. . . .

In the order of their component shares of the Expanded Programme, the Food and Agriculture Organization of the United Nations takes first place, having been allocated over the first fifteen years roughly one-quarter of the resources. It is not surprising that this should have been so, given the traditional reliance of the developing countries in general on farming, animal husbandry, fisheries and forestry both for the sustenance of their populations and for the purposes of external trade—and given the absence in most of them of the means of bringing about either large-scale and rapid modernization of these basic activities or the transformation of their economies through manufacturing and other industries. It was not altogether lightly said on behalf of the FAO at the inception of the Expanded Programme, in justification of its first place under the then automatic system of allocation of resources, that the father of mankind according to one widely-held conception was, after all, a gardener. The assistance which the FAO has been called upon to provide for the "gardeners" of today has been spread fairly evenly over the agency's broad range of competences: land and water development, ranging from soil and irrigation surveys to the manufacture of farm tools and food processing techniques; plant production and protection; animal production and animal health; rural institutions and services; fisheries, nutrition and home economics; forestry and forest products; agricultural economics, covering development programmes and policies, marketing and distribution, and statistical services, and the use of atomic science in food and agriculture.

The United Nations, as the second most important provider of assistance under the Programme, using about one-fifth of its resources, serves mainly in four special fields of clearly proved need in the developing countries. These, in brief, cover firstly general economic surveys and advice on economic planning and programming; the survey, use and management of such natural resources as minerals, energy and water; industrial development; cartographic services; transport development; trade promotion and marketing; public finance and the institutional aspects of the financing of economic development. Secondly, the United Nations provides assistance and training in the organization and programming of economic, demographic and social statistics. A third field is the vital one of public administration in all its aspects and at all its levels; and a fourth comprises important elements in social advancement, such as the planning of social development, social factors in economic programmes, studies of levels of living, estimates of population and manpower, community development, the planning and building of housing, the organization and administration of social services, and training in all these activities.

The well-recognized relationship between disease and poverty, and therefore between public health activities and economic development, indicates in the developing countries generally a need for health assistance so large as to have maintained for the World Health Organization the next most prominent place in the Expanded Programme, its share of the resources ranging between 17 and 22 per cent over the years. WHO divides its EPTA activities, which supplement and extend its regular programmes of assistance and advice to health administrations and institutions, between public health services (administration, maternal and child health, nursing, social and occupational health, organization of medical care, health education, nutrition, radiation health, dental health, mental health, statistics, laboratories and environmental sanitation); action against communicable diseases (malaria, tuberculosis, venereal diseases and others, veterinary public health and epidemiology); and professional and technical education and training.

Ignorance also goes hand-in-hand with poverty, and the universal need for the improvement and expansion of education at some or all levels provides the setting for another major field of technical assistance. The responsibilities and competences here of the United Nations Educational, Scientific and Cultural Organization have given it the next most important share of the resources of EPTA, on a scale that his risen over the years to about 16 per cent of the total resources. The assistance given by UNESCO in the field of education proper covers over-all educational planning, school organization, the training of teachers and educators, technical and vocational education, adult education and youth activities, the eradication of illiteracy and the extension of educational opportunities for girls and women. In matters of science, UNESCO provides assistance in the teaching of pure and applied sciences, the establishment and operation of scientific instrument centres, the organization of scientific research, scientific and technical documentation, and the social sciences. It assists also in the development and operation of mass communication services, libraries and museums.

A pioneer in its own right in technical assistance work, having launched advisory services on labour and social problems as long ago as 1919, the International Labour Organisation has been allocated about one-tenth of the resources of EPTA for types of assistance both supplementary to its regular activities and new in themselves. Its activities have embraced the broad fields of the development of human resources and social institutions and the improvement of conditions of life and work, with vocational training in its various forms taking by far the largest place and accounting, together with manpower organization and planning, for roughly one half of its EPTA resources. Training covers all levels: basic instruction for the unskilled, the upgrading of existing more or less skilled labour, the training of foremen and supervisors and of instructors for training at all levels. Manpower organization and planning includes such matters as the organization of employment services, but the widespread adoption in recent years of comprehensive economic development planning has created an increasing demand for assistance in the assessment of manpower resources and requirements, the formulation of manpower utilization policies and the determination of employment objectives in economic development. The ILO also provides assistance in management development and the improvement of productivity, and several schemes started with EPTA funds have developed into Special Fund-assisted projects. Assistance relating to conditions of life and work includes advice on wages policy, occupational safety and health, social security, labour administration and statistics, workers' education and rural development. A field of growing importance is that of cooperatives and handicrafts and small-scale industries.

The other agencies taking part in the Expanded Programme have provided more narrowly specialized services on a much smaller scale than the others. The International Civil Aviation Organization gives advice on and training in civil aviation administration, air navigation, ground services, flight safety, air transport and aerodrome and airport development; the World Meteorological Organization in the over-all planning and organization of meteorological services and in the practical application of meteorological information to various fields of human endeavour such as water resources development, agriculture, civil aviation, shipping and engineering; the International Telecommunication Union in telephone, telegraph and radio communications; the International Atomic Energy Agency in many aspects of the development and use of nuclear power and research and in the applications of radio-isotopes in agriculture, medicine, industry and hydrology; and the Universal Postal

Union in postal administration and urban and rural postal services. The newest participant, the Inter-Governmental Maritime Consultative Organization, is ready to meet requests for assistance under the Expanded Programme for assistance in its own special field of ocean shipping.

In some of those fields where overlapping is apparent, there is an obligation upon the agencies, and they have evolved practical means of meeting it, for all necessary co-operation in providing the services required: between WHO and FAO, for example, in matters of nutrition, between UNESCO and the ILO in some aspects of training, and between IAEA and FAO in the use of radio-isotopes for agriculture. Again, there are aspects of economic development planning—basically the field of the United Nations—which involve the competences of several other agencies. Jurisdictional disputes do occur between agencies, but they are increasingly rare and far outnumbered by the cases of collaboration. This may go far in projects calling for a team of experts in different fields, where both the planning and the manning of the project require the agencies concerned to work especially closely together. Moreover, for such joint projects, as well as some of the larger projects of individual organizations, the latter often use their own resources as well as those of the Expanded Programme, and in several projects they are able to combine their efforts with material assistance from UNICEF, the World Food Programme or the Freedom from Hunger Campaign, or from bilateral sources. . . .

CHANGES IN EMPHASIS

The respective shares, indicated above, of the Participating Organizations in the resources of the Expanded Programme afford a rough guide to the relative importance of the various fields of endeavour to the countries whose requests for assistance essentially shape the Programme. For reporting purposes, the Technical Assistance Board also classifies the components of the Programme according to the nature of the activities, independently of the identity of the agencies carrying them out. These fall under 50 different headings, arranged in ten major groups, representing 50 specific fields of economic and social development in which assistance is given. Like the agency shares of the Programme, these "fields of activity" have shown surprisingly few major changes in emphasis over the years in a global sense, although within some individual country programmes there were marked adjustments after the abolition in 1955 of fixed allocations of resources to the organizations. Agricultural production has held its position as the most important single major field of activity, representing close on one-quarter of the Programme. Health services come next. The most noticeable recent trend has been increased activity in assisting Governments in the formulation of development plans, including basic surveys of resources and the building up of administrative services as well as advice on planning methods. The least dynamic trend has taken place in the field of industrial development, a situation that has constituted a paradox in the face of the importance placed upon such assistance by the governing bodies.

Within this variety of fields of activity there has been an equal variety of country, subregional, regional and interregional assistance projects. There have been expert missions ranging from brief one-man assignments to team assignments of long duration or in several phases; study, fact-finding and survey missions; advisory missions; demonstration missions; training and education missions; and so forth. There have been fellowship programmes for experts' counterparts; fellowships not related to expert assistance; seminars, training courses long and short, and study tours in advanced as well as in developing regions.

The years have brought some significant changes in emphasis among types of projects. Some of these changes have arisen from developments in technical methodology; others reflect broad phases in the life of the Programme or broad lessons derived from experience in its operation. Thus, there was in the first years some emphasis on survey and advisory missions. This was understandable, since on the one hand assistance could not be developed in a vacuum, and on the other hand Governments frequently felt the need to draw on outside expertise in the appraisal of problems and the formulation of programmes of action. Such survey and advisory missions continued to have a place in the general order of things when fresh geographical ground was broken, as recently in Africa, or in certain technical fields in which advisory assistance has been and will continue to be essential. There has even been noted in recent years a certain new wave of survey and advisory missions, intended to permit a fresh stocktaking and if necessary a re-orientation after a lapse of years, and in some cases to help in the formulation of national schemes or projects possibly qualifying later for assistance from the Special Fund or from the international financial agencies. But, by and large, from a quite early date a dominant role has been assigned to essentially "practical" projects, directed toward the execution of action programmes already conceived with or without international assistance. Such projects may deal with the establishment of institutions, the creation or improvement of skills, the more efficient functioning of administrations; they may aim to cut particular or local Gordian knots or to contribute to the orderly implementation of national development planning. A growing emphasis on institution-building and, as a corollary, on the training of counterpart staff and other national cadres has been reflected in the case of some Participating Organizations in a higher proportion of relatively long-term projects. In recent years, this trend has been modified appreciably by the graduation of a number of substantial long-term projects from EPTA to Special Fund assistance.

LEADERSHIP IN THE SPECIALIZED AGENCIES*

N ow that the Office of the United Nations Secretary-General, and with it the entire conception of an independent, internationally responsible civil service, have become the storm center of heated political controversy, the task of studying the problem of executive leadership in the United Nations family has assumed paramount importance. In this pursuit, it no longer suffices to concentrate exclusively on the Office of the Secretary-General. Our experience in international administration is far broader and more varied. In Montreal, Rome, Paris, Geneva, and Vienna, there have emerged over the years small but compact nuclei of a nascent world loyalty—the Directors-General and the Secretariats of the United Nations Specialized Agencies. These important members of the United Nations family are not simply miniature replicas of the central body in their administrative structures. Indeed, the patterns are quite multi-faceted. Some precede by several decades the founding of the United Nations. Most important, the rich treasury of experience of the Specialized Agencies in developing an international civil service may better illuminate the problems now confronting the central body and may even indicate ways of surmounting the present crisis.

The Specialized Agencies in the United Nations family may be roughly divided into two groups. The first group, whose major purpose is chiefly to broaden and facilitate communication among nations, includes the Universal Postal Union (UPU), the International Telecommunication Union (ITU), the International Civil Aviation Organization (ICAO), the World Meteorological Organization (WMO), and the Inter-Governmental Maritime Consultative Organization (IMCO). Some of these, like UPU and ITU, antedate the creation of the United Nations. Others, like IMCO, did not come into existence until years after the ratification of the United Nations Charter. But all are today part of the United Nations system and are based on the common premises that good "housekeeping" and good communications among nations might decrease the dangers of war.

It is less easy to generalize about the Specialized Agencies in the second group. For lack of a better term, they may be called the "welfare" agencies, in the sense that each is intended to improve world economic, social, and cultural conditions and thus build defenses for the peace. The oldest of these, the International Labor Organization (ILO), is to better conditions

---

* Commission to Study the Organization of Peace, "Executive Leadership in the United Nations Family," *The United Nations Secretary-General: His Role in World Politics*, Part III, 14th Report, January 1962. By permission of the Committee to Study the Organization of Peace.

of labor throughout the world on the assumption that the equalization of labor standards is a necessary condition of peace. The Food and Agriculture Organization (FAO) hopes to raise nutritional levels and improve argricultural technology. The World Health Organization (WHO) is based on the premise that the health of all peoples is fundamental to the attainment of peace and security. Hence, the objective of the agency is the attainment by all peoples of the highest possible level of health. The United Nations Educational, Scientific, and Cultural Organization (UNESCO) was established by its framers because they believed that nations' ignorance of one another's ways and lives was a common cause of distrust leading to war. Hence, UNESCO is to advance understanding among nations through research and the exchange of scholars and scientists. The International Bank for Reconstruction and Development (IBRD) was to bind up the wounds of war through loans for the reconstruction of devastated areas and to better the chances of peace by granting loans for the development of resources in the lesser developed countries. The International Monetary Fund (IMF) aids peace through the promotion of exchange stability and the use of a fund to support weak currencies. The International Finance Corporation (IFC) is to promote the growth of productive private enterprise in the technologically lesser developed countries of the world. Finally, the International Atomic Energy Agency (IAEA), an autonomous member of the United Nations family established in 1957, is to consecrate the energy of the atom to the cause of peace.

While all the above thirteen Agencies are members of the United Nations system, they have nevertheless developed their own unique organizational pattern. Each has its own membership policy. Some, like the Bank and the Fund, do not include the Soviet bloc countries; others, like UPU, ILO, UNESCO, and WHO are virtually universal in their inclusiveness. Many comprise nations or territories which are not members of the United Nations. Some nations have withdrawn from, and then rejoined, the Specialized Agencies. The Soviet bloc countries, for example, boycotted ILO, UNESCO, and WHO for almost a decade, but decided to rejoin in the mid-1950's. Each Specialized Agency has its own constitution and its own executive and deliberative bodies. Each elects a chief administrative officer as Director-General or as Secretary-General. Each has evolved in a tradition of independence and has maintained only the loosest relationship to the United Nations. Several Agencies have come to provide valuable testing grounds for experimentation in different patterns of international administration. Almost all illuminate the problems and progress in the development of an independent international executive in the Office of the United Nations Secretary-General.

*   *   *   *   *   *   *

In several ways, the institutional pattern of the Agencies related to the

UN roughly resembles that of the central body. Typically, there is a General Conference comprising the entire membership which fulfills the deliberative function. The executive body is usually quite large, ranging from twenty-three members in the case of IAEA to as high as forty in ILO. This body nominates the Director-General, usually by a two-thirds vote. The nominee is then confirmed by the General Conference by a simple majority vote. The Director-General has the right to appoint his staff. In so doing, he must maintain the highest standards of efficiency, competence, and integrity and secure the widest possible geographical distribution. The average Specialized Agency Secretariat has about five hundred members.

If we focus on the Directors-General and their Secretariats, however, several important departures from the United Nations pattern immediately become apparent. In the first place, there is no Great Power veto governing the election of a Director-General. The election of most Directors-General has been marked by a remarkable absence of friction. With one notable exception, the election of Dr. Sigvard Eklund as Director-General of the International Atomic Energy Agency in 1961, a high degree of harmony has usually prevailed. This is particularly astounding in the light of the fact that all the Agency Directors-General with one exception (an Indian heads the FAO) are nationals of Western countries. This may be partially attributable to the fact that in all cases a considerable amount of informal consultation and negotiation preceded the actual election. For example, the candidatures of Mr. Sterling Cole for the IAEA post and of Dr. Vittorino Veronese for UNESCO were discussed for over a year before the final confirmation by the General Conference took place. In the case of Dr. Eklund, as will be seen more fully below, such prior consultation was conspicuously absent. As a rule, there is much less voting per se in the Specialized Agencies than in the United Nations. As a technique for solving serious differences on candidates for the post of Director-General, it has been used only as a last resort.

A second departure from the United Nations pattern resides in the powers of the Directors-General. None of the Specialized Agencies provides anything comparable to Articles 98 and 99 of the United Nations Charter. Nevertheless, almost all the Directors-General have taken a leaf from Mr. Hammarskjöld's conception of his Office and have repeatedly made policy recommendations to their governing bodies. Their record of effectiveness has been a mixed one. Director-General Morse of the ILO attempted to continue in the tradition of his dynamic predecessor, Albert Thomas. His proposals usually had a favorable reception. Director-General Sen of the FAO originated the "Freedom from Hunger" campaign which was adopted by the organization in 1959. Director-General Candau of the WHO immediately dispatched teams of doctors and large quantities of medical supplies to the Congo without awaiting specific authorization from the governing bodies.

Mr. J. Donald Kingsley, Director-General of the International Refugee Organization, a non-permanent Specialized Agency which terminated operations in 1952, advocated the passage of the United States Displaced Persons Act. The prodding was successful and the Act became law in 1948. On the other hand, there have been some unsuccessful cases of policy initiative. Dr. Julian Huxley, the first Director-General of UNESCO, vainly tried to convince the General Conference to adopt his principle of evolutionary humanism as a point of departure for the bridging of world ideological differences. Indeed, when this mission failed, he resigned from office. Similarly, Mr. Torres Bodet resigned as UNESCO Director-General in 1952 when the General Conference refused to approve his budget. And Mr. Sterling Cole, the first Director-General of the International Atomic Energy Agency, vainly protested against the proliferation of bilateral and regional atomic power arrangements which were by-passing and threatening to undermine the United Nations Agency.

As far as the staffing of the Specialized Agency Secretariats is concerned, the pattern of geographical representation follows the United Nations model rather closely. But the Agency Secretariats tend to be more intergovernmental and less international in character than the United Nations Secretariat. That is to say, member nations are less inclined to release their citizens as permanent career civil servants to the Specialized Agencies. There has developed a tendency on the part of many of the new nations to recall staff members after a relatively short period. This is not surprising since many of the qualities needed in the Secretariats are the very qualities needed even more badly at home: scientific, medical, agricultural, and technical training. This factor has often made adequate geographical representation difficult to attain. Atomic experts, for example, are in short supply in the developing countries. The new nations are loathe to relinquish their services to an international organization like the International Atomic Energy Agency. As a result, nationals from the technologically more advanced nations have tended to fill most of the leading posts in the IAEA Secretariat. No easy solution to this dilemma seems possible.

On the whole, the Directors-General of the United Nations Specialized Agencies have been one step ahead of governments in their approach to international problems, but as a rule have moved at the same rate and in the same direction as the governments and thus have not lost contact with them. Whenever they have not been followed, they have tended to stop and sometimes, if necessary, have withdrawn altogether as did Dr. Huxley from UNESCO. Hence, the Secretariats have been able to supply a degree of policy leadership without infringing on the rights of their governing bodies. None of the Directors-General has ever become detached from the governmental organs or taken on a life and personality distinct from the governments and the Member States. For better or for worse, none of them has ever used broad discretionary powers to the extent to which Mr. Lie and

Mr. Hammarskjöld had seen these implied in the United Nations Charter. But almost all of them have followed the example of the Secretary-General part of the way.

To some extent, of course, the Directors-General of the Specialized Agencies have had an easier time of it than their counterparts in the United Nations. The storms of political controversy blow more furiously around the Office of the UN Secretary-General. But it must not be forgotten that many of the activities of the Specialized Agencies are also deeply permeated with political significance and often arouse the passions of governments just as deeply. The East-West cold war has been very much in evidence in the Agencies. The erratic behavior of the Soviet bloc with regard to membership was largely motivated by political considerations. In the wake of Premier Khrushchev's attack on the Office of the Secretary-General, ripples were felt in all the Agencies. The "troika" proposal was formally introduced in only one of them, however—UNESCO—where it failed to get any support. The second cold war, over the liquidation of colonialism, has also been felt as the new nations have been swelling the membership of the Agencies. Since many of the Agencies are "supply" organs of goods and services, a tug-of-war has often resulted between the "producer" and the "consumer" powers. In this twofold struggle, the Directors-General have, on the whole, demonstrated an amazing degree of balance, resiliency, and vision. In the difficult task of serving conflicting interests, they have managed not only to follow, but sometimes to lead as well.

At least some of the success of the Specialized Agencies is attributable to an ingrained habit of continuous consultation and confrontation at all levels of the policy-making process. The tripartite system of representation of the ILO is a case in point. The ILO Governing Body consists of twenty members representing governments, ten representing employers, and ten representing workers. Hence, the Director-General has the opportunity to be in constant touch not only with the member governments themselves, but with important non-governmental groups in international society as well. Even where this pattern is not formalized, representation tends to be broad. In almost all the Agencies, government delegates, scientists, educators, and technical experts work side by side. WHO, FAO, UNESCO, and IAEA are cases in point. The net result of this pattern is less emphasis on outvoting the opposition and more on multi-level negotiation; fewer efforts to form majorities and more to convince reluctant minorities.

There are exceptions, of course, but they are rare and tend to confirm the rule. The most significant one was the election of a successor to Mr. Sterling Cole, Director-General of the International Atomic Energy Agency whose term expired in 1961. The United States proposed a Swedish national, Dr. Sigvard Eklund, as Director-General and defended the candidate largely on grounds of his excellent scientific qualifications. The Soviet Union, India, and the African states supported the candidacy of Dr. Sudjarwo, a national of Indonesia. In a bitter attack on the United States position, the Soviet Union advanced the view that since the first Director-General had been an American, the second should not be a national from a Western power; moreover, since the Agency operated largely for the benefit of the lesser developed nations, an Asian or African should be in a leading position; and finally, the Soviet delegate deplored the lack of consultation over the appointment of a successor to Mr. Cole. The IAEA General Conference was deeply split on the issue. Although Dr. Eklund's appointment was confirmed by a vote of 46 to 16 with 5 abstentions, the incoming Director-General faced a resentful minority comprising the Soviet bloc, India, and several other members of the Afro-Asian group. What is significant in this episode within the general context of the Agencies related to the UN is not the rightness or wrongness of the charges and counter-charges, but the fact that the mechanism of consultation had broken down, that unanimity had not been reached, and that a profound cleavage was created which threatened the very life of the Agency as a vital instrument for the creation of international order. In that sense, the IAEA case is atypical and, it is hoped, will remain so.

What conclusions, then, may we draw from the experience of the Specialized Agencies for the benefit of the United Nations?

As far as the Specialized Agencies in general are concerned, two observations seem to be warranted. In the first place, the Agencies have demonstrated the truth, so cogently expressed by Gunnar Myrdal, that no major international problem can be solved by majority vote. There has developed a tendency in the General Assembly in recent years to build majorities *against* the opposition rather than to improve procedures of negotiation *with* the opposition. To be sure, some differences cannot be surmounted and voting must then be resorted to, but it has been resorted to with far too much facility in the United Nations. On the whole, the Specialized Agencies have worked much harder to reach unanimous or near-unanimous agreement than the delegates in the United Nations Organization.

As a result of this habit, most of the Agencies have come to be more than merely barometers of the climate in the outside world. To a considerable degree, they have managed to create a climate of their own, and in some cases, have even contributed to a general climatic improvement. Voting may be a satisfactory way of resolving differences in a situation in which there prevails a fundamental political consensus, but not in an international forum deeply divided by conflicting passions and ideologies. In that sense, the United Nations might well study the negotiation and representation techniques evolved in the Specialized Agencies.

So far as the international executive is concerned, three observations are in order. First, the Specialized Agencies have demonstrated that the single administrative head has worked well and can work even better in the future.

But much of this success has depended on the practice of the Directors-General of remaining in constant touch with member governments at all stages of the policy-making process. Indeed, one of the reasons why the Soviet Union has not introduced the "troika" proposal into more than one of the Agencies may well be the assurance that greater sensitivity to minority positions has been manifested by Directors-General in the Agencies than has been the practice in the policy organs of the United Nations. The Soviet response to being constantly outvoted in the Security Council and the General Assembly has been the attempt to extend the veto power to the Office of the Secretary-General.

One of the most serious difficulties of the international executive is the problem of staffing the Specialized Agencies with first-rate personnel who make the international civil service a career. At this point, first-rate staff is so badly needed in the developing countries that these new nations are reluctant to let their best people go to the United Nations, let alone the Specialized Agencies. As a result, insofar as the developing countries are concerned, the choice so far has been between staffing the Agencies with first-rate personnel who insist on returning home after short periods, or second-rate persons whom governments are willing to let go. If the principle of geographical distribution is to be maintained and if the injunction of the Charter only to employ men and women of the highest efficiency, competence, and integrity is to be observed, then a massive educational campaign must be launched in those countries which have no tradition of an impartial national civil service, let alone an impartial international civil service. The Specialized Agencies themselves, foremost among them UNESCO, might well participate in this task. Failing this, the secretariats of the future will continue to be partly intergovernmental and partly international.

Finally, what about the role of the chief administrator in an international organization? Is the time ripe for the "Thomas Doctrine" and its "Hammarskjöld Corollary"? Men of judgment differ fundamentally on this point. Mr. Hammarskjöld clearly conceived of the Office of the Secretary-General as endowed with the right to exercise political judgment and to provide leadership in case of deadlock. In a sense, he conceived of it as the beginning of international statesmanship and saw his duty in providing the political initiative in that direction. But Guillaume Georges-Picot, former Assistant Secretary-General, sees the matter quite differently. Mr. Hammarskjöld's conception of the Charter, implies M. Georges-Picot, tends to detach the Secretariat from the member governments, and leads it to become contemptuous in relation to the member states, their policies and their delegations. It is far better, in his opinion, to take a step backwards in case of discord and reestablish a consensus, even if it has to be found at a lower level.

In the resolution of this debate, the experience of the Specialized Agencies can be of great help. On the whole, they have struck a good balance. Most of the Directors-General have found that if they outdistance their governing bodies too far, they doom themselves to ineffectiveness. But they have also learned the equally important lesson that if they provide no policy leadership at all, they doom their organization to sterility. In this ability to strike the correct balance between initiative and withdrawal, between determined leadership and sensitivity to the needs and demands of the member nations, lies the key to a successful international executive in the United Nations family.

CENTRALIZATION AND DECENTRALIZATION IN THE UNITED NATIONS ECONOMIC AND SOCIAL ACTIVITIES

W. R. Malinowski*

❊   ❊   ❊   ❊   ❊   ❊   ❊

The Charter envisaged the United Nations as a centralized organization both at the intergovernmental and at the Secretariat level.

The intergovernmental organs established by the Charter are global in character.[1] From the legislative history it would seem that the same principle may have been intended to underlie Article 68 of the Charter which provides for the setting up of subsidiary organs by the Economic and Social Council (ECOSOC). This Article is, however, so broadly formulated that it was considered by the Council (and by the General Assembly) an adequate basis for the establishment of its regional organs, which have become an integral part of the United Nations institutional framework. In the years 1947–1948 the Economic Commissions for Europe (ECE), Asia and the Far East (ECAFE), and Latin America (ECLA) were established, followed ten years later by the creation of the Economic Commission for Africa (ECA).

* W. R. Malinowski, "Centralization and Decentralization in the United Nations Economic and Social Activities," *International Organization*, Vol. 16, 1962, pp. 521–541. Copyright 1962, World Peace Foundation. By permission of *International Organization*.

W. R. Malinowski is Secretary of the United Nations Economic and Social Council and has served on the UN Secretariat in various capacities since 1946.

[1] The functions or the terms of reference of each organ give it its global character. Except for the General Assembly which comprises all Members, other UN organs are of limited membership. The Charter does not envisage UN regional bodies. The only reference to "regional arrangements or agencies" is contained in Chapter VIII and concerns "matters relating to the maintenance of international peace and security" (Article 52).

The process of decentralization (or regionalization) at the intergovernmental level was virtually complete. Outside the geographical scope of the regional commissions remained only the Middle Eastern countries, the Pacific Islands, and North America. In 1959, the Secretary-General, in the *Introduction* to his annual report on the work of the Organization, referred to the "United Nations system of regional co-operation." The degree of decentralization at the intergovernmental level may be judged by the main provisions of the terms of reference of the regional commissions which in this respect are all more or less identical. They open with the statement (paragraph 1) that the Commission shall act "within the framework of the policies of the United Nations and subject to the general supervision of the Economic and Social Council. . . . " The second paragraph of the terms of reference empowers the Commission "to make recommendations on any matter within its competence directly to the governments of the members or associate members concerned, to governments admitted in a consultative capacity and to the specialized agencies." It requires the Commission, however, to "submit for prior consideration by the Economic and Social Council any of its proposals for activities that would have important effects on the economy of the world as a whole." With the limitation referred to above, the regional commissions, by their terms of reference, became autonomous or quasi-autonomous, subject to the submission to the parent organ once a year of a full report on their "activities and plans, including those of any subsidiary bodies" (paragraph 18). So far the Council has never suggested that any regional commission had gone beyond the framework of the policies of the United Nations[2] and year after year the Council has limited its action with regard to regional commissions to taking note of their annual reports and endorsing their work programs. At the same time, on no occasion has any regional commission submitted for the Council's prior consideration any of its proposals for activities that "would have important effects on the economy of the world as a whole," although recommendations such as those on economic integration or common markets could hardly avoid having consequences outside the geographical area of a particular commission. The Council has, of course, power to disapprove the commissions' decisions and to make recommendations to them. As the parent body, it can change their terms of reference and even resolve to abolish them just as it established them. In practice the autonomy of the regional commissions, within the policies established by the General Assembly and ECOSOC, has become even more complete than their terms of reference would suggest. The strength of the commissions is based primarily on a de facto not on a legal status; it stems from the almost completely inclusive character of their membership within their respective regions,[3] from their tendency to act by

[2] The commissions are regularly informed by the Secretariat of the decisions and policies established by the General Assembly and by ECOSOC and its functional commissions.

agreement rather than by voting (this applies especially to the older-established commissions and their subsidiary bodies); from a varying but marked degree of regional consciousness, solidarity, or "regional nationalism"; and, last but not least, from the self-imposed discipline which leads members of the UN regional commissions to behave in their respective commissions in a way expected of UN Members; i.e., in accordance with the principles of the UN Charter and the decisions of the General Assembly and ECOSOC.[4] The strength of the regional commissions is also due to the practical nature of their activities which stem from their terms of reference; these terms of reference emphasize (paragraph 1) not deliberative functions but initiation of and participation in measures for facilitating concerted action for economic development, including its social aspects. The regional commissions were the first United Nations bodies specifically authorized to perform operational functions which they have developed within their limited resources. They have, in particular, placed emphasis on cooperative intra-regional efforts through functional committees, meetings of experts, seminars, technical and economic conferences, dissemination of statistics, economic and technical information, and establishment of regional standards within global standards in various fields of their activity. The Commissions were also authorized [paragraph 1(d)] to render advisory services to individual countries "provided that such services do not overlap with those rendered by other bodies of the United Nations or by specialized agencies"; they were also asked to assist the Council at its request in discharging its functions within their regions in connection with any economic problems, including problems in the field of technical assistance [paragraph 1(e)]. This point is of special significance because the competence of the commissions is so broadly defined in their terms of reference that it covers any field in which the United Nations renders technical assistance.

[3] The membership of the regional commissions was broadened by provisions for associate membership and by the participation of governments in a consultative capacity. In the latter capacity any member of the United Nations can participate in the work of any regional commissions, thus limiting the danger of regional exclusivity or parochialism.

[4] It is noteworthy that David L. Gordon of the International Bank for Reconstruction and Development, in a paper entitled "Regional Approaches to Economic Development," prepared for delivery at the 1960 Annual Meeting of the American Political Science Association, September 8–10, 1960, comes to the following conclusions:

> The need for global consultation and institutions is in no way reduced by the trend of regionalism. On the contrary, in the absence of a strong framework of agreed purposes, regional arrangements might become merely instruments of international economic throat-cutting. Only if such a framework exists to discipline these destructive potentialities can regional approaches fulfil their promise of helping to tame the anarchic forces of nationalism and to bring the weight of less-developed countries to bear toward a better balance and accommodation with the industrial powers.

The UN uniquely provides such "a strong framework of agreed purposes."

It is a matter of record that for many years the activities of the regional commissions have received more enthusiastic support in the deliberations of the principal organs of the Organization (ECOSOC and Second and Third Committees of the General Assembly) than many of the activities carried out in implementation of decisions of the global organs themselves. It is also a matter of record that at one time or another the commissions have pioneered in a number of important fields, e.g., trade cooperation, common markets and integration, planning economic development, training development personnel, and transfer of technology. In these fields decisions of the principal organs of the United Nations initiating global policies and activities were frequently taken only after a measure of success had already been achieved at the regional level. In a world dominated by the political tensions of the "Cold War" and in a period of the emancipation of the peoples of entire continents, a measure of intergovernmental cooperation at least in the economic and social fields may be easier to achieve in the regional than in the global context.

While at the intergovernmental level decentralization (or regionalization) has been far advanced in economic and social activities, the Secretariat's organization has remained essentially centralized. The terms of reference of the regional commissions provide that the Secretary-General shall appoint the executive secretary of each commission and that its staff shall form part of the United Nations Secretariat (paragraph 17). The commissions' administrative budgets are financed from United Nations funds (paragraph 16). The secretariats of the regional commissions form part of the Department of Economic and Social Affairs. The executive secretary of each commission, although of the rank of under-secretary, normally reports to the under-secretary at United Nations Headquarters who is in charge of the whole department. In performing their duties the executive secretaries act on behalf of the Secretary-General. In all respects, except as regards the location of the duty station, the status of the staff of the regional commissions corresponds to that of Headquarters staff. At the Secretariat level, there is no decentralization in the sense that there is at the intergovernmental level; rather, there is a geographical deconcentration of staff.

The functions of the staff of each regional secretariat vis-à-vis its commission are defined in the rules of procedure which the commissions were authorized to adopt (paragraph 15). In no respect, however, does this limit the authority of the Secretary-General over regional staff. The differences, if any, between Headquarters and regional staff arise not from differences in status but rather from differences in general outlook and professional experience, as the geographical distribution of staff varies from office to office. Long service either at Headquarters or in a regional office may also have an impact on staff, as interchange of staff between offices has so far been rather limited. At the same time differences such as those above are eliminated or at least tempered to the extent that the staff adheres to the code of behavior of international civil servants formulated in the staff rules and regulations which are mandatory for the entire staff whether stationed at Headquarters or in the regional offices. Generally, the staff of each office takes pride in and has some sense of identification with that particular office; this does not conflict in any way with loyalty to the United Nations. In the case of the staff of regional commissions, the sense of identification with a patricular region may be intensified by the geographical distribution. . . . International civil servants who are nationals of countries of a region in which they serve usually develop more easily than others a dedication to the interests of that particular region. Dedication to the development of a particular region, both among the members of a commission and among its staff, is in fact one of the advantages of a regional approach within the United Nations; it may indeed be at the root of the success of regional activities.

*   *   *   *   *   *   *

The organization of regional secretariats reflects the diversity of each commission's activities. Through the years regional staff have undoubtedly acquired a knowledge and experience of and *expertise* in the problems of each region and its countries; they have evolved techniques and methods of approaching these problems in a regional context; they have developed ties with many local officials and experts and have gained their confidence. The annual debates of the commissions, as well as of the General Assembly and of ECOSOC, testify that the regional commissions have become the preferred instruments for intergovernmental cooperation and, through their secretariats, for operational (executive) action by the United Nations in each region.

As early as in 1952 the General Assembly declared that

the regional economic commissions have become effective instruments of international economic cooperation and, for that reason, should continue to play an important part in the work of stimulating co-ordinated economic development in their respective regions and should co-operate in the efforts of the countries to that end. . . .

The budgetary appropriations noted also testify to the governments' views.

Parallel to the development of regional organs and their activities, a new international service was born which in concept and importance has overshadowed many other activities. The United Nations mission to Haiti in 1948 gave impetus to the General Assembly decision on Technical Assistance for Economic Development; it was followed in 1949 by the establishment of the Expanded Program of Technical Assistance (EPTA).[5] A new dimension had been added to international cooperation: a multilateral mechanism for the dissemination of modern techniques essential for development. As a responsibility of the United Nations, it was free from extraneous considerations and the exploitation associated in the past with colonial and political penetration, with direct foreign investment and, since the war, with bilateral aid which had not always been without "strings attached." The program of technical assistance has developed considerably in the past decade. It has brought thousands of individual experts and teams of experts from developed to less developed countries. It has also brought a growing number of experts from one less developed country to another, especially from those that are closest to achieving self-sustained growth. As conceived, the program was to be directed and supervised by the General Assembly and ECOSOC, the latter acting through its Technical Assistance Committee (TAC). At the Secretariat level the Technical Assistance Board (TAB) was established, composed of a representative of the Secretary-General and of representatives of the executive heads of the specialized agencies participating in the program. The TAB secretariat is headed by an executive chairman of undersecretary rank provided by the United Nations. At the country level it acts through the TAB resident representatives who maintain relations with governments and perform a variety of coordinating and administrative functions.[6] Within the policies established by intergovernmental bodies and in accordance with procedures and decisions of TAB, and using resident representatives as permanent agents in the field, each participating organization directs and administers its own part of the program.[7]

What follows is an attempt to evaluate the organization and administration of the technical assistance rendered by the United Nations. It aims to illustrate a trend toward integration of the program in the Department of

[5] David L. Gordon, op. cit., thinks that regional groupings may "have a useful rôle to play in the allocation and administration of development aid," inter alia, "by transferring a part of the onus for dealing with aid requests from the donors to the recipient nations themselves. . . ." He goes so far as to express doubts as to whether the central machinery of the UN is free from suspicion on the part of recipients of aid. He says:

> Even the UN and its specialized agencies, although their position in relation to less-developed countries differs substantially from that of individual aid-giving nations, suffer in some degree from this handicap. Inevitably they acquire most of their funds, their predilections and their personnel from the industrial countries and hence appear, to some extent, as agents of the latter.

[6] The functions of resident representatives are described by C. Hart Schaaf in "The Role of Resident Representative of the UN Technical Assistance Board," International Organization, Autumn 1960 (Vol. 14, No. 4), pp. 548–562.

[7] A recent study gives an extensive account of the working of these complex field activities. See Walter R. Sharp, Field Administration in the United Nations System: The Conduct of International Economic and Social Programs, published under the auspices of the Carnegie Endowment for International Peace (London: Stevens & Sons Ltd., 1961), p. xiv, 570.

Economic and Social Affairs at UN Headquarters and a simultaneous trend toward decentralization of technical assistance operations to the secretariats of the regional commissions.

The responsibility for United Nations technical assistance was entrusted to the Technical Assistance Administration (TAA) established in July 1950 as a department of the Secretariat and headed by a director-general reporting directly to the Secretary-General. The TAA was separate from the Department of Economic Affairs and the Department of Social Affairs at Headquarters,[8] as well as from the secretariats of the regional economic commissions. This separation has had far-reaching consequences, and the past decade has marked a long series of efforts at the intergovernmental and secretariat level to overcome them. It has meant the substantial insulation of the TAA administrators from the knowledge and experience in the economic and social fields accumulated at Headquarters and by the regional secretariats; it has also resulted in too much reliance by TAA on outside experts hired for limited periods of time for field duties. It tended to deprive TAA of the advice of competent policy-making personnel at UN Headquarters and in regional offices, and in turn it has deprived TAA experts hired on an *ad hoc* basis of much assistance from regional staffs with extensive knowledge and experience of local conditions.

*   *   *   *   *   *   *

The dichotomy between economic and social activities on the one hand and the technical assistance operations of the United Nations on the other hand appeared increasingly paradoxical especially because the specialized agencies never divorced their substantive departments and regional offices from their technical assistance operations.

After 1950 the regional commissions restated several times their pleas for reorganization and decentralization of the TAA operations. TAA began submitting reports to ECAFE and ECLA on its activities in their respective regions. These commissions included in their programs numerous projects which it would not have been possible to implement without TAA resources (e.g., study tours) or which otherwise would have been deprived of the advice of experts from advanced countries (e.g., seminars, technical conferences, training courses). Eventually, TAA agreed to support selected regional projects but continued to deny the regional secretariats' role in the country programs. The evolution of the country programs of technical assistance increasingly militated in favor of cooperation with the substantive units of the Secretariat. As long as the emphasis was on services of individual experts advising a government within the limits of their specialties, TAA administrators could locate such experts and assign them to a country. The growing need for relating technical assistance to the development

[8] Early in 1955 the two departments were merged into the Department of Economic and Social Affairs.

requirements of a country and selecting "strategic" areas for implementation of development plans in which limited TAA resources would have maximum impact could only be met with the assistance of the substantive units of the Secretariat. Gradually, more extensive use of substantive staff at Headquarters followed.

In 1954, the Secretary-General established a Secretariat Survey Group which studied the organization and operation of the Secretariat. In 1955, the Group, in its second report to the Secretary-General,[9] concluded that

the regional commissions and their staff, for their part, have been largely detached from technical assistance activities in countries in which they work, to which they themselves occasionally provide technical advisory services, and in which they have come to be regarded as the regional economic arms of the United Nations.

This is an anomalous situation in which the substantive resources of the Secretariat as a whole have clearly not been used to the utmost advantage in the development of the technical assistance programme. . . .

Accordingly, the Secretariat Survey Group recommended that "additional advisory responsibilities" be given to the Department of Economic and Social Affairs, including the secretariats of the regional commissions in order to help the TAA. The Group was of the view that this "would materially assist both to improve the services rendered to governments as also to assure the maximum and most economical use of resources. . . ."

❊ ❊ ❊ ❊ ❊ ❊ ❊

Thus, decentralization involves: (1) a measure of autonomy, (2) maintenance of a unified United Nations policy, and (3) emphasis on the provision of direct assistance to governments. By authorization of the General Assembly an experiment in partial decentralization was carried out in the years 1956–1958 by outposting to the ECLA secretariat a small group of TAA program officers. Of the three points made by the Advisory Committee, the second and third were met. The first point—"a measure of autonomy"—was, however, ignored; there was no delegation of authority to the outposted officers or to the executive secretary who supervised them. Accordingly, all decisions, including those of routine day-to-day administration, had to be referred to Headquarters, thus increasing the paperwork and causing delay. In spite of mounting bureaucracy, the Latin American governments were satisfied with the "direct assistance" rendered to them by the joint ECLA/TAA operation. The experiment was, however, terminated at about the time of the merger of TAA with the Department of Economic and Social Affairs. The three conditions for successful decentralization formulated by the Advisory Committee had proved inseparable.

After extensive debates at more than one session, the General Assembly, at its thirteenth session (1958), authorized the amalgamation of TAA and

9 "Organization of the Secretariat—Report of the Secretary-General's Survey Group," November 15, 1955, No. 55–27697.

the Department of Economic and Social Affairs. The merger was accomplished in February 1959. The reorganized TAA became a bureau of the consolidated Department of Economic and Social Affairs; all other units of the Department, each in its field, became involved in technical assistance under the unified responsibility of the Under-Secretary for Economic and Social Affairs and the Commissioner for Technical Assistance. Most of the research activities of the department received new impetus and gradually became oriented toward practical research needed for carrying out operational programs to the benefit of direct assistance to governments.

The General Assembly decided to merge the two departments, not only to remove an anomalous situation at Headquarters, but also because of the detachment of the regional commissions and their secretariats from technical assistance activities. However, it became clear soon after the merger that the centralization of technical assistance in one Headquarters department had not been followed by a significant measure of decentralization of the program to the regional offices. Gradually, however, progress was made on a project-by-project basis. Delegation to ECLA of responsibility for advisory groups to governments and the greater authority entrusted to it for economic development training courses were steps forward. Designation of the ECAFE secretariat as the executive agent on behalf of the United Nations for the development of the Lower Mekong River Basin was another example of the progress made. Delegation to the Secretariat of ECA of responsibility for the statistical survey of Africa showed that the staff of the "youngest" commission could carry out a complicated technical assistance assignment. There was, however, no reorganization designating the regional secretariats as instruments (or executive arms) of the Organization for technical assistance activities in their respective regions. Operation of the program as a whole remained centralized. It is not surprising, therefore, that since the merger, decentralization [became] one of the issues before ECOSOC and the General Assembly.

*   *   *   *   *   *   *

When will the decision of the General Assembly [to provide for decentralization] be implemented fully and what is its bearing on the United Nations field activities? These questions may be in some measure clarified by certain additional considerations.

First and foremost, there is a question of capacity. The UN Secretariat is facing an urgent need to increase its research and operational capacity. The programs at Headquarters and in the regions have in past years developed without an adequate expansion of staff. Indeed, the capacity to service technical assistance projects may even have been relatively reduced as a result of qualitative improvement in the services provided, i.e., many more staff hours are now required per project than in the initial years. In the 1960's, further growth of the programs is likely and further qualitative improvement in programming and in servicing is imperative. Most countries have embarked or intend to embark on the preparation of both comprehensive and sectoral development plans; isolated services formerly rendered under the programs are being increasingly replaced by longer-term and more systematic assistance involving preparation, continuous revision, and implementation of plans. The capacity of the Headquarters Department is further taxed by the need to cooperate with the Special Fund in its pre-investment activities. The United Nations acts as the executing agent for a large number of pre-investment projects which are related to its research and technical assistance activities. Emphasis by Member governments on accelerated industrialization will also lead to a considerable expansion of the work of the department both at Headquarters and in the regions.

✻   ✻   ✻   ✻   ✻   ✻   ✻

In addition, the Department of Economic and Social Affairs has so far been responsible, as the executing agency, for thirty-two Special Fund projects for which earmarkings were made by the Governing Council of the Special Fund in the amount of gross projects costs of $29.5 million.

The Department of Economic and Social Affairs at Headquarters is the largest substantive department of the United Nations Secretariat, though it is rather small in relation to its growing tasks. In an organization which is obliged to cope with thousands of operational details continuously emerging from hundreds of projects initiated and executed in all parts of the world, there may be a stage of growth beyond which efficiency is likely to be impaired. In such circumstances, a measure of decentralization of administration on a functional basis, on a geographical basis, or on both, may offer advantages. In fact, as pointed out earlier, the United Nations developed in the 1950's the geographical framework for such an administrative reform: in the four main parts of the world there are regional offices each of them approximately one-fourth the size of the Headquarters establishment; they are far from having reached the optimum size of efficient operational units: they are, therefore, not likely soon to reach the point of diminishing returns well known in over-centralized administration. The use of regional secretariats with relatively small additions to their staff would considerably increase the capacity of the United Nations to carry on operational activities and at the same time could bring about a further increase in efficiency; at Headquarters, because it would permit due concentration on policy formulation and guidance, on central administration and financial management and control, on coordination, and on research into problems requiring a global approach; in the regions, because they are closer than is Headquarters to the field operations,[10] because they have better knowledge than Headquar-

[10] E.g., from a regional office the cost of a trip to a country in the same region usually amounts to a few hundred United States dollars or less; from Headquarters it is usually more, and sometimes much more, than a thousand dollars.

ters can have of local conditions and, last but not least, because, their work being limited to only one region, they should be able to render "tailor-made" services to governments requesting assistance more easily than a large establishment.

Of various reforms, administrative decentralization is perhaps the hardest to carry out, no less in international than in national administration. Conscious and subconscious resistance to it has to be overcome by the very same people who have to carry out the reform, thus changing their own habits, functions, and positions and acknowledging that others could do what they have done well heretofore. The psychological factors are superimposed on administrative difficulties and intertwined with doubts and risks inherent in any change. The expected growth of the operational programs, the need to increase the capacity for handling them and the existing network of regional offices, all seem to point in the direction of change, quite apart from political pressures arising from decisions of the UN regional commissions and the UN principal organs.

There can be no doubt that, in the 1950's, in addition to questions of administrative merit or necessity, decentralization also had a political connotation; it was a policy favored by the less developed countries, especially new members of the UN who after gaining independence wished that UN assistance be channelled through regional bodies in which they had special confidence and with which they had a sense of greater identification than with the central administration of the United Nations. International solidarity in a global sense often follows rather than precedes regional solidarity, as expressed in regional associations. Within the UN the regional commissions have become symbols of such associations.

As in the case of many UN decisions, the unanimity behind General Assembly Resolution 1709 (XVI), January 4, 1962, reflects a compromise and perhaps more than one current or undercurrent of opinion. Although the vast majority favors regionalization and decentralization of the operational programs, there seems to be little doubt that some advanced countries and some major contributors to the programs entertain doubts, if not reservations, regarding the scope and perhaps even the wisdom of decentralization. There may be political motivations for such opinions; there may be considerations of efficiency as against the uncertainty of any untried scheme that might shift the center of gravity from Headquarters to the faraway regional offices placed in the underdeveloped regions and largely staffed by nationals of the countries of those regions; there may be fear that operations administered from regional centers might lose central direction and control and the undisputed benefits that stem from the global character of the multilateral programs; there may be fear that decentralization would reduce the proportion of experts from some developed countries in favor of others, or in favor of a larger proportion of experts from less developed countries. Such fears and doubts seem to disregard the principle of a centralized Secretariat which stems from the Charter; the locating of part of the staff of the Secretariat in regional offices is, of course, in no way in conflict with this principle. Such fears and doubts do not seem to take account of the admittedly successful operation of regional commissions which is now recognized no less by developed than by underdeveloped countries. In any case, if political arguments against decentralization were based on the different balances of forces existing in earlier years in the General Assembly and in the regional commissions, by the 1960's they had lost their validity.

V

EXTERNAL ASPECTS OF ORGANIZATION

CHAPTER **13**

PEACE KEEPING

Having completed our examination of the internal aspects of policy, procedure, and problems of the United Nations, we are now in a position to examine the Organization in external terms. Although these two perspectives have distinguished the internal from the external in a somewhat arbitrary manner, most students of the subject would probably agree that the more common focus, on the external operations, cannot genuinely be comprehended without a sound grasp of how the UN functions. But in looking at the external activities of the UN we need to be mindful of two things: (1) the Charter provisions and early practices are a major source of information of what the Organization was expected to be and do, but (2) every institution changes as new members and new problems come along. This requires a frequent re-evaluation to determine what new directions are developing and to ascertain whether current demands and expectations remain consonant with the original and the modified conditions. Of course, it is possible for some states to expect the Organization to conform to the initial conditions and other states to expect it to conform to new expectations. This produces organizational schizophrenia, a not uncommon disease in institutions where some members want change and others prefer the status quo.

Such conditions exist in part because the Organization is varied in membership and thus has many different kinds of demands placed upon it. This schizophrenia may also be explained in part because people are sometimes inconsistent and want incompatible ends. For this reason it is good to look at the multitude of activities carried out by the Organization in terms o; both the initial and the current picture.

In his article, "United Nations Use of Military Force," Inis Claude, Jr. attempts, in a limited area, just such a study. He feels firmly the need to revamp our expectations regarding the United Nations and its ability to perform one of the major functions that was originally expected of it— providing collective security for its members. Claude's article, which was written at the time the Congo episode was drawing to a close, focuses primarily on the question of keeping the peace and the need to alter our expectations regarding the service the UN can provide. His examination proceeds from collective security to peace keeping as he outlines the prerequisites of both.

We shift from a general discussion to a specific examination of peace keeping. In the articles by Herbert Nicholas and Hans Morgenthau we have on the one hand an exposition of two peace-keeping missions, the Suez and the Congo, and on the other a critique of peace keeping. The prerequisites of peace keeping are considered in light of present-day political attitudes.

Nicholas explains why the first major peace-keeping mission was so widely received at the outset, pointing to the assumption on the part of a number of states, including the British and French, that the mission would achieve for each state what it wanted out of the crisis. This helped augur well for its success initially as did the fact that many of the parties concerned were unwilling to make of the issue a casus belli. *When the ONUC force for the Congo was established it became clear that only in a rudimentary sense could UNEF be its model, despite the latter's success. But the geographical and political conditions associated with the Congo required many departures from the older pattern. And the ambiguity about the authority and objectives of ONUC, as the author points out, soon aggravated the difficulties. He concludes, nevertheless, that the Congo mission may be construed as a success and points out three lessons that should be learned from that experience.*

Hans Morgenthau's general commentary, "Political Conditions for an International Police Force," first takes up the question of the role and the prerequisites for the successful functioning of a domestic police force. Then, by comparing a national and international society he discusses the problems that would confront an international police force. He concludes that although there is little reason to believe that such a force could play the role many of its advocates want in a world of sovereign states, in a world of complete disarmament such a role would not be inappropriate. This situation is so remote, however, that Morgenthau's views regarding an international police force must be classified as pessimistic.

Clearly little benefit and much harm can come from continuing to assume that a function such as collective security can still be a primary obligation of the Organization. Later, in Chapter 16, we will see that such a perception of the Organization is precisely that held by many Americans. Yet Claude points out that this expectation was futile right from the beginning so far as the major powers were concerned. Can this task, nevertheless, be fulfilled by the Organization when less powerful states are involved in a crisis of large enough proportions to threaten the peace? How can the larger states be encouraged to permit collective security when they themselves are not direct participants in controversies? Would it be considered inequitable if collective sanctions were imposed only in those disputes involving small states? Of course, one might ask how sanctions could even be applied to the less dangerous controversies unless the small states were willing to approve them and the large were at least not unwilling.

As for Morgenthau's critique: does the evidence indicate that such a pessimistic conclusion is warranted? And, if it does, are there any means which might increase the possibility of international police service? Would it help to earmark certain troops for this responsibility and in peacetime to give them operations and tours abroad under foreign military leadership to increase their potential as an international force? If this would help, could such forces be used in collective-security operations or would they essentially have to be consigned to peace-keeping missions?

Of course, one needs to see the problem in terms of its financial aspects as well, and to ask which states would be willing to provide the extra funds for such training. However, the fact that the troops are only special-duty troops on periodic tours and training exercises for international service would minimize the cost.

Finally we come to one of the most critical problems and dilemmas confronting the international community and the UN—the tendency for more and more crises to start out with the characteristics of civil conflicts. As long as this continues the UN's potential will be if not nullified, greatly weakened, for ostensibly the UN may not enter matters which are essentially domestic in nature. And what basic standards ought the Organization use in these controversies, particularly civil wars? Is it enough to seek an end to the fighting? Are there further objectives the UN should assume such as proposing or imposing a solution? Clearly the authors of the selections in this chapter *are correct when they indicate that one of the major purposes of the Organization needs to be given much more consideration than it has had heretofore.*

FURTHER READINGS

Larus, Joel, *From Collective Security to Preventive Diplomacy: Readings in International Organization and the Maintenance of Peace and Security.* New York: John Wiley and Sons, 1965.

McVitty, Marion H., *Wanted: Rules to Guide UN Peace-Keeping Operations of the Future,* New Federalist Paper No. 1, *United World Federalists.* Washington, D.C.: 1965.

Russell, Ruth B., *United Nations Experience with Military Forces—Political and Legal Aspects.* Washington, D.C.: The Brookings Institution, 1964.

Sohn, Louis B., "The Role of the United Nations in Civil Wars," *Proceedings of the American Society of International Law,* 1963, pp. 208–216.

UNITED NATIONS USE OF MILITARY FORCE

Inis L. Claude, Jr.*

There are two possible ways of approaching the question of the purposes of the United Nations. One is to concentrate on the Charter—to treat this formal constitutional document as an authoritative and meaningful expression of the goals which the world organization seeks to achieve and toward which it must be presumed to be working. The Charter, of course, was not handed down from on high, but was formulated by states. Thus, this approach appears to suggest that the Charter was, in 1945, a valid statement of a real consensus among the original members as to what the UN should be and do. As for the present, it suggests that the same conception of the UN is held by the expanded membership of the organization—that the consensus has been widened but not substantively altered—or, alternatively that the UN is an entity sufficiently autonomous to function in accordance with the original consensus whether or not that consensus, or any consensus, still prevails among its members.

The second approach is to focus upon the political interests and purposes of the members of the UN—to proceed upon the assumption that the words of the Charter are less determinative than the policies of the states. Following this approach, we may expect to find that the purposes of the organization are not fixed, but are continuously redefined as states develop new agreements among themselves as to what ends they wish or expect the UN to serve. Moreover, we may expect to find that the organization's purposes are as ambiguous as they are mutable, for it is altogether unlikely that the members have ever been, are now, or ever will be in full agreement concerning the uses to which this international instrument should be put. In these terms, the explorer of the UN's purpose must wrestle with change and conflict, renouncing the expectation of finding the purposes of the organization conveniently spelled out for him.

Adopting the first course, we may ask what the Charter says with respect to the use of military force. What are the purposes to which 51 states ostensibly subscribed in 1945 and which they, along with 59 additional states,

* Inis L. Claude, Jr., "United Nations Use of Military Force," *Journal of Conflict Resolution*, Vol. 7, 1963, pp. 117–125. Copyright 1963 by the University of Michigan. By permission of the *Journal of Conflict Resolution*.

Inis L. Claude, Jr. is Professor of Political Science at the University of Michigan, a member of the board of editors of *International Organization*, and the author of many articles and books including *Swords into Plowshares*.

now purport to regard as appropriate and acceptable? The UN is intended to discourage the irresponsible national use of military force—aggression, in short. It recognizes the legitimacy of defensive action by victims of attack and by other states which may wish to join in that reaction to aggression, but it undertakes to make such defense unnecessary by making offensive action unlikely. In a variety of ways, the UN undertakes to prevent aggression. Its purpose is to deprive states of anything to fight about—by inhibiting the development of, and promoting the elimination of, conditions that might make for conflict, and by facilitating the settlement of difficulties that have reached the critical "dispute" stage. By promoting disarmament negotiations, the organization [and the member states] express the urge to deprive themselves and each other of anything to fight with. Thus far, this analysis suggests that the UN is concerned with the use of force by states, acting on their own. The Charter goes on, however, to say something about the use of force by the UN, or, more accurately, by states acting under its auspices. The two subjects are closely interrelated; provisions calling for the use of force by or on behalf of the UN are integral parts of the scheme for inhibiting aggressive national action and thereby reducing the necessity for individual or collective defensive action. The Charter purports to classify the national use of force under three headings: that which is required, that which is prohibited, and that which is permitted. Insofar as it requires members to provide coercive support for the world organization, the Charter adopts the view that the responsible use of force for international purposes is the ultimate antidote for the irresponsible use of force for national purposes.

The Charter does not in fact go very far in this direction. It pays lip service to the ideal of erecting a collective security system, which would promise to cope with any prohibited use of force by invoking the requirement of collective resistance. But it does not attempt to provide for the actual creation or operation of such a system. At most, it contains a plan for developing a system under which the UN may mobilize collective action against minor aggressors in circumstances which find the major powers unanimously disposed to support or at least to tolerate such action. The crucial provisions pertinent to this scheme, Articles 43 and 45, which contemplate agreements on military contingents to be placed at the disposal of the Security Council by states, have become dead letters but have not been formally erased. The Charter does not, it should be emphasized, either provide or promise a system for UN action or UN sponsored action to repress aggression launched or supported by any of the major powers. The famous veto clause of Article 27 expresses the founding fathers' rejection of the attempt to require member states to join forces under the UN banner for resistance to great-power aggression; the "individual or collective self-defense" clause of Article 51, a permissive clause, expresses the judgment of the founding fathers as to what can and must be done under such circumstances. The Charter, in short, prohibits but does not purport to prevent the most dangerous sort of aggression—that undertaken by or under the auspices of a major power.

We might summarize this reading of the Charter by saying that it speaks much more decisively about the use of force by states than about the use of force by the UN. The purpose of the UN is to discourage the irresponsible, disruptive use of force by states. The organization itself is to use, or to sponsor the use of, force only when—or if—the great powers concur in the implementation of Articles 43 and 45 and subsequently in Security Council decisions regarding particular cases.

Shifting to the second of the approaches to analysis of the purposes of the UN discussed at the beginning, which stresses the policies of states rather than the words of the Charter, one may express doubts as to whether the statesmen who drafted the Charter were as unanimously and as unreservedly dedicated to the creation of an effective peace-preserving organization as they said they were. Equally, one may doubt whether the purposes stated in the Charter are in fact the purposes which all or most member states now wish the UN to pursue and hope that it may realize. There is conflict over the purposes for which the organization is to be used—conflict deriving not from differing interpretations of the Charter but from differing national interests, or conceptions of national interests.

There is no difficulty in securing general condemnation of aggression in the abstract, and agreement that the UN should discourage, if not effectively prevent or suppress, aggression. In concrete terms, however, one state's aggression is always another state's "legitimate use of force to defend vital national interests." What states really want is the imposition of effective international restraint upon the military ventures of "others," not of themselves or of states intimately associated with themselves. It can hardly be imagined that the Soviet Union wishes the UN to be capable of inhibiting Communist conquest of Laos. India presumably does not regret that the organization failed to protect Goa against Indian invasion. The United Arab Republic does not aspire to make the UN an effective guarantor of the integrity of Israel. The United States would have limited enthusiasm for the project of making the UN a bulwark against any possible American attack against Cuba. With respect to its own resorts to force, actual or potential, every state wants to secure at least the tolerance of the UN, even better the blessing of the UN, and at best such substantial support and reinforcement as the organization might provide.

States vary, of course, in their ability and disposition to use force for the promotion or protection of their interests as they see them. They vary also in the degree to which they conceive their interests as compatible with a stable world order in which respect for the territorial integrity and political independence of all states is enshrined and effectuated as a basic principle. I would argue, for instance, that Washington's view of the national interest of the United States is much more compatible with and conducive to that kind of global system than Moscow's view of the interests and purposes which Soviet policy is to serve. I do not suggest that all states are equally bellicose and aggressive. Nevertheless, it seems to me quite clear that every state has to contemplate the possibility that it might, under some circumstances, feel impelled to take military action that would seem to it absolutely necessary for the protection of vital national interests but might not be regarded as legitimate by the political organs of the UN. States do contemplate this possibility; consequently, they do not genuinely commit themselves without reservation to the proposition that they will never resort to force in the face of international disapproval expressed through the UN; consequently, they are not ultimately dedicated to the purpose of enabling the UN—that is its member states—to control the unilateral resort to military action by any and all states, including themselves.

If I am correct in attributing this attitude to states, then it follows that states must have reservations about conferring upon the UN an extensive legal competence and actual capability to exercise a coercive function. One does not fully endorse the principle of the international use of force unless one fully repudiates the policy of the national use of force, for it must be presumed that a militarily effective UN might frustrate one's [own] state in its efforts to safeguard its vital interests—interests which the state may regard as justifying the national use of force but which a sufficient number of the members of a UN political organ might not so regard.

I submit that this is the actual situation today. We must resist the temptation to take too seriously the simple proposition that the world is divided into two groups of states, one of which (including, most prominently, the Soviet Union) opposes the strengthening of the UN, and the other of which (led by the United States) favors the development of that organization as an international repository of coercive authority and power.

It is easy enough to demonstrate that the Soviets oppose that development. It is perhaps less self-evident that the United States does not favor that development. I would argue, however, that the record shows that the United States favors a UN which can give permissive endorsement and lend moral and perhaps more tangible varieties of support to military actions which we regard as necessary and legitimate; I look in vain for evidence that the United States wished to equip the UN with either the formal competence or the effective capability to prevent this country and its allies from fighting whenever we may feel it necessary to fight, or to require us to fight when we are not disposed to do so. In the case of Korea, the UN gave an international blessing to, and stimulated the mobilization of multilateral support for, a military reaction to Communist aggression which we felt impelled to undertake. We valued this marginal assistance, and attempted, in the Uniting for Peace plan, to maximize the possibility that such international aid might be rendered to upholders of similarly worthy causes in the future. This was, however, a far cry from endorsing the actual creation of, or expressing the willingness to accept the onerous obligations of, a full-fledged collective security system. The United States has subsequently supported the quasi-military interventions of the UN in the Middle East and the Congo, but these can hardly be characterized as manifestations of, or even as preliminary approaches to, the establishment of a UN capacity to use international military force to squelch illicit national resorts to force.

* * * * * * *

The purpose of this paper is not to speculate about what the world would be like if it were utterly different from what it is. Focusing on the existing situation and the existing global institution, let us ask what role can reasonably be assigned to the UN in the military-security field.

First, there is the question of the possible use of the UN as a military instrument for dealing with great-power aggression; in our terms, this refers to the possibility of the organization's serving as a defensive bulwark against aggressive action launched by, or supported by, the Soviet Union or Communist China. My response to this is quite negative. We rely, quite properly in my judgment, upon our national power and our alliances for security against this threat. The UN was not designed to cope with this sort of problem, and I see no point in criticizing the organization for not doing what it was not supposed to do, or in regretting its inability to do what it was, from the start, constitutionally debarred from attempting to do. Nor do I see any point in trying to transform the UN into an organization appropriate for this role. The UN is not a NATO, and if we undertake to make it a kind of super-NATO, we may sacrifice its values as a global institution without in fact succeeding in making it a valuable free-world institution. We need not choose between global and free-world organizations. We have both kinds, and we need both kinds, to perform different types of functions. If NATO is defective, the answer is to improve NATO, not to attempt to convert the UN into a NATO-like institution.

* * * * * * *

Secondly, we might ask whether the UN has a significant capability for dealing militarily with clashes between states which lie outside the alignments of the Cold War and the spheres of interest of the major Cold War antagonists. This is precisely what the UN was intended to have, as is indicated by the plan for making national units available for use by the Security Council, stated in Article 43 of the Charter. The question, then, is whether this plan can or should be revived, or a different scheme be substituted for it. The outlook is not encouraging. The early negotiations regarding the implementation of Article 43 indicated that neither the Western powers nor the Soviet Union trusted the other to participate loyally, without ulterior motives, in a collective UN force. Since this mutual distrust has become stronger rather than weaker, it seems perfectly evident that any anti-aggression force assembled by the UN would have to exclude units from the major powers and their most intimate allies. This observation suggests a major limiting factor—the pervasiveness of the Cold War. It is extremely difficult to conceive of an international conflict in our time which the Western and Soviet blocs would not regard as at least potentially related to their competitive struggle; in virtually any case that can readily be imagined, UN military action against an aggressive state would be likely to evoke conflicting reactions from the Soviet Union and the United States. Even though these powers might be excluded from participation in the action, they might well find themselves at odds concerning the propriety of the action, the identity of aggressor and victim, and the nature of the political result which the UN should endeavor to promote. The world is too small to provide a wide zone of indifference between the major contestants. In short, an attempt by the UN to deal coercively with almost any conflict would probably be assimilated to an attempt to deal coercively with great-power struggles.

* * * * * * *

What if the UN were equipped with a permanent military force of its own, a force designed to defeat aggressors, and thus ceased to be dependent upon the willingness of states to contribute, or to permit others to contribute, military contingents for UN actions? This possibility seems to me to have no relevance to the problem of restraining great powers. Military power must rest upon a base—[a] territorial, demographic, social, political, economic, industrial, [or] scientific base. The only base capable of producing and sustaining a military establishment able to match that of a great power is another great power. Concretely, only the United States—or, more broadly, the Western coalition—is able to generate the force required to balance that possessed by the Sino-Soviet bloc. The United States, or the Western coalition, might be rechristened the United Nations, but the change would be both literally and figuratively nominal. The UN is not a New World which can be called in to redress the balance of the old.

Might such a UN force be relevant to the problem of restraining minor aggressors? . . . Who will control the force? Against what state will it be used in a given situation? For what purpose will it fight? Toward what political result will it press? Neither great nor small powers will be indifferent to such issues, or be satisfied with the simple-minded answer that the UN will exercise policy direction and will use the force to achieve the purposes stipulated in the Charter. . . . A UN armed force must be based upon thin air unless it is grounded in dependence upon the very states over which it is supposed to exercise independent authority. Whatever power a UN force might wield would be, in effect, borrowed national power. This is to say that the establishment of a UN force for countering aggression would not in any real sense represent the creation of an autonomous central authority, emancipated from dependence upon the support and cooperation of states and able to function coercively without regard to the policies and attitudes of states.

It might be argued that, given the new technology of warfare which enhances the significance of ready striking power, the problem of the power base has lost, or is losing, its importance. Thus, the UN might gain an impressive military status simply by acquiring a stock of missiles and nuclear warheads, without the necessity of developing the supportive foundations traditionally required by a military establishment. . . .

Moreover, the project of equipping the UN with a self-contained nuclear striking force involves imposing upon the organization all the difficulties and dilemmas associated with the doctrine of massive retaliation. An international military establishment designed to maintain peace and security would require military versatility, the capacity for flexible and graduated response, to the same degree that a major national force requires it. To assert this is to deny that the problem of the power base can be circumvented by providing the UN with a stock of ready-made instruments of thermonuclear destruction and to reaffirm the dependence of the UN upon its member states. A permanent UN military force for combating aggression is not a substitute for the willing collaboration of states, but simply one of the possible vehicles for such collaboration.

❈ ❈ ❈ ❈ ❈ ❈ ❈

We might find some clues in a perusal of the record of the organization. I think we can set aside the Korean case. Here, the UN endorsed and encouraged joint action against Communist aggression, and came to be clearly associated with one side in what was obviously a major episode of the East-West conflict. The initial enthusiasm for putting the UN into this kind of role, so sharply at variance with the original conception of the UN expressed in the Charter, quickly died away. By the end of the Korean War, the UN was being pushed—by the United States, among other members—into the position of a third party, disengaged from the conflict. It has been vigorously pulled in that direction in subsequent years, as its neutralist members have grown in numbers. . . .

More promising clues are to be found in the string of cases which have involved the use of military personnel under UN auspices for purposes other than doing battle with aggressors—for supervising truces, patrolling borders or armistice lines, observing the degree to which rival parties respect agreed arrangements for stabilizing their relationships, and the like. These cases include UN interventions in the Palestine and Kashmir cases, in Lebanon, and—most notable—in the Suez and Congo crises. These are peace-stabilizing, or peace-keeping, or peace-restoring operations, efforts to aid disputant states in the implementation of political resolves to avoid the outbreak or the renewal of military conflict; they are not measures for the international

defeat of determined acts of aggression. We may take UNEF and the
military operation in the Congo as the outstanding instances of this sort of
UN enterprise.

*   *   *   *   *   *   *

[The late Secretary-General of the UN, Dag Hammarskjöld], drew the
conclusion that "the main field of useful activity of the United Nations in its
efforts to prevent conflicts or to solve conflicts" should be defined as that of
taking action to fill vacuums in areas of conflicts outside of, or marginal to,
the zones already clearly involved in the Cold War struggle, so as to minimize the tendency of—or to diminish the incentive for—great powers to move
competitively into those situations. Thus, he hoped that the organization
might prevent the widening and aggravation of the bloc conflicts. . . .

Two points are crucial to the theory of preventive diplomacy:

1. The kind of operation which is envisaged, designed to seal off a zone
of trouble from the competitive instrusions of the East and the West, is
dependent upon the active or the passive consent of both the major contestants in the Cold War. . . . The theory rests upon the assumption that
conflict of interest breeds a limited community of interest, particularly in
the thermonuclear era. Rival parties have a common interest in preventing
their conflict from degenerating into uncontrollable violence. This common
interest does not suggest that the conflict is unreal, or is not fundamental
and deep-seated, or is diminishing in intensity. Quite the contrary, it arises
precisely because the conflict is a basic one; the community or mutuality of
interest is a function of the intensity of the conflict of interest.

*   *   *   *   *   *   *

2. The function of preventive diplomacy is essentially neutralist in
character. It does not involve neutral mediation in disputes and conflicts
between the Cold War blocs—that is also an important political potentiality
of the UN, but it falls under a different heading, and it calls for diplomatic
or legal techniques rather than military or quasi-military instrumentalities.
Rather, preventive diplomacy as such involves neutral interposition between
contestants, using military personnel under UN direction as agents for
achieving the neutralization of a trouble spot—i.e., for insulating the area
against the intrusion of Cold War competition.

*   *   *   *   *   *   *

It appears that the only significant military function which may reasonably
be attributed to the UN is that suggested by the theory of preventive
diplomacy—the conduct of operations, analogous to UNEF and ONUC, designed to assist the great powers in keeping the Cold War cold. This can be
done for the great powers only if they are agreed in wanting it to be done,
and only if each of them is confident that the UN will genuinely promote

the neutralization of trouble spots, not act in the interest of the other. . . .
If the United States and the Soviet Union can join in accepting and even in
valuing the performance of this role by the UN, it seems to me that the
organization may contribute significantly to the stabilization of the global
situation. If they cannot, the UN may yet contribute valuable services in
other realms, but I see no important role for it with respect to the use of
military force under international auspices.

UN PEACE FORCES AND THE CHANGING GLOBE:
THE LESSONS OF SUEZ AND CONGO

Herbert G. Nicholas[*]

*   *   *   *   *   *   *

It is perhaps true that the UNEF idea owed some of its immediate acceptance to the fact that it was imperfectly understood: Britain and France in
particular hoped to see the force act as the agent of the United Nations in
implementing the six-point recommendations on a Canal settlement announced by Mr. Hammarskjöld on October 12, 1956, while Israel hoped to
see it remedy her grievances about transit through the Canal and the Gulf
of Aqaba. If true, however, this remains a marginal consideration. UNEF
was created basically because no interested power could impose a solution
alone, and all powers, great and small alike, preferred an internationally
contrived and controlled solution to a conflict which could develop dangerously into a wider war. Negative considerations pointed the same way;
neither of the two alliances, the Warsaw Pact or NATO, felt their vital
interests threatened (however much, briefly, Britain and France may have),
and neither Israel nor Egypt, on reflection, wanted a fight *à outrance* then
and there.

To see these as the underlying factors that made UNEF possible is not to
depreciate the efforts of Lester Pearson and the other representatives who
came to be known at the United Nations as the "fire brigade," or the role of
the Secretary-General and the Secretariat. "Factors" by themselves do not
stop wars; they have to be assessed and manipulated by human beings. If

[*] Herbert G. Nicholas, "UN Peace Forces and the Changing Globe: The Lessons of
Suez and Congo," *International Organization*, Vol. 17, 1963, pp. 321–337. Copyright
1963, World Peace Foundation. By permission of *International Organization*.

Herbert G. Nicholas is a fellow of New College, Oxford, and Nuffield Reader in the
Comparative Study of Institutions at the University of Oxford. He is the author of
The United Nations as a Political Institution and *Britain and the U.S.A.*

courage, perseverance, diplomatic skill, imagination, and personal prestige had not existed in the right quarters at the right moment in 1956, the resulting drift and confusion would have required more than a UNEF to remedy them.

The celebrated conditions of UNEF laid down by the Secretary-General in his two reports of November 4 and 6, 1956,[1] were the necessary preconditions of its existence and also set the limits to what it might achieve. No one except the Soviet bloc states and the convicted trio of Britain, France, and Israel was willing to enlist in a United Nations force with coercive powers; no one was willing to fight Egypt or Israel, or possibly both simultaneously, in order to impose a just settlement—whatever that would have been—on these old combatants. Once this was recognized, it followed inevitably that the United Nations force could have only the function of facilitating the invaders' withdrawal, of maintaining a minimum of order in the transitional phase from war to armistice, and, finally, of keeping the local combatants, Israel and Egypt, at arms' length. The element of force was, strictly speaking, minimal. It was military only in being composed of soldiers; its functions were fewer even than those of a normal civilian police corps. Police exist to prevent crime and enforce the law as well as to preserve the peace, but UNEF has no powers to prevent anything save the most blatant frontier violations. Its role is pacific and passive. It is essentially interpository in character, a moral United Nations presence given physical embodiment on a scale sufficiently extensive to guarantee that neither side can aim the slightest blow at the other without involving itself by that very act in larger, international consequences. Ever since the cease-fire and withdrawals were effected, UNEF has been in fact a larger and more physically impenetrable UNTSO.[2]

In this capacity its success is undoubted. It has not only achieved its immediate objectives; it has also kept the peace between Egypt and Israel ever since, both in the large and obvious sense and in that of reducing to a previously unknown level the number of incidents along the border. This has been due to many factors besides the efficiency and loyalty of the force. Though the basic local antagonisms remain, nothing has occurred to provoke another 1956 flare-up, while the great power outsiders have all for various reasons been tolerably content not to stoke up the fires of Egyptian-Israeli animosity. Then again there has been a simplicity, a straightforwardness

---

[1] UN Documents A/3289 and A/3302. The conditions were later codified in Document A/3943. In summary, these principles were:

  (i) No permanent member of the Security Council or any "interested" government should contribute contingents.

  (ii) The force should not be used to affect the military or political outcome of the dispute.

  (iii) Its arms should only be used in self-defense.

  (iv) It should not be stationed on a state's territory except with that state's consent.

[2] United Nations Truce Supervision Organization which was in the area prior to the Israeli attack under the command of General Burns [ed.].

about UNEF's role, rare in international affairs, which has helped it greatly. Its task is only to patrol a strip of desert, for the most part totally uninhabited, where it can exercise its simple function with a minimum risk of offending the susceptibilities of its host country or of anyone else. . . .

Finally, the Arab-Israeli rivalry for all its intensity is basically parochial in scale. Outside the Moslem world few countries feel themselves deeply committed to one side or the other. This has made it comparatively easy to recruit for the force contingents whose nationality does not involve them in any serious risk of partisanship or even in accusations of partisanship. . . .

In consequence, the difficulties of the force have been virtually confined to the familiar problems of finance. These, of course, reflect the fact that what was originally welcomed as a solution to an emergency has now become an apparent permanency. The fireman has turned into the lodger. . . . [The situation has] created a precedent and left a legacy of practical experience in the organizing and operating of a United Nations force.

When this legacy was drawn on in the Congo, it was in circumstances that soon made one wonder how far UNEF could properly be regarded as a precedent for the United Nations operation in the Congo (ONUC).[3] To take the simplest factor first, in place of the sealing off of a desert peninsula as in Suez, the Congo crisis required the insulation of an almost land-locked subcontinent, as well as the internal policing of that same huge area. Similarly, whereas UNEF had only to keep two organized and accountable states apart, ONUC had the double task of excluding outside intervention and creating internal viability. While UNEF could operate in an area physically free from complicating interests or inhabitants, no United Nations operation in the Congo could possibly avoid contact with Congolese life at every point —and in circumstances where any contact (or indeed no contact) inevitably involved interference. Finally, whereas it was relatively easy to construct a UNEF out of the contributions of disinterested states, disinterestedness was a much harder quality to command where the Congo was concerned. (What is more, for reasons of incipient Pan-Africanism and color consciousness it was, when discovered, by no means so obviously welcome.) At the very outset all these complications presented a formidable challenge to ONUC; before it had been long in operation, others, and worse, arose for which there was no precedent in the annals of international organization or in the records of international law.

*   *   *   *   *   *   *

There was from the beginning an ambiguity about the authority and objectives of ONUC which reflected the anomalous position of the Congo itself,

[3] In the interests of convenience I have used "ONUC" throughout to refer to the United Nations military force in the Congo, although strictly speaking, of course, it applies to the important civilian operation as well.

a state so newly independent that the *Loi Fondamentale* designed to author-ize its constitution had not yet been ratified by the body appointed to do so, the Congolese parliament. In part, ONUC was a routine response to a routine request from a new state for technical assistance; what was novel was that it was for *military* assistance, a category hitherto unknown in United Nations technical aid circles. Simultaneously, however, it was an appeal for United Nations protection against the reintroduction of Belgian troops into the territory of an ex-colony now independent and also, from the United Nations point of view, a necessary safeguard against unilateral as-sistance pouring in from rival sides in the Cold War. ONUC's role from the outset was consequently a dual one—the provision of both internal and external security. . . .

Nevertheless the Secretary-General took the view that the principles which he had laid down for UNEF were equally valid for ONUC. As he told the Security Council on July 13, 1960,

The United Nations Force would not be authorized to action beyond self-defence[4] . . . . They may not take any action which would make them a party to internal conflicts. . . . The selection of personnel should be such as to avoid complications because of the nationalities used. . . . This does not . . . exclude the use of units from African States, while . . . it does exclude . . . troops from any of the permanent members of the Security Council.[5]

In saying this, the Secretary-General could hardly have been unaware, even at this early stage of the operation, that the problems presented by the Congo were vastly different from those of Suez. His emphasis on UNEF principles in the Congo context must therefore have reflected, as was surely right, a concern for the context of international politics within which the problems of the Congo would have to find their solution, if at all.

As every UN debate from the July 13 Security Council meeting onward showed, the gravest differences of opinion existed among Member States as to what kind of settlement, what kind of Congo indeed, should be aimed at—differences, moreover, not merely between the Soviet bloc and the West but also within the West, within the Afro-Asian group, and even within the ranks of the Africans themselves. Even before Katanga's secession or the

---

[4] How strictly this was originally interpreted can be seen in the wording of the leaflet distributed by Dr. Bunche and General von Horn to all members of ONUC on their arrival in the Congo:

You serve as members of an international force. It is a peace force, not a fighting force.

The United Nations has asked you to come here in response to an appeal from the Government of the Republic of the Congo. Your task is to help in restoring order and calm in this country which has been so troubled recently. You are to be friendly to all the people of this country. Protection against acts of violence is to be given to *all* the people, white and black.

You carry arms, but they are to be used *only* in self-defence. You are in the Congo to help *everyone*, to harm no one.

[5] Security Council *Official Records* (15th year), 873rd meeting, July 13, 1960, p. 5.

outright clash between Kasavubu and Lumumba, these differences were violent enough to guarantee that, if the United Nations attempted to formulate a positive policy for ONUC, it would not merely provoke a clash of opposites; it would reveal the lack of *any* clear majority consensus. (This was precisely what did happen in December 1960.) The only way to avert such a clash was to insist on the principle of non-interference and its corollary of no initiative in the use of force.

... In Suez and Gaza there were always local police forces to whom UNEF could turn over any violators of the peace who came its way. In the Congo such entities hardly existed, yet ONUC itself had no powers to arrest or even disarm the mutineering elements of the *Force Publique*. Such a power eventually was given, and critics have argued that the biggest error of the whole Congo operation was not to have given it at the very beginning. This may be so, but two things have to be remembered. First, in a continent hypersensitive about "neo-colonialist" interference and in a country teetering on the edge of mass hysteria, it was important for the United Nations' long-term mission to preserve the image of itself as a pacific agent seeking only to help Africans to help themselves. Secondly, although some states that contributed to the force, e.g., Ghana, were willing, even eager, to have their troops employed forcefully, others would have refused contributions to a force which was involved in the killing of Africans even in the best of causes and even at the hands of other Africans. When, later on, resolute measures were taken, certain states did seek to withdraw in protest.

But, of course, more was involved than clashes with the *Force Publique*. The issue of force or no force merged into the issue of interference or non-interference. Non-interference was even less possible in practice than abstention from force, because the mere presence of ONUC was interference. Non-interference, however, was also a more indispensable principle because there was no agreed alternative to put in its place. . . .

It was also true that the United Nations accepted the unity of the Congo as axiomatic and secessionist activities as illegal. It explicitly rejected Katanga's claim to independence. Nevertheless, it never laid on ONUC the task of enforcing Congolese unity or ending Katangese independence. These objectives were to be secured by conciliation, moral pressure, or, at most and not until very late in the day, economic and financial sanctions. Moreover, since ONUC had a positive obligation to prevent civil war, it was as opposed to the central government's forcible occupation of Katanga as to Katanga's forcible secession.

In all these senses the United Nations was impartial. Within the framework of Congolese unity it was for the Congolese to decide who should rule and how. But in almost all the actual power contests of Congo politics the United Nations could not avoid taking decisions which favored one side or the other.

* * * * * * *

The cross-currents set up by factional fighting inside the Congo and intervention from outside complicated the Congo operation in two other respects. In six years of operation UNEF has had little difficulty in holding its national contingents together or in maintaining equable relations with its host government. ONUC speedily ran into trouble on both fronts. Dag Hammarskjöld's decision to make ONUC a predominantly African force was certainly a right one; no other course would have secured the indispensable moral backing in Africa or the African votes in the United Nations. But it was impossible for a force so composed to be completely disinterested. Each contributing state had strong views on every Congo issue, and every decision that ONUC had to make imposed a strain on its loyalties. Looking back over the fiercely troubled course of the Congo since July 1960 one is truly impressed to see how well in such circumstances the conglomerate ONUC has held together. Nonetheless, it is instructive to notice how and where the bonds of loyalty chafed.

Thus in September 1960 ONUC's denial to Lumumba of the use of the radio station and airports provoked Guinea, Ghana, and the United Arab Republic to threaten a withdrawal of their troops and claim a right to place them at Lumumba's disposal. This led the Secretary-General to elaborate the basic principles on which a composite UN force operated, as follows:

Were a national contingent to leave the United Nations Force, they would have to be regarded as foreign troops introduced into the Congo, and the Security Council would have to consider their continued presence in the Congo, as well as its consequences for the United Nations operation, in this light.[6]

This important circumscription of the conditions under which withdrawal could take place was further sharpened the following January when Morocco ordered its brigade to "cease to perform its functions" while remaining in the Congo. The Secretary-General insisted that it could remain only "as an integral part of the United Nations Force" and that any other position would be "untenable."[7] Morocco agreed to its troops remaining under the United Nations flag until repatriation could be arranged, "but if called upon to act against their conscience" they would "feel bound not to accept any decision contrary to the interests of the Congo and of legality."[8] The Secretary-General's own inimitable blend of legal argument, moral authority, and diplomacy in fact prevented most of these threatening checks ever being presented for actual payment, but even so he could not eliminate the enervating effect which they had on the United Nations operation. Whereas UNEF was a force united in a common acceptance of a clearcut task, ONUC

[6] Security Council *Official Records* (15th year), 896th meeting, September 9, 1960, p. 20.
[7] UN Document S/4668.
[8] *Ibid.*

for long periods at a time lacked any agreed purpose, indeed at certain periods was sharply divided within itself. Even if the disagreements of participating governments were not fully reflected in the behavior of their contingents, they could not but impair their full cooperation.

To speak of a "host government" in the context of the anarchy which prevailed for most of 1960 and 1961 in the Congo is to bring out how remote were the realities of the United Nations operation from the language of law and diplomacy in which it had to be clothed. Repeatedly ONUC has found itself not merely at odds but actually at blows with the agents of the government whom it was to "assist" and "consult with," to quote the language of repeated United Nations resolutions. Most of these incidents belong to that level of UN-Congolese relations which had more to do with bizarre bargaining and gang warfare than diplomacy, but some of them raised issues not only important at the time but having possible future significance for United Nations procedure and international law. This was conspicuously true of Kasavubu's attempts to impose impossible conditions on ONUC, particularly in connection with the use of the port of Matadi in March 1961. These led the Secretary-General to issue the following interpretation of their relations:

The relation between the United Nations and the Government of the Republic of the Congo is not merely a contractual relationship in which the Republic can impose its conditions as host State and thereby determine the circumstances under which the United Nations operates. It is rather a relationship governed by mandatory decisions of the Security Council. . . . Only the Security Council can decide on the discontinuance of the operation and . . . therefore conditions which, by their effect on the operation, would deprive it of its necessary basis, would require direct consideration of the Security Council. . . .[9]

Here, obviously, we have a potentially far-reaching modification of the 1956 doctrine requiring the consent of the host state as a necessary precondition of the presence of a United Nations force. Partly this reflects the shift in the source of the mandate from the General Assembly to the Security Council; partly it reflects the distinctive role of a United Nations force called in to provide internal aid as well as external protection.

✻   ✻   ✻   ✻   ✻   ✻   ✻

Any lessons which one may draw from these events while the Congo operation is still proceeding must be tentative. Even so, after two and a half years of ONUC something can be said.

First a *caveat*. It is often said that the Congo is *sui generis*. It certainly differs from any situation the United Nations has had to tackle before, but is it so different from what may arise in the future? As long as underdeveloped countries are in ferment and communist (or other) powers prefer subversion to open aggression, variations on the Congo theme are practically

[9] UN Document S/4389/Add.5.

bound to occur. No doubt also it is true that the United Nations is not designed to cope with such situations; as an international organization it is built on the assumption that viable states are the entities with which it has to deal. This palliates failure, but it cannot excuse inaction. Future Congos cannot be ignored simply because they were not dreamed of in the philosophy of San Francisco. This is not to say that the United Nations ought to get into every situation where internal breakdowns occur; if such crises can be settled without such intervention, so much the better. But if they threaten international peace and security, the United Nations cannot side-step them on any narrowly legalistic ground.

*   *   *   *   *   *   *

Certain other conclusions also follow. If one asks why, despite all its difficulties, ONUC has been able to function as well as it has, or—to concede everything to its critics—to function at all, the answers are threefold. First, because the West, and in particular the United States, has been willing to foot the financial bill. . . .

The second reason for ONUC's survival is the general willingness of most of the states variously described as "nonaligned," "neutralist," or the "fire brigades," to support the operation by their votes and often by their contributions. In this the role of the Afro-Asians has been crucial. . . .

This dependence has often seemed to be personified in their support of the Secretary-General and has even been ascribed to a personal confidence in Dag Hammarskjöld. But to see it entirely in these terms is to mistake the man for the institution. It is not by an accident of personality that the creation and functioning of UNEF and ONUC have been linked so closely with the office of the Secretary-General. It is because any sustained executive functions, however limited, can only be discharged in an organization like the United Nations by its Secretariat, a body which the Secretary-General at once leads and personifies. Only the Council and the Assembly are capable of authorizing a United Nations force, but if the history of Suez and the Congo demonstrates anything, it is that they are utterly incapable of running it. . . .

There is a logical connection between the Soviet opposition to ONUC and its advocacy of the "troika." An equivalent logic dictates that no future United Nations force is conceivable for which executive authority is not delegated to a Secretary-General willing and able to act when his "parliamentary" overlords are deadlocked. An advisory committee may abate his loneliness; it cannot relieve him of his responsibility and should not seek to curb his authority. If the office seems dangerously potent, as so developed by Dag Hammarskjöld and as apparently now operated by U Thant, the weapons of negation and frustration are at hand in the Security Council, the General Assembly and, behind both, in the financial deliberations of the

Fifth Committee. Those who wish to use them, however, should do so with a full awareness of the consequences. Nothing in the experience of Suez and the Congo suggests that an international force is exempt from the workings of the inexorable rule that he who wills the end must will the means as well.

POLITICAL CONDITIONS FOR AN INTERNATIONAL POLICE FORCE

Hans J. Morgenthau*

A police force, domestic or international, must meet two requirements: it must be reliable, and it must be effective. While obviously it cannot be effective if it is not reliable, it can be reliable without being effective, and it is for this reason that the two prerequisites must be distinguished. A police force, in order to be reliable, must be loyal to the political authorities and share their conceptions of law and justice. A police force, in order to be effective, must stand in a certain relation of power to that fraction of the population which is likely to call forth police action by breaking law.

The police within the state are the instrument of a central authority which is supposed be be endowed with a will culminating in decision, and it is these decisions that the police are called upon to put into practice. In legal terms the police have the function of enforcing the laws; in political terms they have the function of upholding the authority of the government; in social terms they have the function of protecting a status quo as defined by the laws and expressed in the government's policies. In a well-ordered society the police are but rarely called upon to enforce a change in the status quo; the enforcement of new race relations against groups committed to an outlawed status quo is a case in point in our society. In revolutionary societies, on the other hand, the police force is the main weapon with which a revolutionary minority imposes its will upon a recalcitrant population.

It follows that the police force will be reliable in the performance of its functions only if it has either forged [itself] into so disciplined an instrument

* Hans J. Morgenthau, "Political Conditions for an International Police Force," *International Organization*, Vol. 17, 1963, pp. 393–403. Copyright 1963, World Peace Foundation. By permission of *International Organization*.

Hans J. Morgenthau is Distinguished Professor of Political Science and Modern History at the University of Chicago and director of the Center for the Study of American Foreign Policy. He is the author of *Politics Among Nations, In Defense of the National Interest,* and numerous other works.

of the government's will that it will execute whatever orders it is given regardless of content, or else if its convictions and interests are at the very least not openly at odds with those of the government. Thus the police force, knowingly or without knowing it, is bound to be deeply involved in the political controversies of the society in which it operates.

Lenin maintained, correctly against his opponents within the Marxist camp, that the dictatorship of the proletariat could not afford to take over the enforcement agencies of its bourgeois predecessor and use them for its own purposes; forged for the purpose of maintaining the rule of an exploiting minority over the exploited majority, they could not be so used. Instead the proletariat had to create its own police, open and secret, appropriate to the special tasks of a new society. During certain periods of violent labor struggles in our society, the police force, regardless of the legal merits of the case, tended to enforce the law for the protection of members of racial minorities. In certain regions of the United States they have habitually used their power to deprive such members of their rights through positive action. During the crisis at the University of Mississippi in 1962, state and federal police tried to enforce incompatible legal rules and conceptions of justice. Wherever a society is rent by deeply felt controversies, even though they do not lead to open violence, the political preferences of the police are likely to color the performance of its function.

On a lower level of motivation the police, frequently individually and sometimes collectively, have yielded to the temptation of private gain and neglected to enforce the law against certain types of violations, of which traffic, gambling, vice, and housing code violations are outstanding. If this corruption occurs on a massive scale, the police may transfer their loyalty altogether from the legal government to another, private one in the form of a crime syndicate. The police in our society remain a reliable instrument of law enforcement because normally no more than an insignificant number of them will be opposed to the legal order they are called upon to enforce.

The reliable performance of its functions by the police force within the state is thus not a simple technical matter to be expected with mechanical precision. Quite the contrary, it depends upon political, social, and moral conditions which may or may not be present in individual members of the police or the police force as a whole. These conditions must be created and maintained through a continuous effort of the political authorities. In other words, the functioning of a police force depends not only upon its internal technical qualities, but also upon the political, social, and moral climate within which it operates. If the latter is not favorable, the former will avail little.

The effectiveness of a police force is determined, aside from its reliability, by the power relation that exists between itself and the recalcitrant fraction of the population. For the police to be effective, that power relation must meet three prerequisites.

Of all the citizens of a particular society only a very small fraction must be engaged at any one time in breaking the law. If large numbers of citizens simultaneously break the law, as they [have] with regard to gambling, the police force, although it meets the standards of reliability, ceases to be an effective agency of law enforcement. Second, however great the differences in power are within a given society, the combined power of law-abiding citizens must be distinctly superior to any combination of even the most powerful lawbreakers. If it is otherwise, as in the case of the medieval feudal lord and his modern counterpart in the form of private concentrations of economic power, the police are bound to be almost as impotent as the citizenry at large. Finally, the police force must be manifestly capable of coping effectively with all foreseeable threats to the legal order. This obvious capability serves to deter attacks upon the legal order that go beyond the piecemeal violations of individual legal rules. In other words, its visible readiness for effective action makes its actual employment in good measure unnecessary.

This quality of unchallengeable superiority, aside from being the result of the reputation for reliability, is a function of the two other prerequisites. In consequence the government is able to rely upon a numerically small and lightly armed police force to maintain law and order. In the absence of these prerequisites the state would need a numerous and heavily armed police force in order to meet frontal attacks upon the legal order itself. That is to say, the state would need an army rather than a police force, and the relations between government and people would be tantamount either to civil war or a military dictatorship.

In sum, then, our fundamental proposition is that the problems with which an international police force must come to terms are posed by the peculiar character of the international society since that character affects both the reliability and effectiveness of the force.

✻   ✻   ✻   ✻   ✻   ✻   ✻

The reliability of an international police force is a function of the legal order and the political status quo it is called upon to uphold. Yet the enforcement of an international legal order and the protection of an international status quo present a police force with problems quite different from those the national police has to solve. Great international conflicts which lead to the violation of international law and conjure up the danger of war and therefore call for the intervention of an international police force are typically the ones in which the survival of the existing order and of the political status quo is at stake. The task which the international police force must here perform is not the defense of the legal order and of the political status quo against piecemeal violations, but against an all-out attack. What is at stake here is not the enforcement of a particular legal rule, but the survival of the legal order itself.

✻   ✻   ✻   ✻   ✻   ✻   ✻

What distinguishes an international police force from a national one is, then, the lack of an automatic commitment to a particular legal order and political status quo. Such a commitment can be taken for granted, at least normally and except for piecemeal or marginal deviations, in a national police force. It cannot be taken for granted in an international one, but must there be created and re-created and maintained for each issue. The task an international organization faces in fashioning a police force for a particular issue parellels that of a group of nations seeking political and military support for a particular status quo. The international police forces which have been organized by the United Nations have reflected both the composition and the political and military character of the two-thirds majorities of the General Assembly to which they owed their existence. That is to say, no nation which did not support the police action by its vote in the Security Council or General Assembly supplied contingents for the police force, and of those who so supported it only a small minority supplied contingents. The contributions of these nations were a manifestation of their political interests and military capabilities.

*   *   *   *   *   *   *

This situation would not be materially affected by arms control or limited disarmament. At best the control and limitation of national armaments might increase the effectiveness of an international police force in conflicts among major powers, provided that the stabilization and decrease of national armed forces were to go hand in hand with a corresponding increase in the strength of the international police force. Without the latter proviso, arms control and disarmament might well have an adverse effect upon the effectiveness of an international police force; for they might adversely affect the ability and willingness of national governments to put armed forces at the disposal of an international organization. The best that can be expected from arms control and limited disarmament is a change in the distribution of armed strength between national forces and the international police force in favor of the latter. But the basic political issue bearing upon the reliability of an international police force will continue to make itself felt even in a partially disarmed world; for such a world would still be a world of sovereign nations.

The situation would be radically different in a totally disarmed world. Total disarmament can no more be envisaged in isolation from the over-all structure of international relations than can an international police force. Total disarmament requires as its corollary the existence of a supranational authority capable of committing organized force to the defense of the legal order and the political status quo. In other words, total disarmament and world government go hand in hand. They complement each other. In a totally disarmed world the problem of an international police force ceases to exist and reappears in the form—new in its dimensions and old in its substance—of the police of a world government.

CHAPTER 14

PEACEFUL
CHANGE

The concern for the various aspects of peaceful change is one of the most important differences between the United Nations and the League of Nations. This is not to say that some of the interests or programs presently associated with the UN were not in evidence before. But certainly the great emphasis placed on economic and social needs in the present UN had no counterpart in earlier experiments in international affairs. This observation can be made a fortiori with regard to human rights.

In an excerpt here from a very extensive study, "Human Rights in the United Nations," by Myres S. McDougal and Gerhard Bebr, the UN programs are traced to their historical antecedents. McDougal and Bebr put forth as axiomatic the need for all peoples to have as a part of their cultural milieu the same minimal standards of human rights and security. Despite this they conclude that our present international society is not characterized so much by cooperative efforts to achieve those minimal needs as it is by tendencies to divide into opposing garrisoned blocs. The authors trace the effort to develop a UN human rights program and discuss the meaning of the Universal Declaration of Human Rights and the Genocide Convention, pointing out the difference in legal status of these two documents. In most of the rest of the article, much of which has had to be omitted here for lack of space, McDougal and Bebr deal with the proposed Covenant on Civil and Political Rights and the proposed Covenant on Economic, Social, and Cultural Rights, and the problems of their enforcement. They are frank to acknowledge the difficulties of enforcement and suggest that the greatest help in the problem will come from investigations, reports, and recommendations "publicized for the sanction of world opinion." Is this too weak a reed to rely upon? Part of the answer to this question may be seen in the near future if the International Convention on the Elimination of all Forms of Racial Discrimination is ratified. It was unanimously adopted in the 20th session of the United Nations General Assembly, but the speed of ratification and the willingness of states to comply with the major provisions will be indicators of the importance which the elimination of racial discrimination holds for its signers. Certainly, significant changes have occurred in the public's acceptance of civil rights within the past three decades, but it is possible we have reached the point when the partial and evolutionary approach is no longer adequate and acceptable to those who demand change now in the name of justice and democracy.

Peaceful change has likewise been sought under other labels. To meet the increasing demands for greater security and well-being, governments have been pressured to provide social-welfare programs of many kinds for almost a century. But much of this development has taken place within the past 35 years and has been primarily in the Western-European, Anglo-Saxon, and Socialist countries. In much of the "Tiers-monde," struggles for social and economic improvement have only a very recent history with very limited results. It is, therefore, very understandable that to such countries the United Nations stands for something quite different, in the main, from what it does to many of its original members.

To reveal both the nature of the difficulties and the efforts to reduce the many problems that beset much of mankind, we have included one excerpt from a document of the Economic and Social Council, one from a document of the Department of Economic and Social Affairs, one from a report by the Secretary-General, and an article by George Woods, "The Development Decade in Balance."

Our excerpt, "Recent Social Trends," was taken from a 1966 ECOSOC study, "Report on the World Social Situation." This report clearly indicates the unevenness of development in the 1960's, with gains in education, food production, and health, but with many of these gains cancelled by alarming increases in population and unemployment. The report points out the specific obstacles which have acted as deterrents to development, for ex-

ample, the instability of world markets and the excessive concentration of wealth within many countries.

In the study by the Department of Economic and Social Affairs, "Five-Year Perspective, 1960–1964," from which we took "Economic Development and Social Change," stress is placed on the interrelationship of economic and social factors as shown in the effect of the relative decline in food resources during a time of increasing demands for consumer goods and hopes for urban employment. These pressures interact in such a way as to create tremendous problems of unemployment, inadequate housing, poor sanitation, and unstable family conditions with consequent increases in crime. And efforts to overcome these difficulties through industrialization tend, initally, to increase them. Furthermore, the costs of overcoming the problems of illiteracy, poor health, and grossly inadequate housing are much more than the countries involved are capable of meeting.

Some of the experience gained from the industrialization efforts in the advanced capitalist countries of the West have taught us what to avoid. Furthermore, it is clear, as the report points out, that "in the process of change old institutions and methods of handling social problems will be lost before new ones can be established to replace them."

The tremendous burden of illiteracy reflects the great difficulty in knowing where to begin with many of these problems. For example, teachers are badly needed and to avoid unnecessary obstacles established leaders' positions often need to be supported. But the latter are not always willing to submit to the task of being put through a formal learning program, and, in any case, learning does not come easily at an older age. If, however, the emphasis on education is on that younger age group, who are more amenable to learning, the time lag before they are able to utilize that training and benefit society is very great. But concentration on the older generation means the younger one may have its learning potential seriously limited.

In the Secretary-General's Report, "Reappraisal of the Role of the Social Commission," from which our excerpt is "United Nations Operational Programmes in the Social Field," the Secretary-General provides a brief survey of the magnitude of resources available for economic and social progress. He points out one of the interesting innovations in financing community-development programs—the use of food through the World Food Program—and finds that the program is an incentive to groups to help in local projects and neighborhood improvement efforts. As a matter of fact, one gains through this report an appreciation of the great variety of the forms of assistance the UN provides. And the emphasis on regional approaches is again brought out very clearly.

George Woods, President of the International Bank for Reconstruction and Development, in a succinct study, "The Development Decade in the Balance," delineates very sharply the reasons for the increasing economic gaps between the poor and the rich nations. The twentieth century is here for some nations, but for others, struggling to get a foothold in technological and *scientific development, the twentieth century is yet to arrive. The Development Decade was designed to help meet this growing need and to offset the growing gap. But, despite its good beginning, it has not done so. As a matter of fact, the picture has grown so bleak that it is a wonder that antagonism between North and South is not greater. Fortunately, however, social values have clearly begun to change so that now, in contrast to earlier years, many people, associations, and nations assume they have a responsibility to aid in the alleviation of impoverished conditions. This attitude continues to have a leavening effect within the UN. The number of institutions created to administer to these needs has grown considerably since 1945, the newest being the UN Trade and Development Board, established in 1964 at a conference concerned with commodity problems and the international flow of capital. The problem of debt management and improved agricultural production continues to plague much of the underdeveloped world, and in Woods' opinion the conditions of the developed countries are such that the richer countries ought to greatly increase their contributions to these programs.*

Should we be satisfied with functional programs merely on the basis of reducing or wiping out serious economic and social problems, or should we insist that to this gain be added an acknowledgment of the source from which the help came? If those receiving the aid are unaware of its true source, will loyalties become transferred, as the functionalists hope, from the state to the international organization when basic human benefits are seen to derive from sources other than the state? Perhaps the UN's position of not being concerned with such an issue is indeed a wise one, and yet can the institution really develop a meaningful hold in people's minds if they are unmindful of the work it is doing? This is not to say that these manifold activities are not intrinsically of great merit, but only to raise the question of one of the assumptions and expectations associated with functionalism.

In his historical study, "The Trusteeship System of the United Nations (1945–1960)," J. W. Brügel, the author of the sixth selection in this chapter, points to the many changes that have occurred in attitudes on colonialism. From a position favoring colonialism before World War I, many people shifted to the idea of international trusteeship in the post-World War I period, and eventually to a belief that peoples in trusteeships should be aided in obtaining their independence as quickly as possible. Brügel discusses the different grades of League Mandates and compares them to the UN's trusteeships, all of which have had the same classification except for the United States' Strategic Trusteeship in the Pacific.

Here again we note the important changes which have developed and which may be defined as indications of greater responsibility toward the conditions of life of other peoples. This has been generally true in all the Trusteeships with the obvious exception of South Africa, which has refused to cooperate with the Trusteeship Council.

Perhaps this broad acceptance should be attributed in large part to the constitutional composition of the Council, which has contained an equal number of states without trusts to administer and states with trusts. But it also should be credited to the energy of the General Assembly's Fourth Committee, which has exercised its jurisdiction over the administration of Trusts very zealously. And finally one must note that the right to receive petitions and petitioners was certain to make the trusteeship concept a more noble one, but its operation a more difficult and more limited one in length of time. The success it has had has considerably enhanced the prestige of the undertaking.

To credit the UN alone with the achievement of independence of the many trust areas and colonies which are now sovereign states would be giving the Organization more credit than it is due. But certainly the pressures came from within the UN as well as without, and as its ranks were swelled by these new members such interests and demands were increased. What has been the reaction of the older members to this phenomenon? Has the difference in viewpoint between the anti-colonialists and those who tolerated or supported colonialism increased or diminished as a result of these changes? This has been the subject of inquiry by Edward T. Rowe in "The Emerging Anti-Colonial Consensus in the United Nations." Rowe has carried out his investigation on an empirical basis by examining voting records over a number of years on relevant issues. Unfortunately, this very fine statistical analysis has, because of space limitations, had to be eliminated and only the conclusions are presented here. But these conclusions are important as an aid to understanding the views of a large number of members on the need to end colonialism. However, the consensus on this issue which Rowe reports has significance, it would seem, beyond this. The interpretation that one could draw regarding the UN in general is that as increasing demands are made to reach agreement on issues for which strong moral cases can be made, opposition on the issues tends to disappear rather than to become entrenched, thereby helping not only to resolve the problems but also to strengthen the Organization.

FURTHER READINGS

Hagras, Kamal M., *United Nations Conference on Trade and Development.* New York: Frederick A. Praeger, Inc., 1966.

Murray, James N., Jr., *The United Nations Trusteeship System.* Urbana: University of Illinois Press, 1959.

HUMAN RIGHTS IN THE UNITED NATIONS

Myres S. McDougal and Gerhard Bebr[*]

For its goals the United Nations program is heir to all the great historic movements for man's freedom (including the English, American, and French revolutions and the events they set in train), to the enduring elements in the tradition of natural law and natural rights and in most of the world's great religions and philosophies, and to the findings of contemporary science about the interrelations of simple respect for human dignity and all other individual and community values. It is familiar history how rudimentary demands for freedom from despotic executive tyranny have gradually been transformed into demands for, and provision of, protection against not only the executive but all institutions or functions of government and even private oppression, and how early demands for the barest "civil liberties," embodied in the most primitive conception of rule by "law," have burgeoned into insistence upon comprehensive "human rights"—that is, into demands for effective participation in all community value processes upon which minimum civil liberties depend. This history can be traced in the changing relation of the individual to the state, from the absolutist state through the liberal or "laissez-faire" state to the emerging conception of political organization as an instrument of all values, with government of, by, and for all people. From demands for physical security and inviolability of the person, with freedom from cruel and inhuman punishment and arbitrary detention, may be noted a progression to demands for freedom of expression and opinion, of conscience and worship, and of meeting and association. With the impact of industrialization, large-scale concentration of economic power, and urbanization, and the attendant ills of exploitation, unemployment, and inadequate housing, medical care, education, and so on, came not unnaturally demands for improved working and health conditions, fair and adequate wages, access to education and skill acquisition, and protection against the hazards of sickness, unemployment, old age, and the like. Today the recognition is

[*] Myres S. McDougal and Gerhard Bebr, "Human Rights in the United Nations," *American Journal of International Law*, Vol. 58, 1964, pp. 603–641. Copyright © 1964 by the American Society of International Law. By permission of the *American Journal of International Law*.

Myres S. McDougal is Sterling Professor of Law at Yale University School of Law and a member of the board of editors of the *American Journal of International Law*. He is an associate author of *Studies in World Public Order*.

Gerhard Bebr was formerly a lecturer in law at Yale University School of Law. He is a frequent contributor to the *American Journal of International Law*.

general, and demands are made accordingly, that "liberty" requires "the ordering of social and economic conditions by governmental authority."

It is in response to the ever increasing demands of people everywhere for greater access to, and wider sharing of, basic values, of the kind so impressionistically indicated above, that the United Nations program for human rights is being framed and implemented. For more systematic exposition and appraisal of the specific content of the United Nations formulations, these growing, common demands of people may be conveniently categorized in terms of certain particular values, as follows:

the wide sharing of *power*, both formal and effective, including participation in the processes of government and of parties and pressure groups and equality before the law;
the fundamental *respect* for human dignity which both precludes discriminations based on race, sex, color, religion, political opinion or other ground irrelevant to capacity and provides a positive recognition of common merit as a human being and special merit as an individual; the *enlightenment* by which rational decisions and other choices can be made, including freedom of inquiry, opinion, and communication;
equal and adequate access to *wealth* processes, to opportunities for work and to the resources and technology necessary to the production of goods and services for maintaining rising standards of living and comfort;
the opportunity to achieve health and *well-being*, and the inviolability of the person, with freedom from cruel and inhuman punishments and positive opportunity for the development of talents and enrichment of personality;
opportunity for the acquisition of the *skill* necessary to express talent and to achieve individual and community values to the fullest;
opportunity for *affection*, fraternity, and congenial personal relationships in groups freely choosen;
freedom to choose standards of *rectitude* and responsibility, to explain life, the universe, and values, and to worship as may seem best;
and, in sum, a *security* which includes not merely freedom from violence and threats of violence, but also full opportunity to preserve and increase all values by peaceful, non-coercive procedures.

Though it is for these values that men have long framed constitutions, established and administered governments, and sought an appropriate formulation of principle and balancing of power, the United Nations program seeks to extend this effort to more people, in a vaster area, at higher levels of authority, and "with a grander vision and on a more comprehensive scale" than hitherto attempted.

CONDITIONS UNDER WHICH THE UNITED NATIONS SEEKS ITS GOALS

The conditions under which the United Nations seeks its human rights goals may be described most generally in terms of two trends of contradictory impact: the first and most comprehensive trend is that toward an ever tightening global interdependence of all peoples in securing their basic values, and it is the increasing recognition by peoples of this interdependence that is the dynamic and integrating stimulus behind the human rights program; the interfering trend is that toward the relative bipolarization—or perhaps, more recently, tripolarization—of the world's power structures, which, with its rising crisis in security and continuously more imminent portents of violence, increases the unwillingness of active decision-makers in nation states to loosen controls over individuals and, hence, threatens the whole human rights program, as well as most of man's values and institutions, with disaster.

The major outlines of peoples' contemporary interdependences are only too clear. More than 150 years ago Kant wrote:

The intercourse, more or less close which has been steadily increasing between the nations of the earth, has now extended so enormously that a violation of the right in one of the parts of the world is felt all over it.[1]

Today accelerating changes in technology, in population growth, in the demands and identifications of peoples, and in techniques of organization multiply by many times the intensity of this interdependence. In an earth-space arena of ever increasing dimensions and of hydrogen and atomic bombs, as well, perhaps, as of other new instruments of unimaginable destructiveness, it needs little emphasis that no people can be secure—even in the minimal sense of freedom from violence and threats of violence—unless all peoples are secure. . . . Most broadly and rationally conceived, the "human rights" and "security" of any people and all peoples may in fact be said to be not merely "interdependent" but identical; the different words are but alternative ways of describing the same aspirations and interrelations of people.

It is not, however, rational co-operation in the peaceful pursuit of interdependent values, but rather the trend toward bipolarization or tripolarization, and contending systems of public order with nation states organizing themselves into "garrisoned camps," that today most conspicuously dominate the world arena. The growth of great power blocs, with several of the dominant Powers insisting upon the inevitability of world dominion by totalitarian measures, the destructive potentialities of the newly developed weapons, and the continued incidence in many parts of the world of ignorance, disease, poverty, and exploitation, with their attendant political instabilities, all combine to create general expectations of rising insecurities and more comprehensive violence. These expectations of imminent violence both increase the ordinary difficulties in co-operation between nation states and facilitate processes within nation states deeply inimical to human rights. As lines between probable combatants are more and more sharply drawn, proposals for co-operation between nation states for the promotion of

[1] Kant, *Perpetual Peace* 142 (Smith ed., 1917).

"human rights" or "security" or any other value are appraised in terms, not of possible long-range effects in an ever receding peaceful world, but rather of immediate impact on fighting effectiveness. . . . In this context it is small wonder that the United Nations' human rights program exhibits some of the symptoms of incipient paralysis.

❊   ❊   ❊   ❊   ❊   ❊   ❊

THE ORIGINS AND SCOPE OF THE UNITED NATIONS PROGRAM

International co-operation in the days of the League of Nations produced no comprehensive program for the protection of human rights. The emphasis in President Wilson's Fourteen Points, in the 1919 Peace Treaties, and in the "Minorities Treaties" was not upon the rights of individuals but upon the rights of nations and of minority groups within nations. The principal emphasis upon the rights of individuals was in the Japanese proposal to the Peace Conference, a proposal subsequently rejected, for equality of treatment of aliens. An elementary international protection to individuals was offered by the Minority Treaties—especially the important German-Polish Convention concerning Upper Silesia—but this protection was achieved only through identification with a national minority group.

Stimulated by the mounting evidences of a new barbarism and by the need to clarify war aims, Allied official pronouncements and declarations began, however, early in World War II unmistakably to emphasize the individual and his rights. In his famous "Four Freedoms" speech to the United States Congress on January 6, 1941, President Roosevelt included freedom from want and freedom from fear, along with freedoms of expression and of worship, in "four essential human freedoms" upon which world order should be founded, and his broad conception of human liberties was later confirmed, in the Atlantic Charter and in the Declaration by the United Nations, as embodying specific war and peace aims. . . .

The United Nations Charter explicitly recognizes that the maintenance of "international peace and security" and the protection of human rights are today interdependent, if not identical, purposes; announces the promotion of human rights as one of the major aims of the new organization; and imposes upon both Member states and the organization a clear legal obligation to promote the increased protection of human rights. This structure of purpose and obligation is outlined in various provisions of the Charter. In the Preamble, the "peoples of the United Nations," not merely the Member states, reaffirm their "faith in fundamental human rights" and "in the dignity and worth of the human person." Article 1 includes among stated purposes the achievement of

international cooperation in solving international problems of an economic, social, cultural, or humanitarian character, and in promoting and encouraging respect for human rights and for fundamental freedoms for all without distinction as to race, sex, language, or religion.

Article 13 orders the General Assembly to "initiate studies and make recommendations" for the purpose of

promoting international cooperation in the economic, social, cultural, educational, and health fields, and assisting in the realization of human rights and fundamental freedoms for all without distinction as to race, sex, language or opinion.

Article 55, seeking "the creation of conditions of stability and well-being which are necessary for peaceful and friendly relations among nations," includes among the purposes of "international economic and social co-operation" the promotion of "universal respect for, and observance of, human rights and fundamental freedoms for all without distinction as to race, sex, language, or religion"; and in Article 56

All Members pledge themselves to take joint and separate action in cooperation with the organization for the achievement of the purposes set forth in Article 55.

Article 62 empowers the Economic and Social Council to "make recommendations for the purpose of promoting respect for, and observance of, human rights and fundamental freedoms for all," and Article 68 orders the Council to "set up commissions in economic and social fields and for the promotion of human rights." Article 76 stipulates that "basic objectives" of the international trusteeship system are, *inter alia,* "to encourage respect for human rights and for fundamental freedoms for all" and, it is worth note, "to encourage recognition of the interdependence of the peoples of the world." . . .

The first major implementation of the Charter provisions came with the Universal Declaration of Human Rights, drafted after two years of study by the Commission on Human Rights established under Article 68 of the Charter by the Economic and Social Council, and approved, without dissenting vote, by the General Assembly on December 10, 1948. This Declaration was not designed or proposed as an enforceable treaty obligation, but rather as a broad clarification and recommendation of policy. It was intended, as the General Assembly proclaimed it,

as a common standard of achievement for all peoples and all nations, to the end that every individual and every organ of society, keeping this Declaration constantly in mind, shall strive by teaching and education to promote respect for these rights and freedoms and by progressive measures, national and international, to secure their universal and effective recognition and observance, both among the peoples of member states themselves and among the peoples of territories under their jurisdiction.

The rights stipulated in the Declaration are most comprehensive. They include, among many items, not only provision for equality of treatment with respect to all rights and freedoms set forth in the Declaration, "without distinction of any kind, such as race, colour, sex, language, religion, political or other opinion, national or social origin, property, birth or other status," and the traditional personal liberties such as freedom and security of person, right to a fair trial, and freedom of thought, expression, opinion, religion, assembly, association, and movement, but also certain more recently emerging political, economic, and social claims, such as those to nationality and freedom to change nationality, to asylum from persecution, to take part in government and to have equal access to public service, to social security and choice of employment, and to education, leisure, participation in cultural life, and an adequate standard of living. Despite its lack of status as enforceable treaty obligation or even as "authoritative interpretation" of such obligation, and despite the imprecision of some of its language, this Declaration has, because of its authoritative community origin and eloquent formulation of the growing common demands of peoples throughout the world, exercised an important influence on subsequent decision-making and prescribing in many world arenas. Its future influence may, because of the increasing importance of General Assembly resolutions as a source of customary law, be even greater.

The Genocide Convention, drafted by a special *ad hoc* committee and revised and approved by the General Assembly on December 9, 1948, should also perhaps be regarded as a measure in implementation of the human rights provisions of the Charter. This convention was designed as enforceable treaty obligation after 20 ratifications, and became operative on January 12, 1951, though the major Powers have been slow to ratify. Framed to complement the Nuremberg verdict, which restricted "crimes against humanity" to "inhumane acts, in connection with the planning or waging of aggressive war,"[2] the Genocide Convention makes the intentional destruction "in whole or part" of "a national, ethnical, racial, or religious group as such" an international crime. Acts which constitute genocide include "killing members of the group," "causing serious bodily or mental harm to members of the group," "deliberately inflicting on the group conditions of life calculated to bring about its physical destruction in whole or in part," "imposing measures intended to prevent births within the group," and "forcibly transferring children of the group to another group. . . . For enforcement, the contracting parties undertake to enact necessary domestic legislation and to provide effective penalties, with trial before

a competent tribunal of the State in the territory of which the act was committed, or by such international penal tribunal as may have jurisdiction with respect to those Contracting Parties which shall have accepted its jurisdiction.

The most important measures yet projected in the fulfillment of the Charter provisions are, however, the two proposed Covenants, one on Civil

[2] Office of United States Chief of Counsel of Prosecution of Axis Criminality, Nazi Conspiracy and Aggression, Opinion and Judgment (1947); 41 A.J.I.L. 172 (1947).

and Political Rights and the other on Economic, Social, and Cultural Rights, designed as comprehensive definition in the form of treaty obligation of the principal human rights with respect to which Member states are today willing to permit and undertake appropriate international implementation. . . .

The original plan was for a single Covenant on Human Rights, but in ordering two separate covenants the General Assembly recognized that there are many fundamental differences between traditional civil and political rights and the newly emerging claims to economic, social, and cultural benefits—differences in the degree of precision with which definitions and standards can be formulated, differences in appropriate modes of implementation, ranging from judicial enforcement and general legislation through many forms of community and private action, and differences in the resources available and time required for achievement of specified standards.

*   *   *   *   *   *   *

Throughout both Covenants runs explicit recognition that the protection of human rights is "the foundation of freedom, justice, and peace in the world," and taken in sum, despite all omissions and ambiguities, it is obvious that the two Covenants represent a most substantial achievement in prescribing, for implementation by appropriate national and international authority, both new protection for individual human rights and the general conditions of a free, peaceful, and abundant world society.[3]

ENFORCEMENT MEASURES PROPOSED

The most difficult problem still confronting the framers of the United Nations' human rights program is that of devising effective procedures for enforcement. Since the two Covenants are designed as treaty obligations and contain express promises by the parties to enact all necessary legislation and take other appropriate measures to secure the stipulated rights, any failures in performance that can be proved will of course make available to the other parties to the Covenants all the sanctions that are ordinarily available for violation of treaty obligation. The representatives of the Soviet Union and its satellites have contended from the beginning that no

---

[3] Certainly the completion and ratification of the two Covenants, as presently proposed, by the nation-states of the world could not rationally be construed to worsen such conditions. Both Covenants provide that no provision "may be interpreted as implying for any state, group or person any right to engage in any activity or perform any act aimed at the destruction of any of the rights and freedoms recognized herein or at their limitation to a greater extent than is provided for in this Covenant," and that there shall be "no restriction upon or derogation from any of the fundamental human rights recognized or existing in any contracting state pursuant to law, conventions, regulations or custom on the pretext that the present Covenant does not recognize such rights or that it recognizes them to a lesser extent." See Art. 5 of both Covenants.

other measures of enforcement are needed or admissible, and that the establishment of any special international machinery for the implementation of human rights prescriptions would be an invasion of the "domestic jurisdiction" and "sovereignty" of nation states. The other Members of the United Nations have, however, rejected this argument and many proposals have been made for new machinery of implementation.

With respect to the Covenant on Economic, Social and Cultural Rights, early proposals reflected the general expectation that, since achievement is to be "progressive" over a period of time, implementation will be sought, not by complaints and hearings, but rather by an elaborate series of reports and comments, with performance being sanctioned by the attendant publicity. Provisions to this effect were included in Articles 17–25 of the draft Covenant as finally submitted for approval in 1954 by the Commission on Human Rights to the Third Committee of the General Assembly.

With respect to the Covenant on Civil and Political Rights, the proposals made involve a more radical break with traditional reliance upon the initiative of nation states, and include provision for complaints, investigation, hearings, and agreement to abide by decisions in particular instances of international authority. A brief survey of the various proposals reveals a gradual shift in attitude from emphasis upon negotiation and conciliation to more realistic conceptions which recognize the individual human being as a formal "subject" of international law as well as an effective participant in the world power process, and seek to confer upon him the competency effectively to claim his own rights.

＊   ＊   ＊   ＊   ＊   ＊   ＊

Of the various enforcement proposals, . . . the least satisfactory one, which confines the proposed Human Rights Committee largely to the function of "good offices" between contending nation states, was, with a few changes, incorporated in Articles 27–48 of the draft Covenant as finally adopted by the Commission. The proposed Committee, deprived of the authority to receive petitions from individuals and from non-governmental organizations, could scarcely be expected to achieve an effective enforcement of human rights.

＊   ＊   ＊   ＊   ＊   ＊   ＊

It needs no emphasis that the difficulties inherent in the problem of enforcement will not be easily resolved. The establishment of effective procedures would mean substantial changes in the distribution of power between Member states and the United Nations, and, within Member states, between active decision-makers and the individual human being. Changes of such magnitude are seldom quickly achieved, as is further evidenced by the United States policy announced in 1953, that it does not intend to become a party to the proposed draft Covenants or to any other conventions on human rights. The maintenance of this position by one of the world's most powerful and influential nations has tended to diminish the enthusiasm and hopefulness with which delegates of other nations have approached the task of drafting the two Covenants and has resulted in the United States' relatively passive rôle in the discussion of the Covenants and its general policy of abstention from voting on the articles.

It should be noted, however, that, simultaneously with this announcement, the United States delegates proposed to the Commission on Human Rights that it undertake three new major activities. This proposal was later adopted by resolutions of the Economic and Social Council and approved in part by the General Assembly, thus establishing three new programs, which has added a different and important dimension to the United Nations' work on human rights. The first of these provides for triennial reports by Member states to provide the Commission with information as to the progress achieved and the difficulties encountered in each country in the matter of human rights. The second program entails a series of comprehensive global studies of specific rights enumerated in the Universal Declaration of Human Rights. The third and perhaps most successful of the new programs established advisory services for the implementation of human rights. The services offered take essentially three different forms: the organization of seminars on various specific human rights; the provision of expert advice for countries which request aid in the solution of problems involving human rights; and provision of fellowships for responsible representatives of countries to visit other member countries for the purpose of studying the techniques used there for the protection of human rights.

❖   ❖   ❖   ❖   ❖   ❖   ❖

CONCLUSION

As grand as is the vision which inspires the United Nations human rights program and as indispensable as such vision may be to the achievement of a free, peaceful, and abundant world society, it is improbable in the present world context of bipolarized and other bloc power and of imminent expectations of violence, that startling new progress can be quickly effected on a global scale either in the acceptance of new authoritative prescriptions about human rights or in the establishment of workable enforcement measures. The degree to which Universal Declaration of Human Rights, with its broad prescriptions of the essential rights of a free society has captured the loyalties and imagination of peoples and decision-makers offers, however, a certain opportunity. Persuasive argument has been made that the early decision that the existing Commission on Human Rights is not authorized to act upon specific complaints from individuals and groups not only is not required by the provisions of the United Nations Charter but is even in contravention of such provisions. This decision could be reversed by the General Assembly. The Commission on Human Rights might then hear some, or as many as possible, of the numerous complaints submitted to it each year, investigate the complaints to the extent it can or that the offending state will permit, and make recommendations in terms of the policies described in the Universal Declaration. The cumulative impact of a series of investigations and recommendations, publicized for the sanction of world opinion and any other sanctions that may eventually be made available, might not be wholly without effect, and certainly such activity could serve only to enhance the loyalties of freedom-demanding peoples to the Organization.

RECENT SOCIAL TRENDS*

Judged by growth in national income, the performance of the developing countries as a whole would appear to have declined in the early 1960's.[1] National income is admittedly but a crude indicator of social progress partly because of shortcomings in the method of computation itself and partly because of the number of important aspects of development, especially social aspects, that are not adequately reflected by it. But the general picture it gives is supported by other available data, including the most recent data on the world labour situation, which show a further improvement in the industrialized countries in 1965 but a continued lack of progress in the developing countries.[2] In most industrialized countries, unemployment has declined or has been stabilized at extremely low figures so that, in general, it has ceased to be a serious problem in these countries except for certain categories of persons, especially older workers displaced by sectoral declines or technological changes; rises in money wages have generally exceeded rises in consumer prices. In the developing countries, on the other hand, the figures, while incomplete, agree in showing hardly any improvement: the level of unemployment and under-employment remains high, employment

* United Nations Economic and Social Council, Social Commission, 17th Session, "Report on the World Social Situation." E/CN.5/402, February 28, 1966, pp. 1–14.

[1] The growth in developing countries as a whole slowed down from an average annual rate of 4.5 per cent in 1955–1960 to 4 per cent in 1960–1963. See document E/4059 on trends in world production and trade. The average annual *per capita* income increased by only about $5 in the developing countries between 1960 and 1962, but by almost $100 in the developed market economies (E/4071, p. 4).

[2] See the 1965 edition of the ILO *Yearbook of Labour Statistics*. The conclusions stated here are derived from an ILO analysis of the statistics collected for that publication.

possibilities are far from sufficient to absorb excess man power, and in certain cases there have been substantial increases in the cost of consumer goods.

A similar picture is found in agriculture, especially food production. Thus, in most of the developing world, domestic food production in recent years has either failed to keep pace with, or has only barely exceeded, the growth in population. Preliminary estimates prepared by the Food and Agriculture Organization show the production of food per person in 1964–1965 exceeded the average for the years 1952/53–1956/57 by 14 per cent in the developed countries but by only 1 per cent in the developing lands.[3] Merely to keep pace with the expected world population increase without any improvement in diets would require total food supplies to be almost doubled by the year 2000, but present dietary levels in the developing countries are so inadequate that actual needs for expansion are far greater than this.

A detailed analysis will reveal—as noted in previous reports on the world social situation—that there are significantly different rates of growth in different parts of the developing world and in different sectors of development. The picture thus presented contains both light and shadow; some sectors like education and health have continued to register impressive gains while others such as agriculture, employment and housing have tended to lag seriously behind expectations and requirements. Moreover, certain important innovations, such as changes in the school system, will require a comparatively long period in which to have their full impact upon the development process.

Yet it is an inescapable fact that, in spite of national and international efforts, the rate of progress in the low-income countries in recent years has been a disappointment. Compared with hopes and expectations, the effort at development has been a failure, though not a complete failure. The discrepancy between the aspiration and the reality is perhaps due in part to an exaggerated and unrealistic aspiration; but primarily it raises the question whether the development efforts, both national and international, have been sufficient—and in the right direction.

OBSTACLES TO DEVELOPMENT

There are many different interpretations offered of the painfully slow progress of the developing countries towards the goal of improved living conditions. No single factor can be identified as the cause; the obstacles to development are multiple, complex, and inter-acting. The very adjustments in attitudes, institutions and ways of life that a society has made to its poverty constitute obstacles to the eradication of that poverty. Moreover,

[3] FAO *The State of Food and Agriculture 1965*, p. 15.

as frequently noted, the elements of a low standard of living—bad health, malnutrition, illiteracy, low income, etc.—act as forces that impede the raising of levels of living, each restraining progress in the others. The present report will not attempt a world-wide review of conditions in these separate social sectors, but it is appropriate at this point to call attention to certain other factors that appear as major obstacles to improvement of social conditions in developing countries.

Foreign trade and financing have been shown in recent years to be of crucial importance to the developing countries in affecting rates of economic and social progress. The uncertainty and instability of export incomes, the difficulty of access to developed markets, the structural bias of the world economy towards the interests of the industrialized wealthy countries, and the lessening dependence of the latter countries upon non-industrialized countries for various primary products—these are obstacles that constantly threaten the efforts of the developing nations to acquire the foreign exchange needed for economic growth and concomitant social progress. The situation has been complicated by a leveling off since 1961 in the flow of international assistance and capital to the developing countries, at least so far as public transfers from the advanced market economies are concerned.

Besides these external constraints, there are internal political and social realities that have limited the possibilities of growth. There is hardly a region of the world where urgent tasks of development have not had to be deferred or abandoned because of political instability or the prior claim of the military on resources. A number of Governments have been overthrown in recent years amid charges of corruption, misuse of public funds, and self-aggrandizement or group aggrandizement at the expense of national development. It cannot be assumed that a public political posture favouring development, even when backed by elaborate development plans and machinery, always has the necessary political will for development behind it. Nor can it be assumed that those with the political and economic power to innovate are necessarily interested in applying the resources of science and technology to the problems of development.

While it is now commonplace to stress the essential role played by institutional reforms in economic and social development, it is almost as common to observe the wide disparity between what is declared to be necessary and the reforms actually carried out—or carried out successfully. Restoration of sovereignty over natural resources, land tenure reform and redistribution of wealth are among the principal structural reforms cited as necessary not only to greater social equality but also to increased economic output. Yet in wide areas there has been perseverance of traditional social structures involving marked disparities of status and income and the absence of a dynamic or expanding mass consumption and accompanying social change. The concentration of wealth in relatively few hands is not regarded today even as an effective means of securing a high level of domestic private investment, in view of the prevalence of luxury consumption, transfer of funds abroad and investment in ways that contribute little or nothing to growth of production.[4]

Present policies in a number of developing countries call for tax reforms, including progressive income taxes, bringing a higher proportion of the large incomes into the public sector, where they may be used either for economic investment or for expansion of the high-priority social programmes. However, progressive income taxes have proved extremely difficult to collect, except for salaried employees.[5] For the most part, however, developing countries still rely heavily on indirect taxes for the financing of these measures, a form of taxation that tends to fall regressively on the lower-income groups. To the extent that this is true, the various social programmes so financed do not represent a form of income redistribution; they may even involve in practice a distribution of benefits away from the lowest-income groups (whose articles of consumption are taxed to support them), towards the relatively well-organized, better off and more articulate urban minorities that are able to take best advantage of the programmes. The chief beneficiaries of public housing expenditures, for example, are often public employees or relatively wealthy groups that can meet requirements regarding rentals, mortgage payments, etc.—rather than dwellers in shantytowns and rural and urban slums. Many governments have become sharply aware of the widespread social and economic inequalities which exist in their midst and current commitments call for the extension of public social action in a more equitable fashion to the whole population, including the rural masses and the urban marginal strata; measures to correct internal regional imbalances can also be found in some national development plans.

If progress in some of these fields has been less than might be desired, it should not be a matter of too great surprise, for what, in effect, is involved in some countries is the requirement that the people possessed of the major wealth, land and political power should pass and enforce laws that would appear to diminish their own power and influence, and this is not readily done.

[4] The way in which some countries use their potential economic surplus has been described as a principal obstacle to their rapid economic growth. "It [potential economic surplus] is absorbed by various forms of excess consumption of the upper class, by increments to hoards at home and abroad, by the maintenance of vast unproductive bureaucracies and of even more expensive and no less redundant military establishments." (Paul Baran, *Political Economics of Growth*, New York, 1957, p. 228.)

[5] A common explanation given by businessmen in some developing countries of their reluctance to pay high income taxes is that government bureaucracies are already overswollen with surplus employees who create numerous regulations and red tape to justify their jobs, but thereby impede business activity and may necessitate a heavy outflow in the way of bribes if the businessman is to carry through an undertaking.

Perhaps one of the most significant events in the past few years has been the world-wide attention given to the implications for development of accelerating population growth.[6] The precise nature of the interaction between population growth and development and the consequent implications for policy are still under debate, but it is clear that an increasing number of developing countries have become deeply concerned with the question how they can improve their living standards when a substantial increase is required in the national product each year merely in order to maintain existing standards. Meanwhile, within individual countries the massive movement of population from the countryside to the cities continues unabated with little prospect of employment for more than a fraction of the newcomers.

The high rates of population increase derive from the maintenance of very high levels of fertility combined with levels of mortality that have declined sharply since the 1940's.[7] General improvement in living conditions appears to be no longer a prerequisite for substantial reductions of high morbidity and mortality and, as a consequence, the mortality rate has lost much of its former validity as an index of a country's economic and social well-being. Since the Second World War, a number of developing countries have succeeded in reducing their previously high mortality primarily by the application of new technology, such as vector control and mass immunization, without commensurate progress in classical medical services, sanitation, education, level of living, etc. The achievements of the new technology

[6] Mid-1964 populations by region and their 1960–63 average annual rates of increase were as follows:

REGION	POPULATION (in millions)	ANNUAL RATE OF INCREASE (percentage)
Latin America	237	2.8
Africa	304	2.5
South Asia	943	2.4
Oceania	17	2.2
East Asia	840	1.4
Northern America	211	1.6
USSR	228	1.6
Europe	440	0.9

Countries in which the 1958–62 annual rates of population growth were at least 3 per cent include: Albania (3.2), Brazil (3.4), China (Taiwan) (3.6), Ecuador (3.2), Guatemala (3.2), Israel (3.5), Republic of Korea (3.3), Federation of Malaya (3.2), Mexico (3.1), Morocco (3.0), South Africa (3.2), Philippines (3.2), Thailand (3.0), and Venezuela (3.4). (United Nations Office of Public Information, Population Background Paper No. 1 (Rev.), August 1965, "World Population Trends.")

[7] Around 1960, gross reproduction rates averaged 2.6–2.7 and crude birth rates averaged 41–42 per 1,000 population for the developing regions. Corresponding averages for the more advanced regions were 1.4 and 22 per 1,000. There were no developed countries for which the gross reproduction rate exceeded 2.0 and no developing countries for which the rate was less than 2.0 (A/6101, Para. 8).

have been especially evident in the development of efficient methods of prevention and cure of certain communicable diseases (for example malaria and yellow fever) whereas others (tuberculosis and worm infections, for instance) have proved less amenable to mass control in the developing countries.[8] The different status of scientific knowledge in the various fields of health, as well as differences in the priorities accorded programmes by Governments, obviously has much to do with the relative effectiveness of these programmes; nevertheless, it is worth noting that in the case of some of the more intractable diseases a complex interplay of environmental factors, living conditions and personal habits and attitudes is involved in their prevention and treatment in addition to the technical problems posed.

Whereas the conditions necessary for a reduction in mortality and morbidity are relatively well known—if not always easy to implement—the factors determining fertility levels are subject to considerable uncertainty. There appears to be a general inverse association between fertility and the level of development, but it is also evident that the relationship is a complicated one and, as yet, not very well understood.

Uncertainty about the dynamics underlying the behaviour of fertility rates is matched by diversity of opinion regarding the appropriate population policies to be pursued. Not all countries are convinced of the necessity or desirability of public action to moderate population growth and argue that large-scale family planning programmes represent a diversion of scarce resources from the primary task of promoting development; it is suggested that fertility will decline of its own accord in response to accelerating urbanization, higher levels of employment, the spread of education, and improvements in the status of women, and that attempts to introduce family limitation in the absence of such economic and social changes will result in failure.

A number of Governments have affirmed the importance of national policies to limit births but have failed to follow through with the necessary measures or have implemented them in a very indifferent manner. Some countries have very active programmes but no explicit national policy. Since, in general, the countries that have the most severe population problems—arising from heavy pressure of existing population on land and resources—are already disposed towards family planning, or are

[8] See, for example, Social Progress Trust Fund, *Fourth Annual Report 1964*, p. 143. In a study of an urban tuberculosis control programme in India, for instance, it was found that whereas BCG vaccination had been shown to be applicable on a mass scale, the other principal tool in tuberculosis control—chemotherapy—"has yet to be shown to be operationally feasible on a mass scale." Only about one-third of the patients studied in the programme had been adequately dealt with, largely because of administrative and organizational shortcomings, in the opinion of the authors of the study. See D. Banerji and Stig Andersen, "A Sociological Inquiry into an Urban Tuberculosis Control Programme in India," in *Bulletin of the World Health Organization*, Vol. 29:5, 1963.

moving in that direction, questions of implementation and possibilities of innovations in contraceptive technology will play an important role in the future.[9]

For the coming decade, at least, population policy can hardly be a significant factor in easing the demand for more jobs, more houses, more food and more places in schools. In the meantime, policies intended to influence internal distribution of populations are likely to demand considerable attention.[10] In practically every region of the world urban population has been increasing at twice the rate of increase of total population, with most of this growth concentrated in the principal cities and metropolitan areas, some metropolitan areas having experienced annual rates of growth as high as 8 per cent. The serious social dislocation produced by this urban expansion in the form of unemployment, underemployment, housing shortages and inadequate public services, has often been described and the most recent information adds little to what has been said before. One of the more widely generalized consequences of the inability to absorb a rapidly growing labour force into the economy is the spread of various marginal makeshift ways of livelihood, both in the countryside and in the cities, and there is a serious danger that this "marginal" population will continue to grow, will become increasingly mobile and rootless in its search for a minimum livelihood, and that it will increasingly concentrate on the periphery of the larger cities where its numbers and greater opportunities of playing a political role will compel increasing public attention to its needs and demands.

The problem affects individuals of all ages, but the implications of such environments are especially grave for youth, whose numbers entering the labour force in the developing countries, as a result of population growth, are mounting at a rate substantially faster than urban industry can absorb— or is expected to absorb in the future under present plans and projections. A number of countries are attempting to cope with this problem through the recruitment of unemployed youth to serve for one or two years in various forms of service corps that undertake public works projects and may also offer instruction in literacy and vocational training. With some notable exceptions, however, these schemes have had only limited success as yet and, for the most part, are still hardly beyond the stage of discussion.

Side by side with the problem of surplus labour is that of scarcity of skills. This is universally observed to be a major obstacle to social progress in the developing countries. A large part of international assistance is concerned

[9] The problem is also being approached through indirect methods, such as raising the minimum age of marriage. One indirect approach that has been proposed is the formation of national development armies for public works and vocational training, which would recruit youths of both sexes between the ages of 17–25, the most prolific child-bearing years.

[10] The United Nations is initiating a research-training programme in regional development which will include special consideration of questions of population distribution and urbanization in the context of development.

with it. The labour that is surplus is either uneducated and unskilled or without the requisite skills (the "educated unemployed").

Chronic shortages of skilled manpower for economic and social development have helped to focus attention on the frequent lack of correspondence between the "output" of a country's educational system and the country's actual manpower needs. The result has been a concern to correct this imbalance through the systematic analysis of manpower needs and the planned adaptation of education and training programmes in order to meet the needs (or to create the capacity to meet them). In fact, human resources planning —as this activity has come to be known in its broader aspects—now occupies a position of central importance in the theory of development planning, though remaining something of a rarity in the actual development plans of countries.

In discussion [of] the problem of scarcity of skilled personnel, a distinction must be made between what a country "needs" in a general sense for its social progress and what it can—and will—in fact absorb under prevailing circumstances. Thus, there is no doubt that most developing countries need many more doctors and nurses to raise their level of health. But in a number of these countries, a sizable proportion of trained physicians—estimates range up to 50 per cent—emigrate and establish their practices in more developed countries where incomes and facilities are much better. A similar picture holds with regard to scientists, engineers, and other categories for whom an international market exists. If the home country meets the international level of income and facilities, then income inequality is further increased in the developing country.

A somewhat related problem exists with regard to rural-urban location within countries. Technicians, professional people and management personnel do not like to locate with their families in impoverished rural areas lacking adequate educational facilities, cultural facilities and other amenities, and in which they must either live at a relatively low-income level or be conspicuously different from the villagers. This kind of problem has proved to be an obstacle to decentralization of industry in some of the developing countries. Another aspect is the tendency of professional people like doctors to crowd the modern sector of the capital cities, to the point of unemployment, while in the countryside where needs are so great, services are sparse or lacking. This is another example of the way in which poverty perpetuates itself. While efforts have been made to deal with this problem— as through requirements of one or two years' rural service on the part of certain categories of professionals, especially if they received State assistance in their training—in general, it remains unsolved in most developing regions (as does the similar problem that the brightest and most ambitious young people in a backward rural area, who could contribute most to its future development, tend to be the first to leave it).

ECONOMIC DEVELOPMENT AND SOCIAL CHANGE
IN THE LESS DEVELOPED COUNTRIES*

Economic and social elements are closely interwoven and constantly inter-acting in the process of development. This is quite evident in the current phenomenon of urbanization in less developed countries. The pressure of population and the poverty of agriculture, together with the attraction of urban consumer goods and hopes for urban employment, have led in recent years to a tremendous migration from the countryside. Cities of under-developed countries are growing at a violent rate, with consequent difficulties in a number of fields—employment, housing, transportation, sanitation, family stability, juvenile delinquency, and others. The urban population has in fact generally grown faster than have industry and employment oppor-tunity. Improvement of this situation will depend upon the development of both agriculture and industry, as well as upon the organization of various social services and the introduction of physical planning to prevent a growth of slums and congestion that may otherwise prove irremediable in the future.

Industrialization itself requires far-reaching changes in the nature, quali-fications, and mode of life of the labour force, and in social institutions and attitudes. It may be held back by failure to achieve such changes; it may also push ahead and force certain changes upon a society that is unprepared to assimilate them. Some of the problems that accompanied the proletariza-tion of the labour force in the early stage of industrial development in Western Europe and North America are now being faced to a growing degree in Asia, Africa and Latin America. If a repetition of the worst experiences of industrialized countries is to be avoided, positive measures must be taken to achieve a better integration of economic and social development. One obvious need is for training and orientation of labour so that it may become adapted to the new situation. Another need is for the development of social institutions that will provide organized means of dealing with the problems in question.

It is now more widely recognized that the welfare of labour depends not only on the size of its share in the national product but also on the growth of that product—that is, upon an expanding economy. Economic development is thus a requirement for any substantial advance in labour welfare. The miserable wages or other income now received in the less developed countries would not be greatly improved if the total wealth were

* United Nations, Department of Economic and Social Affairs, "Five-Year Perspective, 1960–1964" (Geneva, 1960), Part I, pp. 7–38.

redistributed. There is a very real problem of maldistribution, it is true, with conspicuous consumption often existing side by side with all too conspicuous poverty; but there is not enough total income to make redistribution, through wage policies, social security, etc., a sufficient answer to labour's problem. Accordingly, there is a growing interest in means by which labour can contribute to increased productivity; also a need to reconsider labour policies that may demonstrably operate against the growth of production.

At the same time, it is recognized that substantial economic advance cannot be achieved with a labour force that is unstable, illiterate, untrained, ill-fed, badly housed and debilitated by disease. There is a growing body of opinion that investment in human resources may prove as productive in the end as investment in capital equipment, although it is obvious that both are essential for any large-scale economic development.

The economic and the social aspects of development are particularly intertwined in the agricultural sector where the family is simultaneously a unit of economic enterprise and a social institution. This is one reason for the importance attached to efforts at simultaneous economic and social change through comprehensive programmes like community development.

One other problem involving complex interaction of economic and social elements deserves mention here, namely inflation. Experience shows [that] economic development is often accomplished by inflation, although the relationship is by no means simple. Higher wages without corresponding increase of production can promote inflation if the costs are passed on to consumers, rather than absorbed by management or used to stimulate greater efficiency of production. Even if accompanied by higher productivity, however, higher wages in one sector, e.g., industry, can be associated with inflation under certain circumstances if there is not a corresponding increase in production in other sectors, such as agriculture and public and private services. Some of the measures used to control or counteract inflation can slow down development. Higher prices of food and other necessities can undermine benefits provided by improved wage measures and render social security largely ineffectual. There are wide disagreements on policies to deal with inflation in relation to development.

PROBLEMS OF WELFARE POLICY AND INSTITUTIONAL CHANGE

A tendency towards a dual economy is characteristic of many countries in process of industrialization: a modern industrial sector is growing side by side with a technologically backward sector. The contrast is often visible and striking. Incomes and welfare are relatively high in the former, relatively low in the latter sector. The minority of the workers that have been absorbed into the modern sector may acquire training, certain welfare benefits by virtue of their employment, and the protection of labour legislation, of social security and of trade unions; they may benefit from existing public housing projects. Many others, however, live on the fringes of this modern sector. They are often casual unskilled workers, illiterate and poor, with little social protection other than what they derive from friends and relatives. They may be engaged in street trades or employed in small workshops which do not observe the labour laws and regulations applied to the larger undertakings. Still greater numbers live in rural areas where the welfare and security of the individual are provided almost exclusively by the family group and often at a very low level for all.

Modern vocational training and employment service facilities are required by the technologically progressive sector of the economy if it is to secure the manpower resources necessary for further economic growth and to provide growing employment opportunities to the population. Regulation and inspection of working conditions is necessary in order to protect those workers who have become committed to industrial work. Some forms of social security are needed for people who have become exclusively dependent on wage earning employment for their own and their family's welfare. At the same time such measures may not, during the initial stages of economic growth, directly benefit those who have not yet become absorbed into the technologically advanced sector; and this constitutes a challenge to contemporary labour and social welfare policy. More attention needs to be given to the development of policies and institutions designed to help the numerous lowest income groups of the urban population.

In the field of social services for the needy and for the family, some of the methods evolved in modern industrialized societies are similarly inadequate to deal with the problems of the numerous poor in the underdeveloped countries. Financial relief in the form of cash is, in general, not possible, even if it were desirable as a regular policy in those countries. Individualized case-work methods for dealing with the needy are not practicable when the latter are to be counted in thousands or millions; trained case-workers for programmes of such magnitude are simply not available. The type of approach to social welfare that is based on the concept that the individual, if in need, has a right to various kinds of public assistance established by law cannot be transferred to areas where public resources for assistance are practically non-existent. The construction of custodial homes—homes for children, the aged, the mentally defective, etc.—also cannot be a very satisfactory solution for countries that do not have the resources to construct them in more than token numbers. Even in the developed countries, it may be noted, custodial institutions are no longer regarded as the most desirable method of dealing with the problems in question, and more emphasis is being placed upon strengthening the facilities of the normal family and community.

There is a danger that in the process of change old institutions and methods of handling social problems will be lost before new ones can be established to replace them. The traditional ties of family and community are apt to be weakened or destroyed by urbanization and industrialization, but the countries in question may not be able to take over the expensive welfare institutions and methods of modern industrialized States (whether or not they are otherwise appropriate). The result may be that neither home, community nor State cares for the child who needs care. This situation calls for a new look at the methods of dealing with populations undergoing transition, including the question of promoting institutional arrangements of a transitional nature. It also points to the fundamental need faced by the less developed countries for the maintenance of family stability and community organization through the period of transition to modernization—even as the structure and environment of the family and community are changing. If this can be done, many of the worst social and human consequences of transition can be avoided, or at least tempered.

The question of institutional change is, in general, a matter of special urgency for populations moving from rural to urban life; for agrarian populations under antiquated systems of land tenure; and for indigenous populations that are held back by institutional and cultural factors and isolated from the rest of the society and economy. Institutional change is delicate and difficult—the failure of land reform projects in some countries, owing to a collapse of productivity, and the failure of co-operatives to take root in many less developed areas, bear evidence of this. At the same time, the marshalling of individual energies through institutions and group organizations in projects of mutual aid and self-help may be the only means of making use of human capital—the chief form of capital in the under-developed regions.

HOUSING

Housing is an area where some form of organized self-help is badly needed. Wretched housing conditions—dwellings devoid of the most elementary facilities and unfit for human habitation or even domestic animal habitation—are prominent features of nearly all under-developed countries, and can be found in some of the most advanced countries. The efforts of the post-war years have failed to make a visible dent in the housing situation in the poorer countries. Rapid population growth and urbanization have aggravated the difficulties; peripheral shanty towns often seem to spring up overnight and may create even worse health problems than central urban slums. A major difficulty lies in the fact that housing is not a field where modern technological advances have been able to achieve rapid progress for the masses of people in less developed areas. The provision in such areas of adequate dwellings by current methods of construction would consume the greater part of the world's total investment capital. It is clear that, in dealing with slums and shanty-town conditions, not only remedial but also preventive measures are called for, which go far beyond the present conventional methods.

HEALTH

On the other hand, certain modern techniques of public health have been applied in economically under-developed areas with striking success, leading to reductions in mortality rates more marked than the progress in many other fields of economic and social development. Nevertheless, the world health situation has a long way to go before it reaches the level that is technologically possible. Some millions of people still die each year from diseases that can in principle be controlled or wiped off the earth today, and many more are incapacitated by them. Infant mortality rates—which are a fairly good indicator of general health conditions—reach the level of 200 or more per 1,000 live births in many of the under-developed countries, while in some of the most advanced countries they have been reduced to twenty per 1,000. If the world level were reduced to twenty, over 16 million children under one year of age who now die each year would survive.

The disease picture varies considerably with the level of social and economic development; the under-developed areas are characterized by a high prevalence of communicable diseases, while in the developed areas cancer, rheumatism and mental and heart diseases have replaced the communicable diseases as the most pressing problems.

In the under-developed countries, a substantial amount of the mortality and sickness of children, particularly in the vulnerable years of early childhood, is also due to malnutrition—insufficient food and the wrong kind of food—as well as various forms of intestinal diseases resulting from unsanitary conditions. Although the extent of malnutrition is not known with any degree of exactness, its presence among children in many areas is evident to the eye and its after-effects in adult life are extensive. The problem is not only the inadequate production and distribution of food, but also faulty consumption habits arising from ignorance.

One important aspect of the world's health picture is the fact that more than half of the world's population remains without the most elementary sanitary facilities—safe water and facilities for the sanitary disposal of human wastes. Another factor is the lack of medical personnel. While in highly developed countries the ratio of physicians to population is approximately 1 to 1,000, in the rest of the world it varies between 1 to 5,000 and 1 to 50,000. The problem is further aggravated by the general ignorance of the public in matters of health, which in turn is related to general levels of education, attitudes towards scientific explanations, availability of means of communication, etc. There is also a clear link between health and the economic situation, with influences operating in both directions.

Thus while it is true that for the control of certain diseases, like malaria, the problem is primarily one of finance to obtain equipment, and of administrative organization to carry out the campaign, in most aspects of health a great deal more is required. For some diseases, the methods of prevention and effective control have yet to be discovered and here the crucial need is for research. This is true, for example, of certain tropical diseases, rheumatic diseases, cancer, cardiovascular diseases, etc. The very process of industrialization is also throwing up a number of new health problems calling for constant research.

EDUCATION

Educational needs of the less developed countries are intimately related to almost all the other needs described above. Education is not only an important means of economic development, for example, but also a powerful ally in the understanding and improvement of health conditions. It is an essential means by which people become capable of exercising their civic rights and political responsibilities—a matter of particular importance to newly developing States. Above all, education is a human right and an end in itself, concerned with the intellectual and emotional development of the individual.

Precisely because education is a human right, the goal of universal and compulsory primary education is often given a high priority. Yet a balanced view of national, social and economic needs suggests that it is also essential to expand and diversify secondary education. This is partly because of the need for well-trained primary school-teachers and technically competent personnel in industry, commerce and agriculture, and partly to provide the basis for higher education as well as an efficient government service. Similar considerations apply to show the need for institutions of higher education, both universities and technological institutes. Further, an effective educational system should reach adults as well as children and youth. The illiterate masses of people in the less developed countries need a minimum of education in some practical form to enable them to improve their living conditions and adjust to the modern world.

All of this serves to emphasize the grave problems and the obstacles to educational advance arising from an insufficiency of funds for the construction and equipment of schools and for the recruitment and training of teachers, administrators and other personnel needed to cover these various fields. There are also problems of making the most effective and strategic use of such funds as may be available to national and local authorities who are responsible for the development of a country's educational system. Thus, one of the most difficult policy questions that the less developed countries face lies in planning the rhythm of development of education at its various levels and in allocating scarce resources—not only to the different levels (primary, secondary, higher) but also to the different fields of education (general education, technical education, study of the humanities, study of engineering, medicine, law, etc.). The patterns of requirement no doubt differ from country to country. One fairly common difficulty may, however, be mentioned: the fact that a dearth of various categories of technically trained personnel required for the economic and social development of the country is often found existing simultaneously with unemployment among secondary and higher education graduates who cannot find the white-collar jobs that they seek. In general, the situation calls for closer attention to the relation between education policy and development policy.

Questions of distribution of expenditures and of balanced growth are, of course, not peculiar to education. They are to be found in relation to every social field—as, for example, in the question of the appropriate pattern of expenditures on various types of health service in less developed countries. There is also the more general and even more difficult question of the appropriate level and distribution of public expenditure for the total field of economic and social development in the less developed countries—a question that concerns both national policy and international policy, and in regard to which more will be said later on in this report.

UNITED NATIONS OPERATIONAL PROGRAMMES IN THE SOCIAL FIELD*

The reappraisal of the work of the Social Commission requires not only a review of United Nations objectives in the social field and the planning of its work programme in a way which provides adequate attention to the major issues of social development, but also a review of the operational programmes which provide the instruments for translating ideas and recommendations into practical realities in the Member States, particularly in the developing countries.

. . . These [operational programmes] include the United Nations Development Programme, the United Nations Children's Fund (UNICEF), and the World Food Programme (WFP) as well as the regular budgets of the United Nations and most of the specialized agencies which provide for advisory services or aid to Member States. Due to the complexities of reporting, including the variety of classification systems and the inherent difficulty in segregating economic and social projects, it is not possible at

* United Nations Economic and Social Council, Social Commission, 17th Session, "Reappraisal of the Role of the Social Commission." Report of the Secretary-General, E/CN.5/400, February 16, 1966, pp. 42–50.

this time[1] to give an accurate over-all picture of the total resources directly available to the United Nations family for assistance in the social sectors as defined in the foregoing chapters of this report. However, it may be useful to indicate the general magnitude of resources available for all fields of activity in the major funds for 1966: the United Nations Development Programme has received pledges and contributions of $147.7 million against a target of $200 million; and the World Food Programme has pledges of slightly over $200 million against a three-year target of $275 million; and the anticipated income for UNICEF is estimated at $35 million. Compared to these resources, the contributions from the regular budgets of the United Nations and the specialized agencies are modest: e.g., the United Nations included in its budget for 1966 a total of $6.4 million for assistance in economic development, social welfare, and public administration.

An analysis of the Expanded Programme of Technical Assistance (EPTA) over the past five years (1960–1964) indicates that 16.6 per cent of the funds went to health services; 13.6 per cent to education; 5.4 per cent to vocational education and training; 1.4 per cent to housing, building and planning; 1.4 per cent to social welfare and social security; 1.2 per cent to community development. These proportions compare with 20.9 per cent in the same period to agricultural production; 15.7 per cent to development planning; 8.2 per cent to power, transport and communications; 6.2 per cent to industrial production.[2]

The Special Fund has greatly augmented the resources allocated to agriculture, natural resources development and industrial development. It has also approved sixty-eight projects in education and eight in housing, building and planning. Allocations to all other social sectors have been modest; the last Governing Council (January 1966) has for the first time approved a grant to one national training centre for community development and one regional centre for population studies.[3]

Since its purposes are directed toward improving the total welfare of the child, UNICEF, on the other hand, is completely devoted to social purposes. Its major allocations continue to be in the field of child health, but since 1958, increasing attention has been given to education, nutrition, welfare, mothercraft and homecraft activities. In recent years, some funds have

[1] These questions are under active consideration by the United Nations and the agencies in conformity with Economic and Social Council resolution 1090 D (XXXIX) and it is expected that such information will be available to the Council at its forty-first session in July 1966.

[2] *Fifteen Years and 150,000 Skills: An Anniversary Review of the United Nations Expanded Programme of Technical Assistance,* United Nations publication, Sales No.: 65.I.18.

[3] Report of the first session of the Governing Council to the forty-first session of the Economic and Social Council (document E/4150).

also been allocated for increasing the interest and education of development planners in the problem of planning for children and youth. In the fields of special interest to the Bureau of Social Affairs, more than $5,300,000 has been allocated to seventy projects in fifty-nine countries.

During the last three years, an additional resource has become available through the World Food Programme (WFP); as a result, food aid has been used to support projects, particularly in the field of community development, and housing, building and planning. In the former field it has taken the form of awards of incentive premiums to local groups with a view to encouraging them to work in an undertaking of local interest and concern, and on which they would not have otherwise worked; in the latter field it has taken the same form, especially for self-help housing and neighbourhood improvement, but it has also served as part payment of wages in kind. As of 31 December 1965 there were fourteen WFP projects in the field of community development. . . .

The "regular" programmes vary widely in size and purposes among the United Nations agencies, but in the case of the United Nations itself, the budget contribution of $6.4 million, of which about $2 million [is] allocated for projects in the social field, is particularly important in supporting regional and inter-regional projects approved by the regional and functional commissions, helping countries in formulating long-term technical co-operation and Special Fund projects, evaluating development projects at critical stages, and supplementing resources from the Expanded Programme of Technical Assistance in more specialized fields such as family and child welfare, rehabilitation of the handicapped, and social defence. It is also possible to provide very modest resources to encourage co-operation among industrialized countries under this heading (e.g., the European Social Welfare Programme).

The principles upon which these programmes are based have not changed significantly since the Social Commission recommended the adoption of the first technical assistance programme of the United Nations (the Advisory Social Welfare programme transferred from the United Nations Relief and Rehabilitation Administration [UNRRA] in December 1946). They were set out more fully in Economic and Social Council resolution 222 A (IX) and General Assembly resolution 304 (IV) to ensure that technical assistance should be given only on the basis of governmental requests, in the form which each country desired, and without any considerations of a political nature. There were also criteria for the selection of experts to ensure not only technical competence but also understanding and integrity, and the spelling out of the obligations as well as rights of requesting Governments.

The forms of this assistance are well established—individual experts, teams of advisers, fellowships and scholarships, study tours, workshops and seminars, and supply of demonstration equipment and technical literature have become the standard methods employed by the regular and expanded programmes of technical co-operation. A full account of the forms preferred by Governments, as well as the geographic distribution of the services, the countries of origin of the experts, the placement of the fellows, etc., is given to the Economic and Social Council annually in reports of the Secretary-General (for the United Nations regular programme) and by the Technical Assistance Board for the Expanded Programme of Technical Assistance (now to become the Inter-agency Consultative Board under the United Nations Development Programme).

An extension of advisory services on a regional basis has been provided over the past several years by the development of a system of regional advisers. The use of regional advisers, stationed at the headquarters of the regional economic commissions, has permitted making their services available for short-term missions to countries within the respective regions, to provide assistance or follow-up on earlier recommendations or to evaluate progress in the fields of their competence. It has also permitted their collaborating with advisers concerned with problems of industrial and agricultural development, with a view to establishing regional projects which are comprehensive in nature and ensuring that the economic and social aspects of the requirements of Governments are taken into account. Thus, in 1965 regional advisers were assigned in the fields of housing, building and planning, social welfare, and community development to the Economic Commission for Africa; in the fields of population, community development, and physical planning to the Economic Commission for Asia and the Far East; in the fields of social development, community development, and housing, building and planning to the Economic Commission for Latin America; and in the fields of population, community development, and town planning to the United Nations Economic and Social Office in Beirut.

In many instances these regional advisers, as well as those assigned to countries, were assisted by associate experts made available by several Governments which have agreed to provide such supplementary assistance. This latter arrangement is advantageous to the recipient Governments, the donor Governments and the United Nations, since the former receives assistance free of cost and as an addition to that which has been programmed; the donor Government provides an opportunity for its nationals to receive valuable training and experience; and the United Nations is enabled to expand the volume of its technical assistance activities without additional cost. Thus, during the period 1958-1964, twenty-five associate experts [were] assigned to projects in the social field, while on 1 January 1965, requests for twenty-seven associate experts were pending.

A related development to that of the regional advisers has been the appointment of inter-regional advisers who, working out of United Nations Headquarters, can provide assistance and advice upon request similar to that provided by the regional advisers, but on a world-wide basis. The programme, which became fully operative in 1965 with the appointment of two inter-regional advisers on social development planning and programming, one on youth and related problems, and three in the field of housing, building and planning, has already permitted the United Nations to be of assistance to Governments in those instances where the requests are for short-term consultations and advice. The inter-regional advisers should, in the period ahead, prove effective in aiding Governments in developing technical assistance programmes as well as Special Fund projects of a more comprehensive nature. They will also become involved in advising on the execution of long-term development plans and in the evaluation of social development projects.

The possibilities provided by the Special Fund to provide a larger component of equipment, as well as pre-investment surveys and technical training, have been particularly important in fields such as housing, building and physical planning where advisory services alone could not make a significant impact.

UNICEF also has provided elements lacking in the technical assistance programmes—the equipment and supplies for maternal and child health and welfare centres, milk for school lunch programmes and seeds for school gardens, tools for vocational education, and stipends for local trainees for child welfare programmes. As noted above, these possibilities have greatly enhanced the work of family and child welfare advisers sent under the technical assistance programmes. Food aid extended through the World Food Programme has worked in much the same way particularly in community development and housing and urban development programmes.

A most encouraging note in recent years has been the requests submitted by Governments seeking United Nations assistance in the evaluation of programmes in the social field, particularly in the area of community development and social welfare training. The reliance upon United Nations experts to undertake the evaluation of programmes closely related to the objectives of their national development plan is an indication of the Government's appreciation of United Nations standards and a willingness to rely on the Organization in determining the quality of their programmes. The Economic and Social Council has launched its own series of over-all evaluation reports for a limited number of countries in the past two years.

✿   ✿   ✿   ✿   ✿   ✿   ✿

In broad lines, the changes in administrative and financial arrangements in the technical assistance programmes have all been in the direction of decentralization: first, in giving more authority to the receiving country to determine its priorities within the regular budget allocations as well as within country targets established by the Technical Assistance Committee;

second, by strengthening the position of the resident representative of the Technical Assistance Board; and third, in giving the regional economic commissions the deciding voice in determining priorities in regional projects of the United Nations. The Special Fund and the World Food Programme also rely heavily on the receiving country and the resident representatives. UNICEF has its own set of field representatives who follow similar principles and guidelines in their relations with recipient Governments.

THE DEVELOPMENT DECADE IN THE BALANCE

George D. Woods*

"Hope," said Sir Francis Bacon, "is a good breakfast but it is a poor supper." The 1960s began with hope for the economically underdeveloped countries, but it is becoming uncertain how they will end. Unless the Development Decade, as President Kennedy christened it, receives greater sustenance, it may, in fact, recede into history as a decade of disappointment. The amount of finance moving from the developed to the underdeveloped world is not rising; and the present trend is for the growth of the low-income countries slowly to lose momentum.

Almost two-thirds of the world's population live in underdeveloped countries; but they have only one-sixth of the world's income. The condition of mankind can be outlined quickly with a few brutal statistics. Defining countries with a per capita income of under $100 as very poor, those with a per capita income of from $100 to $250 as poor, those with a per capita income between $250 and $750 as being of middle income, and those with a per capita income of more than $750 as the high-income countries, here is how the world's people are distributed:

Very Poor	990 million	Middle-Income	390 million
Poor	1,150 million	High-Income	810 million

Just how poor the approximately two-thirds of the world in the Very Poor and Poor Countries are is illustrated by comparing their per capita income of

* George D. Woods, "The Development Decade in the Balance," *Foreign Affairs,* Vol. 44, January 1966, pp. 206–215. Reprinted by special permission from *Foreign Affairs,* January 1966. Copyright by the Council on Foreign Relations, Inc., New York.

George D. Woods is President of the International Bank for Reconstruction and Development.

less than $250 with the average per capita income of $1,400 in the Common Market countries (population: 175 million), and the United States' (population: 194 million) per capita income of about $3,000.

The underdeveloped countries are seeking to enter the twentieth century, but many of them, in some respects, have not yet reached the nineteenth. Many still need to achieve the preconditions of industrialization, including stable government, an acquisitive outlook and technical capacity. The price of admission to industrial society, moreover, is much higher than it was a century ago. Technology is costlier, capital requirements are greater, established producers are harder to overtake in world commercial competition.

The aim of the Development Decade is for the underdeveloped countries, as a group, to reach a yearly rate of economic growth of 5 percent. In the period 1950–54, the rate of increase in their gross national product did approximate that figure. But in 1955–60 it dropped to 4.5 percent; and in 1960–64 it was 4 percent. When allowance is made for population growth, per capita income in about half the 80 underdeveloped countries which are members of the World Bank is rising by only 1 percent a year or less. Even to keep abreast of recent high rates of population growth is not a negligible achievement, but it is far from sufficient. The average per capita income in this lagging group is no more than $120 a year. At a 1 percent growth rate, income levels will hardly reach $170 annually by the year 2000. In some countries they will be much lower.

This is crude arithmetic. But its implications are plain and sobering. If present trends are allowed to continue, there will be no adequate improvement in living standards in vast areas of the globe for the balance of this century. Yet, over the same period, the richer countries will be substantially increasing their wealth. In the United States, for example, the present per capita income of about $3,000 a year will, if it continues to grow at the current per capita rate, reach about $4,500 by the end of the century. In other words, one group's per capita income will increase over this period by $50, while America's will increase by about $1,500.

As the gap widens intolerably, one is bound to wonder when the fine sentiments so eloquently and so often expressed by leaders in all the industrial nations will give way to positive action to help raise the living standards of the developing countries at a much faster rate. For how much longer can the industrial nations justify the relatively low place that development finance has hitherto been accorded in their list of priorities?

An important difference between economic development in the twentieth century and past times is that today the rich nations have accepted a measure of responsibility for the progress of the poor. Outside the Soviet and Chinese blocs, a score of countries—including Israel and the Sheikhdom of

Kuwait—have institutions for granting aid to other countries, and these institutions are constantly evolving in the direction of greater professionalism and efficiency. In the past two years, for example, Canada, the Netherlands, Sweden and the United Kingdom have all reorganized their aid effort to bring a fuller weight of knowledge and experience to bear on development problems.

Since the war, very imposing machinery of multi-national and international organizations also has been built to promote economic growth. The old Marshall Plan organization in Europe has acquired a world-wide outlook in its reincarnation as the Organization for Economic Coöperation and Development (O.E.C.D.), an important center for coördinating the policies and techniques of the aid-giving countries. The development fund associated with the European Economic Community has opened its horn of plenty to the lands of Africa. A development bank has been established to serve the interests of the Latin American countries, and the Inter-American Committee for the Alliance for Progress (C.I.A.P.) is establishing priorities for the financing of Latin American development. A regional African bank, owned entirely by African states, has called up its first capital; and an Asian development bank promises to become a reality in 1966.

The World Bank has shared in this evolution, to a point where it would scarcely be recognized by the founders who wrote its charter just over 20 years ago. Originally intended to operate chiefly as a guarantor of loans by others, the Bank from the beginning has been a lender on its own account. In the fiscal year which ended last June 30,[1] it lent more than $1 billion. Since its creation, the Bank has given birth to two affiliates: the International Finance Corporation (I.F.C.), established in 1956 to specialize in the financing of productive private projects in the underdeveloped countries; and the International Development Association (IDA), established in 1960 to make development finance available on special terms to countries too poor to borrow at conventional rates of interest and repayment. From being purely a lending institution, the Bank has widened its activities to include, amongst other things, a substantial program of technical assistance, designed to improve the quality of development programing in its member countries and to assist them in drawing up specific development projects for financing.

Other patterns of bilateral and multilateral coöperation are taking form. Among the most promising are the groups, consisting of aid-giving countries and international financial agencies, organized to coördinate the flow of finance and technical assistance to particular underdeveloped countries. Groups of this kind now exist for eleven countries; two (for Greece and Turkey) organized by the O.E.C.D., one (for Ecuador) by the Inter-American Development Bank, and the remainder (for India, Pakistan,

[1] 1965 [ed.].

Colombia, Malaysia, Nigeria, Sudan, Thailand and Tunisia) by the World Bank (in company with IDA). Others are in prospect.

Each consultative group has one essential objective; to increase productivity by accelerating economic growth. Its members seek to accomplish this purpose in several ways. In the first place, the arrangement is designed to provide the several aid-givers with informed, objective analyses of the country's needs for external finance and technical assistance—not only the amounts it could effectively use, but also the appropriate terms of financing and the purposes that deserve priority. Second, the group aims at enhancing the developing country's ability to invest by helping in the planning of development, in the preparation and screening of projects and by advising on administrative or financial problems and the like. It also undertakes, in coöperation with the recipient country, a continuous assessment of progress, and attempts to work out agreed solutions to development problems as they arise. We expect that these consultations will encourage the coöperation and mutual trust that is so necessary between the providers of finance and those who receive it, and we hope that a more adequate and assured flow of finance will be the result.

On a more general plane, the concerns of the industrial and the underdeveloped countries are brought together in the working committees of the new United Nations Trade and Development Board, created as a result of the U.N. Conference on Trade and Development (UNCTAD) in 1964. Among the accomplishments of this meeting was the focusing of attention on some of the major problems of the underdeveloped world—among them, the "commodity problem" and the necessity for a continuing and adequate flow of capital to the developing countries.

Of the 80 or so underdeveloped countries of the world, more than 30 depend for more than half their foreign-exchange earnings on exports of a single crop or commodity, and many others are heavily dependent on exports of only two. The rate at which the underdeveloped countries can invest in their own growth depends very largely on how these commodities fare in international trade; what their exports earn brings the developing world four times as much foreign exchange as loans, grants and direct investments from abroad.

But as a source of income, primary commodities are notoriously fickle. Fluctuations of production and demand may cause export earnings to swing up or down by as much as 50 percent in a single year. The long-term trend of commodity earnings, however, is that they decline as a proportion of world trade. Over the years 1950–62, the export income of the underdeveloped countries rose by an annual average of only 3.5 percent—not enough, by itself, to sustain adequate imports of the equipment and materials the low-income countries must have for economic progress.

The slow and uncertain growth of export earnings exerts pressures leading to fiscal imbalance, inflation and stagnation of constructive effort; it retards development, upsets continuity of investment and diminishes the impact of external finance. In the medium term, the commodity problem may be mitigated by international commodity agreements. In the short term, some way has to be found of cushioning a developing country against the effect of a sudden drop in export earnings on which it has been relying for the financing of its development plan. In the long run—a span that may stretch for a generation or more—the solution must be for the developing countries to diversify their production to a wider range of goods; and the industrial nations, as a matter of trade policy, must show a more hospitable attitude toward the exports of the developing nations.

. . . both the high-income and the underdeveloped countries need to give renewed and purposeful attention to this problem. Two initiatives in which the World Bank is joining should eventually help. The first is a study, organized jointly by the International Coffee Organization, the U.N. Food and Agriculture Organization and the Bank. The study will examine the needs of coffee-producing countries to diversify into other lines of production which would impart greater strength and stability to their economies, and will try to identify the possibilities that they have for doing so. A dozen countries in Latin America and Africa depend on coffee as a major source of export earnings; and coffee exhibits some of the worst features of the commodity problem.

*   *   *   *   *   *   *

The continuing need of the underdeveloped world for an adequate flow of external capital is given added urgency by what might be called the "debt explosion." In 1956, the outstanding international debt of the low-income countries, stemming from public sources or carrying governmental guarantees, was estimated at just under $10 billion. In 1964, it reached an estimated $33 billion. Because of rising interest rates and the accumulation of short-term debt, the amount of money needed each year to service this debt climbed even faster. From 1956 to 1964, it rose over four times, from $800 million to $3.5 billion.

The external debt of many developing countries, of course, was bound to rise rapidly. These countries were newly independent; they had little debt to begin with, but increased it rapidly as they plunged with energy and enthusiasm into economic development. At the same time, there was much unwise borrowing—brought about in part, it should be added, by the proffering of credit from the industrial nations for an unrealistically short term and in some cases for purposes of little economic value.

In any case, the underdeveloped countries as a whole must now devote more than a tenth of their foreign-exchange earnings to debt service; and the figure is still rising. These levels of debt service are dangerously high. They mean that a good part of the countries' foreign-exchange resources must be devoted to servicing previous obligations rather than to new productive development.

*   *   *   *   *   *   *

The solution of the debt problem is within the power and the means of the developed countries. They can ease their own terms, and they can dispense finance through other channels. One of the latter is the Bank's affiliate, IDA, the major international institution for transferring capital to the low-income countries on concessional terms. IDA's clients so far comprise 29 of the poorest nations; its credits are extended free of interests (although there is a small service charge) and for a term of 50 years. Principles similar to those of the Bank are followed by IDA in appraising projects and negotiating credits. The same high standards have to be met; only the terms are different. There is no separate IDA staff; the Bank's experts are IDA's experts, and over the years the Bank has assembled a multi-national professional staff of high quality and with a wealth of experience to handle the growing range of responsibilities in the development field.

Unlike the Bank, however, IDA cannot raise funds by borrowing in the capital markets, and its earnings are miniscule. By far the largest part of its resources has originated from the governments of the high-income countries —from their initial subscriptions and from later contributions—and these resources have been supplemented at the close of each of the last two fiscal years by transfers of $50 and $75 million from the Bank's net income. The total of convertible funds so far at the disposal of IDA has amounted to just under $1.7 billion. . . .

The prime ingredient of economic progress in the underdeveloped countries is their own effort in mobilizing and using their own resources. It is this effort, fundamentally, which determines the rate of growth; it is this effort which provides a basis for external assistance to be received and used effectively.

In many of the underdeveloped countries, economic performance must be greatly improved. Many can take more effective measures to increase the mobilization of capital through taxation and through incentives to investment, both domestic and international. It is urgent to cut down some of the biggest items of waste—excessive military expenditures, prestige projects, inefficient administration and subsidies to public services that should be self-supporting. Measures are widely needed to keep excessive population growth from devouring the hard-won gains of development. Recent technical advances and birth-control methods have proved dramatically effective in pilot projects and give real hope that, for example in India, the growth in population may at last be slowed down. Nearly all the developing countries can redouble their efforts to overcome the lag in agricultural productivity. Agriculture, now generally recognized as the most vital economic sector, is generally the most feeble. And yet, in those places where land reform and the difficult transition from ancient to modern agricultural methods are being effected, hope for solid improvement in productivity runs high.

* * * * * * *

Despite differences in the achievements of individual developing nations, and despite some discouraging failures among them, the underdeveloped countries as a group are growing in their ability to carry out investment. Their development institutions are becoming more firmly established, education and skills are spreading, administrative and managerial abilities are improving, and program and project planning is becoming more effective.

* * * * * * *

A preliminary study made by the World Bank staff, utilizing available data and their own experienced judgment, suggests that the developing countries could put to constructive use, over the next five years, some $3 to $4 billion more each year than is currently being made available to them. It may be tempting to suggest that these countries accommodate themselves to what is currently available, on the grounds that it would be a mistake to increase the flow until the recipients had learned more about the effective uses of external resources and considerably diminished their present level of indebtedness. But neither an improvement in the handling of investments nor a constructive easing of the debt burden will be achieved simply by holding down the level of the flow of external resources.

. . . The need therefore is for more action now, and there can be no doubt that, in spite of all the problems and difficulties, the basic economic and financial position of the high-income countries is strong enough to support such an increase.

From every point of view, the time is now ripe for the capital-exporting countries to come to a major and irrevocable decision about development assistance. A vast store of knowledge and experience in development—a whole new technology—is at their disposal; there is no lack of able professionals ready to apply it; the need for its application grows daily more insistent; the industrialized world has itself voiced acknowledgment of the urgency of the situation. With so much already done, and so much still left to do, it would be unthinkable for the richer nations, by their inaction, to let the developing world lose hold of its hard-won gains and lose sight of its ultimate goals.

THE TRUSTEESHIP SYSTEM OF THE
UNITED NATIONS (1945-1960)

J. W. Brügel*

An area of activity of the United Nations which has received little attention by the public but which nevertheless is of significance has reached a decisive turning point which justifies a look backward and a summary. The trusteeship system which in 1946 was created as a successor to the mandate system has lost a great part of its functions much earlier than was expected. This has come as a result of a very dramatic development: "away from colonialism," particularly as it has affected Africa. But the circumstances under which this has occurred have created new, difficult, and unforeseen problems with which the International Community will have to deal.

THE MANDATE SYSTEM OF THE LEAGUE OF NATIONS

The idea of a certain international responsibility for the administration of colonial areas was realized for the first time in the form of the mandate system within the framework of the League of Nations. Article 22 of the Covenant of the League of Nations announced the principle that the welfare and development of the areas under the mandate system respresents a "sacred trust of civilization." Only the former German colonies and parts of the former Ottoman empire were placed under a mandatory administration, in which, after the First World War, at a time when all hopes attached themselves to the League of Nations, many opponents of colonialism saw the best possibility of its gradual transformation. Out of this arose, for instance, the demand which was incorporated in the colonial program of the Socialist International as adopted by the international congress in Brussels in 1928 that the mandate system should be extended, as a means of international control, to all colonies. It is characteristic of the change which had occurred in the meantime that the British socialists, which had earlier fought for this idea in Brussels didn't come back to it after the end of the Second World War but made direct grants of independence to the colonies instead of

* J. W. Brügel, "The Trusteeship System of the United Nations (1945–1960)," *Europa Archiv*, Vol. 15, 1960, pp. 683–694. Translation by Professor Max Mark. By permission of *Europa Archiv* and J. W. Brügel.

J. W. Brügel is a former Czechoslovakian civil servant who has been working in London since 1947 as a writer on international affairs, international law, and contemporary history.

using the detour of an internationalization of administration. The covenant of the League of Nations made a distinction, according to the degree of the maturity of the various areas, between three categories of mandates (A, B, and C). In the case of the A mandates, the activity of the mandatory power was restricted to advice and assistance to a state whose independence was close at hand. The B mandates transferred the administration to the mandatory power whereas, in the case of the C mandates, the administration of an area became an integral part of the mandatory power. The following territories were made a part of the system:

A MANDATES

COUNTRY	MANDATORY POWER
Iraq	Great Britain
TransJordan	Great Britain
Palestine	Great Britain
Syria & Lebanon	France

B MANDATES

Cameroons	Divided—Great Britain & France
Togo	Divided—Great Britain & France
Tanganyika	Great Britain
Ruanda & Urundi	Belgium

C MANDATES

Southwest Africa	Union of South Africa
West Samoa	New Zealand
New Guinea	Australia
Nauru	Australia in the name of the Empire
South Sea Islands, Marianas, etc.	Japan

The League of Nations carried out its role of supervision over the mandatory system with the assistance of a Permanent Mandate Commission which consisted of experts and not representatives of states. The Mandate Commission examined the reports of the mandatory powers, dealt with the petitions from individual persons and non-governmental organizations. With the exception of Palestine, all areas under Mandates of Category A achieved their independence before the establishment of the trusteeship system. The mandate for Palestine ended on May 14, 1948 with the British renunciation of its continuation and the declaration of independence by Israel. No attempt to integrate the country into the trusteeship system was made.

THE PROVISIONS OF THE CHARTER OF THE UNITED NATIONS

In February 1945 at Yalta, it was decided that the conference to be convened for San Francisco, April 25, 1945, to work out the final version of the United Nations should also deal with the provisions for the trusteeship system. The draft of Dumbarton Oaks contained nothing in this respect. It was considered necessary to make provisions for the future of the mandates but at the same time the opportunity was envisioned to include all the other colonial territories in the system. In San Francisco, there was an agreement on the Chapters 11, 12, and 13 of the Charter. Chapter 11 enlarged the concept of sacred trust to include all areas which as yet had not become independent and for the first time established a responsibility (somewhat limited) of all colonial powers to the International community. Chapter 12 contains the provisions of the trusteeship system. Chapter 13 deals with the provisions for the Trusteeship Council as an organ of control over the functioning of the system.

"STATES DIRECTLY CONCERNED"

From the version of the agreement among Roosevelt, Churchill, and Stalin at Yalta, the formulation was taken over into the wording of the charter that before the General Assembly can agree to accept a trusteeship agreement between the United Nations on one hand and individual members on the other, there must be an agreement between the states directly concerned *(les Etats directement intéressés)*. The charter provides only one possible reference in this respect which lends itself to meaningful interpretation of who belongs in this group. A mandatory power, which itself is a member of the United Nations, must be treated as "directly concerned." The lack of clarity about the circle of those who are directly concerned has constituted from the beginning, a point of disagreement within the United Nations which at no time was resolved and which if not skirted, would have jeopardized the whole trusteeship system. The Soviet Union insisted that the circle of directly concerned states be precisely defined. She would have liked to see, for obvious reasons, that all members of the Security Council would be covered by this provision. With the exceptions which will be discussed below, the trusteeship agreements which were later approved by the organs of the United Nations were negotiated by the former mandatory powers and then negotiated with states which the mandatory powers considered as being "directly concerned." No uniform standard was applied in this respect. The Soviet Union considered the approval of the individual agreements by the General Assembly in 1946 and 1947 as illegal. Consequently, the Soviet Union denied the legality of the Trusteeship Council in which the Council Charter gave her a permanent seat, and boycotted its work until April 1948. From thereon it engaged in the very opposite tactics, namely its use as a platform for propaganda. After an activity of nearly 20 years of the trusteeship system, the reference to this old conflict can have today only the signifiance of a historical reminiscence. Since the agreement of "directly concerned states" is also a prerequisite for a change of existing trusteeship agreements, it cannot be excluded that the conflict will erupt again in the future. Fortunately, however, the fears of Toussaint[1] have proved to be without foundation, namely that the conflict could also make it difficult to end an agreement and thereby jeopardize the independence of an area which had been under the trusteeship system.

The Charter does not make the old distinction between three categories and uniformly speaks of the trusteeship territories, but the Charter introduces a new concept—that of strategic areas about which we will talk separately. The goal of the trusteeship system is—in addition to the general ideas of peace, security, and respect for human rights—the development toward self-rule and independence in accordance with the special conditions of each individual territory. Trusteeship agreements can be concluded for the former mandatory territories for territories which, as the result of the Second World War had to be yielded by the "enemy countries" and for areas which the states which administer colonies voluntarily place under the system. A case of this kind has up to now never taken place. Except for Southwest Africa and Palestine, all mandates which at the time of the coming into force of the Charter still existed, were transformed into trusteeships.

In the case of Southwest Africa, this was made impossible by the constant refusal of the government of South Africa to conclude a trusteeship agreement over that area and to give to the United Nations a say as it is provided for in agreements of this kind. At this point, it is certainly of interest that the mandate was originally given to his Britannic majesty for and on behalf of the government of the Union of South Africa. . . .

"THE STRATEGIC AREAS"

Another innovation of the Charter is the possibility of declaring a certain trusteeship area or part thereof to be of strategic significance. In this case, the place of the General Assembly of the United Nations which has to approve the trusteeship agreement and to which the trusteeship powers are responsible is taken by the Security Council. The reason for this is obvious. In the General Assembly, there is no veto of the great powers. The Trusteeship Council which, in general, assists the General Assembly also assists in this case the Security Council to which it has to refer the reports of the trusteeship powers together with its own observations. Here is a certain anomaly because of the two institutions of equal standing, the Trusteeship Council is subordinate to the other in this particular case. Practically speaking, this has had less significance than was thought of in the beginning. Only in one particular case was a trusteeship area designated as a strategic area. This concerns approximately 96 islands in the Pacific Ocean (Marianas,

[1] C. E. Toussaint, "The Trusteeship System of the United Nations," London: Stevens and Sons, Ltd., 1956, p. 194.

Carolinas, Marshall Islands) which were German colonies before the First World War and which were administered as mandated territories by Japan up to their occupation by the United States in 1945. The Security Council accepted on April 2, 1947 a trusteeship agreement which was worked out by the United States according to which this area was transferred to the United States as trusteeship. The United States at the same time received the power to close certain areas for reasons of security even to representatives of the United Nations. Apart from this, there is no distinction from other territories under the trusteeship system.

Interestingly enough the Soviet Union, to the great surprise of all, placed no obstacles in the way of this enhancement of the American military potential. The representative of the Soviet Union at that time and present Foreign Minister, Andrei Gromyko, supported the assignment of these islands to the United States and justified his support by saying that the power of the United States had "played a decisive role in the victory over Japan and the United States in the war with Japan had made incomparably greater sacrifices than the other allied powers." The United States deferred to the request of the Soviet Union to omit provisions which were a part of other agreements and which also were part of the mandate for these islands in the South Pacific, namely, that these areas be administered as "an integral part" of the trusteeship power. More far-reaching changes which the Soviet Union requested were rejected. However, the Soviet Union abstained from voting on the controversial points; she made no use of her veto and finally voted for the convention as a whole. Though it is true that at this particular period (April 1947) the East-West conflict had not yet fully broken out, it is also true that the Soviet Union had made use of her veto quite extensively prior to that time and had also already boycotted the Trusteeship Council. Under these circumstances the attitude of the Soviet Union on the issue of the islands in the Pacific was unusual and remained an isolated case.

SOMALILAND AND JERUSALEM

Only in a single case was the area of an "enemy country" of the Second World War transformed into a trusteeship. This happened because there was a certain dilemma. In the disposition of the former Italian colonies, there was no alternative but to transfer the administration of Italian Somaliland to Italy. This concession to Italy was limited by the provision that the area after ten years would have to achieve independence. In addition, an advisory committee was established composed of Egypt, Colombia, and the Philippines in order to assist Italy. Because of the Soviet veto, Italy was not a member of the United Nations at that time and was not represented in the U.N. negotiations on the trusteeship agreement. This created a number of complications which were resolved only at the end of 1955 when all the obstacles for complete participation of Italy within the United Nations had been removed.

Another attempt to establish an international regime in an area of political tension of the world came to naught. In accordance with the decision to partition Palestine, the Trusteeship Council received the assignment to work out a statute for a permanent internationalization of the city of Jerusalem. To meet the objection that an international regime of a permanent nature was contrary to the idea of the trusteeship system, that is the ultimate establishment of independence in this case, reference to the provisions of the Charter on trusteeships was avoided. The Trusteeship Council honored the request which was submitted to it and worked out a statute which would have given it the supervision over the administration of Jerusalem. The political development and first of all the refusal of Israel and Jordan to agree to such a solution made it impossible to pursue this plan further. It was buried when a decision for adjournment failed on December 15, 1950 to receive the necessary two-thirds majority in the General Assembly.

THE TRUSTEESHIP COUNCIL

The Trusteeship Council as the executive organ of the General Assembly on questions of trusteeships does not have, in contrast to the Security Council and the Economic and Social Council, a definite number of members. It must consist half of trusteeship powers and half of such states which do not have trusteeships under their control. In addition to this, the Charter guarantees a seat to each of the 5 great powers. The latter so far has been meaningful only for the Soviet Union and China; the others are or have been trusteeship powers themselves.[2] In addition to this, there are elected for periods of three years a number of states for the purpose of maintaining a balance between these two categories of members. The Trusteeship Council discharges its duties of supervision over the activities of the trusteeship powers in various ways: through the critical treatment of the reports and oral additions which are submitted to it through the dispatch of missions to the individual trusteeship territories, through giving a hearing to the representatives of the peoples of the areas concerned, and through the examination of petitions.

The great decisions in respect to territories whose administration is under

---

[2] However, on April 27, 1960, the French-administered Trust Territory of Togoland attained independence, whereupon France ceased to be a member of the Trusteeship Council by virtue of administering a Trust Territory. It did, however, remain a member of the Council by virtue of being a permanent member of the Security Council which did not administer any Trust Territories. In 1965 there were eight members of the Council: four administering members—Australia, New Zealand, United Kingdom and the United States; three permanent members—China, France and the Soviet Union; and one elected member—Liberia.

the supervision of the Trusteeship Council have regularly been taken outside the area of activity of the United Nations. For instance, the Trusteeship Council was concerned for a number of years with the demands of Ewe people for national unity through the unification of the trusteeship areas of French Togo and British Togo. But in the end, the establishment of the Republic of Togo (that is the area previously administered by France and the area which after the plebescite of British Togo acceded to Ghana) placed before the Council a *fait accompli*. The system which has been established by the Charter has proved itself, not in the great issues but in the permanent control over the development in the Trusteeship areas. And it could have proved itself even better in the interest of the peoples concerned if the Cold War had not affected the work of the Council. The Cold War atmosphere manifested itself in the criticism which the Soviet Union leveled against the Trusteeship Powers. Its purpose was obviously sheer propaganda and it amounted to a complete denial of any positive achievement on their part. The reaction of the Trusteeship Powers was confined to seeing to it that the Soviet Union would not be represented in any of the missions sent to the Trusteeship territories. (Except for the Soviet Union, no other Communist country has been a member of the Trusteeship Council.) The conditions for the work of this body were extremely unfavorable; it has to be appreciated in particular in this connection that the honest endeavor to get to know the opinions and desires of the peoples of the Trusteeship system was often vitiated because their various representatives expressed diametrically opposed opinions. In the face of all this, the Trusteeship Council has done a creditable job. It has not confined itself to the superficial examination of reports. It could not have done this simply because of the presence of such members as India and Burma. When we speak about a creditable job let us add here that the job was hardly noticed by the public, let alone received a proper recognition. In a formal sense, the Trusteeship relationship may be distinguishable by degree only from a colonial administration which accepts an international responsibility. But in fact the Trusteeship Council has always seen to it that in all cases where the Charter provides opportunities for it to exercise a certain influence, the economic, social and cultural standard was improved and that the road to self-government and independence was opened.

In some form or other, all Trusteeship agreements carry provisions which make possible the introduction or the application of the laws of the Trusteeship powers. In a general sense, this attachment to a larger unit is in the interest of the Trusteeship areas themselves. However, they must maintain their identity if the opportunity to become independent is not to be undercut. It has become the task of a special sub-committee of the Trusteeship Council for "administrative unity" to examine whether in a concrete case both positions which in many ways are contradictory are taken into account.

THE RIGHT TO PETITION

Only for the area of the Trusteeship system has the Charter realized the right of petition for individuals and organizations. And from the beginning, this opportunity to bring before the Council requests and complaints has been amply used. In this way, the treatment of petitions became one of the most important areas of activity of the Trusteeship Council. In view of the enormous number of petitions[3] which came before it or were submitted to the visiting missions, a [Standing Committee on Petitions] for the purpose of sifting the material was established. The fear that the work of the Council would be blocked by the avalanche of generally irrelevant complaints proved to be in the main without foundation. It is true that the petitions which were submitted required an enormous amount of work because of the necessity of preparatory work, the need to inquire of the states against which complaints were lodged, and the job of final disposition. Many petitioners came forth with very general wishes whose fulfillment was not within the purview of the organ to which the complaints were addressed. They had a certain value in providing a barometer of feelings, but could not lead to any action. Innumerable petitions requested of the United Nations things which could have been dealt with through an appeal to the local authorities. Many, however, directed their attention to serious matters which otherwise would not have come to the attention of the international community. The Trusteeship Council does not act as a court which is in a position to announce verdicts of guilty or not guilty. Nevertheless the decisions which the Council has made after dealing with each individual petition have been of great significance. The liberal practice in admitting complaints and the thorough airing of even the most trivial complaints have contributed to strengthening the confidence of the peoples of the Trusteeship territories in the United Nations. . . .

[With only three trust territories remaining under the International Trusteeship System and a consequent reduction in its work, the Trusteeship Council decided at its 29th session to change its rules of procedure so as to abolish its Standing Committee on Petitions. The Council itself now examines all petitions of which there were only nine at the 29th session. The reduction in the number of petitions may indicate that the remaining trust territories are proceeding in a peaceful and satisfactory manner toward the attainment of the objectives of the international trusteeship system. Also because of the lightened work load, the Council agreed to meet for a single regular session each year to be convened during the month of May, instead of for two regular sessions previously held each year.

Between 1946 and 1950 eleven territories, located in Africa and in the Pacific Ocean, with approximately 20 million people, were placed under the

[3] At its 26th and longest session (14 April–30 June, 1960), the Council dealt with 1,971 petitions relating to general questions [ed.].

Trusteeship system. By the end of 1965 only three trust territories remained —New Guinea, administered by Australia; Nauru, administered by Australia on behalf of Australia, New Zealand, and the United Kingdom; and the Trust Territory of the Pacific Islands (a strategic area), administered by the United States. For these remaining territories, the Trusteeship Council has urged that "realistic targets" be set to reflect "a proper sense of urgency for the rapid and planned advance" of the territories. New Guinea and the Pacific Islands can look forward to independence as a distant prospect. Nauruans, however, are faced with resettlement since the tiny island's phosphate deposits, upon which the population depends for its existence, will be exhausted within the next forty years.]

The Trusteeship system as it was conceived in 1945 [is now] restricted to some relatively unimportant islands in the Pacific Ocean. However, at the same time, as the example of the Congo demonstrates, a new form of international Trusteeship arises, in which there is no longer a Trusteeship power, but in which the international community participates directly in the development of states involving nations which so far lack a history. This new form of Trusteeship will make use of the active participation primarily of those members which are not burdened by a past of having been colonial powers.

THE EMERGING ANTI-COLONIAL CONSENSUS IN THE UNITED NATIONS

Edward T. Rowe*

Any attempt to characterize the changes which the world has undergone since the end of World War II would be incomplete without treating the emergence of millions of the world's population from colonial status to independence. "Nations," as Rupert Emerson writes, "have arisen from the ashes of empire." While not all of the colonial regimes have been so reduced, relatively few remain; and for these few the future seems to be fairly short.

Many factors have played a part in this emergence of formerly colonial

* Edward T. Rowe, "The Emerging Anti-Colonial Consensus in the United Nations," *Journal of Conflict Resolution*, Vol. 8, 1964, pp. 209–230. Copyright 1964 by the University of Michigan.

Edward T. Rowe is Assistant Professor of Political Science at the University of Connecticut. He was a Woodrow Wilson Fellow at the University of Michigan from 1959 to 1960.

areas. Although the tasks of specifying all those factors and determining their relative importance will occupy students for many years to come, it appears certain that some recognition must be given to the activities of the United Nations. At the very least, the UN has provided one of the arenas within which colonial issues have been raised and debated. And whatever assessment is made of the effectiveness of many UN actions on colonial issues, certainly the number and scope of such actions have increased almost steadily from the time of the UN's establishment. Less clear, however, is whether or not there has been any general acceptance of these activities or any widespread agreement on colonial issues. Has there been a continuing or widening gap between the colonial and anti-colonial states? Or can we speak of the development of some degree of anti-colonial consensus in the United Nations?

In the past, at least, most writers discerned no such consensus. Generally, the implicit or explicit argument has been that increasingly vehement anti-colonialism had caused a polarization of positions and consequently a barrier to UN effectiveness. Whether this polarization was caused by the demands of the newly emergent nations or by the extreme positions taken by the Soviet Union, it was a phenomenon that most students of international relations believed to be characteristic of the debate on colonial issues.

Without necessarily questioning the accuracy of this type of argument when it refers to earlier periods, the present time seems especially appropriate for a reconsideration of the problem. The rapid decline in the number of areas still under colonial control and the corresponding increase in the number of states having international relevance have brought considerable change to the international environment. In the first place, insofar as these new states have an anti-colonial orientation, the possibility of success in the United Nations of any proposals which are not anti-colonial may be expected to decline. In the second place, the increase in the number of states to which the colonial powers must appeal if they are to gain support in areas other than those involving colonial issues might be expected to produce greater concessions. In the third place, and perhaps most important, the decline in the number of territories under colonial control may be expected to produce a decline in the importance attached to issues in this area, thus making concessions considerably less painful.

*   *   *   *   *   *   *

[These findings seem to indicate, both] with regard to colonial issues generally and with regard to specific issues, increasingly uniform, anti-colonial voting on issues before the United Nations. They also indicate that, with only a few exceptions, the members of the UN, including the colonial powers, now accept a more extensive role for the United Nations in the area of colonialism and related issues than those members were willing to accept in the past. Little has been said concerning the expansion of the

United Nations' anti-colonial activities. But, within the context of such expanded activities, fewer states now take an extremely pro-colonial position than was the case during earlier sessions of the UN. With the exception of South Africa and Portugal, and possibly of Spain (although Spain, as we have seen, has also made some concessions), the colonial powers in particular seem more willing now than they were in the past to accept an expansive interpretation of what the UN may do.

This general finding conflicts somewhat with one of the observations commonly made by writers on the United Nations and colonialism—i.e., that the decline in moderation among the anti-colonial states produces a general reaction among the colonial powers uniting them behind pro-colonial positions. While the latter has occasionally been the case on particular issues, over time and with regard to a whole series of issues it does not seem to be accurate. On the contrary, during the last few sessions at least, the increasingly extreme character of the anti-colonial proposals put forward has been accompanied by the colonial powers moving closer to the anti-colonial majority. It should be noted, however, that such observations were generally made at a time when they may have been more accurate. That is, our results do show that, for a period during the 1950s, a number of the colonial powers were somewhat more extreme than either earlier or later; and this can be partially explained by the less moderate anti-colonial position. Since the latter became even less moderate during later sessions, however, the explanation is inadequate. It may be that a more important factor was the possibility of successfully opposing the anti-colonial proposals—that is, being able to gain enough support to defeat some of those proposals. This was more of a possibility before 1958 than it has been since that year. In the early years of the UN the position of the colonial powers was secure enough and the number of states taking an extremely anti-colonial position small enough that only moderate proposals involving extensive concessions to the colonial powers could be expected to receive adequate support. As the number of anti-colonial states increased, however, through both changes in the positions of various states and additions to UN membership, it was by threatening nonparticipation and exhibiting a high degree of unity that the colonial powers were able to rally enough support from the more moderate states to alter or defeat anti-colonial measures. The extraordinary increase in the number of anti-colonial states in recent years has dated even this tactic, in the sense that using it would for the most part simply mean isolation and repeated defeat for the colonial powers and their associates.

There are undoubtedly a large number of other factors which help explain recent changes. For one thing, the extreme positions of South Africa and Portugal may play a role that those positions did not play earlier. During recent sessions, for instance, the representative of the United Kingdom has several times spoken of his government's desire to be dissociated from the policies of certain other states—the context of the statements being such that the references were obviously to Portugal and South Africa. Futhermore, one cannot ignore the fact that so many of the areas which seemed firmly under colonial control a few years ago are now independent. With fewer interests involved, concessions to anti-colonial sentiments in the United Nations are certainly easier to make. In the case of Belgium, for instance, there seems to be every reason to suspect that recent changes in her positions are closely related to the fact that the Belgian Congo, Rwanda, and Burundi are now independent. Also, the admission of so many newly independent states to the United Nations has not only increased the voting strength of the anti-colonial states but, related to this, heightened the priority to be assigned to eliminating the last vestiges of colonialism. For these and other reasons, a pro-colonial position has become both less tenable and a liability to the mobilization of support for aims not related to colonial issues. The colonial powers can ignore the actions taken by the UN, which they occasionally do; they can oppose the actions but later cooperate, as they also occasionally do; or they can attempt to cooperate in the formulation of proposals in order both to gain concessions in other areas and to keep the proposals from being unacceptably extreme.

The choices which are made by the colonial powers are at least partially determined by the "Cold War." The fact that most of the colonial powers have policy aims arising out of the Cold War which are essentially unrelated to the question of colonialism is probably one of the most important factors helping to determine their positions on colonial issues. Since the Soviet Union takes an extremely anti-colonial position, since the colonial powers are generally concerned with the policies and allegiances of former colonies, and since the end of colonialism is in sight in any case, it is probable that the recent changes we have seen are only the beginning of even more radical changes in the positions of most of the colonial powers.

With the end of colonialism in sight, of course, these changes become less meaningful. All of the sizable trust territories, for instance, are now independent; and only a few large non-self-governing territories remain. Against Portugal and South Africa, however, it would appear that the UN membership will be increasingly united behind increasingly vehement proposals. In addition to this, it may well be that some of the precedents which have been and are now being established through activities in the colonial area will be important for the development of UN activities in other areas. The possibilities of finding procedural and other arrangements for cooperative action in the area of colonial issues which might be transferred to other areas will probably increase as there is increasing consensus with regard to colonial disputes. In short, cooperation and agreement in this area may increase the chances for the successful transfer of experiences to other areas. It seems clear, of course, that cooperation in one area of UN activities cannot be used to predict accurately the degree of cooperation that may be expected in another area. At the same time, where the forces producing conflict and cooperation are similar between different areas of activity, there should be both similarities useful for prediction and potentialities for the transfer of cooperative arrangements. At the very least, there would be a basis for useful comparative studies. Because of the decline in the importance of colonial issues, it is probably in these ways that our findings in this study have most potential significance for our understanding of future United Nations activities.

CHAPTER **15**

DISARMAMENT: PAST PROBLEMS AND PRESENT PROSPECTS

Man's concern with the need to control violence through many methods including disarmament is an ancient one. In the Old Testament Isaiah's vision may be construed as a plea for disarmament when he says, "and they shall beat their swords into plowshares, and their spears into pruning hooks." And one also may recall the philosophers' assumptions that man once lived in a state of nature which he gave up when he formed a government in order to remove the violence and turmoil of his life. In addition, history can point to the Hague Conferences called at the end of the last century and the beginning of this one to attempt to reach some agreement on disarmament. Some success during the period between World War I and World War II, particularly in naval disarmament, was achieved. However, because of the advent of nuclear weapons it is clear that the need to conclude a disarmament agreement has now assumed propor-

470

tions beyond those of any period in the past, which means that the UN is again confronted with a task of formidable proportions.

Dr. Bogdan Babović deals with these efforts to achieve disarmament in his article, "Disarmament and International Community." He discusses the effort from the First Hague Conference through the League period as well as the technological changes which have increased the urgency of finding some solution to the arms problem. However, as Dr. Babović notes, the United Nations Charter seems not to have gone much farther than the League in the establishment of legal obligations in this sphere, stressing, rather, collective security as a means to maintain peace. Hence, he is quite right in saying that so far as the Charter is concerned, international legal obligations have not been revised on the right to manufacture and to own arms. Even the Test-Ban Treaty, which was signed after his article was written, does not involve any modification in this legal obligation, being concerned only with testing. Thus, we are confronted with the paradox that the right to manufacture arms exists, but the right to use them, except in self defense, does not. If the prohibition against using arms is to be made meaningful, the author argues, then the right to manufacture them must be modified.

Daniel Cheever examines the subject of disarmament from a perspective that has been badly needed. Much of the writing on disarmament does not reveal the role and impact the UN has had. In "The UN and Disarmament," Cheever evaluates the Secretary-General's optimism in 1964 that greater progress had occurred in the search for disarmament during the past year than had occurred since the beginning of the Organization's history. Certainly he was right if one considers the lack of success toward disarmament since the Baruch Plan was adopted in 1946—a meaningless General Assembly approval inasmuch as the Soviet Union refused to join the majority. (As a matter of fact, this may be considered the first in a series of votes which were to become hollow victories for the United States.) The difficulty of each side's trying to find a formula which would both guarantee its own security and be acceptable to the other side was magnified for many years by the Soviet Union's insistence, and the United States dogged refusal, to bring the Chinese Communist representatives into the discussion. The question of inspection—when and by whom—has plagued the negotiations from the start. It has been clear for several years that technological developments in detecting tests ought to have diminished the degree of uncertainty as to what the other side is doing.

The other needs which were eventually recognized as interdependent were the establishment of a reliable collective-security system and a pacific settlement system, both of which, however, have seemed out of reach. Hence the emphasis has been on the development of unilateral and multilateral nuclear responses, by nations which at the same time continue to speak of the horror of nuclear war.

Despite these failings, disarmament continues to be one of the perennial hot issues before the UN. And although the Assembly may have grown too large to be useful as a negotiating forum, it has been more useful than other groups simply by keeping the pressure on the major powers to try to make meaningful concessions. Both the United States and the Soviet Union at least have recognized the importance of this forum and have been eager to provide convincing arguments in behalf of their own positions. The views of the Soviet Union and other countries have been included in this chapter in order to provide interpretations other than those of Western writers for the causes of the difficulties standing in the way of disarmament. One of these views is an excerpt of an article which appeared in a Soviet journal published for Western consumption. The others are speeches delivered in the First Committee of the General Assembly from 1957 to 1963. Included in these is the first proposal for a denuclearized zone put forth in a famous speech made by the Polish Foreign Minister Adam Rapacki. In almost all of these speeches one gets a strong sense of deep emotional response to the disarmament stalemate, and an inkling of the great frustration felt by many people over its continuation.

It was suggested earlier that collective security will remain a chimera unless a significant level of disarmament is reached. Is there a reciprocal relationship here? Is it likely that states will be willing to disarm to any appreciable extent unless they feel certain that, should their own security be threatened, they will have some international force available to come to their rescue? The question thus becomes: How much of the difficulty in achieving a disarmament agreement stems from the need to find a substitute for protection which the state is normally expected to provide? We might also ask if disarmament in nuclear weaponry is really enough, or if conventional weapons must not also be included. Certainly if an iron-clad inspection system could be found in which human inspectors had the right to visit and search, a right too remote to be considered seriously, the fear of cheating would be greatly reduced. But without some unlikely agreement such as that, nuclear disarmament is bound to make the Western nations, and especially the United States, continue to feel insecure because of their disadvantage in conventional land armies. Therefore, except perhaps in the psychological realm, what benefits can be seen in proposals that are "half-way houses"?

Finally, it must be asked again whether a genuine effort has really been made by any of the parties involved in disarmament, or whether each side merely puts forth proposals which it knows in advance the other cannot accept because they were designed in the first place to put the proposer at an advantage? And, in connection with this, are the major states keeping in mind the powerful countries which are not engaged in the discussions, but which must be kept in consideration? Can any useful agreement be reached without careful attention to the reactions and positions of France and Mainland China?

FURTHER READINGS

Bechhoefer, Bernhard G., "The Disarmament Deadlock: 1946–1955," *Current History*, Vol. XLII, May 1962, pp. 257–266.

Ikle, Fred C., *Alternative Approaches to the International Organization of Disarmament*. Santa Monica, Cal.: The Rand Corporation, 1962.

Scott, William A., and Withey, Stephen B., *The United States and the United Nations: The Public View*. New York: Manhattan Publishing Company, 1958.

Spanier, John, and Nogee, Joseph L., *The Politics of Disarmament*. New York: Frederick A. Praeger, Inc., 1962.

DISARMAMENT AND INTERNATIONAL COMMUNITY

Bogdan Babović*

The demand for a general disarmament constitutes one of the basic elements of the international order whose purpose is to abolish war as an instrument of national policy in international relations. This demand already appeared attractive enough in the XIXth century to be included in the agenda of official international meetings, particularly of the First Hague Peace Conference of 1899. At that time there was hope among the peoples of the world that a way to abolish war and armaments would be found. However, the Conference yielded very poor results with respect to disarmament. The Conference only adopted a resolution expressing the desire that Military Budgets should be reduced for the sake of increasing the material and moral welfare of mankind. On the other hand, efforts were made to humanize wars by means of elaboration and adoption of legal rules of warfare. The Second Hague Peace Conference did not prove any more successful with regard to the question of reducing armaments. Moreover, some attempts were made to delete the question of disarmament from the agenda of the Conference, but they failed. This time again the final result was embodied in a resolution sponsored by the British Delegation, noting that the military budgets of the States had considerably increased from 1899 to 1907 and inviting the Governments to reconsider the question seriously.

Neither the first nor the second Conference was primarily concerned with disarmament. Their result, therefore, cannot be described as complete failure, which would have been the case had they been concerned only with disarmament. The very approach to the question by the delegates was wrong in the sense that instead of dealing more fully with immediate causes of war, they dealt primarily with its consequences. This might have been caused by the fact that under the international law of the time war was permitted and there was no trend toward a prohibition of the resort to force in international relations.

The Covenant introduced a new method for handling the problem of disarmament. In addition to the provisions for the reduction of armaments required for the maintenance of world peace, the Covenant endeavored to

* Bogdan Babović, "Disarmament and International Community," *Yugoslav Review for International Law*, Vol. 7, 1960, pp. 233–239. By permission of Bogdan Babović and the *Yugoslav Review for International Law*.

Bogdan Babović is a senior research fellow at the Institute of International Politics and Economy, University of Belgrade, Yugoslavia.

organize what was later called "collective security" aimed at creating the necessary conditions and the feeling of security among the States which had to reduce their armaments. Furthermore, some of the Covenant's provisions, while not prohibiting war in an absolute manner, subjected its outlook to the observance of a certain procedure of peaceful settlement of disputes. The last fact meant that positive international law was taking its course toward the prohibition of resorting to force in international relations. Consequently, the end of World War I and the appearance of the first World Peace Organization constitute the beginning of a new era in the attitude of international law to war, the era where the idea of disarmament had to play the most decisive role. International law enters a new stage. In accordance with its function to regulate relationships among States, it had to play a specific role in prevention and suppression of illegal use of force. It also had to determine whether and when such a use of force was taking place.

This new attitude to war and use of force lays special stress on the system of collective security, the idea of collective action of all the members of the League against the State that violates the law, undermines international order and breaks world peace. The idea of collective security and the tendency toward peaceful settlement of international disputes, leads to the demand for disarmament, i.e., to a limitation and reduction of armaments and armed forces of States. This goal should be reached through the conclusion of one or more appropriate international agreements. Such agreement or agreements should be integrated into the international legal order which should, in the first place, express the tendency toward suppressing force and promoting peaceful coexistence of nations.

If the failure of earlier efforts to attain some results in the field of general disarmament are attributed partly to the fact that there was no adequate framework for negotiations, i.e., no international organization, the emergence of the League of Nations, an organization formed for the specific purpose of developing cooperation among States and ensuring peace and security, gave permanency to the efforts for disarmament and rendered them indispensable. This is due to the fact that under the existing conditions the problem of disarmament has become inseparable from the problem of peace and that the efforts directed at the settlement of the former cannot be separated from the settlement of the later.

Since the League's main task was to maintain international peace established after World War I, it is only natural that disarmament had to constitute the core of its preoccupations. There can be no doubt that disarmament has become closely linked with every attempt to organize peace on a universal basis and to build up an international system of collective security. Viewed from the perspective of the present development of international relations, the demand for disarmament has been favorably received, and the drafting of the necessary instruments and the settlement of the problem of disarmament has become one of the basic tasks of the organization of the international community. This progress, if we may call it so, is remarkably demonstrated by the fact that during the Second Hague Conference only twenty-five minutes were devoted to the question of disarmament while endless discussions on the subject took place in the League of Nations, and no time is spared on discussions on disarmament in the United Nations.

Apart from the theoretical discussion on the subject whether disarmament is *per se* a method appropriate enough for solving the problem of peace, it is certain that all adequate solutions of organizing international order must also include disarmament as one of its constituent elements. This is confirmed by the first of the three principles set forth in Article 8 of the League's Covenant. According to this principle the Members recognize "that the maintenance of peace requires the reduction of national armaments to the lowest point consistent with national safety and the enforcement by common action of international obligations." It is also embodied in the first resolution of U.N. General Assembly (41/1), which was unanimously adopted by all Member-States. The resolution deals with the guiding principles for the regulation and reduction of general armaments and it stresses the need to regulate and reduce general armaments and armed forces as soon as possible for the sake of strengthening international peace and security.

The desire to ensure international peace by means of common and organized efforts is combined with the endeavours to bring about disarmament not only because it is but logical that a limitation and reduction of armament considerably contribute to a lessening of tension in the world but also because of the general belief that it is an evidence of a greater or lesser stability in international relations.

The League of Nations started to treat the question of disarmament in a new way, but without success. Disarmament efforts were made outside of the League as well. All the activities in this field were very rich in words, but very poor in results. The history of the League's activities in the field of disarmament offers nothing but indisputable evidence of a constant wrestling of the organization with the problem of priority, namely whether disarmament is a mere result of the long process of organizing peace or is it, on the contrary, its starting point?

The Charter of the United Nations marks a new stage in the evolution of the attitude of the international community and the conceptions of international law toward the problems of war and peace. This came as a result of the development of international relations in which an essential component is formed by the process of economic integration of the world. This integration requires new forms of international cooperation. Under classical international law, war was considered as a normal phenomenon, a legal institute, an attribute of State sovereignty, or a legitimate means by which

States enforce their rights and interests. The Covenant of the League of Nations provided some restrictions in this respect but still did not prohibit war as an institute of international law. The Charter, however, treats the question of disarmament, i.e., the prohibition of war, in a much more rigorous form than the Covenant and even the . . . Briand-Kellogg Pact which went far beyond the point reached in 1919. Under the Charter of the United Nations, war as an instrument of national policy does not exist. On the contrary, it is qualified as international crime. The planning, initiation and waging of war is to be prevented through collective action undertaken by the Organization.

This evolution of the general attitude to war has been dictated by the progress of science and technology. This gave rise to what can be described as physical interdependence of the world, as well as a trend toward wide international economic integration. It further shows that the development of technology in general, and particularly of military techniques endowed war with such effects and consequences as were increasingly hard to limit or attenuate. From the standpoint of international law, it has therefore become increasingly difficult to consider war as "another instrument of policy" of one State with regard to another. On the other hand, "despite differences and crises, the growing measure of organization of international community offered not only new and more perfect means for a peaceful settlement of disputes; it indicated the possibilities for a centralization of international legal sanctions which could progressively replace self help at least in its most rudimentary aspects."

The Charter does not *in ipsis verbis* impose any obligation on the Members of the United Nations regarding disarmament or reduction of their armaments. On the contrary, it provides for "effective collective measures" for the maintenance of peace, by providing for a rather effective and a comparatively highly centralized system of collective measures for the prevention and suppression of the use of force in international relations. It assigns, moreover, the United Nations the task to regulate the question of disarmament. The discharge of this task is entrusted both to the General Assembly (Article 11, para. 1) and the Security Council (Article 26). The General Assembly carries out this task as part of its general competence to consider principles of international cooperation. On the other hand, in order to promote the maintenance of international peace and security with the least division of the world's human and economic resources for armaments, the particular responsibility of the Security Council consists in formulating plans for the establishment of a system for the regulation of armaments. These plans are to be submitted to the Members of the United Nations for approval. Consequently, the United Nations did not reserve for itself the right to determine, carry out and supervise the armament of States in general: it could just appraise, recommend and prepare its limitation and reduction, whereas the final word would be left to the States themselves. Therefore, one could say that the classical rule of international law still applies, namely that armament is a prerogative of sovereign national States, and that the international community cannot deprive them of that prerogative without their consent. This is why some authors have concluded that the attitude of international law toward the disarmament problem has not changed in its essence.

However, if there is no legal rule binding upon the States to disarm, there are guiding principles in the Charter against excessive armament as contrary to the principles upon which the United Nations is based. Among these fundamental principles we should stress the obligation of settlement of disputes by peaceful means and of refraining from the threat or use of force against the territorial integrity or political independence of other States whether or not Members of the Organization. It is illogical that States which solemnly assumed the obligation to act in accordance with these principles should be engaged in a ruinous and portentous armaments race which can at any time result in a general conflagration and universal destruction.

In this connection it should be mentioned that the right to wage war (*ius ad bellum gerendi*) does not exist, the States being deprived of it by the Charter. Hence, if the legal rule on the abolishment of the right to wage war (subject to exception in the case of self-defense) has been incorporated into international law, then it is logically necessary and at present highly urgent to undertake and accelerate the adoption of the rules prohibiting the possession of facilities for an unlimited waging of wars. In absence of these rules, the outlawry of war, although an institute of positive international law, would mainly remain a platonic declaration without any considerable effect. War cannot be excluded, at least not with certainty, by means of any international legal obligations or written arrangements until the unlimited right to arm and, consequently, the mighty armed forces no longer exist, the latter being a permanent and potential danger to peace.

The present-day world is faced with a legally abnormal situation. There is a legal prohibition of war under which the States are no longer entitled to resort to and wage war nor to use any force in their international relations. But, unfortunately, there is still no ban on the production and use of means for waging wars. In other words, the States are deprived of a right which used to represent the ultimate prerogative of their sovereignty, but they are left in full possession of the means to enforce that right, despite the existence of the general organization of a universal character whose task is to maintain international peace and security, and whose Members are bound to settle *all* their disputes by peaceful means "in such a manner that international peace and security, and justice, are not endangered" (Article 2, para. 3). The Charter offers to the Members the necessary machinery for the said settlement of disputes.

THE UN AND DISARMAMENT

Daniel S. Cheever*

In 1964 Secretary-General U Thant asserted

that more significant progress in achieving some measures of disarmament has taken place since the summer of 1963 than in all the years since the founding of the United Nations.

The evidence cited included five achievements: 1) the coming into force in October 1963 of the Moscow Treaty, a partial test-ban treaty banning nuclear-weapons tests in the atmosphere, in outer space, and under water to which more than 100 states had subscribed by 1965; 2) the establishment of the direct communications link between Moscow and Washington; 3) the resolution of the General Assembly to ban nuclear and other weapons of mass destruction from outer space;[1] 4) the unilateral reductions of the military budgets of the Soviet Union and the United States; and 5) the mutual cutbacks in production of fissionable material for military purposes by these two countries and the United Kingdom.

Our inquiry here will have a threefold objective: to evaluate the Secretary-General's unguarded optimism in the perspective of twenty years' experience in disarmament negotiations, to examine the role assigned to the United Nations in major disarmament proposals, and to analyze the use and influence of the Organization as a disarmament forum. The term "disarmament" will be used throughout except in cases where the use of a more analytically precise term such as "arms control" becomes necessary. It is our thesis that disarmament negotiations in the United Nations have made progress to the extent that they have followed the principles of the Charter. Taking disarmament and peacekeeping experience together, there is some evidence that with the partial test ban and the impasse on the financing of peacekeeping operations, developments in the United Nations have come nearly full circle in twenty years. There has been a progression

* Daniel S. Cheever, "The UN and Disarmament," *International Organization*, Vol. 19, 1965, pp. 463–483. Copyright 1965, World Peace Foundation.

Daniel S. Cheever is Professor of International Affairs in the Graduate School of Public and International Affairs at the University of Pittsburgh and a member of the Board of Editors of *International Organization*. He and Field Haviland, Jr. are coauthors of *Organizing for Peace*.

[1] General Assembly Resolution 1962 (XVIII), December 13, 1963. Also see General Assembly Resolution 1963 (XVIII), December 13, 1963.

from the initial premise in the Charter that the management of force in international relations requires the consent and collaboration of the major powers, through an unmapped land of near utopian proposals and enforcement actions by the General Assembly designed to obligate great and small powers alike, back to a grudging acceptance of the Security Council and the rule of big-power unanimity. This is not to say that all the major powers are agreed on disarmament matters. France and Communist China not only have refused to subscribe to the partial test-ban treaty but remain apart as well from the Conference of the Eighteen-Nation Committee on Disarmament, facts that by themselves outweigh the "achievements" noted by Secretary-General U Thant.

✻   ✻   ✻   ✻   ✻   ✻   ✻

IMPLICATIONS OF MAJOR PROPOSALS FOR THE UNITED NATIONS

From the outset the role of the United Nations as a control organization has been at issue in disarmament negotiations. The Baruch Plan of June 1946, presented by the United States to the UN Atomic Energy Commission, included a proposal to establish by treaty an International Atomic Development Authority to own, operate, manage, and license all facilities for the production of atomic energy. To insure that atomic energy would be used solely for peaceful purposes the Authority was to have freedom to carry on inspections on a continual basis in all countries and was to manage its affairs by majority vote. By insisting that violations of the new control agreement should be met by "swift condign" punishment unhampered by the Security Council veto, Bernard M. Baruch was saying in effect that the security and disarmament provisions of the Charter were obsolete before they were tried. All states would be disarmed as far as atomic weapons were to be concerned, and a single world authority would have the only atomic potential. The United States, however, would not be required to disarm until the Authority's control mechanism was in full operation with the result that its atomic advantage over the Soviet Union would be preserved until the international monopoly was established. Other governments in effect were asked to accept the "sacred trust" which President Harry S. Truman declared the United States would hold for all mankind until international controls had been established. The proposed Authority was thus to receive information from the United States in a series of "stages" of which only the last would include both control over atomic weapons and the secret data pertaining to them.

Had the United States not been so preoccupied with the actual role of United Nations bodies in atomic energy control, it would not have been necessary for Bernard Baruch to stress with such emphasis the veto issue in the UN Atomic Energy Commission. While there was to be no formal amendment of the Charter itself, a new threat to mankind was held to demand a new body with unprecedented authority to be specified in a new treaty. Similarly, any serious breach of the treaty would be such an unprecedented threat to the peace as to require immediate punishment. Because this would not be forthcoming if enforcement action by the Security Council could be thwarted by the veto, the proposed treaty would modify the Security Council voting formula on matters arising as a result of breaches of the treaty. The United States, in short, sought to retain the United Nations while at the same time urging the establishment of what in effect was limited world government to enforce atomic disarmament. While the Charter's enforcement provisions were to stand as they were, a new treaty would have effectively altered Article 27 in atomic energy matters.

The Soviet Union chose to stand by the original Charter and its unanimity principle. Soviet Ambassador Andrei Gromyko countered with two proposals that were diametrically opposed to the United States position. Two conventions were to come into force simultaneously, one to outlaw the production and use of atomic weapons and the other to organize the work of the UN Atomic Energy Commission to facilitate the exchange of scientific information for peaceful purposes. Arms control was to be enforced primarily by *national* governments under the general supervisory powers of an International Control Commission which would have the right to conduct only limited and "periodic" inspection of declared plants and facilities. The Soviet proposals would have had the effect of disarming the United States before an effective control system had been established by requiring the prior destruction of nuclear stockpiles. The enforcement of control measures, moreover, was to be decided only by agreement of the Security Council's permanent members.

. . . The result was a compromise in the form of a resolution on the "Principles Governing the General Regulation and Reduction of Armaments" carried unanimously in the 1946 General Assembly. The Security Council was instructed to seek practical measures to reduce and regulate armaments, to expedite the work of the UN Atomic Energy Commission in controlling atomic weapons, and to provide armed forces under Article 43 of the Charter. The resolution in addition urged the withdrawal of armed forces from territories beyond national frontiers. Most important for the relationship of United Nations bodies to armaments control organization was the seeming agreement on the principle that an international control system, including regulation, inspection, and reduction of conventional armaments, with special organs to enforce the system, should be established within the Security Council's framework. This agreement on principles, however, could not paper over the fundamental disagreement between the Western powers and the Soviet bloc. The former continued to insist on a control system including inspection and verification before they were ready to countenance major steps toward disarmament while the latter pressed for prior outlawing of atomic weapons and reduction of *all* weapons without effective international control by means of inspection. The relationship between these points of view to the balance of military forces in the East-West struggle need not be elaborated here. Suffice it to say that the concern of each side to gain military advantage over the other through disarmament negotiations has prevented the implementation of these principles in a twenty-year period. Although the Security Council followed the Assembly's mandate by establishing a UN Commission for Conventional Armaments in February 1947 consisting of the governments represented on the Council, no progress was made since the membership was divided 9-2 on the fundamental issues involved.

A NEW INITIATIVE. . . . the establishment of the Disarmament Commission . . . in effect consolidated the UN Atomic Energy Commission and the UN Commission for Conventional Armaments. Like the UN Atomic Energy Commission, the new body included in its membership all the Security Council members plus Canada. It was directed to prepare a draft treaty for Security Council and Assembly approval for the regulation, limitation, and balanced reduction of all armed forces and all armaments, for the elimination of all weapons adaptable to mass destruction, and for effective international control to insure the prohibition of atomic weapons and the use of atomic energy for peaceful purposes only. However, progressive and continuing *disclosure* and *verification* of all armed forces and all armaments, including atomic armaments, remained as a first and indispensable step in the new disarmament program, a provision that presumably provoked the five negative votes of the Soviet bloc.

The second step was the readiness of the Soviet Union and the Western allies to negotiate the following year as members of the five-power Subcommittee of the Disarmament Commission. . . . The principal difficulty was Communist China. When the Western states suggested that the members of the Subcommittee should be the Soviet Union, the United States, the United Kingdom, France, and Canada, the Soviet Union acquiesced only after urging unsuccessfully the addition of Czechoslovakia, India, and Communist China. The inclusion of the latter was totally unacceptable to the United States and was to continue to remain so for many years to come. In time the exclusion of Communist China would lend an air of unreality to any discussions that seemed to be seriously concerned with disarmament. In 1953, however, it could perhaps be argued that neither Chinese government was "principally involved" in disarmament matters.

That disagreement on substantive matters continued despite the subcommittee device is clear from the fact that throughout its life until the final deadlock and adjournment in 1957, the two sides were unable to resolve their major differences on how to implement the objectives listed in repetitive Assembly resolutions. The Western majority continued to emphasize "verification" and "inspection" as elements of a control system that was to be fully operative before any prohibition of atomic weapons was to be put into effect. The Soviet Union, after receding from its initial position that atomic weapons should be banned first and controls established second, remained adamant on another point: that there must be no interference "in the domestic affairs of states" by an international control organ. With no agreement either on the control measures to be established or on means of enforcement in the event of violation of such measures, there could be little specific discussion of the relationship of control organs to the United Nations.

COLLECTIVE ENFORCEMENT VERSUS FREEDOM OF ACTION. Lawrence S. Finkelstein has stressed the point that two principles of arms control and disarmament enforcement have been in competition from the beginning: collective enforcement by the United Nations or some other international body on the one hand, and resumed freedom of national action in the event of information indicating the breach of a control treaty on the other hand. This point had already been at issue when Mr. Baruch chose to emphasize the abolition of the veto whereas a previous United States study, the Acheson-Lilienthal Report, which had served as a "foundation" for the Baruch proposals, had stressed the point that violations of an atomic energy control agreement would provide a period of time as a margin of safety during which states would be free to take whatever measures, individual or collective, that seemed necessary for their safety. By emphasizing freedom of national action rather than international sanctions, after the disclosure of a break in an arms control treaty, the control problem becomes simplified and the relationship of control organs to the Organization becomes less important. It was the principle of resumed freedom of action, coupled with the essential scientific achievement of national inspection or self-inspection of nuclear testing throughout the world, which made possible the partial test-ban treaty in 1963. On the evidence of the 1965 test episode in the Soviet Union the principal international control element was an information flow and its correct interpretation by the governments involved. The scientific contribution to the political problem of arms control has been to devise at least the beginning of a control technology that may be acceptable in the current stage of international relations in which the major governments continue to resist supra-national institutions. The implied sanction in such a control system is national action which a state party to an arms control treaty is free to follow once it has detected a violation. It may, of course, protest the violation in an international forum such as the General Assembly in order to gain support for and legitimization of its national enforcement and defense measures, as the United States sought to do in the Cuban confrontation of 1962.

Given the nature of the proposals before it, the Disarmament Commission and its five-member Subcommittee could make little progress toward agreement between 1953 and 1957. At no time was it possible to demonstrate a compensating gain in international control to make up for the freedom of action that would have been lost by acceptance of a control arrangement. Rather extreme proposals for the cessation of weapons tests, the elimination of nuclear stockpiles, the termination of nuclear production, and "open skies" over agreed inspection zones to eliminate "surprise attacks" were calculated constantly in terms of politico-military advantage. This was particularly the case with "disengagement proposals" relating to a zone of limited armaments in Central Europe with nuclear armaments specifically prohibited, proposals that had for their objective not general disarmament but the continued nuclear disarmament of Germany and the withdrawal of United States military power from Europe.

The UN was moved to the forefront in a closely related set of negotiations, however, dealing with the control of the peaceful uses of atomic energy. In 1953 United States President Dwight D. Eisenhower presented an "atoms for peace proposal" before the General Assembly in which he suggested that cooperation in the peaceful uses of atomic energy could contribute to the prevention of atomic energy for military purposes. Subsequent negotiations under United Nations auspices led to the establishment of the International Atomic Energy Agency (IAEA) in 1957.

DISARMAMENT AND PEACEKEEPING. In retrospect it is clear that the five governments were negotiating under a major handicap throughout the entire four-year period. The United Nations security system was obviously inadequate. Because the second attempt to establish a universal collective security system had failed to meet the major demands thrust upon it, regional security arrangements had become necessary. The result was that disengagement proposals ran afoul of the obvious importance of NATO and the Warsaw Pact in maintaining both a European and a world military balance. The United Nations could make only a modest contribution in checking the Suez fiasco which may well have confirmed the British and French governments in their intentions to develop nuclear forces of their own. As with the League experience, disarmament once again seemed impossible to achieve without a dependable collective security system.

Although the inadequacy of the collective security system had been obvious from the day the Charter came into force, a new factor in world politics, however, has served to maintain disarmament as a national goal. Nuclear capacity to "overkill" has brought safety to no nation and maintaining the "balance of terror" has hindered the pursuit of national goals such as economic development. Statements by the heads of government of even the nuclear powers to the effect that war had become "unthinkable" and that no nation was safe from a nuclear holocaust seem to have been made with serious intent to negotiate arms control proposals and not solely for propaganda effect. Weapons became so destructive during the 1950's that a safeguard arms control agreement contained the possibility of providing greater national safety by stabilizing the balance of terror. Yet arms control negotiations isolated from discussion of the pacific settlement of disputes and international peacekeeping proved futile just as they had in the League. This line of thought brought governments back to the problem of peacekeeping which already had been linked closely to armaments regulation in the Charter.

On February 18, 1960, Secretary of State Christian A. Herter outlined before the National Press Club what was to be the theme of the subsequent United States' Proposals for General and Complete Disarmament. The purpose of negotiations would be

to cut national armed forces and armaments further and to build up international peacekeeping machinery, to the point where aggression will be deterred by international rather than national force.

He went on to relate disarmament to a conception of world order. The United States would seek "to create universally accepted rules of law . . . backed by a world court and by effective means of enforcement—that is, by international armed force." He continued his discussion of a world disarmed of national forces with the statement that "a useful framework and a considerable body of experience already exists in the United Nations."

The United States statement was a rejoinder to a Soviet proposal made by Premier Nikita Khrushchev to the General Assembly during the previous September which also had urged "general and complete disarmament." Whether to call a bluff or for substantive intent, the United States was emphasizing the circumstances that were essential to make this possible. Where the Soviet leader had emphasized the horrors of war and new opportunities for economic development following disarmament, he had scarcely mentioned the United Nations. He chose to stress partial measures such as an "atom-free" zone in Central Europe, the abolition of military bases in foreign states, and the conclusion of a nonaggression pact between the members of NATO and the Warsaw Treaty Organization rather than the buildup of a United Nations peacekeeping capacity. The United States rejoinder was that general disarmament was impossible unless the UN had the capacity to keep the peace.

. . . In an "Outline of Basic Provisions of a Treaty on General and Complete Disarmament in a Peaceful World," submitted on April 1962 and amended in August 1963, the United States has urged the development of "arrangements" for the establishment of a United Nations Peace Force after a reduction of weapons specified in Stage I and to take effect in Stage II. By Stage III of arms reduction the parties to the Treaty would progressively strengthen the United Nations Peace Force established in Stage II until it had sufficient armed forces and armaments so that no state could challenge it.

The Soviet Union, in turn, submitted a draft "Treaty on General and Complete Disarmament Under Strict International Control" to the General Assembly in September 1962 and added amendments as late as February 1964 following discussion in the Conference of the Eighteen-Nation Disarmament Committee, which under Article 37 would obligate all parties to the Treaty to "conclude agreements with the Security Council" for the provision of "armed forces, assistance and facilities."[2] Where the United States draft contemplated various ways of achieving a United Nations Peace Force, including "the experience of the United Nations" as well as the "feasibility of concluding promptly the agreements envisaged in Article 43," the Soviet Union stayed closer to the Charter. The Soviet proposals specify in Article 18, paragraph 2, that national forces designated for the United Nations "shall form part of the national armed forces of the States concerned and shall be stationed within their territories." It would appear that before all the contemplated forces could actually be available to the United Nations in time of need, the veto must be hurdled in the Security Council, and the governments concerned must agree to release their troops. When the forces were actually being used by the Security Council, moreover, it is clear that they would be under the command of a "troika" since the command would be

composed of representatives of the three principal groups of States existing in the world, each to be represented equally with decisions to require the assent of all three groups.

The difference between the two proposals would appear to be both basic and familiar. In stressing previous United Nations experience with peacekeeping, the United States as well as those Members which have already taken steps to designate part of their armed forces as international police forces have indicated they are ready to build on the lessons gained by the United Nations forces in Egypt and in the Congo which were enabled to operate outside the veto. The Soviet Union, on the other hand, continues to emphasize unanimity and has extended its skepticism of the impartiality of international administration to the command of the United Nations forces. France has refused to pay for the troops in the Congo for closely related reasons.

THE PROBLEM OF A CONTROL ORGANIZATION. Proposals for test bans and disarmament since 1958 have included consideration of proposed control organs but have been obscure on the relationship of such organs to the United Nations itself. A contemplated control organization to supervise a comprehensive nuclear test ban was evidently expected to enter into an "appropriate relationship with the United Nations" rather than to be an integral body of the Organization. When the comprehensive effort was

2 Current Disarmament Proposals as of March 1, 1964 (New York: World Law Fund, 1964).

abandoned, the partial test ban was enabled to sidestep this issue, as already noted, owing to the acceptability of its self-enforcing features.

Both proposals under consideration at the Conference of the Eighteen-Nation Committee on Disarmament provide for the establishment of an International Disarmament Organization (IDO), similarly conceived with similar structures and with functions consisting principally of inspection and verification. Differences appear in the manner by which IDO will reach decisions and relate to the United Nations. The Soviet draft prescribes in Articles 41 and 42 that both the General Conference and the Control Council of IDO will reach decisions on procedural matters by a simple majority vote and on substantive matters by a two-thirds majority. The United States draft says . . . the determination of whether each stage has been carried out is to "be made by affirmative vote of two-thirds of the members of the Control Council, including at least the United States and the Union of Soviet Socialist Republics." There is a further stipulation that IDO and its inspectors "have unrestricted access without veto to all places as necessary for the purposes of effective verification."

As in the case of the proposed United Nations forces, the differences in the two proposals with respect to the relationship of IDO to the United Nations would appear to be crucial. Both drafts indicate unmistakably that the new body is to be established within the framework of the United Nations. The Soviet draft requires IDO to report to the General Assembly and the Security Council much in the manner of a specialized agency reporting to the Assembly and the Economic and Social Council (ECOSOC). In the event of a violation of the disarmament treaty the Soviet version specified . . . :

All questions connected with the safeguarding of international peace and security which may arise in the course of the implementation of the present Treaty, including preventive and enforcement measures, shall be decided by the Security Council in conformity with its powers under the United Nations Charter.

From this it is quite evident that states (Members of the Organization), and not the Organization itself, are to be the effective centers of enforcement decision making, that the control agreement will or will not appear to provide adequate safeguards to the extent that its obligations are self-enforcing rather than enforceable by an international institution, and that the control organization is to be closely linked to the United Nations.

❖   ❖   ❖   ❖   ❖   ❖   ❖

THE UN AS A DISARMAMENT FORUM

Although it is difficult to assess the role of the United Nations as a disarmament forum, there appear to be correlations, on the one hand, between the political orientation of the Organization's membership and the substance of disarmament proposals and, on the other hand, between the size of the Organization and the extent to which its principal organs, particularly the General Assembly, are used as negotiating forums. The establishment of an analytical framework to discover and test such correlations would be useful for the study of international organization and would also shed light on disarmament diplomacy. However, since a thorough study of this nature is beyond the scope of the present analysis, only a few general conclusions can be drawn from the rather obvious juxtapositions between the progress of disarmament negotiations and the size and composition of the General Assembly.

The Security Council may be quickly disposed of since it has played scarcely any role in disarmament discussions despite the Charter's mandate that it should formulate plans "for the establishment of a system for the regulation of armaments." . . .

The Secretariat has played a useful if inconspicuous role by providing services which have been drawn upon even by non-United Nations bodies such as the Eighteen-Nation Disarmament Committee. The Secretary-General has taken important initiatives on a number of occasions by suggesting how to influence the course of disarmament discussions. He pressed for the reestablishment of a United Nations negotiating forum when he suggested in 1958 that the General Assembly "might wish to define its attitude toward the results of the Conference of Experts and to consider the primary objective of balanced world-wide disarmament."

It is the Assembly, however, that has become the significant forum as both major and minor powers have sought to mobilize support for their points of view. Blocs have tended to loosen at times in disarmament debate as the confrontation between nuclear and nonnuclear powers has developed.

* * * * * * *

The United States appears to have misjudged the political atmosphere in the Assembly on the disarmament question in 1957 when it sought to mobilize support against the Soviet Union after a deadlock in the five-nation Subcommittee. Twenty-four Members were enlisted as cosponsors of a United States resolution, and no effort was made to compromise with the Soviet Union which had submitted two counterproposals. While the latter were defeated at the price of 25 abstentions, the United States resolution carried only after repeated efforts by the Latin American states, India, Norway, and Pakistan to mediate between the nuclear powers and to urge the United States not to press for all or nothing. In their efforts to mobilize support, major powers have been confronted instead by Assembly pressures to compromise.

With respect to the size of the Organization, the history of disarmament since the Second World War suggests that the Assembly has often been thought to be too unwieldy a body for fruitful negotiations. Even at the start, the United Nations Atomic Energy Commission was accepted unanimously by the membership as an appropriate body for serious, continuing negotiations. The establishment of the UN Commission for Conventional Armaments in 1947 and the consolidated Commission for the Control of Armaments and Armed Forces in 1952 presumably reflected the same conviction. . . .

What appears to be significant with respect to the problem of size is that all arms control and disarmament negotiations were held in the United Nations bodies until the breakdown of discussions in the Disarmament Commission's Subcommittee in 1957. Since that time negotiations have been carried on principally in non-United Nations bodies, and the shift in the negotiating forum corresponded with the approximate doubling of United Nations membership that began in 1955.

*   *   *   *   *   *   *

The effect of such vigor [in the Assembly concerning disarmament] is to pressure the major powers to continue negotiations. Only France, owing to its preoccupation with becoming a full-fledged nuclear power, has remained largely impervious. Even when disarmament negotiations shift to non-United Nations bodies such as the Eighteen-Nation Disarmament Conference, however, reports of success or failure are demanded in the General Assembly. To say that Assembly pressure brought about the partial test ban would probably be to ascribe too much to its influence. When the three major nuclear powers felt that it was in their self-interest to accept such a ban, however, they had Assembly resolutions to legitimize their agreement. It may not be too much to assume that they welcomed this support in their respective differences with France and Communist China.

CONCLUSIONS

It is in a sense beside the point to ask whether disarmament negotiations are making progress. Whether they are or not, they will continue because nations' interests are perceived constantly in terms of war and peace. What is more, a forum as wide and visible as the General Assembly reinforces the place of disarmament discussions as a continuing feature of the international political landscape. Specific interests and foreign policy goals are sought in the United Nations through disarmament policy. This state of affairs applies to lesser powers as well as to the Great Powers, if to a lesser degree. India, Canada, and Yugoslavia, to take but three examples, have been influential in disarmament matters at one time or another and have utilized the United Nations to mobilize support for their points of view. Indeed, with the increasingly "dysfunctional" character of massively destructive weapons, a premium is necessarily placed on disarmament diplomacy as a continuing international process.

Another straw in the wind indicates that the two major nuclear powers may both be moving back toward the original United Nations notion of collective security. While continuing to insist, perhaps beyond the bounds of prudence, that the cost of peacekeeping forces were expenses of the Organization which the Members were obligated to bear in amounts determined by the General Assembly, the United States nonetheless indicated its readiness to utilize the Security Council to a greater extent for the future mobilization of international forces. It is too early at the time of writing to know whether this change of emphasis will be reflected in the United States position at the Eighteen-Nation Disarmament Conference scheduled for resumption at Geneva in the spring of 1965. A more serious roadblock, of course, is the nonparticipation of France and Communist China either in the Eighteen-Nation Conference or, along with Cuba, in the partial nuclear test ban.

Efforts to make the United Nations or UN-related bodies the center of action for armaments control or for disarmament negotiations have been fraught with difficulties. The General Assembly is too unwieldy for serious negotiations. The concept and authority of the United Nations itself as an international organization are now too much the subjects of controversy for it to be able to monopolize disarmament discussions or armaments control. On the other hand, the Organization cannot avoid being heavily involved no matter how great the efforts to curb its role. For one thing, progress toward disarmament depends heavily on concurrent progress toward an international legal order. No international disarmament organization of itself can make the peace by transforming the nature of international relations. While progress toward disarmament can theoretically and perhaps practically hasten the approach of an international "community," disarmament, like the community itself, appears to be more the result than the cause of achievements in other areas of pressing concern such as the settlement of outstanding political differences by the major powers and the achievement of human rights and economic development.

The United Nations will continue to be involved for another reason. Disarmament is seldom considered as an isolated problem. Disarmament policies are linked closely with other political strategies the implementation of which is sought frequently in the General Assembly owing to the broad scope of its concerns and the size of its membership. This may well explain why the Soviet Union seeks a full-scale public debate on disarmament by the entire UN membership prior to the resumption of "private" discussions in the Eighteen-Nation Disarmament Conference in Geneva at a time when the United States is in the quagmire of "counterinsurgency" in Vietnam.

Finally, the most tenable conclusion to be drawn from twenty years' experience is that disarmament discussions have been fruitful in limiting the armaments race to the extent that they adhere to the Charter principle of big-power unanimity. Admittedly, this is scant comfort in the quest for peace.

U.N.: ROSTRUM, FORUM, ARENA

M. Lvov*

The Soviet programme for general and complete disarmament spreads all the disarmament measures over three stages.

At the *first stage* it is proposed to destroy all the means of delivering nuclear weapons (rockets, bombers, submarines and surface ships carrying nuclear weapons, and atomic artillery), dismantle all foreign bases and withdraw all foreign troops in other countries, reduce the armed forces of states and carry out a number of other disarmament measures.

At the *second stage*, to ban nuclear weapons and destroy all their stockpiles, and also the stockpiles of all other types of mass destruction weapons, and make a further reduction in the armed forces of states.

At the *third stage*, to complete the disbandment of the armed forces and destruction of armaments, dissolve all military organisations, and stop military training and budget appropriations for military purposes.

❋   ❋   ❋   ❋   ❋   ❋   ❋

However, the delegates of the U.S.A., Britain, Italy and Canada in the 18-Nation Committee alleged that the Soviet proposal to do away with delivery vehicles and foreign bases at the first stage would upset the balance, deprive the NATO countries of security, and prevent the U.S.A. from fulfilling its allied commitments to NATO's European members, "in case of need." They also said that the Soviet proposals did not provide any guarantee against possible aggression by any side in the process of disarmament.

There is actually no ground for such assertions either from the military-strategic or the political standpoint, and the delegations of the Soviet Union and the other Socialist countries in the Committee proved this on every

M. Lvov, "U.N.: Rostrum, Forum, Arena, Disarmament Problems at the 18th General Assembly," *International Affairs* (Moscow), November, 1963, pp. 10–15.

M. Lvov is a frequent contributor to *International Affairs*, a journal of the Soviet Union which publishes articles in English on foreign affairs.

point. However, the U.S.A. and its NATO allies would not budge and refused to get down to a businesslike examination of the Soviet proposals. Moreover, they tried to counterpose the American programme to the Soviet programme for general and complete disarmament.

The main feature of the American "disarmament programme" is that it spreads out the elimination of nuclear weapons delivery vehicles over the three stages (one-third at each stage), without actually making any provision either for the dismantling of foreign military bases in other countries or the destruction of nuclear weapons as such.

There is no doubt that if the American programme were implemented, its first and chief result would not be disarmament but strategic advantages for the Western Powers to the detriment of the security of the Soviet Union and the other Socialist countries. In effect, according to the American programme the Soviet Union would have to abandon, at the very first stage of disarmament, a considerable part of its most powerful rockets which constitute the backbone of its defence, while the U.S.A. would retain intact its whole system of military bases along the borders of the Socialist community, with their means of delivery and nuclear components targeted to strike at key points in the Soviet Union and the other Socialist countries.

Naturally, it would not do to seek agreement on the basis of such American proposals. The 18-Nation Committee found itself in an impasse. The Western Powers tried, quite groundlessly, to place the blame for this on the Soviet Union, whose programme, they alleged, did not devote enough attention to the security of states.

The Soviet Government, in an effort to set the talks going once again, announced at the 17th General Assembly last year that it was prepared to meet the Western request for additional guarantees of security for all states in the process of disarmament. With that end in view, it proposed that when nuclear weapons delivery vehicles were destroyed at the first stage, an exception should be made for a strictly limited agreed number of intercontinental, anti-missile and anti-aircraft rockets with nuclear warheads which could be retained by the U.S.S.R. and the U.S.A. on their own territories until the end of the second stage of disarmament, that is, until nuclear weapons as such were completely destroyed. There is, of course, no special need for this "rocket umbrella," but the Soviet Government has agreed to let it be in order to remove the obstacle raised to negotiations by the Western Powers in the form of additional guarantees of security.

In the subsequent talks in the Committee, the Soviet delegation specified its proposal, showing that the "rocket umbrella" should be powerful enough to deter any aggressor who would try to use the situation in the course of disarmament for its own treacherous ends, but should not, upon the other hand, be such as to lend itself to use for the contrary purpose, namely, as a weapon of aggression.

It looked as though the way to agreement had been cleared. The Western Powers could not but recognise the constructive nature of the Soviet proposal for the "rocket umbrella" or the "mutual deterrent missile force," as it came to be known in the West. Still, the U.S.A. and its allies insisted that even this Soviet proposal did not entirely solve the problem of security and did not create the necessary confidence in the process of disarmament, especially in the third stage.

❊   ❊   ❊   ❊   ❊   ❊   ❊

Nevertheless, the Soviet Government, wishing to preclude every possibility of Western references to the security problem as a pretext for rejecting disarmament, told the 18th General Assembly that it agreed that the U.S.S.R. and the United States should retain a "rocket umbrella" not only until the end of the second, but of the third stage of general and complete disarmament.

In putting forward this proposal, Andrei Gromyko said:

With the U.S.S.R. and the U.S.A. retaining a limited number of rockets, the problem of confidence in the process of disarmament is found to be solved even with the most suspicious approach on the part of the sceptics in the West who have been inventing all kinds of things simply to obstruct the way to disarmament. We hope that our partners in the talks will examine the Soviet Government's new proposal in a spirit of striving for agreement.

The third Soviet proposal made at the General Assembly—a ban on the orbiting of vehicles with nuclear weapons on board—is likewise timely and constructive. The world is aware of the existence of two "generations" of nuclear weapons vehicles, namely, bombers and rockets. Orbital nuclear weapons could well be the third "generation." They would be suspended above the heads of men as a death sentence with an unspecified date of execution. The Soviet Government's proposal is aimed at preventing this third "generation" of nuclear weapons vehicles from ever seeing the light of day.

In making this proposal, the Soviet Government reaffirmed its readiness and desire to reach agreement on a number of other measures aimed at curbing the arms race, especially in nuclear weapons, strengthening international confidence and easing tensions, even before general and complete disarmament is implemented. Among them are the establishment of nuclear-free zones in various parts of the world, conclusion of a non-aggression pact between the NATO and the Warsaw Treaty countries, prevention of the further spread of nuclear weapons, measures to prevent surprise attack, and reduction of the military budgets of states.

Coupled with the Moscow Nuclear Test Ban Treaty, this system of measures to reinforce peace put forward by the Soviet Government could do a great deal toward making the life of nations more peaceful and adding to their confidence in the future.

SPEECHES IN THE UN ASSEMBLY ON DISARMAMENT

MR. RAPACKI (POLAND)*

In our view, the special responsibility conferred upon the great Powers under the Charter in no way limits the responsibility and the role of the smaller countries; every nation has its particular facilities for developing its relations with other nations and we feel that each nation should use them in such a way as to contribute, to the greatest extent possible, to the development of constructive co-operation, the restoration of mutual confidence and the *rapprochement* of all peoples.

✿ ✿ ✿ ✿ ✿ ✿ ✿

The key issue before the twelfth session of this Assembly is disarmament. This is not the first time that the United Nations has had to deal with it. Toward the close of the last session, most delegations represented here expressed optimism as to the possibility of the discussions held that year leading at least to a preliminary agreement. Unfortunately, the results of the work of the Sub-Committee of the Disarmament Commission fell short of that expectation.

✿ ✿ ✿ ✿ ✿ ✿ ✿

The second obstacle to the Sub-Committee's progress was the insistence of the Western Powers that concrete measures for disarmament should be conditional on the simultaneous solution of other controversial international problems.

Finally, the third obstacle arose from the opposition of the Federal Republic of Germany and from considerations relating to the remilitarization of Western Germany.

✿ ✿ ✿ ✿ ✿ ✿ ✿

In my comments here, I should like especially to stress the importance of the [disarmament] question for the most vital interests of Poland. So far as we are concerned, armaments are primarily related to the situation in Europe, in the territory of Germany on Poland's borders.

✿ ✿ ✿ ✿ ✿ ✿ ✿

We are against the dividing of Europe into opposing military blocs. Our views regarding the North Atlantic Treaty are well known. Every Polish

* UN General Assembly, 12th Session, *Official Records*, Plenary Meetings, 697th Meeting (October 2, 1957), pp. 235–238.

494

citizen judges NATO primarily in relation to its policy in the German question. In the face of the danger which Western Germany's armaments within NATO represent for our country and for other European countries, Poland and its allies were forced to conclude the Warsaw Treaty, which safeguards our country's security until such time as an effective system of collective security is established instead of the present division of Europe. We want such a system and will help to achieve it to the best of our ability.

* * * * * * *

Hence I should like on behalf of my Government to make the following statement: In the interest of Poland's security and of a relaxation of tension in Europe, and after consultation with the other parties to the Warsaw Treaty, the Government of the People's Republic of Poland declares that if the two German States should consent to enforce the prohibition of the production and stockpiling of nuclear weapons in their respective territories, the People's Republic of Poland is prepared simultaneously to institute the same prohibition in its territory.

I am convinced that if that could be achieved, we would at least have made the first step toward solution of a problem which is vital not only to the Polish people and the German people and their mutual relation, but to the whole of Europe and to all peoples of the world.

MR. BERSTEIN (CHILE)*

He wished to speak in the general debate, firstly, because nuclear testing was driving mankind to the brink of destruction and his delegation felt morally bound to help in the search for a solution of the problem, rather than sit back passively and watch the power struggle between the two blocs; and secondly, because the march of events had caused his country to lose its faith that the great Powers alone could settle current problems.

The grave dangers to the human race created by nuclear testing were recognized by everyone, in particular by the nuclear Powers themselves. In the report of the United Nations Scientific Committee on the Effects of Atomic Radiation, eminent scientists had expressed their concern for the fate of present and future generations, and had recommended the final cessation of nuclear tests. Yet more than one hundred nuclear bombs had been exploded during the past year.

The great Powers had pledged themselves under the Charter of the United Nations "to take collective measures for the prevention and removal of threats to the peace" (Article 1, paragraph 1), to "settle their international disputes by peaceful means" (Article 2, paragraph 4); in addition,

* UN General Assembly, 17th Session, *Official Records*, First Committee, 1249th Meeting (October 16, 1962).

they had pledged themselves, in the Preamble to the Charter, "to save succeeding generations from the scourge of war," "to practise tolerance and live together in peace with one another as good neighbors" and "to ensure, by the acceptance of principles and the institution of methods, that armed force shall not be used, save in the common interest." That pledge had been the basis for granting the great Powers permanent seats in the Security Council and the so-called "right of veto." It was evident, however, that the great nuclear Powers had not fulfilled their solemn pledges. They were threatening each other with the most deadly and destructive weapons, they were endangering the physical health of those same succeeding generations whom they had promised to save from the scourge of war, and they had stressed the paramountcy of national interests, of so-called "national security," in defiance of the interests of the international community. For that reason, his delegation was now obliged to speak quite plainly.

He attached little importance to the accusations exchanged and the self-justificatory statements made by the nuclear Powers. The question [of] who was actually responsible for the failure to reach agreement on the suspension of nuclear tests was of no real interest; the point was to find a solution, or at least the beginning of a solution, to the problem; for the common man was blaming the nuclear Powers, without exception, for the existing state of affairs, and was judging them all by the same standards. While that might be unjust, it was a fact, and resulted inevitably from the fear and terror existing in the world. The common man asked how far the power for destruction would increase; why there were so many tests if no one intended to use the bombs manufactured on the basis of them; and how long the great nuclear Powers would keep mankind in its present state of insecurity.

The great nuclear Powers bore a tremendous responsibility. On behalf of a small nation, he appealed to all of them to find some solution; to find some way of living together and letting others live; to fulfill the pledges they had made in signing the Charter of the United Nations. He was certain that the great Powers could not remain deaf to the anguished appeals addressed to them from all corners of the earth and from within their own countries. The undoubted desire for peace among the people of the United States, the United Kingdom and the Soviet Union had surely been a cause of the changes recently made in their Governments' positions, which, while still opposed, were no longer irreconcilable. . . .

The greatest obstacle to agreement was clearly the distrust between the two great blocs: one side did not trust the other to live up to its pledges, while the second did not trust the first to make proper use of the proposed controls. His delegation believed that the non-nuclear countries should make a united effort to dispel that climate of distrust. If such an effort bore no fruit, his Government believed that as a partial interim measure, denuclearized zones should be established in various parts of the world, and it believed that Latin America should be such a zone. The Latin American countries would be called upon to pledge themselves not only not to acquire nuclear weapons, but also to refuse them if they were offered.

MR. PAZHWAK (AFGHANISTAN)*

Neither logic nor even technical consideration could be of much help in solving the problem under discussion if it was considered from a purely political and military viewpoint. The problem was primarily a humanitarian one, and its solution was dependent on a humanitarian approach to the whole question. It was regrettable that that approach had not prevailed in the past; however, the United Nations should concentrate not on past history but on the present situation and the future of mankind.

＊　＊　＊　＊　＊　＊　＊

No matter what the justification might be, the nuclear arms race was contrary to the interests of international peace and security. One of the most serious facts was that the United Nations seemed to be becoming accustomed to the idea of the destruction of humanity, for it had gradually become much calmer in the expression of its concern, during a period in which the race in testing nuclear and thermo-nuclear weapons had been accelerated. The United Nations should strongly condemn that race and reject the reasons put forward to justify it. That would not be moral pressure; it was a duty on the part of the non-nuclear Powers in the interests of the whole world.

The division of the non-nuclear world into two camps was as foolish as the continuance of the nuclear tests. Every country had the right to conclude alliances in order to ensure its security, but his delegation could not understand how countries could join the camp of annihilation of mankind and not join the camp of humanity in the interest of its survival. The United Nations should unanimously urge [the former] to bring to an end at once their destructive activities. The nuclear Powers should have no allies on this issue.

Since in the event of a nuclear war there would be neither security nor victory for either side, and neither would dominate or even survive, the only possible explanation for the nuclear arms race was the lack of confidence among the great Powers. The solution then was to urge them to have confidence at least in the United Nations, where it was precisely those Powers that were in some respects the privileged ones. . . .

Summarizing his Government's views on the question, he said that the United Nations, on behalf of the people of the world, should: first, express its deep concern over the continuance of any tests in any environment; second, strongly condemn policies which would allow further continuance of any nuclear or thermo-nuclear tests; third, declare that no nation had

* UN General Assembly, 17th Session, *Official Records*, First Committee 1251st Meeting (October 18, 1962), pp. 38–39.

the right to test; fourth, demand from the nuclear Powers the cessation of all tests and a pledge to the world that the tests would not be resumed in any circumstances; fifth, declare that the gradual and partial process of the cessation of nuclear tests would ultimately not be effective and that all tests would be discontinued immediately; sixth, urge the nuclear Powers to refrain from following any policies that would result in the spreading of nuclear weapons to countries which did not possess them at the present time; seventh, urge the nuclear Powers to enter into negotiations during the current session in order to reach an agreement on the technical aspects of the matter, particularly on effective measures of international inspection and control, on the basis of the joint memorandum of 16 April 1962 and in the light of the views expressed in the First Committee's discussion of the present item; eighth, urge all nuclear Powers to declare jointly that the use of nuclear weapons would be considered a crime against humanity as a whole and that such weapons would not be used under any circumstances; ninth, urge all nuclear Powers to enter into negotiations, as a further step for the achievement of general and complete disarmament, and to destroy all nuclear weapons which already existed.

MR. HAY (AUSTRALIA)*

The problem posed by nuclear armaments was unodubtedly of vital importance. . . . However, nuclear weapons were not the only means of mass destruction: in this statement in the Assembly's general debate (1226th plenary meeting), the Australian Minister for External Affairs had described an air attack carried out during the Second World War when in about fourteen hours "conventional" bombs had devastated 1,600 acres and killed twice as many people as had the first atomic bomb. Thus, disarmament must cover all forms of weapons.

For that reason, his country approached the various proposals for nuclear-free zones with caution. His Government considered that in present circumstances such a zone in Australia's own region, for example, would be illusory and indeed dangerous, since it would disturb the existing strategic balance and increase the risk of aggression. Nevertheless, the Australian Government did believe that the establishment of nuclear-free zones might ease tension in certain areas and limit the spread of nuclear weapons, provided that four basic requirements were met. The first requirement was that any arrangement for the creation of a nuclear-free zone must enjoy the unanimous support of the countries concerned; otherwise the basis for such a zone simply did not exist. The second requirement was that the establishment of a nuclear-free zone should not upset the over-all strategic balance, both nuclear and conventional, in the area, due regard being paid also to the

*UN General Assembly, 18th Session, *Official Records*, First Committee, 1321st Meeting (October 30, 1963), pp. 60–61.

strength and policies of countries adjacent to the area or having commitments or strategic needs in it. Thirdly, there must be adequate provision for verification and control; all States [and] parties must have grounds for confidence that the provisions of the agreement would be respected by all nations, both within and without the zone. The difficulties involved varied from region to region. On land, no reliable means of detecting hidden nuclear weapons yet existed, while at sea the detection of nuclear-armed submarines, for example, was likely to present insoluble problems. Fourthly, there must be no nuclear targets in the zone, either because of the physical characteristics of the countries in it or because outside nuclear Powers agreed to observe denuclearization of the zone.

Proposals for denuclearized zones in many parts of the world had been made from time to time, and Australia had carefully studied the question of the establishment of such a zone in the area of Asia and the Pacific from the standpoint of the four requirements just enumerated. Firstly, all the States concerned would have to agree to refrain from manufacturing, storing or testing nuclear weapons. If the area were defined to include part of the territory of one or more of the major nuclear Powers and the mainland of China, it seemed unlikely, in view of the existing world situation and the proclaimed intentions of the Peking regime, that unanimity would be secured. Secondly, the prohibition of nuclear weapons in that area would create a serious imbalance, owing to the enormous manpower resources and capacity for conventional warfare of Communist China. Thirdly, proper verification and control would be impossible in such a vast area, especially if large expanses of ocean were included. Fourthly, nothing short of general and complete disarmament would ensure the absence of nuclear targets in the area.

The Australian Government consequently did not consider that under existing conditions a nuclear-free zone in the area of Asia and the Pacific could satisfy those four requirements, although it would be fully prepared to see similar proposals for other areas considered on their merits. But in any event, nuclear-free zones were neither an ideal nor a final solution, and their implications required careful study.

MR. PALAR (INDONESIA)*

In his delegation's view, there was much value in the Soviet proposal for a non-aggression pact between the NATO and the Warsaw Treaty countries. Technical collateral measures such as those he had just mentioned would have no effect if the political atmosphere was not favourable; for that reason, measures should be taken to ease the tensions of the cold war. The Western Powers, however, did not seem to be convinced that such a pact

*UN General Assembly, 18th Session, *Official Records*, First Committee, 1328th Meeting (November 5, 1963).

would be in their interest at present. The chief obstacle preventing Western consent was the problem of the status of the German Democratic Republic. The West feared that the Soviet Union might use the proposed pact to bring about the formal confirmation of the German Democratic Republic as an independent State, an eventuality which the Federal Republic of Germany declared it would never accept. But there were some indications that the Soviet Union might be willing to come to an arrangement under which the question of the status of East Germany would be side-stepped. If that proved to be the case, his delegation would strongly urge the West to make concessions in its turn. The problems caused by the division of Germany must be resolved if any significant progress was to be made in disarmament negotiations, and they would have to be resolved by the States responsible for creating the situation in the first place. In any event, the issue could not be allowed to hinder the progress of disarmament.

A favourable political climate for the solution of cold-war issues and for the accomplishment of general disarmament could be created by achieving some progress toward agreement on collateral measures and a comprehensive test ban treaty. He had already stated (1317th meeting) during the debate on the question of nuclear tests that any progress made on collateral measures would encourage the three nuclear Powers to refrain from further testing and, conversely, that negotiations on a comprehensive test ban would help to bring about agreement on collateral measures. The influence exerted in the matter by pressure of public opinion could not be overestimated. . . .

Until the three nuclear Powers provided convincing evidence of their intention to renounce the use of nuclear weapons and to disarm, France would never renounce its desire to become a nuclear Power, or consent to join in the disarmament negotiations. It was therefore urgent to take immediate steps to convince France of the genuineness of the "detente" between East and West on disarmament matters.

In the case of the People's Republic of China, the problem was different, since that country had been excluded by other States from the disarmament negotiations. There were signs, however, of a swing of public opinion in favour of co-operation with the People's Republic of China. It was difficult to imagine its participation in disarmament negotiations without a reconsideration by the Western Powers of their position on the status of Taiwan —which was a prerequisite for, among other things, the solution of the question of Chinese representation in the United Nations. It was reasonable to hope that the realities of the situation would be appreciated, but in view of the urgency of the matter, it might be possible to reach some interim solution which would enable the People's Republic of China to participate in the disarmament negotiations at the proper time. Some use might, for example, be made of the fact that the Eighteen-Nation Committee was not wholly a creation of the United Nations; its composition, it would be recalled, had been decided by the United States and the Soviet Union in joint consultation and had then been endorsed by the General Assembly in resolution 1722 (XVI). Thus, it should be possible for those two Powers to invite the People's Republic of China to participate in the discussions. If they felt that the balance in the Eighteen-Nation Committee might be disturbed by the presence of the People's Republic of China, they could perhaps bring in two additional countries—say, one Western Power and one non-aligned Power. In any case, even if the problem of Chinese representation in the United Nations had not been solved by that time, the Peking Government might perhaps be able to accept an invitation from a committee that was not technically a United Nations body. Of course such an invitation would be tendered only when the present negotiations on collateral measures and a comprehensive test ban treaty had approached a successful conclusion. The pressure of world public opinion and the need for bringing the People's Republic of China to the forum as soon as possible would probably force the Powers now negotiating to reach a stage of significant agreement within a year.

CHAPTER **16**

THE PUBLIC AND THE UNITED NATIONS

One of the far-reaching objectives of the United Nations and hopes of its creators and supporters is to influence men's minds in the direction of increased friendliness and understanding toward the people of other lands. However, attitudes toward the UN itself are also considered important because of the assumption that the Organization is and ought increasingly to be a major factor in influencing men's minds. Hence it is important for us to know what the prevailing opinions are about the UN and its activities, and to know to what extent these opinions have shifted over a period of time. Ideally we ought to know the answers to these questions from the viewpoints of the people of all countries, or at least of major states. But it is not possible to report on all of this, particularly the latter, because no polls have been taken of opinions on identical, or even similar, questions in any wide-scale coordinated survey. To provide the results of surveys whose questions are unrelated would be pointless. Hence the best we are able to do is to provide here the results of one of the most recent studies of public opinion in the United States.

Alfred D. Hero, Jr. in "The American Public and the UN: 1954–1966" indicates that a number of changes in American opinion seem to have developed since the last major study of attitudes toward the UN was made in 1954. These changes continue in the direction of support for the UN and for multilateral approaches to problems in international relations in general. And, while it is true that opinions seem to shift as the international scene takes on a bleaker or rosier view, support for the UN's efforts as well as for the United States' continued participation in the UN remains high. The polls indicate that many Americans would even be willing to accept drastic changes in policy with regard to key issues, as, for example, the seating of a Chinese Communist delegation, strengthening the UN's role in world affairs by authorizing it to send inspectors to different countries to check on the size of armed forces, and giving the UN authority to perform in some respects as a world government.

Hero points out what many have recognized for some time: that responses to those questions do not always reflect a consistent set of attitudes. True, support for the UN is strong and so is support for increasing its powers and encouraging its work in aiding international organizations to achieve peaceful settlements of disputes. At the same time, many Americans support escalation of United States force to solve the present Viet Nam crisis. Yet, the possibility of turning that problem over to the UN also has widespread support. Further inconsistency seems to be revealed regarding the seating of a Chinese Communist delegation; some people who would counsel United States withdrawal if the Chinese Communists should be seated nevertheless favor Presidential initiative to have them admitted.

Despite these apparent inconsistencies, the over-all results of these polls seem to indicate that over the years support for the UN has not diminished among Americans, and that despite the adversities facing the Organization and the recognition that the rosy expectations of the founding days were unrealistic, support has generally increased. This support appears to be even greater than it is for NATO and other military associations of which the United States is a member.

We said initially that it is unfortunate that the opinion surveys are not world-wide. We might add that it is also unfortunate such polls have not been taken of our government elite. For although we are able to make some judgments about the opinions of some government officials on a limited number of specific policy positions in comparison to poll responses, we do not have any way of comparing the officials' responses on a variety of alternative positions. Of course, despite the anonymity of the respondents, candor might still be lacking. Yet it would be desirable to be able to test what is frequently asserted: that the public is often ahead of its leaders in terms of flexibility and willingness to try new approaches.

We might ask ourselves that unpardonable question for democratic societies: Does it make any difference what the public believes? Do we have evidence to indicate that, except in wartime, public opinion on foreign-policy questions is strong and influential? Do we know that foreign-policy issues are important to many publics? Furthermore, what ought government positions be with regard to public-opinion polls on crucial questions? In the United States we are told that President Johnson is an avid reader of polls. Does this interest appear to exist among other chiefs of state? And does avid reading indicate that the polls have influence? Many of these questions demand more careful study than they have generally been given. Until such studies have been made we can only hope that more informed publics will develop than presently exist and that they will provide support for the Organization in fair weather and, especially, in foul.

FURTHER READINGS

Almond, Gabriel A., *The American People and Foreign Policy*. New York: Frederick A. Praeger, Inc., 1960.

Cohen, Bernard C., *The Press and Foreign Policy*. Princeton: Princeton University Press, 1963.

THE AMERICAN PUBLIC AND THE UN: 1954–1966

Alfred O. Hero, Jr.[*]

The United States and the United Nations: The Public View, a book by William A. Scott and Stephen B. Withey,[1] analyzed trends in American opinion toward the United Nations during its first eight years, as indicated by national surveys and opinion polls.

Since 1954 a number of significant developments have taken place which may have modified opinion in the United States with respect to the world body. Whereas formerly the U.S. had typically been able to rely on majority votes in the General Assembly in support of its preferred policies, this balance has changed. The number of Member States has about doubled since 1954, the new additions being primarily former colonial areas, underdeveloped, nonaligned in the Cold War, and non-Caucasian in race. Two Western European Secretaries-General have been succeeded by an Asian from such a less-developed, neutralist country. While most representatives of these new Member States have by no means voted for the most part against the West, more recent General Assemblies have been less inclined than their predecessors to support the policies of Western Europe and North America. A number of other developments may likewise have influenced American reactions to the U.N.—the Suez intervention, the paucity of effective U.N. action relative to the Soviet suppression of the Hungarian revolt, the Congo affair, the troika debates, the controversy over financing of peacekeeping operations, the growing likelihood of a majority vote in the General Assembly favorable to the seating of the People's Republic of China, and so forth.

This article examines national survey and related evidence pertinent to more general developments in American public opinion toward the United Nations system from 1954 through mid-1966. This discussion will initially examine national distributions of opinion, then relationships of opinions on

* Alfred O. Hero, Jr., "The American Public and the UN: 1954–1966. This study is based on survey tabulations made by Louis Vexler of the Gallup Organization and the staffs of the Roper Public Opinion Research Center of Williams College and the Survey Research Center of the University of Michigan.

Alfred O. Hero, Jr. is managing editor of International Organization, executive secretary of the World Peace Foundation, and author of "Foreign Aid and the American Public."

1 New York, Carnegie Endowment for International Peace, 1958.

various aspects of the U.N. to one another and to views on other spheres of foreign policy, and later the relative incidence of major patterns of opinion on the world organization among particular demographic, social, and political groups.

GENERAL APPROVAL

Scott and Withey discovered that no more than 13% of the American public felt the U.S. should withdraw from the U.N. from the time of ratification of the Charter by the U.S. Senate until the last survey reported, in 1954.[2] Table I indicates that this minority decreased still further after

TABLE I

"*Do you think our government should continue to belong to the U.N., or should we pull out of it now?*"

DATE	NORC* NO.	(N)	STAY IN	PULL OUT	NO OPINION DON'T KNOW
Aug. '55	(374)	(1262)	88%	5%	7%
Apr. '56	(386)	(1224)	88	6	6
Nov. '56	(399)	(1286)	87	6	7

"*Do you think the United States should give up its membership in the United Nations, or not?*"

DATE	AIPO† NO.	(N)	STAY IN	GET OUT	NO OPINION DON'T KNOW
Jan. '62	(654)	(1543)	86%	9%	5%
Nov. '63	(679)	(1636)	79	8	13

* *National Opinion Research Center* [ed.].
† *American Institute of Public Opinion* [ed.].

the Korean War, ranging from 5% to 6% in 1955 and 1956 respectively. In a similar poll by the American Institute of Public Opinion (AIPO) the minority who would have the U.S. "give up its membership in the United Nations" declined from between 12% and 14 % in 1951 to 9% in early 1962 and 8% in late 1963 (Table I).

Asked how important they thought it was for the United States "to try to make the United Nations a success," Americans who felt it "very important" rose from 77% in October 1952 to between 85% and 88% from the fall of 1956 to the winter of 1959, followed by a decline, to 79% in late 1963. Those who felt it "not so important" declined from 6% in 1952 to between 2% and 4% after the fall of 1956 (Table II).

2 *Ibid.*, pages 10–17.

TABLE II

"How important do you think it is that we try to make the United Nations a success—very important, fairly important, or not so important?"

DATE	AIPO NO.	(N)	VERY IMPORTANT	FAIRLY SO	NOT SO IMPORTANT	NO OPINION DON'T KNOW
Oct. '52	(507)	(3114)	77%	10%	6%	7%
Nov. '56	(575)	(1502)	85	8	3	4
Dec. '59	(622)	(1527)	88	7	2	3
Oct. '60	(637)	(1589)	83	8	2	7
Jan. '62	(654)	(1543)	83	9	4	4
Nov. '63	(680)	(1552)	79	8	4	8

"Do you think the United States should give strong support, or only a little support to the United Nations?"

DATE	AIPO NO.	(N)	STRONG SUPPORT	A LITTLE SUPPORT	NO OPINION DON'T KNOW
Dec. '54–Jan. '55	(541)	(1445)	72%	16%	12%

Queries about the quality of performance of the U.N. and the satisfaction or dissatisfaction with the organization also revealed increasingly favorable images of the international body after the armistice in Korea (Table III).

TABLE III

"In general, do you think the United Nations is doing a good job, or a poor job, in trying to solve the problems it has had to face?"

DATE	AIPO NO.	(N)	GOOD OR FAIR	POOR JOB	NO OPINION DON'T KNOW
July '54	(534)	(1549)	59%	26%	15%
Oct. '55	(554)	(1500)	80	10	10
Nov. '56	(575)	(1502)	77	11	12
June '62	(659)	(1512)	78	15	7
Nov. '63	(680)	(1552)	80	7	13
July '64	(695)	(1569)	81	7	12

"In general, are you satisfied or dissatisfied with the progress the U.N. has made so far?"

DATE	NORC NO.	(N)	SATISFIED	DISSATISFIED	NO OPINION DON'T KNOW
Oct. '54	(364)	(518)	62%	25%	13%
Aug. '55	(374)	(1262)	74	17	9
Nov. '56	(399)	(1286)	72	20	8

Similarly small minorities have felt that the headquarters of the U.N. should be located outside the United States. In late 1946, only 10% would have the "permanent United Nations headquarters move to some other nation"; 69% preferred that it remain in this country.[3] Asked in the summer of 1948, "Because the United States has not offered to lend $65 million to the U.N. to build its headquarters, some U.N. officials want to move the headquarters to Europe. Do you think it would be a good thing or a bad thing for the U.N. to move to Europe?" Only 10% thought it would be a "good thing" if the U.N. were moved to Europe, 61% that it would be a "bad thing," and 16% said it would make no appreciable difference, or words to that effect.[4] By the end of 1952, during the Korean War, the minority who felt "we would be better off if the U.N. headquarters were in some other country" had increased slightly, to 12%, those who believed it made little difference whether it were moved or not had grown to 26%, and those who thought it "a good thing for the U.S. to have the U.N. headquarters in our country" had declined to 51%.[5]

No comparable query has been posed during recent years. The public was asked in the fall of 1960, "It has been suggested that the headquarters of the U.N. be moved from the United States to some neutral country like Switzerland. Would you, yourself, favor or oppose having the U.N. headquarters moved to some other country?" At that time 17% favored such a move, while 61% opposed it,[6] but only a minority of those who agreed that U.N. headquarters should be moved to a neutral country like Switzerland were hostile to the organization or its supposed influences in this country. Thus, most of the 17% who favored such a move also felt that the world body had done at least a "fair job in trying to solve the problems it has had to face" and that it was at least "fairly important" to make the U.N. a success.

When asked why they preferred that the United States withdraw from the U.N., the small minorities who have agreed with that view have most frequently mentioned the supposed expense to the United States of its membership and their assumption that this country pays a disproportionate share of the expenses of the organization. Next most frequently mentioned has been the opinion that the U.N. has not accomplished anything. The reason given third most often has been that the communist powers have too much influence there. Only infinitesimal minorities—less than one percent of the national population—have typically mentioned the strength of the colored, or the less developed, or the neutralist countries in the international organization.[7] The reasons given by those who would withdraw from the U.N. have not differed substantially in the 1960's from those offered in the late 1940's, before the entry of most of the Asian and African Member States.

  [3] AIPO 384, 11–14–46 (3029).
  [4] AIPO 421, 7–10–48 (3147).
  [5] NORC 334, 12–29–52 (1291).
  [6] AIPO 637, 10–18–60 (1589).
  [7] AIPO 679, 11–8–63 (1636).

MEMBERSHIP OF THE COMMUNIST POWERS

Shortly before the Communist attack on South Korea, 41% of the American public thought that "if the U.N. should be reorganized leaving out Russia and all communist-dominated countries . . . the U.N. would be better able to keep the peace of the world," 39% felt it would be less able to do so, and 6% said it would make no difference (Table IV). When the same query was posed two months after the initiation of the invasion of South Korea, those who felt the U.N. should be reorganized without the U.S.S.R. mounted to 50%, those who felt it would be less able to keep the peace without the communist powers as Member States fell to 29%, and those who believed it would make no difference rose to 10%. However, by June 1955, those who believed the world body could keep the peace better without these countries as Member States had fallen to 35%—less than was the case before the war began—those who thought the U.N. would keep the peace more effectively with them as Members rose to 45%—more than before June 25, 1950—and those who replied that it would make no difference had fallen to 4%.

The number who would admit Communist China to the United Nations has consistently been much smaller than that who would prefer that the U.S.S.R. and its East European allies remain Members.

Although 40% of the American public in the spring of 1954 said they would "be willing to let Communist China become a member of the U.N., provided they agree to a satisfactory settlement in both Korea and Indo-China,"[8] the minorities who favored admitting her when no such provisos were mentioned have been sharply smaller. Only 11% approved "of letting Communist China become a member of the United Nations" (Table IV), and two months later only 7% thought "Communist China should be admitted as a member of the United Nations" (Table IV). At no time between 1950 and early 1964 did more than one American out of five favor admission of Communist China.

However, these findings might lead to underestimates of the acquiescence that would probably be forthcoming should the U.S. government change its public opposition to Communist Chinese membership to one of at least conditional acceptance. Public reactions would, of course, depend on the general tone of the modified public stance and the forcefulness and skill with which the new policy was brought to public attention. But when the public was asked in the late spring of 1964 about their probable reactions to a possible suggestion by the President "that we let Communist China join the United Nations," 31% of those 72% of Americans who knew that Mainland China was ruled by a communist regime replied that they would definitely favor, or at least probably favor this proposition,

[8] NORC 355, 4–22–54 (1207). A month earlier, fifty percent would not have admitted Communist China even under such conditions.

TABLE IV

"Would you approve or disapprove of letting Communist China become a member of the United Nations?"

DATE	NORC NO.	(N)	APPROVE	DISAPPROVE	DEPENDS	DON'T KNOW NO OPINION
Nov.–Dec. '53	(349)	(1301)	12%	74%	6%	8%
Mar. '54	(353)	(535)	11	79	5	5
Sept. '56	(393)	(1263)	17	73	5	5

"Do you think Communist China should be admitted as a member of the United Nations?"

DATE	AIPO NO.	(N)	YES	NO	DON'T KNOW NO OPINION
June '50 (before Korea)	(456)	(1450)	11%	58%	31%
June '54	(533)	(1587)	7	78	15
Aug. '58	(603)	(1563)	20	63	17
Mar. '66	(726)	(1500)	25	55	20

and 53% said they would definitely or probably oppose it (Table V). Two years later, in March 1966, 56% of Americans said they would "favor admission of Communist China if it would improve United States-Communist Chinese relations," only 28% replied that they would be opposed under such conditions (Table V).

Thus, a change in official posture of the U.S. toward acquiescence in Chinese membership under certain conditions (e.g., the regime on Formosa remaining a member as well, though perhaps not a permanent member of

TABLE V

"Now the President of the United States might decide that it was in our best interests to take certain new actions with regard to Communist China. For each thing I mention, would you tell me how you would feel about it if the President suggested that action? Suppose the President suggested that we let Communist China join the United Nations?" SRC survey of May-June 1964 (1501). This question was posed only to the 72% (1088) of the public who knew that Mainland China is ruled by a Communist government.

Definitely in favor	13% ⎱ 31%
Probably in favor	18 ⎰
Probably against	13 ⎱ 53%
Definitely against	40 ⎰
No opinion	15
Not ascertained	1

"Would you favor admission of Communist China if it would improve United States-Communist Chinese relations?" AIPO survey of March 1966 (N > 1500) cited in Gallup Political Index, *Report No. 4, Sept. 1965, p. 12.*

Yes	56%
No	28
No Opinion, Don't Know	16

the Security Council) would significantly reduce the negative impacts of her entry on public attitudes toward the U.N. in this country if American citizens were not prepared for this development. However, widespread opposition to membership for the Peking regime has not necessarily implied equally widespread sentiment that the United States should withdraw from the world organization should such transpire. At no time since the Communists gained control of the [Chinese] mainland has a majority felt the U.S. should withdraw from the U.N. if their government became a Member.

Even at the height of Communist Chinese attacks on American troops in Korea, more Americans felt "the U.S. should go along" with a majority decision "to give Communist China a seat on the U.N. Security Council if the Chinese agree to stop fighting in Korea" than believed it should not. Asked whether "the United States should resign its membership in the United Nations . . . (if) a majority of the other members . . . vote to

TABLE VI

"Suppose a majority of members of the U.N. decide to admit Communist China to the United Nations. Do you think the U.S. should go along with the U.N. decision or not?"

DATE	AIPO NO.	(N)	GO ALONG	DO NOT	NO OPINION DON'T KNOW
July '56	(567)	(2105)	39%	44%	17%
Sept. '61	(650)	(>1500)	44	39	17
Jan.–Feb. '64	(684)	(1631)	39	44	17
Feb. '65	(706)	(1568)	49	35	16
Mar. '66	(726)	(>1500)	49	31	20

"Some people say that if Communist China gets into the United Nations, we ought to get out of the United Nations. Other people say that if Communist China gets into the United Nations, we should stay in and make the best of it. Do you have an opinion about this or not? (If yes): How do you feel about this?" (Asked only of the 72% of Americans who knew that Mainland China is controlled by a Communist regime.) SRC survey of May–June 1964 (1501 cases, of whom 1088 were asked this question).[10]

U.S. should stay in U.N. with Red China	75%
U.S. should get out	5
No opinion	14
Other; answer not clear	3
No reason given	3

admit Communist China," only 25% in mid-1954 felt it should, 59% that it should not, and by a year later the former had declined to only 14%.[9]

By the late spring of 1964 only 5% of the 72% of those adult Americans

[9] AIPO 534, 537, July 1954, May 1955, respectively. [For other surveys on the question see Table VII.]

[10] Reported in "The American Public's View of U.S. Policy Toward China: A Report Prepared for the Council on Foreign Relations by the Survey Research Center, University of Michigan," New York, Council on Foreign Relations, 1964, p. 24.

who knew a Communist government controlled most of China would have us "get out" if Mainland China became a Member State.

When this 5% were asked why they felt we should "get out," only 41% of them (2% of all those who knew a Communist regime controlled the Mainland) indicated that they held generally hostile views about the U.N., unrelated to China's admission. Twenty-one percent said the U.S. would be outvoted or would lose influence, 12% that the U.N. could not accomplish anything if Communist China were in it, 9% that the U.S. should have nothing to do with Communist China, in the U.N. or elsewhere, 9% mentioned financial problems connected with Communist China's admission, 9% [gave] other miscellaneous reasons, and 9% gave no reasons.[11]

KEEPING THE PEACE

Scott and Withey observed that the vast majority of Americans—four out of five—regarded the prevention of war as the primary or virtually only purpose or function of the U.N. system, and that only one American out of five mentioned any other objectives or purposes, such as those of the International Court of Justice, the I.B.R.D., ECOSOC, or the Specialized Agencies.[12]

Although no statistically comparable queries have been posed since 1954, it is clear that peace keeping has remained the overriding purpose of the U.N. in the minds of the American public.

Thus, when asked to describe the "good" and "bad points" of the organization in early 1962, to an overwhelming degree the outstanding "good" point mentioned was its role in the prevention of war. Only a minority mentioned any other "good point."[13] Moreover, only minorities of the American public have said they have even heard of the Specialized Agencies, and only very small minorities have been able to define their activities.[14] "Success" for the U.N. has continued in most American minds to mean largely preventing military hostilities, and especially World War III.

---

[11] "The American Public's View of U.S. Policy Toward China: A Report Prepared for the Council on Foreign Relations by the Survey Research Center, University of Michigan," New York, Council on Foreign Relations, 1964, p. 24.

[12] Scott and Withey, op. cit. pp. 38–39.

[13] AIPO 654, 1–9–62 (1543).

[14] Paucity of knowledge about UNESCO in 1953 and again in 1955 provides one indicator. In April 1953 only 30% of the public replied in the affirmative to the query, "Have you heard or read about UNESCO," in August 1955, affirmative replies to the same query were but 31%. Further asked, "What do you understand to be the main purpose of UNESCO?", only 11% in 1953 and 10% in 1955 could provide even a vague general correct description of the organization's purpose, role, or activities. However, among the minorities who said they had heard of it, clear majorities both times—71% and 57% respectively—said they had a "favorable impression" of UNESCO's work and only 11% and 15% respectively replied their impressions of its activities were "unfavorable." See NORC 339, 4–1–53 (1291), and NORC 374, 8–4–55 (1300).

The proportion of the public who have believed that the world body would succeed in the purpose has varied with the perceived general state of international affairs, and particularly of relations of the United States and its allies with the Communist world. When the level of tensions between our government and the governments of our allies on the one hand and the Communist powers on the other seemed to rise, increasing numbers of Americans anticipated another world war within the next several years, and the number who believed the U.N. would not "succeed," or that its "chances for keeping peace" were not good, or the like, also grew.

Thus in the spring of 1955, shortly prior to the Summit meeting in Geneva, 64% thought "the United Nations Organization will succeed in spite of the disagreements which come up," and only 20% that "these disagreements are so serious that the U.N. will fail." [15] By early 1957, however, shortly after the suppression of the Hungarian uprising and the intervention of the U.N. to halt Anglo-Franco-Israeli military actions against the Nasser regime in Egypt, only 42% felt "as things stand today . . . the chances of the U.N. for keeping the peace are good"; 37% thought they were only "fair," and 20% considered them poor.[16] . . .

Nevertheless, after 20 years, in June 1965, 59% of the American public thought "if the United Nations had not been in existence . . . there would likely have been another world war"; only 25% said they felt the U.N. had not had any significant role in preventing such a catastrophe.[17]

Remarkably large numbers of Americans have continued to favor further strengthening of the powers of the U.N. in order that it might be more effective in preventing war, including even Charter revision amounting to world government.

Thus, in the fall of 1953 only 3% of adult Americans felt "the United Nations Organization is too powerful . . . as things stand now," 58% believed it "not powerful enough," and 22% "about as powerful as it should be."[18] In late 1951, 66% favored "a system of inspection whereby a group of inspectors from the United Nations Organization could go into any country, including the United States, to see if it actually was keeping down the size of its armed forces"; in early 1956, 56% replied likewise to the same question.[19] In July 1953, 41% of the public agreed that "the United Nations should be strengthened to make it a world government with power to control the armed forces of all nations, including the United States"; two years later, in the spring of 1955, 42% agreed in reply to the identical query (Table VII). Provided with six alternatives for achieving peace in the summer of 1953 and again ten years later, only 6% in 1963

15 NORC 370, 3–11–55 (1225).
16 AIPO 577, 1–15–57 (1494).
17 AIPO 712, 6–2–65 (1639).
18 NORC 348, 9–24–53 (526).
19 NORC 314, 11–22–51 (1237), and NORC 382, 1–26–56 (1238).

TABLE VII

"Do you think the United Nations should or should not be strengthened to make it a world government with power to control the armed forces of all nations, including the United States?"

DATE	AIPO NO.	(N)	SHOULD	SHOULD NOT	NO OPINION DON'T KNOW
March '51	(473)	(2104)	49%	36%	15%
July '53	(518)	(1454)	41	46	13
March '55	(545)	(1555)	42	45	13

contrasted with 9% a decade before chose the isolationist alternative, 22% versus 21% would "continue to work along with the United Nations just about as we have been, gradually trying to make it better as time goes on," 39% versus only 35% previously felt "we should immediately get behind *strengthening* the United Nations and do everything necessary to give it more power and authority than it has—enough to actually keep even a

TABLE VIII[*]

"While everyone seems to agree that peace is an important thing, there are a good many different views as to how to bring it about. Here are some different ideas . . . Will you . . . tell me which one you come closest to agreeing with?"

SELECTED AS BEST WAY TO BRING ABOUT PEACE:	JULY 1963 N (3007)	JULY 1953 N (3502)
We shouldn't get tied up in any *more* alliances or joint commitments with other countries and we should aim at getting out of as many as we can as soon as we can.	6%	9%
We should continue to work along with the United Nations just about as we have been, gradually trying to make it better as time goes on.	22	21
We should start now working toward transforming the United Nations and do everything necessary to give it more power and authority than it has—enough to actually keep even a strong nation from starting a war.	39	35
In addition to continuing with the United Nations, we should also unite with the friendly democratic countries into one government in which each member nation would in effect become a state, somewhat like the different states in this country.	6	6
We should start now working toward transforming the United Nations into a real world government of *all* nations of the world, in which every nation would in effect become a state, somewhat like the different states in this country.	11	11
Some of these ideas are good, but we won't get any of them working in time to prevent war, so we'd better not rely on them.	6	7
Don't know or no answer.	10	11

[*] *From "A Study of Attitudes Concerning Closer Ties Among Democratic Nations," New York, Elmo Roper Assoc., mimeographed, September 1963, vi.*

strong nation from starting war," 6% on both occasions would continue with the U.N., and also form a federal state with "friendly democratic countries," and 11% both in 1963 and 1953 would transform the U.N. into a "world government" (Table VIII).

Queries over the period since the early 1950's about international military forces under U.N. control have not been identically worded and therefore responses have not been strictly comparable.

In October 1950, 83% thought the United States should agree "to provide troops, along with those of other countries, to help stop an aggressor" under a suggested plan that Member States "keep troops ready at all times to be sent anywhere in the world where trouble breaks out"—more or less the "Acheson plan" which the U.S. introduced in the General Assembly about that time.[20]

In early 1958, 66% agreed that the proposal "to build up the United Nations Emergency Force to a size great enough to deal with 'brush fire' or small wars throughout the world" was "a good idea"; only 15% said it sounded like a "poor idea" to them. Informed that the "present number of men in the U.N. Emergency Force is 10,000," and asked if they would "like to see it built up into an army of at least 100,000, or more," 51% of the public said they would, only 26% that they would not. However, only 38% favored elimination of the veto in the Security Council whereby "the U.N. Emergency Force could be prevented from going into a troubled area"; 33% felt the Security Council veto should remain operative.[21] Finally, in early 1958, the summer of 1960, and again in January 1961, only minorities of Americans felt the U.N. Emergency Force should be made up only of personnel from "small countries"; more than not favored inclusion of "volunteers from such large countries as the U.S. and Russia."

The degree of support for the general idea of a U.N. Emergency Force large enough to deal with limited wars remained relatively stable throughout the late 1950's into the mid-1960's. The proportion of the public favorable to this suggestion rose somewhat with the advent of the Congo disorders shortly after the independence of that territory from Belgian control, to 72% in July 1960, but declined to 62% by the spring of 1964 and returned to 66% in mid-1964—the same level as six and a half years before.

THE U.N. AND AMERICAN POLICY

The American public in recent years has been at least as willing as its federal officials to see the U.N. involved in international matters in which the United States has had a major interest. The major exception has been multilateral administration of foreign aid—even relatively inexpensive technical assistance—through the world body. During the Korean War, in the

20 Scott and Withey, p. 100.
21 AIPO 595, 2–12–58 (1474).

summer of 1952, only 36% of the public was willing to channel any part of Point 4 assistance to "backward countries" through the U.N., and only one American out of six would spend all of it through the U.N. Although by March 1955 Americans favorable to aid to such countries had increased from 73% to 79%, the number who would route at least "some" such aid through the international organization had fallen to 31%, and those who would put all such assistance at the disposal of the multilateral institution had declined from 16% to 11% (Table IX).

TABLE IX

"In general, do you think it is a good policy for the United States to try to help backward countries in the world to raise their standard of living, or shouldn't this be any concern of our government?" Those who replied "a good policy" were further queried, "Do you think the money we put up for such a program should be handled entirely by our government, or should some of it be spent through the United Nations Organization, or should all of it be spent through the United Nations Organization?"

DATE & NORC	(N)	GOOD TO HELP	NO CONCERN	NO OPINION DON'T KNOW	OUR GOVT.	SOME THRU UN	ALL THRU UN	NO OPINION DON'T KNOW
Aug.– Sept. '52								
(329)	(1297)	73%	23%	4%	34%	20%	16%	3%
March '55								
(370)	(1225)	79	18	3	43	20	11	5

However, the increasing influence of underdeveloped, mostly nonaligned countries in the U.N. did not result in lessening of public support for U.N. involvement in most other international issues in which the U.S. had an important interest. At the time of the Suez crisis, 88% thought "it would be a good idea . . . to have the Suez question come up before the United Nations Organization"; only 6% were opposed.[22] Several months later, 39% agreed that the U.N. should apply "sanctions, or penalties, . . . against Israel . . . if she does not withdraw from the Gaza Strip and Aqaba"; only 28% disagreed; and 38% ventured no views.[23] among the 72% of the population who said they had followed the news about Quemoy and Matsu "and the threat of all-out war between the United States, China, and Russia over these islands" in September 1958, 91% indicated they would "like to see the U.S. try to work out a solution to this problem in the United Nations before we get more involved in a military way in the fight over these two islands" and 61% agreed with the suggestion "that Formosa be neutralized, that is, put under the protection of the United Nations."[24] Only 6% opposed the first line of action and 19% the second.

22 NORC 393, 9–13–56 (1263).
23 AIPO 579, 2–26–57 (1531).
24 AIPO 604, 9–8–58 (1522).

The next March, during a period of accentuated tension between the Soviet Union and the West over Berlin, 41% agreed that the "Berlin problem be turned over to the United Nations," while only 23% felt it could "be handled better outside the United Nations." [25] Two years later, several weeks prior to the closing of the border and erection of the wall between East and West Berlin, 81% of the American public thought an effort should be made by the U.N. to "try to settle the Berlin dispute" and only 12% opposed entry of the U.N. therein. Moreover, 40% said they felt the U.N. could actually settle this dispute if it attempted to do so. Even among the 40% who thought the U.N. could not in fact settle this dispute, a majority felt it should try to do so.[26]

Fifty-eight percent of the public approved in July 1964 of the suggestion "that a U.N. Army deal with the problems of Southeast Asia and Vietnam" and only 19% disapproved.[27] The distribution of opinions on this proposition was approximately the same just before the initiation of the bombings of North Vietnam in early 1965, when 60% approved and 20% disapproved of introduction of international forces under U.N. auspices into this troubled area.[28] During the rapid build up of U.S. forces and the bombings of North Vietnam in the summer of 1965, 74% approved of asking "the United Nations to try to work out its own formula for peace in Vietnam"; only 12% disapproved.[29] When the 66% who had "heard or read that the problem of Vietnam is being taken up by the U.N." in February 1966 were queried about their sentiments on "having the U.N. try to work out a solution," 89% favored this idea and only 7% opposed it. Moreover, 32% even thought the U.N. would "be able to bring about a peaceful settlement of differences in Vietnam" while 48% said they did not believe it would.[30]

Furthermore, although only small minorities have possessed much information about U.S. policies and behavior in the World organization, large majorities have apparently approved of whatever they have perceived to be our basic postures there. Thus, even though majorities had voted against him for President in 1952 and again in 1956, only 11% of the American public in late 1962 disapproved "of the way Adlai Stevenson is handling his job as ambassador to the U.N." while 62% approved. Even among self-declared Republicans, only 19% disapproved as contrasted with 56% who approved of Stevenson's performance as U.S. permanent representative to the United Nations.[31]

25 AIPO 611, 3–2–59 (1532). Thirty-six percent either said they had not "heard or read anything about the recent trouble with the Russians over Berlin" or ventured no views on the possible role of the U.N. in this controversy.
26 AIPO Release of 8–2–61.
27 AIPO 695, 7–21–64 (1569).
28 AIPO Release of 2–17–65.
29 AIPO 715, 8–3–65 (>1500).
30 AIPO 724, 2–8–66 (1567).
31 AIPO 666, 12–11–62 (>1500).

THE U.N. IN THE CONTEXT OF FOREIGN POLICY GENERALLY

The U.N. and active U.S. collaboration therein have fared very well indeed with the American public in comparison with most other aspects of their government's policies in international affairs. Barely half the public favored foreign aid as a general idea during the late 1950's and 1960's and majorities of those venturing opinions have felt that the amount of our foreign assistance should be reduced significantly, if not stopped entirely, that particularly aid to unaligned and communist regimes should be cut, and that aid should be kept on a year-to-year basis. Only minorities have favored reductions of tariffs, liberalizations of quotas, and lowering of barriers to trade generally. Even the majorities who have favored continued U.S. participation in N.A.T.O. and intercultural exchange programs have been smaller than those favorable to the U.N. and to active U.S. participation within it.

Thus, many Americans who have held generally favorable views of the U.N. would cut foreign aid and discontinue reductions of barriers to foreign imports, and considerable minorities harboring pro-U.N. opinions would even withdraw from N.A.T.O., reduce intercultural exchanges, especially with Communist countries, and adopt "tougher" postures toward the Communist world than those pursued by our government. A considerable number in the mid-1960's would bomb the major cities of North Vietnam and otherwise escalate the war in Southeast Asia. The small minorities of Americans who would withdraw from the U.N., who have considered it unimportant to try to make the U.N. a success, who have felt it has done a "poor job," or the like have for the most part been general isolationists and have opposed most other forms of international cooperation as well.

Inconsistencies between opinions on the U.N. and views on other fields of foreign affairs have been even more widespread than those among opinions on different aspects of the U.N. itself. Thus, correlations between activist or "internationalist" thinking on the U.N. and views favoring other multilateral cooperation have on the whole been lower than those among views on the world organization itself. Although linkages of pro-U.N. attitudes with support for international cooperation in other fields have typically been statistically significant, they have not been particularly close.

In late 1956 those who felt Communist China should be admitted were only slightly more inclined than those opposed to agree that Congress should appropriate about the same amount, $4 billion, as that voted "during recent years" to assist other countries and "help prevent their going Communistic" —among the former, 62% favored aid at the magnitude indicated while 29% opposed it, whereas among the latter only 59% favored while 30% opposed it.[32]

However, by the late spring of 1964, 62% of those definitely for Chinese

[32] AIPO 576, 12–12–56 (1540).

TABLE X*

	PAID NO ATTENTION & UNINFORMED	FAVOR PEKING'S ADMISSION	OPPOSE, BUT [PREFER] U.S. STAY IN IF [PEKING] ADMITTED	DON'T KNOW IF [U.S. SHOULD] STAY IN OR NOT, DEPENDS	GET OUT	DON'T KNOW IF PEKING SHOULD BE ADMITTED
(N)	(428)	(219)	(483)	(70)	(101)	(147)
Negotiate differences with Communists:						
Yes	47%	81%	70%	68%	51%	69%
Depends	2	3	3	4	2	3
Refuse to deal with them	20	4	9	10	27	8
Don't know & no interest	31	12	18	18	20	20
Freer trade with Communists:						
Allow Americans to trade	20	41	28	26	23	26
Depends	3	6	5	5	4	4
Forbid trade	45	29	42	43	47	42
Don't know & no interest	32	24	25	26	26	28
Chances of staying out of war:						
Getting better in recent years	25	39	30	27	26	27
About same	47	47	48	47	45	47
Getting worse	20	10	18	19	20	18
Don't know/no opinion	8	4	4	7	9	8
Foreign economic aid:						
Give help	41	67	57	50	48	56
Depends	13	16	21	20	32	16
Each country make own way as best [it] can	26	12	16	23	17	10
Don't know & no interest	20	5	6	7	3	18

* SRC 473, September–November, 1964 (1571).

519

TABLE XI*

	ADMIT PEKING TO U.N.	SHOULD NOT [ADMIT PEKING]	DON'T KNOW & NO OPINION	GO ALONG WITH MAJORITY ON PEKING	DON'T [GO ALONG WITH MAJORITY]	NO OPINION & DON'T KNOW
In general:						
For foreign aid	64%	57%	45%	65%	50%	48%
Against it	30	36	26	29	41	28
No opinion & don't know	6	7	29	6	9	24
Foreign aid request of President for $3.4 billion:						
Congress should increase	7	6	6	6	8	3
Decrease	46	54	30	50	55	32
Keep same	40	31	31	37	29	30
No opinion & don't know	7	9	33	7	8	35
Would like to see trade between U.S. & Japan.						
Increased	32	22	20	31	19	20
Decreased	16	20	18	17	20	18
Kept same	46	50	34	45	52	33
No opinion & don't know	6	8	28	7	9	29

* AIPO 706, 2–17–65 (>1500).

Communist entry into the U.N. contrasted with but 42% of those definitely against it favored a compromise agreement with Peking to neutralize all Vietnam. Conversely, only 38% of the former versus 48% of the latter would use U.S. combat forces in South Vietnam "if necessary."[33] The following fall Americans who would admit Peking as a Member State were the most likely to agree that 1) our leaders should "sit down and talk to the leaders of the Communist countries and try to settle our differences," 2) our government should allow "our farmers and business men . . . [to] do business with Communist countries as long as the goods are not used for military purposes," 3) our "chances of staying out of war" had been "getting better . . . during the last few years," and 4) our government should "give aid to other countries if they need help" (Table X). Those who opposed Chinese Communists entry but would have the U.S. remain a member if Peking were admitted were next most inclined to favor these propositions, those who would withdraw were still less apt to do so, and those who said they had paid no attention to "what kind of government most of China has" and did not know that Communist China was not a Member of the U.N. were least favorable of all to these views. Similarly in early 1965, those who would admit Communist China to the U.N. or would go along with a majority vote on the matter were more inclined to approve of foreign aid as a general idea, to support the sum requested for aid by the President of the Congress, and to favor expansion of trade with Japan than were others who opposed her admission and, particularly, those who would not go along with a majority of the General Assembly if it voted favorably on Peking's entry (Table XI).

---

[33] "The American Public's View of U.S. Policy Toward China," p. 54.

PART VI

THE LEGAL WORLD

CHAPTER **17**

THE LAW OF INTERNATIONAL ORGANIZATION

In this chapter we shall attempt to examine two aspects of international organization: (1) the United Nations as a law-making agency and (2) the legal position and status of the delegates. Implicit in statements about the Organization is the view that laws are made by courts and legislatures and that the UN, being neither, does not make laws. Such an opinion is commonly expressed because of the awareness that the UN, consisting of sovereign states, cannot be a law-making body. Of course this is a view that has been debated, as has the argument that official positions taken by the UN are reflections of positions previously adopted by its individual members, which the UN makes binding.

Professor Leo Gross in a lengthy analysis, of which we have included only a brief section, indicates in his article, "The United Nations and the Role of Law," that "soft" law (resolutions and declarations) is frequently con-

sidered a precursor of "hard law" (treaties). In regard to the controversy over
the status of resolutions, he holds that the wiser position, and the one commonly accepted within the Organization, is that resolutions are not legally
binding. When they are followed by duly ratified conventions the particulars
may be considered legal obligations; international law is thereby made. Yet
the importance of these resolutions must not be overlooked, for they not
only reflect views of the majority, which may be quite large, but, if reiterated
frequently over a long period of time, indicate expectations of obligations—
a conclusion not to be lightly considered. One may argue that any action
which consistently brings strong and widespread condemnation has the
representative character of law, but the nature of practice and the nature of
protests may not coincide. Gross supports Wolfgang Friedmann's view that
such resolutions are an important link in building new principles of law.

Differences of opinion on this point are frequently thought of as resulting
in large measure from the pressures brought by the newer states, through
UN resolutions, to establish a body of anti-colonial law. And while it is true
that some of the effort to establish UN law comes from such maneuvering,
it is also true that the Soviet Union has been insisting on the codification
of what it calls "the law of coexistence." Edward McWhinney in his article,
"The 'New' Countries and the 'New' International Law: The United Nations'
Special Conference on Friendly Relations and Cooperation Among States,"
is concerned that the West has been overlooking important political and
diplomatic advantages inherent in soft law. Many states today feel that new
law of the soft variety is both vital and binding. To insist on only the traditional sources and methodologies for the establishment of international law
is to insist that new institutions have and can have only a very limited function in the pursuit of solutions to international problems. Furthermore, insistence on traditional sources and methods reflects a complete lack of
sympathy with the fact that the international law of the Western and older
states was formulated at a time when over half of the sovereign actors of
the present world scene were non-existent and thus in no position to affect
the content of that law. McWhinney's plea for a more sympathetic and
flexible approach to the pleas of the states less concerned with tradition is
well articulated and deserving of careful thought. In particular it ought
not to be rejected by the United States in view of its own origins.

In the succeeding article, by Frank Barabas, written before he joined the
UN Secretariat, Barabas discusses "Membership and Representation" and the
distinctions between these two categories. He deals first with the provisions
on membership and the difficulties that have been encountered in defining
its meaning and in allocating responsibilities for admission. In his article he
reveals the efforts made in the Secretariat to draw up ground rules which
pertain to the problem the 1949 Chinese revolution presented. These rules
would establish principles to be followed if the credentials of a body of

*delegates are challenged due to the defeat of the government which ap-
pointed them. The "constitutive law" position was not adopted by the
delegates despite the fact that the United States at that period was quite
willing to consider the issue as procedural. Under the Eisenhower Administration, however, the United States position changed and the problem
remains on the critical list yet. Barabas recognizes that it cannot be solved
as if it were one requiring merely a careful, competent legal analysis. If
such analysis were all that was required, a vote by the credentials committee and a confirmation or repudiation by the Assembly would be all that
was necessary. The fact that this method has not been employed in the case
of China is indicative of the depth of political feeling on the issue. The
author's conclusion, therefore, that the legal problem of Communist China
must be resolved on a political basis is probably a wise assessment. But his
opinion that the government of Communist China will have to modify its
determined opposition not to allow the Nationalists to remain in the UN
ignores the fact that the Nationalists have taken exactly the same position
regarding their rival.*

*The last selection in this chapter provides a study of a little-discussed
but nevertheless important aspect of international organization: the diplomatic status of the representatives of its members. Although the question of
the legal status such representatives hold is comparatively new, it has received
considerable attention at least since the days of the League of Nations. Most
scholars deny the basis and nature of immunities by generalizing from the
status of the regular diplomat. Nevertheless, functionalism is usually considered to be the proper basis for determining immunities for both groups
as well as for determining the nature of their privileges and immunities.
Yet, as Leo Gross writes in "Immunities and Privileges of Delegations to
the United Nations," national representatives are not considered to belong to
a state or even to the chief administrative officer of the Organization. Their
status must be defined by the member states who have created and maintained the Organization, and it is assumed that the provisions which
identify their diplomatic standing are expected to be honored by all members. Clearly, the performance of all countries in terms of these obligations
is important, but of crucial significance is the host country's behavior. The
United States never signed the United Nations General Convention, which
specifies the immunities of the delegates, although most of the other states
did. Instead, the United States signed with the Secretary-General a Headquarters Agreement Act, which is not as comprehensive as the General Convention. Furthermore, the Headquarters Agreement states that in case of
disagreement between the General Convention and the Headquarters Agreement the latter shall prevail. Many situations can arise in which the host
state has an opportunity to exercise a special influence over the functioning
of the members, as, for example, in terms of entry into the United States,*

*termination of an individual's stay, and his freedom of movement and there-
fore possible performance while here. The United States has tended in almost all instances to proceed with caution in such matters and to place major
emphasis on its own security. Gross identifies some of the difficulties which
have arisen because of this approach. The author is critical of the United
States because of its excessive emphasis on national interest in such matters
and believes that the sooner the Organization has a territorial base as a means
of guaranteeing the immunities of its delegates, the sooner will the problems
of the present arrangement be eliminated.*

*If one argues that the United Nations was expected to be and ought to
be a major institution in the search for world peace, would it not be wise to
examine each issue when it is raised to determine its effect on world
peace? If so, is it wise to take the position that resolutions cannot be considered binding but have only a suasive character. Clearly, if members are
alleged to so consider these resolutions, as Gross finds, the scholar can only
plead for a contrary position. But how much of the answer to this question is
determined by the major powers whose opportunity to influence the outcome
in such matters is still large? Would it be desirable for the delegates themselves in the wording of resolutions to indicate that certain resolutions are
expected to be put to national ratifying bodies?*

*Is the reluctance of the United States and other Western states to accept
seriously the growth of the new law doing serious damage to their standing
in international politics by unnecessarily setting them off as less progressive
and less interested in change than the Soviet Union and others?*

*The question of change also raises the China question, and here again
one must ask for a serious look at the issue of representation in the UN.
With increasing numbers of states recognizing the Peoples Republic of
China, and with more and more of the major world controversies being
influenced by China, does an American position adopted in 1950 make much
sense more than a decade and a half later? If the United States feels
the need to have contacts in Warsaw with the Peoples Republic representatives, why are contacts in New York less desirable or necessary? And was
the ability to treat with Soviet officials at the UN during the height of the
Berlin blockade not an asset to the solution of the problem and therefore a
potential lesson for the solution of the war in Viet Nam and other crises with
China?*

*Finally, we may ask if it makes any sense for the United States to con-
tinue to refuse to sign the General Convention? Have we not seen by now
that all the necessary protection we might want we are able to have without
remaining alien in regard to this treaty? And is this refusal not one more
invidious distinction that we maintain between us and the other states in
terms of our obligations to the principles of the Charter?*

FURTHER READINGS

Brown, Benjamin H., and Green, Fred, "Chinese Representation: A Case Study in United Nations Political Affairs." New York: Woodrow Wilson Foundation, 1955, pp. 31–51.

Friedmann, Wolfgang, "The Uses of 'General Principles' in the Development of International Law," *The American Journal of International Law*, Vol. LVII, No. 2, April 1963, pp. 279–300.

Kelsen, Hans, *The Law of the United Nations: A Critical Analysis of Its Fundamental Problems*. New York: Frederick A. Praeger, Inc., 1964.

Weissberg, Guenter, *International Status of the United Nations*. Dobbs Ferry, N.Y.: Oceana Publications, Inc., 1961.

THE UNITED NATIONS AND THE ROLE OF LAW

Leo Gross*

... The resort to the medium of resolutions as a vehicle for the progressive development of international law does not imply that the United Nations has abandoned the medium of the treaty or convention, or in more colloquial terms that the formulation of "hard" law (treaty) has been set aside in favor of "soft" law (resolution or declaration). The United Nations is pragmatic about its choice of media, and sometimes "soft" law is only considered a precursor of "hard" law. Thus, in the field of human rights, pending the completion of the covenants on human rights, the General Assembly adopted several conventions on some specific subjects such as slavery, political rights of women, and consent to marriage. On the other hand, the Assembly adopted the Declaration on the Elimination of All Forms of Racial Discrimination and at the same time requested the Economic and Social Council to give "absolute priority" to the preparation of a draft convention on the same subject.

There are differences of opinion on the significance or role of resolutions or declarations of the General Assembly as sources of international law. It may be observed first of all that where the Assembly has chosen a two-stage approval—first a declaration or resolution, followed by a convention—it has drawn a distinction between the traditional and accepted source of legal obligation, the convention, and the novel and controversial form, the resolution or declaration. The distinction is of vital significance and, it is submitted, should be maintained.

This is not to suggest that the traditional sources of international law should not be kept under continuous review and that their adequacy need not be tested in the light of contemporary developments. There is room for a number of intermediate positions between the two extremes: At one pole of a continuum is the proposition that the General Assembly has a legislative or quasi-legislative function,[1] and at the other pole is the proposition that resolutions of the Assembly are legally not binding. The former view assumes

* Leo Gross, "The United Nations and the Role of Law," *International Organization*, Vol. 19, 1965, pp. 537–561. Copyright 1965, World Peace Foundation. By permission of *International Organization*.

Leo Gross is Professor of International Law and Organization at the Fletcher School of Law and Diplomacy and a member of the board of editors of *International Organization*. He is the author of many journal and law review articles.

[1] Jorge Castañeda, "The Underdeveloped Nations and the Development of International Law," *International Organization*, Winter 1961 (Vol. 15, No. 1), pp. 38–48.

and must assume that where the Assembly adopts resolutions such as those relating to human rights, self-determination, etc., it is merely elaborating principles already accepted as binding by the Members; and, in turn, it assumes further that the Assembly has the power of authentic and binding interpretation.[2] As was pointed out earlier, this view has not been generally accepted, and it is doubtful whether it would be desirable to accept it. The latter position adheres to the original conception of the Assembly as a deliberative body endowed with limited powers and certainly, by design and not by omission, not endowed with legislative prerogatives. The two-stage approach followed by the Assembly is a clear and incontrovertible evidence that the Assembly shares this view of its own powers.

The significance of the resolutions of the Assembly is primarily political. Many are designed to give direction to the Members and the Organization as well. Some resolutions, such as those dealing with outer space, may derive especial significance from the fact that they represent the consensus of the two powers which have a virtual duopoly in that virginal field. Where there is or is claimed to be law, as, for instance, with respect to compensation for the expropriation of property owned by aliens, a resolution of the Assembly, such as that on "Permanent sovereignty over natural resources" may have sufficient force to create or increase uncertainty as to the claimed law without being sufficiently persuasive to create a new rule. In this particular case the international standard according to which the state taking such measures must pay "prompt, adequate and effective" compensation has been under attack for so long and by so substantial a number of states that it could be fairly doubted whether that standard ever was or still is a rule of customary international law. This being so, the resolution of the Assembly proposing merely "appropriate compensation" may be deemed to have administered the *coup de grâce* to the alleged international standard. This conclusion is based not on any assumption of the resolution's having an obligatory character. It may be based more simply on the traditional concept of customary international law according to which a rule requires practice and the *opinio juris*, that is, the manifestation of conviction that the practice has been accepted as binding or obligatory. The debates in the Assembly stretching over a period of years would indicate that this conviction was lacking, that there was no supporting consensus. Thus, as a convenient index for determining the existence or absence of consensus, the debates in the Assembly and the resolutions which it adopts may serve a useful purpose. But consensus without state practice is not productive of a rule of law.

There is a long way from the birth of an idea to its consummation in a rule of law, be it conventional or customary. Resolutions of the Assembly purporting to be of a lawmaking character are certainly "an important link in the continuing process of development and formulation of new principles

[2] *Ibid.*, p. 47; and Manfred Lachs, "The Law in and of the United Nations," *Indian Journal of International Law*, 1960–1961 (Vol. 1), p. 438.

of international law."[3] It has been suggested that the traditional statement of sources of international law in Article 38 of the Statute of the International Court of Justice and the distinction between binding and nonbinding sources "was becoming increasingly irrelevant and unrealistic." This is perhaps too extreme a view, although it may serve a useful purpose to reexamine Article 38, which had been part of the Statute of the Permanent Court of International Justice and was adopted in 1945 without change in the Statute of the new Court, and perhaps to arrange for a reexamining of the sources of international law generally by a committee of governments. Until this is done, however, it may be proper to regard debates in and resolutions of the General Assembly not so much as sources but, in the words of Article 38, paragraph 1 (d), of the Statute "as a subsidiary means for the determination of rules of law." They might rank with, or even ahead of, "the teachings of the most highly qualified publicists" but below judicial decisions.

To close this analysis on a slightly ironical note: The Sixth Committee held a far-ranging debate in which it frequently expressed dissatisfaction with the state of international law, its own modest role in the United Nations, the slow progress of the work of the International Law Commission, and its near starvation in having had referred to it only three out of about 90 items on the agenda of the General Assembly; it noted the attitude of new states toward traditional international law which, having grown up without their participation, has failed to reflect their interests; yet finally, it adopted unanimously a Ukrainian amendment to the pending draft resolution which called for the "strict and undeviating observance [of international law] by all Governments."

THE "NEW" COUNTRIES AND THE "NEW" INTERNATIONAL LAW

Edward McWhinney[*]

Looking back on the history of the coexistence (friendly relations) debate over the past few years, and the general Soviet-Western scientific legal confrontation, the conclusion seems to emerge inescapably that the time

---

[3] Wolfgang Friedmann, *The Changing Structure of International Law* (New York: Columbia University Press, 1964), p. 139.

[*] Edward McWhinney, "The 'New' Countries and the 'New' International Law: The United Nations' Special Conference on Friendly Relations and Co-operation among States," *American Journal of International Law*, Vol. 66, 1966, pp. 1–33. Copyright ©

is ripe for a change in basic Western tactics. Western delegations, both in official inter-governmental arenas, such as those provided by the United Nations specialized commissions and agencies and the General Assembly itself, and also in private, scientific organizations, originally resisted the Soviet campaign for an immediate act of codification, *uno ictu*, of postulated principles of peaceful coexistence. Apart from the evident propaganda objectives that Soviet-bloc jurists were seeking to realize in the period prior to the Soviet-Western *détente* arising from the Cuban nuclear missile crisis of October, 1962, it seemed clear at the time that any list of principles arrived at in this way by purely *a priori* methods would be mere exercises in cloudiness and semantic confusion, flowing from the normative ambiguity existing between the different legal systems to be involved in any such grand declaration or code. But the Western insistence, instead, on pragmatic, empirical, problem-oriented, step-by-step methods, involving the induction of any principles of coexistence (friendly relations) from the main tension-issues of current Soviet-Western relations and their concrete resolution, necessarily involved a correlative obligation to be ready and willing actively to apply such methods—in a word, to take part in the dialogue. It would be a pity if the impression were to emerge that an originally legitimate and methodologically valid Western response to an, on the whole, originally rather clumsy and somewhat unscientific Soviet legal campaign in behalf of coexistence, were only a device or stratagem for defeating or delaying the pressures and aspirations of the "new" countries for the progressive re-writing of old international law doctrine to meet the revolutionary changes in the world community since World War II.

The fact is, of course, that the larger part of the world, including a majority of the "new" countries, is civil law in legal background, and does not have the same distrust of abstract general formulations or codes that Western common lawyers have. It is right for common lawyers to continue to insist on the empirical, problem-oriented approach to inter-systems accommodations; I do not see how, however, we can avoid taking note of, and cataloguing in detailed listings or codes, any general principles or rules of inter-systems relations induced by these non-abstract, thoroughly empirical, methods. It is a pity, in this regard, that the main Western countries' positions in the Mexico City Special Committee seemed to be so generally defensive, with the main initiatives for "new" international law-making coming from the Socialist bloc and the uncommitted countries. Part of the difficulty may have come from the fact, already mentioned, that the Western countries, apparently in an endeavor to downgrade the Mexico City conference, either sent only fairly junior personnel as their

1966 by the American Society of International Law. By permission of the *American Journal of Law*.

Edward McWhinney is Professor of International and Comparative Law at the University of Toronto and is editor of *Law, Foreign Policy and the East-West Détente*.

representatives or else hamstrung them by denying them *pleins pouvoirs* as to the day-by-day negotiating and by insisting on a continual reference back to head office for instructions and approval. It seems unfortunate, for example, that the United States Delegation was so peremptorily over-ruled by Washington in their accord to the compromise draft on the prohibition of force, especially where the generality of the legal language concerned would hardly seem to warrant Washington's fears as to the possible exclusion of "hot pursuit." It seems equally unfortunate that the Canadian Delegation, apparently for reasons of lack of affirmative instructions and authority, had to maintain such a sustained silence throughout the Mexico City sessions. All this threw an unfair responsibility on certain Western delegations, most notably the United Kingdom Delegation, to present basic Western positions; and the United Kingdom Delegation in any case had to carry the extra burden of defending itself against "colonialist" charges.

It is clear that, in the light of continuing Soviet-bloc pressure, and also the new interest of the uncommitted Afro-Asian countries and the Latin American countries, there is a fairly general impatience with the slowness and delays of existing bodies concerned with the revision or rewriting of old international law doctrine. In the new mood of international law-making and codification, therefore, it behooves the West to take part in the dialogue with *élan* and imagination, and to develop theories in the international law area which will adequately reflect the dynamic relationships between positive law and social change which are regarded in North American law schools as axiomatic for internal law purposes. We need to project affirmatively, in these new international arenas concerned with the "new" international law, our own revolutionary legal tradition and its inherent capacity to continue to adapt traditional, customary international law creatively to meet new conditions in the world community.

As a second point, we have probably been too literalistic in our approach to the traditional "sources" of international law, and in our insistence, in Austinian positivistic fashion, that only that is law and therefore legally binding which emerges from such pre-existing, recognized sources. Traditional international law is silent, for example, as to the exact status, in terms of lawmaking authority and potential, of U.N. General Assembly resolutions, or the conclusions of United Nations committees, or the opinions or votes of international scientific legal conferences or reunions. Perhaps General Assembly resolutions that have unanimity or at least substantial inter-systems support behind them can be assimilated to traditional sources of international law as, in effect, "instant customary international law;" perhaps they can be taken as evidence of "the general principles of law recognized by civilized nations," recognized as an approved source in Article 38(1) (c) of the Statute of the World Court. Perhaps conclusions of international scientific legal conferences can be accepted as being "teachings of the most highly qualified publicists" and therefore as "subsidiary means for the determination of rules of law," in terms of Article 38 (1) (d). However that may be—and the Soviet-bloc literature in favor of expanding the legal significance of these new approaches to international lawmaking is becoming quite substantial by now—it is clear that, as with the principle of the non-orbiting of nuclear weapons in space vehicles, which does not fit easily into any of the traditional categories of "sources," we may in the end accept certain principles as being law simply because they are generally rational and reasonable and rest on a sufficient inter-systems consensus. In this respect, they may be said to become law in the legal realists sense simply because they are generally accepted as such and acted upon, without worrying too much about whether or not they fit into *a priori* categories or definitions of "sources."

As a third point, it seems clear that some traditional Western-based intellectual approaches to world peace and relief of international tensions will either need considerable revision or else are doomed to political failure under present conditions. The "World Rule of Law" campaign, for example, which, as one of its cardinal points, rests on the extension of the compulsory jurisdiction of the World Court, runs counter to a widespread feeling on the part of uncommitted countries as much as of the Soviet bloc that it is a Western-dominated or at least "unrepresentative" body. The most direct remedy for any such feelings, as Western delegations to the Mexico City Special Committee rightly pointed out, is for all countries to take a more active part in the periodic elections to the Court. Yet a basic dilemma remains. The "new" countries are not so much concerned with ascertaining or restating existing international law doctrine as with rewriting it; in effect, with legislating.

A more "representative" World Court, resulting from a far greater politicization of the processes of election than the present rather casual horse-trading methods and exchanges, would inevitably be under pressure from certain quarters to exercise some of the policy-making, "legislative" functions of the United States Supreme Court. Would the cause of relief of international tensions be better served by an "activist" World Court on the American model, rather than by a more deliberately restricted and restrained final tribunal on the English or French pattern, taking note of the fact that there hardly exists in the world community today a sufficient inter-systems consensus of a range and degree paralleling that national minimum consensus that has made the American court's policy-making politically viable? It seems clear that more thought is needed here before formulating any overly categorical Western institutional positions or preferences as to the arenas for international lawmaking. For, in the light of some of our second thoughts over the merits of political primacy for the General Assembly in U.N. peacekeeping operations, in the wake of the abortive Western-sponsored Article 19 and U.N. Expenses proposals, it is important to remember that the institutional preferences one successfully asserts today may be those that one has to live with tomorrow. Certainly, Western reaction back to the Security Council in the face of an increasing "politicization" of the General Assembly, suggests some caution on the issue of insisting on sponsoring judicial settlement of disputes in priority to all other forms of peaceful settlement. The clear preference of the Soviet bloc and the uncommitted countries, in this regard, for direct ne- gotiation as the prime mode of peaceful settlement, may thus have more relation to the realities of present-day international life and necessary inter-systems accommodations than Western delegates were prepared to concede in Mexico City.

As a fourth point, the opposition of Soviet-bloc countries and also un- committed countries at Mexico City to any notion of an overriding "world law" or "world government" seems to have been rooted essentially in strict notions of state sovereignty which have traditionally bulked larger in Soviet-bloc legal thinking than in our own; and it is certainly not an op- position to international law as such. In fact, in its necessary opposition also to any notion of postulated, *a priori*, pre-eminent legal principles, this particular position of the Soviet bloc and uncommitted countries seems to tie in with the Western-sponsored emphasis on the *a posteriori*, empirical approach to international law and inter-systems accommodation, and on the avoidance of abstract, holistic formulae in favor of a general problems- orientation. Within the terms of reference of the Mexico City conference, there is obviously considerable room for further debate and discussions, and, even more obviously, for further intellectual refinement and qualification. Just what, for example, is the relationship *inter se* of the four principles discussed at Mexico City—prohibition of the threat or use of force; peaceful settlement; non-intervention; sovereign equality? Are they all juridically equal, or is there in fact a hierarchy of legal principles, with some principles being juridically superior to others and thus prevailing in the event of con- flict between them? For example, would the principle of prohibition of threat or use of force rank before all others, in a concrete problem-situa- tion, as a sort of super-eminent legal principle or *jus cogens?* As with the earlier Soviet-bloc campaign for an immediate codification of the law of peaceful coexistence, it becomes apparent that the mere iteration of any such principles could only be a beginning, and not the end, of legal inquiry.

It is already apparent in the Mexico City discussions that, once inquiry proceeds at a level of concrete cases and problems, there is no longer a monolithic unity of Soviet-bloc attitudes. For the smaller Soviet-bloc countries—certainly Yugoslavia and perhaps also Rumania—would clearly rank the principles of non-intervention and sovereign equality before the others. The Soviet Union, perhaps, would favor the principle of the pro- hibition of the threat or use of force in any conflict with the other prin- ciples. Faced with a showdown, for example, between the principle of prohibition of the threat or use of force and the principle of sovereign equality, it is difficult to believe that the Soviet Union, any more than the United States, could concede that deference to sovereign equality involves sanctioning indiscriminate proliferation of nuclear weapons to smaller countries simply because the major Powers may have them. It is not impossible, either, in this nuclear weapons context, to envisage a possible future conflict between the principle of prohibition of threat or use of force and the principle of non-intervention.

And thus, as long as the dialogue continues, the opportunities for fruitful Western scientific legal contributions to the great debate also continue. It is to be hoped that, recognizing that the Soviet bloc itself is saddled with its own defensive attitudes, as revealed in the Mexico City debates, stemming from a certain timorousness in regard to vigorous competition with the West in the field of intellectual ideas and information and communications generally and in the field of trade and commercial intercourse, the West will try to make its own fresh intellectual initiatives, fully capturing the spirit of our own insistence, in our law schools, on the dynamic, revolutionary character of law as a response to rapidly changing societal conditions and social expectations in the community for which it exists.

MEMBERSHIP AND REPRESENTATION

Frank Barabas[*]

. . . According to the United Nations Charter, only states can become Members of the Organization. A dispute over representation can arise only when more than one government claims to represent a single state, as in the case of China. The distinction is illustrated clearly in the case of India which in 1947 was granted full independence and split into two dominions. The new Dominion (now Republic) of India was regarded as the continuation with a new government of the old state, and simply had to send new credentials . for its delegation to the UN, while Pakistan had to apply for admission as a new state. . . .

[*] Frank Barabas, "Membership and Representation," *Journal of International Affairs*, Vol. 9, 1955, pp. 31–38. Copyright © 1955 by the board of editors of the *Journal of International Affairs*. By permission of the *Journal of International Affairs*.

Frank Barabas has been employed with the United Nations since 1955. He has been the information officer of the Office of Public Information of the United Nations since 1965. From 1960 to 1961 he was a member of the United Nations team in the Congo Operation.

The second distinction between membership and representation concerns the criteria which the United Nations must apply in each case. According to Article 4 of the Charter, "Membership in the United Nations is open to all ... peace-loving states which accept the obligations contained in the present Charter and, in the judgment of the Organization, are able and willing to carry out these obligations." Since neither the Security Council nor the General Assembly details the reasons for its action on a membership application, no clear jurisprudence has grown up concerning the meaning of the Charter criteria. In Council debates on individual applicants, various Members have thought a large number of facts relevant. As to an applicant's statehood, these points, among others, have been raised: the possession or lack of frontiers, foreign occupation of the applicant's territory, relations with a former sovereign, independent management of foreign policy, defense arrangements with other powers, recognition of the applicant by Members, and the maintenance of diplomatic relations with other states. In connection with an applicant's acceptance of and ability and willingness to carry out Charter obligations, reference has been made to these matters: internal political structure, fulfillment of treaty obligations, compliance with Security Council resolutions, and close association with Franco–Spain.

Most subjective of the criteria for membership is the term "peace-loving," the use of which in a legal text is open to criticism. The authors of the Charter justified it as a compromise between a long list of standards which a state would have to meet and no political criteria at all. In practice the points raised in connection with this term have included the following: conduct during World War II, continued existence of a technical state of war, compliance with UN recommendations, instigation of border incidents, and willingness to settle border disputes peacefully.

At the very first Security Council discussion of membership applications from eleven states in August, 1946, the United States proposed the admission of all "to accelerate the achievement of universality of membership." The Soviet Union objected to the admission of states en masse on the ground that applicants had to be examined individually. The same arguments continued to be advanced, but [later] it [was] the United States which oppose[d] simultaneous admission and the Soviet Union which insist[ed] on it. . . .

Confronted with this Soviet attitude, the General Assembly asked the International Court of Justice for an opinion whether members were "juridically entitled" to base their votes for or against applicants on conditions other than those laid down in Article 4 of the Charter. In May, 1948, by nine votes to six, the Court answered in the negative, adding specifically that consent to admission could not rest on the condition that a group of states be admitted simultaneously. Four justices dissented, holding that the very fact that applications were handled by the two top political organs of the United Nations underlined the importance of political considerations, even beyond those listed in the Charter, in dealing with membership questions. The Court's opinion is of little practical value, however, since there is no way of challenging the reasons advanced by a state in opposition to a membership application. No amount of Charter interpretation can replace the need for political agreements on this problem.

Contrasted with standards for membership and the many issues which various states have regarded as relevant to them is the complete lack of criteria in the Charter for settling a dispute over representation. Many people, including high United States officials who ought to know better, have confused the issue of Chinese representation by referring to the legally irrelevant Charter provisions governing membership, stressing particularly that the Chinese Communists are the opposite of peace-loving. However accurate a description of the Communist regime this may be, it must be recalled, first, that the Peiping Government is not applying for membership, and second, that the Charter, perhaps paradoxically, does not require members to *continue* to be peace-loving. Membership is open to "peace-loving" states, but once a state is admitted there is no requirement anywhere that it continue to meet this test. In fact, in the case of the fifty-one original Members, including China, the standards of Article 4 were never applied. Expulsion can be brought about by the same procedure as admission, but the criteria are different. A state must have "persistently violated" the principles of the Charter before it can be expelled, and even then expulsion is permissive, not mandatory. In any event, a permanent member of the Security Council like China can veto its own expulsion.

The need for criteria in settling controversies over representation was felt by some states soon after the first and only such dispute reached the United Nations in January, 1950, when the Soviet Union left the Security Council over the China issue. Legal experts of the Secretariat drew up a "secret" memorandum so controversial that parts of it soon leaked to the press. The study sought to deduce appropriate standards from the Charter requirement that applicants for membership must be able and willing to carry out the obligations of membership. In the event of a continuing revolution, the argument ran, the government which was in fact able to direct the resources and people of the state in fulfillment of those obligations was the one which ought to represent the state in the United Nations. Consequently, the only two criteria relevant to such an issue were said to be (1) whether the new government exercised effective authority within the territory of the state, and (2) whether it was habitually obeyed by the bulk of the population.

By the time the General Assembly discussed the overall question of representation in October, 1950, the Chinese Communists had intervened in Korea. Most Members were unwilling to agree that a revolutionary regime could automatically gain representation by fulfilling the simple conditions set forth in the Secretariat study, although substantially the same criteria

were advanced by the United Kingdom, with the addition of the notion
that control over the population and resources should appear to be permanent. Latin American republics led the group which called for standards for
representation substantially more stringent than those applied to applicants
for membership, including the following: the general consent of the population; ability and willingness to achieve the purposes of the Charter, to
observe its principles and to fulfill the international obligations of the state;
respect for human rights and fundamental freedoms; and acquisition of political authority through internal processes. So diverse were these standards
and so varied the views of representatives that the Ad Hoc Political Committee, after referring the matter to a subcommittee, gave up the attempt
at enumeration and sent to the Assembly a resolution drafted in vague
terms which reflected the lack of agreement. It was adopted in plenary
session of the General Assembly by 36 votes to 6, with 9 abstentions, as a
recommendation that:

whenever more than one authority claims to be the government entitled to represent a Member State in the United Nations and this question becomes the subject
of controversy in the United Nations, the question should be considered in the
light of the Purposes and Principles of the Charter and the circumstances of each
case . . .

No further United Nations action has been taken along these lines.

Another source of confusion is the connection between recognition of a
government by Member States and its representation in the United Nations.
Use of the word "recognition" in its non-legal sense has sometimes obscured
the fact that the United Nations is incompetent to recognize any government
in the technical meaning of the term. The Secretariat analysis rightly
pointed out that general recognition by Members was not a prerequisite for
representation. Depending on the legal theory a state adheres to, the two
acts may rest on entirely different standards. For this reason, there need be
no inconsistency between withholding recognition from a new regime and
voting to admit its representatives to the United Nations. Nevertheless, that
situation is unlikely to arise since a state like the United States which on
moral grounds refuses to recognize a government is generally unwilling to
give its support to representation of that regime in the United Nations, if
only to avoid the appearance of inconsistency. On the other hand, some
states which recognize the Peiping Government, notably the United Kingdom, have abstained on the Chinese representation issue since the Chinese
intervention in Korea, arguing that it was politically unwise to give China's
seat to the Communists at the moment. The General Assembly formally
distinguished between representation and recognition by declaring that its
attitude on the former "shall not of itself affect the direct relations of
individual Member States with the State concerned."

One concept frequently mentioned in membership discussions which is also politically relevant to the dispute over Chinese representation is the principle of universality. The log jam over membership applications limits not only the geographical but the political scope of United Nations activities. The Organization labors under this handicap in its relations with the Chinese mainland. In both cases it is important to recall that a world organization should mirror world politics, however sordid the other fellow's politics may appear. Nevertheless, to ignore the merits of particular applicants or the facts of particular situations is clearly unwise. Aggression against the United Nations, for instance, cannot be deemed politically irrelevant to an issue of representation simply because it is legally irrelevant. Reconciling universality and selectivity is either impossible or fruitless in a vacuum. Not principles alone but facts and prospects of the individual case should determine policy.

The third difference between the questions of membership and representation is in the procedure by which the two are dealt with in the United Nations. The Charter is clear on the method of handling membership applications. The Security Council must make a positive recommendation, which is subject to the veto, to the General Assembly, which then decides the question by a two-thirds majority. . . . A number of attempts, especially by Latin American states, to circumvent the veto have been unavailing in the face of the unambiguous Charter provisions.

Disputes over representation technically come within the scope of procedure for handling credentials of delegates. Approval of credentials was regarded from the beginning as a procedural matter to be settled independently by each of the principal organs of the United Nations. Credentials for representatives on each principal organ are issued by a head of state or minister of foreign affairs and are sent to the Secretary-General. In the General Assembly they are examined by a nine-member Credentials Committee, whose reports are passed on to the Assembly for approval. The Security Council does not formally approve credentials unless there is a challenge. When the issue of Chinese representation arose, the need for some procedure common to all organs became obvious. Otherwise, an anomalous situation could arise in which, for example, one of two competing regimes could be represented in the Council and the other in the Assembly. An Indian proposal to require the Council to obtain the views of all other members on such a dispute before it took a decision was set aside until the Assembly could take up the matter of coordinating United Nations procedure.

In a resolution of December, 1950, the General Assembly rightly regarded itself as the most appropriate organ to set United Nations policy on representation disputes. It recommended that "when any such question arises, it should be considered by the General Assembly," or by the now defunct Interim Committee when the Assembly is not in session. But getting organs with differing membership to comply with Assembly decisions is another matter. The resolution was unable to say more than this:

Recommends that the attitude adopted by the General Assembly or its Interim Committee concerning any such question should be taken into account in other organs of the United Nations and in the specialized agencies . . .

* * * * * * *

The admission of Peiping, long regarded at the United Nations as merely a matter of timing, may well not be settled as a simple representation issue. The nations which have been referring to Communist China as an inevitable fact of life may be coming to realize that Chiang Kai-shek's government is equally a reality entitled to representation. The problem then becomes one of how to seat the first without unseating the second and, especially, of how to determine who gets the Security Council veto. A compromise along these lines will not only save face on all sides but will result in greater equity. It cannot easily be achieved, however, without some improvement in Mao Tse-tung's international behavior and a softening of his determination to destroy the Nationalists at all costs.

IMMUNITIES AND PRIVILEGES OF DELEGATIONS TO THE UNITED NATIONS

Leo Gross*

* * * * * * *

INSTRUMENTS GOVERNING THE STATUS OF DELEGATIONS

The status, rights and privileges of delegations to the United Nations at its Headquarters are governed by several international instruments:

1. The Charter of the United Nations, in particular Article 105;
2. The General Convention on the Privileges and Immunities of the United Nations adopted by the General Assembly on February 13, 1946; and
3. The Agreement between the United Nations and the United States regarding the Headquarters of the United Nations of June 26, 1947.

* Leo Gross, "Immunities and Privileges of Delegations to the United Nations," International Organization, Vol. 16, 1962, pp. 483–520. Copyright 1962, World Peace Foundation. By permission of International Organization.

Leo Gross is Professor of International Law and Organization at the Fletcher School of Law and Diplomacy and a member of the Board of Editors of International Organization. He is the author of many journal and law review articles.

In addition there are several United States statutes which bear on the subject:

1. The International Organizations Immunities Act of 1945 as amended in 1952 (Public Law 291); and
2. The Joint Resolution authorizing the President to bring into effect the Head-quarters Agreement, approved August 4, 1947 (Public Law 357).

There are also several relevant executive orders and laws of the State of New York and of the City of New York.[1] Principles of customary international law may have to be drawn on to fill gaps, to provide appropriate rules of construction of the applicable instruments, and to determine the relation between the municipal instruments of the United States on the one hand, and the Charter, the General Convention, and the Headquarters Agreement on the other. Concerning the latter point there should be no ambiguity: in case of conflict between international law and municipal law the former ought to prevail. And there need be no doubt that this would be so if a dispute between the United Nations and the United States were submitted to the arbitral tribunal provided for in Section 21 (a) of the Headquarters Agreement or if the International Court of Justice were asked for an advisory opinion on a legal question relating to such a dispute as provided for in paragraph (b) of Section 21. However, no dispute has ever been submitted to settlement in accordance with this procedure. Such problems as have arisen have been ironed out in negotiations between the Secretary-General and representatives of the United States. . . .

The multiplicity of instruments is the source of more than one anomaly. The United States International Organizations Immunities Act was enacted on December 29, 1945, well in advance of the General Convention and the Headquarters Agreement, both of which were intended to implement the general principles enunciated in Article 105 of the Charter. The United States legislation was never amended to bring it into line with the instruments adopted by the General Assembly in virtue of its powers under Article 105, paragraph 3.[2] Another anomaly is that the United States which through its Government and the Congress invited the United Nations "to locate the seat of the United Nations Organization within the United States" has failed to accede to the General Convention which is the basic instrument concerning the privileges and immunities of the United Nations. It was certainly not anticipated that the host country would persistently decline

---

[1] All these instruments are conveniently available in the United Nations Legislative Series: *Legislative Texts and Treaty Provisions concerning the Legal Status, Privileges and Immunities of International Organizations* 1959 (U.N. Publications Sales No.: 60. v. 2) pp. 128–173, 183–193, 204–217. Hereafter referred to as *Legislative Texts*. This work is the source of all references to relevant national and international instruments in this paper.

[2] C. Wilfred Jenks, *International Immunities* (London: Stevens, 1961), p. 11. Jenks notes that the United Kingdom did so amend its legislation.

to accede to the Convention which had been accepted by a majority of Members including the Soviet Union. The interdependence between the General Convention and the Headquarters Agreement was always recognized. Thus in Resolution 259 (111) of December 8, 1948, the General Assembly declared that the Headquarters Agreement and the General Convention "are complementary . . . since *these instruments taken together* are intended to define the status of the United Nations in the country where these headquarters are located" and that "if the United Nations is *to achieve its purposes and perform its functions effectively,* it is essential that the States Members should unanimously approve the provisions of the said Convention." . . .

The Headquarters Agreement does indeed "incorporate by reference" in Section 13, paragraph (*b*)3 and paragraph (*d*), the corresponding provisions, specifically and generally, of the General Convention which bear directly upon the subject here under consideration. More importantly still, Section 26 provides explicitly:

The provisions of this agreement shall be complementary to the provisions of the General Convention. In so far as any provision of this agreement and any provisions of the General Convention relate to the same subject matter, the two provisions shall, wherever possible, be treated as complementary so that both provisions shall be applicable and neither shall narrow the effect of the other; but in any case of absolute conflict, the provisions of this agreement shall prevail.

This clause calls for some observations. First of all it makes abundantly clear that both the United Nations and the United States Department of State assumed that the United States would promptly accede to the General Convention. This accession has not been forthcoming after nearly a decade and a half, apparently for reasons of a political character which have nothing to do with the question of immunities and privileges of representatives. Secondly, the incorporation by reference is unconditional; that is, the General Convention may be regarded as binding upon the United States even without formal accession. Such a construction, resting upon the relevant sections of the Headquarters Agreement, particularly Section 26, has not been adopted in practice but is perfectly tenable juridically. Political considerations have probably made the adoption of such a construction both impractical and undesirable.

. . . Committee [IV/2 of Commission IV at the San Francisco Conference] deemed it inadvisable to spell out in detail the necessary immunities and privileges but, it declared, "If there is one certain principle it is that no member state may hinder in any way the working of the Organization or take any measures the effect of which might be to increase its burdens, financial or other."

This fundamental principle applies to the Organization but it must equally apply to the Secretariat, the Members, and their representatives, without whom the Organization could not operate of all. Any national restrictions, controls, or administrative rulings, whether general or particular, which would impede the effective and independent functioning of the Organization or any of its organs, would seem to be incompatible with that principle. To be sure, the modern approach to immunities and privileges favors the functional test. But the test must be the free and independent exercise of its functions by the Organization. And this test may be applied by national authorities and by the Organization itself, but ultimately and authoritatively it should be construed by the organs which are entrusted with the international control, that is, the arbitral tribunal and the International Court of Justice in accordance with the provisions of the General Convention and the Headquarters Agreement.

This construction of the primacy of UN objectives clearly raises the issue of national internal security and national interest of the host country. The almost continual influx of representatives of Members, at its peak for General Assembly sessions, and the residence in the territory of the United States of a substantial number of members of permanent missions to the United Nations and of members of the Secretariat inevitably pose a problem of national security for the United States. Are considerations of national internal security of the United States on the same plane as, or even superior to, the principle of the freedom and independence from national control and interference of the United Nations? And there is another question: can the United States as the host country derive any advantage from its position as the grantor of entry visas and residence privileges in order to promote its national interest? May the United States, more precisely, in retaliation for treatment accorded its own national diplomatic representatives in certain Members' countries impose, as it does, corresponding restrictions on the representatives of those Members to the United Nations?

An indication of United States policy can be seen in the following: the United States restricted to a minimum the scope of applicable international regulations by refusing to accede to the General Convention and by attaching a sweeping reservation to the Headquarters Agreement which it did accept. The resulting situation then appears to be as follows: the privileges and immunities of members of the Secretariat of the United Nations are not governed by any international instrument, apart from the Charter, to which the United States is a party. Their status is subject to unilateral United States legislation, notably the International Organizations Immunities Act of December 29, 1945, Public Law 291, and the Immigration and Nationality Act of 1952, Public Law 414. The status, privileges, and immunities of representatives of Members are governed by Public Law 291 as well as Public Law 357 of August 1947 which is the Joint Resolution authorizing the President to bring into force the Headquarters Agreement. Section 6 of Public Law 357 is in the nature of a unilateral reservation of national security and is not part of the arrangements between the United States and the United Nations.[3] Public Law 357, which incorporates the Headquarters Agreement insofar as representatives of Member States are concerned, governs explicitly and subjects to the reservation only the [representatives'] transit to and from the Headquarters district but not their privileges and immunities which are provided for in the General Convention to which the United States is not a party. The status, privileges, and immunities of members of permanent delegations to the United Nations are governed by the Headquarters Agreement but subject to the reservation in Public Law 357; they may also be subjected to Public Law 291. The General Convention does not deal specifically with resident representatives but there is no reason why the general principles regarding the representatives of Members should not also apply to resident representatives. . . .

SOME SPECIAL PROBLEMS

ACCEPTANCE OF MEMBERS' REPRESENTATIVES. Section 8 (a) of Public Law 291 provides:

No person shall be entitled to the benefits of this title unless he (1) shall have been duly notified to and accepted by the Secretary of State as a representative, officer, or employee; or (2) shall have been designated by the Secretary of State, prior to formal notification and acceptance, as a prospective representative, officer, or employee.

Whatever the meaning of subsection (2) may be, it is clear from subsection (1) that the enjoyment of the privileges and benefits of Members' representatives is conditioned by prior notification to and acceptance by the Secretary of State. Public Law 291 specifies the privileges afforded such representatives with respect to entry into and departure from the United States as well as their immunity from suit and legal process for their official acts. Clearly notification of such persons is a necessary condition for the enjoyment of such privileges and immunities and for inclusion in the "Bluebook" published every two months by the United States Mission to the United Nations in cooperation with the Protocol Division of the United Nations. By analogy to the Diplomatic List issued by the Department of State with respect to the Diplomatic Corps in Washington, inclusion in the Bluebook is *prima facie* evidence of status.

The requirement of acceptance or approval as a condition for the enjoyment of privileges and immunities by representatives of Members is a different matter altogether. Does the entry of such representatives depend upon the approval by the Secretary of State? Clearly the analogy which comes to mind is the procedure of *agréation* provided for diplomatic representatives accredited to the President of the United States. The representa-

[3] It is not reprinted in the *Legislative Texts* although it was included in the *Handbook on the Legal Status, Privileges and Immunities of the United Nations,* Document ST/LEG/2, September 19, 1952, pp. 292 ff.

tives of Members, however, are not accredited to the government of the United States in any way or in any sense. *Agréation* implies prior approval and national control. It has its traditional place and significance in connection with diplomatic representatives of foreign states who are to transact business with the United States government. Representatives of Members to the United Nations have no business to transact with the United States. Representatives to meetings of the General Assembly or to other organs of the United Nations bear credentials which are scrutinized by those organs. Permanent delegates, although they present their credentials to him, are not accredited to the Secretary-General, for this would imply control and the right to reject persons appointed by Members. No such right has been conceded by the sovereign Members to the Secretary-General.

*   *   *   *   *   *   *

It should be noted in this connection that neither the General Convention nor the Headquarters Agreement provides for accreditation to the United Nations or the Secretary-General or the Secretary of State as a condition of privileges and immunities. Accreditation is specifically required as [a] condition of entry only for representatives of the press, radio, film, or other information media. Section II of the Headquarters Agreement provides that such representatives shall be "accredited by the United Nations . . . in its discretion after consultation with the United States." Neither of the international instruments provides for prior approval by the Secretary of State.

From the point of view of the United States the requirement of approval may serve both national interest and internal security. For it is the basis for prior control of the entry into the United States of representatives of Members who on one ground or another are not deemed acceptable to the United States. On the other hand, the requirement would seem to be incompatible with the independence of the Organization which is necessary for the effective exercise of its functions and the fulfillment of its purpose.[4]

*   *   *   *   *   *   *

SOJOURN IN THE UNITED STATES AND THE QUESTION OF RECIPROCITY. . . . The freedom of movement in the territory of the United States is limited for resident representatives of the Soviet Union, the Ukrainian SSR, the Byelorussian SSR, Albania, Hungary, Romania, and Bulgaria. They may move freely in the area lying within a twenty-five mile radius of Columbus Circle on Manhattan Island. For travel outside this area they are required to notify the Department of State and obtain its permission. These restrictions are reciprocal in nature and were imposed as a result of restrictions placed on

[4] [The author states that] Mrs. Gunnar Myrdal, a prominent official of UNESCO, was first denied the necessary visa by United States authorities but was eventually admitted. Remarks by Mr. Sterner (Sweden), ECOSOC Official Records (16th Session), pp. 249–256.

United States diplomatic personnel in the countries of the missions concerned. They are communicated to the missions by formal notes from the Department of State.

The issue to be considered here is that of reciprocity. That this principle prevails in diplomatic practice is not doubted. It applies on a bilateral basis. The relations between the United States and missions to the United Nations are not based on the traditional bilateral relationship. Reciprocity in the application of restrictive measures is intended as a retaliatory measure to induce the state which first imposed restrictions to remove them. By applying retaliatory measures to permanent missions to the United Nations as well as to the diplomatic missions accredited to it, the United States brings to bear additional pressure upon the state concerned, against which that state cannot retaliate. This advantage accrues to the United States from its unique position as host to the United Nations headquarters. But its legal position vis-a-vis missions is regulated by the Charter, the General Convention, and the Headquarters Agreement, and unless a legal basis is found in these instruments, there is none.

The United Nations Charter provides no more support than the General Convention for reciprocal and discriminatory treatment. The Headquarters Agreement does not provide for reciprocity. . . . Thus none of the three applicable international instruments can be involved in this matter. As the Swiss Federal Council, which is host to the European Headquarters of the United Nations and several specialized agencies declared: reciprocity cannot apply with respect to international organizations.

*   *   *   *   *   *   *

Public Law 291, the International Organizations Immunities Act, is the source of such privileges and immunities as the United States unilaterally confers upon *ad hoc* representatives. Excepting entry privileges, Section 7 (*b*) recognizes only immunity "from suit and legal process relating to acts performed by them in their official capacity and falling within their functions as such representatives." This is a far cry from normal or full diplomatic privileges and immunities and those specified in the General Convention. And even these exiguous privileges and immunities are dependent upon notification to and acceptance by the Secretary of State. Moreover, they can be terminated at will by the Secretary of State.

Resident representatives, by comparison, enjoy normal diplomatic privileges and immunities in virtue of Section 15 of the Headquarters Agreement. These would include all those listed in the General Convention for representatives of Members generally and include also those excluded therein, i.e., the exemption from excise and sales taxes. This exemption forms part of the usual privileges accorded diplomatic envoys by customary international law and is recognized in Article 34 of the Vienna Convention on Diplomatic Relations. The omission of *ad hoc* representatives in the provisions of the

Headquarters Agreement devoted to immunities and privileges is traceable to the assumption that the United States would, as host country, naturally accede to the General Convention. In view of the resistance of the United States it would seem to be imperative to fill the gap by an amendment of, or an additional protocol to, the Headquarters Agreement. The fact that no incidents have arisen or that their occurrence has not reached the public is no argument against making explicit the privileges and immunities of representatives. To do so would afford protection to the representatives, clarify their status in possible litigation before courts, and safeguard the United States from possible criticism at home and abroad.

TERMINATION OF PRIVILEGES AND IMMUNITIES

. . . Analogies to diplomatic envoys are necessarily misleading as there is no analogy of the relation between the host state on the one hand and representatives of Members to the United Nations on the other and the relationship between a sending and receiving state in case of customary diplomatic envoys. This is confirmed by the fact that the General Convention is silent on the subject and accords no right of termination to the state which acts as host to meetings of United Nations organs. Clearly the independent exercise of their functions would be jeopardized if the host state could unilaterally and at its discretion terminate and thereby prevent them from exercising the function entrusted to them by the Member States. That is the meaning of Article 105, paragraph 2, of the Charter. However, absence of an express stipulation does not necessarily prevent or remove misunderstanding. . . . In any event the practice of declaring an envoy *persona non grata* cannot be applied to [an] *ad hoc* representative or a resident representative of a Member who is in the two categories of persons expressly included in Section 13 (*b*)(3), the reason being that such persons are not accredited to the United States. . . . Deportation of representatives of Members invested with diplomatic immunities and privileges would be a most unusual step, for nothing in the Headquarters Agreement gives the United States the right to deprive such representatives of their diplomatic character; this position is founded upon the Agreement and the General Convention, which for this purpose and in this context, must be regarded as incorporated by reference in the Agreement.

However, the United States reserved the right of unilateral action in Public Law 291, the International Organizations and Immunities Act, Section 8 (b) which reads as follows:

Should the Secretary of State determine that the continued presence in the United States of any person entitled to the benefits of this title is not desirable, he shall so inform the foreign government or international organization concerned, as the case may be, and after such person shall have had a reasonable length of time, to be determined by the Secretary of State, to depart from the United States, he shall cease to be entitled to such benefits.

SUMMING UP

. . . In the present context of international relations the problem of the immunities and privileges of delegates to the United Nations is in final analysis only one aspect, albeit an important one, of the coexistence of the United Nations and the prevailing nation-state system. The International Court of Justice found unanimously that the United Nations "at present the supreme type of international organization" was "a subject of international law" and in "the possession of a large measure of international personality and the capacity to operate upon an international plane." In so doing the United Nations operates on the same plane as and concurrently with the states. It is not essential that all subjects of international law be established on a territorial basis. It is not a question of principle but rather one of functional necessity. The time may not yet have come when the United Nations will be face to face with this necessity, but it is certainly not far off. If it is to function as an effective and reasonably independent actor in the international arena, it will have to get from the Member States the necessary territorial base. Without it, its functional independence and freedom from control or interference by any one Member government will always be precarious.

PART **VII**

APPENDIXES

APPENDIX A

CHARTER OF THE UNITED NATIONS*

WE THE PEOPLES OF THE UNITED NATIONS DETERMINED

to save succeeding generations from the scourge of war, which twice in our lifetime has brought untold sorrow to mankind, and

to reaffirm faith in fundamental human rights, in the dignity and worth of the human person, in the equal rights of men and women and of nations large and small, and

to establish conditions under which justice and respect for the obligations arising from treaties and other sources of international law can be maintained, and

to promote social progress and better standards of life in larger freedom,

AND FOR THESE ENDS

to practice tolerance and live together in peace with one another as good neighbors, and

to unite our strength to maintain international peace and security, and

to ensure, by the acceptance of principles and the institution of methods, that armed force shall not be used, save in the common interest, and

to employ international machinery for the promotion of the economic and social advancement of all peoples,

HAVE RESOLVED TO COMBINE OUR EFFORTS TO ACCOMPLISH THESE AIMS.

Accordingly, our respective Governments, through representatives assembled in the city of San Francisco, who have exhibited their full powers found to be

* Signed at the United Nations Conference on International Organization, San Francisco, California, June 26, 1945. Department of State Publication 2353, Conference Series 74.

in good and due form, have agreed to the present Charter of the United
Nations and do hereby establish an international organization to be known as
the United Nations.

CHAPTER I

PURPOSES AND PRINCIPLES

Article 1

The Purposes of the United Nations are:

1. To maintain international peace and security, and to that end: to take
effective collective measures for the prevention and removal of threats to the
peace, and for the suppression of acts of aggression or other breaches of the peace,
and to bring about by peaceful means, and in conformity with the principles of
justice and international law, adjustment or settlement of international disputes or
situations which might lead to a breach of the peace;

2. To develop friendly relations among nations based on respect for the
principle of equal rights and self-determination of peoples, and to take other
appropriate measures to strengthen universal peace;

3. To achieve international cooperation in solving international problems of an
economic, social, cultural, or humanitarian character, and in promoting and encouraging respect for human rights and for fundamental freedoms for all without distinction as to race, sex, language, or religion; and

4. To be a center for harmonizing the actions of nations in the attainment of
these common ends.

Article 2

The Organization and its Members, in pursuit of the Purposes stated in Article
1, shall act in accordance with the following Principles.

1. The Organization is based on the principle of the sovereign equality of all
its Members.

2. All Members, in order to ensure to all of them the rights and benefits resulting from membership, shall fulfill in good faith the obligations assumed by them
in accordance with the present Charter.

3. All Members shall settle their international disputes by peaceful means in
such a manner that international peace and security, and justice, are not endangered.

4. All Members shall refrain in their international relations from the threat or
use of force against the territorial integrity or political independence of any state,
or in any other manner inconsistent with the Purposes of the United Nations.

5. All members shall give the United Nations every assistance in any action it
takes in accordance with the present Charter, and shall refrain from giving assistance to any state against which the United Nations is taking preventive or enforcement action.

6. The Organization shall ensure that states which are not Members of the
United Nations act in accordance with these Principles so far as may be necessary
for the maintenance of international peace and security.

7. Nothing contained in the present Charter shall authorize the United Nations to intervene in matters which are essentially within the domestic jurisdiction of any state or shall require the Members to submit such matters to settlement under the present Charter; but this principle shall not prejudice the application of enforcement measures under Chapter VII.

Chapter II

MEMBERSHIP

Article 3

The original Members of the United Nations shall be the states which, having participated in the United Nations Conference on International Organization at San Francisco, or having previously signed the Declaration by United Nations of January 1, 1942, sign the present Charter and ratify it in accordance with Article 110.

Article 4

1. Membership in the United Nations is open to all other peace-loving states which accept the obligations contained in the present Charter and, in the judgment of the Organization, are able and willing to carry out these obligations.

2. The admission of any such state to membership in the United Nations will be effected by a decision of the General Assembly upon the recommendation of the Security Council.

Article 5

A Member of the United Nations against which preventive or enforcement action has been taken by the Security Council may be suspended from the exercise of the rights and privileges of membership by the General Assembly upon the recommendation of the Security Council. The exercise of these rights and privileges may be restored by the Security Council.

Article 6

A Member of the United Nations which has persistently violated the Principles contained in the present Charter may be expelled from the Organization by the General Assembly upon the recommendation of the Security Council.

Chapter III

ORGANS

Article 7

1. There are established as the principal organs of the United Nations a General Assembly, a Security Council, an Economic and Social Council, a Trusteeship Council, an International Court of Justice, and a Secretariat.

2. Such subsidiary organs as may be found necessary may be established in accordance with the present Charter.

Article 8

The United Nations shall place no restrictions on the eligibility of men and women to participate in any capacity and under conditions of equality in its principal and subsidiary organs.

CHAPTER IV

THE GENERAL ASSEMBLY

Composition

Article 9

1. The General Assembly shall consist of all the Members of the United Nations.
2. Each Member shall have not more than five representatives in the General Assembly.

Functions and Powers

Article 10

The General Assembly may discuss any questions or any matters within the scope of the present Charter or relating to the powers and functions of any organs provided for in the present Charter, and except as provided in Article 12, may make recommendations to the Members of the United Nations or to the Security Council or to both on any such questions or matters.

Article 11

1. The General Assembly may consider the general principles of cooperation in the maintenance of international peace and security, including the principles governing disarmament and the regulation of armaments, and may make recommendations with regard to such principles to the Members or to the Security Council or to both.
2. The General Assembly may discuss any questions relating to the maintenance of international peace and security brought before it by any Member of the United Nations, or by the Security Council, or by a state which is not a Member of the United Nations in accordance with Article 35, paragraph 2, and, except as provided in Article 12, may make recommendations with regard to any such questions to the state or states concerned or to the Security Council or to both. Any such question on which action is necessary shall be referred to the Security Council by the General Assembly either before or after discussion.
3. The General Assembly may call the attention of the Security Council to situations which are likely to endanger international peace and security.
4. The powers of the General Assembly set forth in this Article shall not limit the general scope of Article 10.

Article 12

1. While the Security Council is exercising in respect of any dispute or situation the functions assigned to it in the present Charter, the General Assembly

shall not make any recommendation with regard to that dispute or situation unless the Security Council so requests.

2. The Secretary-General, with the consent of the Security Council, shall notify the General Assembly at each session of any matters relative to the maintenance of international peace and security which are being dealt with by the Security Council and shall similarly notify the General Assembly, or the Members of the United Nations if the General Assembly is not in session, immediately the Security Council ceases to deal with such matters.

Article 13

1. The General Assembly shall initiate studies and make recommendations for the purpose of:

a. promoting international cooperation in the political field and encouraging the progressive development of international law and its codification;

b. promoting international cooperation in the economic, social, cultural, educational, and health fields, and assisting in the realization of human rights and fundamental freedoms for all without distinction as to race, sex, language, or religion.

2. The further responsibilities, functions, and powers of the General Assembly with respect to matters mentioned in paragraph 1 (b) above are set forth in Chapters IX and X.

Article 14

Subject to the provisions of Article 12, the General Assembly may recommend measures for the peaceful adjustment of any situation, regardless of origin, which it deems likely to impair the general welfare or friendly relations among nations, including situations resulting from a violation of the provisions of the present Charter setting forth the Purposes and Principles of the United Nations.

Article 15

1. The General Assembly shall receive and consider annual and special reports from the Security Council; these reports shall include an account of the measures that the Security Council has decided upon or taken to maintain international peace and security.

2. The General Assembly shall receive and consider reports from the other organs of the United Nations.

Article 16

The General Assembly shall perform such functions with respect to the international trusteeship system as are assigned to it under Chapters XII and XIII, including the approval of the trusteeship agreements for areas not designated as strategic.

Article 17

1. The General Assembly shall consider and approve the budget of the Organization.

2. The expenses of the Organization shall be borne by the Members as apportioned by the General Assembly.

3. The General Assembly shall consider and approve any financial and budgetary arrangements with specialized agencies referred to in Article 57 and shall examine the administrative budgets of such specialized agencies with a view to making recommendations to the agencies concerned.

Voting

Article 18

1. Each member of the General Assembly shall have one vote.

2. Decisions of the General Assembly on important questions shall be made by a two-thirds majority of the members present and voting. These questions shall include: recommendations with respect to the maintenance of international peace and security, the election of the non-permanent members of the Security Council, the election of the members of the Economic and Social Council, the election of members of the Trusteeship Council in accordance with paragraph 1 (c) of Article 86, the admission of new Members to the United Nations, the suspension of the rights and privileges of membership, the expulsion of Members, questions relating to the operation of the trusteeship system, and budgetary questions.

3. Decisions on other questions, including the determination of additional categories of questions to be decided by a two-thirds majority, shall be made by a majority of the members present and voting.

Article 19

A Member of the United Nations which is in arrears in the payment of its financial contributions to the Organization shall have no vote in the General Assembly if the amount of its arrears equals or exceeds the amount of the contributions due from it for the preceding two full years. The General Assembly may, nevertheless, permit such a Member to vote if it is satisfied that the failure to pay is due to conditions beyond the control of the Member.

Procedure

Article 20

The General Assembly shall meet in regular annual sessions and in such special sessions as occasion may require. Special sessions shall be convoked by the Secretary-General at the request of the Security Council or of a majority of the Members of the United Nations.

Article 21

The General Asssembly shall adopt its own rules of procedure. It shall elect its President for each session.

Article 22

The General Assembly may establish such subsidiary organs as it deems necessary for the performance of its functions.

CHAPTER V

THE SECURITY COUNCIL

Composition

Article 23

1. The Security Council shall consist of eleven Members of the United Nations. The Republic of China, France, the Union of Soviet Socialist Republics, the United Kingdom of Great Britain and Northern Ireland, and the United States of America shall be permanent members of the Security Council. The General Assembly shall elect six other Members of the United Nations to be non-permanent members of the Security Council, due regard being specially paid, in the first instance to the contribution of Members of the United Nations to the maintenance of international peace and security and to the other purposes of the Organization, and also to equitable geographical distribution.

2. The non-permanent members of the Security Council shall be elected for a term of two years. In the first election of the non-permanent members, however, three shall be chosen for a term of one year. A retiring member shall not be eligible for immediate re-election.

3. Each member of the Security Council shall have one representative.

Functions and Powers

Article 24

1. In order to ensure prompt and effective action by the United Nations, its Members confer on the Security Council primary responsibility for the maintenance of international peace and security, and agree that in carrying out its duties under this responsibility the Security Council acts on their behalf.

2. In discharging these duties the Security Council shall act in accordance with the Purposes and Principles of the United Nations. The specific powers granted to the Security Council for the discharge of these duties are laid down in Chapters VI, VII, VIII, and XII.

3. The Security Council shall submit annual and, when necessary, special reports to the General Assembly for its consideration.

Article 25

The Members of the United Nations agree to accept and carry out the decisions of the Security Council in accordance with the present Charter.

Article 26

In order to promote the establishment and maintenance of international peace and security with the least diversion for armaments of the world's human and economic resources, the Security Council shall be responsible for formulating, with the assistance of the Military Staff Committee referred to in Article 47, plans to be submitted to the Members of the United Nations for the establishment of a system for the regulation of armaments.

Voting

Article 27

1. Each member of the Security Council shall have one vote.

2. Decisions of the Security Council on procedural matters shall be made by an affirmative vote of seven members.

3. Decisions of the Security Council on all other matters shall be made by an affirmative vote of seven members including the concurring votes of the permanent members; provided that, in decisions under Chapter VI, and under paragraph 3 of Article 52, a party to a dispute shall abstain from voting.

Procedure

Article 28

1. The Security Council shall be so organized as to be able to function continuously. Each member of the Security Council shall for this purpose be represented at all times at the seat of the Organization.

2. The Security Council shall hold periodic meetings at which each of its members may, if it so desires, be represented by a member of the government or by some other specially designated representative.

3. The Security Council may hold meetings at such places other than the seat of the Organization as in its judgment will best facilitate its work.

Article 29

The Security Council may establish such subsidiary organs as it deems necessary for the performance of its functions.

Article 30

The Security Council shall adopt its own rules of procedure, including the method of selecting its President.

Article 31

Any Member of the United Nations which is not a member of the Security Council may participate, without vote, in the discussion of any question brought before the Security Council whenever the latter considers that the interests of that Member are specially affected.

Article 32

Any Member of the United Nations which is not a member of the Security Council or any state which is not a Member of the United Nations, if it is a party to a dispute under consideration by the Security Council, shall be invited to participate, without vote, in the discussion relating to the dispute. The Security Council shall lay down such conditions as it deems just for the participation of a state which is not a Member of the United Nations.

CHAPTER VI

PACIFIC SETTLEMENT OF DISPUTES

Article 33

1. The parties to any dispute, the continuance of which is likely to endanger the maintenance of international peace and security, shall, first of all, seek a solution by negotiation, enquiry, mediation, conciliation, arbitration, judicial settlement, resort to regional agencies or arrangements, or other peaceful means of their own choice.

2. The Security Council shall, when it deems necessary, call upon the parties to settle their dispute by such means.

Article 34

The Security Council may investigate any dispute, or any situation which might lead to international friction or give rise to a dispute, in order to determine whether the continuance of the dispute or situation is likely to endanger the maintenance of international peace and security.

Article 35

1. Any Member of the United Nations may bring any dispute, or any situation of the nature referred to in Article 34, to the attention of the Security Council or of the General Assembly.

2. A state which is not a Member of the United Nations may bring to the attention of the Security Council or of the General Assembly any dispute to which it is a party if it accepts in advance, for the purposes of the dispute, the obligations of pacific settlement provided in the present Charter.

3. The proceedings of the General Assembly in respect of matters brought to its attention under this Article will be subject to the provisions of Articles 11 and 12.

Article 36

1. The Security Council may, at any stage of a dispute of the nature referred to in Article 33 or of a situation of like nature, recommend appropriate procedures or methods of adjustment.

2. The Security Council should take into consideration any procedures for the settlement of the dispute which have already been adopted by the parties.

3. In making recommendations under this Article the Security Council should also take into consideration that legal disputes should as a general rule be referred by the parties to the International Court of Justice in accordance with the provisions of the Statute of the Court.

Article 37

1. Should the parties to a dispute of the nature referred to in Article 33 fail to settle it by the means indicated in that Article, they shall refer it to the Security Council.

2. If the Security Council deems that the continuance of the dispute is in fact likely to endanger the maintenance of international peace and security, it shall decide whether to take action under Article 36 or to recommend such terms of settlement as it may consider appropriate.

Article 38

Without prejudice to the provisions of Articles 33 to 37, the Security Council may, if all the parties to any dispute so request, make recommendations to the parties with a view to a pacific settlement of the dispute.

CHAPTER VII

ACTION WITH RESPECT TO THREATS TO THE PEACE, BREACHES OF THE PEACE, AND ACTS OF AGGRESSION

Article 39

The Security Council shall determine the existence of any threat to the peace, breach of the peace, or act of aggression and shall make recommendations, or decide what measures shall be taken in accordance with Articles 41 and 42, to maintain or restore international peace and security.

Article 40

In order to prevent an aggravation of the situation, the Security Council may, before making the recommendations or deciding upon the measures provided for in Article 39, call upon the parties concerned to comply with such provisional measures as it deems necessary or desirable. Such provisional measures shall be without prejudice to the rights, claims, or position of the parties concerned. The Security Council shall duly take account of failure to comply with such provisional measures.

Article 41

The Security Council may decide what measures not involving the use of armed force are to be employed to give effect to its decisions, and it may call upon the Members of the United Nations to apply such measures. These may include complete or partial interruption of economic relations and of rail, sea, air, postal, telegraphic, radio, and other means of communication, and the severance of diplomatic relations.

Article 42

Should the Security Council consider that measures provided for in Article 41 would be inadequate or have proved to be inadequate, it may take such action by air, sea, or land forces as may be necessary to maintain or restore international peace and security. Such action may include demonstrations, blockade, and other operations by air, sea, or land forces of Members of the United Nations.

Article 43

1. All Members of the United Nations, in order to contribute to the maintenance of international peace and security, undertake to make available to the Security Council, on its call and in accordance with a special agreement or agreements, armed forces, assistance, and facilities, including rights of passage, necessary for the purpose of maintaining international peace and security.

2. Such agreement or agreements shall govern the numbers and types of forces, their degree of readiness and general location, and the nature of the facilities and assistance to be provided.

3. The agreement or agreements shall be negotiated as soon as possible on the initiative of the Security Council. They shall be concluded between the Security Council and Members or between the Security Council and groups of Members and shall be subject to ratification by the signatory states in accordance with their respective constitutional processes.

Article 44

When the Security Council has decided to use force it shall, before calling upon a Member not represented on it to provide armed forces in fulfillment of the obligations assumed under Article 43, invite that Member, if the Member so desires, to participate in the decisions of the Security Council concerning the employment of contingents of that Member's armed forces.

Article 45

In order to enable the United Nations to take urgent military measures, Members shall hold immediately available national air-force contingents for combined international enforcement action. The strength and degree of readiness of these contingents and plans for their combined action shall be determined, within the limits laid down in the special agreement or agreements referred to in Article 43, by the Security Council with the assistance of the Military Staff Committee.

Article 46

Plans for the application of armed force shall be made by the Security Council with the assistance of the Military Staff Committee.

Article 47

1. There shall be established a Military Staff Committee to advise and assist the Security Council on all questions relating to the Security Council's military requirement for the maintenance of international peace and security, the employment and command of forces placed at its disposal, the regulation of armaments, and possible disarmament.

2. The Military Staff Committee shall consist of the Chiefs of Staff of the permanent members of the Security Council or their representatives. Any Member of the United Nations not permanently represented on the Committee shall be invited by the Committee to be associated with it when the efficient discharge of

the Committee's responsibilities requires the participation of that Member in its work.

3. The Military Staff Committee shall be responsible under the Security Council for the strategic direction of any armed forces placed at the disposal of the Security Council. Questions relating to the command of such forces shall be worked out subsequently.

4. The Military Staff Committee, with the authorization of the Security Council and after consultation with appropriate regional agencies, may establish regional subcommittees.

Article 48

1. The action required to carry out the decisions of the Security Council for the maintenance of international peace and security shall be taken by all the Members of the United Nations or by some of them, as the Security Council may determine.

2. Such decisions shall be carried out by the Members of the United Nations directly and through their action in the appropriate international agencies of which they are members.

Article 49

The Members of the United Nations shall join in affording mutual assistance in carrying out the measures decided upon by the Security Council.

Article 50

If preventive or enforcement measures against any state are taken by the Security Council, any other state, whether a Member of the United Nations or not, which finds itself confronted with special economic problems arising from the carrying out of those measures shall have the right to consult the Security Council with regard to a solution of those problems.

Article 51

Nothing in the present Charter shall impair the inherent right of individual or collective self-defense if an armed attack occurs against a Member of the United Nations, until the Security Council has taken the measures necessary to maintain international peace and security. Measures taken by Members in the exercise of this right of self-defense shall be immediately reported to the Security Council and shall not in any way affect the authority and responsibility of the Security Council under the present Charter to take at any time such action as it deems necessary in order to maintain or restore international peace and security.

CHAPTER VIII

REGIONAL ARRANGEMENTS

Article 52

1. Nothing in the present Charter precludes the existence of regional arrangements or agencies for dealing with such matters relating to the maintenance of

international peace and security as are appropriate for regional action, provided that such arrangements or agencies and their activities are consistent with the Purposes and Principles of the United Nations.

2. The Members of the United Nations entering into such arrangements or constituting such agencies shall make every effort to achieve pacific settlement of local disputes through such regional arrangements or by such regional agencies before referring them to the Security Council.

3. The Security Council shall encourage the development of pacific settlement of local disputes through such regional arrangements or by such regional agencies either on the initiative of the states concerned or by reference from the Security Council.

4. This Article in no way impairs the application of Articles 34 and 35.

Article 53

1. The Security Council shall, where appropriate, utilize such regional arrangements or agencies for enforcement action under its authority. But no enforcement action shall be taken under regional arrangements or by regional agencies without the authorization of the Security Council, with the exception of measures against any enemy state, as defined in paragraph 2 of this Article, provided for pursuant to Article 107 or in regional arrangements directed against renewal of aggressive policy on the part of any such state, until such time as the Organization may, on request of the Governments concerned, be charged with the responsibility for preventing further aggression by such a state.

2. The term enemy state as used in paragraph 1 of this Article applies to any state which during the Second World War has been an enemy of any signatory of the present Charter.

Article 54

The Security Council shall at all times be kept fully informed of activities undertaken or in contemplation under regional arrangements or by regional agencies for the maintenance of international peace and security.

CHAPTER IX

INTERNATIONAL ECONOMIC AND SOCIAL COOPERATION

Article 55

With a view to the creation of conditions of stability and well-being which are necessary for peaceful and friendly relations among nations based on respect for the principle of equal rights and self-determination of peoples, the United Nations shall promote:

    a. higher standards of living, full employment, and conditions of economic and social progress and development;

    b. solutions of international economic, social, health, and related problems; and international cultural and educational cooperation; and

    c. universal respect for, and observance of, human rights and fundamental freedoms for all without distinction as to race, sex, language, or religion.

Article 56

All Members pledge themselves to take joint and separate action in cooperation with the Organization for the achievement of the purposes set forth in Article 55.

Article 57

1. The various specialized agencies, established by intergovernmental agreement and having wide international responsibilities, as defined in their basic instruments, in economic, social, cultural, educational, health, and related fields, shall be brought into relationship with the United Nations in accordance with the provisions of Article 63.

2. Such agencies thus brought into relationship with the United Nations are hereinafter referred to as specialized agencies.

Article 58

The Organization shall make recommendations for the coordination of the policies and activities of the specialized agencies.

Article 59

The Organization shall, where appropriate, initiate negotiations among the states concerned for the creation of any new specialized agencies required for the accomplishment of the purposes set forth in Article 55.

Article 60

Responsibility for the discharge of the functions of the Organization set forth in this Chapter shall be vested in the General Assembly and, under the authority of the General Assembly, in the Economic and Social Council, which shall have for this purpose the powers set forth in Chapter X.

CHAPTER X

THE ECONOMIC AND SOCIAL COUNCIL

Composition

Article 61

1. The Economic and Social Council shall consist of eighteen Members of the United Nations elected by the General Assembly.

2. Subject to the provisions of paragraph 3, six members of the Economic and Social Council shall be elected each year for a term of three years. A retiring member shall be eligible for immediate re-election.

3. At the first election, eighteen members of the Economic and Social Council shall be chosen. The term of office of six members so chosen shall expire at the end of one year, and of six other members at the end of two years, in accordance with arrangements made by the General Assembly.

4. Each member of the Economic and Social Council shall have one representative.

Functions and Powers

Article 62

1. The Economic and Social Council may make or initiate studies and reports with respect to international economic, social, cultural, educational, health, and related matters and may make recommendations with respect to any such matters to the General Assembly, to the Members of the United Nations, and to the specialized agencies concerned.

2. It may make recommendations for the purpose of promoting respect for, and observance of, human rights and fundamental freedoms for all.

3. It may prepare draft conventions for submission to the General Assembly, with respect to matters falling within its competence.

4. It may call, in accordance with the rules prescribed by the United Nations, international conferences on matters falling within its competence.

Article 63

1. The Economic and Social Council may enter into agreements with any of the agencies referred to in Article 57, defining the terms on which the agency concerned shall be brought into relationship with the United Nations. Such agreements shall be subject to approval by the General Assembly.

2. It may coordinate the activities of the specialized agencies through consultation with and recommendations to such agencies and through recommendations to the General Assembly and to the Members of the United Nations.

Article 64

1. The Economic and Social Council may take appropriate steps to obtain regular reports from the specialized agencies. It may make arrangements with the Members of the United Nations and with the specialized agencies to obtain reports on the steps taken to give effect to its own recommendations and to recommendations on matters falling within its competence made by the General Assembly.

2. It may communicate its observations on these reports to the General Assembly.

Article 65

The Economic and Social Council may furnish information to the Security Council and shall assist the Security Council upon its request.

Article 66

1. The Economic and Social Council shall perform such functions as fall within its competence in connection with the carrying out of the recommendations of the General Assembly.

2. It may, with the approval of the General Assembly, perform services at the request of Members of the United Nations and at the request of specialized agencies.

3. It shall perform such other functions as are specified elsewhere in the present Charter or as may be assigned to it by the General Assembly.

Voting

Article 67

1. Each member of the Economic and Social Council shall have one vote.
2. Decisions of the Economic and Social Council shall be made by a majority of the members present and voting.

Procedure

Article 68

The Economic and Social Council shall set up commissions in economic and social fields and for the promotion of human rights, and such other commissions as may be required for the performance of its functions.

Article 69

The Economic and Social Council shall invite any Member of the United Nations to participate, without vote, in its deliberations on any matter of particular concern to that Member.

Article 70

The Economic and Social Council may make arrangements for representatives of the specialized agencies to participate, without vote, in its deliberations and in those of the commissions established by it, and for its representatives to participate in the deliberations of the specialized agencies.

Article 71

The Economic and Social Council may make suitable arrangements for consultation with non-governmental organizations which are concerned with matters within its competence. Such arrangements may be made with international organizations and, where appropriate, with national organizations after consultation with the Member of the United Nations concerned.

Article 72

1. The Economic and Social Council shall adopt its own rules of procedure, including the method of selecting its President.
2. The Economic and Social Council shall meet as required in accordance with its rules, which shall include provision for the convening of meetings on the request of a majority of its members.

CHAPTER XI

DECLARATION REGARDING NON-SELF-GOVERNING TERRITORIES

Article 73

Members of the United Nations which have or assume responsibilities for the administration of territories whose peoples have not yet attained a full measure of self-government recognize the principle that the interests of the inhabitants of these territories are paramount, and accept as a sacred trust the obligation to promote to the utmost, within the system of international peace and security established by the present Charter, the well-being of the inhabitants of these territories, and, to this end:

a. to ensure, with due respect for the culture of the peoples concerned, their political, economic, social, and educational advancement, their just treatment, and their protection against abuses;

b. to develop self-government, to take due account of the political aspirations of the peoples, and to assist them in the progressive development of their free political institutions, according to the particular circumstances of each territory and its peoples and their varying stages of advancement;

c. to further international peace and security;

d. to promote constructive measures of development, to encourage research, and to cooperate with one another and, when and where appropriate, with specialized international bodies with a view to the practical achievement of the social, economic, and scientific purposes set forth in this Article; and

e. to transmit regularly to the Secretary-General for information purposes subject to such limitation as security and constitutional considerations may require, statistical and other information of a technical nature relating to economic, social, and educational conditions in the territories for which they are respectively responsible other than those territories to which Chapters XII and XIII apply.

Article 74

Members of the United Nations also agree that their policy in respect of the territories to which this Chapter applies, no less than in respect of their metropolitan areas, must be based on the general principle of good-neighborliness due account being taken of the interests and well-being of the rest of the world, in social, economic, and commercial matters.

CHAPTER XII

INTERNATIONAL TRUSTEESHIP SYSTEM

Article 75

The United Nations shall establish under its authority an international trusteeship system for the administration and supervision of such territories as may be placed thereunder by subsequent individual agreements. These territories are hereinafter referred to as trust territories.

Article 76

The basic objectives of the trusteeship system, in accordance with the Purposes of the United Nations laid down in Article 1 of the present Charter, shall be:

a. to further international peace and security;

b. to promote the political, economic, social, and educational advancement of the inhabitants of the trust territories, and their progressive development towards self-government or independence as may be appropriate to the particular circumstances of each territory and its peoples and the freely expressed wishes of the peoples concerned, and as may be provided by the terms of each trusteeship agreement;

c. to encourage respect for human rights and for fundamental freedoms for all without distinction as to race, sex, language, or religion, and to encourage recognition of the interdependence of the peoples of the world; and

d. to ensure equal treatment in social, economic, and commercial matters for all Members of the United Nations and their nationals, and also equal treatment for the latter in the administration of justice, without prejudice to the attainment of the foregoing objectives and subject to the provisions of Article 80.

Article 77

1. The trusteeship system shall apply to such territories in the following categories as may be placed thereunder by means of trusteeship agreements:

a. territories now held under mandate;

b. territories which may be detached from enemy states as a result of the Second World War; and

c. territories voluntarily placed under the system by states responsible for their administration.

2. It will be a matter for subsequent agreement as to which territories in the foregoing categories will be brought under the trusteeship system and upon what terms.

Article 78

The trusteeship system shall not apply to territories which have become Members of the United Nations, relationship among which shall be based on respect for the principle of sovereign equality.

Article 79

The terms of trusteeship for each territory to be placed under the trusteeship system, including any alteration or amendment, shall be agreed upon by the states directly concerned, including the mandatory power in the case of territories held under mandate by a Member of the United Nations, and shall be approved as provided for in Articles 83 and 85.

Article 80

1. Except as may be agreed upon in individual trusteeship agreements, made under Articles 77, 79, and 81, placing each territory under the trusteeship system, and until such agreements have been concluded, nothing in this Chapter shall be construed in or of itself to alter in any manner the rights whatsoever of any states or any peoples or the terms of existing international instruments to which Members of the United Nations may respectively be parties.

2. Paragraph 1 of this Article shall not be interpreted as giving grounds for delay or postponement of the negotiation and conclusion of agreements for placing mandated and other territories under the trusteeship system as provided for in Article 77.

Article 81

The trusteeship agreement shall in each case include the terms under which the trust territory will be administered and designate the authority which will exercise the administration of the trust territory. Such authority, hereinafter called the administering authority, may be one or more states or the Organization itself.

Article 82

There may be designated, in any trusteeship agreement, a strategic area or areas which may include part or all of the trust territory to which the agreement applies, without prejudice to any special agreement or agreements made under Article 43.

Article 83

1. All functions of the United Nations relating to strategic areas, including the approval of the terms of the trusteeship agreements and of their alteration or amendment, shall be exercised by the Security Council.

2. The basic objectives set forth in Article 76 shall be applicable to the people of each strategic area.

3. The Security Council shall, subject to the provisions of the trusteeship agreements and without prejudice to security considerations, avail itself of the assistance of the Trusteeship Council to perform those functions of the United Nations under the trusteeship system relating to political, economic, social, and educational matters in the strategic areas.

Article 84

It shall be the duty of the administering authority to ensure that the trust territory shall play its part in the maintenance of international peace and security. To this end the administering authority may make use of volunteer forces, facilities, and assistance from the trust territory in carrying out the obligations towards the Security Council undertaken in this regard by the administering authority, as well as for local defense and the maintenance of law and order within the trust territory.

Article 85

1. The functions of the United Nations with regard to trusteeship agreements for all areas not designated as strategic, including the approval of the terms of the trusteeship agreements and of their alteration or amendment, shall be exercised by the General Assembly.

2. The Trusteeship Council, operating under the authority of the General Assembly, shall assist the General Assembly in carrying out these functions.

CHAPTER XIII

THE TRUSTEESHIP COUNCIL

Composition

Article 86

1. The Trusteeship Council shall consist of the following Members of the United Nations:

a. those Members administering trust territories;

b. such of those Members mentioned by name in Article 23 as are not administering trust territories; and

c. as many other Members elected for three-year terms by the General Assembly as may be necessary to ensure that the total number of members of the Trusteeship Council is equally divided between those Members of the United Nations which administer trust territories and those which do not.

2. Each member of the Trusteeship Council shall designate one specially qualified person to represent it therein.

Functions and Powers

Article 87

The General Assembly and, under its authority, the Trusteeship Council, in carrying out their functions, may:

a. consider reports submitted by the administering authority;

b. accept petitions and examine them in consultation with the administering authority;

c. provide for periodic visits to the respective trust territories at times agreed upon with the administering authority; and

d. take these and other actions in conformity with the terms of the trusteeship agreements.

Article 88

The Trusteeship Council shall formulate a questionnaire on the political, economic, social, and educational advancement of the inhabitants of each trust territory, and the administering authority for each trust territory within the competence of the General Assembly shall make an annual report to the General Assembly upon the basis of such questionnaire.

Voting

Article 89

1. Each member of the Trusteeship Council shall have one vote.

2. Decisions of the Trusteeship Council shall be made by a majority of the members present and voting.

Procedure

Article 90

1. The Trusteeship Council shall adopt its own rules of procedure, including the method of selecting its President.

2. The Trusteeship Council shall meet as required in accordance with its rules, which shall include provision for the convening of meetings on the request of a majority of its members.

Article 91

The Trusteeship Council shall, when appropriate, avail itself of the assistance of the Economic and Social Council and of the specialized agencies in regard to matters with which they are respectively concerned.

CHAPTER XIV

THE INTERNATIONAL COURT OF JUSTICE

Article 92

The International Court of Justice shall be the principal judicial organ of the United Nations. It shall function in accordance with the annexed Statute, which is based upon the Statute of the Permanent Court of International Justice and forms an integral part of the present Charter.

Article 93

1. All Members of the United Nations are *ipso facto* parties to the Statute of the International Court of Justice.

2. A state which is not a Member of the United Nations may become a party to the Statute of the International Court of Justice on conditions to be determined in each case by the General Assembly upon the recommendation of the Security Council.

Article 94

1. Each Member of the United Nations undertakes to comply with the decision of the International Court of Justice in any case to which it is a party.

2. If any party to a case fails to perform the obligations incumbent upon it under a judgment rendered by the Court, the other party may have recourse to the Security Council, which may, if it deems necessary, make recommendations or decide upon measures to be taken to give effect to the judgment.

Article 95

Nothing in the present Charter shall prevent Members of the United Nations from entrusting the solution of their differences to other tribunals by virtue of agreements already in existence or which may be concluded in the future.

Article 96

1. The General Assembly or the Security Council may request the International Court of Justice to give an advisory opinion on any legal question.

2. Other organs of the United Nations and specialized agencies, which may at any time be so authorized by the General Assembly, may also request advisory opinions of the Court on legal questions arising within the scope of their activities.

CHAPTER XV

THE SECRETARIAT

Article 97

The Secretariat shall comprise a Secretary-General and such staff as the Organization may require. The Secretary-General shall be appointed by the General Assembly upon the recommendation of the Security Council. He shall be the chief administrative officer of the Organization.

Article 98

The Secretary-General shall act in that capacity in all meetings of the General Assembly, of the Security Council, of the Economic and Social Council, and of the Trusteeship Council, and shall perform such other functions as are entrusted to him by these organs. The Secretary-General shall make an annual report to the General Assembly on the work of the Organization.

Article 99

The Secretary-General may bring to the attention of the Security Council any matter which in his opinion may threaten the maintenance of international peace and security.

Article 100

1. In the performance of their duties the Secretary-General and the staff shall not seek or receive instructions from any government or from any other authority external to the Organization. They shall refrain from any action which might reflect on their position as international officials responsible only to the Organization.

2. Each Member of the United Nations undertakes to respect the exclusively international character of the responsibilities of the Secretary-General and the staff and not to seek to influence them in the discharge of their responsibilities.

Article 101

1. The staff shall be appointed by the Secretary-General under regulations established by the General Assembly.

2. Appropriate staffs shall be permanently assigned to the Economic and Social Council, the Trusteeship Council, and, as required, to other organs of the United Nations. These staffs shall form a part of the Secretariat.

3. The paramount consideration in the employment of the staff and in the

determination of the conditions of service shall be the necessity of securing the highest standards of efficiency, competence, and integrity. Due regard shall be paid to the importance of recruiting the staff on as wide a geographical basis as possible.

CHAPTER XVI

MISCELLANEOUS PROVISIONS

Article 102

1. Every treaty and every international agreement entered into by any Member of the United Nations after the present Charter comes into force shall as soon as possible be registered with the Secretariat and published by it.

2. No party to any such treaty or international agreement which has not been registered in accordance with the provisions of paragraph 1 of this Article may invoke that treaty or agreement before any organ of the United Nations.

Article 103

In the event of a conflict between the obligations of the Members of the United Nations under the present Charter and their obligations under any other international agreement, their obligations under the present Charter shall prevail.

Article 104

The Organization shall enjoy in the territory of each of its Members such legal capacity as may be necessary for the exercise of its functions and the fulfillment of its purposes.

Article 105

1. The Organization shall enjoy in the territory of each of its Members such privileges and immunities as are necessary for the fulfillment of its purposes.

2. Representatives of the Members of the United Nations and officials of the Organization shall similarly enjoy such privileges and immunities as are necessary for the independent exercise of their functions in connection with the Organization.

3. The General Assembly may make recommendations with a view to determining the details of the application of paragraphs 1 and 2 of this Article or may propose conventions to the Members of the United Nations for this purpose.

CHAPTER XVII

TRANSITIONAL SECURITY ARRANGEMENTS

Article 106

Pending the coming into force of such special agreements referred to in Article 43 as in the opinion of the Security Council enable it to begin the exercise of its responsibilities under Article 42, the parties to the Four-Nation Declaration, signed at Moscow, October 30, 1943, and France, shall, in accordance with the provisions of paragraph 5 of that Declaration, consult with one another and as occasion requires with other Members of the United Nations with a view to such joint action on behalf of the Organization as may be necessary for the purpose of maintaining international peace and security.

Article 107

Nothing in the present Charter shall invalidate or preclude action, in relation to any state which during the Second World War has been an enemy of any signatory to the present Charter, taken or authorized as a result of that war by the Governments having responsibility for such action.

CHAPTER XVIII

AMENDMENTS

Article 108

Amendments to the present Charter shall come into force for all Members of the United Nations when they have been adopted by a vote of two thirds of the members of the General Assembly and ratified in accordance with their respective constitutional processes by two thirds of the Members of the United Nations, including all the permanent members of the Security Council.

Article 109

1. A General Conference of the Members of the United Nations for the purpose of reviewing the present Charter may be held at a date and place to be fixed by a two-thirds vote of the members of the General Assembly and by a vote of any seven members of the Security Council. Each member of the United Nations shall have one vote in the conference.

2. Any alteration of the present Charter recommended by a two-thirds vote of the conference shall take effect when ratified in accordance with their respective constitutional processes by two-thirds of the Members of the United Nations including all the permanent members of the Security Council.

3. If such a conference has not been held before the tenth annual session of the General Assembly following the coming into force of the present Charter, the proposal to call such a conference shall be placed on the agenda of that session of the General Assembly, and the conference shall be held if so decided by a majority vote of the members of the General Assembly and by a vote of any seven members of the Security Council.

CHAPTER XIX

RATIFICATION AND SIGNATURE

Article 110

1. The present Charter shall be ratified by the signatory states in accordance with their respective constitutional processes.

2. The ratification shall be deposited with the Government of the United States

of America, which shall notify all the signatory states of each deposit as well as the Secretary-General of the Organization when he has been appointed.

3. The present Charter shall come into force upon the deposit of ratifications by the Republic of China, France, the Union of Soviet Socialist Republics, the United Kingdom of Great Britain and Northern Ireland, and the United States of America, and by a majority of the other signatory states. A protocol of the ratifications deposited shall thereupon be drawn up by the Government of the United States of America which shall communicate copies thereof to all the signatory states.

4. The states signatory to the present Charter which ratify it after it has come into force will become original Members of the United Nations on the date of the deposit of their respective ratifications.

Article 111

The present Charter, of which the Chinese, French, Russian, English, and Spanish texts are equally authentic, shall remain deposited in the archives of the Government of the United States of America. Duly certified copies thereof shall be transmitted by that Government to the Governments of the other signatory states.

IN FAITH WHEREOF the representatives of the Governments of the United Nations have signed the present Charter.

DONE at the city of San Francisco the twenty-sixth day of June, one thousand-nine hundred and forty-five.

PROTOCOL OF ENTRY INTO FORCE OF THE AMENDMENTS TO ARTICLES 23, 27 AND 61 OF THE CHARTER OF THE UNITED NATIONS ADOPTED BY THE GENERAL ASSEMBLY RESOLUTIONS 1991 A AND B (XVIII) OF 17 DECEMBER 1963

WHEREAS Article 108 of the Charter of the United Nations provides as follows:

Article 108

Amendments to the present Charter shall come into force for all Members of the United Nations when they have been adopted by a vote of two thirds of the members of the General Assembly and ratified in accordance with their respective constitutional processes by two thirds of the Members of the United Nations, including all the permanent members of the Security Council.

WHEREAS the General Assembly of the United Nations adopted on 17 December 1963, in accordance with the said Article 108, the amendments to Articles

23, 27 and 61 of the Charter of the United Nations as set forth in resolutions 1991 A and B (XVIII),

WHEREAS the requirements of the said Article 108 with respect to the ratification of the above-mentioned amendments were fulfilled by 31 August 1965, as shown in the Annex to this Protocol, and the said amendments entered into force on that day for all Members of the United Nations.

AND WHEREAS the text of Articles 23, 27 and 61 of the Charter of the United Nations as amended reads as follows:

Article 23

1. The Security Council shall consist of fifteen Members of the United Nations. The Republic of China, France, the Union of Soviet Socialist Republics, the United Kingdom of Great Britain and Northern Ireland, and the United States of America shall be permanent members of the Security Council. The General Assembly shall elect ten other Members of the United Nations to be non-permanent members of the Security Council, due regard being specially paid, in the first instance to the contributions of Members of the United Nations to the maintenance of international peace and security and to the other purposes of the Organization, and also to equitable geographical distribution.

2. The non-permanent members of the Security Council shall be elected for a term of two years. In the first election of the non-permanent members after the increase of the membership of the Security Council from eleven to fifteen, two of the four additional members shall be chosen for a term of one year. A retiring member shall not be eligible for immediate re-election.

3. Each member of the Security Council shall have one representative.

Article 27

1. Each member of the Security Council shall have one vote.

2. Decisions of the Security Council on procedural matters shall be made by an affirmative vote of nine members.

3. Decisions of the Security Council on all other matters shall be made by an affirmative vote of nine members including the concurring votes of the permanent members; provided that, in decisions under Chapter VI, and under paragraph 3 of Article 52, a party to a dispute shall abstain from voting.

Article 61

1. The Economic and Social Council shall consist of twenty-seven Members of the United Nations elected by the General Assembly.

2. Subject to the provisions of paragraph 3, nine members of the Economic and Social Council shall be elected each year for a term of three years. A retiring member shall be eligible for immediate re-election.

3. At the first election after the increase in the membership of the Economic and Social Council from eighteen to twenty-seven members, in addition to the members elected in place of the six members whose term of office expires at the end of that year, nine additional members shall be elected. Of these nine additional members, the term of office of three members so elected shall expire at the end of one year, and

of three other members at the end of two years, in accordance with arrangements made by the General Assembly.

4. Each member of the Economic and Social Council shall have one representative.

NOW, THEREFORE, I, U THANT, Secretary-General of the United Nations, sign this Protocol in two original copies in the Chinese, English, French, Russian and Spanish languages, of which one shall be deposited in the archives of the Secretariat of the United Nations and the other transmitted to the Government of the United States of America as the depository of the Charter of the United Nations. Copies of this Protocol shall be communicated to all Members of the United Nations.

DONE AT THE HEADQUARTERS OF THE UNITED NATIONS, NEW YORK, this thirty-first day of August, one thousand nine hundred and sixty-five.

DATE OF ADMISSION OR MERGER OF MEMBER NATIONS AS OF 20 SEPTEMBER 1966

MEMBER	DATE OF ADMISSION
Afghanistan	19 November 1946
Albania	14 December 1955
Algeria	8 October 1962
°Argentina	24 October 1945
°Australia	1 November 1945
Austria	14 December 1955
Belgium	27 December 1945
°Bolivia	14 November 1945
°Brazil	24 October 1945
Bulgaria	14 December 1955
Burma	19 April 1948
Burundi	18 September 1962
°Byelorussian SSR	24 October 1945
Cambodia	14 December 1955
Cameroon	20 September 1960
°Canada	9 November 1945
Central African Republic	20 September 1960
Ceylon	14 December 1955
Chad	20 September 1960
°Chile	24 October 1945
°China	24 October 1945
°Colombia	5 November 1945
Congo (Brazzaville)	20 September 1960
Congo (Democratic Republic of)	20 September 1960
°Costa Rica	2 November 1945
°Cuba	24 October 1945
Cyprus	20 September 1960

Source: United Nations Office of Public Information
° Original member. (There are 51 in all.)

MEMBER	DATE OF ADMISSION
*Czechoslovakia	24 October 1945
Dahomey	20 September 1960
*Denmark	24 October 1945
*Dominican Republic	24 October 1945
*Ecuador	21 December 1945
*El Salvador	24 October 1945
*Ethiopia	13 November 1945
Finland	14 December 1955
*France	24 October 1945
Gabon	20 September 1960
Gambia	21 September 1965
Ghana	8 March 1957
*Greece	25 October 1945
*Guatemala	21 November 1945
Guinea	12 December 1958
Guyana	20 September 1966
*Haiti	24 October 1945
*Honduras	17 December 1945
Hungary	14 December 1955
Iceland	19 November 1946
*India	30 October 1945
*Iran	24 October 1945
*Iraq	21 December 1945
Ireland	14 December 1955
Israel	11 May 1949
Italy	14 December 1955
Ivory Coast	20 September 1960
Jamaica	18 September 1962
Japan	18 December 1956
Jordan	14 December 1955
Kenya	16 December 1963
Kuwait	14 May 1963
Laos	14 December 1955
*Lebanon	24 October 1945
*Liberia	2 November 1945
Libya	14 December 1955
*Luxembourg	24 October 1945
Madagascar	20 September 1960
Malawi	1 December 1964
Malaysia	16 September 1963
Maldive Islands	21 September 1965
Mali	28 September 1960
Malta	1 December 1964
Mauritania	27 October 1961
*Mexico	7 November 1945
Mongolia	27 October 1961
Morocco	12 November 1956
Nepal	14 December 1955
*Netherlands	10 December 1945
*New Zealand	24 October 1945

* Original member. (There are 51 in all.)

MEMBER	DATE OF ADMISSION
°Nicaragua	24 October 1945
Niger	20 September 1960
Nigeria	7 October 1960
°Norway	27 November 1945
Pakistan	30 September 1947
°Panama	13 November 1945
°Paraguay	24 October 1945
°Peru	31 October 1945
°Philippines	24 October 1945
°Poland	24 October 1945
Portugal	14 December 1955
Romania	14 December 1955
Rwanda	18 September 1962
°Saudi Arabia	24 October 1945
Senegal	28 September 1960
Sierra Leone	27 September 1961
Singapore	21 September 1965
Somalia	20 September 1960
°South Africa	7 November 1945
Spain	14 December 1955
Sudan	12 November 1956
Sweden	19 November 1946
°Syria	24 October 1945
Thailand	16 December 1946
Togo	20 September 1960
Trinidad and Tobago	18 September 1962
Tunisia	12 November 1956
°Turkey	24 October 1945
Uganda	25 October 1962
°Ukrainian SSR	24 October 1945
°USSR	24 October 1945
°United Arab Republic	24 October 1945
°United Kingdom	24 October 1945
United Republic of Tanzania	2 November 1964
°United States	24 October 1945
Upper Volta	20 September 1960
°Uruguay	18 December 1945
°Venezuela	15 November 1945
Yemen	30 September 1947
°Yugoslavia	24 October 1945
Zambia	1 December 1964

° Original member. (There are 51 in all.)

583

APPENDIX C
ORGANIZATIONAL CHART OF THE UNITED NATIONS

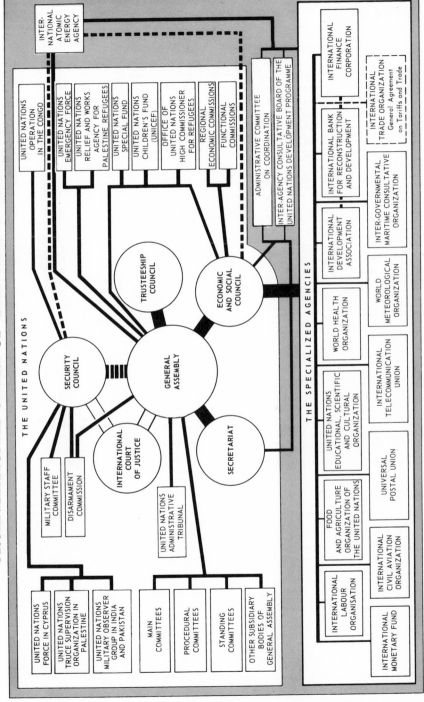

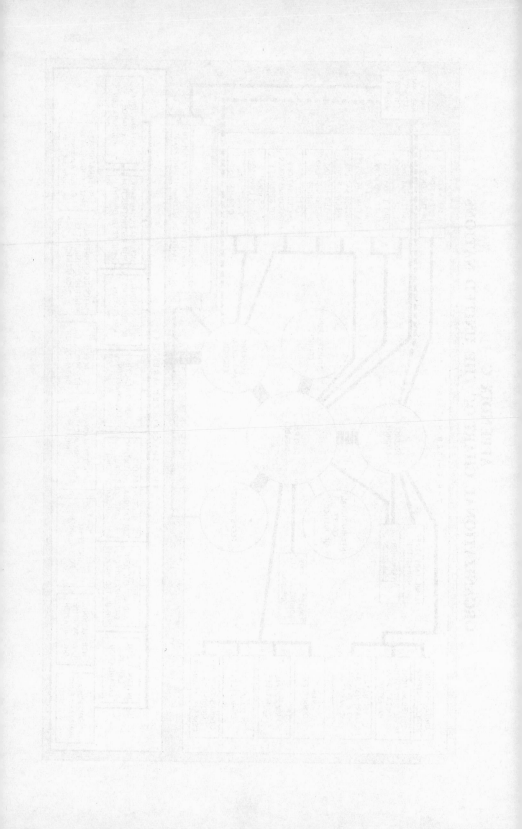